T0325550

THE HISTORY OF
ECONOMIC THOUGHT IN THE

PEOPLE'S REPUBLIC
OF CHINA

www.royalcollins.com

THE HISTORY OF ECONOMIC THOUGHT IN THE
PEOPLE'S REPUBLIC OF CHINA

The Development and Transformation
of Modern China's Economic Thought
(1949–2019)

———

ZHAO XIAOLEI

Books Beyond Boundaries

ROYAL COLLINS

The History of Economic Thought in the People's Republic of China:
Development and Transformation of China's Economic Thought (1949–2019)

Zhao Xiaolei

First published in 2022 by Royal Collins Publishing Group Inc.
Groupe Publication Royal Collins Inc.
BKM Royalcollins Publishers Private Limited

Headquarters: 550-555 boul. René-Lévesque O Montréal (Québec) H2Z1B1 Canada
India office: 805 Hemkunt House, 8th Floor, Rajendra Place, New Delhi 110 008

Original Edition © Capital University of Economics and Business Press

ISBN: 978-1-4878-0859-4

To find out more about our publications, please visit www.royalcollins.com.

Preface

In October 2009, I published a key book on China's Eleventh Five-Year Plan, *The History of the Economic Thought in the People's Republic of China (1949–2009)*. Ten years later, in October 2019, I published a key book on the Thirteenth Five-Year Plan, *The History of the Economic Thought in the People's Republic of China: Development and Transformation of China's Economic Thought (1949–2019)*. The latter follows the former in terms of academic thought and research methods and the selection and application of ideological materials, particularly the ideological materials from the 1950s to 1970s, and offers new designs in system construction, structural arrangement, and research content, building the framework system for the construction of the mainstream form of economic thought in the People's Republic of China, the evolution of the mainstream form of economic thought in the People's Republic of China, and the transformation of the mainstream form of economic thought in the People's Republic of China. It takes the theoretical composition of economic thought in the People's Republic of China and the exploration and development of socialist political economy with Chinese characteristics as the main theoretical line and studies the development and evolution of China's economic thought from 1949 to 2019.

In terms of the construction of the mainstream form of economic thought, in the 1950s, the theoretical composition of economic thought in the People's Republic of China took the Marxist political economy as the guide and Soviet Union's socialist political economics and Western economics as the reference. At the beginning of the 21st century, the main form of economic thought in the People's Republic of China underwent a transformation. Marxist political economy remained the guiding principle, but more emphasis was placed on its combination and integration with China's reality, that is, the "Sinicization of Marxism," while Western economics remained as the reference, but with more emphasis placed on the beneficial part of the market economy's operation and regulation. The socialist political economics of the Soviet Union as the reference was replaced by the "localized" thought of Chinese practice, Chinese characteristics, and Chinese experience. The theory of socialism with Chinese characteristics is the main theoretical line of the transformation of the mainstream form of economic thought. The theory of socialism with Chinese characteristics includes the development of Marxism in China, the positive reference of Western economics, and the localization and practical elements based on China's national conditions, practice, and development. The development and transformation of economic thought over the past seventy years reflects China's development and transformation from a key aspect and records the development track and achievements of the thought, theory, policy, and system.

In the process of writing this book, Wang Chuang was in charge of the data and text collation for several chapters, Han Lijuan of the technical statistics and collation of Chapter 16, and Shen Chenyan of the text input and the sorting of the electronic edition.

On the occasion of the 60th anniversary of the founding of the People's Republic of China, Capital University of Economics and Business Press asked me to write *The History of the Economic Thought in the People's Republic of China (1949–2009)*. On the occasion of the 70th anniversary of the founding of the People's Republic of China, Capital University of Economics and Business Press asked me to write *The History of the Economic Thought in the People's Republic of China – Development and Transformation of China Economic Thought (1949–2019)* and applied for the key book on the Thirteenth Five-Year Plan. I would like to thank the Capital University of Economics and Business Press for its attention to this academic topic, president and editor-in-chief Yang Ling's planning and broad support, my meticulous editor, Xue Jie, and other scholars for their excellent work in editing and publishing this book.

ZHAO XIAOLEI

June 2019, Shanghai University of Finance and Economics

Contents

PART ONE
The Construction of the Mainstream Form of Economic Thought
in the People's Republic of China (1950s–1970s)

PART TWO
The Evolution of the Mainstream Form of Economic Thought of the People's Republic of China (1980s)

PART 3

**The Transformation of Mainstream Economic Thought
in the People's Republic of China (1990s–2010s)**

An Investigation into the Development of Economic Thought in the People's Republic of China (1949–2019)

1. On the Development of Economic Thought in the People's Republic of China from the 1950s to the 1970s

After the founding of the People's Republic of China in 1949, China gradually formed an economic ideological paradigm and theoretical system with the Marxist and Soviet socialist political economy as the main substance. During the thirty years of development from 1949 to 1979, some important thoughts and theories were produced within this basic framework, and their theoretical understanding and policy views had a profound impact on future development.

From the perspective of development characteristics, there were generally two guiding principles for development in this stage of economic thought. One was to inherit the transmission and research of Marxist economics in China after the May 4th Movement, which was manifested in the extensive, in-depth study of the classic works of Marxist economics and the application of those principles to analyze socialist economic problems. The other was the introduction of Soviet socialist political economics based on Stalinist theory, which was manifested in the systematic introduction to the theory of Stalinist socialism and the *Textbook of Political Economics* compiled by the Institute of Economics of the Soviet Academy of Sciences, along with its coverage of Chinese economics teaching and research. These two development principles were not unconnected, but were interwoven and interacted with each other. During this period, the debates on some important issues in China's economic and ideological communities, as well as some brilliant ideas generated in the course of these debates, arose from the investigation and study of problems from different angles of the two development principles. For example, in the early days of the founding of the People's Republic of China, Mao Zedong published many works of economic theory, such as "Fighting for the Basic Improvement of China's Financial and Economic Situation," "On the Issue of Agricultural Cooperation," "On the Ten Major Relations," and "On the Proper Handling of Contradictions Among the People," formulating a strategic plan for the overall development of socialist industrialization and economic construction. These expositions of Mao Zedong were based on the use of principles of Marxist economics to analyze and study real economic problems. At the same time, they also fully absorbed and drew lessons from the theory and practice of the socialist economic construction of the Soviet Union, and then put forward some innovative and developmental ideas, which had a profound impact on the development of China's economic thought. For example, the debates on some important economic theoretical issues in this period, such as the object of political economics, the relationships between productivity and production and between politics and economy, the basic economic law of socialism, the law of value under the socialist system and commodity production, distribution according to work, and agriculture as the basis of the national economy were basically carried out within the framework of these two development principles. In addition, some outstanding theoretical viewpoints produced during this period, such as Mao Zedong's discussion on the relationship between industrialization and agricultural modernization, Li Pingxin's discussion on productivity economics, Wang Yanan's discussion on socialist political economics employing the system of *Das Kapital,* Ma Yinchu's "new population theory," and Sun Yefang's discussion on economic system reform, also followed the two development principles arising from the mutual discussion and debate on relevant issues.

In this stage of development, especially from 1949 to 1957, China's economic and ideological circles were relatively active, with various ideas, theories, and viewpoints debated one after another, creating an atmosphere of "a hundred schools of thought contending." However, after the late 1950s, with the gradual establishment of the guiding ideology of "taking class struggle as the key link" in social and political life, the study of economic theory was greatly affected, and the active situation began to fade. Under the guidance of Marxist economic theory, the academic thought of objective scientific research on socialist economic issues was suppressed and attacked, while the academic thought of unilateral, dogmatic, rigid understandings and applications of socialist theory, which took Soviet theory as the model, occupied a dominant position and gradually developed in extreme directions. During the Great Leap Forward, from 1958 to 1960, the study of political economy began to have more political color, while the academic tones gradually faded. Under the guidance of the policy line (general line) of a one-sided pursuit of rapid economic growth, economic theorists discussed the relationship between politics and economy, between calls for "more, faster, better, and more economical" and economic laws, and between political demands and economic interests. Judging from the discussion, the majority opinion was that politics was primary and the economy was secondary. It was believed that economic and other professional work should serve the politics of the proletariat and that politics should govern the economy. Although some scholars proposed that politics should be implemented in production and business, those opinions were criticized under political pressure at that time. With the economic adjustment and the sharp political struggle after the Great Leap Forward, the tendency of "politics alone" in the study of economic theory became even more serious, going to the greatest extreme in the Cultural Revolution.

In May 1966, China entered the special historical period of the Cultural Revolution, during which social economy, culture, education, and science suffered a catastrophe, basically moving into a state of stagnation. During this period, in fact, there was no economic research. Some so-called "economic theories" twisted and distorted Marxist economics on some basic issues, merely for political purposes. For example, in the struggle of ideological and theoretical circles criticizing the "productivity-alone theory," bourgeois rights, distribution according to work, commodity economy, and the law of value, some fallacies that violated or even "fixed" scientific socialist economic theory bewitched people's minds and disrupted their thinking and behavior. During this period, extreme leftist economic theories were mainly presented in the book *Socialist Political Economy,* collated by Zhang Chunqiao and Yao Wenyuan in Shanghai. After that, some learning pamphlets centering around the book were published across the nation, which were the fruits of the economic thought at this stage. After the end of the Cultural Revolution in 1976, ideological and theoretical circles were still confined by this extreme leftist concept, and there was no substantial loosening in the field of economic research. This situation did not change until the Third Plenary Session of the Eleventh CPC Central Committee was held in December 1979.

2. On the Development of Economic Thought in the People's Republic of China in the 1980s

After the Third Plenary Session of the Eleventh Central Committee of the Communist Party of China was held in December 1978, China's ideological and academic circles gained vigorous development vitality, and its economic thought entered a stage of comprehensive development. Judging from the development characteristics, there were generally two development principles in this stage of economic thought. One was the study and research of Marxist economics, which was combined with the practice of China's economic reform to further enrich Marxist economics in the construction of basic theories. The other was the introduction, research, and application of modern Western economics. The latter development principle first emerged in the early 1980s, and it showed a strong development momentum. By the end of the 1980s, it had converged and integrated with the former, initially showing the trend of integrating Marxist economic research with modern Western economic research. For example, a series of breakthroughs and innovations, including the relationship between the planned economy and market regulation, the theory of socialist commodity economy, the theory of the combination of the planned economy and market regulation, and the theory of the reform of state-owned enterprises, were put forward and founded based on Marxist economic theory, absorbing and drawing upon the reasonable factors in Western market economy theories. Another example was the economic phenomena that occurred in the process of China's economic system reform and economic development in the 1980s, such as fiscal deficit, inflation, industrial structure adjustment, agricultural labor transfer, unemployment, the growth of the non-state-owned economy, and the emergence and development of factor markets, especially the financial and securities markets. As China was in the transitional period from a planned economy to a socialist commodity economy, and in the "primary stage of socialism" as well, neither the traditional socialist economic theory, the classical Marxist economic theory, nor the Western neoclassical economic theory could work effectively on its own. It was necessary to integrate and blend all of these theories to offer a reasonable, accurate explanation for the economic phenomena in that special social environment and economic conditions. As a final example, in terms of the composition of economic researchers, most economists at that time had a theoretical basis of Marxist economics and basic training in Western economics to varying degrees. They saw through their analysis of China's economy that it was not enough to settle China's economic reform by merely sticking to the established conclusions of Marxist economics, and innovations were much needed. They also realized that simply relying on Western economics would fail to accurately analyze and explain China's economy, so more scientific analysis and borrowing were essential.

In addition, the integration of Marxist economics and Western economics in this period also highlighted the transformation of economic research methods. Before the 1980s, China's economic research mainly adopted the approach of normative analysis, focusing on the construction of abstract theories and laws based on logical reasoning, while neglecting the interpretation and analysis of actual economic life. In the 1980s, with the introduction of Western economics and the growth of a new generation of economists, the empirical analysis method of economics was gradually popularized and adopted. This research method claimed to eliminate value evaluation and aimed to explain "what the real economic operations are like." However, due to the typical thought patterns of Chinese economists and the characteristics of institutional change in China's economic development, truly empirical analysis was rare, and a large number of studies still had a touch of strong normative analysis.

However, the empirical analysis method was given increasing intersection and iteration with normative analysis methods and was gradually integrated into the mainstream. One of the outstanding manifestations of this was the rapid spread and wide application of the structural analysis of development economics and the institutional analysis of new institutional economics in China. As structural analysis and institutional analysis have the methodological characteristics of the combination of normative and empirical and also met the practical needs of China's economic system reform and innovation, they were extremely applicable.

One of the main manifestations of the prosperity and development of China's economic thought in this period was the urgent need of economic reform and development for economic theories, the unprecedented liveliness of the economic circles, the emergence of a large number of economic research findings, and the endless emergence of academic views. According to a catalogue of economics works collected in the *Overall National Bibliography*, the *New National Bibliography*, and the *Overall National Economic Science Bibliography*, 692 works on theoretical economics (including 469 books and 223 translated works) were published in China (excluding Hong Kong, Macao, and Taiwan) during the thirty years from 1949 to 1979. In the ten years between 1980 and 1989, China published 4,040 economic theory books (including 3,463 works and 577 translated works). In addition, numerous economics journals and papers were published in the 1980s. In this stage of development, the academic exchanges between China and other countries were also unprecedented. Academic exchanges on economics with Western Europe, America, Eastern Europe, international organizations, and developing countries were carried out in a comprehensive way, greatly promoting the development of China's economics research and opening its economic thought to the world. In particular, in October 1987, the Thirteenth National Congress of the Communist Party of China set the reform goal of building a "socialist planned commodity economic system." The in-depth discussion in China's economic community on the relationship between socialism and the commodity economy and between planned regulation and market regulation in the socialist commodity economy had innovative significance in both theory and practice.

In the 1980s, there were still many discussions on the principles, concepts and definitions of Marxist economic theory, but increasingly, they were closely tied to the actual economy. The greatest significance of the theory of the primary stage of socialism, which was put forward and continuously improved in the 1980s, was that it had a fresh understanding of and research on socialism based on China's actual national conditions. It not only laid a new theoretical foundation for the research and development of China's socialist political economy, but also provided a scientific basis for the state to formulate proper lines, guidelines, and policies. From the perspective of research methods, normative analysis remained the primary approach, but due to the needs of actual economic research and the influence of Western economics, the method of focusing on statistical data and even empirical analysis started to gain attention. In terms of academic atmosphere, the style of general, dogmatic, and policy-based interpretation was suppressed, and the practical, objective scientific attitude was steadily encouraged. The study of Marxist economic theory in China was in nature firmly rooted in economic science.

During this period, the scope of research into Marxist economic theory was relatively wide and could be divided into several categories. One was the continuation and extension of some lingering historical issues, which mainly included the basic law of the socialist economy, the law of the planned development of the national economy, and the law of distribution according to work. The second was to conduct new research on and offer new expressions of some original theories and concepts from a new perspective and connotation, which mainly included the reform of the socialist ownership system, the socialist economic law system, the relationship between the plan and the market in the socialist economy, the reform of state-owned enterprises, industrial structure, and industrial policies, and so on. The third was to study some new economic and theoretical issues and bring them into the Marxist economic system, which mainly included the fluctuation of the socialist economic cycle, inflation, economic development strategies, regional economies, knowledge value theory, the stock economy, enterprise theory, the socialist commodity economy, and the socialist market economy.

Beginning in the 1980s, the research and revision of the socialist political economy system in China's economic and ideological circles entered a new stage of development. In the early 1980s,

China published a number of monographs on the socialist political economy, but the system and substance remained unable to shake off the impact and framework of the Soviet theory. In September 1984, the Institute of Economics of the Chinese Academy of Social Sciences organized a "symposium on the system of socialist political economy" to discuss the establishment of a theoretical system of the socialist political economy. The meeting held that, from the perspective of published works on the socialist political economy, some traditional paradigms had been broken through in terms of system, structure, and content, but great innovation had not yet been made in grasping the research objects of the socialist political economy, understanding the essence of socialist economic relations, and changing research methods. Beginning in the mid-1980s, with the deepening of economic reform, new ideas and propositions emerged which required economic circles to offer demonstration and explanation. The socialist political economy needed to bring these new major issues into its own system to comprehensively reflect the essence of the socialist economy. For example, after the proposition of the socialist planned commodity economy was put forward, theoretical circles generally believed that the basic viewpoint that the socialist economy was a planned commodity economy on the basis of public ownership had to be carried out in the theoretical analysis of the entire economic process of socialist production, distribution, exchange, and consumption, and the viewpoint of socialist product economic theory should be completely abandoned so as to make the socialist political economy system reflect the practice of socialist reform and the current economic situation. Further, the proposition of the primary stage of socialism showed that China's socialism was based on an underdeveloped economy and developed under a specific economic system, and the economic system changed with the development of productive forces. Therefore, merely understanding the essence of the socialist economic system without studying the development and change of this system could not fully grasp the characteristics of the socialist economy. In addition, the theory of commodity production and commodity exchange in the socialist economy was a major change in the system structure of the socialist political economy, but if there was no fundamental change in the concept and paradigm, it was difficult to explain this issue in a scientific way.

The textbooks and treatises on the socialist political economy published in the 1980s shared a common theoretical thread: the theory of the socialist commodity economy. In order to construct the system of the socialist political economy with the theory of the socialist commodity economy as the main line, it was necessary, under the guidance of the basic principles of Marxism and in combination with the practice of China's socialist economic development, to carry out scientific exploration, research, and innovation in the theoretical category, content structure, analysis methods, and other areas. The formation of such a theoretical system would be an innovation of economic theory, putting forward a number of axiomatic basic assumptions of human nature and human behavior on the basis of public ownership as the main body, and based on these assumptions, carrying out empirical analysis of the economic activities of a socialist society and people's economic behaviors and developing a set of corresponding concepts, categories, and theoretical frameworks, and in this theoretical framework, explaining the interest relationship of people in the public ownership economy and the behavior relationship and mechanism generated for the pursuit of interests, and then further explaining the relationship between this behavior relationship and mechanism and between resource allocation and income distribution.

In the 1980s, the introduction, dissemination, research, and application of Western economics entered a stage of great development. In order to introduce and study Western economics on a large scale, in September 1979, the Chinese Society for the Study of Foreign Economic Theories was established in Beijing. In 1980, a lecture on foreign economics was held in Peking University. The topics included microeconomics, macroeconomics, economic growth theory, development economics, regional economics, mathematical economics, econometrics, input-output analysis, economic prediction theory and methods, and other topics. In total, sixty lectures were held over the course of two years, and the participants included college and university teachers, researchers from various institutions, and senior cadres of different ministries and commissions. When the program was over, the course books were published in collections, and a number of corresponding popular reading materials were published as well.

In the first half of the 1980s, the introduction and research of Western economics were mainly based on classical and neoclassical economic theories. Among them, some important works of the post-Keynesian mainstream school were introduced and studied. For example, the American economist Paul Samuelson's *Economics* was the representative work of the contemporary post-Keynesian mainstream school, which was very popular in China. Most colleges and universities regarded it as the designated reference book for economics majors. During this period, the works of other non-mainstream schools, such as the monetary school and the supply-side school, were also translated and studied by scholars. However, these schools advocated "reviving" traditional economic liberalism, and their theories and policies were not quite applicable to China, which took the "planned commodity economy" as the reform goal at that time. Many scholars believed that the theories of these schools were relatively poor and their policies were too simple to replace the Keynesian School. There were some, however, who held that those theories made up for the weaknesses in Keynes' theory and thus could be included in the Western mainstream economics.

In the second half of the 1980s, the introduction and research of Western economics shifted the focus to the theory of economic growth and development economics. Meanwhile, the introduction and research of national economic management and enterprise management theory also emerged as a focus. Economic growth theory and development economics, with their theoretical characteristics more appropriate for the economic status of developing countries, as well as strong empirical and comparative analysis characteristics in the analytical methods, had a wider impact on China's economic and ideological circles. In addition, economic growth theory and development economics held that in developing countries, industrialization was basically initiated by the government, coupled with the low degree of marketization and socialization of the economy and the slow accumulation of modern factors. Therefore, in order to achieve rapid economic development, it was necessary to go through a stage of strengthening national intervention. This policy proposition was also in line with the preferences of Chinese academics and decision makers.

In the late 1980s and early 1990s, the introduction and research of Western economics was characterized by the introduction and study of property rights theory and new institutional economics. New institutional economics in Western countries started to burgeon in the 1920s and 1930s, gradually maturing in the 1960s and 1970s. It was part of the frontier discipline of economics. The research and application of this theory in China's economic circles not only had important value in theory and analysis methods, but also narrowed the gap between China's economic research and the development of world economics, indicating that China's introduction, research, and application of Western economics made great strides forward on the original basis.

3. On the Development of the Economic Thought in the People's Republic of China in the 1990s

In the 1990s, the development principle of China's economic thought was seen in some aspects of Marxist economics research, explanation, and innovation, and in the introduction, research, and application of modern Western economics, and these two development principles further converged and merged. Although the distinction was clear, it was not distinctly divided. In October 1992, the Fourteenth National Congress of the Communist Party of China established the goal of China's economic system reform, which was to establish and improve the socialist market economic system on the basis of adhering to public ownership and distribution according to work as the main body and other economic components and distribution methods as supplements. The research on the topic of the socialist market economy further illustrated the requirements of the times for the effective combination of Marxist and Western economics.

On the basis of the development in the 1980s, the study of China's economic thought in the 1990s gradually deepened. For example, the study of Marxist economics was not only the interpretation of classical works, but also the criticism of the "Soviet paradigm" by returning to standard Marxist economic principles and concepts. The main purpose was to grasp the theoretical system of Marxist economics fully and accurately and to push forward this open theoretical system so that it could be applied to the actual economy (including the contemporary capitalist economy and socialist economy in the reforms) and have stronger explanatory power and guiding significance. In this process, some theoretical elements and concept categories and the innovation of analytical methods were generated. In addition, the reporting and application of Western economics were further developed. The introduction of theory was no longer scattered, but more closely involved in the entire theoretical system and the overall school of thought. The fundamental theory was more accurately grasped, the basic analysis tools were applied more skillfully, and the new frontier disciplines of the development of modern economics were further introduced and understood. The borrowing and application of modern Western economics for reference was more rational and practical. With the deepening of China's economic market-oriented reform, the application value of Western economics to explain and predict actual economic operations became more evident. Another example was the integration of Marxist and Western economics in China in the 1990s. The characteristics of Western economics in terms of research objects, basic hypotheses and theoretical frameworks, and the research methods that sought to make every economic category do quantitative analysis had a profound impact on China's economic ideological circles. In addition, the highly abstract force, rigorous logical reasoning, and thorough analysis of economic and interest relations among people in social and economic life went beyond Western economics. From this perspective, the integration of the two theoretical systems in the 1990s was not only the intersection and absorption of several categories and concepts (such as adding the categories of equilibrium price, opportunity cost, utility function, consumption function, multiplier principle, market equilibrium, etc.) in the textbooks of socialist political economy, but also the drawing upon, intersection with, and integration of the basic theoretical framework, analysis methods, and basic category system. It was true that Marxist and Western economics were two distinct theoretical paradigms. Although they both study human social and economic issues, due to different theoretical perspectives, their research objects and methods, basic category system, theoretical framework, and content were quite different. This difference was not the difference between various schools in the same theoretical system, but the difference between the two theoretical systems. From the perspective of scientific development, although the two theoretical systems met and integrated in China in the 1990s, they were not integrated into the same framework.

In brief, in the 1990s, Chinese economists developed China's economic thought to a new level with more solid professional training, more rational thinking, and more in-depth research.

In the late 1980s and early 1990s, China's economy entered the period of "governance and rectification." The main issues discussed and studied by economic and ideological circles were the reform of the state-owned system, inflation, the speed of economic growth, and the orientation and path of economic system reform. In 1992, Deng Xiaoping's talk during his Southern Tour prompted Chinese economic and ideological circles to become active again. From the perspective of economic thought, the theoretical innovation in Deng Xiaoping's talk mainly focused on two issues. One was the scientific summary of the essence of socialism, pointing out that the essence of socialism was to liberate and develop productive forces, eliminate exploitation and polarization, and ultimately achieve common prosperity. The other was the exposition of the socialist market economy, which held that the fundamental difference between socialism and capitalism did not lie in whether it was planning- or market-dominant. A planned economy was not equal to socialism, as capitalism had plans, while the market economy was not equal to capitalism, as socialism similarly had a market, thus planning and the market were both economic means. In the first half of the 1990s, Chinese economic and ideological circles mainly discussed these two issues and other basic theoretical issues deriving from them. They conducted a great deal of research work and published many valuable findings.

The important theoretical issues discussed and studied in this period included the essence of socialism, the standard of productive forces, the ownership and the dominant position of public ownership, the private economy and the joint-stock economy, the nature of the market economy (capitalist or socialist), the property right reforms of state-owned enterprises, and the path of economic reform. These were not new propositions, but because the development of China's economic thought was restricted by strong ideological and political factors, these basic theoretical issues were constantly raised and discussed in different ideological and political environments.

Although frequent discussions may have failed to make different or opposite views converge, and even aroused hot-tempered assaults, they helped eliminate some conceptual and ideological barriers and pushed forward the development of economic theory research.

In addition to these fundamental theoretical issues, the economic and ideological circles also carried out in-depth study on the law of economic operation research. In the first half of the 1990s, China's continuous rapid economic growth led to serious inflation. On June 24, 1993, the Central Committee of the Communist Party of China and the State Council jointly issued the Opinions on the Current Economic Situation and Strengthening Macro-control, which began to implement macro-control over the national economy. In this economic context, people in the economic community aired their respective views on topics such as inflation, unemployment, economic growth, the bubble economy, and macro control means, and they published a series of research results. A considerable part of these achievements were valuable for policy advisory and played an important role in the formulation and implementation of macroeconomic policies.

In the second half of the 1990s, with the deepening of China's economic market-oriented reform, relying on their solid knowledge of Marxist economics and Western economics, a group of young and mid-career economists studied the development of China's economic thought and put forward some fundamental issues concerning the development of economic thought from a new perspective, such as the modernization of Chinese economics, China's economic roots, the Chinese School of economics, and China's transitional economics. Some scholars regarded the socialist political economy, the mainstream of China's economic thought guided by Marxism, as "traditional economics." They thought that the defects of traditional economics in theory and method were responsible for its failure to explain and predict the economic reality, pushing it into a serious crisis. The crisis of traditional theory provided an opportunity for the modernization of economics, making it necessary to summarize and criticize the traditional theory so as to open up its own development path and create and develop new theories. Some scholars believed that China's economic thought was based on the integration of classical economics, modern economics, Marxist economics, and Chinese traditional economic thought and that China's economics should have its own independent cultural value and the "practical value" of serving China's economy. As China's market-oriented reform furthered, some economists put forward the concept of "transitional economics," a theory of the transition from a planned economy to a market economy which could be taken as a branch of institutional transformation theory. Scholars in other countries studied the social and economic system changes in Russia and other Eastern European countries, attempting to summarize the general framework of the transition from a planned economy to a market economy. Inspired by this, some Chinese scholars (including overseas Chinese scholars) took China's economic reform process as their research subject and explored the track and characteristics of China's market-oriented reform. Because China's reform path had distinct characteristics compared with those of Russia and other Eastern European countries, the sustained rapid economic growth aroused the great interest of economists at home and abroad after the reform. Therefore, China's "transitional economics" was considered to be very promising, and many people even asserted that if a theoretical framework could be provided with standard economic language and methods for the furtherance of in-depth research into China's economic reform after the adoption of the reform policy, the results would have universal value.

Since the mid-1990s, another important landscape in the field of economics has been the emphasis on the study of the history of economic theories and the retrospection of the cultural characteristics and humanistic implications of China's economic thought. This phenomenon is related to the vigorous rise of academic history research in China since the 1990s. The rise of the study of academic history was not only a cultural reflection on the "end of the century," but more importantly, it showed the mature trend of Chinese philosophy and social science research and reflected the serious thinking of Chinese intellectuals on the academic value and essence, as well as the rational exploration of academic humanities and cultural tradition. From the perspective of economics, some scholars investigated the characteristic thought of China's economic theory against the background of traditional Chinese ideology and culture and explored its historical and cultural traditions, while others examined the historical blending of Chinese and Western academic cultures from the perspective of world economics history, trying to prove the due position of ancient Chinese economic thought in the history of world economic theories, and still others were committed to correcting the biased "Scientism" of economics to turn it back to the track of the classical "Humanities" academic norms. It aimed at elevating economics from empiricism and instrumental rationality to "ideology" – the logical form of scientific rationality, or at least to include humanities. The publishing of research on this academic history showed that China's academic research was gradually aligning itself with international academic circles in terms of academic norms, subject classification, knowledge system, academic language, analytical methods, and other aspects of an academic nature and expression, demonstrating the requirements of the times for further strengthening academic exchanges between China and foreign countries and for academic integration with the rest of the world.

In the 1990s, the introduction, research, and application of Western economics presented a new scene. First, throughout the 1990s, new institutional economics was a hot spot in the introduction and research of Western economics. There were specific reasons why new institutional economics attracted great attention in China from the perspective of methodology. Western classical and neoclassical economics generally regarded economic growth as a function of capital investment and technological progress. In this sort of model, the property right and economic systems were viewed as an established factor or exogenous variable. New institutional economics believed that institutional innovation had a great impact on economic development and that modern society relied on the property right mechanism or property right system, which could provide effective incentives or constraints to reduce waste, so that scarce resources could be effectively allocated. This theory held that institutional change (rather than technological change) was the more essential source of income growth, and it introduced institutional change as an endogenous variable into the analytical framework of modern economics. This theory was of great significance and application value to China in the process of institutional change.

Second, in the 1990s, Chinese economic and ideological circles attached great importance to the introduction of the cutting edge theories of Western economics, such as endogenous economic growth theory, information economics and incentive theory, game theory, public choice theory, resource economics, enterprise capital structure theory, option pricing theory, capital market efficiency theory, auction theory, neoclassical economics, new institutional economics and development, and other cutting edge theories of economics. Admittedly, compared with the development of foreign economics, there was still a big gap in the introduction of and research on cutting edge disciplines of Western economics in China. Unlike the situation in which Chinese economic circles favored the Keynesian mainstream school in the 1980s, after the 1990s Neo-liberal economic theories, such as those of the modern monetary school, the rational expectation school, and the London School, aroused great interest among Chinese economists, especially Hayek's economic theory, which was highly commended by some young and mid-career economists, and quoting Hayek's remarks became the fashion. On the one hand, this situation was related to the "revival" of liberal economics or conservative economics in Western countries after the 1980s. On the other hand, it was also the reflection of some Chinese economists' ideas of accelerating market-oriented reform and reducing government intervention in the economy. The popularity of neo-liberal economics in China implied that people were beginning to doubt whether economic modernization could be achieved by relying on government management and intervention and whether centralized decision-making was contrary to the process of democratization. From the perspective of the development of China's economic thought, this was a change worthy of attention.

Finally, in the mid and late 1990s, great progress was made in the application of Western economics. Many economists used the theories, methods, and analytical tools of Western economics to study China's economy. This tendency of "Westernization" was seen in most of the literature on China's economy and economic reform. In some research literature, the theory and method of Marxist and Western economics were used at the same time, peacefully coexisting. This situation in economic research was consistent with the trend of the integration and development of Marxist and Western economics in China, analyzed alongside the development principles mentioned above.

It is true that there remained different views on Western economics. In the second half of the 1990s, there was a great debate about Western economics in China. In view of the attitude of many young and mid-career economists toward Western economics and their "Westernization" complex, based on the viewpoint and position of defending Marxist economics, other economists used the tools of class analysis to criticize the class vindication of Western economics and the defects of some assumptions, categories, and theories and to point out that merely copying Western economics would not solve China's economic problems, nor could China's economic development follow the path of Western economics. Rather, China should adhere to Marxism and develop a socialist political economy. The opposing view was that the theory and method of traditional socialist political economy were weak in explaining real-world economic operations, and the "laws" it revealed were not quite relevant to social and economic activities. This view held that the development of China's economic thought should thus shift from the revision to the criticism and reconstruction of the system and advocated using the basic assumptions, theoretical framework, and research methods of Western economics to construct Chinese economics, and even opposed the proposition of "Chinese economics" and "Western economics" altogether. This academic debate was not only a normal phenomenon but also a manifestation of a high level of academic freedom.

4. On the Development of Economic Thought in the People's Republic of China in the Early 21st Century

In early 21st century, the development of China's economic thought presented some new characteristics. First, economic theory research gave more attention to the hot issues of China's industrialization development and economic reform, such as macroeconomic operations and control, regional economy and regional planning, monetary policy and income distribution, and the agricultural economy and rural construction. The development of the social economy put forward more urgent requirements for economic theory's functions of interpretation and prediction. In addition, the debate over ideas in economic ideological circles switched from a conceptual debate to economic policy and even the reform path. With the intensification of Reform and Opening Up, the social strata were divided, the income gap widened, and the social contradictions intensified at some points, which led to debate in economic and ideological circles over whether to adhere to the Reform and Opening Up policy, to the development of socialist market economy to achieve common prosperity, or to attribute some contradictions in the process of social and economic development to the production relations and economic system constructed by Reform and Opening Up. Both sides of the debate tried to influence high-level decision-making and the process of Reform and Opening Up. Finally, the introduction and application of Western economics gave closer attention to cutting edge theories, such as theoretical innovation of the "new economy," theories of behavioral finance and mathematical finance, modern monetary theory, modern enterprise financing theory, the financial bubble theory, new economic geography and new trade theory, and human capital and income distribution theory. These economic theories were not only cutting edge, but also met the actual needs of China's economic and social development, reflecting the theoretical frontier and policy application characteristics of China's introduction of Western economics.

From the perspective of policy, at the beginning of the 21st century, the Communist Party of China held the Sixteenth National Congress (in November 2002) and the Seventeenth National Congress (in October 2007), and the CPC Central Committee and the State Council formulated the Tenth Five-Year Plan for national economic and social development (2001–2005) and the Eleventh Five-Year Plan (2006–2010). The Sixteenth National Congress of the Communist Party of China established the important thought of the "Three Represents," alongside Marxism, Leninism, Mao Zedong Thought, and Deng Xiaoping Theory, as the guiding ideology that the Communist Party of China must adhere to for a prolonged period and put forward the goal of building an overall moderately well-off society. The Third Plenary Session of the Sixteenth Central Committee of the

Communist Party of China (in October 2003) adopted the Decision of the Central Committee of the Communist Party of China on Several Issues Concerning the Improvement of the Socialist Market Economic System, a programmatic document guiding the reform of China's economic system. The Sixth Plenary Session of the Sixteenth Central Committee of the Communist Party of China (in October 2006) adopted the Decision of the Central Committee of the Communist Party of China on Several Major Issues Concerning the Construction of a Harmonious Socialist Society, which launched a specific comprehensive deployment for the construction of a socialist harmonious society proposed at the Sixteenth National Congress of the CPC, the Fourth Plenary Session of the Sixteenth Central Committee, and the Fifth Plenary Session of the Sixteenth Central Committee. The Seventeenth National Congress of the Communist Party of China comprehensively expounded the scientific connotation, spiritual essence, and fundamental requirements of the scientific outlook on development, unanimously agreed to put the scientific outlook on development into the Party Charter, and put forward new requirements for achieving the goal of building an overall moderately prosperous society. The report of the Seventeenth National Congress of the Communist Party of China emphasized that the key to achieving the development goal of building a moderately prosperous society by 2020 was to make significant progress in accelerating the transformation of the mode of economic development and improving the socialist market economic system. It was necessary to improve the understanding of the laws of the socialist market economy, give full play to the basic role of the market in the allocation of resources, and form a macro-control system conducive to scientific development. On December 18, 2008, the CPC Central Committee held a meeting to commemorate the 30th anniversary of the Third Plenary Session of the Eleventh CPC Central Committee. It affirmed the important position and great significance of the Third Plenary Session of the Eleventh CPC Central Committee, summarized the great achievements and experiences of Reform and Opening Up and socialist modernization construction over the previous thirty years, and clearly pointed out the direction of further promoting the cause of Reform and Opening Up. These guiding ideology, principles, and policies not only put forward new content for the study of economic thought and economic theory, but also opened up a new theoretical realm for China's economic thought.

From 2008 to 2009, the world economy encountered the most serious financial crisis since the beginning of the 21st century, and also the most serious financial and economic crisis since the Great Depression of the 1930s. The global financial crisis triggered by the US subprime mortgage crisis not only impacted the free market economic system, but also challenged liberal economic thought. After the financial crisis, many scholars in China and abroad believed that the economic system and development model of the United States and the West were out of date. Some even put forward the view that the capitalist market economy was on the verge of extinction, and that China's economic system and development model could save the world.

The world financial crisis in 2008 had a considerable impact on the development of China's economic thought as well. One of the core issues was whether the cognition of the theoretical system of the market economy was reversed and whether the direction of China's reform would change. If the nature of the financial crisis was the failure of the market economy, then China's reform goal of establishing a socialist market economy must be revised. In terms of the relevant views in 2008 and 2009, most of the commentators offered a rational analysis and determined that China could not doubt the fundamental market economic system because of the problems in it. Financial crisis, economic crisis, and economic cyclical fluctuations were the normal operation of the market economy, and in response to these economic crises, human society could improve the market economic system through system design, instead of returning to the regulatory economy and planned economy system. In 1929, the collapse of the American stock market triggered the world economic depression in the 1930s. The US government promulgated the Securities Act in 1933 and the Securities Exchange Act in 1934, and established the Securities Regulatory Commission, granting it great power. In 1940, the Investment Company Act and the Investment Advisory Act were promulgated. These laws perfected the market economy system and made the United States the most developed market economy in the world. In 1990, the US economy accounted for about 50% of the world's economy, and in 2008 it still accounted for 23.1%. The market economy was, then, the most efficient economic system designed by human society to that point, although it was not perfect. There was no other way for China to enable nearly 1.4 billion people to live a prosperous life except to develop the market economy.

The world financial crisis in 2008 also triggered additional thinking on the level of China's economic thought, raising the question of whether China's export-oriented economic growth model would be sustainable after Reform and Opening Up. The export-oriented economy relied on exports and international markets (especially the markets of developed countries), forming an international trade and economic relationship between Chinese production (the so-called "world factory") and consumption of Western countries. After the financial crisis, many theorists pointed out that the growth of an economy highly dependent on foreign trade and insufficient domestic demand was unsustainable. China's economy was a big country's economy, and the basis of sustainable economic growth was domestic demand. Therefore, it was important to expand domestic demand, build a consumption-oriented society, and transform the growth mode into domestic demand-oriented economic growth. China lacked the basic social systems needed by a consumer society, such as a social security system, a medical and health system, and a national education system, so it was important for the government to strive to increase the supply of relevant public goods, which was also an important institutional condition for China to become a modern country. The discussion on China's economic growth mode and economic development goal resulting from the financial crisis indicated that the thinking of China's economic ideological circles was profound, fully embodying the social function of "experiencing the world in the practice" of economics. However, from the perspective of economic empirical analysis, China's economic growth model was fundamentally determined by considerations such as factor endowment conditions, the international division of labor system, and China's institutional conditions. In order to discuss the transformation of economic growth mode, it was necessary to construct an analytical framework under these constraints and derive reliable and explanatory conclusions from it.

In October 1992, the report of the Fourteenth National Congress of the Communist Party of China put forward that the goal of economic system reform was to establish and improve the socialist market economic system. The purpose was to make the market play a fundamental role in the allocation of resources under the macro-control of socialist countries and to allocate resources to the links with better benefits. In October 2003, the Third Plenary Session of the Sixteenth Central Committee of the Communist Party of China passed the Decision on Several Issues Concerning the Improvement of the Socialist Market Economic System, which put forward the objectives and tasks of improving the socialist market economic system and demanded that the basic role of the market in the allocation of resources be given greater play. In October 2007, the report of the Seventeenth National Congress of the Communist Party of China proposed that in order to promote the sound, rapid development of the national economy, it was necessary to deepen the understanding of the law of the socialist market economy, give better play to the basic role of the market in the allocation of resources, and form a macro-control system conducive to scientific development. With the advancement of the reform of the socialist market economy system, the research on resource allocation optimization became an important manifestation of the transformation of China's economic thought research in the early 2000s. Resource allocation and efficiency analysis had always been a central topic in economics. The general process of economic activities was to produce products and services and to meet the basic needs and development needs of human society through exchange. Economic empirical research aimed to analyze how to improve the efficiency of resource allocation and further meet the needs of human society under the assumption of scarcity of resources (economic scale). Efficiency analysis formed the basis of microeconomics, because the main idea of effective resource allocation could be expressed in the simplest form of a linear production activity analysis model. Therefore, economic efficiency and resource allocation efficiency were synonyms. When studying the efficiency of an economic system, the main concern was whether the resources were optimally allocated between different production purposes, so as to meet people's various needs to the maximum extent. China's economic circles took resource allocation as the main research objective, which would inevitably lead to more empirical research methods.

In the first decade of the 21st century, the establishment and improvement of the socialist market economy was the main line of economic system reform and of research on economic theory. It was a process moving from a non-market economy to a market economy, and the corresponding period was an economic transition or shifting period. China's economy in the transition or shifting period had its own characteristics in terms of system, which included 1) traits of an economic foundation and conditions in the transition from a planned economy to a market economy, 2) the growth and decline and coordination between a traditional economy and a modern economy in the transformation of a dual economic structure, 3) the contradiction, combination, growth, and decline of planned regulation and market regulation in economic operations, 4) traits of economic activities such as production, distribution, exchange, consumption, and investment in the process of the transformation of the system, and 5) traits of the relationship between the government and the market in the system transformation. Determined by these characteristics, China's economic system faced the problem of a "double failure," that is, both market and government failure. On the one hand, the market system was not perfect, the market mechanism was not developed, and the market could not fully and effectively regulate the allocation of resources and economic operations. On the other hand, the regulatory effect of the planned mechanism was gradually weakened, but the role of the government in the market economy needed to be transformed, and the government's social management and macro-control functions needed to be more effective. This "double failure" was a unique institutional risk in the period of economic transition. Therefore, in the process of market-oriented reform, how to better play the role of the government was not only a reform task, but also an important topic for economic research. Market economy and government intervention complemented each other. On the one hand, economic, scientific, and effective government intervention provided an important guarantee for the healthy operation of the market economy. On the other hand, the sound market system, the standardization of market transactions, and the development of the market mechanism were the basis for improving the efficiency of government intervention. In the reform of the socialist market economy system, in order to develop the market economy, it was important to reduce administrative intervention to the economy, while the imperfection of the market economy system needed to resort to administrative means, thus curbing the natural formation and development of the market system. In discussing the market economy, it was important to study the goals, means, and effects of government intervention under the conditions of an underdeveloped market in theory, system, and operation, so as to realize the basic, decisive role of the market in the allocation of resources and give better play to the role of the government.

In the early 2000s, the exploration of the socialist political economy system made some progress. In April 2004, the project of Marxist theoretical research and construction was launched, the textbook compilation project of *Introduction to Marxist Political Economy* was launched, and a research group was set up. The textbook was put into nationwide use. The compilation and publication of the textbook was the basic work in the theoretical research and textbook construction of a political economy with Chinese characteristics.

In the early 2000s, China's economy grew rapidly. From 2000 to 2010, the average growth rate of the GDP was 10.36%. From the perspective of policy, rapid growth required China to build on the basis of improving the quality, optimizing the structure, and increasing efficiency, while taking a path of national economic development with both higher speed and better benefits. However, rapid economic growth and overheated aggregate demand also caused economic fluctuations, so the business cycle became a hot research field. In economics, the two concepts of growth and cycle were closely linked. Generally speaking, the market economy would fluctuate periodically. Empirical research on the world economy showed that the length of a business cycle was about eight to ten years. Although the increase of labor productivity brought about by the "new economy" made the economy grow continuously, the "new economy" could only deform the cycle, but not make it disappear. Due to the fluctuation of the technology industry cycle and the volatility of venture capital, the potential impact of the "new economy" was great. However, it was also argued that the interfering factors leading to economic fluctuations mainly came from the government's economic policies, especially monetary policies. In the long run, due to the existence of rational expectations, the change of money supply was expected, the price level would change correspondingly, and the actual money supply would remain unchanged, so such policies were invalid. But in the short term, if the change of money supply was not expected, it would cause economic fluctuation. In particular, when the price system was not perfect and the interest rate marketization was not realized, the information asymmetry caused by the money supply would have a great impact on the economy.

5. On the Development of Economic Thought in the People's Republic of China in the First Decade of the 21st Century

In November 2012, the report of the Eighteenth National Congress of the Communist Party of China issued a complete definition of socialism with Chinese characteristics, including the path of socialism with Chinese characteristics, the socialist system with Chinese characteristics, and the socialist institution with Chinese characteristics, which were unified in the great practice of socialism with Chinese characteristics. The Eighteenth National Congress of the Communist Party of China put forward the goal of building an overall moderately well-off society and comprehensively deepening Reform and Opening Up by 2020. It was necessary to speed up the improvement of the socialist market economic system and comprehensively intensify the reform of the economic system. The core issue of economic system reform was to deal with the relationship between the government and the market, give full play to the basic role of the market in resource allocation to a greater extent and in a wider scope, improve the open economic system, and promote more efficient, fair, sustainable economic development. The report of the Eighteenth National Congress of the Communist Party of China (CPC) for the first time described the core issues of economic system reform as it dealt with the relationship between the government and the market, more respect for market laws, and gave better play to the role of the government, making it clear that the improvement of the open economic system was an important part of the improvement of the socialist market economic system, reflecting the requirements for the interaction between the deepening of economic reform, the expansion of opening up, and the intensification of reform.

In November 2013, the Third Plenary Session of the Eighteenth CPC Central Committee adopted the Decision of the CPC Central Committee on Several Major Issues on Comprehensively Deepening the Reform, proposing that the overall goal of expansive deepening of reform was to improve and develop the socialist system with Chinese characteristics and promote the modernization of the national governance system and capacity. Economic system reform was the key point of overall deepening of reform. The core issue was to handle the relationship between the government and the market, so that the market could play a decisive role in the allocation of resources and give better play to the role of the government. The decision expressed the core issue of economic system reform to make the market play a decisive role in resource allocation and better play the role of the government, and it clearly defined the responsibilities and functions of the government.

In October 2017, the report of the Nineteenth National Congress of the Communist Party of China stated that socialism with Chinese characteristics had entered a new era, which was the new historical orientation of China's development. The main social contradiction in China had been transformed into the contradiction between the people's growing need for a better life and unbalanced, inadequate development. The thought of socialism with Chinese characteristics in the new era further clarified that the overall goal of comprehensively deepening the reform was to improve and develop the socialist system with Chinese characteristics and promote the modernization of the national governance system and capacity. The Nineteenth National Congress of the Communist Party of China proposed the implementation of the new development concept and the building of a modern economic system. The construction of a modern economic system included six tasks: 1) deepening the supply side structural reform, 2) accelerating the construction of an innovative country, 3) implementing the rural revitalization strategy, 4) implementing the regional coordinated development strategy, 5) accelerating the improvement of the socialist market economic system, and 6) promoting the formation of a new pattern of comprehensive opening up. In regards to speeding up the improvement of the socialist market economic system, the report of the Nineteenth National Congress of the Communist Party of China made it clear that the reform of the economic system must focus on the improvement of the property rights system and the market-oriented allocation of factors, so as to realize effective incentive of property rights, free flow of factors, flexible price response, fair and orderly competition, and survival of the fittest enterprises. It was necessary to deepen the reform of the commercial system, break the administrative monopoly, prevent market monopolies, speed up the market-oriented reform of factor prices, relax the access restrictions of service industries, and improve the market supervision system.

In the first decade of the 21st century, with the process of China's Reform and Opening Up, especially the process of improving the socialist market economic system, the social practice of expanding the opening up and deepening the reform provided many practical subjects and new requirements for economic research and promoted the sustained prosperity and development of China's economic thought.

With the advancement of the reform of the socialist market economy system, the optimization of resource allocation continued to be the main substance of China's economic research in the first decade of the 21st century. China's economic thought, especially the socialist political economy, involved the important transformation performance of the main research object or research content turning to resource allocation. This performance not only showed that China's economic research was closer to real economic operations under the guidance of the social practice of Reform and Opening Up, but also demonstrated the transformation of research methods of the socialist political economy, to a certain extent. Economic empirical research aimed to study how to improve the efficiency of resource allocation and meet the needs of human society to a greater degree under the assumption of a scarcity of resources. China's economic thought and socialist political economy took resource allocation as the main research objective, which was a demonstration of the transformation from normative research to empirical research.

The reform of state-owned enterprises involved the micro structure of the socialist market economy, which remained the focus of policy and theoretical research in the first decade of the 21st century. From August 2014 to July 2018, the Central Committee of the Communist Party of China and the State Council issued 11 documents on the reform of state-owned enterprises, including the Reform Plan for the Salary System of the Principal Persons in Charge of the Central Management Enterprises (on August 18, 2014); Some Opinions on Upholding the Party's Leadership and Strengthening the Party's Construction in Deepening the Reform of State-owned Enterprises, and On Strengthening and Improving the Party's Construction Opinions on Supervising and Preventing the Loss of State-owned Assets in Enterprises (June 5, 2015); Guiding Opinions of the CPC Central Committee and the State Council on Deepening the Reform of State-owned Enterprises (September 13, 2015); Guiding Opinions on Defining and Classifying the Functions of State-owned Enterprises (October 13, 2015); State-owned Assets Supervision and Administration Commission of the State Council on Capital Management, the Plan to Promote the Transformation of Functions (December 5, 2016); the Implementation Plan for the Corporate System Reform of Central Enterprises (June 26, 2017); the Opinions on Reforming the Wage Determination Mechanism of State-owned Enterprises (March 28, 2018); the Guiding Opinions on Strengthening the Assets and Liabilities Constraints of State-owned Enterprises, and Regulations on Personnel Management of the Leaders of Central Enterprises (May 11, 2018); and Implementation Opinions on Promoting Pilot Reform of State-owned Capital Investment and Operating Companies (July 30, 2018). In the first decade of the 21st century, especially after the Nineteenth National Congress of the Communist Party of China, the key direction of the reform of state-owned enterprises was to continuously deepen the reform of the system and mechanism, including the reform of state-owned assets management systems focusing on state-owned capital investment and operating companies, the reform of property rights structure and system focusing on the reform of mixed ownership, and the reform of legal entity governance structure and management system with the focus on the corporate system. Regarding the reform of state-owned enterprises, economic circles carried out research from different angles and methods and put forward many viewpoints. From the perspective of the institutional framework of the market economy, the main line of the study can be summarized as follows: on the basis of vigorously promoting market construction, the guarantee of system reform is given in law and policy, so that the ownership structure, property right structure, enterprise system, and state-owned asset management system can be adjusted and reformed in a timely way, which is related to the degree of economic marketization development and the optimization of resource allocation so that economic operation requirements are consistent.

The report of the Eighteenth National Congress of the Communist Party of China clearly defined handling the relationship between the government and the market as the core issue of the economic system reform, making it clear that deepening the reform of administrative examination and approval was one of the main tasks to promote the reform of the political system, and clearly defining the transformation of government functions was central to social management and public services. This reflected the reform requirements for the acceleration of the improvement of the socialist market economic system and the greater, wider play of the basic role and decisive role of the market in resource allocation. Thus, under the condition of the socialist market economy, the transformation of government functions, innovation, and improvement of macro-control became the main topics of economic thought research in the first decade of the 21st century. Chinese economists generally believed that in the process of China's transition from a planned economy to a socialist market economy, the development of the market system needed a long historical stage, and the micro basis and institutional conditions for the allocation of resources by price mechanism needed to be improved gradually. Under such conditions, in order to avoid a major shock in the process of economic and social transformation, to maintain stable and rapid economic growth, and to implement favorable guidance for economic and social development, the government needed to strengthen and improve macro-control and better play its role.

There were three kinds of research methods in the field of economic thought. The first was policy interpretation, the second was normative research, and the third was empirical research on a certain topic. The views of the discussion differed and even conflicted, but they were all based on the understanding and vision of China's socialist market economic system reform, with a strong touch of localization. The consensus in the discussion was that the transformation of government functions should include both action and inaction. Action meant that the government should undertake its own responsibilities, such as increasing investment in social fields, human capital investment, ensuring social equity and justice, playing a fundamental role in providing public goods and services, and ensuring the equalization of social public services. The results suggested that the ratio of government public service expenditure to total government expenditure increased by 1 percentage point, and the resident consumption rate increased by 0.2 percentage point. Inaction meant that the government should reduce its intervention in micro economic activities, especially in the market access side, relax regulations, break monopolies, reduce examination and approval, improve the efficiency of supervision during and after the event, and improve the efficiency of economic operations.

From the Seventeenth, Eighteenth, and Nineteenth National Congress of the Communist Party of China, major adjustments were made in the economic development strategy, the core element of which was for China to shift from a high-speed growth stage to a high-quality development stage and realize the transformation of the development mode of optimizing the economic structure and transforming the growth momentum. Economic development, economic growth, structural adjustment, and development transformation had always been hot issues in China's economic circles. With the proposal of development strategy and new development concept in the new era, the research on this topic deepened in the first decade of the 21st century. An important topic in the discussion was the relationship between investment and consumption. In the discussion on the transformation of China's economic development, a common view was that an important part of economic transformation and development was to transform economic growth from investment driven to consumption driven. In terms of economic policy, it was important to implement corresponding leverage and measures to increase residents' income and expand domestic demand, so that China's economic growth could change from mainly relying on investment to mainly relying on consumption. This view was not very accurate in theory. Consumption was very important, and could even be considered the purpose of economic development, but consumption was not a variable of production function, nor an element of economic growth, so there was no concept of consumption driving economic growth in economic theory. The most important variable determining consumption was income (disposable income). The consumption function represented the level of consumption expenditure at each income level. It was income growth (economic growth) that determined consumption level, not consumption level that determined economic growth, and it was the level of disposable income that determined the consumption level of residents. The level of disposable income was determined not only by the structure of the national income distribution, but also by economic growth. Economic theory states that capital accumulation and investment are the main sources and driving forces of economic growth. Under the condition of fixed investment efficiency, physical capital investment is the main factor of income and social welfare growth. Assuming the efficiency of economic system (resource allocation efficiency) is fixed, the determinants of economic growth are capital accumulation (investment), labor, and technological progress. Under certain conditions, these three elements can to a certain degree be substituted, but in the process of productivity formation, capital investment plays a key role. Both the improvement of labor productivity and technological progress depend on the support of capital investment. Investment determines the growth rate of physical capital stock in the economy, which in turn determines the long-term economic growth and production rate. There are only two kinds of production factors, capital and labor, in the function of production. In a developing economy, due to the shortage of capital and labor force, the incremental capital-output ratio is relatively low, while that in an advanced economy is relatively high.

This indicates that with the development of a country's economy, under the condition of a fixed investment efficiency rate, the incremental capital-output ratio tends to rise. One implication of the policy is that to maintain the continuous growth of the economy, it is necessary to push it to grow from the stage of underdevelopment to that of development, with the incremental capital-output ratio increasing. On the whole, China remains in the primary stage of socialism and in the process of industrialization and urbanization, even in the early 2020s. At this stage of economic development, the increase of capital goods accumulation (investment) is necessary. If China is unable to keep the steady growth of per capita investment level, productivity will decline, and the economy will not continue to grow. For both the improvement of labor productivity and technological progress, investment is fundamental. In particular, there is a large number of new labor employment every year, so there must be corresponding investment growth to provide production equipment and technical means. The key link in China's economic transformation and development is not to reduce the investment rate, but to follow the law of the market economy, allocate and use capital more effectively, improve investment efficiency, and make an equal amount of capital promote more national income growth. The report of the Nineteenth

National Congress of the Communist Party of China accurately defined structural adjustment and reform as supply side structural reform, taking it as the main line of implementing the new development concept and building a modern economic system, which was in line with the development status and transformation development requirements of China. In order to solve the structural contradiction between supply and demand imbalance, only by promoting the supply side structural reform, putting the focus of economic development on the real economy, and taking improving the quality of the supply system as the main direction of attack would significant improvement in the quality of China's economic development be made, which would better meet the people's growing needs for a better life.

In the first decade of the 21st century, China's socialist political economy construction entered a new stage. On November 23, 2015, at the CPC Central Committee Politburo Collective Learning Conference, Xi Jinping pointed out that based on its national conditions and development practice, China should reveal new characteristics and new laws, refine and summarize the regular results of its economic development practice, upgrade practical experience to systematic theory, and constantly open up a new realm of contemporary Marxist political economics. On May 17, 2016, Xi Jinping hosted a Forum on Philosophy and Social Sciences, emphasizing the need to speed up the construction of philosophy and social sciences with Chinese characteristics. In accordance with the ideas of establishing a foothold in China, drawing upon the experience of other countries, digging into history, grasping the contemporary, care for humanity, and facing the future, China should strive to build its philosophy and social sciences with its own guiding ideology, discipline system, academic system, and discourse. The system fully embodied Chinese characteristics, style, and mindsets. After Xi Jinping's speeches on China's Marxist political economics, philosophy, and social sciences with Chinese characteristics were published, economic academic circles launched a heated discussion on the topic of China's socialist political economy. The research involved the research object, logical starting point, fundamental method, theoretical attributes, guiding principle, and historical setting of the socialist political economy with Chinese characteristics and its position, theoretical source, practical basis, scientific connotation, theoretical innovation direction, and system construction evolution, among other similar topics. The general understanding presented in the literature was that the development performance, development path, and structural contradictions in China's Reform and Opening Up and the construction of socialism with Chinese characteristics were difficult to explain with the theory and paradigm of Western economics. It was thus important to combine China's development practice, national characteristics, and institutional conditions, develop Marxist economics under the guidance of Marxist economic principles, scientifically learn from Western economics, and construct a socialist political economy with Chinese characteristics.

Both a Marxist political economy and modern Western economics have their own conceptual and discourse systems, on which a theoretical system is formed. The two economic systems are different in conceptual and discourse systems, but they both originated from British classical political economy, so their conceptual and discourse system are cross blended. From the meaning of "original problem" or "genetics," a key topic is how to construct the conceptual and discourse systems of Chinese socialist political economy. Economics is a social science that explains economic phenomena and reveals laws of economic activities. As long as the economic phenomena and economic activities of human society have common features, economics will also have universal concepts, categories, discourses, and theories.

However, due to the different historical, economic, cultural, and political conditions of each economic society, there are differences in economic phenomena and economic activities, which reflect the differences in economic concepts, economic categories, economic discourse, and economic theory, each of which have their own characteristics. For this reason, the conceptual and discourse systems of the socialist political economy related to the socialist market economy are derived from Marxist political economy and Western market economy theories, combined with the practice of China's socialist market economy. In terms of discourse system and analytical framework, it is not only universal and general, but also necessarily different and unique. It should have good explanatory and prediction functions for China's socialist market economy, and it must be able to carry out international exchanges on the level of theoretical form.

PART ONE

The Construction of the Mainstream Form of Economic Thought in the People's Republic of China (1950s–1970s)

CHAPTER 1

The Constitution of Economic Thought and Theory in the People's Republic of China

1.1 Guidance of Marxist Political Economics

1. Introduction of Marxist Political Economics Before 1949

According to the research in academic circles, the time when Chinese people learned the terms Marxism and socialism can be traced back to the end of the nineteenth century. Some scholars defined some activities of the period between 1896 and 1904 as the earliest stages of the introduction of Marxist economic theory into China, including the early records of the Western socialist movement by Chinese people, the introduction of European socialism by Westerners in China, and the translation of Marxist theory.[1] The first complete translation of Marxist economic works published in China was Engels' *Socialism from Utopia to Scientific Development*, translated by Shi Renrong. It was originally serialized in the *New World* semimonthly in Shanghai in 1912 under the title "Ideal Socialism and the Implementation of Socialism." The New Culture Movement started in 1915 and the May 4th Movement in 1919 promoted the spread of Marxism in China. The New Culture Movement emphasized science and democracy and sought to expand this ideological concept from ideological fields to the construction of a new social moral foundation, code of conduct, and even social system. As an important factor, the New Culture Movement inspired the May 4th Movement in 1919. The May 4th Movement was mainly a patriotic movement with

---

1. Tan Min, *Looking Back on History: the Pre-history of Marxist Economics in China*, vol. 1 (Shanghai University of Finance and Economics Press, 2008), 85–143.

young students forming the main body, but it also carried the scientific and democratic demands of the New Culture Movement and spread the spirit of that movement into a wider social class. *New Youth*, which was founded in 1919, said in its inaugural declaration that the ideal new era and new society would be honest, progressive, positive, free, equal, creative, beautiful, good, peaceful, loving and helping each other, and with each person working and enjoying life and the entire society being happy.[2] The May 4th Movement and the October Revolution in 1918 led to a greater demand in China for the spread of Marxism in the field of ideological liberation and social change. In May 1919, the *Beijing Morning Post* (Supplement) started a column on "Marxist Studies," edited by Li Dazhao, and serialized the full translation of *Employed Labor and Capital,* which was the second complete translation of Marxist economic works in China.[3] In 1920, some Marxist research groups appeared in China, forming the basis for intellectuals at that time to become interested in Marxism and conduct research and begin disseminating Marxist ideas.[4] In 1921, the Communist Party of China was founded. Marxist parties in the true sense began to appear in China, and Marxist theory began to spread systematically in China. According to incomplete statistics, from the 1920s to 1940s, there were 222 translated works of Marxist economic theory, including a few classic philosophical ones, 48 in the 1920s, 110 in the 1930s, and 64 in the 1940s. Some classic works of Marxist economics, such as *Das Kapital, Value, Price and Profit, The Origin of Family Private Property and the State, Anti-Dühring, History of Surplus Value Theory,* and some works by Lenin, such as the *Development of Russian Capitalism* and *Imperialism,* were translated and published.[5]

After the founding of the People's Republic of China in 1949, Marxism became the guiding ideology for the construction and development of China's politics, economy, culture, and society. The introduction and research of Marxist political economics became more systematic and comprehensive, and ultimately became the main theoretical source and research content for the economic thought of the People's Republic of China.

2. The Guidance of the Basic Principles of Marxist Political Economics in China's Economic Thought

The basic principles of Marxist political economics include the surplus value theory and the scientific socialism theory. The theory of surplus value derives the theory of labor value from the abstract analysis of commodity production and reveals the basic contradiction of commodity production on the basis of scientific labor value theory. Labor value theory is the basic theory

---

2. Zhou Cezong, *The May 4th Movement: Ideological Movements in Modern China* (Stanford University Press, 1967), 174–175.

3. Hu Jichuang, *Outline of the History of Modern Chinese Economic Thought* (China Social Sciences Press, 1984), 433–436.

4. Arif Dirlik, *Anarchism in the Chinese Revolution* (Guangxi Normal University Press, 2006), 189.

5. Ding Shouhe et al., *From the May 4th Enlightenment to the Spread of Marxism* (Sanlian Bookstore, 1979), 162.

of Marxist political economics. Marx states that "to stamp an object of utility as a value is just as much a social product as language. The recent scientific discovery, that the products of labor, so far as they are values, are but material expressions of the human labor spent in their production, marks, indeed, an epoch in the history of the development of the human race."[6] The theory of surplus value reveals that the basic conditions of surplus value production are labor becoming commodity, the unity of labor process and value increment process in capitalist production process, the attribute and movement process of capital production relations, the historical trend of capital accumulation, the internal contradiction of capital accumulation, and the basic contradiction of the capitalist mode of the socialization of production and the means of production. The contradiction between the private ownership of humanism reveals that "the limitations and the merely historical, transitory character of the capitalist mode of production, [and] testifies that for the production of wealth, it is not an absolute mode, moreover, that at a certain stage it rather conflicts with its further development."[7]

The two theoretical cornerstones of scientific socialism are historical materialism and surplus value theory. The concept of historical materialism "is a revolutionary discovery not only for economics but also for all historical sciences."[8] Historical materialism reveals that the contradiction between productive forces and production relations and between the economic base and superstructure is the fundamental driving force of social development. The contradictory movement between productive forces and production relations constitutes the internal motivation of social development, while the contradiction between productive forces and relations of production leads to the change of mode of production. Human society will inevitably develop from capitalist society to socialist and communist society. The theory of surplus value reveals that the only purpose of capitalist production is to produce and increase surplus value. It stipulates the nature of capitalist production, distribution, exchange, and consumption. With the development of the basic contradiction of capitalist mode of production, it is an inevitable law of social and historical development that the social possession of the means of production must be realized in order to meet the requirements of production socialization. The theory of scientific socialism reveals and clarifies that it is an inevitable trend for human history to replace capitalism. The basic contradiction of capitalism determines that capitalism will inevitably perish, and the development of capitalism creates the material premise for the realization of socialism. It is a long and tortuous historical process for socialism to replace capitalism, and as Marx notes, "No social order ever perishes before all the productive forces for which there is room in it have developed; and new, higher relations of production never appear before the material conditions of their existence have matured in the womb of the old society itself."[9] The theory of scientific socialism also predicts and envisages future society. Based on the principle of historical materialism, the theory of scientific socialism discusses the law of the development of human society and holds that human society

---

6. Marx and Engels, *Complete Works of Marx and Engels,* vol. 23 (People's Publishing House, 1972), 91.

7. Marx and Engels, *Complete Works of Marx and Engels,* vol. 25 (People's Publishing House, 1974), 289.

8. Marx and Engels, *Selected Works of Marx and Engels,* vol. 2 (People's Publishing House, 1995), 38.

9. Marx and Engels, *Selected Works of Marx and Engels,* vol. 2 (People's Publishing House, 1995), 33.

is a historical process of progression from a lower to a higher stage. As a negation of the private property system, communism is also a long process of development. Communist society develops on the basis of capitalist productive forces. Marx notes, "But these defects are inevitable in the first phase of communist society, as it is when it has just emerged after prolonged birth pangs from capitalist society. Right can never be higher than the economic structure of society and its cultural development conditioned thereby."[10] On the basis of the continuous development of social productive forces, there is a gradual development to the advanced stage of communism. The essence of future society is the all-round development of human beings. *The Communist Manifesto* states, "In place of the old bourgeois society, with its classes and class antagonisms, we shall have an association in which the free development of each is the condition for the free development of all."[11] It further points to "the *marche generale* [general path] imposed by fate upon every people, whatever the historic circumstances in which it finds itself, in order that it may ultimately arrive at the form of economy which will ensure, together with the greatest expansion of the productive powers of social labour, the most complete development of man."[12]

The mainstream form of economic thought in the People's Republic of China has followed the two basic principles of the surplus value theory of Marxist political economics and the theory of scientific socialism when constructing its theoretical main line of the development stage. The theory of surplus value is mainly used to guide the research and analysis of the capitalist social economy, to grasp the general laws of the occurrence, development, and extinction of capitalism, and to grasp some laws of capitalist economic operation. The scientific socialist theory is mainly used to guide the research and analysis of the socialist social economy and to grasp the development law and present situation of socialist society, especially the socialist economy, and the development characteristics in different stages of development.

3. The Concept of the Basic Principles of Marxist Political Economics as the Main Content of Chinese Economic Thought

The concept of surplus value theory includes commodity and commodity production, labor and labor value theory, commodity and currency, the law of value, the historical trend of commodity production development, conditions of surplus value production and its relation to capital, the historical trend of capital accumulation, the basic contradiction between capital accumulation and the capitalist mode of production, the capitalist economic crisis and capital movement process, the distribution of surplus value, the general law of socialized production, the trend of socialized production, and capital socialization. This conceptual system involves commodity, the two factors of commodity, the duality of labor in producing commodity, the basic contradiction of commodity production, the determination of commodity value, social necessary labor time,

---

10. Marx and Engels, *Selected Works of Marx and Engels,* vol. 3 (People's Publishing House, 1995), 304.
11. Marx and Engels, S*elected Works of Marx and Engels,* vol. 1 (People's Publishing House, 1995), 294.
12. Marx and Engels, *Complete Works of Marx and Engels,* vol. 19 (People's Publishing House, 1963), 130.

the source of creating commodity value, commodity and currency, the substance and function of the law of value, commodity fetishism, labor commodity, labor processes, and value increment processes. It encompasses absolute surplus price value and relative surplus value, capital and capital composition, primitive accumulation of capital, capital accumulation and capital concentration, capital circulation and turnover, total social capital, the transformation form of capital and average social profit, loan capital and interest, land ownership and land rent, social production and consumption, and the main proportion in the realization of social reproduction. These main concepts constitute the concept system of surplus value theory and the theoretical framework of Marxist political economics. These concepts are the main content of the economic thought of the People's Republic of China, especially its socialist political economics. Of course, in different historical stages, the study of these concepts has differed in terms of theoretical depth and the degree of connection with the real economy.

The concept of scientific socialism theory includes productivity and relations of production, economic base and superstructure, the transformation of the production mode and development of human society, class and class struggle, the basic contradiction of capitalism, the private and social possession of the means of production, socialism and the proletarian revolution, the dictatorship of the proletariat, and the development stage of future society. These main concepts constitute the conceptual system of scientific socialism theory and are an important part of Marxist political economics. The theory of scientific socialism is connected with the theory of surplus value. Historical materialism and the theory of surplus value are the two theoretical cornerstones of the theory of scientific socialism. The theory of surplus value reveals the nature of capitalist production, distribution, exchange, and consumption, reveals the basic contradiction between the socialization of capitalist production and private possession of the means of production, and explains that it is an inevitable law of social historical development that the requirements of socialization of production must be met and the social ownership of the means of production must be realized. Chinese economic thought takes the concept of scientific socialist theory as the main research content. Through the research and deduction of the concept, it is evident that human society is a process of development from a low-level stage to a high-level stage, and it is an evolution process from non-comprehensive development to comprehensive development. It is the essential requirement of future society to realize the comprehensive, independent development of all humans.

1.2 The Socialist Political Economics of the Soviet Union as a Reference

1. Lenin's Political Economic Thought on Building Socialism

Lenin's new economic policy and socialist economic policy have had a long-term impact on China's economic thought. The basic content of the new economic policy was to replace the surplus grain collection system with a grain tax, mobilize farmers' enthusiasm for production, promote the recovery and development of agricultural production, and consolidate the industrial and agricultural alliance economically. It further aimed to change the practice of general nationalization of ownership, allow private enterprises to support the development of small-scale peasant economy, vigorously develop commerce, promote the circulation of industrial and agricultural products to meet the needs of urban and rural areas, strengthen international economic cooperation, make use of foreign funds, and introduce advanced Western technology and management methods, which were conducive to the recovery of the national economy.[13] Lenin's thought on the agricultural cooperative policy and the policy of realizing industrialization and electrification in the socialist economics had a significant influence on the formation of the mainstream form of China's economic thought. Lenin put forward a plan of using cooperatives to transform agriculture and lead peasants to the socialist path. He thought that in the Soviet Union, "since political power is in the hands of the working-class, since this political power owns all the means of production, the only task, indeed, that remains for us is to organize the population in cooperative societies."[14] The forms of cooperatives Lenin discussed included production cooperatives, credit cooperatives, sales cooperatives, and consumption cooperatives. He held that they provided a better way to carry out independent operations, with the family as the basic unit. Lenin attached great importance to industrialization and electrification, and he proposed that communism was the Soviet regime plus the electrification of the whole country, and that the only real foundation for building a socialist society was big industry. Only when the country had realized electrification and laid the technical foundation for modern large industry in industry, agriculture, and transportation could it gain total victory.[15] These ideas espoused as part of Lenin's economic policies were basically transformed into the practice of socialist construction in the Soviet Union, which not only had an important impact on China's economic thought, but also on China's socialist construction from the 1950s to the 1960s.

2. Stalin's Exposition on Socialist Political Economics

(1) On the Law of Socialist Political Economics
Stalin's work *Economic Problems of Socialism in the USSR* mainly focused on the economic laws under the socialist system. As for the nature of the economic law under the socialist system, Stalin emphasized the objective nature of the law of political economics under the socialist system, saying, "The same must be said of the laws of economic development, the laws of political economy—whether in the period of capitalism or in the period of socialism. Here, too, the laws of economic development, as in the case of natural science, are objective laws, reflecting processes

---

13. National Cadre Training Textbook Compilation and Review Guiding Committee, *Basic Issues of Marxism Leninism* (People's Publishing House, 2002), 345–346.

14. Lenin, *Selected Works of Lenin*, vol. 4 (People's Publishing House, 1995), 767.

15. Lenin, *Selected Works of Lenin*, vol. 4 (People's Publishing House, 1995), 796–797.

of economic development which take place independently of the will of man. Man may discover these laws, come to know them and, relying upon them, utilize them in the interests of society, impart a different direction to the destructive action of some of the laws, restrict their sphere of action, and allow fuller scope to other laws that are forcing their way to the fore-front; but he cannot destroy them or create new economic laws."[16] Stalin emphasized that Marxism holds that scientific laws are the reflection of objective processes that are not transferred by human will. People cannot change or abolish these laws, and they certainly cannot make or create new scientific laws. But the economic law has its own way of moving, which is not permanent, but changes with the changing conditions. Stalin goes on to say, "One of the distinguishing features of political economy is that its laws, unlike those of natural science, are impermanent, that they, or at least the majority of them, operate for a definite historical period, after which they give place to new laws. However, these laws are not abolished, but only lose their validity owing to the new economic conditions and depart from the scene in order to give place to new laws, laws which are not created by the will of man, but which arise from the new economic conditions."[17] Under the socialist system, the laws of political economics include that the relations of production must be suitable for the laws of the nature of productive forces and the laws of planned (proportional) development of the national economy. These are all objective laws, reflecting the regularity of the process of economic life that does not depend on the people's will. On the basis of expounding the law of socialist political economics, Stalin defined the basic law of the socialist economy. Its main characteristics and requirements are "the securing of the maximum satisfaction of the constantly rising material and cultural requirements of the whole of society through the continuous expansion and perfection of socialist production on the basis of higher techniques."[18] Stalin's exposition on the nature of the economic law under the socialist system and the basic economic law of socialism profoundly influenced the study of the socialist political economics in China. This influence is not only reflected in the research on socialist economic law system, but also in the dialectical unity of political economics research methods.

(2) Commodity Production Under the Socialist System

Stalin systematically discussed the law of commodity production and value under the socialist system in his *Economic Problems of Socialism in the USSR*. On the issue of commodity production under the socialist system, Stalin disapproved of the opposition of commodity production to public ownership and the linkage between commodity production and capitalism, saying, "Commodity production must not be regarded as something sufficient unto itself, something independent of the surrounding economic conditions. Commodity production is older than capitalist production. It existed in slave-owning society and served it, but did not lead to capitalism. It existed in feudal

---

16. Stalin, *Economic Problems of Socialism in the USSR* (People's Publishing House, 1952), 3.
17. Stalin, *Economic Problems of Socialism in the USSR* (People's Publishing House, 1952), 3.
18. Stalin, *Economic Problems of Socialism in the USSR* (People's Publishing House, 1952), 31.

society and served it, yet, although it prepared some of the conditions for capitalist production, it did not lead to capitalism. Why then, one asks, cannot commodity production similarly serve our socialist society for a certain period without leading to capitalism, bearing in mind that in our country commodity production is not so boundless and all-embracing as it is under capitalist conditions, being confined within strict bounds thanks to such decisive economic conditions as social ownership of the means of production, the abolition of the system of wage labour, and the elimination of the system of exploitation?"[19] According to *Economic Problems of Socialism in the USSR,* the reason for the existence of commodity production in the socialist economy was that the public ownership of the means of production had not yet been implemented, but only a part of the means of production was publicly owned. There were two basic forms of socialist production in the economy, state ownership by all the people and collective farms. Therefore, socialist commodity production was not ordinary commodity production, but special commodity production. It involved the commodities produced by the united socialist producers (the state, collective farms, and cooperatives), and its activities were limited to personal consumer goods. Obviously, it must not develop into capitalist production, and it was destined to serve the development and consolidation of socialist production together with its "monetary economy."[20] Stalin's discussions on the reasons for the existence of commodity production in the socialist economy (the exchange of ownership by the people and collective ownership), the scope of commodity production (limited to individual consumer goods), and the relationship between commodity circulation and monetary economy were discussed by Chinese economic and ideological circles from the 1950s to the 1970s, and even into the 1980s, and they formed the main theoretical basis and main topics of the relationship.

(3) On the Law of Value Under the Socialist System

Regarding the law of value under the socialist system, Stalin clearly pointed out that where there are commodities and commodity production, there cannot be no law of value, but under the socialist system, the scope of the law of value is limited. First of all, the law of value plays an important role in the circulation of commodities, the role of regulator within a certain range. In terms of socialist production, the law of value has no regulatory significance, but it has an impact on production. Because the consumer goods needed to compensate for the labor consumption in the production process are produced and sold as commodities and the goods are affected by the law of value, the enterprise's economic accounting, profit problems, cost problems, price problems, and other issues will be affected by the law of value, which has a practical significance. Stalin acknowledged the limited role of the law of value in the socialist economy, but stressed that the scope of the role of the law of value in the socialist economy was strictly limited, and it was especially unable to play the role of production regulator. He observed that "the law of value can be a regulator of production only under capitalism, with private ownership of the means of

---

19. Stalin, *Economic Problems of Socialism in the USSR* (People's Publishing House, 1952), 11.
20. Stalin, *Economic Problems of Socialism in the USSR* (People's Publishing House, 1952), 13.

production, competition, anarchy of production, and crises of overproduction. They forget that in our country the sphere of operation of the law of value is limited by the social ownership of the means of production, and by the law of balanced development of the national economy, and is consequently also limited by our yearly and five-yearly plans, which are an approximate reflection of the requirements of this law."[21] Stalin's exposition on the law of value under the socialist system also had a profound impact on China's economic thought. From the 1950s to the 1970s, research on the law of value under the socialist system in China's economic and ideological circles mainly focused on the status and role of the law of value in the socialist planned economy, the interaction between the law of value in the socialist economy and the law of planned and proportional development of the national economy, and the effect of the law of value on production and distribution in the socialist economy. The function of circulation was basically the category in *Economic Problems of Socialism in the USSR*. The argument that the law of value plays a limited role in the socialist economy also had an impact on China's economic policies and macro-control policies in the period of the planned economy.

(4) Industrialization Theories in Socialist Countries

Stalin's thought on industrialization in socialist countries arose from Lenin's thought on indus-
trialization and electrification and his theory of "two parallel and opposite world markets." For a socialist country with limited industrial development and an economic blockade from Western countries, it was necessary to implement independent industrialization. He wrote, "Encircled as it is by capitalism, the land of the dictatorship of the proletariat cannot remain economically independent if it does not itself produce instruments and means of production in its own country, if it remains stuck at a level of development where it has to keep its national economy tethered to the capitalistically developed countries, which produce and export instruments and means of production. To get stuck at that level would be to put ourselves in subjection to world capital."[22] Stalin's theory of industrialization in socialist countries especially emphasized "the production of the instruments and means of production," that is, the development of heavy industry. He said, "The keynote of the development of our national economy is industrialisation, the strengthening and development of our own heavy industry. This means that we have already established and are further developing our heavy industry, the basis of our economic independence."[23] Stalin's thought and policies on industrialization in socialist countries, such as developing an independent industrial system, giving priority to developing heavy industry, realizing industrialization at a high speed, and relying on internal accumulation of industrialization funds, all had an important influence on China's economic thought and industrialization policies.

---

21. Stalin, *Economic Problems of Socialism in the USSR* (People's Publishing House, 1952), 18.
22. Stalin, *Selected Works of Stalin,* vol. 1 (People's Publishing House, 1979), 462.
23. Stalin, *Selected Works of Stalin,* vol. 1 (People's Publishing House, 1979), 462–463.

3. The Framework of the Textbook of Political Economics Compiled by the Institute of Economics of the Soviet Academy of Sciences

(1) The Framework of Socialist Political Economics

The Chinese version of the *Textbook of Political Economics* compiled by the Institute of Economics of the Soviet Academy of Sciences was divided into two volumes. The first included "The Object of Political Economics," "Pre-capitalist Mode of Production," and "Capitalist Mode of Production," which was basically the same framework as *Das Kapital*. The second volume included "Socialist Mode of Production." In 1979, the Sanlian Bookstore reprinted the second volume according to the revised edition in 1960 for internal distribution for research purposes. According to Lenin and Stalin's socialist policy thought and the Soviet Union's socialist practice, the Soviet Union's *Textbook of Political Economics* constructed the socialist political economics framework. Under the guidance of the socialist mode of production, the book was divided into two parts. One was "The Transitional Period from Capitalism to Socialism," and the other was "Socialist National Economic System." The first section discussed the basic characteristics of the transitional period from capitalism to socialism, socialist industrialization, the socialist transformation of agriculture, and the establishment of a socialist national economic system. The second part included "The Public Ownership of the Means of Production and the Nature of Socialist Relations of Production," "The Basic Economic Law of Socialism," "The Law of Planned and Proportional Development of the National Economy," "Social Labor Under the Socialist System and the Law of Continuous Growth of Labor Productivity," "The Law of Commodity Production, Value, and Currency Under the Socialist System," and "The Economic Law of Distribution According to Work and Wages Under the Socialist System." It also included "Economic Accounting and Profit, Cost, and Price," "Economic Basis of Collective Farming System," "Commerce Under the Socialist System," "State Budget, Credit, and Currency Circulation Under the Socialist System," "Socialist Reproduction and National Income," "Gradual Transition from Socialism to Communism," "World Socialist Economy," and other topics. The socialist national economic system made a qualitative and normative analysis of the socialist national economy from the abstract concepts of production relations and basic economic laws, and it gradually involved the micro level of economic operation such as labor, production, currency, distribution, circulation, cost and price, and the macro level of economic operations such as the national budget, currency circulation, reproduction, and national income. The analysis and discussion of economic operations was more related to the real economy of the Soviet Union at that time, and it had a practical basis. The last two parts were normative analysis. One was the normative analysis of the transition from socialism to communism, and the other was the normative analysis of the world socialist economic system according to Stalin's two world systems and two world markets.

The *Textbook of Political Economics* was the first textbook that systematically discussed the socialist mode of production and constructed the framework of socialist political economics. It was guided by the basic principles and methods of Marxist historical materialism, inherited Lenin and Stalin's exposition on the socialist production mode and economic operation, and combined with the first socialist country in human history's economic practice and linked with the socialist construction practice of China and other socialist countries at that time, it established the socialist political economics system. Socialist political economics was the political economics of the socialist economic system, and the socialist economic system was the core element in defining socialism. In contrast to the capitalist economic system, the socialist economic system has the following characteristics:

1) Under the socialist system, the means of production is manifested in two forms of public property, that is, workers represented by socialist countries or represented by collective farms, other cooperative enterprises, and cooperative organizations. Therefore, the products of labor also belong to the workers. Under the capitalist system, the means of production are private property, most of which belong to capitalists and landlords. Therefore, most of the labor products belong to the capitalists and landlords.

2) The socialist economic system eliminates the phenomenon of exploitation. The purpose of production is to improve the welfare of workers and meet their growing material and cultural needs. The distribution principle of material wealth is stated as "each according to his ability and to his work." The capitalist economic system means that the proletariat and the masses of working peasants are forced to work for capitalists and landlords, and the purpose of production is to make the exploiting class rich.

3) Socialist production develops in a planned, uninterrupted way on the basis of advanced technology. The continuous growth of people's welfare is the driving force for expanding production and the guarantee for avoiding the crisis of overproduction and unemployment. The development of the capitalist mode of production is spontaneous, which inevitably leads to the crisis of overproduction and an increase in unemployment.

As a result, socialism is a system based on public ownership of the means of production. Under this system, exploitation has been eliminated and production has been expanded in a planned way on the basis of high technology in order to continuously improve the welfare of the people. At the same time, under the socialist system, the principle of distribution according to work should be realized.[24]

The historical process of the socialist mode of production (including the transition period from capitalism to socialism, the socialist national economic system, and the gradual transition from socialism to communism) in the *Textbook of Political Economics,* as well as the political and economic system established on the basis of the socialist national economic system, have been China's economic thought for many years.

---

24. Institute of Economics of the Soviet Academy of Sciences, *Textbook of Political Economics* (Sanlian Bookstore, 1979), 83–84.

(2) Basic Economic Law of Socialism

The *Textbook of Political Economics* put forward that with the emergence and development of socialist relations of production, new economic laws – the basic economic law of socialism, the law of planned and proportional development of the national economy, the law of continuous improvement of labor productivity, the law of distribution according to work, the law of socialist accumulation, and other laws – had emerged and developed. Since commodity production still existed under the socialist system, the law of value still played a role in the socialist economy, and various categories related to the law of value were still in place. The new economic conditions formed under the socialist conditions changed the nature of commodity production and circulation and restricted their scope of action.[25]

The basic socialist economic law was the most important determinant of the socialist economic law. The characteristic of the basic socialist economic law was the continuous expansion and perfection of production on the basis of advanced technology, so as to fully meet the needs of all members of society and allow them to develop in an all-round way. The basic economic law of socialism was the law of the development of the socialist mode of production, because it determined the purpose of socialist production and the means to achieve it. The basic economic law of socialism determined the development of socialist production and the improvement of the material welfare and cultural level of workers.[26]

China's economic thought and socialist political economics took the socialist basic economic law and related categories defined in the *Textbook of Political Economics* as a reference for developing the system of the socialist economic law to guide socialist economic construction. In China's description of the main social contradictions, it also referred to the connotation of the basic socialist economic laws defined in the *Textbook of Political Economics*.

(3) The Law of Planned and Proportional Development of the National Economy

It is a socialist economic law that the national economy develops in a planned and proportional way. The basic characteristics of this law are that the law of planned and proportional development of the national economy requires that the development of all economic departments be subject to the unified planned leadership of society and that a certain proportion should be maintained among all departments of the national economy. The nature of the proportion in the socialist economy is determined first of all by the requirements of the basic socialist economic law and by the necessity of ensuring that socialist production continues to rise rapidly on the basis of advanced technology and that the people's welfare is constantly improved. Among the most important proportions of national economic development, the first is the correct proportional relationship between production of the means of production and production of the means of consumption. The correct proportional relationship between the two major categories of social production

25. Institute of Economics of the Soviet Academy of Sciences, *Textbook of Political Economics* (Sanlian Bookstore, 1979), 122–123.

26. Institute of Economics of the Soviet Academy of Sciences, *Textbook of Political Economics* (Sanlian Bookstore, 1979), 132–140.

requires that the departments of the means of production give priority to development, and that the development of heavy industry and its core machinery manufacturing industry be prioritized. Secondarily, the growth of departments producing consumer goods should meet the needs of the people's economic growth. The important proportion of national economic development also includes the correct proportion of industry and agriculture, the proportion of accumulation and consumption, and the distribution of socialist production.[27] The essence of the so-called various proportions is the allocation of resources among various sectors of the national economy, between the two major categories of production and consumption and between regions. According to the *Textbook of Political Economics,* rational and economic utilization of resources is one of the conditions to ensure the continuous and rapid development of production. The law of resource allocation in the socialist economy is the law of planned and proportional development of the national economy.

The law of the planned and proportional development of the national economy should be reflected through the implementation of the economic plan. It is the most important feature of the organization economic function of socialist countries to implement planned leadership over the national economy. The first condition for correctly planning the socialist economy is to master and make good use of the law of planned development of the national economy. According to the objective law of such development, it is possible to correctly plan social production and formulate plans that fully reflect this law. The work of national economic planning includes product cost, price, monetary income and expenditure of enterprises, national income and its distribution in monetary form, commerce, credit, and finance. The law of value and commodity currency levers should be used in the planning work. Through money and credit, it is possible to oversee whether the use of investment is economic and reasonable and supervise the implementation of the plan of reducing product cost, increasing production profits and internal economic accumulation.[28]

The law of planned and proportional development of the national economy and its related exposition have been the core of the study of China's socialist political economics and the main theoretical basis of economic policies in the period of the planned economy. In 1953, China implemented the First Five-Year Plan. From 1951 to 1954, the First Five-Year Plan was compiled by the Central Financial and Economic Commission and the State Planning Commission. Chen Yun was responsible for the preparation of the plan. The First Five-Year Plan included the proportion of agriculture and industry, the proportion of light industries, the proportion of heavy industry departments, the proportion of industrial development and railway transportation, the balance between fiscal revenue and expenditure, and the balance between purchasing power and commodity supply. This was practice drawn from the *Textbook of Political Economics* on the planned and proportional development of the national economy in China.

---

27. Institute of Economics of the Soviet Academy of Sciences, *Textbook of Political Economics* (Sanlian Bookstore, 1979), 144–150.

28. Institute of Economics of the Soviet Academy of Sciences, *Textbook of Political Economics* (Sanlian Bookstore, 1979), 152–154.

(4) Law of Distribution According to Work

The *Textbook of Political Economics* clearly points out that distribution according to work is the economic law of socialism. The economic law of distribution according to work requires that products be distributed directly according to the quantity and quality of each laborer's work. Equal pay for equal work should be implemented for all citizens in a socialist society, regardless of age, race, gender, or nationality. Labor remuneration in industry and agriculture is to be based on this law. The wage standard under the socialist system is formulated according to the economic law of distribution according to work. According to the requirements of the economic law of distribution according to work, the wages of every worker and employee depend on the quantity and quality of his labor. If the quantity and quality of labor are equal, the wages should be equal. Under the socialist system, due to the law of commodity production and value, wages must take the form of money. According to the basic economic law of socialism and the law of distribution according to work, a socialist country determines the wage fund and the wage level of all kinds of workers in a planned way during each period. According to the needs of distribution according to work, the *Textbook of Political Economics* also lays out the design for the overall differential and reward level of labor remuneration, the quota of labor, and the wage grade system, along with the piecework wage system and the hourly wage system.[29] The law of distribution according to work has long been one of the main fields in the study in Chinese socialist political economics and economic thought. The relevant expositions in Soviet textbooks served not only as theoretical references, but also as the main basis for formulating economic policies.

1.3 Reference to Western Economics

1. Introduction of Western Economics Before 1949

Western mercantilism and industrialization thought influenced foreign thought on big machine industry and "learning from the West," "making foreign products," "revitalizing commerce," and "enriching the people and strengthening the country," which emerged in the 1860s. In the 1880s, a group of early bourgeois reformists in China began to spread Western economic knowledge. Later, Kang Youwei, Liang Qichao, Yan Fu, Sun Yat-Sen, and others systematically translated, introduced, studied, and expounded Western classical economic thought and modern economic thought. From the 1880s to the eve of the May 4th Movement in 1919, China published about forty books on Western economics, of which about 2/3 were compiled by Chinese scholars, and 1/3 were translated, mainly from Japanese. However, from the 1920s to 1940s, the number of economic works translated from Western countries increased greatly, while the number of those

---

29. Institute of Economics of the Soviet Academy of Sciences, *Textbook of Political Economics* (Sanlian Bookstore, 1979), 205–210.

coming from Japan gradually decreased.[30]

From the 1930s, more works of Western economic theory were written by Chinese scholars, but their quality was not good. At that time, there were many independent lectures on Western economics, but few reached the publishing level or sold well. It was not until the late 1940s that several Western economic works with higher academic standards were published. From the 1880s to the 1940s, the introduction and dissemination of Western economic theory in China progressed slowly, but on the whole, the academic research level in this field was not high, and even the translation and introduction of Western economic theory was not complete and systematic.[31]

From 1949 to the end of the 1970s, the introduction and research of Western economic theory was very limited. According to statistics, from 1949 to 1979, only 68 economic works were translated from Western countries, of which 52 were British or American. Original works of classical economics accounted for a large proportion of these works.[32]

2. The Influence of Western Economics on the Transformation of Traditional Chinese Economic Thought

(1) The Transformation of Chinese Economic Thought from Pre-science to Science

In his *Outline of the History of Modern Chinese Economic Thought,* Hu Jichuang drew a line of demarcation between Chinese economic thought before and after the May 4th Movement in 1919. The May 4th Movement was a kind of exogenous new ideological form to replace the old original ideological form. Its observation of all things aimed to use a point of view and testing method that had never been before. In terms of cultural scholarship, this exogenous factor defeated China's original cultural and academic tradition, which was independent of the world on the surface, but in fact, it integrated Chinese cultural scholarship with the world's scientific and cultural scholarship, become part of this milieu, and worked with the people of the world to jointly promote the development of human civilization. Hu Jichuang observed that in the economic thought in the historical period from the Opium War in 1840 to the 1911 Revolution, although some economic thought was introduced from the West, traditional Chinese economic thought still held considerable power. After the 1911 Revolution, traditional Chinese economic thought had in fact withdrawn from the historical stage and was replaced by foreign economic theories. Especially after the May 4th Movement in 1919, traditional Chinese economic thought became a relic of history, viewed only as something of the remote past.[33]

---

30. Hu Jichuang, *Outline of the History of Modern Chinese Economic Thought* (China Social Sciences Press, 1984), 382–383.

31. Hu Jichuang, *Outline of the History of Modern Chinese Economic Thought* (China Social Sciences Press, 1984), 384–387.

32. Zhao Xiaolei, *Outline of the History of Economic Thought of the People's Republic of China (1949–2009)* (Capital University of Economics and Business Press, 2009), 427–429.

33. Hu Jichuang, *Outline of the History of Modern Chinese Economic Thought* (China Social Sciences Press, 1984), 378–381.

According to Hu Jichuang's analysis, from the middle of the nineteenth century, China's economic thought underwent a transformation from traditional, pre-scientific economic thought to become a modern economic science. In the style of the *Outline of the History of Modern Chinese Economic Thought,* the economic thought from 1840 to 1919 was called "economic thought," while that from 1919 to 1949 was called "economic science." The "Hu Jichuang boundary" was the transformation of Chinese economic thought from a traditional paradigm to a modern one. The basic point of this demarcation was a "new scientific starting point, scientific classification system, and scientific analysis method." The May 4th Movement spread the scientific classification system and the scientific analysis method, which had been widely used in the world in various ideological fields, rapidly and forcefully, finally achieving success and making them generally recognized as indisputable principles. This allowed China to better sort out its cultural heritage and correctly introduce and digest foreign advanced scientific knowledge, so as to make new contributions to the civilization of all mankind under new conditions.[34]

The "Hu Jichuang boundary" defined the transformation of Chinese economic thought from the traditional pre-scientific paradigm to the modern scientific paradigm. Its basic point was the transformation of research methods – the adoption of scientific classification system and analytical methods. Based on the transformation of research methods, this paradigm change was also reflected in two important aspects, the international discourse system and the emergence of the "professional community" of economists. Hu Jichuang pointed out that compared with other social sciences, economic science should be a science with a wide range of connotations and the most complex categories. Continuing with the traditional notion of "proper governance for financial management" and "wealth deriving from more production and less consumption" would limit China's ability to adapt to economic life in the real world. In order to engage in the exchange of international economic practice and theory, it was necessary to have a common principle that could be aligned in many specific models and theoretical categories. Otherwise, it would be impossible to communicate,[35] and those engaged in economic science research and practicing the international discourse system would be a group of professional economists. In the 2,000 years before the May 4th Movement, although many thinkers put forward some valuable economic views, they did not specialize in economic research, so no one was worthy to be called an ancient economic thinker.[36]

Hu Jichuang emphasized that the ideological, academic, and cultural changes brought about by the May 4th Movement were driven by exogenous factors. However, from the perspective of China, this was a process of "integration." On the one hand, favorable scientific external factors were used to serve China's cultural development, and on the other was the integration of

---

34. Hu Jichuang, *Outline of the History of Modern Chinese Economic Thought* (China Social Sciences Press, 1984), 378–381.

35. Hu Jichuang, *Outline of the History of Modern Chinese Economic Thought* (China Social Sciences Press, 1984), 378–381.

36. Hu Jichuang, *Outline of the History of Modern Chinese Economic Thought* (China Social Sciences Press, 1984), 378–381.

Chinese and foreign cultural studies in the field of science. Chinese cultural studies integrated into the world's scientific and cultural studies through scientific paths and became a part of the world's scientific civilization. Therefore, the core element of the transformation of economic thought and cultural academic paradigm revealed by the "Hu Jichuang boundary" was science. Through scientific thinking, scientific methods, the scientific discourse system, and the scientific professional community, the transformation from economic thought to economic science was begun.

(2) Comparison Between Pre-science and Science

Hu Jichuang pointed out that before Western economics became a science in the mid-eighteenth century, China's classical economic thought could be compared with the economic thought of any country in the world at that time, and the more it went back to ancient times, the more this was true. After a kind of science formulated in modern economics, it developed rapidly, while Chinese classical economic thought basically stagnated and fell behind modern economics. The reason for this phenomenon was that China's economic thought had not realized the transformation to science. Hu Jichuang analyzed that China's economic thought of the 3,000 years from the pre-Qin period to the middle of the nineteenth century were purely Chinese classical economic thought. It had its own unique logic system, expression, and terminology, which were quite different from Western economic thought. Although the themes of social and economic phenomena such as commodities, production, commerce, currency, capital, finance, and so forth studied by Chinese and Western economic thought were roughly the same in ancient and modern times, and in China and in ancient Athens,[37] the economic thought of ancient Greece was directly related to modern economics, so its thinking mode and terminology were basically the same. However, ancient Chinese economic thought had always established a system independent of the Western economic thought tradition with its unique way of thinking and terminology. From the perspective of the pre-science stage of political and economic study, although ancient Chinese economic thought had developed independently over a long period and had no direct or obvious connection with Western economic thought, they both studied the same objective things. Certain commodity production, trade, currency, and other phenomena were common in ancient China and the ancient West. The only difference was that the terms used to express them and even the analysis methods were different. For example, it was necessary to abandon the narrow Eurocentrism of Western thought and investigate from the perspective of the whole world, adding the achievements of ancient Chinese economic thought to the study of the history of ancient economic thought.[38] However, after the transformation of Western economic thought into an economic science in the middle of the eighteenth century, classical Chinese economic thought basically stagnated and lagged behind modern economics. From the middle of the nineteenth

---

37. Hu Jichuang, *A Compendium of the History of China's Economic Thought* (China Social Sciences Press, 1981), 472.

38. Hu Jichuang, *The Prehistory of Political Economics* (Liaoning People's Publishing House, 1988), 26–27.

century to the beginning of the 20th century, in order to consolidate its dominant position in the field of ideology, China's inherent classical economic thought once resisted the spread of Western economics, but Western economics quickly excluded classical Chinese economic thought from every aspect.[39]

Because China's classical economic thought had not been transformed into economic science for such a long period, Hu Jichuang analyzed the mode of production, economic relations, and geographical conditions. He said that the rapid development of economic theory and the rapid growth of the monetary economy within a country were closely related to various international economic relations. Under the natural economic and geographical conditions of ancient China, if there were no drastic economic changes, classical economic thought could continue for a long time without a paradigm transformation.[40] In fact, Chinese and foreign academic circles extensively discussed the reasons traditional Chinese thought patterns were relatively weak in analytical philosophy and empirical sciences. From the perspective of historical materialism, the root cause was attributed to the mode of production and the natural environment on which the mode of production depended. With the different natural environments, the different ways of obtaining a basic means of living, and the different modes of production, economic structure, and social structure, the thought patterns of different nationalities or civilizations were different. Only when there was an independent form of civilization could there be an independent form of thinking and learning. The form of civilization and thinking could be pluralistic, but science was unique, because the essence of things was unique. The understanding of the essence of things and the thinking of the definition required that the concept system be unitary and the discourse system normative, commensurable, and unified. In other words, only scientific thinking (epistemology and the methodology of science) could approach the objective essence, and science was the only way to know truth. Here, the formalization of "paradigm" elements such as concept system, discourse system, and logical form was very important and became the tool of cultural and academic exchange and the technical path of scientific universality. Thus the economic thought of ancient China, though advanced in the pre-scientific era, was gradually excluded from the mainstream economic thought of the world and even replaced by modern economic science due to the lag of its paradigm transformation, which made it impossible to communicate with the cultural and academic fields of other civilizations in the world.

3. Western Economics as a Clue to the Development of China's Modern Economic Thought

From the 1950s to the 1970s, the introduction and dissemination of Western economics in China did not continue the development trend of the 1930s and 1940s. After 1949, the attitude of China's economic and ideological circles toward Western economics followed Marx's evaluation. Marx

---

39. Hu Jichuang, *A Compendium of the History of China's Economic Thought* (China Social Sciences Press, 1981), 472–473.

40. Hu Jichuang, *A Compendium of the History of China's Economic Thought* (China Social Sciences Press, 1981), 472–473.

divided Western bourgeois economics into "classical political economics" and "vulgar economics." Marx's so-called classical political economics was in contrast to the work of all "economists who, since the time of William Petty, have investigated the real internal framework of bourgeois relations of production, as opposed to the vulgar economists who only flounder around with the apparent framework of those relations."[41] Marx writes of "classical political economy, beginning with William Petty in Britain and Boisguillebert in France, and ending with David Ricardo in Britain and Sismondi in France."[42] According to Marx's classification, Western classical political economics included the economic theory of Adam Smith, the physiocratic school represented by Quesnay and Turgot, and the theories of some economists such as Locke, Hume, and Jones. Following Marx's evaluation, from 1949 to 1970s, China introduced and studied some representative works of Western classical political economics and conducted a critical study of the theories of some important Western economists and economic schools from the perspective of the history of political economics. From the 1950s to the 1970s, among Chinese economic circles, "except for the classical economics and early vulgar economics analyzed by Marx, there was almost no knowledge of the Western economic theories which emerged since the end of the nineteenth century. Even if a few works related to them were published, most of them were vague with a completely negative attitude toward Western theories."[43] This evaluation basically explained the introduction and research status of Western economics in China before the end of the 1970s. From the 1950s to the 1970s, there were two clues to the development of China's economic thought. First was the dissemination and research of Marxist economics, followed by the introduction and research of Soviet Socialist political economics. Western economics did not constitute a development guide for Chinese economic thought.

In the 1980s, China began to introduce Western economics broadly and systematically. In the 1980s, the introduction and research of Western economics mainly focused on classical and neoclassical economics theories, the most important of which were the introduction and research of important works of the post-Keynesian mainstream school. In the 1990s, the characteristics of the introduction and research of Western economics were mainly focused on the introduction and research of Western New Institutional Economics and property rights economics. In the 1980s and 1990s, research on Western economics in China's economic and ideological circles began gradually and made great achievements. From the 1990s to the beginning of the 21st century, the introduction and research of Western economics continued the development momentum of the 1980s and 1990s, especially the systematic introduction and research on some cutting edge theories, such as new political economics, information economics, new liberalism economic thought, new economic growth theory, new trade theory, endogenous economic growth theory, behavioral economics, regulatory economics, new economic geography, public economics, and macro-econometrics.

---

41. Marx and Engels, *Complete Works of Marx and Engels,* vol. 23 (People's Publishing House, 1972), 98.
42. Marx and Engels, *Complete Works of Marx and Engels,* vol. 13 (People's Publishing House, 1972), 41.
43. Hu Jichuang, "Preface," in *Western Economic Theory after 1870* (Economic Science Press, 1988).

With the introduction of and research on Western economics, the evaluation of Western economics in China also changed, from the basic negation of the 1950s to the 1970s, to the recognition of the duality of Western economics. On the one hand, it was considered to be the property of bourgeois ideology, especially neo-liberal economics, which advocated the *laissez faire* capitalist economic system, and was not universal. On the other hand, it was also of referential significance to the construction and development of the socialist market economy, because many theories of Western economics reflected some bases of the modern market economy. This law was scientific to some extent. In line with the above situation, after the 1980s, the development direction of China's economic thought changed. The first development guide was the study and research of Marxist economics, which was combined with China's economic reform practice to carry out theoretical innovation, further enriching and developing Marxist economics in terms of basic theoretical construction. The other development guide was the introduction, research, and application of modern Western economics. This second guide began to appear in the 1980s, but showed a strong momentum of development and gradually integrated with the first development guide. From that time, Western economics became one of the theoretical components of China's economic thought.

CHAPTER 2

The Formation and Characteristics of the Mainstream Form of Economic Thought in the People's Republic of China

2.1 The Category System of the Mainstream Form of Economic Thought

1. Category System Within the Framework of Marxist Historical Materialism

Historical materialism is the basis of the Marxist theoretical system and its world outlook, and it serves as the foundation for the methodology of Marxist philosophy and economics. Marxist historical materialism reveals the position and role of human social practice, especially material production, in human social life and historical development and reveals that "all social life is essentially practical."[1] Material production is the primary, basic form of human social practice. There must be two relations in the process of material production. One is the relationship between man and nature, and the other is the social relationship between people. A mode of production is composed of these two relations, the dialectical relationship between productivity and production relations. In the contradictory movement between productive forces and relations of production, productive forces play a decisive role, and relations of production are subject to productive forces. Marx states, "We thus see that the social relations within which individuals produce, the social relations of production, are altered or transformed with the change and development of the material means of production and of the forces of production. The relations of production

---

1. Marx and Engels, *Selected Works of Marx and Engels,* vol. 1 (People's Publishing House, 1995), 56; National Cadre Training Textbook Compilation and Review Committee, *Basic Issues of Marxism Leninism* (People's Publishing House, 2002), 25–26.

in their totality constitute what is called the social relations or society, and, moreover, a society at a definite stage of historical development, a society with peculiar, distinctive characteristics."[2] Production relation is the decisive factor in the social structure. It is the economic foundation of society and the foundation of the superstructure of a country and its ideology.

Within the framework of historical materialism, the categories related to political economics include the research object of political economics, productive forces and relations of production, the social mode of production, the economic foundation and superstructure, the social economic form, the social economic system, and other areas. From the 1950s to the 1970s, these categories were the main components of China's economic thought category system, and also the main subject of its economic theory research. The object of political economics, productive forces and relations of production, and their relations were discussed and studied in depth during this period.

The object of political economics was likewise discussed in the Soviet Union. Before the 1920s, it was generally believed that only the commodity economy, which developed spontaneously, was the object of political economics, and in a socialist society, political economics would die out. This view was denied in the Soviet Union in the late 1920s and early 1930s. There was a debate over whether the object of political economics should include productivity.[3] In the first half of the 20th century, Chinese economists discussed the research objects of economics and political economics in the process of studying Marxist economics. At first, according to Marx and Engels, the research object of political economics was defined as production relations. In 1952, Stalin clearly pointed out in his work *Economic Problems of Socialism in the USSR* that the research object of political economics was the people's production relations, that is, economic relations. From that time on, this view was generally accepted and gradually tended to extremes. The relationship of production was discussed abstractly from the development of social productive forces. In 1959, China's economic and ideological circles put forward the view that productivity should also be included as a research object of political economics. It was held that the relationship between production and productivity should not be separated mechanically. At any stage of historical development, there could be no production relationship independent of productivity. Productive forces and relations of production were always both contradictory and unified. As the content and form of production, they constituted the material basis of society. In any social form, at any stage of historical development, there would be no productive relations that existed independent of productive forces, nor would there be one-sided isolated productive forces without the relations of production. Therefore, political economics not only took production relations as its research object, but had to combine the nature of production relations, analyze and synthesize the nature of productivity of various social and economic forms, and further study the differences and junction

---

2. Marx and Engels, *Selected Works of Marx and Engels*, vol. 1 (People's Publishing House, 1995), 345.

3. Editorial Department of *Economic Research* and *Economic Trends, Debates on Important Issues of Political Economics Since the Founding of the People's Republic of China (1949–1980)* (China Financial and Economic Publishing House, 1981), 1–2.

points between the nature of productivity and the nature of production relations.[4] After this point of view was advanced, there was great discussion in theoretical circles. The central question was whether the research object of political economics should include productivity and what should be included in the relation of production as the research object of political economics. At that time, many views disagreed with the prospect of making productivity the research object of political economics. They believed that political economics did not study the structure and movement law of productive forces, but regarded productivity as the material basis for the movement and development of production relations, the material conditions for the emergence, development, and decline of material production relations, and the results of production relations and their functions. The purpose of political economics studying productivity was not to explain the movement law of productivity itself, but to clarify the law of development and change of production relations. Political economics was to study the social aspect of production in the unity of productive forces and relations of production, that is, the social relations of production. But it was important to avoid taking productivity as the research object of political economics as a result. During the discussion, some critics also suggested that the research object of political economics was the mode of production, which was the unity of opposites of productivity and production relations. The debate on this issue went through many ups and downs, until it finally reached a climax in the late 1970s.[5]

There were two theoretical bases adopted by the research objects of political economics discussed by Chinese economic and ideological circles from the 1950s to the 1970s. One was Engels' statement in *Anti-Dühring*, noting that political economics was a science that studied the conditions and forms of production and exchange in various human societies and the corresponding distribution of products. The second was Stalin's definition in *Economic Problems of Socialism in the USSR*. He stated, "The province of political economy is production, the economic relations of men. It includes: a) the forms of ownership of the means of production, b) the status of the various social groups in production and their inter-relations that follow from these forms, or what as Marx notes, 'they exchange their activities,' and c) the forms of distribution of products, which are entirely determined by them. All these together constitute the province of political economy."[6] Undoubtedly, the research object or focus of Marxist political economics was social production relations. Marx's important contribution was to reveal the capitalist production relations contained in commodity, capital, value, and surplus value, and to clarify the development law of capitalist society. However, the category of production relations in Marxist historical materialism was related to productive forces, which could not be separated from the

---

4. Editorial Departments of *Economic Research* and *Economic Trends, Debates on Important Issues of Political Economics Since the Founding of the People's Republic of China (1949–1980)* (China Financial and Economic Publishing House, 1981), 2–15.

5. Editorial Departments of *Economic Research* and *Economic Trends, Debates on Important Issues of Political Economics Since the Founding of the People's Republic of China (1949–1980)* (China Financial and Economic Publishing House, 1981), 2–15.

6. Stalin, *Economic Problems of Socialism in the USSR* (People's Publishing House, 1952), 58.

productive forces when investigating the relations of production. Moreover, productivity was the prerequisite for the study of production relations. In other words, the thesis could only exist if the relations of production and productivity were separated. Therefore, the thesis was not a well-defined problem, and there was no conclusion that it was well-defined. However, in the course of the debate, scholars conducted in-depth studies on the relations of production, productivity, mode of production, and the nature and research methods of political economics, which promoted the theoretical understanding and academic levels in the field. The discussion and research on the category of productive forces and relations of production included the substance of relations of production and the dialectical unity of relations of production and productive forces. One school of economic thought, historiography, adopted Stalin's definition, which was that the relations of production included the ownership of the means of production, exchange relations, and product distribution forms. Other views held that the relations of production, as the object of political economics, should include not only the relations of production, distribution, and exchange, but also the social relations in the field of consumption, such as the consumption level of different classes and different social groups, the relationship between collective consumption and individual consumption, and the relationship between consumption and production and between distribution and exchange.[7] There were other differing opinions, such as the notion that as the research object of political economics, the relations of production were, first of all, the narrow sense of production relations, especially the ownership of the means of production, and secondarily, distribution relations and exchange relations. The ownership of the means of production determined people's position in production and the mode of distribution of products. In distribution, the proportion relationship between accumulation and consumption must first be dealt with, and then consumption and consumption level could be discussed. In the process of production, distribution, and exchange, consumption was regarded as "need" and "necessity," as the elements that would act on the starting point and cause the whole process to start over again. Therefore, it was unnecessary to separate consumption as a research object of political economics.[8] The consumption relationship was an indispensable link in the relations of production. "However, since it is determined by production and further determined for distribution and exchange, generally speaking, the analysis and study of production, distribution, and exchange also includes the issue of the consumption relationship. From this point of view, it is possible not avoid mentioning the consumption relationship."[9]

Productive forces and relations of production were two important categories of Marxist economics. Combined with the socialist nature of China's production relations and the backward situation of productivity development at that time, this issue had even more practical significance. The research and discussion on this issue mainly focused on 1) the key elements of productive forces, 2) the decisive factors in productive forces, 3) the nature of productive forces, 4) the

---

7. Jiang Xuemo, "On Labor Form and Other Issues," *Academic Monthly*, no. 4 (1962).

8. Yang Changfu, "Two Issues on the Object of Political Economics," *Academic Monthly*, no. 7 (1962).

9. Gu Shutang, "Objects and Production Relations of Political Economics," *New Construction*, no. 8 (1962).

driving force for the development of productive forces, 5) the laws governing the development of productive forces, 6) the relations of production should be adapted to the nature of the productive forces, and 7) the contradiction between advanced socialist relations of production and backward productive forces. Although these discussions were very heated, they were basically conceptual debates. Regarding which elements of productivity to include, there was a debate between "two elements" and "three elements." According to the viewpoint of "three elements," productivity included three elements: 1) laborer, 2) means of labor, and 3) object of labor. As a production level or labor productivity, productivity was the result of labor process. The simple elements of labor process were purposeful activities or labor itself, labor objects, and labor materials, which referred to the simple elements of productivity. Especially with the development of modern science and technology, the object of labor played an important role in the revolution of productive forces.[10] According to the view of "two elements," productivity and labor process were two concepts which cannot be equated. Labor processes should have both active factors (labor force and production tools) and object factors (labor object). Since productivity was a kind of "force," it could only include dynamic factors, not object factors. Productivity reflected the relationship between society and natural forces, and it included the ability of society to conquer nature. It could only include laborers and production tools. The object of labor was the object of productive forces. It was the object to the productive forces and the place where the productive forces depended and played their roles, but it was not productivity itself. Another point of view was that the "two elements" and "three elements" should be dialectically unified, that is, the unity of "quantity" and "quality" of productivity. There were also views on whether production management and labor organization also belonged to the category of productivity, and whether science and technology were also elements of productivity.[11] The discussion on the relationship between production and productive forces was carried out under the umbrella of the research object of political economics.

After the Cultural Revolution began in 1966, the normal development guideline of Marxist economic theory was interrupted. At that time, there was no theoretical research, but more borrowing and distorting words and concepts of Marxism to serve political purposes.

During the period of the Cultural Revolution, one-sided focus on the relations of production and criticism of the theory of "productivity only" had a great impact on the theoretical and practical economic work. After 1976, theorists first discussed this issue. It was generally believed that the contradiction between productivity and production relations and between economic base and superstructure was a common contradiction in all stages of human society. The unity of productive forces and relations of production was the unity of opposites. First, productivity determined the relations of production, and the degree and level of development of productive

---

10. Editorial Department of *Economic Research* and *Economic Trends*, *Debates on Important Issues of Political Economics Since the Founding of the People's Republic of China (1949–1980)* (China Financial and Economic Publishing House, 1987), 32.

11. Editorial Department of *Economic Research* and *Economic Trends*, *Debates on Important Issues of Political Economics Since the Founding of the People's Republic of China (1949–1980)* (China Financial and Economic Publishing House, 1987), 34–35.

forces determined the nature and types of production relations. Productivity was the decisive material force of social development, but the relationship of production had a significant adverse effect on productivity. The decisive role of productive forces on production relations mainly lay in the fact that productivity determined the nature of production relations and that productive forces determined the transformation of production relations. Many views held that the productive forces determined the relations of production, which should be suitable for the nature of the productive forces. The relations of production here not only referred to the relations of production that lagged behind the development of productive forces, but also included the "advanced" relations of production beyond the stage of the development of productive forces. Any relations of production incompatible with the development of productive forces would hinder the development of productive forces. In short, in the relationship between productive forces and relations of production, it was generally recognized that the decisive role of productive forces was more emphasized, and that the development of history was ultimately determined by productive forces. Although the reaction of the relations of production to the productive forces could not be ignored, it was important not to equate the role of productive forces in determining the relations of production and the economic base determining the superstructure with the decisive effects of the relations of production on the productive forces and the superstructure on the economic base, because there were fundamental differences between the two. The decisive role of productive forces on the relations of production and the economic base on the superstructure was fundamental and general, while the decisive role of relations of production on productivity and superstructure on economic foundation was the product of specific conditions, and the emergence of specific conditions was the result of economic development.[12]

A representative viewpoint in the period of the Cultural Revolution held that the socialist relations of production had both socialist and capitalist attributes, and the capitalist factor was "bourgeois rights." In criticizing this argument, economic theorists offered an analysis from the perspective of the evolution of the social forms of capitalism, socialism, and communism. Capitalist commodity exchange was equal value exchange, and socialist distribution according to work was equal labor exchange. The principle they were based on was the principle of equal labor exchange. According to this principle, both sides of the exchange were equal. This equal right was the symbol of bourgeois rights. Marx abstracted the common point of capitalist commodity exchange and socialist distribution according to work, that is, equal rights embodied in the principle of equal labor exchange, and called them bourgeois rights, which was meant in an abstract sense. Moreover, compared with the bourgeois rights in capitalist society, a socialist society reserved bourgeois rights with the common characteristics of formal equality and de facto inequality, but they were different in nature and had fundamentally different social attributes. The original bourgeois rights reflected the exploitation and exploited relationship between capitalist

---

12. Xue Muqiao, *Theoretical Issues in the Socialist Economy* (People's Publishing House, 1979); Wu Zhengkun, "The Decisive Role of Productive Forces in Historical Development," *Red Flag*, no. 1 (1978); Yu Shaobo and Xiang Qiyuan, *On the Rule that Production Relations Must be Suitable for the Nature of Productive Forces* (Shandong People's Publishing House, 1980).

and employed labor in the capitalist mode of production. The de facto inequality reflected by the bourgeois rights under the condition of socialist public ownership was relative to communism and was the right relationship between socialist laborers. Generally speaking, in socialist society, the relationship between equal amount of labor and equal amount of labor exchange was the economic relationship on which bourgeois rights depend, which objectively determined the existence of bourgeois rights.

In the early 1980s, China's economic and ideological circles were still arguing about the research object of political economics and the concept of productivity and production relations.[13] By the end of 1980s, the views of Soviet economics on the research object of political economics had changed. In 1988, the Soviet Union published the *Textbook of Political Economics,* which revised the traditional definition of the object of political economics research. It said, "political economics is a science about the relations of production and its development law," and offered a new definition, "political economics studies production relations from the unity of production relations, productivity, and superstructure."[14] This made it clear that the research object of political economics included not only production relations, but also productive forces. Since the end of the 1980s, the view that the object of political economics was mainly production relations but also included productivity has become the consensus of Chinese economic ideological circles.

Within the framework of historical materialism, Chinese scholars and economic theorists have discussed such topics as the law that the relations of production must be suitable for the nature of productive forces, the relationship between opposites and unity as seen in socialist relations of production and productive forces, the relationship between productive forces, relations of production and modes of production, economic basis and superstructure, and the evolution of social and economic forms and systems. Marxist historical materialism included two remarkable characteristics, one dialectical and the other practical. Marxist theory was not satisfied with explaining the world, but also aimed to change the world. Marx says, "Philosophers have hitherto only *interpreted* the world in various ways; the point is to *change* it."[15] And he says that "for the real communist, it is a question of overthrowing the existing state of things."[16] From the perspective of methodology, empirical analysis was generally used to explain things, that is, to answer "what is," while to change things, normative research methods were generally used to answer "what should be." In philosophy, explaining the world was the epistemology of the object acting on the subject, while changing the world was the epistemology of the subject acting on the object, that is, the epistemology of practice. The discussion and research on the category system of Marxist historical materialism in China's economic and ideological circles basically adopted the

---

13. Xiang Qiyuan and Yu Shaobo, "On the Elements of Modern Productive Forces," *On China's Economic Issues,* no. 5 (1980); Cai Jianhua, "On the Nature of Productivity in Corporate Management," *Economic Research,* no. 9 (1980); Wei Xinghua and Li Kaiming, "On the Content and Other Issues of Productivity," *Philosophical Research,* no. 11 (1980).

14. V. A. Medvedev et al., eds., *Political Economics* (China Social Sciences Press, 1989), 37.

15. Marx and Engels, *Selected Works of Marx and Engels,* vol. 1 (People's Publishing House, 1995), 57.

16. Marx and Engels, *Selected Works of Marx and Engels,* vol. 1 (People's Publishing House, 1995), 75.

standard research method. In many cases, it involved debate of concepts, even of a certain word, and it formed views from different perspectives and different dimensions of understanding. The influence of this methodology was even more profound in the study of China's economic thought.

2. The Category System Within the Framework of Marxist Surplus Value Theory and Scientific Socialism Theory

The theory of surplus value was an epoch-making achievement of Marx's work. Scientific socialism was based on this idea as its starting point, and it developed with this central idea.[17] Since the theory of surplus value was an analysis of the capitalist economy and the mode of production and evolution trend of capitalist society, and because socialism evolved on the basis of the development of capitalism, in the study of socialist political economics, the relevant categories of surplus value theory were related to those of scientific socialism theory, which together constituted the category system of the mainstream form of Chinese economic thought, which was mainly reflected in two theoretical areas. One was the discussion and research on the law of commodity production and value under the socialist system and was related to the concepts of commodity and commodity production, commodity and currency, law of value, determination of the quantity of commodity value, necessary labor time, and the historical trend of commodity production development. The other was the discussion and research on the distribution of labor in relation to labor and labor value theory, the condition of the generation of surplus value, surplus value production and capital, labor commodities, labor process and the process of value accumulation, and the duality of labor in the production of commodities.

In 1957, Chinese theorists began to discuss commodity production and commodity exchange under the socialist system. In April 1959, the first National Theoretical Seminar on commodity production and the law of value under the socialist system was held in Shanghai. About 250 theoretical and practical personnel from economic departments, institutions of higher learning, and scientific research institutions participated in the conference. Nearly 80 papers and investigation reports were submitted to the conference, with discussion focusing on the socialist system commodity production, law of value, piece wage, and distribution according to work. This was the largest academic conference between the founding of the People's Republic of China and the late 1950s. The period before and after the meeting marked the first climax of discussion on the theory of the socialist commodity economy. According to incomplete statistics, from the end of 1958 to July 1959, nearly 300 articles on the law of commodity production and value under the socialist system were published in major newspapers and periodicals across the country.

Theoretical research on commodity production and exchange under the socialist system mainly focused on 1) the reasons for the existence of commodity production under the socialist system, 2) whether the means of production exchanged between state-owned enterprises were commodities, 3) whether the exchange between the state and the employees of state-owned

---

17. Marx and Engels, *Selected Works of Marx and Engels*, vol. 3 (People's Publishing House, 1995), 548.

enterprises was commodity exchange, and 4) whether socialist commodity production was a new type or an old form that would produce capitalism. One of the central questions was the reason for the existence of commodity production under the socialist system. At that time, there were several opinions. First, there was general agreement with Stalin's book *Economic Problems of Socialism in the USSR,* which was decided by the coexistence of two socialist ownership systems (ownership by the people and collective ownership). Second, it was widely accepted that distribution according to work was the reason for the existence of commodity production.[18] Third, it was understood that the difference in economic interests was the fundamental reason.[19] Fourth, it was agreed that individual ownership of part of labor or private ownership of labor was the reason for the existence of commodity production.[20] It should be pointed out that research at that time broke through the frame of Stalin's theory and made a step forward in the scientific interpretation of the socialist commodity economy. The coexistence of two kinds of public ownership could not explain the fundamental reason for the existence of socialist commodity production from the substantive level, but it needed to be further explored. However, the discussion at that time was mainly conducted from the perspective of production relations, and rarely from the perspective of productivity and the development of the social division of labor. Therefore, some new views or theories were not convincing.

The theoretical research on the law of value under the socialist system mainly focused on defining the law of value, the status and role of the law of value in the socialist planned economy, and the relationship between the law of value in the socialist economy and the law of planned and proportional development of the national economy. Regarding the first question, there were three main points of view. One was that the law of value was the law of the whole process of the existence and movement of value. Value was the social necessary labor itself materialized in commodities, which was not unique to the commodity economy. Social necessary labor reflected the concept of the "quantity" of value, while the "quality" of value was the relationship between production cost and utility. A socialist society attached importance to the concept of value, which meant that it attached importance to economic effects. The second was that the law of value was the law determined by value, that is, the amount of social necessary labor determined the value of commodities. Third, the law of value was the law of equivalent exchange, that is, the price of goods tended to be consistent with the value of an inevitable trend.[21] On the second and third questions, there were three different representative views. The first view was that the socialist economy was "governed by the law of planned and proportional development, and the law of value could

18. Yu Liangxin, "On the Causes of Commodity Production in Socialist Society," *Ta Kung Pao* (January 27, 1957).

19. Zhang Chaozun, "The Necessity and Characteristics of Internal Commodity Production Under Socialist Ownership by the People," *Teaching and Research*, no. 6 (1959).

20. Wang Xuewen, "Commodity Relations and the Law of Value Under the Socialist System," *Economic Research*, no. 5 (1959).

21. Editorial Department of *Economic Research* and *Economic Trends*, *Debates on Important Issues of Political Economics Since the Founding of the People's Republic of China (1949–1980)* (China Financial and Economic Publishing House, 1981), 165–169.

only play an auxiliary role." For the production and allocation of products managed by the state through direct planning, the law of value was only used as a tool for economic accounting, while for the production and circulation of products managed by the state through indirect planning, the state still needed to use the law of value to regulate within a certain range, and the production and circulation of products beyond the scope of national plan management mainly allowed the law of value to progress spontaneously. The state could only have a certain degree of influence. With the expansion of the scope of planning management, the scope of the law of value would be further restricted.[22] The second opinion held that "the socialist economy is the contradictory unity of the planned economy and economic accounting," and "if we overemphasize one side of planning and negate the relationship between value and price and the impact of price on production distribution and product transfer, thus denying the role of economic accounting, the improper practice of trying to stipulate everything with planning will occur. This will hinder the development of the social economy."[23] The third opinion was that planning and statistics should be practiced on the basis of the law of value. The basic content and function of the law of value was to promote the development of social productive forces by determining the value by the average amount of necessary labor of society and to regulate or distribute social production forces, which existed in both socialist and communist societies.[24]

Study of the law of commodity production, commodity exchange, and value under the socialist system held great theoretical significance. It broke through the framework of some traditional theories, delved deep into the socialist economic relations and economic operation itself, and put forward some valuable opinions, playing an important role in the development of socialist economic theory and Marxist economics.

The relationship between socialism and commodity production was an important issue that was subject to heated debate in theoretical circles after the Cultural Revolution. The discussion on this issue provided an important theoretical preparation for the reform of the economic system. At that time, an important understanding was that commodity production needed to be separated from capitalist production relations, demonstrating that commodity production was a coexistence of various social forms, rather than unique to the capitalist mode of production. Among the socialist commodity producers, because of the differences in production and operation conditions, there were also differences in interests. However, under the conditions of public ownership of the means of production and the planned economic system, a large amount of monetary wealth would not accumulate in the hands of a few people through the regulation of various economic mechanisms such as taxation. At the same time, because of the public ownership of the means of production, it was impossible to purchase a great deal of machinery, equipment,

---

22. Xue Muqiao, "The Planned Economy and the Law of Value," *People's Daily*, October 28, 1956; "Further Discussion on the Planned Economy and the Law of Value Regulation," *Planned Economy*, no. 2 (1957).

23. Gu Zhun, "On the Law of Commodity Production and Value Under the Socialist System," *Economic Research*, no. 3 (1957).

24. Sun Yefang, "Putting Planning and Statistics on the Basis of Law of Value," *Economic Research*, no. 6 (1956).

and raw materials. More importantly, in the socialist system, the rights of workers were protected by national laws and they could not be reduced to wage workers. Therefore, socialist commodity production would not be transformed into capitalist production like the production of small commodities.

Related to commodity production was the discussion of the law of value. At that time, it was generally believed that since socialist production was still commodity production, each enterprise must exchange goods according to the principle of equivalent exchange based on the value contained in the commodity. Therefore, the law of value, like other objective economic laws, could not be violated. With regard to the meaning of the law of value in a socialist economy, Sun Yefang believed that Marx and Engels mentioned two different laws. One was the law of value of the capitalist commodity economy, that is, the law of market value. It required that the social average necessary labor quantity contained in commodities must be expressed through commodity exchange and the third commodity, but not directly expressed by calculation. The law of value in another sense referred to the law of value which still played a dominant role in a communist society. It required that the labor contained in the product should not be represented by commodity exchange and the third commodity, and the value should not take the form of exchange value, but could be expressed directly through statistical reports and planning indicators. Sun Yefang further expressed his view that "value determination is the law of value," pointing out that in a capitalist economy, the law of value appeared spontaneously, which eliminated the backward and stimulated the advanced through market competition. In a socialist society, it was important to not allow the law of value to initiate itself, but to consciously save labor time by constantly improving management and technology, so as to achieve maximum economic effect with minimum labor consumption.[25]

Research and discussion on distribution according to work was related to the supply system, wage system, piecework wage system, and bourgeois rights from the 1950s to the 1960s. The key points of the discussion were 1) whether to replace the supply system with the wage system, 2) the advantages and disadvantages of keeping or abolishing piecework wages, 3) the economic conditions for the generation of the law of distribution according to work, 4) distribution according to work and bourgeois rights, and 5) the "duality" of distribution according to work and the principle of socialist material interests. As for the economic conditions for the law of distribution according to work, most in economic and ideological circles believed that 1) it was determined by the level of productive forces, 2) it was determined by socialist public ownership, and 3) it was decided by individual ownership of labor force or part of labor individual ownership. With regard to distribution according to work and bourgeois rights, the majority held that the principle of distribution according to work recognized the differences in laborers' working abilities, which could lead to the unequal distribution of income, and thus was a residual effect of "bourgeois rights." But at the same time, it conformed to the principle of economic and social

---

25. Sun Yefang, *Research on Socialist Economic Issues* (People's Publishing House, 1985); "To Fully Understand Chairman Mao's Exposition on the Law of Value," *Economic Research*, no. 11 (1978).

material interests in the socialist stage, so it could be used as the distribution principle of a socialist society. According to the majority opinion, the principle of distribution according to work and material interests reflected the correct combination of the public interests and personal interests of the working people, which was conducive to improving the enthusiasm of workers in production, the improvement of labor productivity and the continuous growth of socialist production. Therefore, they were the objective economic laws of socialism. It was correct from the perspective of economics that the distribution mode and the principle of material interests were connected with the improvement of labor productivity and the acceleration of social productivity.

The theoretical research in this period also included the problem of socialist ownership, the relationship between politics and economy, the law of planned and proportional development of the national economy, economic accounting, economic structure, price formation, economic effect, population theory, and productivity economics. From 1949 to 1965, though the research and discussion of economic theory were restricted and influenced by historical conditions, social background, and political movements, it was possible to conduct extensive discussion and research on some Marxist economic principles and socialist economic issues with the attitude of academic research and academic discussion and the method of normative analysis, and there was a certain amount of progress.[26]

After the Cultural Revolution, four national symposiums on the theory of distribution according to work were held in April, June, and October of 1977 and October, 1978. During this period, more than 100 relevant articles were published in various newspapers and periodicals, which exceeded previous discussions on this issue in terms of both depth and breadth.

At that time, it was generally believed that distribution according to work was one of the socialist economic laws and part of a socialist distribution system. Distribution according to work was the inevitable result of the common possession of the means of production and the final realization of socialist public ownership. As for the economic conditions of distribution according to work, it was generally believed that the individual ownership of the labor force determined distribution according to work. Part of the labor force was owned by individuals, which was an "intermediate link" between capitalism and mature communism. The existence of distribution according to work showed that the communist way of combining laborers with means of production was not mature and perfect in the socialist stage.

In this discussion, some theorists put forward the idea that under the condition of the commodity economy, the realization of distribution according to work should take enterprises as the main body, and the labor remuneration must be related to the operating results of enterprises. Because under the conditions of the commodity economy, the laborer's "labor" could not be completely and directly expressed as social labor. Generally speaking, their labor was first directly manifested as local labor within the scope of enterprises. Through commodity exchange, it was proven that this kind of labor met the needs of society, so that local labor could be transformed

---

26. Su Xing, "Some Opinions on Studying the Law of Economic Development," *People's Daily*, March 4, 1957; Ping Xin, "On the Nature of Productivity," *Academic Monthly*, no. 6 (1959).

into social labor and become a part of the total labor of the overall society.[27] These viewpoints broke through the original framework and link distribution according to work with the socialist commodity economy, which had a certain innovative quality at that time. The distribution according to work mentioned in Marx's classic works aimed to exclude the relationship between commodity and currency, and directly receive equal remuneration according to equal amount of labor across society. Under the condition of the commodity economy, the labor taken as the distribution standard must be the labor that produced and realized value. Only when the commodity produced by the enterprise realized its value through exchange could the validity and span of the laborer's "labor" be determined. Without the operation effect of the enterprise, there was no basis for the distribution of workers. If distribution according to work led to equalitarianism, it was in contradiction with improving economic efficiency. If distribution according to work was associated with the effectiveness of "labor," it would encourage enterprises to improve economic efficiency and encourage employees to provide more effective labor.

3. The Category System Within the Framework of the Textbook of Political Economics

Many categories in the framework of the *Textbook of Political Economics* intersected with the category system within the framework of Marxist historical materialism and Marxist surplus value theory, especially the category system within the framework of scientific socialism theory, such as the object of political economics, productivity and production relations, commodity production under the socialist system, the role of the law of value under the socialist system, socialist ownership, distribution according to work, and other similar issues. However, from 1950s to 1970s, the basic socialist economic law and the law of planned and proportional development of the national economy within the framework of the *Textbook of Political Economics* were important topics for discussion and research in the field of Chinese economic thought and an important part of the category system of the mainstream form of China's economic thought.

(1) Basic Economic Law of Socialism

The basic economic law of socialism was an important theoretical problem of socialist political economics. The research and discussion on this issue mainly focused on two aspects, whether the basic socialist economic law would work in China's transitional period and the content and expression of the basic socialist economic law. There were four main views on the first aspect. The first point of view was that the basic economic law of socialism was the basic economic law of China in the transitional period. Although the socialist economy had not completely occupied the dominant position in the transitional period, with the increasing development of China's economy and the state's mastery of the economic lifeline, the socialist economy occupied a dominant position in the national economy. It was to develop day by day with the development

---

27. Wang Haibo, Wu Jinglian, and Zhou Shulian, "The Necessity of Closely Linking Part of the Income of Workers with the Operating Conditions of Enterprises," *Economic Research*, no. 12 (1978).

of the national economy and finally replace all non-socialist forms of economy. In this way, the basic economic law of socialism determined the basic economic law of China's transitional period. The second point of view was that the socialist and the capitalist basic economic laws worked simultaneously in China's transitional period. Since there were two modes of production in the transitional period of China, the socialist mode of production and the capitalist mode of production, there were two basic economic laws that worked at the same time. The third point of view was that the transitional period had its unique basic economic law. Since the transitional period was a society, it had its own basic economic laws. Only when the basic economic law in the transitional period had completed its historical task and withdrawn from the historical stage could it give way to the socialist basic economic law across society. The fourth point of view was that all kinds of economic components in the transitional period had their own main laws and regulations. The state-owned economy, cooperative economy, individual economy, and private capitalist economy were the social and economic components in the transitional period. Each economic component had its own main process and major aspects of dominating the economic component because of its own condition.[28]

There were three main views on the second aspect. One was to agree with Stalin's statement of the basic socialist economic laws in his *Economic Problems of Socialism in the USSR*, where he wrote, "Continuous expansion and perfection of socialist production on the basis of higher techniques is the *means* for the achievement of the aim [maximum satisfaction of the constantly rising material and cultural requirements of the whole of society]." The second was to turn to the idea of "developing production and meeting the needs," as proposed by Mao Zedong during the War Against Japanese Aggression, to replace Stalin's statement on the basic socialist economic law. This opinion had great influence in academic circles and it spread widely. The third was to quote the relevant expositions in Marx's *Critique of the Gotha Program*, particularly noting that "public essential value" was the basic economic law of socialism.[29]

At that time, discussion on the basic economic law of socialism was extensive, and some aspects of the study were in-depth. Through discussion and research, the understanding of the basic economic law, the purpose of socialist production, the characteristics of social form in the transitional period, and the relationship between socialist production and consumption further developed. However, the basic economic law was an abstract theoretical concept, and there was no longer a long period of socialist economic development as a practical reference, so most of the research and discussion in this area were purely logical reasoning from concept to concept, lacking investigation, statistics, and empirical analysis of the real economy, while some discussions deliberated in a battle of words. For example, some articles made a large argument

---

28. Editorial Department of *Economic Research* and *Economic Trends*, *Debates on Important Issues of Political Economics Since the Founding of the People's Republic of China (1949–1980)* (China Financial and Economic Publishing House, 1981), 88–92.

29. Editorial Department of *Economic Research* and *Economic Trends*, *Debates on Important Issues of Political Economics Since the Founding of the People's Republic of China (1949–1980)* (China Financial and Economic Publishing House, 1981), 93–98.

on the "main" economic law and the "basic" economic law. One side held that the "main" was not "basic," while the other side held that the "main" was actually "basic," and the two could not be distinguished. This method of normative analysis and the metaphysical academic atmosphere were quite common at that time. After debate on this issue came to an end, some of the participants remarked that many articles were rarely based on the research of Chinese statistical materials, and only a few examples were used to prove some conclusions. The fundamental reason for this phenomenon was that China had yet to learn to use the Marxist research method of proceeding from reality and occupying materials in detail. Therefore, the research objective was not to make a specific analysis of China's specific situation under the guidance of the general principles of Marxism-Leninism, but was often satisfied with adding these principles to real economic life.[30]

At the end of the 1970s, China's economic and ideological circles began to discuss the basic economic laws of socialism. Discussion mainly focused on several topics. The first was a discussion on Stalin's expression of basic socialist economic laws, which was basically correct, but the content was imperfect and needed to be supplemented, or it was basically imperfect and unscientific. The second was a discussion on the connotation of socialist production purpose, while the third addressed the realization of socialist production purpose, such as drawing up the national economic plan in accordance with the basic economic law of socialism, reversing the order of priority for heavy industry, light industry, and agriculture, carrying out reforms in all aspects in accordance with the purpose of socialist production, and organizing socialist circulation in accordance with the requirements of the basic socialist economic law.[31]

(2) The Law of Planned and Proportional Development of the National Economy

The planned and proportional development of the national economy was an important category of the mainstream form of China's economic thought from the 1950s to the 1970s, and an important guiding ideology for economic construction. In economic circles, topics discussed included whether the planned, proportional development of the national economy is an economic law of socialism or a general objective law, the relationship between planned and proportional development, between the law of planned and proportional development and the basic socialist economic law, between the law of planned and proportional development and the law of value, between the law of planned and proportional development and the rapid development of the national economy, as well as the regulatory role of the law of planned and proportional development in the socialist economy. Each topic basically had several different views.[32] By the

---

30. Xiang Qiyuan et al., *Review and Reflection on Socialist Economic Theory* (Jiangsu People's Publishing House, 1988).

31. Editorial Department of *Economic Research* and *Economic Trends, Debates on Important Issues of Political Economics Since the Founding of the People's Republic of China (1949–1980)* (China Financial and Economic Publishing House, 1981), 99–109.

32. Editorial Department of *Economic Research* and *Economic Trends, Debates on Important Issues of Political Economics Since the Founding of the People's Republic of China (1949–1980)* (China Financial and Economic Publishing House, 1981), 110–129.

end of the 1970s, the discussion on the law of planned and proportional development of the national economy was generally related to the law of value. Some held that the law of planned and proportional development and the law of value played a regulating role in the socialist economy. Because the socialist planned economy itself was a combination of a planned and market economy, and the planned nature was the leading one, objectively, the proportional relationship of economic development was jointly regulated by the law of planning and the law of value.[33] There was also a view that the concept of value would not exist in a future communist society (including socialism with single public ownership) in which commodities and money had disappeared, let alone the law of value. The law of planned and proportionate value was adequate to reflect the objective inevitability of the planned distribution and saving of labor time, and there was no need to rely on the law of value.[34]

There were questions regarding which aspects of the economic planning arrangement of the proportion relationship were most significant in actual economic activities. On June 30, 1954, Chen Yun reported to the Central Committee of the Communist Party of China on the formulation of the First Five-Year Plan. Proportional development involved the proportion of agriculture and industry, the proportion of heavy and light industries, the proportion of various departments of heavy industry, the proportion of industrial development and railway transportation, the proportion of supply and demand of technical force, and other issues. The only way to see whether it was balanced was to determine whether it was proportional. Proportionality was balanced, and if it was balanced, it would be proportionate.[35]

2.2 Exploration of the System of Socialist Political Economics

1. The Influence of the Soviet Political Economics System

In the history of world economic theory, socialist political economics was a new discipline that emerged in the early 20th century. Marxist classical writers mainly studied the capitalist economy, but they only advanced some reasoning and ideas on the future socialist economy, without systematic theoretical elaboration. It was not until after the October Revolution in Russia that the Soviet Union, the first socialist country in human history, was established. Before the 1920s, political economics was divided into a "broad sense" and a "narrow sense."

Broad sense political economics was the economics which studied the various social forms of humans, while narrow sense political economics was that which took capitalist society as

---

33. Sun Shangqing, Chen Jiyuan, and Zhang Er, "Several Theoretical Issues on the Combination of Planned and Market-oriented Socialist Economy," *Economic Research*, no. 5 (1979).

34. Liu Duqing, "Law of Value, Law of Planning, Law of Proportional Development," *China Economic Issues*, no. 4 (1979).

35. Li Zhining, *The Economic Canon of the People's Republic of China* (Jilin People's Publishing House, 1987), 142–143.

the research object. At the time, some Marxist theorists believed that economics was a science that aimed to study and that revealed the movement law of the emergence, development, and even extinction of capitalism. Once the capitalist economy was replaced by the socialist planned economy, economics would "end." This view was criticized by Lenin, who pointed out that even in a communist society, there were still two major categories of exchange relations, and political economics would still be needed. From that time, research into socialist political economics began to receive attention from theoretical circles, and it gradually developed into an independent subject with socialist economy as the research object.

In 1952, Stalin published *Economic Problems of Socialism in the USSR*, which can be called the first theoretical work on socialist economy in the history of political and economic theories. In 1954, based on Stalin's theory and system, the Soviet Academy of Sciences compiled and published the *Textbook of Political Economics*, marking the initial establishment of the discipline system of socialist political economics.

The socialist political economics system of the Soviet Union had a profound influence on China. In the 1950s, almost all the textbooks used by Chinese colleges and universities were *Textbook of Political Economics* from the Soviet Union. Every revision of this textbook had a large circulation in China. From the 1950s to the 1960s, a large part of the works on political economics published in China were studied and explained around the system, content, and viewpoints of Soviet textbooks. In the early 1960s, some Chinese economists tried to write a socialist political economics with Chinese characteristics, but due to the limitations of the objective conditions and subjective understanding of economic development, they failed to break through the framework of the Soviet system.

The theoretical system of the Soviet Union's socialist political economics had three basic points. The first was the public ownership of the means of production, the second was the socialist industrialization characterized by giving priority to the development of heavy industry, and the third was the highly centralized planned management system, which ran through the basic economic laws of socialism defined by Stalin.[36] This theoretical system not only had a broad, far-reaching impact on China's theoretical circles, but also on China's socialist construction.

In 1988, the Soviet Union published a new *Textbook of Political Economics*, which revised the object and system of political economics. With regard to the object of political economics, the new textbook revised the traditional definition which stated that "political economics is a science concerned with the relations of production and its development laws," and proposed that "political economics studies relations of production from the unity of production relations, productivity, and superstructure."[37] The object of political economics included not only production relations, but also productive forces. It emphasized that the mode of production should be studied from the dialectical unity of production relations and productive forces. As for

---

36. Institute of Economics of the Soviet Academy of Sciences, *Textbook of Political Economics* (Sanlian Bookstore, 1960).

37. V. A. Medvedev et al., eds., *Political Economics* (China Social Sciences Press, 1989), 37.

the political economics system, the framework of the new textbook centered around the general principles of economic development, the capitalist system, the socialist economic system, and the modern world economy.[38] At the end of the 1980s, when China's economic system reform was developing vigorously, the reflection and negation of traditional concepts, views, and definitions constantly emerged in the study of economic thought. The new textbooks from the Soviet Union had a certain impact on the exploration of China's socialist political and economic system in this period.

2. The Exploration of the Chinese Economics Community

In the 1950s and early 1960s, although the Soviet system dominated the country, the exploration of establishing China's socialist political and economic system in Chinese theoretical circles never stopped, and some important issues were discussed. At that time, the research and exploration mainly focused on two issues, the starting point category of socialist political economics and the main line running through socialist political economics.

(1) Exploration of On Socialist Economics

On Socialist Economics was a main subject that Sun Yefang began to study in the 1950s. In June 1961, he proposed opinions on the first draft of *On Socialist Economics* and the preliminary idea of the second draft.

From 1962 to 1963, some important manuscripts began to form, but it was not finished until Sun Yefang died of illness in 1983. In accordance with his will, the Institute of Economics of the Chinese Academy of Social Sciences collated and revised his relevant manuscripts and speeches and compiled the draft of *On Socialist Economics*, which was published by the People's Publishing House in 1985. This manuscript more completely and accurately reflected the views and theories formed through Sun's long-term research on the socialist part of Marxist political economics, including his exploration of the socialist political economics system.

Sun pointed out that in the research object of political economics, it was necessary to oppose two kinds of biases, the "productivity theory" and the "material and technological foundation theory" and the "fear of productivity theory," which regarded political economics as an illusory thing that did not address specific problems, but aimed only to define from concept to concept, playing word games without solving any problems. Production relations and productivity were the basic contradictions of the social economy, so one could not be ignored to study the other. From the perspective of social and economic development, productivity was the main aspect of the contradiction, but as far as the research object of political economics was concerned, the production relationship was the main issue.

Socialist relations of production were the main research object of socialist political economics, but it was impossible to understand the socialist relations of production from the viewpoint of the

---

38. V. A. Medvedev et al., eds., *Political Economics* (China Social Sciences Press, 1989), 37.

"natural economy" or commodity monetary economy. Sun Yefang advocated study of political economics through the analysis of the objective economic process. The objective economic process was the process of production and circulation, and in general was the process of social production and reproduction. The study of the socialist economic process took the category of the "product" as the logical starting point. The so-called "product" was not a specific thing, but a summary of the production relations between people at the advanced stage of socialist ownership and communism, an abstract category reflecting the internal relations of socialist ownership by the people. Without using abstract analysis, simply studying "products" from different ownership systems and distribution according to work would result in a turn from external causes to internal causes and from commodity and monetary relations to ownership by the people. This would not be appropriate. It was important to instead start with the most essential relationship. Political economics studied the relations of production, and in abstracting the natural attributes of "products," the rest represented the relations of production. After abstracting the different ownership systems and distribution according to work, the rest represented the internal relations of production under ownership by the people. Only from this starting point was it possible to analyze the essential relationship of the socialist economy.

The product category in the socialist economy also had the duality of use value and value. It was of no economic significance to talk only about use value but not value. Since the product had this duality, socialist labor had a similar duality of concrete labor and abstract labor. Only under the premise of the duality of labor was it possible to analyze the relationship between individual labor and social labor and exchange. The duality of labor determined the duality of the production process. The production process of socialist products was the unity of use value manufacturing and value creation. The value of products depended on the consumption of social necessary labor time in the process of product production. In order to calculate the social necessary labor time, it was necessary to compare economic effects and production costs. According to this logic, Sun Yefang proposed that the line of socialist political economics textbooks should be to produce the most products to meet the social needs with the least social labor consumption. This line reflected the purpose of socialist production and also gave the various categories of socialist political economics the necessary internal relations.[39]

Sun Yefang's advanced explorations referred to the framework and methods of Marx's *Das Kapital* to construct the discipline system of socialist political economics, which was different from the *Textbook of Political Economics*. It played an important role in the theoretical history of Chinese socialist political economics and laid a corresponding foundation for future research.

(2) On the Central Issue of Socialist Political Economics

In 1958, Yu Guangyuan published in the Eleventh issue of *Learning* magazine that "meeting social needs to the fullest extent is a central issue in the socialist part of political economics," which explored the system of socialist political economics. Yu Guangyuan pointed out that under the

---

39. Sun Yefang, *Research on Socialist Economic Issues* (People's Publishing House, 1985).

socialist system, the purpose of production was to meet the social needs to the fullest extent. Therefore, it was a central issue in the socialist part of political economics. The material goods that could be used to meet the needs of a society were said to have some use value in political economics. If the center of the capitalist part of political economics was value, then the center of the socialist part of political economics should focus on the use value. Of course, the point was not to study the natural attributes of use value and its utility, but to examine how to produce more, better, and more suitable products with various use values, how to reasonably distribute these products, and how to reasonably consume these products when studying the regularity of the socialist economic movement.

Yu Guangyuan concluded that meeting the growing needs of society to the fullest extent was a line running throughout socialist production. In the socialist part of political economics, how to combine the fundamental purpose of socialist production with the main aspects and main processes of the socialist economy was a central issue in theoretical research.[40]

(3) *The Exploration of* Socialist Political Economics *(Southern Edition)*

In 1979, Sichuan People's Publishing House published a trial textbook entitled *The Socialist Part of Political Economics,* jointly compiled by sixteen southern universities (Fudan University, Nanjing University, Xiamen University, Wuhan University, Sun Yat-sen University, Hangzhou University, Jinan University, Sichuan University, Shanghai Normal University, Shandong University, Guangxi University, Yunnan University, Jiangxi University, Zhengzhou University, Xiangtan University and Anhui Labor University). The textbook pointed out that the socialist part of political economics was an important part of Marxist political economics. The socialist part of political economics took socialist production relations as the research object, and its central task was to analyze the process of socialist production and reproduction according to the reality of socialist construction, clarify the objective law of the development of socialist production relations, and serve socialist economic construction. The theoretical system of the textbook was mainly composed of three chapters which covered the topics of the establishment of socialist production relations, the socialist public ownership of the means of production, and the essence of socialist production, along with production, flow, distribution, and other factors. From the perspective of theoretical expression, this textbook presented the basic view of the Soviet textbook, but it was a complete textbook with its own chapter system, which had a great influence at that time.

(4) *The Exploration of* Socialist Political Economics *(Northern Edition)*

In December 1979, Shaanxi People's Publishing House *The Socialist Part of Political Economics,* jointly compiled by thirteen Northern Universities (Peking University, Renmin University of China, Nankai University, Liaoning University, Hebei University, Shanxi University, Jilin

---

40. Yu Guangyuan, "Meeting Social Needs to the Maximum Extent is a Central Issue in the Socialist Political Economics," *Learning*, no. 11 (1958).

University, Heilongjiang University, Lanzhou University, Ningxia University, Qinghai Normal University, Shaanxi Normal University, and Beijing Institute of Economics). The textbook was chiefly edited by Nankai University and co-edited with Liaoning University. By 1993, the fifth edition of the textbook was published. From the second edition on, it was chiefly edited by Gu Shutang and Song Zexing.

The textbook pointed out that the research object of political economics (socialist part) was socialist production relations. This book studied the relations of production in the underdeveloped socialist stage. The so-called "underdeveloped socialist stage" was characterized by a low degree of socialization of production, two forms of public ownership of the means of production, and even a certain amount of individual ownership. Distribution according to work could not be fully implemented throughout society at this stage.

The basic task of political economics (socialist part) was to clarify the law of socialist economic development. After the establishment of socialist relations of production, the main task of social development changed from emancipating productive forces to developing productive forces under the protection of new production relations. Therefore, the fundamental purpose of political economics (socialist part) in studying the law of socialist economic development was to constantly improve the relations of production and promote the development of productive forces.

The textbook held that the core of socialist economic relations was the material interest relationship within the state and between the collective and the individual, and it took the socialist material interest relationship as an important guide throughout the book. The content of the textbook was divided into five sections and thirteen chapters. The first introduction mainly discussed the development stage and characteristics of socialist society, the second part covered the production process, the third part addressed the circulation process, the fourth part discussed the reproduction process, which was the central part of the book, and the fifth part was about the class struggle in the underdeveloped socialist stage.

In the later revisions of the textbook, based on the changes of historical conditions and the deepening of theoretical research, the teaching material made corresponding adjustments to the research object, theoretical framework, and chapter contents, and finally developed into "political economics of the socialist market economy." The textbook won many awards and had a wide influence in the field of political economics.

2.3 The Theory of Economic Policy in the Transitional Period of Socialism

1. The Definition of the Transitional Period and the Formation of the General Line of the Transitional Period

The Constitution of the People's Republic of China was adopted by the First National People's Congress in 1954. According to the Constitution, this was a transitional period from the founding of the People's Republic of China to the completion of socialism. The starting point of the transitional period was the establishment of a new democratic country after the success of the new democratic revolution. The completion of socialist transformation, that is, the establishment of the socialist system, marked the end of the transitional period. According to this view, the starting point of the transitional period was the establishment of the People's Republic of China, and the completion of the three major socialist reforms in 1956 marked the end of the transitional period.

China's transitional period was different from that discussed by Marx and Engels. Marx and Engels lived in the rising stage of capitalism. Without concrete practice, they could only foresee the development of society according to the development trend of capitalism at that time, and as they noted, "between capitalist and communist society there lies the period of the revolutionary transformation of the one into the other."[41] This period was the first stage of a communist society, that is, the socialist stage in the process of transformation from a capitalist to a communist society. As a transitional period, the socialist society was established on the basis of a highly developed capitalist society. Socialist society and communist society were the products of the basic contradictions of capitalist society. Marx described communist society, saying that "a communist society[…] has *developed* on its own foundations, but, on the contrary, […] it *emerges* from capitalist society; which is thus in every respect, economically, morally, and intellectually, still stamped with the birthmarks of the old society from whose womb it emerges."[42] The task of the socialist stage "is the *declaration of the permanence of the revolution*, the *class dictatorship* of the proletariat as the necessary transit point to the *abolition of class distinctions generally*, to the abolition of all the relations of production on which they rest, to the abolition of all the social relations that correspond to these relations of production, to the revolutionizing of all the ideas that result from these social relations."[43]

Lenin believed that the transitional period referred to by Marx and Engels was a period of proletarian dictatorship, in which "the purpose of the proletariat is to build socialism, eliminate the class division of society, make all members of society become workers, and eliminate the basis of the system of exploiting people by all people." He said, "This object cannot be achieved at one stroke. It requires a fairly long period of transition from capitalism to socialism, because the reorganisation of production is a difficult matter, because radical changes in all spheres of life need time, and because the enormous force of habit of running things in a petty-bourgeois and bourgeois way can only be overcome by a long and stubborn struggle. That is why Marx spoke of an entire period of the dictatorship of the proletariat as the period of transition from capitalism to socialism."[44] Stalin defined the end of the transition period as the basic realization of national industrialization and agricultural collectivization on the basis of leading the practice of Soviet economic construction.

---

41. Marx and Engels, *Selected Works of Marx and Engels*, vol. 3 (People's Publishing House, 1972), 21.
42. Marx and Engels, *Selected Works of Marx and Engels*, vol. 3 (People's Publishing House, 1972), 10.
43. Marx and Engels, *Selected Works of Marx and Engels*, vol. 1 (People's Publishing House, 1972), 479–480.
44. Lenin, *Selected Works of Lenin*, vol. 3 (People's Publishing House, 1972), 857.

Marx, Engels, and others did not study how to enter a socialist society in a country with low productivity like China. The theory of China's transition period was put forward by the leadership of the Communist Party of China headed by Mao Zedong, using existing communist theory and combining it with China's special national conditions and revolutionary situation. Therefore, China's transition period was different from that described by Marx, Engels, Lenin, and Stalin. Mao divided the Chinese revolution led by the Communist Party of China into two stages, the new democratic revolution and the socialist revolution. According to this view, the first step of the Chinese revolution was the new, special bourgeois democratic revolution led by the Communist Party of China. After the victory of the revolution, a new democratic society was established through the joint dictatorship of various revolutionary classes. On the basis of the new democratic society, the socialist society was established through the dictatorship of the proletariat. Mao Zedong pointed out, "This is a transitional period from the founding of the People's Republic of China to the basic completion of socialist transformation."[45] China's special national conditions determined that the transition from a capitalist to a socialist society was not realized, nor that from a semi-colonial, semi-feudal society to a socialist society, but from a new democratic to a socialist society.

In March 1949, in his report delivered at the Second Plenary Session of the Seventh Central Committee of the Communist Party of China, Mao Zedong proposed various policies for promoting the rapid victory of the revolution and organizing this victory. It explained that under a national victory, the focus of the party's work must be shifted from rural areas to cities, and the focus of urban work should be on the recovery of production in the formulation of the basic policies of the Party in politics, economics, and foreign affairs after Liberation. It also pointed to the development direction of China from an agricultural country to an industrial country, and from a new democratic society to a socialist and communist society. At the same time, Mao analyzed in detail the proportion of various economic components in China at that time and the corresponding guiding strategies. On the eve of the founding of the People's Republic of China, the Common Program of the Chinese People's Political Consultative Conference affirmed the basic principles and guidelines of the Second Plenary Session of the Seventh Central Committee of the Communist Party of China, which laid a policy foundation for the proposal of the general line in the transitional period. After three years of construction, by 1952, the national economy had been restored. The output of the main industrial and agricultural products exceeded the highest level before 1949, that is, 20% of the output from 1936. In September 1952, the proportion of the state-owned economy increased to 67.3%, while that of the private sector decreased to 32.7%. This was a significant change compared with that in 1949 when the proportion of the state-owned economy in the total industrial output value was less than half. These achievements provided certain objective conditions for the formal proposal of the general line for the transitional period. Mao Zedong pointed out, "After the downfall of the landlord class and the bureaucratic bourgeoisie, the main contradiction in China is the contradiction between the working class and

---

45. Mao Zedong, *Selected Works of Mao Zedong*, vol. 5 (People's Publishing House, 1972), 89.

the national bourgeoisie, so the national bourgeoisie should no longer be called the intermediate class."[46] This shows that Mao Zedong tended to gradually step into the transformation of the substantive stage of socialism, which laid the ideological foundation for the later general line of the transitional period.

From June 13 to August 13, 1953, the National Financial Work Conference was held. During the meeting, Mao made a preliminary statement on the general line for the transitional period. In August, when Zhou Enlai deliberated on the conclusion drawn by the meeting, Mao stressed that the time for socialist transformation should be "over a fairly long period of time." According to Mao's earlier statement, Zhou Enlai made a more detailed explanation of the definition of the transitional period at the 49th Executive Enlarged Meeting of the first CPPCC on September 8, 1953, saying, "In the transitional period, the socialist transformation of national industrialization, agriculture, handicraft industry, and capitalist industry and commerce was only basically realized, not completely realized. Now, as long as it is basically realized, the transitional period will be over. The length of the transition period depends on whether the country has basically completed industrialization and the socialist transformation of agriculture, handicraft industry, and capitalist industry and commerce. It depends on our efforts."[47]

On September 24, 1953, on the occasion of the fourth National Day, the general line for the transitional period was announced. That December, Mao Zedong pointed out in his *Struggle to Mobilize All Forces to Build Our Country into a Great Socialist Country: Outline of Study and Propaganda of the Party's General Line in the Transitional Period* that this was a transitional period from the founding of the People's Republic of China to the basic completion of socialist transformation. The Party's general line and task in this transitional period was to gradually realize the socialist industrialization of the country and the socialist transformation of agriculture, handicraft industry, capitalist industry, and commerce over a fairly long period of time. This general line was a beacon for all the country's work. Departing from it would lead to both rightist and leftist error.[48]

The general line for the transition period was adopted at the First National People's Congress in 1954 and was included in the Constitution. According to the Constitution, this was a transitional period from the founding of the People's Republic of China to the completion of socialism. The general task of the state in the transitional period was to gradually complete the socialist industrialization of the country and the socialist transformation of agriculture, handicraft industry, capitalist industry, and commerce.

---

46. Mao Zedong, *Selected Works of Mao Zedong*, vol. 5 (People's Publishing House, 1972), 75.

47. Zhou Enlai, *Selected Works of Zhou Enlai*, vol. 2 (People's Publishing House, 1984), 105.

48. Mao Zedong, *Selected Readings of Mao Zedong*, vol. 2 (People's Publishing House, 1987), 704.

2. Economic Analysis of the General Line in the Transitional Period

The essential aim of the general line of China's transition period was to solve the problem of ownership through socialist industrialization and socialist transformation, so as to gradually eliminate the exploitation system and establish a socialist society. Here, industrialization was the economic foundation and material condition of socialist transformation and socialist society, while socialist transformation was the political means of ownership reform, and the purpose of both was to establish a socialist society.

The general line of the transitional period embodied the principles and policies of socialist industrialization and socialist transformation at the same time, with each promoting the other. Mao believed that national industrialization was the "main body," while socialist transformation was its "two wings." He believed that the general line was to solve the problem of ownership, while emphasizing the status of national industrialization. Socialist industrialization provided the economic and material basis for socialist transformation, and socialist transformation provided the institutional guarantee for the realization of socialist industrialization.

The report of the Second Plenary Session of the Seventh Central Committee of the Communist Party of China set the goal of establishing a complete, independent industrial system, which was the first socialist industrialization thought proposed. The Common Program stipulated that China must change from an agricultural country to an industrial country, and the goal of industrialization was set as China's infrastructure policy. The general line of the transitional period established that industrialization was the basic state policy and economic goal of the People's Republic of China. During the First Five-Year Plan period, China concentrated its efforts on carrying out industrial construction with 156 construction units designed with the assistance of Soviet Union as the center and composed of 694 construction units. Through economic construction during the First Five-Year Plan period, China established the initial stage of China's socialist industrialization foundation. Mao Zedong pointed out at the Second Plenary Session of the Seventh Central Committee of the Communist Party of China that the individual agricultural economy must be guided systematically in the direction of collectivization and modernization. The Common Program also had provisions to encourage farmers to voluntarily develop cooperative undertakings and organize supply and marketing cooperatives.

In 1952, the Government Administration Council issued the Decision on Agricultural Production in 1952, calling for the development of temporary mutual aid groups, the promotion of perennial mutual aid groups, and the development of agricultural production cooperatives with land shares. In the spring of 1953, in accordance with the Resolution of the Central Committee of the Communist Party of China on Mutual Assistance and Cooperation in Agricultural Production, all localities, in accordance with the principle of voluntariness and mutual benefit, tried to establish land shares and develop mutual aid and cooperation organizations. At the same time, the resolution called for overcoming the negative, impatient tendencies in agricultural mutual aid and cooperation. In December 1953, the Central Committee of the Communist Party of China passed the Resolution on the Development of Agricultural Production Cooperatives, indicating that agricultural production cooperatives had moved from the trial period to the formal development period. With the continuous increase in the number of various types of cooperatives, the Constitution adopted by the First National People's Congress in September 1954 affirmed the cooperative economy as a socialist economy under collective ownership or a semi-socialist economy under partial collective ownership.

The socialist transformation of capitalist industry and commerce began in 1953. On November 11, 1953, the *People's Daily* published an article entitled "Further Bringing Private Industry and Commerce into the Orbit of State Capitalism," which pointed out that in order to make private industry and commerce suitable for the national construction plan and the needs of the people, it was necessary to change their production relations and business methods. Therefore, it was necessary to encourage capitalist commerce to develop in the direction of state capitalism. On October 9, 1954, the *People's Daily* published an editorial, "Strengthening the Socialist Transformation of Capitalist Commerce," which explained the tasks of state-owned commerce and cooperative commerce in gradually realizing the socialist transformation of capitalist commerce.

At the end of 1955, the government successively approved industry public-private joint ventures. In January 1956, socialist transformation of capitalist industry and commerce peaked. On July 28, 1956, the State Council issued the Instructions on Some Issues in the Socialist Transformation of Private Industry and Commerce, Handicraft Industry, and the Private Transportation Industry, pointing out that vendors who did not participate in the public-private joint venture and cooperative stores should, on the principle of voluntariness, form a cooperative group with decentralized operations and with each bearing profit and loss by stages and industries, and its business was to be composed of state-owned stores and suppliers, marketing cooperatives, or joint venture stores. By the end of 1956, 99% of the capitalist industries and 82% of the private businesses in China had been transformed into socialist institutions, and the ownership transformation of capitalist industry and commerce had been basically completed.

At the end of 1952, the Central Committee of the Communist Party of China put forward the general line for the transitional period. The core of the general line was "One Transformation and Three Reforms," which indicated that over a fairly long period of time, China would gradually realize the socialist industrialization of the country and the socialist transformation of agriculture, handicraft industry, capitalist industry, and commerce. After the leading position of the state-owned economy was established in the period of national economic recovery, the economy of other components also transited to socialism. On July 29, 1953, at the enlarged meeting of the Politburo of the CPC Central Committee, Mao Zedong said, "What are the conditions for the transformation of state capitalism into socialism? First, there are thousands of large socialist factories; second, agricultural cooperation requires mutual assistance and cooperation in a planned, steady, active, and voluntary manner; and third, the internal conditions of state capitalist enterprises, including Party organizations and trade unions, together with our leadership, can ensure that the enterprises are transferred to socialism, that the ownership of capitalists can be cancelled, and that they can be arranged properly. Here, the first step is to change capitalism into state capitalism and to transform independent, unrestricted and free-market capitalism into non-independent, restricted, and capitalism without free markets, that is, state capitalism. The second step is to transform state capitalism into socialism and eliminate classes."[49] The completion of the general task in the general line of the transitional period indicated that the socialist public ownership of the means of production had become the only economic foundation of the state and society, and China's socialist system had been formally established.

3. Discussion on Economic Policy Theory in the Transitional Period

The economic theory in the transitional period mainly involved industrialization and ownership reform theory, and Mao Zedong was the main founder of the economic thought during the transitional period. Both Zhou Enlai and Liu Shaoqi emphasized the consistency between the general line of the transitional period and the new democracy, and they made contributions in the form of some measures that were clear and specific.

In June 1949, Mao Zedong analyzed in detail the reasons China chose Marxism and embarked on the people's democratic dictatorship in his book *On the People's Democratic Dictatorship,* and pointed out that under the people's democratic dictatorship, the country must solve the problem of national industrialization one step at a time. Under the leadership of the working class and the Communist Party, China must steadily move from an agricultural country to an industrial country, and from a new democratic society to a socialist and communist society.[50]

At the beginning of the founding of the People's Republic of China, Party and state leaders realized that the formulation of China's economic policies should start from a clear understanding of the basic national conditions. In June 1950, at the National Committee of the Chinese People's Political Consultative Conference (CPPCC), Mao Zedong stated that after China's economic and cultural undertakings had developed to a certain extent, it would be possible to enter the socialist period calmly and properly. Liu Shaoqi also believed that the new democratic society was a transitional society. This stage was a relatively independent historical stage, different from capitalism and socialism, and it was insurmountable. In 1951, Liu Shaoqi pointed out that the national economy of the new democracy was mainly composed of the state-owned economy, cooperative economy, state capitalist economy, private capitalist economy, small commodity economy, and semi-natural economy. On this basis, Liu's countermeasures were to take the development of the state-owned economy as the main body, establish the cooperative economy generally, closely combine the cooperative economy with state-owned economy, assist independent small producers and lead them to gradually develop toward cooperatives, organize the state-owned capitalist economy, and gradually increase socialist elements in the national economy under the possible conditions. He aimed to strengthen the planning of the national economy, so as to gradually and steadily transition to socialism and to allow the development of

---

49. Mao Zedong, *Collected Works of Mao Zedong,* vol. 6 (People's Publishing House, 1996), 285–287.
50. Mao Zedong, *Selected Works of Mao Zedong,* vol. 4 (People's Publishing House, 1991), 1468–1482.

private capitalist economy within the scope conducive to the national economy and the people's livelihood.[51] Later, Mao Zedong summarized this approach as "giving consideration to both public and private affairs, benefiting both labor and capital, mutual assistance between urban and rural areas, and internal and external exchanges."

Mao attached great importance to the issue of industrialization. He regarded industrialization as the material basis of China's revolution and future, and he believed that only powerful modern industry could consolidate socialism. During the War Against Japanese Aggression, Mao proposed that machine industry was the foundation of a democratic society. He said, "The foundation of a new democratic society is factories (social production, public, and private) and cooperatives (including change of work teams), not a decentralized individual economy. Decentralized individual economy, family agriculture, and cottage industry are the foundation of a feudal society, not the foundations of a democratic society (including old democracy, new democracy, and socialism), which is the difference between Marxism and populism."[52] After the founding of the People's Republic of China, Mao held that "socialist industry is the material basis for socialist transformation of the entire national economy. Only a sufficiently strong socialist industry can attract, reorganize and replace capitalist industry, support socialist commerce, transform and replace capitalist commerce, and transform individual agriculture and handicraft industry with new technologies to most efficiently expand production, accumulate funds produce competent people for socialist construction, and cultivate socialist habits, thus making economic, cultural, and political preparation for the complete victory of socialism."[53]

In addition to the help of the Soviet Union in industrial construction, the guiding policies of industrialization in the transitional period were also influenced by the Soviet Union. In August 1952, entrusted by Mao Zedong, Zhou Enlai and Chen Yun went to the Soviet Union to consult with the Central Committee of the Soviet Communist Party and the Soviet government on the Draft Outline of the Five-Year Plan. Subsequently, the Central Financial and Economic Commission (CFEC) issued the Guidelines on the Preparation of the Outline of the Five-Year Plan and China's Economic Situation and the Tasks and Schedules of the Five Year Construction, emphasizing the importance of industrial construction with heavy industry as the primary focus and light industry as the secondary concern. That December, the Central Committee of the Communist Party of China issued the Instructions on Several Issues Concerning the Formulation of the 1953 Plan and the Outline of the Long-term Plan, which pointed out that the development of heavy industry must be the focus, and the infrastructure construction of heavy industry and national defense industry should first be guaranteed.

In the process of the formation of socialist transformation thought on agriculture, there were two different opinions within the Communist Party of China. One, represented by Mao Zedong, advocated cooperation before mechanization, and the other, represented by Liu Shaoqi, advocated

---

51. Liu Shaoqi, *Selected Works of Liu Shaoqi*, vol. 1 (People's Publishing House, 1985), 428.

52. Mao Zedong, *Collected Works of Mao Zedong*, vol. 3 (People's Publishing House, 1996), 207.

53. Literature Research Office of the CPC Central Committee, *Selected Important Documents Since the Founding of the People's Republic of China*, vol. 4 (Central Literature Publishing House, 1993), 701.

mechanization before cooperation. Liu Shaoqi believed that the main task of the economic recovery period after the founding of the new China was to "abolish the land ownership system exploited by the feudal landlord class and implement the land ownership system of farmers, so as to develop the rural productive forces, develop agricultural production, and open up the road for the industrialization of the new China,"[54] at the beginning of the founding of the new China, the conditions to take steps of shaking private ownership were not yet mature.

Liu Shaoqi's specific strategy was that after the proletariat gained power, he organized supply and marketing cooperatives through voluntary fund-raising in rural areas throughout the country, linked small-scale production of farmers and socialized large-scale industry with it, and carried out collectivism and socialist education on farm cooperatives through Party organizations and Party members in rural areas to foster transformation of small-scale production into large-scale production in the future. He said, "Only with the leadership and help of the working class and the nationalization of industrialization and of the land can collectivization be realized and a large number of machines be supplied to the peasants, so that agriculture can be generally collectivized."[55] "Gradually shaking, weakening, or even denying the private foundation, raising the agricultural production mutual aid organizations to agricultural production cooperatives as a new factor to 'overcome the spontaneous factors of farmers' was said to be a wrong, dangerous, 'utopian rural socialism' idea."[56]

Liu Shaoqi did not agree to abolish rural private ownership by promoting mutual aid and the cooperation movement. Later, his thinking changed. This change was evident in his letter to Stalin on October 20, 1952. On the issue of agricultural transformation, he said in the letter, "In the agricultural industry, after the land reform, we have developed mutual assistance and cooperation among farmers. At present, 40% of the peasants throughout the country have participated in this movement, while 70% to 80% of the peasants in the old liberated areas have taken part in the movement. In addition, thousands of well-organized agricultural production cooperatives and several collective farms have become shareholders, with their land as the capital. We are ready to vigorously and steadily develop this movement in the future, to organize most of China's farmers in agricultural production cooperatives and collective farms in the next ten to fifteen years, and basically realize the collectivization of China's agricultural economy. Mutual aid and the cooperation movement is the main path to rural economic development in China in the future. In the final stage of rural economic collectivization, the measures should be taken to eliminate private ownership of not many rich peasants would depend on the situation at that time."[57]

---

54. Editorial Department, *Selected Historical Materials of China's Land Reform* (National Defense University Press, 1988), 642.

55. Liu Shaoqi, *Liu Shaoqi on the Economic Construction of New China* (Central Literature Publishing House, 1995), 183.

56. Liu Shaoqi, *Liu Shaoqi on the Economic Construction of New China* (Central Literature Publishing House, 1995), 192.

57. Literature Research Office of the CPC Central Committee, *Selected Important Documents Since the Founding of the People's Republic of China*, vol. 3 (Central Literature Publishing House, 1992), 370.

As for the positive role of cooperation, Chen Yun held that there were three ways to increase agricultural production, which included opening up wasteland, building water conservancy, and cooperating with each other, with the fastest results being seen in co-ops at that time. According to past experience, the average output could be increased by 15% to 30%. If it was possible to increase production by 30%, there would be 100 billion *jin* of grain. Only after agricultural cooperation could various measures of increasing production be more effective. Therefore, the cooperative was a way to increase production with less cost and more immediate results, and the state should give more financial support to it.[58]

In July 1955, Mao Zedong criticized the view of shrinking cooperatives in his report On the Issue of Agricultural Cooperation. He said that comrades who held the view of that the cooperative movement should be slowed down were like women with bound feet. After the report was issued, all localities accelerated the process of agricultural cooperation, thus contributing to the leftist mistakes in the movement of the agricultural cooperation, which made the socialist transformation of agriculture deviate from the general line of the transitional period. The later agricultural cooperative movement was established on the basis of backward production, which seriously affected other economic construction work, especially the process of industrialization.

During the period from the second half of 1955 to the end of 1956, the CPC Central Committee overestimated the farmers' consciousness, which led to the rapid development of the cooperation against the wishes of farmers and dampened their enthusiasm for production. On this issue, Deng Xiaoping said, "In the past, the speed of socialist transformation was too fast. I don't think this opinion is unreasonable at all. For example, agricultural cooperation reached a peak in one or two years, a form of organization was not yet consolidated, and it was soon changed. This is the case from the primary cooperatives to the general high-level cooperatives. If we make steady progress, consolidate for a period of time, and then develop, we may do better."[59]

In July 1951, Chen Yun pointed out at the work report meeting of the China Federation of Industry and Commerce that handicraft workshops should join the Federation of Industry and Commerce, but that this should be carried out step by step according to the specific situation in each city. In his letter to Stalin on October 20, 1952, Liu Shaoqi also expressed his views on the development of handicraft co-operatives, saying, "For these handicraft industries, we are ready to help small handicraftsmen organize production cooperatives and encourage handicraftsmen to unite to adopt machine production, and some of them will be crushed by the machine industry. However, the situation among small handicraftsmen is different from that among peasants. We have established or will soon establish Party organizations in the struggle of peasants against landlords, while we generally do not have Party organizations among handicraftsmen. Therefore, we will have more difficulties in reforming the handicraft industry and organizing handicraft production cooperatives, and we may need more time."[60]

---

58. Chen Yun, *Collected Works of Chen Yun*, vol. 2 (Central Literature Publishing House, 2005), 239.

59. Deng Xiaoping, *Selected Works of Deng Xiaoping*, vol. 3 (People's Publishing House, 1983), 276.

60. Literature Research Office of the CPC Central Committee, *Selected Important Documents Since the Founding of the People's Republic of China*, vol. 3 (Central Literature Publishing House, 1992), 371.

From November 20 to December 17, 1953, the third national handicraft production cooperation conference was held, and Zhu De and others made a report. Zhu De pointed out in the report that in the early stage of industrial construction, light industry could not meet the growing needs of the people, and in this case, the handicraft industry would be even more significant. He believed that the socialist transformation of handicraft industries was an indispensable part of the general line of the transition period. The economy of individual handicraft industry should be transformed into collective ownership through cooperation. The organization of handicraft production cooperatives was the only form of organization to transform the handicraft industry's individual economy and help them transition to socialism. Some industrial cooperatives would exist not only in the transitional period, but also in the socialist society.[61]

On December 24, 1954, Zhu De affirmed at the fourth national conference of handicraft industry representatives that the number of handicraft workers entering the cooperatives had increased from 300,000 to more than 1 million, and the total output value had increased from 5 trillion yuan to 11 trillion yuan. He pointed out that the establishment of handicraft cooperatives not only needed the support of the state, but also depended on the masses.[62] On December 31, 1954, in his report Solving the Difficulties in the Production of the Private Handicraft Industry at the national public private joint venture conference, Chen Yun held that the development of handicraft cooperative production should be managed and controlled. He said that the cooperation of handicraft industry should not be carried out too fast, but should be slower.[63]

On July 5, 1955, in the report of the second session of the National People's Congress, Li Fuchun said that the cooperative handicraft industry was related to the fundamental changes in the production and lifestyle of tens of millions of handicraft workers and could not be completed in a short time. It must instead be done through long-term hard work and could be completed through the transition form.[64]

At the end of 1955, there were only 2 million people participating in the handicraft cooperatives. At the provincial and municipal Party Secretary's meeting in January 1956, Mao Zedong stated that the socialist transformation of the handicraft industry was a little slow, but then it developed 3 million people in two months. In March 1956, Mao Zedong said that the transformation of the handicraft industry was still slow, and he demanded that the socialist transformation of the handicraft industry should be completed by 1956, but he stressed that the state should protect the traditional handicraft industry while helping cooperative mechanization and semi-mechanization. "We must have a recovery if we lose what is good for our nation and make it better," he said.[65]

61. Zhu De, *Selected Works of Zhu De* (People's Publishing House, 1983), 320–324.

62. Zhu De, *Selected Works of Zhu De* (People's Publishing House, 1983), 334–335.

63. Chen Yun, *Selected Works of Chen Yun*, vol. 2 (People's Publishing House, 1984), 265–266.

64. Office of *Planning Work in Contemporary China, Major Events of the National Economic and Social Development Plan of the People's Republic of China (1949–1985)* (Red Flag Press, 1987), 72.

65. Mao Zedong, *Selected Works of Mao Zedong*, vol. 5 (People's Publishing House, 1977), 289–291.

In May 1953, on the basis of field investigation, Li Weihan submitted the Issue of Public-Private Relations in Capitalist Industry to the Central Committee. In this report, he suggested that the transformation of capitalist industry should be realized through public-private joint ventures. On July 29, 1953, at the enlarged meeting of the Central Politburo, Mao Zedong pointed out, "During the transition period, we must gradually transition from state capitalism to socialism in the transformation of private capitalist industry and commerce… The transformation mentioned here is not the final step of abolishing the capitalist private ownership and transforming it into a socialist enterprise, but rather, under the condition of recognizing the limited and incomplete private ownership of capitalists, the capitalist enterprises gradually become state capitalist enterprises, that is, under the management of the people's government, and they are connected and combined with the state-owned socialist economy in various ways, as a state capitalist enterprise that is supervised by workers. This kind of capitalism is not capitalism in the general sense, but a new, special capitalism, that is, under the leadership of the working class. It has some socialist characteristics and exists in several different situations… In state capitalism, public private joint ventures are of socialist composition and are semi-socialist. But it is not appropriate to call all state capitalism, such as accepting processing orders, semi-socialism, but it should be said that it has a number of socialist properties."[66]

In September 1953, Mao Zedong explained to several members of the CPPCC the Party's policy on socialist transformation of capitalist industry and commerce during the transitional period, saying, "It is sound policy and method to complete the socialist transformation of private industry and commerce through state capitalism… First of all, it is affirmed that national capitalism transforms capitalist industry and commerce to gradually complete society. It is the only way to transition from socialism to communism." Meanwhile, Mao Zedong criticized the two wrong biases of capitalists and workers, stating, "Some capitalists have kept a great distance from the country, and they still haven't changed their ideas of profit-seeking, while some workers are moving too fast, and they do not allow capitalists to make good use of it. We should educate people in both areas so that they can gradually strive as soon as possible to suit the national policy. Even if China's private industry and commerce basically serve the national economy and people's livelihood, and part of it is for the capitalists, it will go on the track of national capitalism." When it came to private business, he thought that "private business can also implement state capitalism, and it is impossible to simply 'exclude.'"[67]

In November 1955, Chen Yun pointed out that the implementation of public-private joint ventures was the result of economic development. His opinions on the socialist transformation of capitalist industry and commerce involved making overall arrangements for production in all walks of life nationwide, reorganizing or reforming industry, implementing public-private joint ventures across industry, paying the capitalists a fixed interest according to the value of fixed assets, organizing professional companies, and strengthening the leadership under the

---

66. Mao Zedong, *Mao Zedong's Works*, vol. 6 (People's Publishing House, 1996), 285–287.
67. Mao Zedong, *Collected Works of Mao Zedong*, vol. 6 (People's Publishing House, 1996), 291–292.

comprehensive planning of socialist transformation.[68]

At the peak of socialist transformation, Liu Shaoqi pointed out at the Party Committee Working Meeting of Provinces, Municipalities, and Autonomous Regions in November 1955 that "to transform capitalist industry and commerce, we should have a comprehensive plan and not just follow suit, and we should plan and carry out this work step by step."[69]

4. Theoretical Basis and Related Categories of Planned Economy

From the theoretical point of view, the planned economy is considered the embodiment of the socialist production mode and the essential interest relationship of socialist society at the level of economic operations. The planned economy refers to the economic management and operation system, which is based on the public ownership of the means of production by society (the state) according to the requirements of economic and social development in the form of predetermined economic plans or planning to coordinate social interest relations and allocate social and economic resources across society. In speaking of labor time, Marx says, "Its apportionment in accordance with a definite social plan maintains the proper proportion between the different kinds of work to be done and the various wants of the community."[70] From the 1950s to the 1970s, Chinese political and economic circles generally believed that the reason the planned economy was an economic operation system linked with the socialist mode of production was that the requirements of socialized development of socialist economic production and the characteristics of social and economic life determined by the production relations of socialist public ownership made it possible to conform to the social production level across society. It was necessary and feasible to allocate social labor or economic resources consciously, uniformly, and in a planned way. In the socialist mode of production, the public ownership of the means of production eliminated the contradiction between the socialization of production and the private ownership of the means of production, and it eliminated the factors of exploitation and the fundamental conflict of interest in socio-economic relations, interest relations, and distribution relations. The fundamental interests of workers were consistent. In the socialist economy, the consistency of the fundamental interests of workers and the development of the socialization of production connected social and economic activities into a whole to a certain extent. The unity and integrity of the socialist economy, on the one hand, required unified planned management and regulation of social production. On the other hand, it also provided feasible conditions for society to manage and regulate the national economy in a planned, unified way. Therefore, the nature of socialist public ownership determined the characteristics of the socialist social and economic interest relations, and then determined the specific forms of economic management and operation system suitable for this social interest relationship.

---

68. Chen Yun, *Selected Works of Chen Yun*, vol. 2 (People's Publishing House, 1984), 281–293.
69. Liu Shaoqi, *Selected Works of Liu Shaoqi* (People's Publishing House, 1985), 182.
70. Marx and Engels, *Complete Works of Marx and Engels*, vol. 23 (People's Publishing House, 1972), 96.

At the micro level, the planned economic system meant that the production units, as part of the national economy, obeyed the state's planned regulation, guidance, and management. At the macro level, the national economy operated in accordance with the unified plan reflecting the social will and the overall interests of society, striving for balanced development.

The theoretical basis of the planned economy was the law of planned and proportional development of the national economy and the related categories of public ownership of the means of production and distribution according to work. Before the 1970s, Chinese political and economic circles had different opinions on the law of the planned and proportional development of the national economy. Generally speaking, from the logic of normative research, the economic conditions for planned and proportional development were socialized mass production and public ownership of the means of production. Since the socialist economy was a large-scale socialized production and public ownership of the means of production was implemented, planned and proportional development was to be the unique economic law of socialism. There were also views on the separation of "planned" and "according to proportion," which held that "planned" was the subjective will of humans, not an objective economic law, while "proportionality" was a requirement of objective economic development and the economic law of large-scale socialized production. The superiority of the socialist system lay in consciously applying this law to guide economic development.[71] At that time, there were also some views on the relationship between the law of value and the law of planned and proportional development. If the law of value and the law of planned and proportional development reflected the economic law of different social forms, they were contradictory. The law of planned and proportional development was essentially socialist and communist, while the law of value was essentially of the commodity economy and capitalism. The socialist economy was dominated by the law of planned proportional development, but not by the law of value. In a socialist society, the reason the law of value should be used was simply because the state plan could not cover everything, but the law of value could only be used, not serve as the main basis for arranging the proportion of plans.[72] As for the relationship between planned commodity economy and law of value, there were views that both could coexist under socialist conditions. Under the condition of obeying the basic socialist economic law, these two economic laws acted on different aspects and different processes of social production. They restricted each other and reflected the characteristics of social production development from different aspects.[73] The above views and opinions reflected that the political economics research at that time basically adopted the normative research method, logically promoted it from concept

---

71. Editorial Department of *Economic Research* and *Economic Trends*, *Debates on Important Issues of Political Economics Since the Founding of the People's Republic of China (1949–1980)* (China Financial and Economic Publishing House, 1981), 110–113.

72. Yu Lin, "Commodities of Socialist Society," *New Construction*, no. 6, 1965; Xue Muqiao, "Further Discussion on the Planned Economy and the Law of Value," *Planned Economy* (February 1957).

73. Editorial Department of *Economic Research* and *Economic Trends*, *Debates on Important Issues of Political Economics Since the Founding of the People's Republic of China (1949–1980)* (China Financial and Economic Publishing House, 1981), 170.

to concept, had the dialectical characteristics of speculation, and produced abstract conclusions of "what should be." This kind of research method formed a kind of traditional acculturation, which affected the thinking mode and research routine of Chinese economists over a long period. In the 1950s, Chen Yun proposed the idea of "combining the main body and the supplementary mode" of the planned economy and market regulation from the perspective of national economic operations. In September 1956, Chen Yun put forward the idea of combining the planned economy with market regulation in his speech "New Problems After the Basic Completion of Socialist Transformation." He said, "In terms of production planning, the main part of the country's industrial and agricultural products is produced according to the plan, but at the same time, some products are freely produced within the scope of the national economy according to market changes." He went on to add, "Planned production is the main body of industrial and agricultural production. According to market changes, free production within the scope permitted by the state plan is a supplement to planned production."[74] Chen Yun's mode of "combination of subject and supplement" was of operational significance in actual economic operations. At that time, Sun Yefang proposed that the law of planned proportional development and the law of value were the unity of opposites. The planned and proportional development of the national economy must be based on the law of value. It would violate the principle of equal value exchange, and as a result, development would shift to the opposite side of the law of planned and proportional development if we talk about the law of planned and proportional development without the law of value and absolutize planned and proportional development, particularly if we do not regard the proportion of departments as the balance of necessary social labor among various production departments.[75] Sun Yefang's discussion on the relationship between the law of planned proportion and the law of value had theoretical depth, considering the historical conditions at that time.

During the recovery period of the national economy from 1949 to 1952, the basic economic policy of "giving consideration to both public and private affairs, benefiting both labor and capital, mutual assistance between urban and rural areas, and internal and external exchanges" was carried out. Under the leadership of the state-owned economy, all kinds of economic components had their own division of labor and cooperation. The Common Program adopted on September 29, 1949, defined the status and role of various economic components in the national economy and established the basic policies of the Communist Party of China on the non-public sectors of the economy, such as the private sector, foreign capital, and private industry. That is to say, it aimed to make full use of and give full play to the positive role of private capital in the national economy and people's livelihood. At the same time, it was necessary to restrict the unfavorable aspects of the national economy to the national economy and the people's livelihood, and bring the non-public economy onto the right development track, so that all kinds of social and economic components under the leadership of the state-owned economy could divide their work and

---

74. Guan Mengjue, *Chen Yun's Economic Thought* (Knowledge Publishing House, 1984), 65.

75. Sun Yefang, *Some Theoretical Problems of the Socialist Economy* (People's Publishing House, 1979), 12, 13, 331.

cooperate, so as to promote the development of the entire social economy. After 1953, the policy on the non-public economy began to change. At that time, the general line and general task of the socialist transition period aimed "to gradually realize the socialist industrialization of the country and gradually realize the socialist transformation of agriculture, handicraft industry, capitalist industry, and commerce over a fairly long period of time."[76] It was noted that "the essence of the Party's general line in the transitional period is to make the socialist ownership of the means of production the only economic foundation of China and society."[77] From 1953 to 1957, the composition of China's national economy gradually tended to be singular. After 1962, individual industries and other types of economic components in urban and rural areas disappeared from the statistical data, and a single public ownership structure (the people and the collective) was formed. According to the statistics of 1978, the economy owned by the people accounted for 77.6% of the total industrial output value, the collective economy accounted for 22.4%, and the statistics of individual industry and other economic components were zero.[78] From the 1950s to the 1970s, decision-makers and theorists believed that the elimination of private ownership and the implementation of socialist public ownership would inevitably lead to the leapfrog development of social productive forces. Productive forces, relations of production, mode of production, and other categories were important concepts discussed and studied by political and economic circles at that time. It was a common understanding of economic ideological circles and the policy level that the development of productive forces was to be promoted by changing the relations of production. At the same time, the policy and theory of China's socialist transformation were still influenced by the industrialization road, ownership mode, and economic system of the Soviet Union to a certain extent. Mao Zedong pointed out, "The purpose of the socialist revolution is to liberate productive forces. Agriculture and the handicraft industry have changed from individual ownership to socialist collective ownership, and private industry and commerce have shifted from capitalist ownership to socialist ownership, which will inevitably greatly liberate productive forces. In this way, the social conditions have been created for the great development of industrial and agricultural production."[79] In the publicity of this period, the Central Committee of the Communist Party of China also stressed that "only when the transition from private ownership of the means of production to socialist ownership has been completed will the situation be conducive to the rapid development of social productive forces and a technological revolution."[80]

The ownership structure was related to the economic operation system. The single public ownership structure determined that the allocation of resources was realized through centralized decision-making and planned allocation, and the economic system was shown to be a planned

---

76. Mao Zedong, *Collected Works of Mao Zedong*, vol. 6 (People's Publishing House, 1999), 61.

77. Mao Zedong, *Collected Works of Mao Zedong*, vol. 6 (People's Publishing House, 1999), 316.

78. Yang Yonghua, "Empirical Analysis and Theoretical Enlightenment on the Evolution of China's Ownership Structure in the Past 50 Years," *Journal of Tianjin Normal University*, no. 2 (2000).

79. Mao Zedong, *Collected Works of Mao Zedong*, vol. 7 (People's Publishing House, 1999), 1.

80. Teaching and Research Office of the Party History School of the CPC Central Committee, *Reference Materials for the History of the Communist Party of China (8)* (People's Publishing House, 1980), 45.

economy. The multiple ownership structure determined that the allocation of resources was realized through decentralized decision-making and market allocation, and the economic system was represented by the market economy.

Distribution according to work was also an important theoretical category related to the law of planned proportional development of the national economy. Distribution according to work was considered the principle of material benefit distribution under the condition of public ownership of the means of production. Under the condition of public ownership of the means of production, the only factor of production that people used to exchange means of living was labor. It was generally believed that the principle of distribution according to work reflected the combination of the public interests and personal interests of the working people, which was conducive to improving workers' production enthusiasm and meeting the material interests of the working people. Therefore, it was an objective economic law of socialism. But there were some controversies and puzzles in the theory and operation of the category of distribution according to work. In theory, there were different opinions on distribution according to work and equalitarianism, the legal basis of distribution according to work (involving the individual ownership of labor force or part of labor individual ownership), distribution according to work and "bourgeois rights." In operation, the measurement of distribution according to work, distribution according to work and production efficiency, comparison of different types of labor of different nature, and the consideration relationship between distribution according to work and monetary wage were all lacking in scientific and standard-specific methods. Therefore, from the perspective of factor participation in distribution, distribution according to work was a realistic economic category in a sense, because in the planned economic system of public ownership of the means of production, the only exchange condition for workers to obtain means of living was labor. However, from the perspective of economic theory, distribution according to work, as the objective economic law or theoretical basis of the socialist planned economy, had some areas of dispute and contradiction at the level of normative and empirical research.

CHAPTER 3

Research on the Planned Economy and the Economic Development Strategy of the People's Republic of China

3.1 Ownership Structure and the Planned Economic System

1. Formation and Development of the Single Public Ownership Structure

In the early days of the founding of the People's Republic of China, the new democratic economy was mainly composed of five economic components, the state-owned economy, the cooperative economy, the state capitalist economy, the private capitalist economy, and the individual economy, among which the state-owned economy was in the leading position. In the total industrial output value, state-owned and cooperative industries accounted for 34.7%, public-private joint ventures for 2%, and private industries for 63.3%.[1] The state-owned economy accounts for 58% of the country's power generation, 68% of raw coal, 92% of pig iron, 97% of steel, 68% of cement, and 53% of cotton yarn. The state-owned economy also controlled the railways of the entire country, the vast majority of banking businesses and foreign trade, and the economic lifeline of the entire country.[2] During the recovery period of the national economy from 1949 to 1952, the basic economic policy of "giving consideration to both public and private affairs, benefiting both labor and capital, mutual assistance between urban and rural areas, and internal and external exchanges" was carried out. Under the leadership of the state-owned economy, all kinds of

---

1. Liu Guoguang and Dong Zhikai, "Changes of Ownership Structure in 50 Years of New China," *Research on Contemporary Chinese History*, no. 5 and 6 (1999).

2. Jiang Jiajun, You Xianxun, and Zhou Zhenhan, *Economic History of the People's Republic of China* (Shaanxi People's Publishing House, 1989), 59.

economic components had a "division of labor and cooperation, and each had its own place." The state gave priority to the development of the state-owned economy, actively supported the cooperative economy, and encouraged the state capitalist economy. For the private economy, on the one hand, it implemented management policies with the main content of controlling capital, controlling trade, and strengthening the plan, and it restricted the private economy in the areas of activity scope, tax policy, market price, and labor conditions, among others, which was not conducive to the national economy and people's livelihood. On the other hand, the state carried out material exchange between urban and rural areas through adjusting industry and commerce to activate market circulation. In addition, it expanded the processing order and product acquisition of private industry, so that the private economy could obtain normal profits and continue to produce and expand reproduction.

In 1952, the output value of state-owned, cooperative, and public-private joint ventures accounted for more than 50% of the total industrial output value, which was already dominant compared to other economic components. In 1949, the individual economy accounted for about three quarters of the total industrial and agricultural output value. After three years of economic recovery, the proportion of the individual economy decreased. By 1952, the proportion of the individual economy in the total industrial and agricultural output value dropped to about 2/3. At the same time, in accordance with the principle of voluntariness and mutual benefit, farmers and handicraftsmen were called upon to organize and take the road of mutual assistance and cooperation. By 1952, about 40% of the farmers in China had been organized, which was three times more than that in 1950. Among them, there were 8.03 million annual mutual aid groups and nearly 4,000 primary cooperatives. By 1952, there were 3,280 handicraft production cooperatives with 218,000 employees, accounting for 3% of the total number of handicraft workers, and the output value was 246 million yuan, accounting for 3.4% of the total output value of handicraft industry.[3] The proportion of the output value of private industry in the total industrial output value (excluding the handicraft industry) decreased from 63.3% in 1949 to 39% in 1952. In some heavy industry sectors, the proportion of private industry declined even more. In 1952, compared with 1949, electric power decreased from 36% to 6%, coal from 28% to 12%, and pig iron from 8% to 3%. The proportion of the wholesale volume of private commerce decreased from 76% in 1950 to 36% in 1952, the proportion of private retail sales decreased from 83.5% to 57%, and the proportion of private import and export decreased from 33.5% to 7%.[4] From 1949 to 1952, the coexistence of multiple ownership elements sent China's national economy into a recovery period, which provided the material basis for the socialist economic construction begun in 1953 and ensured the successful implementation of the First Five-Year Plan.

From the perspective of China's social and economic structure in 1949, private and non-public sectors of the economy constituted the main body of the national economy, while the

---

3. Chen Wenhui, *An Introduction to China's Economic Structure* (Shanxi Economic Publishing House, 1994), 29.

4. Jiang Jiajun, You Xianxun, and Zhou Zhenhan, *Economic History of the People's Republic of China* (Shaanxi People's Publishing House, 1989), 63–64.

proportion of state-owned economy in the social economy was relatively small. The question of how to correctly deal with a large non-public economy and how to continue to play a positive role in economic construction became the key to the recovery and development of the national economy. The Common Program of the Chinese People's Political Consultative Conference (CPPCC) adopted on September 29, 1949, defined the status and role of various economic components in national economic life and established the basic policies of the state in non-public sectors of the economy, such as the private sector, foreign capital, and the individual sector. At the same time, it was necessary to restrict the side that was not conducive to the national economy and the people's livelihood, bring the non-public economy onto the correct development track, and lead all sorts of social and economic elements to work together under the leadership of the state-owned economy, so as to promote the development of the overall social economy.

In the early days of the founding of the People's Republic of China, the support and utilization of the non-public economy mainly focused on private industry and commerce, especially private industry. Mao Zedong pointed out that the public-private relationship "should be treated differently and plans should be made to deal with it. What is different is that the state-owned enterprises take the leading position and are progressive. We cannot reverse the position, because private industry and commerce are relatively backward… Others should be treated as generally equal."[5] In order to restore and develop production as soon as possible and stabilize the economic order, the Party and the government adopted many policies and measures to stabilize prices, curb inflation, crack down on speculative commerce, balance revenues and expenditures, and unify finance and economics. However, with the implementation of the deflation policy, market money was tight. In the process of rapid economic changes, a large number of industrial and commercial bankruptcies occurred in various places. In this regard, the CPC Central Committee made a timely decision to adjust industry and commerce, and it adjusted public-private relations and labor relations. At the beginning of the founding of the People's Republic of China, private capital played a certain role in the recovery and development of the economy.

In 1953, Mao articulated that the general line and task of the socialist transition period was "to gradually realize the socialist industrialization of the country and gradually realize the socialist transformation of agriculture, handicraft industry, capitalist industry, and commerce over a fairly long period of time."[6] He continued, "The essence of the Party's general line in the transitional period is to make the socialist ownership of the means of production the only economic basis for China and its society."[7] The completion of the socialist transformation allowed China to finally establish the socialist system, and at the same time, to establish the dominant position of public ownership in China's social economy, and the overall national economy was brought onto the track of a planned economy.

---

5. Mao Zedong, *Collected Works of Mao Zedong*, vol. 6 (People's Publishing House, 1999), 61.

6. Mao Zedong, *Collected Works of Mao Zedong*, vol. 6 (People's Publishing House, 1999), 316.

7. Teaching and Research Office of the CPC Central Committee, *Reference Materials for the History of the Communist Party of China (8)* (People's Publishing House, 1980), 45.

After the establishment of the dominant position of socialist public ownership, the issue of how to give full play to the enthusiasm of the individual, private, and other non-public sectors of the economy so that they could become a useful supplement to the public economy, became a concern. Beginning in 1956, with the basic completion of the socialist transformation, the Communist Party of China began to actively explore the socialist road suitable for its own national conditions. In this period, in the ownership structure, the Communist Party of China began to realize the disadvantages of the single form of public ownership and made some beneficial explorations. Before and after the Eighth National Congress of the Communist Party of China, Mao Zedong actively explored the new problems that arose after the establishment of socialist public ownership and made breakthroughs in the understanding of the mode of socialist ownership. Mao Zedong's exploration in this period, especially his understanding of capitalism, was known as the New Economic Policy theory. The content of this thought mainly included Mao's proposal that capitalism could be eliminated, and then be carried out. It initially formed the assumption of constructing the ownership mode with public ownership as the main body and various forms of ownership coexisting. In addition, Mao proposed the construction of the target model of the socialist ownership structure, and he also advocated making full use of the bourgeoisie and absorbing capital personnel to participate in economic work.

In the period of national economic adjustment, as the policy of the individual economy was relaxed, the family sideline industry, handicraft industry, and other forms of individual business were developed to a certain extent, which played an important role in the recovery of the economy and the development of production. After that, with the gradual improvement of the economic situation and the gradual escalation of the expansion of class struggle, the individual economy began to be denied and banned as a spontaneous force of capitalism. Taking the Tenth Plenary Session of the Eighth Central Committee of the Communist Party of China as the turning point, the Party's non-public economic policy underwent fundamental changes. In the political atmosphere in which class struggle was the key link, the private economy was not only regarded as a dissident force of socialism, but the remaining individual economy was also banned as a spontaneous force of capitalism.

At the end of 1952, the Central Committee of the Communist Party of China put forward the general line for the transitional period, with the core of "One Transformation and Three Reforms." At that time, the essence of the general line was to make the socialist public ownership of the means of production the only economic basis for China's state and society. In 1952, the ownership structure of the industrial sector, in terms of the structure of total output value, was 41.5% for the state-owned sector, 3.2% for the collective, 20.6% for the individual, and 34.7% for the others. After that, the state-owned component rose rapidly. In 1957, it was 53.6% state-owned, 19.4% collective, 0.8% individual, and 26.2% other. From 1953 to 1957, China's economic composition gradually tended to be singular, especially after the second half of 1955, when the process of public ownership accelerated rapidly. In 1957, the proportion of farmers participating in agricultural production cooperatives reached 97.5%, and all private industries were jointly operated by the public and the private sector. In the wholesale and retail businesses, the private sector accounted for only 0.1% and 2.7% respectively.[8] After 1957, individual industry and other economic types in urban and rural areas disappeared from the statistical data, leaving only state-owned industry and collectively owned industry. In 1956, the leaders of the Party and the state understood the problem of the rapid development of public ownership at that time, and they formulated relevant policies in 1957 to try to correct them, trying to "learn from the Soviet Union" and establish an economic management system suitable for China's national conditions, but the exploration was soon interrupted. In 1958, more stringent measures were taken to restrict and reform the self-employed industrialists and businessmen. First, they organized to join the cooperatives, except for a few special handicraft industries, and then, the collective industry and commerce were merged into or transferred into state-owned enterprises. In 1958 and 1959, the vast majority of the collective industrial and commercial enterprises was transformed into state-owned enterprises, and the remaining few cooperative stores and cooperative groups basically remained in that form. In fact, they were all under the unified accounting of state-owned enterprises or unified payment of profits and losses according to the management methods of state-owned enterprises. In terms of agriculture, by the end of 1956, 96% of the farmers participated in agricultural cooperatives. Among them, for 88% of the high-level cooperatives, their main means of production, such as land, were collectively owned. In 1957, 97.5% of the farmers participated in agricultural cooperatives, of which 96.2% were senior cooperatives and less than 3% were individual farmers. By 1959, 3% of the individual farmers who remained after the agricultural cooperation had joined the rural people's communes, which were larger and more public than the senior cooperatives. In 1961, there were only about 1 million employees in the individual economy in China.[9] The year 1965 was a turning point. The proportion of state-owned industry was 90%, reaching the highest point in history, and the proportion of collective ownership industry decreased to 9.9%, while other components were less than 0.1%. The proportion of state-owned industries began to decline, while the proportion of industries under collective ownership began to rise. During the Cultural Revolution period, China pursued the pure form of public ownership blindly and one-sidedly. On the one hand, other economic elements besides public ownership were excluded, and the non-public economy was cut off as the "tail" of capitalism. On the other hand, the state unilaterally emphasized the superiority of ownership by the people, underestimated the inevitability of the existence and development of collective ownership, confused the boundaries between ownership by the people and collective ownership, carried out the "upgrading," "poor transition," and "merger" of ownership, and took "large scale and highly public ownership (of the people's commune)" as the standard to judge whether the ownership form was advanced or not, that is, the larger the scope of socialist public ownership, the better, and the higher the degree of public ownership, the better. In 1978, enterprises owned by the people accounted for 77.6% of the country's total industrial output value, and the collective economy accounted for 22.4%. Basically,

---

8. Liu Guoguang and Dong Zhikai, "The Changes of Ownership Structure in the 50 Years of New China," *Research on Contemporary Chinese History*, no. 5 and 6 (1999).

9. Liu Guoguang and Dong Zhikai, "The Changes of Ownership Structure in the 50 Years of New China," *Research on Contemporary Chinese History*, no. 5 and 6 (1999).

there were only two kinds of public ownership in China's economic structure, ownership by the people and collective ownership. The ownership structure of the means of production had become a single public ownership.

Table 3.1 shows the evolution of China's industrial sector ownership economy.

TABLE 3.1 1952–1978 Evolution of China's Industrial Sector Ownership Economy (%)

Year	SOE	Collective Industry	Private Industry	Other Economy
1952	41.5	3.2	20.6	34.7
1957	53.7	19.0	0.8	26.4
1962	87.8	12.2	—	—
1970	87.6	12.4	—	—
1975	81.1	18.9	—	—
1978	77.6	22.4	—	—

Source: Yang Yonghua, "Empirical Analysis and Theoretical Enlightenment on the Evolution of China's Ownership Structure in the Past 50 Years," Journal of Tianjin Normal University, no. 2 (2000).

2. Single Public Ownership and the Planned Economic System

The ownership component gradually formed a single public ownership, which inevitably required centralized decision-making. The government had strong control over the national economy, and planning became the only means of resource allocation. Thus, single public ownership with state ownership as the main body constituted the basis of a highly centralized directive planned economy. Under single public ownership, the planned economy had to be carried out. The formation of the planned economy was mainly the result of market failure (including equity) and the government's pursuit of high-speed economic growth (including national security), and it was conditioned by the government's control over resource allocation. The planned economy could only be built on the basis of single public ownership, which was determined by the nature of both. Because the essence of the planned economy was that the state must be able to directly control the business activities of enterprises and individuals, the collective ownership of the means of production by the state or which the state could control was necessary, and it was understood that the collective ownership under the single public ownership was not real collective ownership, and its ownership was inseparable and inheritable, so that its members would not freely withdraw, transfer, or exercise their power independently, and the government could easily control it. Only by establishing this control was it possible to exclude the market mechanism and establish a top-down planned economy characterized by administrative management.

The planned economic system characterized by high concentration and administrative management as the main mechanism was introduced from the Soviet Union in the early days of the founding of the People's Republic of China (or even earlier in the northeast liberated areas). After comprehensive personnel training and institutional setup, especially after the operation of the First Five-Year Plan (1953–1957), it was completed in the middle and late 1950s. This economic system constituted the main economic system of the People's Republic of China from its founding to 1979.

The transformation from the new democratic economy to the planned economy was based on the rapid development of the state-owned economy and the socialist transformation. It started with the important industries and products related to the national economy and the people's livelihood, and then gradually expanded. In 1949, the government began to set up state-owned grain and cotton gauze companies to organize the purchase and distribution of grain and cotton yarn, and direct distribution was carried out through urban and rural supply and marketing cooperatives and consumer cooperatives, which initially unified the supply, marketing, and distribution of commercial goods. On this basis, the central government unified the domestic and foreign trade of the entire country, established a top-down national specialized company and the China Federation of Supply and Marketing Cooperatives, local cooperatives, and grassroots cooperatives, which mainly led rural commerce, and implemented a system of material allocation and funds withdrawal. In this way, commercial circulation moved toward national unity. It played an important role in the stability of the market and prices, and also provided conditions for centralized and unified material allocation in the planned economy. From 1949 to 1952, the state carried out the planned management of the financial industry and foreign trade, as well as the unified purchase and marketing of a small number of short and important products such as cotton yarn and fabrics. From 1953 to 1956, with the state's implementation of the unified purchase and marketing of major agricultural and sideline products and the socialist transformation of private commerce, planned management basically covered the product market. At the same time, with the basic completion of the socialist transformation, the labor market disappeared. Due to the serious surplus of the labor force in China, China's restrictions on labor mobility and employment were far greater than those of the Soviet Union and Eastern Europe. However, after agricultural cooperation was realized in 1956, the national plan played a guiding role in its production and management. Until the establishment of the people's commune with the integration of the government and society in 1958, the government directly controlled the operation of the rural economy, and the planned economic system was formed.

On October 1, 1949, the Central Financial and Economic Affairs Commission (CFEAC) was established. At that time, the Common Program, which played the role of the provisional constitution, stipulated that the state should regulate the state-owned economy, cooperative economy, individual economy of farmers and handicraftsmen, private capitalist economy and state capitalist economy in the aspects of business scope, raw material supply, sales market, labor conditions, technical equipment, financial policies, and so on. Under the economic leadership, division of labor and cooperation was to be carried out in order to promote the development of the overall social economy. The Central People's government strove to work out a master plan for the recovery and development of the main departments of the national public and private economy at an early date, stipulate the scope of division of labor and cooperation between the central and local governments in economic construction, and uniformly adjust the relationship between the central and local economic departments. At that time, the national economic construction investment was centrally distributed by the CFEAC, and the construction projects were proposed by the central departments and submitted to the CFEAC for approval. The specialized plans drawn up by the central departments were to be implemented with the approval of the CFEAC. The planning bureau not only reviewed the professional plans of each department and grasped their investments, but it also focused on the systematic investigation and study of the economic situation and took the survey results as the basic material for the audit plan. In the winter of 1949, the central government decided to implement the policy of the unified management of national finance and economy. Through the national financial conference held in February 1950, the central government put forward Six Unifications in a mandatory way. These included the unification of fiscal revenue and expenditure, the unification of public grain, the unification of taxation, the unification of establishment, and the unification of trade and banking.

In March 1950, the Government Administration Council promulgated the Decision on Unifying National Financial and Economic Work, which transferred the main powers of fiscal revenue and expenditure, material allocation, currency distribution, and cash management to the central government, forming a management system of centralized revenue and expenditure. This measure quickly stabilized the national economic situation, but it also seriously restricted local mobility. In March 1951, the central government made corresponding adjustments and implemented the system of "dividing revenues and expenditures and managing at different levels," and established the three-level finance of the central, large administrative regions, and provinces. After the abolition of the large administrative regions in 1954, county-level finance was established. This system had obvious vertical subordination. The central government controlled 80% of the fiscal revenue, which was basically a centralized and unified system that provided conditions for the establishment of a planned economic system.

In May 1950, on the basis of the specialized plans of various ministries, the CFEAC tried to compile the Outline of the National Economic Plan for 1950, which made overall arrangements for investment and production in various industries across the country. In February 1951, the Central Committee of the Communist Party of China issued the Inner Party Circular on the Main Points of the Resolution of the Enlarged Meeting of the Politburo of the CPC Central Committee, proposing to establish the idea of "three-year preparation and ten-year planned economic construction." On March 13, 1951, the Government Administration Council approved and issued the first set of national plan forms. On September 15, the CFEAC also formulated the Methods for Drawing up the National Economic Plan, including the methods for the preparation of capital construction plan, production plan, labor plan, material supply plan, transportation, post and telecommunications, and other areas, which meant the basic work of economic planning had made initial progress.

In May 1951, the Planning Bureau of the CFEAC tried to work out the main points of the national economic plan for 1951, which was the first time that China compiled a national economic plan. This plan included an industrial production plan (basically only the central state-owned supply department), agriculture and forestry plan, transportation plan (state-owned part), industrial transportation infrastructure plan (central investment part), and water conservancy construction plan (larger water conservancy projects in which the central government invested). In January 1952, the CFEAC issued the Interim Measures for Capital Construction, aiming at overcoming the inefficiency, decentralization, and confusion of infrastructure construction. The Interim Measures emphasized the importance of planned centralized management and stipulated the following principles: dividing the investment amount of infrastructure units into "above quota" and "below quota," dividing the preparation, examination, and approval of financial budget and capital construction plan into two systems, the central and regional systems, and allocating investment separately.

In January 1952, the CFEAC issued the Interim Measures on the Compilation of National Economic Plans, the first systematic planning system in China. According to the Interim Measures, the planning procedure involved issuing control figures from top to bottom, preparing and submitting draft plans year by year from bottom to top, and then approving plans level by level from top to bottom. The planning system was divided into two systems, the central competent department and the large administrative region. After the plans of the department and the region were prepared respectively, the CFEAC collected and compiled the draft national economic plan. State owned industry and local public industry were enterprises (railways, shipping, posts, and telecommunications were the corresponding units), state-owned trade was the provincial (city) association or grassroots cooperatives, private industry or private commerce was the industrial and commercial administrative organ of each province (city), and agriculture, animal husbandry, and forestry were exclusive or county-level agricultural and forestry departments. As these units were mainly part of the decentralized private economy, only provisional plans were made. All major administrative regions, financial and economic departments of the central government, their subordinate management organs at all levels, and grassroots planning units were to prepare the draft plan in accordance with the prescribed procedures and forms and submit the draft plan for examination and approval in accordance with the prescribed system and time. The Interim Measures also stipulated the lateral relations between the departments and regions. State owned enterprises (including enterprises directly under the central government at all levels of management departments and enterprises entrusted with the management of large administrative regions) mainly allocated control figures and prepared draft plans by departments. However, the control figures allocated by the central competent departments and the draft plans drawn up by the central competent departments were comprehensively studied, and suggestions were put forward for consideration by the central departments and the Central Bureau of Financial and Economic Planning. Draft plans for the region, including all departments of the national economy, all management systems, and all economic components, were submitted to the CFEAC. The Finance and Economy Commission of the region was fully responsible for the planning of local enterprises, leading its subordinate departments and provinces (cities). The Central People's government approved the national economic plan and the plans of the central departments and major administrative regions submitted by the CFEAC, while the central departments approved the plans of the enterprises in charge of the large administrative regions and the management departments at all levels directly under the central government and the plans of the provinces (cities) under the jurisdiction of the regional finance committees.

In November 1952, the Nineteenth meeting of the Central People's Government Committee decided to establish a State Planning Commission.

On February 13, 1953, the Central Committee of the Communist Party of China issued the Notice on the Establishment of Planning Institutions. The circular pointed out that all the national economic departments and cultural and educational departments at the central level were to quickly strengthen the planning work and establish planning institutions for grassroots enterprises and grassroots work departments. The financial and economic committees of major regions, provinces and cities were responsible for the planning work in their respective regions, and they designed separate bureaus or departments under the dual leadership of the financial and economic commissions at the same level and the planning institutions at higher levels. On February 1, 1954, the Central Committee of the Communist Party of China issued the Instructions on the Establishment and Enrichment of Planning Institutions at All Levels, which stipulated that planning committees should be set up in major regions, provinces, and cities (districts), and at the same time, the State Planning Commission was instructed to formulate organizational regulations for planning commissions at all levels. At this time, the national planning organization system was basically completed. Through the top-down planning institutions to implement the management system of combining direct planning with indirect planning, direct and directive plans were issued to state-owned enterprises, and guiding plans were issued to the private economy and agriculture. The adjustment of planning permeated into private and individual economy by means of price, tax, credit, raw material supply, and product purchase and sale.

In September 1954, Article 15 of the Constitution of the People's Republic of China, formulated and adopted at the first session of the First National People's Congress, stipulated that the state must use economic plans to guide the development and transformation of the national economy, so as to continuously improve productivity, improve the people's material and cultural life, and consolidate the independence and security of the country. This was a formal provision in the national constitution that made the planned economy the form of China's economic system. In July 1955, the second session of the First National People's Congress adopted the First Five-Year Plan for the Development of the National Economy of the People's Republic of China. As early as the spring of 1951, the CFEAC began to work out the First Five-Year Plan on a trial basis. By March 1955, the draft of the First Five-Year Plan was worked out.

During the First Five-Year Plan period, China's economic recovery and construction were basically carried out under a highly centralized planned economic system. China established a highly centralized management system in economic operation management, industrial enterprise management, capital construction management, financial management, material management, and price management. During this period, state-owned enterprises and some public-private joint ventures producing state products were directly planned, and the state issued mandatory production targets to these enterprises. The number of industrial enterprises directly managed by various departments of the central government increased from 2,800 in 1953 to 9,300 in 1957, accounting for 16% of the total 58,000 state-owned industrial enterprises in that year, while the industrial output value was close to 50% of the total state-owned industrial output value.[10] From 1953 to 1956, the number of products under the unified management of the State Planning Commission increased from 115 to more than 380. These products accounted for about 60% of the total industrial output value, and the purchase plan of agricultural products generally accounted for about 70% of the total purchase amount.

There were as many as twelve mandatory indicators issued to industrial enterprises. Most of the investment in capital construction projects was directly arranged by the central government. The state implemented a financial management system of unified revenue and expenditure for state-owned enterprises. In addition, in order to strengthen the centralized management of materials, materials were divided into three categories, the first of which involved unified distribution of materials, with production and distribution organized by the State Planning Commission. Second, the production and distribution of materials under the management of the ministry was organized by the competent departments of the State Council. The production and distribution of these materials, which were listed in the state plan and distributed by the State Planning Commission or the ministries of the State Council, were not at the disposal of local governments and enterprises. Third, for local management materials, some were produced and sold by local governments, and most were produced and sold by enterprises. The highly centralized planning management system was determined by the industrial development road and industrialization development strategy at that time, which met the needs of concentrating funds and resources to carry out industrialization construction with heavy industry as the center during the First Five-Year Plan period. The main task of the First Five-Year Plan was to carry out industrial construction centering on 156 construction projects designed with the assistance of the Soviet Union and composed of 694 construction projects above the quota, so as to establish a preliminary foundation for China's socialist industrialization. A total of 11 billion yuan was invested in the construction units designed with the assistance of the Soviet Union over five years, and 1.8 billion yuan was invested in 143 construction units above the quota. In addition to other projects, the total investment in industrial construction over five years was 24.85 billion yuan.[11] Such large-scale construction was in contradiction with China's weak economic foundation, low level of productivity, and very limited national financial, material, and technical resources. This being the case, the highly centralized economic management system could concentrate the social capital, materials, and technical power for the national key construction projects and make them form productive forces relatively quickly. At the same time, in the early stage of construction, in view of the chaotic economic situation, it was also necessary to adopt a strong, highly centralized management system to ensure normal, orderly economic life. Therefore, the highly centralized

---

10. Wang Haibo, *Industrial Economic History of New China* (Economy and Management Publishing House, 1986), 143.

11. *First Five-Year Plan for the Development of the National Economy of the People's Republic of China* (People's Publishing House, 1955), 31.

planning management system in the period of the First Five-Year Plan was considered to have met the requirements of the development of social productive forces and the social and economic conditions of China at that time, and it played an important role in the smooth completion of the First Five-Year Plan.

3. Reform of the Highly Centralized Planned Economy

Although the highly centralized planned economic system in the First Five-Year Plan period helped promote the development of China's industrialization, with the development of economic construction, the highly centralized characteristics of this system with its strong administrative color violated the objective economic law to a certain extent, suppressing the production enthusiasm of local governments, enterprises, and workers, and this began to have a negative impact on economic development. In April 1956, Mao Zedong delivered a report On the Ten Major Relations at the enlarged meeting of the Politburo of the CPC Central Committee. When talking about economic management, Mao Zedong pointed out that in terms of the relationship between the central and local governments, on the premise of consolidating the unified leadership of the Central Committee, it was important to expand local rights, enable the local authorities to do more, and give full play to the enthusiasm of the central and local governments. That May, the State Council held a national institutional meeting to examine the phenomenon of excessive centralization of power and put forward a draft resolution on improving the state administrative system. On September 15, the first session of the Eighth National Congress of the Communist Party of China was held. In his political report, Liu Shaoqi pointed out that it was necessary to correctly combine the enthusiasm of economic departments at all levels of the Central Committee with that of local economic organizations. At the meeting, Li Fuchun delivered a speech entitled "Strengthening the National Planning Work for Socialist Construction." He pointed out that China was not good at combining the unity of the national plan with the flexibility of adjusting measures to local conditions according to suit local needs, nor had it improved the planned economic system in a timely manner according to changes in the situation. The control of capital construction investment was too centralized, and some table indicators were too cumbersome. He further pointed out that in order to adapt to the new situation, appropriate changes needed to be made to the planning system and methods so that the nation's planning work could better meet the general requirements of mobilizing all positive factors to strengthen socialist construction. Therefore, hierarchical management needed to be carried out in the planning system. All the indicators that needed to be unified and balanced by the whole country were to be balanced and arranged by the provinces, cities, autonomous regions, and departments according to their own circumstances and local conditions and reported to the State Council for the record, so that they could be integrated into the national plan. Many other various minor indicators were not suitable, so they could not be specifically included in the national plan. The targets were arranged by local governments or grassroots units themselves, and the state only planned them in macro ways and adjusted them in terms of price policies and sales relations. The indicators included in the national plan were divided into the categories of mandatory indicators, adjustable indicators, and reference indicators.

In June 1957, Xue Muqiao pointed out in his Opinions on the Current Plan Management System that there were two rules for improving the plan management system. One was that the planning management system must combine centralization with flexibility, which had both necessary centralization and necessary flexibility, that is, the principle of "big plan, small freedom" put forward by Chen Yun. Second, the planning management system needed to adopt the principle of unified leadership and hierarchical management and give all departments, regions, enterprises, and institutions a certain degree of autonomy. He believed that it was necessary to make bold reforms of the current plan management system and make corresponding adjustments in the planning indicators, main products, planning scope, and planning cycle, so as to make the planning management more flexible. In August 1957, the State Planning Commission drew up Preliminary Opinions on Improving the Planning Work System. The Opinion pointed out that the basic requirement for improving the planning work was to ensure that the state carried out comprehensive planning and unified leadership for the development of the national economy, and at the same time, it could give full play to the enthusiasm of all ministries, provincial, regional, and municipal people's committees and grassroots units.

In April 1958, the CPC Central Committee and the State Council issued Several Provisions on the Decentralization of Industrial Enterprises, which put forward the general principles of enterprise decentralization. In June 1958, the Central Committee of the Communist Party of China issued the Regulations on the Decentralization of Enterprises, Institutions, and Technical Forces, which further specified the issue of system decentralization. By June 15, 1958, 80% (880 in total) of enterprises and institutions under the central government had been delegated to local management.[12] In August 1958, the Central Committee of the Communist Party of China and the State Council issued Provisions on Improving the Examination and Approval Methods for Design Specifications of Capital Construction Projects above Quota, which decided to delegate the examination and approval authority of design specifications for construction projects above quota, so as to accelerate the development of local industries.

From April 1956 to 1960, China's economic management thought and system underwent a major change, mainly moving from a thought and system that emphasized highly centralized management during the First Five-Year Plan period to one that emphasized appropriate decentralization of management authority, so as to stimulate the enthusiasm of local governments and enterprises and promote the rapid development of industrialization. This reform aimed to make intentional adjustments and improvements to the planned economic system, but it only focused on decentralization and giving power to the local government, not on making the planned management conform to the objective economic law and the actual economic situation. Because these institutional reforms characterized by local decentralization were aimed at realizing the local industrial output value exceeding the local agricultural output value as soon as possible and

---

12. *Xinhua Bimonthly*, no. 13 (1985): 63.

establishing local independence, the effect of this system reform was not satisfactory. After the central system devolved to the central government, the local governments were decentralized at different levels. As a result, management was in confusion, the original subordinate and cooperation relationships were disrupted, and the economic benefits of enterprises decreased. The decentralization of planning power, financial power, and material right and labor management power weakened the ability of macroeconomic control and led to economic disorder. The rapid expansion of the scale of capital construction, the one-sided pursuit of industrial self-contained system in various localities, and the industrial policy of "taking steel as the key link" sent the economy spiraling out of control and into a serious imbalance in both gross and structural aspects, thus causing serious setbacks to the development of the national economy.

4. The Evolution and Efficiency Analysis of the Planned Economy System

In January 1961, the Central Committee of the Communist Party of China issued Some Interim Provisions on Adjusting the Management System. On the basis of summing up the experience and lessons of the Great Leap Forward in the previous three years, the document emphasized the centralization and unification of economic management. It was stipulated in the document that the power of economic management should be concentrated at the Central Committee, the Central Bureau, and the provinces (or autonomous regions and municipalities directly under the central government). In the next two or three years, more power was to be concentrated in the Central Committee and the Central Bureau. All production, capital construction, materials, culture and education, finance, labor, and other work was to follow the principle of "one game of chess and one book of accounts." From that time, the CPC Central Committee and the State Council formulated a series of economic management decrees. With these as the guiding ideology, China's economic system began to change, with concentration as its basic content and mainly involving several aspects.

The first was the centralization of some enterprises out of the decentralization. After the decentralization of the system in 1958, there were only 1,200 enterprises and institutions directly under the central government, but by 1965, including the newly-built enterprises during and after the Great Leap Forward, the number of enterprises and institutions directly under the central government increased to 10,533. The total industrial output value of enterprises directly under the central government accounted for 42.2% of the total industrial output value of the entire country, of which 55.1% belonged to the means of production.[13] Profit sharing and "full credit" were cancelled, and the incentive fund, four expenses allocation, and separate export management of working capital were restored.

The second was the strengthening of the centralized, unified management of the plan. In accordance with the policy of "one game of chess and one book of accounts," the practice of two accounts during the Great Leap Forward period was changed, and the phenomenon in which

---

13. Zhou Taihe, *Economic System Reform in Contemporary China* (China Social Sciences Press, 1984), 418.

the state plan lost its effectiveness was overcome. In the period of adjustment, the state plan was basically returned to a set of planning indicators for the First Five-Year Plan period. Expanding the scope of calculation, the number of industrial products managed by the State Planning Commission was restored from 215 to about 400. The output value of these products accounted for about 60% of the total industrial output value.

The third was the strengthening of the centralized, unified management of capital construction. It was necessary to take back the power of examination and approval of capital construction projects, strictly enforce the procedures for examining and approving capital construction projects, and strengthen the supervision over the allocation of funds for capital construction projects.

The fourth was the strengthening of the centralized, unified management of finance. It was important to centralize state financial power at the central, regional, and provincial (city, autonomous region) levels and reduce the power of special regions, counties (cities), and communes. The ratio of the central government to the local government was changed from five years to one year. It was important to change the proportion and method of retaining profits for enterprises. In 1961, the proportion of retained profits for enterprises nationwide was reduced from 13.2% to 6.9%. Beginning in 1962, state-owned industrial enterprises no longer carried out the profit retention method, but changed instead to the enterprise fund system.

The fifth was the implementation of highly centralized, unified management of material circulation. In 1963, the State General Administration of Materials Management was established to exercise vertical leadership over local specialized material management companies. In 1964, the General Administration of Materials Management was changed into the Ministry of Materials, which organized the supply and marketing of materials in a unified way, forming a unified material management system throughout the country. At the same time, the scope of material management was expanded, and the variety of materials for unified distribution and management was increased. In 1959, the number of materials allocated and managed by the Ministry was reduced to 285, and it was restored to 516 in 1963.

The sixth involved trying to establish trust in some enterprises in industry and transportation. In August 1964, the CPC Central Committee and the State Council, in agreement with the report of the Party group of the State Economic Commission, decided to set up a trial trust in some enterprises in industry and transportation. The organizational form of the trust pilot enterprises was stipulated, and a list of the first batch of twelve pilot units was proposed, of which nine were national and three were regional. In 1965, the national industrial transportation conference discussed and approved the Key Points of Industrial Transportation Work in 1965, and decided to set up six trusts that year, including petroleum industry companies, instrument industry companies, wood processing industry companies, coal industry companies, cotton textile industry companies, and electrical machinery industry companies. The report of the State Economic and Trade Commission pointed out that the industrial transportation company with the nature of a trust was an economic organization under the centralized, unified management of the socialist ownership by the people and an independent economic accounting unit under the unified national plan. The trust was fully responsible for the completion of the national plan and carried out unified management of its branches, factories and mines, and scientific research and design units. The task of the trust was to carry out industrial reorganization according to the principle of specialization and cooperation. Since the trial establishment of the trust was based on China's national conditions and economic means were used to manage the economy, many implementation methods were also feasible at that time. Despite the initial attempt, there were still some problems in the relationship between departments and local governments, but positive economic results were achieved. For example, China Tobacco Company was officially listed in the trust in August 1964. According to statistics from November 1964, the number of cigarette factories in China was reduced from 104 to 61, a decrease of 41%, and the number of employees was reduced from 5,900 to 4,100, a decrease of 31%. The comprehensive production capacity of cigarettes was increased by 17%, the labor productivity was increased by 35%, and the cost of cigarette processing was increased. By 1965, the total profit was 5.6 billion yuan.[14]

After this rectification, China's economic system embarked on a highly centralized track, and centralization of power was further intensified. This played a crucial role in controlling the economic chaos during the Great Leap Forward period and enabled economic adjustments to be carried out effectively. From 1963 to 1965, the total output value of industry and agriculture increased by an average of 15.7% per year, including an average annual growth of 17.9% in the gross industrial output value, 11.1% in the total agricultural output value, 14.7% in the national income, 17.4% in the actual wages of workers, and 15% in the income of farmers.[15] But this time, power was basically administrative, not economic. In other words, the strengthening and hardening of economic management was not based on objective economic laws, nor by means of economic leverage and measures, but with a strong organizational and administrative color.

In February 1969, the National Planning Forum printed and distributed three documents on system reform, including "Preliminary Opinions on the Reform of the Financial Management System (Draft)," "Preliminary Ideas of the Central Departments on the Decentralization of the Enterprise Management System," and "Preliminary Opinions on the Reform of the Material Management System." According to the spirit of these documents, China's economic system underwent another reform with decentralization as its main objective. In the financial system, it was necessary to carry out the financial contract with the expansion of local finance as the main focus. From 1971 to 1973, the system of fixed income, fixed expenditure, and responsibility for revenue and expenditure was implemented. In 1974 and 1975, the system of "keeping income in a fixed proportion" was tested in Northern China, Northeastern China, and Jiangsu Province. In 1976, the system of "linking revenue with expenditure and sharing the total amount" was changed, and the authority of local governments in financial budget and taxation was correspondingly expanded. In the industrial management system, the main task was to decentralize enterprises under the central departments and move to local management. In terms of material management

---

14. Ma Hong, *A Full Account of China's Reform: General Theory Volume* (Dalian Press, 1992), 28.

15. Fang Wen, *Theory and Practice of Socialist Economic System Reform* (CPC Central Committee Party School Press, 1990), 139.

system, the management system was changed based on "rules and regulations" and the material distribution system of "regional balance, surplus transfer out and transfer in" was implemented under the central unified plan. The transfer out and transfer in plans were worked out by the State Planning Commission in conjunction with competent departments, and the remaining materials were managed by the local authorities. In principle, the excess part of the main raw materials and equipment produced by local enterprises beyond the national plan were not to be included in the central unified distribution.

As in the Great Leap Forward period, the decentralization of the system was just a simple decentralization, and there was no comprehensive, deep-seated reform of the entire economic system. In the end, the results were not satisfactory. In September 1970, the State Planning Commission sorted out the main problems of system decentralization reflected by various departments in the work briefing. First, after enterprises were decentralized to the level of provinces and cities, there was a trend of decentralization at different levels, but the management work could not keep up with it, which affected production. Second, some of the products supplied to the entire country were not able to meet the demand after the decentralization. Third, some enterprises, especially the mechanical maintenance enterprises, were unwilling to undertake the tasks assigned by the Ministry. Fourth, some enterprises with national tasks had difficulties in their work. For example, after the port was decentralized, it was difficult for the local government to grasp the overall situation and the port transportation arrangement was difficult. Fifth, after the decentralization of enterprises, some financial systems could not keep up. For example, it was difficult for some budget units to be fully subsidized by local governments after decentralization. Sixth, some provinces reported that central enterprises devolved too much, and they were unable to manage for a while and requested that the process of decentralization be postponed.

These problems in the process of decentralizing the system greatly affected the order and efficiency of economic operation. In addition, the impact of class struggle on production in the Cultural Revolution led to chaos in the country's economic life. Therefore, on February 26, 1973, the State Planning Commission put forward a Notice on Adhering to the Unified Plan and Strengthening Economic Management, which was drafted by Zhou Enlai, and decided to rectify the economic management system. The main contents of the document included adhering to the unified plan, establishing comprehensive balance, and opposing each going its own way. Strict control of the increase of staff and workers and improvement of labor productivity were needed. The power to control the total number of employees and wages was to be controlled by the central government, and the labor force was to be subjected to unified transfer. In capital construction, it was important to concentrate efforts on the war of annihilation and improve the efficiency of investment. Infrastructure projects were to be handled in accordance with procedures. Capital management would be strengthened and financial discipline strictly enforced. Enterprises had to pay taxes and profits in accordance with state regulations. It was necessary to strengthen material management and oppose decentralized overstocking. Strict production discipline and quality control discipline were established, and it was necessary to adhere to the principle of distribution according to work. Large and medium-sized enterprises could not be decentralized at all levels.

The change of product direction of decentralized enterprises had to be approved by the relevant departments of the State Council. It was necessary to strengthen the Party's leadership over economic work and adhere to the unity of politics and business, and it was dereliction of duty for the main person in charge of an enterprise to fail to pay attention to production.[16]

In January 1974, the movement of "criticizing Lin Biao and Confucius" was carried out throughout the country, which seriously affected the economic work and the rectification of the planned system. In 1975, the "counterattack of rightist overturning cases" was launched against Deng Xiaoping. Therefore, the rectification of economic work and the reform of the system were not put on the agenda of the Central Committee, and the economic chaos continued until the end of the Cultural Revolution.

The biggest advantage of the central planning economy was that it could centrally allocate resources and services throughout society at lower cost through the central government's mandatory plan, mobilize the entire society to the maximum extent, and serve some simple and clear objectives of the government at a specific stage, so as to meet the urgent, overwhelming needs of the government on a specific date. American economists Egan Newberg and William Duffy pointed out that the centralized planning system was considered to have several advantages, including 1) the system's directors had a greater ability to achieve their goals, even if their goals were not shared by members of the economic system, 2) there was a greater possibility of rapidly realizing large economic structural changes in order to cope with some unexpected events, 3) the central authorities were more likely to estimate the costs and benefits of any decision in the current year, rather than being limited to short-term costs or benefits, 4) there was the possibility of "internalizing external economic and non-economic conditions," for example, the benefits of youth education and the cost of eliminating pollution caused by factories could be considered from the overall economy, 5) it could obtain better information about the interaction of various decision-making bodies within the overall economic scope, 6) the instructors could concentrate scarce resources, including the personnel who had received scientific and technological education, to focus on the most important fields, and 7) they could achieve the standardization and unification of products and avoid the extreme waste caused by difference.[17] What needed to be affirmed was that in the early days of most socialist regimes, the central planned economic system played a positive role in economic development. First of all, it provided the necessary experience reference for the national economic development into the plan management. Second, the planning system placed importance on industrial development, which prepared the necessary material and technical conditions for the later economic development, and the implementation of the Five-Year Plan played a huge role in accelerating the industrialization process in a short

---

16. Li Zhining, *The Economic Canon of the People's Republic of China* (Jilin People's Publishing House, 1987), 425.

17. Egan Newberg, William Duffy et al., *Comparative Economic Systems: Comparison from the Perspective of Decision-making* (The Commercial Press, 1984).

period of time. Under the condition of a backward economy, it ensured the high accumulation and priority for the rapid development of heavy industry and established a relatively complete independent industrial system and infrastructure. Third, through the extensive allocation of resources, the planning system effectively suppressed social unrest and crisis in the early stages of the establishment of the new regime. In the case of economic backwardness and high accumulation, it ensured the people's basic life and social stability, except in some abnormal periods.

For a long time, whether in theory or in practice, the understanding and implementation of the planned economy was divorced from actual economic development. It was understood that the planned economy was related to the socialist mode of production, but not yet grasped that the development form of the planned economy was related to the development level of the socialist mode of production. In the exposition of Marxist classical writers, the future society would distribute labor to various production departments and organize the production and distribution of society overall through a general plan including the production and circulation of the entire society. Society would link up the balance of total supply and demand completely through this plan. This sort of planned economy needed to have two conditions, the high development of social productive forces and large-scale socialized production and overall society implementing the public ownership of the means of production in a complete sense (i.e. the means of production being directly owned by society), so that the foundation of the commodity economy would no longer exist. At that time, based on the information system and other technical conditions, it was possible to directly calculate the social demand and labor time for producing various products to meet this demand, and then to directly allocate labor according to the proportion without the aid of value or exchange value. However, China's socialist mode of production had obviously not developed to this level. Its socialist economic construction was not carried out on the basis of the full development of commodities, but on the basis of the natural economy and feudal small-scale production. This foundation of social productive forces determined that China's socialist mode of production was not a socialism with highly developed socialized mass production, direct possession of the means of production, and the highly unified economic interests of members of society, as envisaged by classical Marxist writers. Therefore, it did not meet the conditions for the implementation of a highly centralized, unified planned economic system. The result of subjective implementation would only lead to the depression of workers' enthusiasm for production and the lack of efficiency in economic activities.

The planned economic system was adapted to the realistic conditions of China's social and economic development at that time. Faced with economic backwardness, it ensured the high accumulation and priority of the rapid development of heavy industry, established a relatively complete independent industrial system and infrastructure, and at the same time, ensured the people's basic life and social stability in the face of economic backwardness and high accumulation, effectively mobilizing the limited human, material, and financial resources when faced with a material shortage. This large-scale economic construction established the material basis for the consolidation and development of the socialist system in the relatively short period of just over ten years. In the First Five-Year Plan period, after the end of the national economic recovery period, 694 large and medium-sized construction projects and a number of key enterprises were built with 156 projects constructed with the assistance of the Soviet Union as the center, which helped China establish a relatively complete framework for a basic industrial system and national defense industrial system. This accumulated experience laid the foundation for national industrialization.

The planned economy was a kind of economic management and operation system in which subjective decision-making was connected with objective laws. The scientific, effective planned economy had two objective provisions. On the one hand, the plan needed to correctly reflect the law of productivity development and social demand. Any plan divorced from the actual development and market demand would either fail to work or cause confusion in economic life. On the other hand, it was necessary for the government to create a comprehensive plan for the development of the planned economy. Economic means and leverage needed to be used to manage and regulate the economy. Otherwise, the planned system would become invalid and the quality of economic operations would decline.

Throughout China's economic development from the 1950s to the 1970s, both the formulation and implementation of the plan lacked attention to both science and the economy. At the same time, the implementation of the plan basically relied on administrative means, so the purpose and effect of the plan were difficult to achieve. Even if these goals were achieved, what was established was basically a statistical phenomenon on paper, which was quite different from the actual economic situation. China was still in the early stage of industrialization and had not yet reached a high degree of socialization of production. The key to the superiority of the planned economy was to obtain enough information in a timely way and deal with problems promptly, which became the biggest challenge to making appropriate plans. It was difficult for decision makers to obtain enough information in a timely way, not only because of the complexity of the economy itself and the backwardness of the means of production, but also because the information was collected and conveyed by many institutions or personnel. In this process, relevant institutions and personnel naturally filtered or even distorted the information according to their own understanding and preferences.[18] The mandatory plan fettered enterprises, leading to a lack of enthusiasm and initiative in production, which was not conducive to promoting technological progress and innovation. At the same time, there were problems in the formulation of the plan itself. Some scholars used the method of economic statistics to estimate the input-output benefits of China's industrial and agricultural sub-sectors and the national economy from 1957 to 1978 by adding the total value of labor input.[19] At the same time, using the growth index model, the annual growth rate of all input and output was calculated in the planned system period. Both methods showed that under the planned system, the performance of the national economy and the industrial and agricultural sub-sectors was very low, due to the serious disconnect between the formulation and

18. Wu Li, "Reexamination and Evaluation of China's Planned Economy," *Research on Contemporary Chinese History*, no. 4 (2003).

19. Qu Shang, "The Performance of China's Planned Economic System (1957–1978): An Analysis Based on the Comparison of Input-output Benefits," *China Economic History Research*, no. 1 (2008).

implementation of the plan, the lack of incentive mechanism in the economic system, and the low enthusiasm of workers, and this resulted in the low efficiency of resource utilization. In terms of economic performance, the overall efficiency of China's industry declined before 1978, and a higher growth rate was achieved by reducing consumption, increasing the accumulation rate, and increasing the scale of investment. The serious imbalance of industrial structure was mainly manifested in a biased in favor of heavy industry and a light industry that lagged behind. In heavy industry, the general processing and manufacturing industry was biased, and the development of energy and transportation lagged behind. The total grain output increased slowly. In 1976, the per capita annual consumption of grain was only 381 *jin,* even lower than the level of 395 *jin* per capita in 1952. From 1966 to 1976, the per capita income of farmers from collective distribution hovered around 60 yuan, and in 1976, the per capita income of farmers was only 62.8 yuan. There were 250 million people living in poverty in China. From 1966 to 1977, the wage growth of urban workers basically stagnated, the main light industrial products and agricultural and sideline products faced a serious shortage, and the employment situation in cities and towns was grim. At the end of 1970s, there were about 20 million unemployed people in Chinese cities.[20]

In brief, during the 1950s to the 1970s, China's economic system was inefficient, the quality of its economic operations was low, economic fluctuation was large, and the waste of economic resources was serious. The deeper reason is that the economic system and the reality of productivity development is not compatible, as well as the planned economic decision-making is not scientific and non-economic. However, it was undeniable that China's planned economy had adapted to the objective conditions of the social and economic development of that time. The establishment of the planned economic system not only achieved initial economic stability in a short period of time at the beginning of the founding of the People's Republic of China, but also ensured that its limited resources were concentrated in key construction at a low level of economic development, laying a foundation of basic technology and productivity for China's industrialization.

3.2 The Formation and Development of the Strategic Thought on Economic Development from the 1950s to the 1970s

1. On the Concept of Economic Growth and the Economic Development Strategy

In classical Western economics, the growth of the national income has always been regarded as the only important measure of economic development. There has generally been no distinction between "economic growth" and "economic development." Economic development and economic progress have been seen as equivalent to economic growth, that is, a continuous increase of the national income. At the beginning of the 20th century, Arthur Cecil Pigou, one of the main

---

20. Office of the State Economic Restructuring Committee, *Compilation of Documents on Economic Restructuring (1978–1983)* (China Financial and Economic Publishing House, 1984), 10.

representatives of the neoclassical school, established the welfare economics system along the Marshall marginal utility theory system, using Alfred Marshall's Consumer's Surplus concept. Pigou's concept of Economic Welfare refers to the satisfaction of utility related to people's economic life, which cannot be measured directly or indirectly by money, and which has a decisive impact on the total welfare of the entire society.[21] The sum of individual economic welfare forms social economic welfare. Social and economic welfare is represented by the "national divide," that is, the net flow of material and non-material products in a certain period of time. It is the national income expressed in real units. Therefore, to increase economic welfare, it is necessary to increase national income and eliminate uneven distribution. According to the law of diminishing marginal utility, the marginal utility of money held by people with more income is smaller, while that of people with less income is greater. Therefore, even if the national income remains unchanged, the equalization of income distribution can also improve social and economic welfare. However, the most fundamental factor to promote social welfare is to increase the total national income. In order to make the national income produced by a certain amount of a society's production resources reach the maximum value, it is necessary to optimize the allocation of social production resources. It is evident that in welfare economics, the increase of "economic welfare" not only includes the growth of the national income, but also includes the fairness of social distribution and the optimization of resource allocation. From this point of view, the theory represented a new understanding of economic growth and development.

Later, Alfred Clark inherited and developed Pigou's ideas. Pigou believed that as long as it was not hindered by unequal distribution and uncertain transactions, welfare would increase with the increase of material goods and services provided. Clark summed up this proposition. He held that economic progress is brought about by the increase of material goods and service supply (i.e. an increase in production). Production can be calculated by the per capita real gross national product created by unit labor time. Moreover, the increase of per capita real gross national product can be achieved through the productivity of various industries and the distribution of labor supply and capital accumulation. This idea means that "per capita national income" can be used to express "welfare" with a wide range of concepts. This view is still the basic idea held in economic development theory, and "per capita national income" is widely used as an important indicator to measure economic growth. On the basis of the above views, Clark offered a specific description of the content of economic progress and suggested that economic progress is mainly manifested in eight aspects: 1) the growth of production, 2) the progress of technology, 3) the change of industrial structure, 4) the accumulation of capital, 5) the progress of international economic relations, 6) the change of demand structure, 7) the progress of system, and 8) the change of values. Among these, the growth of production is a central phenomenon in economic progress.[22] It is clear that in Clark's explanation, the connotation of economic growth has been

---

21. Arthur Cecil Piguo, *The Economics of Welfare* (Artharcell Macmillan, 1932).

22. Alfred Clark, "Conditions of Economic Progress," in *Western Economic Development Theory* (China Renmin University Press, 1989), 2.

further expanded. However, there is no clear conceptual distinction between economic growth and economic development.

In the 1940s, British economist Roy Harrod abstracted the phenomenon of continuous growth of national income from various phenomena of economic development and put forward a clear concept of economic growth. In 1948, he systematically discussed his economic growth theory and model in his book *Towards a Dynamic Economics*. In the same period, the American economist Evsey Domar likewise carried out similar research, published two papers, *Capital Expansion, Rate of Growth and Employment* and *Expansion and Employment*, and put forward an economic growth model that was basically the same as Harrod's. The publications by Harrod and Domar marked the beginning of modern Western economic growth theory. In modern Western economics, economic growth theory (growth economics) is an independent research field. In the theory of economic growth, the term "economic growth" generally refers to the quantitative growth of a country's economy, mainly expressed by the change of per capita national income. The theory of economic growth mainly studies three topics: 1) whether there is balanced economic growth in the long run, 2) if there is long-term balanced economic growth, what are its dynamic characteristics, and 3) the conditions balanced economic growth must meet. The theory of economic growth takes developed countries' economy as the research object, but its basic methods, theories, and policy propositions are also widely used in the economic research of developing countries.

Economic development strategy was a relatively new concept not only in China, but also in the world. Generally speaking, from the 1950s to the 1960s, in order to eliminate poverty and promote their own economic development and industrialization, some developing countries formulated medium and long-term economic development strategies with industrialization as the core. At that time, it was generally recognized that the key to the transformation of developing countries' economy from underdeveloped to developed was to rapidly increase GNP or per capita national income. Logical reasoning and the examples of developed countries indicated that there was no more effective way to achieve rapid economic growth in addition to the development of modern industry. Therefore, to realize industrialization as the main content and to pursue high-speed economic growth as the goal became the general characteristics of the economic development strategy at that time. However, the implementation of this strategy did not achieve the desired results. Therefore, people began to re-examine the development strategy with a one-sided pursuit of high-speed economic growth as the core and put forward some new ideas on economic development strategy. In this respect, the idea of modern economic growth put forward by Simon Kuznets is typical. Kuznets first emphasized the internal relationship between economic growth and economic development. He said, "The economic growth of a country can be defined as the long-term increase in the ability to provide residents with an increasingly wide range of economic products. This growth ability is based on the corresponding adjustment of advanced technology and the required system and ideology." Based on this understanding, he put forward the concept of modern economic growth. Modern economic growth refers a specific stage in the development of world history, which is different from the feudalism era and commercial capitalism era. Its main characteristics are evident in 1) the high growth rate of output calculated by population and the high growth rate of population, while the growth rate of per capita output is higher than that of the population, 2) the high productivity (including all production) growth, 3) the rapid change of the economic structure, in which the main content is the transfer of labor force from agriculture to industry, from industry to service industry, 4) the rapid change of social structure and ideology related to the change of economic structure, 5) the economic developed countries expanding to all parts of the world with the help of increased technical strength, and 6) the fact that although modern economic growth has a great impact on the world, its spread remains limited in three quarters of the world's population.[23] According to Kuznets, these six characteristics supported the important hypothesis that modern economic growth marked a specific economic era, that is, the process from traditional economy to modern economy and from an underdeveloped state to a developed state, which was essentially the process of industrialization. Taking the concept of modern economic growth as the core of economic development strategy, the characteristics of this strategy were 1) it was no longer one-sided pursuit of high-speed growth of output and output value, but attached importance to the healthy, coordinated development of society and the economy and took improving people's living standard as the main goal, 2) in the theory of economic growth, capital accumulation was no longer emphasized as economic growth, but the only important factor of long-term development was to promote economic growth and improve the quality of economy through technological progress, structural transformation, and the growth of necessary elements input, and 3) linking economic growth with economic system reform and the corresponding political structure reform, so as to achieve coordinated economic and social development.

The concept of the economic development strategy was widely used in China in the early 1980s. From the time the Twelfth National Congress of the Communist Party of China in 1982 formulated the strategy of China's social and economic development by the year 2000, the concept of an economic development strategy was discussed in theoretical circles. The general understandings included 1) the economic development strategy is generally defined as the general and basic principles for realizing the goal of a country's economic development, 2) the strategy of economic and social development is the general principle and policy of a country in the process of developing from a state of low productivity and a backward economy and society to a state of relatively developed productivity and an advanced economy and society, 3) the economic development strategy mainly refers to the economic policies and guidelines adopted by developing countries in order to eliminate economic and social underdevelopment caused by various factors and gradually realize national modernization in the process of transition from backward economic state to modern economic development, and 4) the economic development strategy includes strategic objectives, strategic principles, and corresponding steps, meaning

---

23. Kuznets, "Modern Economic Growth: Discovery and Reflection. Selected Papers on Modern Foreign Economics," in *Association of Foreign Economic Theory Studies*, vol. 2 (The Commercial Press, 1981).

that it refers to a major overall plan and the general strategy of a country.[24] To sum up this understanding, the economic development strategy refers to the overall long-term development goals formulated by a country for its social and economic development, as well as the guidelines, basic principles, and policies and measures to achieve the overall goal.

Although the term "economic development strategy" was widely used in China in the 1980s, since the founding of the People's Republic of China, China had planned and formulated the social and economic development goals for realizing socialist industrialization and modernization from the overall perspective of social and economic development, as well as the related economic policies, plans, and guidelines. These principles, plans, and policies formed a system in theory and guided the development of the national economy in practice. Therefore, they were in fact economic development strategies.

2. Two Ideological Debates on the Speed of Economic Growth in the 1950s

At the Second Plenary Session of the Seventh Central Committee of the Communist Party of China in March 1949, on behalf of the Party Central Committee, Mao Zedong put forward the grand goal of China's socialist industrialization and declared that China's economic heritage was backward, but the Chinese people were brave and industrious, and the victory of the Chinese people's revolution and the establishment of the People's Republic of China, the leadership of the Communist Party of China, and the assistance of the working class from all over the world, mainly the assistance of the Soviet Union meant that China's economic development would not be very slow, but might be quite rapid. China's prosperity would thus eventually be achieved.[25] This was the first time the speed of economic development was discussed from the perspective of industrialization. In the report of the Second Plenary Session of the Seventh Central Committee of the Communist Party of China and in the general line for the transition period put forward by the Central Committee of the Communist Party of China in December 1952, it was estimated that it would take about fifteen years to realize national industrialization, that is, three Five-Year Plans. At the end of 1955, Mao Zedong pointed out in the "Preface to the Socialist Peak in China's Rural Areas" that it was important to constantly criticize right-leaning conservative thought in the aspects of industrial and handicraft production and the scale and speed of infrastructure construction of industry and transportation. China's socialist transformation was completed in 1956. The First Five-Year Plan was successfully completed in 1957. These achievements greatly stimulated the idea of rapid economic development. In December 1957, Liu Shaoqi made

---

24. Huang Fangyi, "A Survey of the Concept of 'Development Strategy,'" *Economic Research*, no. 7 (1982); Yu Guangyuan, "Scientific Research on the Strategic Issues of China's Social and Economic Development," *People's Daily*, August 16, 1982; Zhou Shulian, "Historical Experience in Seriously Studying China's Economic Development Strategy," *People's Daily*, May 2, 1982; Sun Shangqing, "Understanding of China's Economic Development Strategy," *People's Daily*, April 12, 1982.

25. Mao Zedong, *Selected Works of Mao Zedong*, vol. 4 (People's Publishing House, 1968).

a speech on behalf of the Central Committee of the Communist Party of China at the Eighth National Congress of Trade Unions of China. He pointed out, "In fifteen years' time, the output of the most important products of the Soviet Union may catch up with or surpass that of the United States. We should strive to catch up with or surpass Britain in the production of steel and other important industrial products at the same time. In this way, the socialist world will leave imperialist countries far behind."[26]

This guiding ideology promoted the rash practice of being eager for success in industrial production and unilaterally pursuing the rapid growth of output and output value. In 1956, the scale of capital construction (in China's economic statistics, investment in fixed assets included new capital construction and technological transformation of existing enterprises and renewal of fixed assets) was too large, the number of employees increased too much, and the credit breakthrough plan and the financial deficit appeared. In view of this situation, at the Central Working Conference held in May 1956, Zhou Enlai and Chen Yun proposed opposing both conservatism and rashness. This proposal was later affirmed at the Eighth National Congress of the Communist Party of China and was summarized as an economic construction policy that was both anti-conservative and anti-rash, making steady progress in the overall balance. At the first session of the Eighth National Congress of the Communist Party of China held in September 1956, Zhou Enlai delivered a report entitled Suggestions on the Second Five-Year Plan for the Development of the National Economy. He pointed out that the development speed of the national economy should be regulated objectively according to the needs and possibilities, and the plan should be put on a positive, reliable basis to ensure the smooth development of the national economy. During the Eighth National Congress of the Communist Party of China, Bo Yibo put forward the idea of "two, three, and four" proportions in the national economy, that is, in the following few years, under normal circumstances, the proportion of China's accumulated part of national income would not be less than 20% or slightly higher, the proportion of the national budget would not be less than 30% or a little higher, and the proportion of capital construction expenditure in the state budget expenditure would not less than 40% or slightly higher. This would not only ensure the development of China's industry, especially heavy industry, but also ensure the continuous improvement of the people's living standards.[27] The Eighth National Congress of the Communist Party of China pointed out that the contradiction between the people's need for rapid economic and cultural development and the current situation that the economy and culture could not meet the people's needs was the main domestic contradiction. The main task of the people throughout the country was to concentrate on the development of social productive forces, realize national industrialization, and gradually meet the people's growing material and cultural needs. The Proposal of the CPC Central Committee on the Second Five-Year Plan adopted by the Congress stipulated that since China's national economy was still very backward, the proportion

---

26. Liang Xiufeng, "Historical Review and Reflection on China's Economic Construction," *Research on the History of the Communist Party of China*, no. 5 (1989).

27. Office of the Plan for Contemporary China, *Essentials of the National Economic and Social Development Plan of the People's Republic of China (1949–1985)* (Red Flag Press, 1987), 89.

of agriculture was still large, and the people's living standard was relatively low, the proportion of the accumulated part in the national income could not and should not grow too high or too fast.

On January 18, 1957, Chen Yun made a speech entitled "The Scale of Construction Compatible with National Strength" at the meeting of Secretaries of Party committees of provinces, cities, and autonomous regions. He pointed out that the size of construction scale must be compatible with the financial and material resources of the country. Whether it could adapt or not was the boundary between economic stability and instability. As a large country with a population of 600 million, economic stability was extremely important in China. If the scale of construction exceeded the financial and material resources of the state, chaos would occur. If the two were appropriate, the economy would be stable. Of course, if it was conservative, it would hinder the pace of construction. However, it was easier to correct conservatism than rashness. Because there was too much material, it was relatively easy to increase construction. However, due to insufficient financial and material resources, it was not as easy to suppress the construction scale because of insufficient financial and material resources, which would also cause serious waste.[28] This above discussion indicated that after the founding of the People's Republic of China, China had basically formed two guiding ideologies on the issue of economic development speed. One was inclined to pursue a high speed of economic growth and strive to realize industrialization as soon as possible, and the other was that the speed of economic growth should adapt to the national strength so as to achieve coordinated, stable economic development. Judging from the spirit of the Eighth National Congress of the Communist Party of China, the latter guiding ideology was basically affirmed at that time.

However, the anti-rightist movement that began in the summer of 1957 directly affected the guiding ideology of economic construction. At the Third Plenary Session of the Eighth Central Committee of the Communist Party of China, held after the anti-rightist movement, Mao Zedong pointed out in his analysis of the domestic situation, "The contradiction between the proletariat and the bourgeoisie and the contradiction between the socialist road and the capitalist road are undoubtedly the main spear and shield of our society at present. There is a paragraph in the resolution of the Eighth National Congress of the Communist Party of China which states that the main contradiction is the contradiction between the advanced social system and the backward social productive forces. This is not true."[29] This sort of argument based on class struggle had a profound impact on the guiding ideology of China's economic construction. The Third Plenary Session of the Eighth Central Committee of the Communist Party of China (CPC) criticized the "anti-rash advance" in 1956. The plenary session accused the "anti-rash advance" of being "right leaning" and "promoting retreat." In early 1958, the Hangzhou and Nanning meetings convened by the Central Committee of the Communist Party of China, the Chengdu Conference in March, and the second session of the Eighth National Congress of the Communist Party of China in May

---

28. Office of the Plan for Contemporary China, *Essentials of the National Economic and Social Development Plan of the People's Republic of China (1949–1985)* (Red Flag Press, 1987), 97.

29. Mao Zedong, *Selected Works of Mao Zedong*, vol. 5 (People's Publishing House, 1977), 475.

all fiercely criticized the "anti-rash advance." This led to a situation in which the left was seen as better than the right in economic work, the left was preferred to the right, and the right was to be criticized but the left not corrected, which created conditions for the blind pursuit of high-speed construction both ideologically and politically.

On January 31, 1958, on the basis of discussions at the Hangzhou and Nanning Conferences, Mao Zedong put forward the Sixty Articles on Working Methods (Draft). On February 7, the CPC Central Committee transmitted the document to the entire Party. Among them, those closely related to economic work and which had a significant impact included the following: First, there were three accounts on the production plan. The Central Committee had two: one was on the plan to be completed, which was to be issued, and another was a plan for this period, which was not to be issued. There were also two local accounts, the first was the second account of the Central Committee, which was to be completed at the level of the local government, and the second account was the local plan for the future. The evaluation was based on the second account of the central government. Secondly, beginning in 1958, the Party committees of the central government, provinces, cities, and autonomous regions were to focus on industry, finance, and trade. Thirdly, the industrial output value of various localities was to exceed the local agricultural output value within five, seven, or ten years. Fourthly, in the next five to eight years, China would complete the provisions of forty articles of the outline for agricultural development. Fifthly, China would work hard for three years to basically improve the outlook of most areas. Finally, it was important for China to focus the Party's work on technological revolution.[30] This method of "three accounts" laid the ideological foundation for separating itself from reality, from national conditions, and national strength, and for pursuing high targets and high speed. After that, the "leftist" error of impetuosity and rashness in economic construction became the main guiding ideology.

3. The Proposal of the General Line of Socialist Construction and the Decision to Launch the Great Leap Forward

The proposal of the general line of socialist construction went through a process. In 1955, when listening to the work reports of the central financial and economic departments, Zhou Enlai proposed that socialist construction should be increased, and it should be both faster and better. Li Fuchun added that the province should be economical. These opinions were approved by Mao Zedong.[31] In October 1957, Mao Zedong said at the Third Plenary Session of the Eighth Central Committee of the Communist Party of China, "Can we avoid the detour that the Soviet Union has taken and make it faster and better than the Soviet Union's quality? We should strive for this possibility. For example, can we achieve 20 million tons of steel in three Five-Year Plans or more?

30. Office of the Plan for Contemporary China, *Essentials of the National Economic and Social Development Plan of the People's Republic of China (1949–1985)* (Red Flag Press, 1987), 117.

31. Xu Jianhua, "A Preliminary Study on the General Line of Socialist Construction," *Research on the History of the Party*, no. 5 (1981).

It is possible with hard work." He also said, "At first, good quality and economy are intended to restrict 'more' and 'fast.' Good means good quality, economy means spending less money, more means getting more things done, and fast means getting more things done faster. The slogan in nature limits itself, because it requires good quality and less spending. It is impossible and unrealistic to get more things done faster. What we are talking about is seeking truth from facts, which is more, faster, better, economical and more in line with the actual situation rather than being driven by one's own will. We should always strive for more and faster as much as possible, but we are against the wishful 'more and faster.'"[32]

On February 3, 1958, the *People's Daily* published the editorial "To Strive for the Upper Reaches," calling on the people to summon up the revolutionary energy, break all "right leaning" conservative ideas, strive for the upper reaches, and build socialism with more, faster, better, and economical. That March, the Central Committee of the Communist Party of China held a working conference in Chengdu and determined to take the slogan of "summoning energy to strive for the upper reaches, aiming at more, faster, better, and the economy" as the basic substance of the general line of socialist construction. In May, the second session of the Eighth National Congress of the Communist Party of China formally adopted the general line and basic points of socialist construction of "encouraging all effort, striving for the upper level, and building socialism more quickly, better, and more economically." Liu Shaoqi said in the political report, "The Party Central Committee believes that the basic points of the general line of building socialism with full energy, striving for the upper level more quickly, better, and more economically include mobilizing all positive factors to correctly handle contradictions among the people, consolidating and developing socialist ownership by all the people and collective ownership, consolidating the dictatorship of the proletariat and the international unity of the proletariat, and continuing to complete the economic development. With the socialist revolution on the economic, political, and ideological fronts, we should gradually realize the technological revolution and the cultural revolution. Under the condition of giving priority to the development of heavy industry, industry and agriculture should be developed simultaneously. Under the conditions of centralized leadership, comprehensive planning, division of labor, and cooperation, central and local industries should be developed simultaneously, and the development of large enterprises and small and medium-sized enterprises should be carried out at the same time. We should build our country into a great socialist nation with modern industry, modern agriculture, and modern science and culture as soon as possible."

The general line of socialist construction and its basic points, put forward in 1958, were the first official guidelines on economic development in China's socialist construction. This guideline determined the strategic objectives and relevant policy principles of China's economic development, and it was the summary and development of the guiding ideology on economic development after the founding of the People's Republic of China. The defect of this policy was that it ignored the sober understanding of national conditions and national strength, and

---

32. *Xinhua Bimonthly* (November 1958): 7.

that economic development needed to strictly follow objective economic laws and the law of productivity development. These defects were the product of the expanding "left leaning" thought at that time, and they directly led to the Great Leap Forward.

The second session of the Eighth National Congress of the Communist Party of China put forward the general line of socialist construction, and at the same time, it put forward the requirement of catching up with Britain in seven years and catching up with the United States in fifteen years. The meeting emphasized that "the speed of construction is the most important issue before us after the victory of the socialist revolution."[33] The main index of construction speed was the growth rate of gross industrial output value, mainly the growth rate of heavy industry, especially the growth rate of steel output. On June 21, 1958, the *People's Daily* published an editorial entitled "Striving for High Speed," which explained the general line. "To develop China's social productive forces at the highest speed runs through all aspects of the general line," the editorial said. "If we don't seek for high speed, then there's no need to talk about more, faster, better quality, and the economy. In that case, we don't need to work hard or strive for the top. Therefore, it can be said that speed is the soul of the general line... The issue of speed is that of the construction line and the fundamental principle of China's socialist cause... Speed is the central link of more, faster, better quality, and the economy." This view of extreme highlighting of speed deviated from Mao's discussion on the relationship between more, faster, better quality, and the economy at the Third Plenary Session of the Eighth Central Committee of the Communist Party of China.

The second session of the Eighth National Congress of the Communist Party of China deviated from the line of the first session of the Eighth National Congress. It injected theoretical content and form into the one-sided pursuit of high-speed economic growth formed and developed after the founding of the People's Republic of China. In August 1958, the Central Committee of the Communist Party of China held an enlarged meeting of the Politburo in Beidaihe. It was decided that the steel output in 1958 should reach 10.7–11.5 million tons, double that of 1957, and industrial production should first ensure steel production. After the Beidaihe meeting of the CPC Central Committee, a nationwide Great Leap Forward in industrial production and the people's commune movement, which took steel as the key link, quickly set off across the country. Industry, agriculture, transportation, commerce, culture, education, and health all set their own high targets, and they all needed to achieve the Great Leap Forward. This leap forward of all walks of life was centered on doubling the output of iron and steel, that is, what was called "with one horse leading, ten thousand horses galloping," and "with steel as the key link, we should work for an overall leap forward."

The Wuchang Meeting of the CPC Central Committee in November 1958 and the Sixth Plenary Session of the Eighth Central Committee of the CPC in November 1958, recognized the serious consequences of the Great Leap Forward and pointed out that there were two lessons from the Great Leap Forward in 1958. The first was that the speed of national economic development must be based on objective possibility, and the second was that the national economy must be

---

33. *Xinhua Bimonthly* (November 1958): 7.

planned and compared to the development of the system. In both meetings, it was proposed that they should "compress the air," suppress high targets, oppose exaggeration and false reporting of achievements, and demand that economic work be close to and conform to reality.

In July 1959, the Enlarged Politburo Meeting of the CPC Central Committee was held in Lushan. The original topic of the meeting was to further summarize the lessons from 1958 and continue to correct the "leftist" tendency in economic construction. However, the situation in the late period of the conference turned rapidly from rectifying the "left" to an anti-right direction, launching a criticism of the so-called "right leaning" opportunism of Peng Dehuai and others. At the Eighth Plenary Session of the Eighth Central Committee of the CPC in August, a resolution was made to defend the Party's general line and oppose the "right leaning," opportunism, which extended the fight against the "right leaning" to the whole Party and country. The plenary session adopted the Resolution on the Campaign for Increasing Production and Practicing Thrift, which required that the Second Five-Year Plan, originally set for completion in 1962, should be completed in the production of major industrial and agricultural products in 1959, and that effort should be made to catch up with the UK in the output of major industrial products within ten years from 1958. Under the slogan of "anti-right leaning and continuing to leap forward," industrial production, especially heavy industrial production, continued to develop at a high speed in 1959. By the end of the year, the total industrial output value had reached 148.3 billion yuan, an increase of 36.1 per cent over the previous year. The total output value of heavy industry was 86.7 billion yuan, an increase of 48.1%, and the steel output reached 13.87 million tons, an increase of 73.4%.[34]

On January 1, 1960, the *People's Daily* published an editorial entitled "Looking Forward to the 1960s." The editorial pointed out that according to the experience of recent years, China had found three magic weapons, the general line of building socialism, the development speed of the Great Leap Forward, and the organizational form of the people's commune. The editorial called for the establishment of a complete industrial system in the new decade to catch up with or surpass the UK in the output of major industrial products, basically realize the modernization of industry, agriculture, and science and culture, and build China into a great socialist power.

On January 7,1960, the CPC Central Committee held an enlarged Politburo meeting in Shanghai. Under the influence of the spirit of the Eighth Plenary Session of the Eighth Central Committee of the CPC, the conference discussed and formulated the national economic plan of 1960, and it again put forward a high index, with 18.4 million tons of steel as the center. From March 30 to April 10, the second session of the Second National People's Congress was held. At the meeting, on behalf of the State Council, Li Fuchun made a report on the draft national economic plan for 1960. The report proposed that the task of developing the national economy in 1960 was to better implement the general line of the Party's socialist construction and strive for the national economy to continue to leap forward in all areas. On June 14, the *People's Daily* published an editorial entitled "The Dialectical Unity of the High Speed of the Great Leap Forward and the

---

34. *China Statistical Yearbook (1984)* (China Statistics Press, 1984), 225–226.

Planned Proportion," which held that the Great Leap Forward of the national economy in the two years since 1958 proved that high speed and proportion were a dialectical unity in socialist construction. High speed was the main aspect of contradiction and the most important issue in socialist construction. A major task of socialist economic construction was to take the realization of high speed as the guiding ideology and seek the correct proportional relationship to ensure the high-speed development of the national economy. According to the implementation results of the national economic plan in 1960, the accumulation rate was up to 39.6%, and the fiscal deficit was 8.18 billion yuan, which was the most serious since the founding of the People's Republic of China. The output value of heavy industry increased by 25.9% compared with the previous year, agricultural output value decreased by 12.6%, and the consumption level of the entire nation was 13.6% lower than that in 1957.[35]

4. Development Strategy in the Period of National Economic Adjustment

(1) The Decision to Adjust, Consolidate, Enrich and Improve the National Economy

During the Shanghai Conference, held by the Central Committee of the Communist Party of China in June 1960, Mao Zedong wrote a summary of the previous ten years, emphasizing the principle of seeking truth from facts. He pointed out that in 1958 and 1959, quantity had been discussed, but in the future it was important to pay attention to quality, specifications, and variety. It was necessary to put variety and quality first and quantity second. He believed that the planned targets in 1960 should be adjusted and some leeway should remain for the indicators. It was preferable to have less than the actual requirement, and allowing it to become too full would put the country at a disadvantage.[36] In September of that year, in the report on the control figures of the national economic plan of 1961 approved and transmitted by the central government, the eight character policy of "adjustment, consolidation, enrichment, and improvement" was proposed for the first time. In January 1961, the Ninth Plenary Session of the Eighth Central Committee of the Communist Party of China formally established the policy of "adjusting, consolidating, enriching, and improving" the national economy. The plenary session called to use agriculture as the base to set an appropriate reduction of the scale of capital construction, an adjustment of the speed of development, and a push to consolidate, enrich, and improve on the basis of existing victories.[37] In August and September 1961, the CPC Central Committee held a working conference in Lushan to discuss economic issues. At the meeting, Li Fuchun reviewed the experience and lessons of the planning work in the Great Leap Forward and put forward suggestions on the adjustment of the

---

35. *China Statistical Yearbook (1984)* (China Statistics Press, 1984), 223, 225; Office of the Plan for Contemporary China, *Essentials of the National Economic and Social Development Plan of the People's Republic of China (1949–985)* (Red Flag Press, 1987), 163.

36. Liu Suinian et al., *National Economy in the Period of the Great Leap Forward and Adjustment* (Heilongjiang People's Publishing House, 1984), 83.

37. "Communique of the Ninth Plenary Session of the Eighth Central Committee of the Communist Party of China," *Xinhua Monthly News*, no. 2 (1961).

national economy, mainly the industrial sector. He said that in the previous three years, China had overestimated the production capacity of industry, especially heavy industry. As a result, the planned targets were too high, the development speed too fast, and the capital construction front too long. To a certain extent, the normal proportion had been destroyed, production relations had been disrupted, and some productive forces had been destroyed. He emphasized that the central task of the "eight character" policy was adjustment. It was necessary to adjust the proportion of agriculture, light and heavy industries, and the relationship between industries and enterprises. As far as specific arrangements were concerned, industrial infrastructure and production indicators were not only to be withdrawn in a planned way, but also to a sufficient level, leaving room for the general situation to be relaxed. According to the opinions discussed, the meeting drew up the Instructions on Current Industrial Problems issued by the CPC Central Committee, which was printed and distributed to all provinces and municipalities on September 15, stipulating that all industrial departments and enterprises must unswervingly implement the "eight character" policy, focus on adjustment in the next three years, and reduce the industrial production index and construction scale to a reliable level with the greatest determination.[38]

In January 1962, an enlarged Central Working Conference was held. Liu Shaoqi delivered a report on behalf of the Central Committee at the meeting, preliminarily summarized the basic experience and lessons of socialist construction since 1958, and suggested that the main task of the entire Party at that time was to do a steadfast, energetic job of adjustment. Mao Zedong delivered a speech at the meeting, asking for a deeper understanding of the laws of socialist construction on the basis of summing up positive and negative experiences.[39]

(2) On the Theory of Expanding Reproduction

In the late 1950s and early 1960s, the national economy suffered a serious setback due to the Great Leap Forward. Combined with the implementation of the "eight character" policy, theoretical circles carried out a more extensive discussion on the issue of socialist reproduction. The discussion focused on the following three issues.

Extension and connotation. Marx's theory of social reproduction not only divided reproduction into simple reproduction and expanded reproduction, but also divided extended reproduction into extension reproduction and connotation expansion reproduction. There were different views regarding which type of socialist expanded reproduction should be given priority.

One view held that among the forms of social expansion and reproduction, the most obvious manifestation of the characteristics of socialist expanded reproduction was to adopt the extension form of new construction and expansion of capital construction. This was because taking this form could significantly increase production funds, expand production equipment, enrich fixed assets, increase production capacity, increase organic composition, and expand production scale, so as to

---

38. Office of the Plan for Contemporary China, *Essentials of the National Economic and Social Development Plan of the People's Republic of China (1949–1985)* (Red Flag Press, 1987), 174.

39. Liu Suinian et al., *National Economy in the Period of the Great Leap Forward and Adjustment* (Heilongjiang People's Publishing House, 1984), 97–98.

actively improve and increase the material and technical basis of socialist renewable production. Therefore, this form was the most important form of socialist expanded reproduction.[40]

Another view was that the socialist economy was characterized by connotation expansion and reproduction, and the expansion of socialist production scale was mainly carried out according to connotation, because there was always a certain limit to the growth of labor force resources in a certain period of time, and with the increase of the labor force occupied by the non-productive service sector, the new labor resources that could be put into production were also subject to certain restrictions. At the same time, fundamentally speaking, the purpose of socialist production could only be realized on the basis of continuous progress of production technology and by the continuous improvement of social labor productivity. Therefore, the connotation of the expansion of reproduction in the entire socialist expansion of reproduction would gain an increasingly dominant position.[41]

The proportional relationship between accumulation and consumption. Some theorists held that the most fundamental criterion for the appropriateness of the proportion of accumulation and consumption was that it could ensure the continuous, high-speed expansion of socialist reproduction and the gradual improvement of people's living standards. From the perspective of accumulation, in a certain period of time, the increase of accumulated amount had to be less than the increase of the national income. After deducting the consumption funds needed by the newly increased population from the newly increased national income, the remaining part was the maximum limit of increased accumulation. Within this limit, it was necessary to consider using the appropriate portion to improve the current living standard of the people. The minimum limit of accumulation was to expand the funds for reproduction, to at least ensure that the people's living standards would not decline in the years to come. From the perspective of consumption, there were two boundaries. First, the consumption funds could at least ensure that the per capita consumption level was not lower than that in the early stage. Second, the increase of consumption funds could not affect the funds needed for expansion and reproduction.[42] It was also pointed out that the minimum limit of consumption funds was that the average consumption amount calculated by population should not be lower than that in the previous period, while the minimum limit of accumulation funds should be determined according to productive accumulation and non-productive accumulation. The minimum limit of consumption funds and accumulation funds was determined, and the maximum limits of consumption funds and accumulation funds were stipulated respectively. Under the normal development of the national economy, the proportion of consumption and accumulation could only be adjusted within the range of the lowest limit and the highest limit. If the limit was exceeded, the result would not be

40. Qi Qisheng, "On the Dialectical Relationship Between Simple and Expanded Reproduction of Socialism," *Ta Kung Pao* (August 13, 1962).

41. Liu Guoguang, "On the Relationship between Extension and Connotation," *Guangming Daily*, July 2, 1962.

42. Liu Jinlu, "On the Proportional Relationship Between Accumulation and Consumption," *Ta Kung Pao* (January 10, 1962).

to reduce the level of people's consumption, or it would affect the scale of reproduction.[43]

On August 2, 1961, Sun Yefang wrote an opinion and submitted it to Li Fuchun and the Party group of the State Planning Commission. In view of the accumulation rate of more than 40% in the Great Leap Forward and some people's opinions on maintaining the accumulation rate of about 25% during the period of the First Five-Year Plan, Sun Yefang expressed his views. He pointed out, "We can't generally say that the accumulation rate of 40% must be too high, but not normal. The accumulation rate of 25% must be normal but not too much. The question is, first, how much more production, especially income (i.e. national income or net output value) will increase, and second, whether people's consumption level can be improved with the condition of an increasing income. If the income does not increase, or if the income increases little, and people's living standards do not improve or even decrease, then even the 25% accumulation rate will be too high. On the contrary, the accumulation rate of 40% is unnecessarily too high and abnormal. The reason why our accumulation in recent years is too high and abnormal is mainly because the increase of accumulation in recent years is based on a false income report."[44]

The growth rate and proportional development. According to the first opinion, high speed was an objective law, and it should be subject to the requirements of the law of high-speed development in proportion to plans. This point of view was tendentious at that time, and it played a dominant role. The reason was that the high-speed development of the socialist economy was not only objective, but also decisive. In this sense, the relationship between proportion and speed was unified. The purpose of building socialism was to develop the national economy at a high speed to meet the needs of the people. Therefore, the law of high speed was close to the basic economic law of socialism and had an inviolable nature. The relationship between speed and proportion was the relationship between the basic socialist economic law and the law of planned and proportional development of the national economy. In other words, the requirement of reflecting the basic socialist economic law at a high speed was the purpose of planned and proportional development, and reflecting the requirements of the law of planned and proportional development of the national economy in proportion was the means of high-speed development. Means served the purpose and needed to be subject to the requirements of high speed in proper proportions. Various proportions were thus to be studied and determined according to the requirements of high speed, and high speed was the standard to measure whether the proportion is correct or not.[45]

---

43. Yang Jianbai, "On the Internal Relationship Between the Proportion of Agriculture, Light Industry, and Heavy Industry and the Proportion of Consumption and Accumulation," *Economic Research*, no. 1 (1962).

44. Sun Yefang, *Sequel to Some Theoretical Issues of Socialist Economy* (People's Publishing House, 1983), 291.

45. Tian Er and Lu Hanzhang, "Some Views on the Relationship Between High Speed and Proportionality," *Academic Monthly*, no. 8 (1959); Yin Shijie, "The Relationship Between High Speed and Proportional Development of the National Economy." *Theoretical Front*, no. 6 (1959); Shi Yuqian, "On the Relationship Between High Speed and Proportional Development," *Jiangxi Daily*, June 19, 1960; Zhou Ming, "High Speed and Proportional Development of the Socialist Economy," *Chongqing Daily*, July 30, 1959.

According to the second opinion, high speed was not an objective law, but a requirement or principle of work. It should be subject to proportionality, and without proportionality, there would be no high speed, because speed was relative. However, the proportion was different, and once the proportion was violated, it would not only affect speed, but also cause production stoppage. To achieve a high speed, it was important to ensure that the conditions of the basic socialist economic law and the law of planned and proportional development of the national economy were in place. Only through proportion could the national economy develop at a high speed, and speed must be based on proportion. Only by proportion was it possible to achieve comprehensive, lasting high speed, and high speed could not be observed except in proportion. If the proportioned relationship of the national economy was destroyed for the sake of high speed, speed would decline. The more the national economy developed in proportion, the faster that economic development would be.[46]

The third view was that speed and proportion were interdependent, mutually restricting and promoting. If there was no proportion, there would be no high speed. The maximum limit of speed was restricted by the requirement of proportion, and the direction of motion according to proportion was restricted by the requirement of high speed.[47] It was pointed out that the understanding of the contradictory unity between speed and proportion could not be based on abstract concepts in isolation, or speed would always be speed and proportion would always be proportion. But in fact, they were not only interdependent, but also mutually transforming. From the perspective of interdependence, if there was no change in the speed of the development of the entire national economy, there would be no change in the proportion, and if there was no change in proportion, there would be no change in speed. From the perspective of mutual transformation, if speed was the movement of social production in time, then proportion was the movement of social production in space. Speed could be seen as a longitudinal proportion, and proportion could be regarded as various transverse velocities. Crisscrossing, they constituted an overall developing national economy. Therefore, the speed ratio was interdependent and closely linked.[48] This point of view had some original views on the relationship between economic growth and structural adjustment, which was more insightful at that time.[49]

---

46. Yang Yingjie, "On Several Important Economic Laws in a Socialist Society," *New Construction* (December 1962); "On Comprehensive Balance," *Ta Kung Pao* (March 26, 1962); Xue Muqiao, "The High Speed and Proportional Development of the Socialist Economy," *People's Daily*, January 7, 1959; Yang Shaohua, "Learning to Master and Apply the Law of Planned and Proportional Development of the National Economy," *Front Line*, no. 8 (1959); Li Guangyu, "On the National Economy and Views on the Law of Planned and Proportional Development," *Economic Research*, no. 7 (1959).

47. Zhang Qian, "The Meaning of High Speed and Proportionality and Their Relationship," *Academic Monthly*, no. 8 (1959).

48. Bian Jie, "The Relationship Between Speed and Proportion is the Unity of Contradiction," *Academic Monthly*, no. 9 (1959).

49. This view can also be seen in "First Symposium on Economic Theory in 1960," *Endeavor*, no. 3 (1960), and "The Main Arguments on High Speed and Proportional Development," *Academic Monthly*, no. 8 (1959).

(3) The Completion of the Adjustment Task and the Strategic Goal of the Four Modernizations

From 1961 to 1965, China's national economy was in a period of adjustment. In 1962, when industrial production reached its lowest point, it began rapidly rising at an average annual rate of 17.9% from 1963. In 1965, the industrial output value reached 140.2 billion yuan, which was close to the level of 1959 and 1960 and double that of 1957. From 1963 to 1965, the total labor productivity of state-owned industrial enterprises increased at an average annual rate of 23.1%. The profit per 100 yuan of fixed assets was 20.9 yuan, an increase of 134.8% over 1962 and close to the level of 1957 (23.0 yuan). The profit and tax per 100 yuan of capital was 29.8 yuan, an increase of 97.4% over 1962. The profit on annual industrial output value reached 21.3 yuan, an increase of 70.4% over 1962, higher than 17.5 yuan in 1957.[50]

In December 1964, Zhou Enlai said in the government work report delivered at the first session of the Third National People's Congress that the task of adjusting the national economy had been completed and the national economy had been improved overall. In 1965, it was important to continue to complete some unfinished work in the adjustment of the national economy and make preparations for the Third Five-Year Plan, which began in 1966, to meet the all-round upsurge in industrial and agricultural production. In the report, Zhou Enlai put forward for the first time the strategic objectives and steps of building the Four Modernizations. The report said that the main task of developing the national economy in the future was to build China into a powerful socialist country with modern agriculture, modern industry, modern national defense, and modern science and technology in a short period, so as to catch up with and surpass the advanced countries of the world. In order to realize this great historical task, starting from the Third Five-Year Plan, the development of China's national economy could be considered in two steps. The first was to establish an independent and relatively complete industrial system and national economic system after the Third Five-Year Plan period, and the second step was to fully realize agriculture, industry, national defense, and science by the end of the century so that technological modernization would propel China's economy to the forefront of the world.[51]

Zhou Enlai put forward at the meeting the strategic objectives and steps to realize the Four Modernizations, which was the first comprehensive, long-term economic development strategy in the process of China's industrialization. This strategic thought became the guiding principle for China to formulate medium and long-term plans in the next four Five-Year Plans (1966–1985). It had great significance and a far-reaching influence on China's industrialization and economic development. But in theory, this strategy made no substantial change compared with the guiding ideology of the previous period in the pursuit of high-speed economic growth, and there were no objective aspects in the understanding of modernization. Its so-called modernization was a worldwide and historical concept that referred to the development of productivity and society at a higher level on the basis of industrialization. It had some worldwide basic standards (such as the level of per capita national income, the height of industrial structure, the degree of urbanization,

---

50. *China Statistical Yearbook (1984)* (China Statistics Press, 1984), 263, 270.
51. *Xinhua Monthly News*, no. 2 (1965): 4–5.

the level of social science, culture, education, etc.), and these standards were constantly changing with the development of history. Therefore, whether China's economy could take the lead in the world in 2000 and become a modern country depended not only on its own development, but also on the development of other countries. Of course, as the first long-term, comprehensive strategy, it marked a new development in the evolution of China's economic development strategy.

5. The Change of Strategic Thought on Economic Development During the Cultural Revolution

In August 1966, the Eleventh Plenary Session of the Eighth Central Committee of the Communist Party of China passed the Decision on the Cultural Revolution of the Proletariat and determined the thought of "preparing for war, preparing for famine, and serving the people" put forward by Mao Zedong as the basic guiding principle of economic construction during the Cultural Revolution. From that time, "left leaning" thought once again occupied a dominant position in China's economic construction. The Fourth Five-Year Plan with its high indicators stipulated that the industrial growth rate would increase by 12.8% annually during the Fourth Five-Year Plan period. In 1975, steel output would reach 35–40 million tons, an increase of 106–135% over 1970. The hinterland should be built into a powerful strategic rear with relatively complete departments and coordinated development of industry and agriculture. It was important to vigorously develop local "five small" industries and set up large-scale machinery industries. At that time, the plan was known as "a plan for war preparedness and a plan for leaping forward." High indicators led to the rapid expansion of the scale of capital construction. In 1969, investment in capital construction, including industry, was 18.6 billion yuan. In 1970, it increased to 29.5 billion yuan, an increase of 58.6%. In 1971, the total investment in capital construction reached 32.1 billion yuan. The expansion of capital construction led to high accumulation, with an accumulation rate of 23.2% in 1969, 32.9% in 1970, and 34.1% in 1971.[52]

In 1971, Zhou Enlai presided over the daily work of the Party Central Committee and implemented some adjustment measures for industrial construction, mainly to reduce the investment in national defense industry and national defense scientific research. In May 1973, the Central Committee of the Communist Party of China held a working conference and decided to compress and adjust some of the main indicators of the Fourth Five-Year Plan, appropriately slow down the construction speed of the grand third line, and reduce the annual industrial growth rate of 12.8% to 7.7% and the steel output index in 1975 from the original 35–40 million tons to 30 million tons.[53]

In January 1975, the first session of the Fourth National People's Congress was held. In his government work report, Zhou Enlai reiterated the strategic goal of realizing the Four

---

52. *China Statistical Yearbook (1984)* (China Statistics Press, 1984), 32.

53. Wang Haibo, *Industrial Economic History of New China* (Economy and Management Publishing House, 1986), 340.

Modernizations by the end of the 20th century and the two-step strategic strategy put forward by the Third National People's Congress. The report pointed out that the following ten years would be the key decade to realize this two-step plan. The State Council would formulate a Ten-Year Plan, a Five-Year Plan, and an Annual Plan according to the two-step vision. After the meeting, Deng Xiaoping, vice premier of the State Council, presided over the daily work of the Central Committee and the State Council and began to overhaul industry. In June 1975, the State Planning Commission drafted Fourteen Articles of Several Issues on Accelerating Industrial Development. During the discussion, Deng Xiaoping also put forward some important suggestions, such as the need to ensure that agriculture was taken as the basis, introducing new foreign technology and equipment, strengthening the scientific research work of enterprises, rectifying the management order of enterprises, grasping the quality of products, restoring and perfecting rules and regulations, and adhering to the principle of distribution according to work. The State Planning Commission made amendments in accordance with these suggestions, expanding them from fourteen to twenty. Although some issues related to accelerating industrial development (the twenty articles on industry) were not formally written, its basic spirit had a great influence on industrial construction. When a series of rectification projects carried out by Deng Xiaoping began to touch on the ideological line of the Cultural Revolution, after the death of Zhou Enlai on January 8, 1976, the campaign of "criticizing Deng Xiaoping and counterattacking the rightist trend of overturning cases" was launched and the industrial rectification was aborted.

From 1966 to 1976, China's industrial production continued to develop. In 1976, the total industrial output value was 315.8 billion yuan, an increase of 172.6% over 1965, an average annual growth of 9.5%, and a decrease of 2.8 percentage points compared with the average industrial growth rate of 12.3% from 1953 to 1965.[54] The development of industrial production in the ten years of the Cultural Revolution was mainly supported by high accumulation, high investment, and high consumption. In the previous ten years, the total amount of capital construction investment in the industrial sector reached 151.948 billion yuan. In 1975, the fixed working capital of state-owned enterprises was 77.08 billion yuan, an increase of 235% compared with that of 1965, and the number of employees increased by 118%. However, the total industrial output value increased only 113% in the same period. From 1965 to 1976, the profit per 100 yuan of original value of fixed assets of industrial enterprises owned by all the people decreased from 20.9 yuan to 12.1 yuan, the profit and tax realized per 100 yuan capital decreased from 29.8 yuan to 19.3 yuan, the profit realized per 100 yuan output value decreased from 21.3 yuan to 12.6 yuan, and the working capital occupied per hundred yuan increased from 25.5 yuan to 36.9 yuan. Compared with 1965, the average annual real wages of employees in industrial enterprises owned by the people decreased by 8.6% in 1976.[55]

---

54. *China Statistical Yearbook (1984)* (China Statistics Press, 1984), 24.
55. *China Statistical Yearbook (1984)* (China Statistics Press, 1984), 263, 460.

3.3 Comments on the Strategic Theory of Economic Development from the 1950s to the 1970s

1. The Relationship Between Economic Growth and Capital Accumulation

Generally speaking, China's economic development strategy from the 1950s to the 1970s had the characteristics of quantitative growth with a growth of output value as the goal, the increase of accumulation and investment as the means, and the extension and expansion of reproduction as the mode. Its guiding ideology was to pursue high-speed economic growth. Ben Bernanke, an American economist, believed that for a poor country like China, there could never really be "too fast" economic growth. The main problem was that if China tried to increase too fast and lower the current living standard, if the investment choice was inappropriate or if the investment was so chaotic that it could not be supported by finance, then the effort to make the economy grow so rapidly would have the opposite effect.[56] In fact, there was no problem in pursuing high-speed economic growth, especially for economically backward developing countries, and it was important for them to put maximum effort into accelerating their own economic growth rate to catch up with the pace of world development. However, in the most basic sense, the speed of economic growth had to be restricted by capital accumulation.

Capital accumulation as the main driving factor of economic growth has been the prominent view throughout the history of economics. According to classical Western economics, the growth of national wealth mainly depends on capital accumulation. In his book *An Inquiry into the Nature and Causes of the Wealth of Nations,* Adam Smith states that the increase of national wealth is mainly realized through the expansion of industrial production. Once modern industry is established, all industrial equipment will inevitably undergo technological progress and the development of division of labor, so as to improve the productivity of labor and land and reduce production costs. As a result, enterprises save capital (surplus income), and for individual income, a person's frugality is the source of increased capital accumulation. Economic growth is achieved by increasing capital accumulation. Smith's analysis of the relationship between capital accumulation and economic growth is that "[t]he annual produce of the land and labour of any nation can be increased in its value by no other means but by increasing either the number of its productive labourers, or the productive powers of those labourers who had before been employed. The number of its productive labourers, it is evident, can never be much increased, but in consequence of an increase of capital, or of the funds destined for maintaining them. The productive powers of the same number of labourers cannot be increased, but in consequence either of some addition and improvement to those machines and instruments which facilitate and abridge labour; or of a more proper division and distribution of employment. In either case an additional capital is almost always required. It is by means of an additional capital only that the undertaker of any work can either provide his workmen with better machinery or make a more

---

56. Ben Bernanke, "China's Macroeconomic Policy," *Management World,* no. 4 (1989).

proper distribution of employment among them. When the work to be done consists of a number of parts, to keep every man constantly employed in one way requires a much greater capital than where every man is occasionally employed in every different part of the work."[57] Ricardo also believed that economic growth is basically caused by capital accumulation. He observed that the possibility of capital accumulation lies in the increase of income and savings. Therefore, as the growth rate of investment, the capital accumulation rate depends on the savings rate, which in turn depends on the profit rate, and the profit rate is determined by the profit share of income (the ratio of profit to wages). However, Ricardo pointed out that due to the law of diminishing returns in agriculture, and with the social progress and the increase of wealth, the minimum demand for grain is bound to increase, and at the same time, the land will become increasingly barren. Therefore, the price of agricultural products will increase, which leads to the minimum living expenses rising and the increase of the minimum wage and the proportion of profit in the national income. The decline of profit margins is the resulting trend. The decrease of profit rates makes capital accumulation slow down. Once the profit rate drops to the lowest level, the capital accumulation rate will be zero. When the capital accumulation is stagnant and the population remains unchanged, the economy will enter a "static state" and stop growing. This is what Ricardo called the gradual process of economic growth to a "static state."[58]

Marx's theory and mode of social total capital expansion and reproduction was also based on capital accumulation. Capital accumulation aims to convert part of profit or surplus value into capital. It is the source of capital appreciation and expansion and the power of capital production, and therefore the basis of production development and social progress. Engels also pointed out that accumulation is the most important progressive function of society, saying, "The whole development of human society beyond the stage of brute savagery begins on the day when the labour of the family created more products than were necessary for its maintenance, on the day when a portion of labour could be devoted to the production no longer of the mere means of subsistence, but of means of production. A surplus of the product of labour over and above the costs of maintenance of the labour, and the formation and enlargement, out of this surplus, of a social production and reserve fund, was and is the basis of all social, political and intellectual progress. In history, up to the present, this fund has been the possession of a privileged class, on which also devolved along with this possession, political domination and intellectual leadership."[59]

In the theories of economic growth and economic development from the 1950s to the 1960s, a generally accepted view was "capital fundamentalism," which regarded capital accumulation as the only determinant to economic growth. Economic growth was said to be mainly driven by investment growth, while capital shortage was the most important restriction of economic growth. The Harrod-Domar model was the first to make a systematic theoretical exposition of "capital fundamentalism." The Harrod-Domar model generalized the relevant factors of economic

---

57. Adam Smith, *An Inquiry into the Nature and Causes of the Wealth of Nations*, vol. 1 (The Commercial Press, 1972), 315–316.

58. Ricardo, *Political Economics and Taxation Principles* (The Commercial Press, 1976), 78–101.

59. Marx and Engels, *Selected Works of Marx and Engels*, vol. 3 (People's Publishing House, 1972), 233.

growth into three variables, economic growth rate G, capital output ratio K, saving income ratio C, and saving rate S. The model put forward two assumptions, that the propensity to consume and save remained unchanged, and that production technology and capital output ratio remained unchanged. Because K was a constant, the economic growth rate mainly depended on the saving rate, that is to say, under the premise of a fixed capital coefficient, capital accumulation was the only decisive factor of economic growth. In the middle of the 20th century, according to the Harrod-Domar model, some Western economists systematically studied the poverty problem of developing countries and concluded that the stagnation of economic growth and the low level of per capita income were the causes of poverty in those countries, and that the root cause of economic growth stagnation and low-income level lay in the lack of capital and investment. Therefore, capital scarcity was the main constraint on economic growth in developing countries. From the perspective of capital formation[60] and economic development, they put forward that capital formation was the prerequisite for economic growth, the prerequisite for economic "take-off" in developing countries, and the material basis for realizing industrialization. If developing countries wanted to eliminate poverty and realize economic growth and industrialization, they needed to accumulate a good deal of capital and raise investment rates by a large margin. Based on this point of view, the theory of "balanced growth" was developed in Western economic growth theory. The representative works of this theory included Rosenstein-Rodan's *Problems of Industrialization in Eastern and South-Eastern Europe*, Nurkse's *Problems of Capital Formation in Underdeveloped Countries*, and Nelson's *A Theory of the Low-level Equilibrium Trap in Underdeveloped Countries*. This theory held that the key to breaking through the "vicious cycle of poverty" or the "low-level balance trap" of developing countries was to increase savings, expand investment, promote capital formation, and realize economic growth on a large scale. To this end, they designed a balanced development of the "big push" of the integrated industrialization model, requiring large-scale comprehensive investment to achieve industrialization. After that, Lewis's dual economic development model and Rostow's economic growth stage theory emphasized the decisive significance of capital accumulation and productive investment on economic growth. In his 1954 paper "Economic Development Under the Condition of Unlimited Labor Supply," Lewis advanced his famous conclusion that the central issue of economic development was to understand the process of a society from saving and investment of less than 4 to 5% of its national income to voluntary savings reaching more than 12 to 15% of the national income. The reason it became a core issue was that the central fact of economic development was the

---

60. Capital Formation is a specific concept in development economics. It refers to how savings are formed and transformed into investment in capital goods production, and how investment forms a certain type of capital and produces a certain production capacity. Capital formation can be divided into net capital formation and total capital formation. The former refers to the net investment after deducting the depreciation of fixed capital from savings or capital accumulation. It is generally believed that only net investment has an effect on economic growth. The latter refers to the total investment including the renewal of fixed capital, which is equivalent to the general capital accumulation (savings). The commonly used concept of capital formation refers to total capital formation.

rapid accumulation of capital (including the use of knowledge and technology of capital). If the reason savings increased relative to national income could not be explained, then no industrial revolution could be explained.[61]

This theory indicated that capital accumulation was an important factor in determining economic growth. In order to give the national economy a certain degree of growth, it was necessary to maintain a certain accumulation rate. One of the important reasons the industrialization process of old China was slow was the lack of accumulation. It has been estimated that the accumulation rates of China from 1931 to 1936 were −4.1%, 2.4%, −2%, −9%, −1.8%, and 6.4% respectively.[62] Research indicates that in the fifteen years before 1975, the increase of physical capital investment alone accounted for about 50% of the total income growth of nine developed countries. The relatively low investment rate of the United States in 1970 (18% of GDP, one of the lowest among all major industrial countries) is considered to be the main reason the growth rate of the United States has been lower than that of Japan and Western Europe since 1979.

According to the study of middle-income countries such as South Korea, the Philippines, and Mexico, the contribution of the growth of physical capital stock to income growth is about 1/4 and 1/3, aside from the growth of human capital stock. If the estimation is higher, it is as high as 1/2 in poorer countries. This conclusion shows that a society can maintain a fairly large proportion of investment in GDP (15%–25%),[63] so as to maintain a very small income growth rate over a prolonged period. China's economic development strategy also based its economic growth mainly on the increase of accumulation rate, which caused the economy to develop after maintaining a high accumulation rate over a prolonged period. Statistics show that from 1949 to 1980, the total output value of China's industry and agriculture increased from 46.6 billion yuan to 661.9 billion yuan, increasing by 15.1 times, with an average annual growth of 9.4%. The total agricultural output value increased from 32.6 billion yuan to 162.7 billion yuan, an increase of 2.8 times and an average annual growth of 4.4%. The total industrial output value increased from 14 billion yuan to 499.2 billion yuan, increasing by 45.2 times, with an average annual growth rate of 13.2%. The national income increased from 35.8 billion yuan to 363 billion yuan, increasingly by 7.8 times, with an average annual growth of 7.3%, and fiscal revenue increased from 6.52 billion yuan in 1950 to 106.61 billion yuan, an increase of 15.4 times, with an average annual growth of 9.8%. In 1949, China's industrial fixed assets amounted to about 12.8 billion yuan. In 1980, state-owned enterprises owned more than 500 billion yuan of fixed assets, including 370 billion yuan of industrial fixed assets. In 1952, the average annual consumption level per capita was 76 yuan, and in 1979, it was 197 yuan. Excluding price factors, the actual increase was 85%.[64] If there were no long-term high accumulation rate, it would have been impossible for China's economy to make such progress.

---

61. Lewis, *The Theory of Dual Economy* (Beijing Institute of Economics Press, 1989).

62. Wu Baosan, *China's National Income*, vol. 1 (Zhonghua Book Company, 1947), 173.

63. Malcolm, Gillis et al., *Development Economics* (Economic Science Press, 1989), 341.

64. *China Economic Yearbook (1981)* (Economy and Management Publishing House, 1981), iv–3.

2. The Relationship Between Economic Growth and Economic Benefits

First, the contradiction was between high accumulation, high investment, and stability of economic growth. During the period of the First Five-Year Plan, China's accumulation rate was basically 23 to 25%. It was 33.9% in 1958, 43.8% in 1959, 30.8% in the period of the Second Five-Year Plan, 26.3% in the period of the Third Five-Year Plan, 31.3% in 1976, 32.3% in 1977 and 36.5% in 1978. Within the accumulation, the proportion of productive investment was 59.8% in the First Five-Year Plan period, 77.4% in the Second Five-Year Plan period, and 83.2%, 75.4%, and 75.9% in 1976, 1977, and 1978, respectively. In the eighteen years from 1956 to 1973, Japan accumulated 38.8% of GDP and 29.6% of national income, which was lower than the level of China's Second Five-Year Plan, Third Five-Year Plan, and the late 1970s.[65] It can be seen that after the founding of the People's Republic of China, the accumulation rate was generally above 30%, and the investment rate was basically close to 20%, which was higher than the level of 10 to 12% required by Rostow's economic take-off. However, China's economic growth rate was still not fast, and the economy did not take off. For China, a country with a large population, extremely weak economic foundation, and in the initial stage of industrialization, the above accumulation and investment rates were still low. Due to the lack of funds, it was impossible to carry out comprehensive, large-scale investment. Instead, China could only carry out inclined investment, resulting in an imbalance of economic structure and a rise and fall of economic growth, and the degree of stability was extremely low. On average, the growth rate was not high. For example, in the three years of the Great Leap Forward, the average economic growth rate was more than 18%, while in 1961 and 1962, the average rate of economic growth was −21.5%. As a result, the economy during the period of the Second Five-Year Plan did not grow, but declined. For example, from 1953 to 1978, China's total social output value increased by 7.9% every year. The highest growth year was 32.6% (1958), 24.7 percentage points higher than the average growth rate, while the lowest growth year was −33.5% (1961), which was 41.4 percentage points lower than the average growth rate. If there had been enough investment, agriculture and light and heavy industries could have developed in an all-round way. "Taking steel as the key link" could have driven "ten thousand horses galloping." However, if the funds were insufficient, the rapid development of heavy industry would restrict the development of agriculture and light industry, and "taking steel as the key link" would lead to structural imbalance and affect the speed of economic growth. For a country, the accumulation capacity or capital supply capacity of the entire society is fixed in a certain period of time. A scientific economic development strategy should be based on the specific national conditions and national strength, planning the corresponding construction scale and economic growth rate. Ignoring this objective reality and pursuing high speed one-sidedly can only cause economic chaos and a failure to achieve the goal of rapid growth.

---

65. Ma Hong and Sun Shangqing, *A Study of China's Economic Structure* (People's Publishing House, 1981), 52.

Further, there was a contradiction between high accumulation, high investment, and economic benefits. The promotion effect of accumulation and expansion on economic growth needed to be based on economic benefits. In the Harrod-Domar model, the capital coefficient is fixed, that is, the ratio of output driven by a certain capital input is certain, in other words, the investment benefit is certain. However, in China's economic analysis, the benefits of investment and economic activities could not be assumed to be fixed. On the contrary, the low economic benefits were the key reason China did not achieve a higher economic growth rate under the conditions of a higher accumulation rate. According to statistics, the delivery and utilization rate of China's fixed assets was 83.7% during the period of the First Five-Year Plan, 61.4% during the period of the Second Five-Year Plan, and 68.5% from 1952 to 1978. From 1952 to 1978, China's capital construction investment totaled 600 billion yuan, and only 400 billion yuan of fixed assets were formed. The amount of investment needed for each increase of 1 yuan of national income in China was 1.68 yuan in the First Five-Year Plan period, 7.37 yuan in the Second Five-Year Plan period, 2.32 yuan in the Third Five-Year Plan period, 3.76 yuan in the Fourth Five-Year Plan period, and 3.00 yuan in 1976–1978.[66] China's several periods of rising accumulation rate were also the period of the worst economic benefits. It is estimated that in the three years of the Great Leap Forward, the national income lost 180 billion yuan, and in the ten years of the Cultural Revolution, the national income lost about 500 billion yuan.[67] Due to the poor economic benefits, the huge accumulation and investment did not bring about corresponding economic growth.

This analysis shows that the defect of China's economic development strategy lay not in the pursuit of high speed nor in the promotion of high accumulation, but in the lack of objective understanding of national conditions and national strength and one-sided emphasis on accumulation as the only important factor in economic growth under the condition of an extremely low per capita income level. More important was the factor of one-sided pursuit of high speed without ensuring economic benefits. Under the restriction of low per capita income and low economic efficiency, the economic development strategy of high growth, high accumulation, and high investment not only failed to achieve the goal of rapid economic growth, but also caused a series of contradictions in economic life, including the contradiction between industrial development and agricultural development, the contradiction between high accumulation and the improvement of people's living standards, the contradiction between economic construction and resource supply, and the contradiction between the growth of output and output value and the growth of national income, among others. The essence of economic growth is the increase of national wealth and the growth of per capita national income. From the 1950s to the 1970s, China's economic growth seemed not too slow in terms of output value and output, but slower in

---

66. Ma Hong and Sun Shangqing, *A Study of China's Economic Structure* (People's Publishing House, 1981), 52.

67. Compilation Group of the Current Volume, *Learning Materials of the Spiritual Guidance of the Fifth Plenary Session of the Thirteenth CPC Central Committee* (Shanghai People's Publishing House, 1989), 59.

terms of national income. The per capita national income increased from 102 yuan in 1952 to 314 yuan in 1978, with an average annual growth of 3 to 4%.[68] Due to the slow growth of the national income, the country's strength and people's living standards did not improve significantly. The strategic objectives and means of high growth, high accumulation, and high investment resulted in high consumption, low efficiency, and low growth, and the quality of economic development was affected.

---

68. Ma Hong and Sun Shangqing, *A Study of China's Economic Structure* (People's Publishing House, 1981), 730.

CHAPTER 4

China's Socialist Economic Construction and Innovation in Economic Thought

4.1 Mao Zedong's Theory of Socialist Industrialization

1. China's Industrialization Development Path

In 1956, after the socialist transformation of the ownership of the means of production was completed, China entered a new historical period of building socialism on a large scale and in an all-round way. At that time, an important task in economic circles was the exploration of a socialist industrialization development path in line with China's national conditions.

The concept of the industrialization path was put forward by Mao Zedong in *Correctly Handling Contradictions Among the People*, mainly referring to the relationship among the three economic sectors in the process of industrialization. At that time, it was believed that agriculture and heavy and light industry were the main body and foundation of the national economic structure, so the relationship between the three could basically explain the development path of China's industrialization.

From 1956 to 1957, Mao Zedong concentrated the wisdom of the entire Party, combined with China's national conditions, to profoundly analyze the internal relations among the three major economic sectors of agriculture and light and heavy industry in the process of industrialization and creatively put forward the idea of developing industry and agriculture simultaneously in the process of industrialization. In September 1962, the Tenth Plenary Session of the Eighth Central Committee of the Communist Party of China advanced the general policy of developing the national economy based on agriculture and led by industry. In September 1963, the Central

Committee of the Communist Party of China issued On Industrial Development (first draft), which further proposed that the general policy of China's industrialization development was to closely combine industry with agriculture and develop industry and agriculture simultaneously. The relationship between them was based on agriculture and led by industry. This general policy was a concentrated summary of Mao Zedong's theory on the path to industrialization, which marked the formal establishment of China's socialist industrialization path.

Mao Zedong's theory on the path of industrialization contained three economic principles, with agriculture as the foundation of social and economic development, the priority development of the means of production (heavy industry), and the coordinated and balanced development of two major categories of social production.

(1) Agriculture as the Foundation of Social and Economic Development
In the history of economic theory, the school of agriculture first systematically discussed the theory that agriculture is the foundation of the national economy. It was even held that agriculture was the only form of production. When analyzing the production of capitalist land rent, Marx said, "The physiocrats, furthermore, are correct in stating that in fact all production of surplus-value, and thus all development of capital, has for its natural basis the productiveness of agricultural labour... An agricultural labour productivity exceeding the individual requirements of the labourer is the basis of all societies, and is above all the basis of capitalist production."[1] This suggests that agricultural production is the basis of human survival and social and economic development, and the degree of agricultural development determines the development level of industry and other fields. In other words, it is only through how much surplus labor agriculture provides for a society that the social labor occupied by industry and other social fields, as well as the development scale and level related to it, can be determined.

In the 1950s and early 1960s, developing countries formulated industrialization strategies, striving to eliminate poverty and backwardness through industrialization. At that time, in all levels from the government to academic circles, the majority believed that industrial productivity, especially marginal productivity, was high, while agricultural productivity, especially marginal productivity, was low. Therefore, giving priority to the development of industry could improve the marginal productivity of society and increase the total output. The investment efficiency of industry was high, and it was easy to adopt advanced technology, making the output increase rapidly, while the investment efficiency of agriculture was low, which was not easy to estimate. The growth of new technology and output was also slow, and the development of industry could expand the scale of cities, promote urbanization, and quickly improve the per capita income and living standards, while it was difficult for agriculture to achieve this effect. The expansion of industry could absorb a greater employment population, but the labor force in agriculture was at a relative surplus. These were just some of the factors affecting the situation. Under the guidance of this theory, developing countries generally emphasized the development of industry, while

---

1. Marx, *Das Kapital*, vol. 3 (People's Publishing House, 1975), 885.

ignoring the development of agriculture. However, the industrialization process of any country had its own objective laws. The industrial development of many countries was increasingly restricted by backward agriculture. Not only had industrialization not been realized, but agriculture had also regressed, a thought-provoking fact. People began to re-examine the status and role of agriculture in the process of industrialization and rethink the relationship between agriculture and industry. From that time, with the publication of Schultz and other scholars' authoritative works on agriculture, the understanding of the importance of agriculture began to develop.

Therefore, among the industrialization theories of developing countries in the middle of the 20th century, the theory of agriculture as the basis put forward by Mao Zedong was quite scientific, conforming to the objective law of social and economic development. From the perspective of industrialization, this theory analyzed the development relationship among the three major production departments, namely, agriculture, light industry, and heavy industry. It also demonstrated from the perspective of production, exchange, and market that only by strengthening the development of agriculture could industry be developed faster. In this way, it became a great theoretical contribution to China's industrialization theory.

(2) On the Priority Development of the Means of Production (Heavy Industry)

In the middle of the 20th century, the development and evolution of China's industrialization persistently followed the important theoretical basis of Lenin's "priority growth law of the means of production." Mao Zedong's theory of taking the development of heavy industry as the center and giving priority to the development of heavy industry also reflected Lenin's theory. Lenin's law of the fastest growth of the means of production under the condition of technological progress illustrated the trend of industrial development with machine production as the core instead of manual production. In the past, people's understanding of this argument had focused on the faster growth of the means of production. In my opinion, the focus should be on technological progress. Technological progress in the sense of industrialization means that machine labor replaces manual labor. The more advanced technology is, the smaller the component of manual labor is and the greater the component of machine production is. A natural result of this process is the gradual improvement of the organic composition of capital. The improvement of the organic composition of capital means that the demand for the means of production in the form of constant capital constantly expands in social and economic development, which inevitably promotes the rapid growth of the means of production. Therefore, Mao Zedong's theory of taking industry as the leading factor and giving priority to the development of heavy industry precisely grasped the essence of industrialization, defined the development direction of the national economy, and introduced the entire social economy into the mode of production of large machines through the development of industry, so as to realize industrialization.

(3) On the Coordinated, Balanced Development of the Two Major Categories of Social Production

Mao Zedong analyzed the development relationship of agriculture, light industry, and heavy industry from the aspects of capital, technology, raw materials, and the market, and he expounded the idea of close combination of industry and agriculture and simultaneous development of industry and agriculture. The theoretical essence of this thought was the coordinated, balanced development of the two major categories of social production. Marx's theory of the expanding reproduction of social capital clarified the relationship between the means of production and the means of living as conditions, markets, and constraints. The expansion and reproduction of any one of the two categories was inseparable from the other. This is the basic law of all social expansion and reproduction, and it is more essential than the law of rapid growth of the means of production under the conditions of technological progress. Though Marx studied reproduction with the assumption that technology remained unchanged, that is, assuming that the organic composition of capital remained unchanged and that the expansion of production was due to the role of accumulation, this abstract analysis essentially explained the law of balanced growth of the two major categories, which was Marx's basic principle of social reproduction. Mao Zedong's theory of coordinated development of agriculture, light industry, and heavy industry not only reflected the objective requirements of faster growth of heavy industry in the process of industrialization, but also conformed to the objective law of balanced development of the two major categories of social production, so it was a scientific theory. As for China's industrialization practice at that time, one-sided emphasis on giving priority to the development of heavy industry, resulting in the imbalance of the proportion structure of the national economy, was due to the eagerness for success in the guiding ideology and the unilateral pursuit of high speed, which deviated from the established industrialization development path.

2. The Relationship Between Industrialization and Agricultural Modernization

(1) Bringing Agricultural Modernization into the Category of Industrialization

With the development of the theory of world industrialization, there was a change in the understanding of the relationship between industrialization and agricultural modernization. In the middle of the 20th century, many theorists developed a one-sided understanding of the meaning of industrialization, which meant that industrialization was only regarded as the share of industry in the national income and labor allocation continued to rise. After the 1970s, Western economic circles made great progress in understanding the relationship between agriculture and industrialization. They realized that agriculture was not only to provide surplus for industrialization, but also the main content of industrialization. Only when agriculture, like other production sectors, was modernized and agricultural productivity greatly improved could the overall social economy be regarded as industrialized (technically, agriculture had become an "industrial sector").

In July 1955, Mao Zedong issued a report On the Issue of Agricultural Cooperation at the meeting of the Party Secretaries of provinces, cities and autonomous regions, offering a penetrating analysis of the relationship between industrialization and agricultural modernization. He said that in giving priority to the development of heavy industry, it was necessary to develop industry and agriculture simultaneously and gradually realize modern industry and agriculture.

In the past, China often talked about building itself into an industrial country, which actually included the modernization of agriculture. Mao Zedong's exposition clearly brought agricultural modernization into the category of industrialization and clarified the significance of agricultural modernization in the process of industrialization. This thought was prevalent not only in China, but also in the history of the development of the world's industrialization theory, and it was an outstanding achievement.

As agricultural modernization was regarded as an integral part of industrialization, Mao Zedong put forward the proposition of socialist industrialization, and at the same time formed the thought of agricultural modernization related to it. The report On the Issue of Agricultural Cooperation comprehensively expounded the relationship between agricultural modernization and national industrialization, as well as the principles and policies of agricultural modernization. The report pointed out that if China could not first basically solve the problem of agricultural cooperation within the period of about three Five-Year Plans, that is, from small-scale operations using animal farm tools to large-scale operations using machines, China would not be able to solve the contradiction between the annual growth of the needs of commodity grain and industrial raw materials and the low general yield of major crops. It was impossible to complete socialist industrialization that way. Secondly, heavy industry, one of the most important sectors of socialist industrialization, could only use many of its products on the basis of large-scale cooperative operation of agriculture. China was in the process of carrying out not only the revolution from private ownership to public ownership in the social system, but also the technological revolution from handicraft production to large-scale modern machine production, with the two revolutions being combined. In terms of agriculture, under Chinese conditions (in capitalist countries, it was to make agriculture capitalist), there must be cooperation before big machines could be used. This made it evident that China could never separate and isolate industry and agriculture, socialist industrialization, and socialist agricultural transformation. It could not only emphasize one aspect while weakening the others.

From this discussion, it is clear that Mao Zedong's agricultural modernization plan was to realize agricultural mechanization on the basis of agricultural cooperation. To be specific, it meant reforming the backward, feudal small-scale peasant economy and small-scale land management mode in rural areas in line with the development of national industrialization and implementing land management based on collective land ownership. On the basis of the transformation of production relations centered on ownership and management mode, it was important to use developed heavy industry to carry out technological transformation of agriculture, equip agriculture with modern technology and tools, realize agricultural mechanization, and transform China's traditional agriculture into a modern socialist agriculture. This agricultural modernization theory based on the agricultural social reform (agricultural cooperation) and agricultural technology reform (agricultural mechanization) constituted the guiding principle of China's agricultural development from the 1950s to the 1970s, and it had a profound impact on both theory and practice.

(2) Theoretical Analysis of Agricultural Modernization Thought

Mao Zedong's theory of agricultural modernization should be analyzed from three aspects. The first is that in theory, this idea included outstanding views on the relationship between industrialization and agricultural modernization. The history of world economic development suggested that industrialization would inevitably promote the modernization of agriculture. The general development process of agricultural modernization was to change the backward feudal small-scale peasant economy, change small-scale land management into large-scale land management, and implement a reform of agricultural production technology on this basis, so as to greatly improve agricultural productivity. In the development of capitalism, small production was eliminated through the primitive accumulation of capital. The way to reform the small-scale peasant economy in China should not be capitalist, but socialist. That is, the scattered individual farmers should be organized to centralize the land and other means of production for collective management and eventually develop into a large socialist agriculture. This was the basic approach to agricultural reform in the process of socialist industrialization. Therefore, Mao Zedong's theory of agricultural modernization conformed to the law of China's industrialization development, the actual situation of China's rural areas, and the nature of socialist production relations.

Second, the speed of agricultural cooperation, that is, time planning, had a strong subjective color. From the point of view of the relationship between the cooperative and industrialization, Mao thought that the speed of agricultural cooperation should adapt to the steps of industrialization. According to the plan of the CPC Central Committee on the general line for the transitional period, from the founding of the new China to the completion of the Third Five-Year Plan, China needed to basically complete socialist industrialization and the socialist transformation of the handicraft industry, capitalist industry, commerce, and agriculture. There were two bases for Mao's proposal that agricultural cooperation should be completed as soon as possible. One was the experience of the Soviet Union. Mao analyzed in On the Issues of Agricultural Cooperation that the Soviet Union had completed its agricultural cooperation in seventeen years, from 1921 to 1937, and its main work was completed in the six-year period from 1929 to 1934. Therefore, according to the experience of the Soviet Union, it was entirely possible for China to complete its agricultural cooperation in eighteen years. The second was the advantage of cooperation in productivity. Mao pointed out that more than 80% of the 650,000 agricultural production cooperatives that had been established had increased their output, which proved that the productivity of agricultural production cooperatives was higher than that of mutual aid groups and individual households, so it was necessary to accelerate the development of agricultural production cooperatives. In response to the view that the pace of agricultural cooperation was too fast, Mao criticized the situation, saying that this theory did not consider agricultural cooperation and industrialization. In December 1955, Mao drafted for the Central Committee of the Communist Party of China a document entitled Consultation on 17 Agricultural Articles, which required that the advanced form of cooperation should be basically completed in 1960, and strive to be basically completed in 1959. This was seven or eight years ahead of the eighteen years stipulated in the general line for the transition period. In November 1956, Mao delivered a speech at the Second Plenary Session of the Eighth Central Committee of the Communist Party of China, pointing out that the original arrangement was to basically complete the socialist transformation of ownership in eighteen years, which would be promoted quickly. It was written in the draft outline of agricultural development that the advanced form of agricultural cooperation was to be completed in 1985. At the time of writing, it seems that the following winter and spring will see its achievement, which is two or three years ahead of the requirements of the 17 Agricultural Articles. Under the guidance of this ideology, the nature of agricultural cooperation in China has changed from the idea of developing cooperation to improving agricultural productivity, and further to pursuing the rapid transition of ownership and the development of public ownership, taking the people's commune of "large scale and highly public ownership" as its extreme development form. Practice indicates that the elimination of small-scale production is not a subjective planning process, but an objective natural development process, which is fundamentally restricted by the development level of productive forces. Judging from the situation in China at that time, agricultural productivity was still very low after the land reform. On the one hand, this level of productivity determined that it was necessary for farmers to take the path of cooperation, but at the same time, it also determined the long-term, complex, and arduous nature of the transformation of the mode of production. Moreover, China was a country with thousands of years of feudal society. Farmers were deeply influenced by the traditional habits of small-scale production. It would also require a long-term process to change their psychology and concepts and help them adapt to and accept the socialist mode of production. It was for this reason that Mao talked about agricultural cooperation from the perspective of industrialization, which was a very creative theory. However, in terms of the development speed of agricultural cooperation, it was divorced from the actual development level of productive forces and the specific situation of rural areas, and it was characterized by one-sided pursuit of the nature of production relations as quickly as possible.

Third, the basic point of Mao Zedong's theory of agricultural modernization was social reform and the technological reform of agriculture, by which it aimed to realize agricultural mechanization on the basis of agricultural cooperation. Mao Zedong believed that, restricted by China's economic conditions, the time required for technological reform would be longer than that for social reform. It was estimated that it would take about four to five Five-Year Plans, that is, 20 to 25 years, to basically complete the technological reform of agriculture nationwide. From then, the development plan of agricultural mechanization formulated by the Chinese government was required to basically realize agricultural mechanization in 1980. The experience of developed countries showed that agricultural modernization was of course an important aspect of industrialization, but fundamentally speaking, agricultural modernization should have two conditions. The first was that industrial development needed to reach a certain level and have the ability to feed agriculture and carry out a comprehensive technical transformation of agriculture, and the second was that the development of traditional agricultural productivity needed to reach a certain level, which proposed the reform of production technology requirements. The development of agricultural mechanization started in the late stage of industrialization, which was an objective requirement of a highly coordinated industrial structure. In the final analysis, it was the natural process of productivity development. There was a time difference between industrial modernization and agricultural mechanization in Western developed countries. Generally, industry developed to a certain level before agricultural mechanization began. However, in terms of strategic planning, China required the simultaneous development of industrialization and agricultural mechanization, attempting to realize industrial modernization and agricultural modernization simultaneously. Although it came from an urgent desire to change China's backward state, the subjective desire was divorced from objective reality. As a result, not only did the industrialization process have complicated contradictions, but the agricultural mechanization and modernization could also not be realized as expected. On the whole, China's agricultural production was quite backward. The average number of modern agricultural production tools was extremely limited, and the development level of labor productivity and the commodity economy was very low. These facts indicate that although agricultural collectivization was realized in the thirty years after 1949, this collectivization was not based on the corresponding development of productive forces, and in fact was a simple amplification of the natural economy. China's agricultural development thus still faced the grim task of transforming from traditional agriculture to modern agriculture.

4.2 Productivity Theory, Population Theory, and Commodity Theory in the Socialist Economy

1. Productivity Theory and Population Theory

(1) Productivity Theory

Starting from the political economics system of the Soviet Union, the research object or focus of socialist political economics was production relations. However, while emphasizing the study of production relations, Chinese economists also devoted much energy to the study of productivity and obtained important theoretical results. At the end of the 1950s, Li Pingxin proposed a new viewpoint on the nature of productive forces. He believed that productive forces had material, technical, and social attributes. Productivity had its inherent development law and could increase its value in the contradictory movement between it and production relations. Political economics needed to simultaneously study production relations and productivity. This view was a new interpretation of traditional theory. According to traditional theory, material production had two attributes: from the perspective of the relationship between man and nature, it belonged to productivity, while from the perspective of human relationships, it belonged to production relationships. Productivity was the material and technical attribute of production, and the relationship of production was its social attribute. Li Pingxin advanced the view that productivity had material, technical, and social attributes. On the one hand, the composition of the productivity system of every society must rely on many necessary material and technical conditions, which gave it the material attributes suitable for the production needs at that time. On the other hand, it must rely on many necessary social conditions, which gave it the characteristics of labor at that time, and the social attribute of the social nature of production. It was noted that "the nature of productive forces is the sum of its material and technical attributes and the social attributes of productive forces in a certain historical stage," and "to distinguish the nature of productive forces of various social and economic forms, we should not only consider their material and technical attributes." This view further defined the material, technical, and social attributes of productivity. Li said that "the performance and quantity of production tools, traffic conditions, transport organs, factories, workshops, and mines in a certain historical stage, the performance, quantity, and source of raw materials, and the labor skills, processing knowledge, operation methods, production experience, and labor regulated by these factors are the combination of dynamic productivity and general technical level (or science and technology level) that mark the material and technical attributes of productivity in a social and economic form." And, "In a certain historical period, the social status, life outlook, and spiritual function of workers, the general nature of labor, the social nature of production, the nature of labor organization, the purpose and social role of the use of the means of production, the metabolic characteristics of various factors of productive forces, and the various social conditions for the change and development of productive forces taken together determine the social attributes of productive forces of a certain socio-economic form."[2] Although this viewpoint invited different reactions, it made a breakthrough and development in the theory of the connotation, elements, nature, and development law of productivity. Moreover, since the late 1950s, it has been a feature of Chinese economic theory research, attaching importance to the study of productivity. In the 1980s, this research field saw greater development, and it formed a new independent discipline in productivity economics.

Productive forces is a concept of Marxist political economics. The corresponding or similar concepts of Western neoclassical economics are production and productive forces. Neoclassical production theory mainly studies the characteristics of input demand function and output supply function under the assumption of profit maximization in a given production function. It includes two kinds of problems: the technical constraint to describe the range of available production processes and the structure of the market in which the enterprise trades (complete competition, monopoly competition, or complete monopoly, etc.). Productive forces is the ratio of a certain measure of output to a certain index of input. Productivity measures the current situation of technology used by an economy (or industry or firm) in producing goods and services. Therefore, the concept of production and productive forces in neoclassical economics is basically the same as productive forces in Marxist political economics, that is, the material and technical attributes of production. Li Pingxin deduced that productive forces have material, technical, and social attributes, which had certain theoretical value in the level of abstract law and economic philosophy.

---

2. Li Pingxin, On the Nature of Productive Forces," *Academic Monthly*, no. 6 (1959).

(2) Population Theory

In 1953, the People's Republic of China carried out its first census. After that time, the problem of population size attracted the attention of economic circles, and the theoretical research in this field became very active. From the 1950s to the 1960s, China's debate on the issue of population size traced the twists and turns in the history of socialist political economics. With the interference of various political factors, what was originally an academic discussion turned into political criticism. A group of theorists and economists were labeled as "rightists," and the population problem became a taboo topic for a prolonged period. At that time, a few scholars, represented by Ma Yinchu, insisted on a scientific attitude in their own views, and they put forward their original ideas in the form of theories.

According to Ma Yinchu's population theory, the large population and small capital was a key contradiction in China. According to the results of the first census, the population of the country was more than 600 million. In the four years since the founding of the People's Republic of China, the population had increased by 12 to 13 million every year, with a growth rate of 20%. Calculating the population growth rate, it was estimated that the population of China would reach 800 million in 15 years and 1.6 billion in 50 years. Therefore, the biggest contradiction in China was that population growth was too fast and fund accumulation seemed to be too slow. With a large population, overly rapid population growth would cause a series of contradictions.

The first was the contradiction between the large population on one side and capital accumulation and socialist industrialization on the other. In 1956, China's national income was nearly 90 billion yuan, of which consumption accounted for 79% and accumulation only accounted for 21%. Insufficient accumulation would inevitably delay the completion of industrialization. There were also contradictions between the large population and mechanization and automation. If there were too many people, it was impossible to achieve mechanization and automation quickly, and having too large a population would hold back high-speed industrialization.

The second was the contradiction between the large population on one side and agricultural mechanization and farmers on the other. Agricultural labor productivity was far lower than that of industry. To improve agricultural labor productivity, it was important to achieve agricultural electrification and mechanization, greatly increase the use of chemical fertilizer, and improve water conservancy facilities. However, this was in contradiction with insufficient supply and accumulation of funds. Therefore, in order to improve the labor productivity of farmers, it was necessary to accumulate funds on the one hand and control the population on the other.

The third contradiction was between large population and grain, industrial raw materials, labor and employment, and people's livelihood. China had little land and many people, with an average of less than 3 *mu* per capita. (2.7 *mu* per capita in 1955). Although there were 1.5 billion *mu* of wasteland, including rocky mountains, land with no water source, and grasslands that ethnic minorities had depended on for generations, all of which could not be cultivated at all. In addition, with backward industry and limited financial resources, large-scale reclamation could not be carried out for a prolonged period. As far as food was concerned, population control was also indispensable. Most of the raw materials for China's light industry came from agriculture.

With the increase of population, food consumption would inevitably increase, and the area of cash crops would shrink, which would directly affect light industry and indirectly affect heavy industry. In order to improve people's material and cultural living standards, the growth of the means of living must be faster than that of the population.

The fourth contradiction was between the large population and scientific research. It was necessary to first promote the technical equipment of the industrial sector and improve labor productivity as quickly as possible, and then lay the material foundation for scientific research. Although the conditions for scientific work in China had been greatly improved, due to the limitations of the existing industrial level and national financial resources, they could not fully meet the requirements of carrying out research. Therefore, it was also necessary to control the population so as not to let the population growth hold back scientific research.

Fifth was the contradiction between population quantity and quality. The problem of population was not only a matter of quantity, but also of quality. In poor, destitute China, a large population was a great resource, but it was also a great burden. Preserving this great resource and removing the heavy burden could only be done by improving the quality of the population and controlling the population. The quantity and quality of China's population were not commensurate. Now that China had entered the era of atomic energy, it needed to integrate the quality and quantity of the population quickly and appropriately in order to complete the tasks of the age.

Therefore, Ma Yinchu concluded, "Too large a population is our fatal injury. Our socialist economy is a planned economy. If we do not include the population in the planned economy, if we cannot control the population and implement family planning, we will not be a planned economy."[3]

Ma Yinchu's "new population theory" aimed at the argument that "the larger the population, the better." It pointed out that a large population and rapid population growth would cause a series of economic and social contradictions, including contradictions with accumulation, with agricultural mechanization, with food, industrial raw materials, labor, and employment, with people's life, with scientific research, and with population quality. To control the rapid population growth, family planning had to be carried out. Although Ma Yinchu's views were criticized at that time, he linked population growth with economic resources and social production, explored the population law of a socialist society, and explored the relationship between population quantity and population quality, which was an innovation in the development of Marxist economic theory and socialist economics. Moreover, it can be said that it was on the basis of Ma Yinchu's theory that China formulated and implemented the basic national policy of family planning and made remarkable achievements in controlling excessive population growth, improving the quality of the population and people's living standards. It can be argued that this was one of China's great contributions to the development of human society.

---

3. Ma Yinchu, *Selected Economic Papers of Ma Yinchu* (Peking University Press, 1981); *[*NOTE: NOW the spelling Peking is not used here.]Selected Works of Ma Yinchu* (Tianjin People's Publishing House, 1988).

2. Commodities in the Socialist Economy

From the 1950s to the 1960s, research on the law of commodity production and value in the socialist economy was actually an innovative study of socialist production relations and the economic system. The classic works of Marxism did not connect the socialist mode of production with the production of commodities. The theory of the Soviet Union only acknowledged that a socialist society had extremely limited commodity exchange relations. However, China's theoretical research had broken through these frameworks, extensively explored the commodity category of socialist society, the reasons for the existence of commodity production, and whether the means of production exchanged within the economy of ownership by all the people were commodities, and it had advanced many new viewpoints. In the early 1960s, China's economic circles also advanced the idea that the planned economy and the commodity economy should be unified, and that a socialist economy was a planned commodity economy.[4]

(1) Commodity Production in the Socialist Economy

On the reasons for the existence of commodity production in the socialist economy, the most representative opinions at that time were that the coexistence of socialist ownership by all the people and collective ownership was the reason for the existence of socialist commodity production. But Zhuo Jiong suggested the view that the social division of labor determined the production of goods. He held that commodity production was a natural process associated with the social division of labor. As long as there was a social division of labor, there would be commodity production. The commodity determined by the social division of labor was the generality of the commodity, or the commonness of the commodity, and ownership determined the social nature of the commodity, or the characteristics of the commodity. Commodity production under the condition of the socialist system had the nature of socialism. Zhuo Jiong further suggested that the socialist economy was a "planned commodity economy." He held that the planned economy and commodity economy were not mutually antagonistic, mutually exclusive, or incompatible. The commodity economy could serve private ownership and anarchy, as well as public ownership and a planned economy, without any contradiction.[5] When Zhuo Jiong put forward this view in 1961, it was a cutting edge theory. The research on the relationship between the socialist economy and commodity production was an important innovation of Marxist economics created by Chinese economists. It constituted an important theoretical issue in China's socialist political economics, but it did not attract the attention of theoretical circles for some time. In the 1980s, this issue developed into a discussion of socialism, the commodity economy, and the market economy, and it became an important theoretical basis for economic system reform.

---

4. Editorial Department of *Economic Research* and *Economic Trends, Debates on Essential Issues of Political Economics Since the Founding of the People's Republic of China (1949–1980)* (China Financial and Economic Publishing House, 1981).

5. Zhuo Jiong, *On Socialist Commodity Economy* (Guangdong People's Publishing House, 1981).

(2) Socialist Economy and the Law of Value

While discussing the relationship between the socialist economy and commodity production, economic circles also conducted an in-depth study on the relationship between the socialist economy and the law of value. In May 1953, Xue Muqiao published the article "The Role of the Law of Value in China's Economy" in the 9th issue of the *Journal of Learning*. He believed that the national plan could not control the whole national economy without restrictions, but could only play a regulatory role in a certain range and to a certain extent. According to Xue Muqiao's memoir, he realized that in the socialist economy, the role of the law of value could not be denied. The spontaneous function of the law of value had been limited, but the role of the law of value could not be denied. The law of value should still be considered when state-owned industries calculated costs, set prices, and carried out economic accounting. The consumer goods produced by state-owned industries and some means of production to be sold in the market were not only affected by the law of value to a large extent in the process of production, but also to a certain extent regulated by the law of value in the process of circulation.[6] In September 1956, Chen Yun advanced the idea of combining the planned economy with market regulation in his speech "New Problems After the Basic Completion of Socialist Transformation," that is, that planned production was the main body of industrial and agricultural production, and free production within the scope permitted by the state plan according to market changes was the supplement of planned production.

In the discussion of the relationship between the socialist economy and the law of value, Gu Zhun, an economic theorist, made the most important theoretical contribution. In 1998, *Gu Zhun's Collected Works* was published, highlighting the elegant demeanor of this economic theorist who had been obscured by history. In 1957, Gu Zhun was dismissed from the Party and assigned to labor because of his so-called "anti-Soviet speech" in the Sino-Soviet border resource negotiations. After the labor reform, he worked at the Political Economics Research Office of the Institute of Economics, Chinese Academy of Sciences. There, Gu Zhun published his famous paper "On the Law of Commodity Production and Value under the Socialist System." In this paper, Gu Zhun suggested that the socialist economy was the contradictory unity of the planned economy and economic accounting.

Economic planning needed to be supplemented by economic accounting. If one side of the plan was overemphasized, the relationship between value and price was negated, the influence of price on production distribution and product transfer was negated, and to the extent that the role of economic accounting was negated, the disadvantages of trying to stipulate everything with planning would emerge, hindering the development of the social economy. The law of value regulated social production through the economic accounting system. The regulation of the law of value closely linked the material rewards of workers closely to the profits and losses of enterprises, while price became the main tool for regulating production. Because the enterprise would spontaneously pursue production with favorable prices, prices would also rise and fall

---

6. Xue Muqiao, *Memoirs of Xue Muqiao* (Tianjin People's Publishing House, 1996).

spontaneously, and this fluctuation regulated production. Economic planning was not the synthesis of individual plans, but a kind of economic expectation. Therefore, it should be flexible, more inclined to specify some important economic indicators and reduce its specific provisions on the economic activities of enterprises.[7] Gu Zhun's paper completely disagreed with the popular view that the "planned economy is the mainstream, while the regulation of the law of value is only a supplement and will be gradually restricted," and clearly suggested that China needed to make full use of the law of value to regulate the socialist economy, and at the same time limit the regulatory role of economic planning on the economy. At that time, this view was undoubtedly enlightening and innovative, so it was grasped. It is reported that on the eve of his death in 1983, Sun Yefang solemnly declared, "I put forward the law of value in the 1950s, inspired by Gu Zhun's article." Wu Jinglian, Gu Zhun's disciple and a famous economist, called Gu Zhun "the first person to propose the theory of the market economy under socialist conditions."

Another theoretical peak in the discussion of the relationship between socialist economy and law of value was Sun Yefang's "On Value, and on the Position of Value in the Socialist and Communist Political Economics System" published in 1959. In this paper, Sun Yefang argued that the law of value should be the law of the existence and movement of the socially necessary labor which formed the value entity. The concept of value was indispensable in any article on socialist and communist political economics. Without it, it could not be regarded as political economics, nor economics. Therefore, it was important to greatly improve the status of value in the system of socialist political economics. Since the law of value was an objective law, it could not be restricted. It was no less a mistake to restrict the law of value than to cancel or reform the law of value. The importance of Sun Yefang's paper also lay in the fact that the category of production price existed in the socialist economy for the first time, discussed the objective inevitability of transforming value into production price, and pointed out that the objective conditions for the formation of production prices were the production of large machinery and the socialization of production, so as to improve the organic composition of capital and the important role of investment in the development of social production. Socialism could not do without an investment account. Capital profit rate and production price were tools to help make such economic comparison within the scope of the whole national economy and among various departments. Sun Yefang summed up his own logic, saying that the study of economic effects (ultimately summed up as the saving of labor time) was the core of the law of socialist social value. The economic effect mainly included the calculation of investment effect and labor productivity. To study the effect of investment, it was necessary to recognize the average profit rate of capital. The recognition of production prices was an inevitable logical conclusion of capital profit rate.[8]

In addition, Wang Yanan also advocated giving full play to the positive role of the law of value in the socialist economy. He believed that the law of value was the common characteristic of all

---

7. Gu Zhun, "On the Law of Commodity Production and Value Under the Socialist System," *Economic Research*, no. 3 (1957).

8. Sun Yefang, "On Value, and on the Position of Value in the Socialist and Communist Political Economics Systems," *Economic Research*, no. 9 (1959).

social forms of commodity production, not as a negative, but as a positive. Its basic role was to promote production. In the socialist economy, the real function of the law of value was shown in its positive role in improving labor productivity and promoting production. The main problem at the time was not how to prevent its negative destructive effect, but how to give full play to its positive role in promoting production.[9]

These thoughts and theories made important contributions to the development of the Marxist economic system, and they were also important advanced ideological materials for the innovation of China's socialist market economic system in the 1980s and 1990s.

4.3 Chen Yun's Theory on the Operation and Regulation Policy of the Socialist Planned Economy[10]

1. Planned Economic System and Planned Regulation Theory

On October 1, 1949, the Central Financial and Economic Affairs Commission (CFEAC) was established. The CFEAC was an organization under the unified leadership of the National Finance and Economy Council. It was composed of the former Ministry of Finance and Economics of the Central Committee and the Northeast Financial and Economic Office. Its director was Chen Yun, its deputy directors were Bo Yibo and Ma Yinchu (Li Fuchun was added after 1951), and its secretary general was Xue Muqiao. At the same time, the Central Bureau of Financial Planning was set up as a subordinate organ of the CFEAC, which was mainly responsible for the comprehensive handling of daily financial and economic work in the early days of its establishment.

In the early days of the founding of the People's Republic of China, the CPC Central Committee tended to establish a unified, planned economic system in economic management. At that time, the Common Program, which played the role of the provisional constitution, stipulated that the state should regulate the state-owned economy, cooperative economy, individual economy of farmers and handicraftsmen, private capitalist economy, and state capitalist economy in terms of business scope, raw material supply, sales market, labor conditions, technical equipment, fiscal policy, and financial policy so that under the leadership of the national economy, division of labor and cooperation should be carried out to promote the development of the overall social economy. The central people's government needed to strive to work out a master plan for the recovery and development of the main departments of the national public and private economy as early as possible, stipulate the scope of the division of labor and cooperation between the central and local economic departments, and regulate the interaction between the central and local economic

---

9. Wang Yanan, "Giving Full Play to the Positive Role of the Law of Value in China's Socialist Economy," *People's Daily*, May 15, 1959.

10. In this section, the time limitation on Chen Yun's research on the socialist planned economy operation regulation policy was 1985. Because Chen Yun's thought is a system with strong continuity, it is not suitable to make a rigid separation before and after Reform and Opening Up.

departments. At that time, national economic construction investment was centrally distributed by the CFEAC, and the construction projects were proposed by the central departments and submitted to the CFEAC for approval. The specialized plans drawn up by the central departments were implemented with the approval of the CFEAC, and in addition to auditing the professional plans and mastering the investment of various departments, the Planning Bureau of the CFEAC also concentrated on the systematic investigation and study of China's economic situation as the basic material for the audit plan.

In September 1954, the Constitution of the People's Republic of China, formulated and adopted at the first session of the First National People's Congress, stipulated that the state use economic plans to guide the development and transformation of the national economy, so as to improve the people's material and cultural life and consolidate the independence and security of the country. This was a formal provision in the national constitution that instituted the planned economy as the form of China's economic system. In July 1955, the second session of the First National People's Congress adopted the First Five-Year Plan for the Development of the National Economy of the People's Republic of China.

In the spring of 1951, the CFEAC began to work out the First Five-Year Plan. In August 1952, the CFEAC drew up a draft outline of the First Five-Year Plan. In 1953, the CFEAC, together with the State Planning Commission and departments of the Central Committee and major regions, made several revisions to the outline of the Five-Year Plan with reference to the Opinions of the State Planning Commission of the Soviet Union. In April 1954, the Central Committee set up an eight-member group headed by Chen Yun to compile the outline of the Five-Year Plan and began to work out the overall plan. By March 1955, the first draft Five-Year Plan was prepared. The Central Committee of the Communist Party of China revised the draft and submitted it to the second session of the First National People's Congress for deliberation and decision.

Chen Yun was the main decision-maker and executor in the formation of China's planned economy system, and since 1949, he had put forward the idea of the planned economy. During the period of economic recovery after the founding of the People's Republic of China, he said, "In the past, social production was unplanned. Now, we have a plan. This is a means to gradually eliminate anarchy."[11] He went on, "We want to develop a planned economy. If we only plan for the public sector and do not include many private production plans, the national economic plan will not be carried out."[12] Chen believed that the connotation or principle of the planned economy was proportional development. In 1954, he pointed out in Notes on the First Five-Year Plan that "the principle of proportional development must be observed, but the specific proportion among production departments will not be the same in each country or even in each period within a country. A country should, according to its economic situation at that time, stipulate the proportion in its plan. It is hard to say how much is right. The only way is to see if it is balanced.

---

11. Chen Yun, *Selected Works of Chen Yun*, vol. 2 (People's Publishing House, 1995), 93.
12. Chen Yun, *Selected Works of Chen Yun*, vol. 2 (People's Publishing House, 1995), 93.

Proportionality is balance. If it is balanced, it will be proportionate in general."[13] In 1957, Chen Yun pointed out in his speech "Issues for Attention After the Improvement of the System," "We must strengthen the work of balancing the entire country. Because economic units are decentralized, without overall balance, there is no planned economy."[14] In 1961, Chen said at the coal work symposium that "the socialist economy has a plan, that is, it is proportional. In proportion, it depends not only on the current year, but also on five years, ten years, and sometimes even twenty or thirty years."[15] From the perspective of macro-economic operations, the purpose of Chen Yun's proportional development was the comprehensive balance of the national economy. He noted, "The so-called comprehensive balance is in proportion. When in proportion, it is balanced. No one department can leave other departments. Proportionality is an objective law. If we do not follow it, we will not be able to do it well."[16]

The planned, proportional development of the national economy was the theoretical basis of the planned economic system. On the basis of analyzing the crisis of overproduction in the capitalist economy under the regulation of the market mechanism, Marx conceived that the economic system associated with the socialist mode of production is the planned economy, saying that labor-time's "socially planned distribution controls the correct proportion of the various labor-functions to the various needs."[17] In 1952, Stalin put forward the law of planned (proportional) development of the national economy in his *Economic Problems of Socialism in the USSR*. Economists in China and the Soviet Union regarded this as the law of the socialist economy. Chen Yun's concept of planned, proportional development of the national economy was basically carried out in this theoretical framework. The practice of China's planned economy from the 1950s to the 1970s suggested that it was difficult to achieve "proportionality" or "comprehensive balance" by means of planning, because it was impossible for the subjective economic plan to link up with the balance of social aggregate supply and demand, regardless of the actual economic basis or technical means. However, historical analysis indicated that with the constraints of China's economic and institutional conditions in the middle of the 20th century, Chen Yun's notion of planned, proportional development of the national economy conformed to the general requirements of macroeconomic equilibrium, and thus had theoretical value.

2. Planned Economy and Free Production

After 1953, the malpractice of the highly centralized planned economic system began to appear, especially in the implementation of the policies of planned purchase, planned supply, and unified purchase and sale, so that the quality and variety of industrial products decreased and could

---

13. Guan Mengjue, *Chen Yun's Economic Thought* (Knowledge Publishing House, 1984), 52.

14. Guan Mengjue, *Chen Yun's Economic Thought* (Knowledge Publishing House, 1984), 52.

15. Guan Mengjue, *Chen Yun's Economic Thought* (Knowledge Publishing House, 1984), 52.

16. Chen Yun, *Selected Works of Chen Yun*, vol. 3 (People's Publishing House, 1995), 211.

17. Marx and Engels, *Complete Works of Marx and Engels*, vol. 23 (People's Publishing House, 1975), 96.

not meet the social demand to an increasingly serious degree. On January 25, 1956, speaking at the third Supreme State Conference on the Socialist Transformation of Private Industry and Commerce, Chen Yun pointed out, "The situation in which we cannot maintain good variety and quality occurred after the unified purchase and sale. Because we have no competition, everything is purchased by the state. As a result, we are willing to mass produce goods and are not willing to produce fewer but better-quality goods."[18] Chen Yun believed this problem could only be solve through letting the market play its role with a little profit and competition incentive. He said, "We should not only implement the planned economy, manage the market well, and oppose speculation, but also avoid destroying the market. If we don't take this path, we can't find another, better way."[19] At the Eighth National Congress of the Communist Party of China in September 1956, Chen Yun delivered a speech entitled "New Issues After the Climax of Capitalist Industrial and Commercial Transformation," pointing out that "after the decisive victory in the socialist transformation of capitalist industry and commerce, some measures taken by the state economic departments to restrict capitalist industry and commerce in the past few years have become unnecessary. Not only are these measures basically no longer needed today, but they were not without shortcomings at that time."[20] The measures mentioned by Chen Yun included that state-owned commercial enterprises must implement the method of processing and ordering, alongside the unified purchase and exclusive sale of capitalist industries. It also included the notion that the circulation of commodities relied on the "distribution" of goods by state-owned trading companies in accordance with the administrative system, and that strict market management limited the purchase and trafficking of private merchants, which meant that agricultural and sideline products were monopolized by supply and marketing cooperatives or state-owned shops. In view of the drawbacks of the highly centralized planned economy system, Chen Yun said that "in running industry, commerce, and the handicraft industry, we should serve consumers, plan for consumers, and consider the convenience of consumers in order to enliven the market, increase the variety and quantity of products, increase the enthusiasm of producers, and meet the needs of the people's market."[21] Therefore, specific adjustment measures were proposed, covering five aspects.

The first was the relationship between purchase and sale. Instead of processing and ordering for industry, it was important to select and buy instead. For business, goods were not to be sent or matched from top to bottom, any unit could purchase goods from any place. The second was a price policy. In the future, China needed to adopt a policy of quality goods at favorable prices, low quality goods at low prices, and high quality at good prices. The third was the form of organization. It was wrong to blindly centralize and calculate profits and losses in industry, commerce, and the handicraft industries. The national market was to be supported by a free market. The fourth focused on market management. Market management was dead, but it was

18. Chen Yun, *Selected Works of Chen Yun*, vol. 2 (People's Publishing House, 1995), 261.
19. Chen Yun, *Selected Works of Chen Yun*, vol. 2 (People's Publishing House, 1995), 335.
20. Chen Yun, *Selected Works of Chen Yun*, vol. 3 (People's Publishing House, 1995), 4.
21. Chen Yun, *Collected Works of Chen Yun*, vol. 3 (Central Literature Publishing House, 2005), 99.

important for the country to live. It was impossible to rely on the commercial sector alone. Banks, railways, and the post and telecommunications departments should make corresponding changes. Plan management was the fifth issue. At the time, some of the plans were a dead end, and the rest were very uncertain. In the future, the system of planning and statistics should be changed, with a "big plan" balanced by "small freedoms."[22] On the relationship between planning and freedom, Chen Yun offered further analysis, saying, "No matter how big or small, not all plans can work. Individual production is the complement of collective ownership. Only 25% is free market, with 75% purchased by the state. If we do not have this 25% freedom, we will die. This 25% freedom is necessary. It should be big plans and small freedoms. Capitalist countries are small plans and big freedoms. They are large, and productivity and production relations are not compatible, while small entities such as a factory are planned. We have big plans and deal with specific issues accordingly. We need big plans and small liberties. At present, we can't plan big or small."[23]

Chen Yun's idea of adjusting the highly centralized planned economy was accepted by the Eighth National Congress of the Communist Party of China. The Resolution on Political Reporting issued by the Eighth National Congress of the Communist Party of China stipulated that the socialist unified market should take the national market as the main body, with a free market under the leadership of the state within a certain range as a supplement to the national market. The Proposal on the Second Five-Year Plan for the Development of the National Economy (1958–1962), adopted by the Eighth National Congress of the Communist Party of China (CPC), proposed that China should implement a method of grading and pricing according to quality in the procurement of industrial products and implement the method of purchasing some products, while reserving and appropriately developing the free market under the leadership of countries outside the national market.[24] These thoughts advanced by Chen Yun played a positive role in adjusting the development of the national economy at that time.

From the 1950s to the 1960s, Chinese theorists discussed the relationship between the law of planned, proportional development and the law of value. At that time, many arguments held that planned, proportional development was the objective law of a socialist economy, and it was contradictory to the law of value. But there were also some who held that the law of value and the law of planned, proportional development could coexist under socialist conditions, and even that the law of planned proportionality and the law of value were a the unity of opposites.[25] Chen Yun advocated the implementation of planned economic regulation, but his long-term practice of leading economic management made him realize that production planning could not cover

22. Chen Yun, *Collected Works of Chen Yun*, vol. 3 (Central Literature Publishing House, 2005), 99–101.

23. Chen Yun, *Collected Works of Chen Yun*, vol. 3 (Central Literature Publishing House, 2005), 103.

24. *Documents of the Eighth National Congress of the Communist Party of China* (People's Publishing House, 1956), 86, 91.

25. Editorial Department of *Economic Research* and *Economic Trends, Debates on Essential Issues of Political Economics Since the Founding of the People's Republic of China (1949–1980)* (China Financial and Economic Publishing House, 1981), 120.

the entire social economy in every aspect. In September 1956, Chen Yun said in his speech "New Problems Following the Basic Completion of Socialist Transformation" that "I think the socialist economic situation will be like this: in terms of industrial and commercial operation, state operation and collective operation will be the main body of industrial and commercial industry, but there will also be a certain number of individual operations. This type of individual management is the complement of state management and collective management. With regard to the production plan, the main part of the national industrial and agricultural commodities are produced according to the plan, but at the same time, some products are freely produced within the scope of the state permission according to market changes. Planned production is the main body of industrial and agricultural production, and free production within the scope permitted by the state according to market changes is a supplement to planned production." He went on to say, "In the socialist unified market, the state market is its main body, but there is a free market under the leadership of the state within a certain range. This kind of free market is under the leadership of the state and serves as a supplement to the national market. Therefore, it is an integral part of the socialist unified market."[26]

Chen Yun's theory of coordination between the planned economy and free production to a certain extent aimed to recognize the market mechanism's regulation on the social economy, although this regulation only played a complementary role. Chen Yun regarded the overall national economy as a plate structure. As far as the market was concerned, the socialist unified market was a plate, the national market was its main body, and the free market under the leadership of the state was its supplement. As far as social production was concerned, production according to plan was the main body and free production according to market changes was the supplement. Economic planning regulated planned production and the national market, and the market mechanism regulated the free market and free production. Compared with the highly centralized, unified, and all-inclusive planned economic system, Chen Yun's theory was more in line with the social and economic reality of China at the time, and it offered some innovation in the scope of the theory of the planned economy.

3. The Theory of System Reform Based on the Planned Economy and Supplemented by Market Regulation

(1) On the Relationship Between the Planned Economy and Market Regulation

In a speech on March 8, 1979, Chen Yun talked about planning and market issues. He pointed out that the drawback of the previous planning system was that there was only a plan in proportion, and there was no market regulation. The so-called market regulation aimed to adjust according to the law of value. He believed that the economy of the whole socialist period must have two parts, the planned economy (the planned part according to the proportion) and market regulation (not making plans and allowing it to produce according to the changes of market supply and demand,

---

26. Chen Yun, *Selected Works of Chen Yun*, vol. 3 (People's Publishing House, 1995), 13.

that is, the part with "blind" regulation). The first part was basic and necessary, while the second part was subordinate and secondary, but necessary. He pointed out that in the future economic adjustment and system reform, the proportional adjustment of the planned economy and market regulation would account for a large proportion.[27]

In October 1984, the Third Plenary Session of the Twelfth Central Committee of the Communist Party of China adopted the Decision of the Central Committee of the Communist Party of China on the Reform of the Economic System. The Decision clearly pointed out that the socialist planned economy must intentionally be based on and apply the law of value. It was a planned commodity economy on the basis of public ownership. On this basis, the Decision further clarified the direction of China's economic system reform, pointing out that in order to fundamentally change the economic system that constrained the development of productive forces, it was important to conscientiously sum up China's historical experience, carefully study the actual situation and development requirements of China's economy, and at the same time, absorb and learn from all the reflections of the world today, including developed capitalist countries. It was necessary to establish a socialist economic system with Chinese characteristics, full of vigor and vitality, and promote the development of social productive forces. This was the basic task of China's economic system reform.

On September 23, 1985, Chen Yun delivered a speech at the National Congress of the Communist Party of China. He pointed out that the reform of the socialist economic system was the self-improvement and development of that system. The purpose of economic restructuring was to develop productive forces and gradually improve the people's living standards. The rural reform had achieved obvious results. The general direction of urban economic system reform was correct, and concrete steps and measures were being explored. It was important to take steps and look at it, summing up previous experience when needed. It was necessary to persist in carrying out the reform well. Chen Yun believed that from the perspective of national work, the planned economy was the main task, and market regulation was the supplement. This remains relevant today. A guiding plan is not equal to market regulation. Market regulation means that production is carried out according to the changes of market supply and demand without planning, that is, blind regulation. Planning is the main basis of macro control. Only by doing well in macro control is it possible to enliven the microcosmic and make it live, but not be disorderly.[28]

In the 1980s, China's economic system reform was carried out around the relationship between the planned economy and market regulation, with the purpose of establishing an economic operation and management system that not only embodied the essential characteristics of the socialist production mode, but also conformed to the basic laws of the commodity economy. Chen Yun's idea of the "planned economy as the main part and market regulation as the supplement" in

---

27. *Selected Important Documents Since the Third Plenary Session of the CPC Central Committee* (People's Publishing House, 1982), 65; Chen Yun, *Selected Works of Chen Yun*, vol. 3 (People's Publishing House, 1995), 244–247.

28. *China Economic Yearbook (1986)* (Economy and Management Publishing House, 1986), 1–26; Chen Yun, *Selected Works of Chen Yun*, vol. 3 (People's Publishing House, 1995), 350.

this period was a continuation of his theory of the planned economy and free production as main and auxiliary structures proposed in the 1950s and 60s, but it had developed in two aspects. The first was his emphasis that market regulation was to reflect the role of the law of value, and even that mandatory plans and guiding plans could not be separated from market demand and should respect objective economic laws. The second was that the relationship between planning and the market was no longer a simple "plate structure," and not only should the proportion of planned economy and market regulation be adjusted promptly, but they were also "classic bird cages." Chen Yun pointed out that "invigorating the economy is to invigorate it under the guidance of the plan, not without the guidance of the plan. This is just like the relationship between a bird and a cage. A bird can't be pinched in one's hand. If it is pinched in the hand, it will die. If it wants to fly, it can only fly in the cage. If birds are to enliven the economy, then cages are national plans."[29] This was different from the 1950s and 60s, when free production was only a supplement to the deficiencies of the planned economy. It recognized that planning and market, as means of regulating the economy, could be combined, but market regulation was still supplementary, and it could not be separated from the guidance of the plan and the scope of the national plan. In October 1987, the report of the Thirteenth National Congress of the Communist Party of China proposed the establishment of a socialist planned commodity economic system. It emphasized that the planning work must be based on the commodity exchange and the law of value. The scope of action of the plan and the market covered the whole of society. Generally speaking, the new economic operation mechanism was to be the mechanism of "the state regulating the market and the market guiding enterprises." This system and mechanism design was related to Chen Yun's idea of combining a planned economy with market regulation.

(2) The Mode of Economic Operation with the Planned Economy as the Main Factor and Market Regulation as the Supplement

In October 1984, the Third Plenary Session of the Twelfth Central Committee of the Communist Party of China adopted the Decision of the Central Committee of the Communist Party of China on the Reform of Economic System. Before the concept of the planned economy as a planned commodity economy on the basis of public ownership, the policy viewed the planned economy as the main and market regulation as the supplement, which was the guiding principle of China's economic system reform. The central link of the reform at this stage was to reform the planned economic system and strengthen the effective management and guidance of the state to the national economy. According to the principle of the planned economy as the main factor and market regulation as the supplement, three management methods – mandatory plan, guiding plan, and market regulation – were adopted according to different enterprises, products, and tasks. At that time, the dominant idea was to improve the planned economy through reform, which was in line with what Chen Yun had said, noting that reform was the self-improvement

29. Chen Yun, *Selected Works of Chen Yun*, vol. 3 (People's Publishing House, 1995), 320.

and development of the socialist system. According to this reform idea, a new definition of the economic system was formulated.

China's planned economy was not a market economy. Production and exchange, which were regulated spontaneously and blindly through the market, were limited to small commodities, three types of agricultural and sideline products, and service repair industries, which played an auxiliary role in the overall national economy.

The planned economy was not equal to mandatory planning. Both mandatory planning and guiding planning were concrete forms of the planned economy. At that time and for a long time to come, it was important to gradually reduce mandatory planning and expand the guiding plan.

The guiding plan was mainly regulated by economic means, and the mandatory plan also needed to consider the role of economic law, especially the law of value. The plan was to be realized through the law of value and serve the plan through the law of value.[30]

In the design of such an economic system and mode of economic operation, the planned economy was not only the main body, but also the core of reform. The key point of the reform was to divide the planned economy into mandatory planning and guiding planning. What was more important was to make it clear that both the guiding plan and the mandatory plan should be regulated by economic means, and the role of economic law should be considered. This idea of direct connection of the planned economy with economic law and the law of value became the first theoretical resource of the reform mode of the socialist planned commodity economy and the combination of the planned economy and market regulation in the second half of the 1980s.

---

30. *Ten Years of China's Economic System Reform* (Economy and Management Publishing House, 1988), 41.

CHAPTER 5

The Mainstream Form of Economic Thought in the People's Republic of China and the Reference to Western Economic Theory

5.1 An Overview of the Introduction of Western Economic Theories from the 1950s to the 1970s

1. Research and Evaluation of Western Classical Political Economics

The introduction and dissemination of Western economic theory in China began earlier than that of Marxist economic theory. In the 1880s, a group of early bourgeois reformists in China began to spread some Western economic ideas. After that, Kang Youwei, Liang Qichao, Yan Fu, Sun Yat-Sen, and other bourgeois reformists and revolutionaries systematically translated, introduced, studied, and expounded Western classical economic thought and modern economic thought. From the 1880s to the 1940s, the introduction and dissemination of Western economic theories in China was ongoing, but on the whole, the academic research level in this field was not high, and these theories were not translated and introduced completely and systematically. According to textual research, at that time, most of the students who went abroad to study economics chose applied economics instead of taking basic principles as their major. The introduction and research of the basic theory of Western economics were affected, and research results with original ideas in theory were rare.[1] According to another study, with the adjustment of colleges and departments in China's universities in 1952, the construction of economic departments in Chinese universities

---

1. Hu Jichuang, *Outline of the History of Modern Chinese Economic Thought* (China Social Sciences Press, 1984), 416–422.

abandoned the tradition of Western bourgeois economics and turned to the academic system of the Soviet Union. Aside from some universities (such as Peking University and Wuhan University) that were allowed to retain some courses and teachers on Western bourgeois economics, most colleges and universities canceled and replaced these subjects with Marxist economic theory reformed and explained by the Soviet Union, and the economics teaching system was constructed accordingly.[2]

Marx divided Western economics into "classical political economics" and "vulgar economics." Marx's so-called classical political economics "refers to all such economics since William Petty. This kind of economics, contrary to vulgar economics, studies the internal relations of bourgeois production relations."[3] "In England, classical political economics began with Petty and ended with Ricardo, while in France, it began with Boisguillebert and ended with Sismondi."[4] According to Marx's classification, Western classical political economics included the economic theory of Adam Smith, the physiocratic school represented by Quesnay and Turgot, and the theories of economists such as Locke, Hume, and Jones.

With Marx's evaluation, the attitude and evaluation of Chinese economic and ideological circles toward Western classical political economics were relatively objective and pertinent. The emergence and development of Western classical political economics took place from the mid-seventeenth century to the first half of the nineteenth century. This was exactly the stage of the occurrence and development of the capitalist system. Classical political economics reflected the interests of the bourgeoisie in the early stage of capitalist development. It sought to offer theoretical explanation on how to increase wealth under the capitalist system, discussed the law of wealth production and distribution, and demonstrated that capitalist production was superior to feudal production. Classical political economics adapted to the requirements of the new bourgeoisie to expand capitalist production, strongly opposed the state's intervention in economic life, and put forward the concept of laissez faire economics. In exploring the economic law of capitalism, classical political economics eliminated the influence of mercantilism. For the first time, it transferred its theoretical research from the field of circulation to the field of production and made a preliminary analysis of the internal relations of capitalist production relations, thus making political economics an independent science.

Classical political economics laid the foundation of labor value theory. Petty first came to the conclusion that the value of a commodity, which he called its "natural price," was determined by the amount of labor consumed in the production of goods. But in Petty's theory, there was no clear distinction between value and use value, value and exchange value, or value and price. The physiocratic school did not put forward the theory of labor value, but it realized that under the condition of full, free competition, exchange was equivalent. Smith developed the theory of labor value and clearly suggested that labor was the real standard by which to measure the exchange

2. Liu Wei, "Developing Socialist Political Economics with Chinese Characteristics in the Combination of Marxism and Chinese Practice," *Economic Research*, no. 5 (2016).

3. Marx and Engels, *Complete Works of Marx and Engels*, vol. 23 (People's Publishing House, 1972), 98.

4. Marx and Engels, *Complete Works of Marx and Engels*, vol. 13 (People's Publishing House, 1975), 41.

value of all commodities. However, this theory was far from complete, because he also believed that the value of a commodity was determined by the amount of labor purchased or dominated by the commodity in exchange. This led Smith astray, and thus led to the so-called "Smith doctrine" that value was composed of wages, profits, and land rent. Smith's theory of value was pluralistic, but labor value theory still played a leading role in his overall theory. Ricardo criticized Smith's error and insisted on the correct view that commodity value was determined by the necessary labor time spent in producing goods. However, he only paid attention to the analysis of value quantity, while lacking an understanding of value entity and value form. In particular, he could not explain scientifically how the exchange between capital and labor and the same amount of capital gets the same amount of profits could be consistent with the law of value, which were two major contradictions that his value theory could not resolve.[5]

Classical political economics studied surplus value. According to Petty, land rent was the total surplus over the production cost, and interest (money rent) was the rent that money lenders such as landlords should get, since they had the ability to buy land. Therefore, in his discourse, land rent was the real form of surplus value. The physiocratic school correctly proposed a basic argument that only labor producing "pure products" (surplus value) was productive. Because this theory emphasized that "pure products" were created in the field of production, research on the origin of surplus value was transferred from the field of circulation to the field of direct production, laying a foundation for the analysis of capitalist production. However, the physiocrats only regarded agriculture as productive labor, so they only recognized land rent as the form of surplus value. Smith broke through the one sidedness of physiocratic theory and suggested that general social labor was what created value, regardless of the specific form of labor. Surplus value was not only a form of land rent, but also a form of profit, rent, and interest. Ricardo further studied surplus value. His theoretical contribution mainly lay in the quantity of surplus value, the nature of land rent, existing conditions, and the law of change.

Classical political economics studied the reproduction of total social capital. Quesnay's *Economic Table* was the first attempt to explain the whole process of capitalist reproduction, which was an outstanding innovation in the field.

From the perspective of Marxist political economics, the most important scientific contribution of classical political economics lay in, first, the fact that it had laid the foundation of labor value theory, and second, that it had studied surplus value and its various specific forms on the basis of labor value theory. Although these studies were not sufficient and thorough, they were critically inherited by classical Marxist writers. On a foundation that was completely different from bourgeois classical political economics, Marxist theorists created a truly scientific proletarian political economics. In addition to various scientific factors and being limited by historical conditions and class position, Western classical economics included many wrong or vulgar views. These vulgar views were inherited by later bourgeois economists and developed into a vulgar economics defending the capitalist system.

---

5. Wang Yanan, *Selections of Bourgeois Classical Political Economics* (The Commercial Press, 1965).

2. Understanding and Evaluation of Western "Vulgar Economics"

What Marx called "vulgar economics" in the West referred to the economics used to defend the capitalist system. This theory regarded the capitalist system as a natural, absolute, and eternal form of social production in accordance with human nature, and it studied some features of the capitalist economy. Marx pointed out that for political economics, "[I]t was thenceforth no longer a question, whether this theorem or that was true, but whether it was useful to capital or harmful, expedient or inexpedient, politically dangerous or not. In place of disinterested inquirers, there were hired prize fighters; in place of genuine scientific research, the bad conscience and the evil intent of apologetic."[6] For Western "vulgar economics," Chinese economic and ideological circles at that time held a critical attitude, and their evaluation was basically negative.

From the 1950s to the 1960s, China successively translated some Western "vulgar economics" works. In 1963, the Commercial Press published the *Anthology of Bourgeois Vulgar Political Economics,* which introduced Western economic theory after the Ricardo school. According to these materials, China's economic and ideological circles commented on "vulgar economics."[7]

Jean Baptiste Say of France and Thomas Robert Malthus of England were the first two economists to vulgarize Adam Smith's doctrine. Say derived his three factors of production (labor, capital, and land) and three kinds of remuneration (wage, interest, and land rent are the remuneration of labor, capital, and land respectively) from the Smith doctrine (the value of commodities consists of wage, profit, and land rent), which completely concealed the essence of capitalist exploitation. Malthus distorted the true source of profit by drawing on Smith's other view that the value of goods depended on the labor available to buy, and concluding that his profit lay in the fact that goods were bought cheap and sold at a high price. Britain's James Muller and John Ramsay McCulloch were vulgarizers of Ricardian economics.

From the 1920s to the 1930s, the Ricardo school disintegrated. A group of economists, represented by Nassau William Senior of England, Frederic Bastiat of France, and Henry Charles Carey of the United States, attacked classical political economics and beautified the capitalist system. In the 1840s, the German School of history began to take shape. Its pioneers were Georg Friedrich List, and the main representatives were Wilhelm Georg Friedrich Roscher and others (known as the old historical school) and Gustav von Schmoller (called the new historical school and "forum socialism"). They opposed the theories of Smith and Ricardo, denied that there were universal economic laws, and believed that the task of economics was only a description of historical processes. In the 1870s, William Stanley Jevons of England, Manley E. Leon Valla of France, and Carl Menger of Austria successively published the theory of final utility, the theory of ultimate unit utility, and the theory of marginal utility. These subjective utility theories were used to oppose Marx's theory of labor value and surplus value. Among them, the Austrian school founded by

---

6. Marx and Engels, *Complete Works of Marx and Engels,* vol. 23 (People's Publishing House, 1975), 98.

7. Lu Youzhang, Li Zongzheng, and Wu Yifeng, *Bourgeois Political Economics* (People's Publishing House, 1975).

Carl Menger had the greatest influence. Their theory of marginal utility value and the theory and method of quantifying subjective utility with "marginal analysis" were called the "marginal revolution" in the history of economic theory.

At the end of the nineteenth century and the beginning of the 20th century, there appeared the Cambridge school represented by Alfred Marshall, the American school represented by John Bates Clark, and the American institutional school represented by Thorstein Bunde Veblen. These theories reflect the signs of various collections of vulgar economic theories. In the 1930s, against the backdrop of the world economic crisis, Keynes' macroeconomics arose. In order to stimulate "effective demand" and eliminate economic crises, Keynes advocated the implementation of "regulated capitalism" with state intervention, and reformed the traditional economic theory of liberalism, a move called the Keynesian Revolution. After the Second World War, some economists added some supplements and amendments to Keynesian theory, forming the post-Keynesian mainstream school. At the same time, some other schools and theories, such as incomplete competition theory, welfare economics, neo-liberal economics, the monetary school, economic growth theory, and development economics, developed to varying degrees.[8]

5.2 Research on the Introduction of the History of Western Classical Political Economics and Economic Theory

1. On the Introduction of Classical Western Political Economics

After 1949, China's earliest introduction of classical Western political economics was *Selected Works of Bourgeois Classical Political Economics* edited by Wang Yanan, which was published by the Commercial Press in 1965 and revised in 1979. The second edition was later published, with Wu Feidan serving as chief editor and Wu Chunwu and Liu Bai'ao as co-editors. *Selected Works of Bourgeois Classical Political Economics* introduced the life, main ideas, and academic status of the main representatives of classical British and French political economics, such as Petty, Boisguillebert, Quesnay, Turgot, Smith, Ricardo, Sismondi, and others. In their important economic works, chapters reflecting their basic theories were selected to allow the Chinese economic community to have some understanding of the main thread and basic generalizations of classical Western political economics. The selected works of Petty include chapters 1, 2, 3, 4, 5, 10, 12 and 14 of *Treatise of Taxes an Contributions,* chapters 2, 5 and 10 of *Verbum Sapienti,* the original preface and chapters 1, 2, 4, 5, 10 of *Political Arithmetick,* and *Quantulumcunque Concerning Money*. Boisguilbert's works included the second and third parts of *La Détail de la France,* the introduction, the first, fourth and seventh chapters of the first part, and the second, third and fourth chapters of the second part of *The Case for Deregulation of Grain Markets,* and the second and third chapters of *Theory of Money, Circular Flow, Effective Demand, and Distribution*

---

8. Hu Jichuang, *Western Economic Theories Since 1870* (Economic Science Press, 1988).

of Wealth. Quesnay's works included *Economic Table, Explanation of the Economic Table, Analysis of Economic Table, Important Investigation* and *General Principles of Economic Management in Agricultural Countries.* Turgot's main work in translation was *Reflections on the Formation and Distribution of Wealth.* Smith's works included the main parts of the first, second and fourth chapters of *An Inquiry into the Nature and Causes of National Wealth.* Sismondi's works included the preface to, the main parts of the second, third, fourth and seventh chapters of *New Principles of Political Economy,* part of the preface to *The Study of Political Economy,* and the thirteenth and sixteenth papers on the value theory.[9]

At that time, Chinese economic and ideological circles studied classical Western political economics from the viewpoint, standpoint, and method of Marxist economics, mainly from the value theory, surplus value theory, capitalist social reproduction theory, and distribution theory. Generally speaking, Petty's main contribution to political economics was that he first put forward some basic viewpoints on labor value theory. He distinguished the "natural price" (i.e. value) from the market price. He thought that value was determined by the labor time spent in the production of the commodity, and the amount of value was inversely proportional to the labor productivity of the commodity. He put forward the view that "land is the mother of wealth, and labor is the father of wealth." On the basis of labor theory of value, he examined the economic categories of wages, land rent, interest, and money.

Boisguilbert's main contribution also lay in putting forward some basic viewpoints of labor value theory. When he analyzed the value of agricultural products and production costs, he attributed the exchange value of commodities to labor time. He explored the "real value" behind the market price. He believed that under the condition of free competition, if an industrial sector invested too much labor, resulting in too many products and lowering prices, some labor would withdraw from the department. By contrast, if an industrial sector invested too little labor, resulting in insufficient products and rising prices, a part of labor would be transferred to the department. In this way, labor would be distributed to various industrial sectors in accordance with the correct proportion, so that the "real value" (that is, the exchange value) would be determined by the labor time.

The center of Quesnay's economic theory was the "pure product" theory, which held that agriculture was the only production sector. Only agriculture could increase material wealth and produce "pure products" (that is, the balance of agricultural products after deducting production costs). His economic philosophy was "L'Ordrenaturel," and the way to realize "natural order" was laissez faire economic policy. Another outstanding contribution of Quesnay was the creation of the *Economic Table,* which offered a systematic analysis of the reproduction process of social capital for the first time. Marx stated that it was "was an extremely brilliant conception, incontestably the most brilliant for which political economy had up to then been responsible."[10]

---

9. Wang Yanan, *Selected Works of Bourgeois Classical Political Economics* (The Commercial Press, 1965).

10. Marx and Engels, *Complete Works of Marx and Engels,* vol. 26, bk. 1 (People's Publishing House, 1975), 366.

On the basis of Quesnay's three classes (the productive class, the landowner's class, and the unproductive class), Turgot further divided the productive class and the unproductive class into the working class and the capitalist class and described the characteristics of these two classes. He examined in detail five ways of using capital: buying land, using land, engaging in industrial production, operating commerce, and lending money. At the same time, the basic income of a capitalist society was divided into wage, profit, interest, and land rent. Through the in-depth investigation of capitalist production relations, Turgot developed the system of the physiocratic school to the highest level.

Smith's *An Inquiry into the Nature and Causes of the Wealth of Nations* established a complete political and economic system for the first time. He introduced the basic hypothesis of the "economic man." Under this assumption, he described the ideal capitalist economic order, an "economic man" whose activities of pursuing personal interests would promote the growth of social welfare through the regulation of an "invisible hand." For the first time, Smith systematically discussed the basic principles of the labor theory of value. He believed that labor was the real measure of the exchange value of all commodities. He distinguished simple labor from complex labor, examined the relationship between "natural price" (value) and market price, and analyzed the role of the law of value. He divided the classes of capitalist society into three classes, the working class, the bourgeoisie, and the landlord class. He studied the three kinds of income of the three classes, wages, profits, and land rent. He pointed out that profit and rent were a deduction of the value created by labor, thus involving the source of surplus value.

Ricardo's *On the Principles of Political Economy and Taxation* was most representative of the interests of the industrial bourgeoisie in the period of British Industrial Revolution. It was also the representative work with the most scientific arguments in British classical political economics. Ricardo's important contribution to economics was that he adhered to and developed the theory of labor value, and thus analyzed the performance of class opposition in capitalist society in distribution relations. He criticized Smith's dualistic theory of value and insisted that the value of a commodity depends on the labor consumed in production. He first put forward the concept of necessary labor and explained the determination of commodity value. Ricardo regarded clarifying and studying the law of wealth distribution among social classes as the main subject of political economics. The core of the theory of distribution was actually the production and division of surplus value. Therefore, he investigated the categories of wages, profits, and land rent, and first systematically analyzed the two forms of differential rent. Marx called Ricardo the "last great representative" of classical British political economics.

Sismondi's contribution to political economics was the analysis of the contradiction of capitalism and an explanation of the inevitability of the overproduction crisis. He pointed out that the consumption of workers could only realize this part of the value of wages, while capitalists and landlords would not consume all the surplus value. What's more, the products of a year were paid by the income of the previous year. In order to obtain profits, the capitalists kept expanding production. If this year's production exceeded last year's income, not all the products could be realized. In addition, under the condition of free competition, in order to occupy the market, reduce production costs, and try to lower wages, more goods were produced as surplus. Having no foreign market would inevitably lead to an economic crisis of overproduction.[11]

2. A Study on the Introduction of the History of Western Economic Theories

From the 1950s to the 1960s, Chinese economic and ideological circles not only introduced Western economic theories from the perspective of classical political economics, but also critically studied the theories of some important Western economists and economic schools from the perspective of the history of political economics. "Histories of bourgeois political economics" published at that time systematically introduced the Western mercantilist economic theory, the emergence, development, and termination of classical political economics, and the emergence and development of vulgar economics. Compared with the introduction of classical Western political economic theory, the introduction of the "history of bourgeois political economics" was more in-depth and systematic, and it paid attention to the continuity of theory. More importantly, most of these works were devoted to the introduction and critical study of bourgeois vulgar political economics, so that Chinese economic circles could appreciate the general situation of Western economics after Ricardo and understand some new theories.

In addition to mercantilism and classical political economics, the research scope of the history of bourgeois political economics included German Historical School, marginal utility theory, quantitative economics school, the American institutional school, Marshall's economic theory, Chamberlain and Robinson's monopolistic competition theory, Keynesian economics, economic growth theory, welfare economics, econometrics, and input-output analysis. At that time, the purpose of studying these Western economic theories was to criticize them. For example, there were the three basic propositions of new welfare economics: the individual – not others – is the best judge of his own welfare; social welfare depends on the welfare of all the individuals who make up society, rather than on anything else; and if at least one person is better off and no one is worse off, the situation of the overall society will be better. At that time, Chinese scholars criticized each of these ideas. The first proposition aimed "to publicize the bourgeois egoism, to advocate the bourgeois creed that the pursuit of personal happiness and welfare is human nature, and to promote bourgeois individualism." The purpose of the second proposition was to "attempt to deny that human society is the sum of all kinds of relations among people based on productive forces and relations of production, to deny that human nature is the sum total of social relations, and to obliterate class division and class opposition, so as to describe the nature of the bourgeoisie as human nature and pretend that the happiness and welfare of the bourgeoisie is the general happiness and welfare of society." The third proposition involved "concealing the class exploitation relationship in capitalist society. The monopoly bourgeoisie is in fundamental

---

11. Xu Dixin, *Dictionary of Political Economics*, vol. 1 (People's Publishing House, 1980); Wang Yanan, *Selected Works of Bourgeois Classical Political Economics* (The Commercial Press, 1965); Lu Youzhang, Li Zongzheng, and Wu Yifeng, *Bourgeois Political Economics* (People's Publishing House, 1975).

opposition to the interests of the proletariat and the masses of the working people. A small number of monopolistic capitalists are based on the poverty and bankruptcy of the majority of the people. In a capitalist society, there has never been a state in which some people 'get better' and no one 'goes down.'"[12]

As for Harrod's theory of economic growth, commentators at that time said, "Harrod's fallacy about the long-term development trend of capitalist economy and its causes completely avoids the development trend of capitalist economic reality in the imperialist stage, but abstractly lists all kinds of possibilities. It seems that in the period of imperialism, in addition to the long-term stagnation trend, there may also be long-term prosperity and a stable growth trend. This cannot but be refuted mercilessly by historical facts. Capitalism has never experienced long-term prosperity and stable growth, and its economic development has always been intermittent from crisis to upsurge, and then from upsurge to crisis." And, "On the issue of the causes of stagnation, Harrod fully exposes the reactionary face of defending monopoly."[13]

Another example is the criticism of Marshall's demand theory. It was noted that "Marshall's demand theory is completely antithetical to science, because demand does not depend on people's subjective wishes, but on the amount of national income and its distribution among different classes. Marshall deliberately avoids these most important factors that determine the change of demand under the capitalist system. Starting from psychological factors, Marshall fabricates the fallacy of the law of diminishing demand price, completely covers up the decisive role of class antagonism of distribution on demand under the capitalist system, and covers up the basic contradiction of capitalism, and its resulting contradiction between the unlimited expansion of production and the relatively narrow consumption of the ability to pay of the working masses."[14]

Although these critical remarks are marked by their times, they also reflect the degree of mastery of Western economic theories by Chinese economists of that day. Due to the failure to understand Western economic theory from the aspects of analytical methods (truthful analysis), basic assumptions (such as the "rational person" hypothesis), and basic concepts (such as Marshall's "law of demand"), there was a suspicion that the criticism of Western economic theory was far-fetched, and some aspects were even irrelevant.

From the 1950s to the 1970s, China's research on the introduction of the original works of Western economics mainly focused on the works of classical Western political economics and some important works of "vulgar economics." The translation and publication of these original works provided the basic conditions for the study of Western economic theories by Chinese economic circles at that time.

---

12. Lu Youzhang, Li Zongzheng, and Wu Yifeng, *Bourgeois Political Economics* (People's Publishing House, 1975).

13. Lu Youzhang, Li Zongzheng, and Wu Yifeng, *Bourgeois Political Economics* (People's Publishing House, 1975).

14. Lu Youzhang, Li Zongzheng, and Wu Yifeng, *Bourgeois Political Economics* (People's Publishing House, 1975).

In the 1950s, the Chinese versions of the original works of Western economic theories generally included Keynes' *The General Theory of Employment, Interest, and Currency* (Sanlian Bookstore, 1957), Chamberlain's *Theory of Monopolistic Competition* (Sanlian Bookstore, 1958), Menger's *Principles of Economics* (The Commercial Press, 1958), Veblen's *Theory of Business Enterprise* (The Commercial Press, 1958), Hansen's *Fiscal Policy and Business Cycles* (Shanghai People's Publishing House, 1959), Clark's *The Distribution of Wealth* (The Commercial Press, 1958), Moore's *Dynamic Complement to Pure Economics* (The Commercial Press, 1959), Bohm-Bawerk's *Capital and Interest* (The Commercial Press, 1959), and Thomas Mann's *Britain's Wealth from Foreign Trade* (The Commercial Press, 1959).

The Chinese translations published in the 1960s included Turgot's *Reflections on the Formation and Distribution of Wealth* (The Commercial Press, 1961), Hansen's *The Economy of the United States* (The Commercial Press, 1962), Liszt's *The National System of Political Economics* (The Commercial Press, 1961), Robinson's *Economics of Imperfect* (The Commercial Press, 1961), Malthus's *Principles of Political Economy* (The Commercial Press, 1962), Say's *Overview of Political Economy* (The Commercial Press, 1963), William Petty's *Treatise of Taxes and Contribution, Verbum Sapienti,* and *On Currency* (The Commercial Press, 1963), Sismondi's *New Principles of Political Economy* (The Commercial Press, 1964), Marshall's *Principles of Economics* (The Commercial Press, 1964), Veblen's *The Theory of the Leisure Class* (The Commercial Press, 1964), Bohm-Bawerk's *The Positive Theory of Capital* (The Commercial Press, 1964), and Hansen's *Economic Issues of the 1960s* (The Commercial Press, 1964). The Chinese versions published in the 1970s included Adam Smith's *An Inquiry into the Nature and Causes of the Wealth of Nations* (The Commercial Press, 1972). In addition, in 1963, The Commercial Press published *Selected Works of Bourgeois Vulgar Political Economics*, which introduced Schmoller's *The General National Economic Outline*, Roscher's *The National Economics System*, Bastiat's *The Economic Harmony*, and Muller's *The Outline of Political Economics*.

Chinese economists also studied Western economic theories by using original works in foreign languages. The original English works introduced at that time included Leontief's *The Structure of the American Economy, 1919–1939* (1951), *Econometrics* (1963), *Research on American Economic Structure* (1953), Valavanis's *Econometrics* (1959), and Robinson's *Economic Philosophy* (1963), Samuelson's *Economics* (1961), Lerner's *The Economics of Control: Principles of Welfare Economics* (1949), Hansen's *Fiscal Policy and Business Cycles* (1941), Hayek's *The Principles of Liberal Social Order* (1960), Graaf's *Theoretical Welfare Economics* (1957), Ritter's *The Review of Economic Studies* (1960), Reder's *Studies in the Theory of Welfare Economics* (1948), Pigou's *Industrial Fluctuations* (1929), *The Economics of Welfare* (1938), and *Theory of Unemployment* (1933), Catlin's *The Progress of Economic: a History of Economic Thought* (1962), Rostow's *The Stages of Economic Growth* (1960) and *The Takeoff into Self-Sustained Growth* (1964), Harrod's *Towards a Dynamic Economics* (1956), Domar's *Essays in the Theory of Economic Growth* (1957), Dillard's *The Economics of John Maynard Keynes* (1955), Hejland's *Multiple Equilibria* (1954), Joseph Alois Schumpeter's *History of Economic Analysis* (1961), Galbraith's *American Capitalism: the Concept of Counterforce* (1952), Stonier and Hague's *Textbook of Economic*

Theory (1964), Marshall's *Industry and Trade* (1927), Clark's *The History of Economic Thought* (1927), Walras's *The Elements of Pure Economics* (1926), and Senior's *An Outline of the Science of Political Economy* (1951).[15]

During the thirty year span of the 1950s to the 1970s, China generally introduced some original Western economic theories. In the study of Western classical political economics and "vulgar economics," Chinese economists also quoted many comments and evaluations in the works of Marx, Engels, and Lenin, and they conducted a critical study of Western economic theories, with the evaluation from the classic works of Marxism as their guiding ideology.

---

15. Information Center of News Publishing Committee and Chinese Version Library, *National Bibliography (1980–1996)* (Zhonghua Book Company).

PART TWO

The Evolution of the Mainstream Form of Economic Thought of the People's Republic of China (1980s)

CHAPTER 6

From the Economic Ideology of the Socialist Planned Economy to the Socialist Planned Commodity Economy

6.1 The Evolution of the Mainstream Form of Economic Thought

1. Theoretical Basis of the Planned Economy and the Evolution of Policy Theories

From the theoretical perspective, the planned economy is the embodiment of the characteristics of the socialist production mode and the essential interest relationship of a socialist society at the level of economic operation. The planned economy refers to the economic management and operation system, based on the public ownership of the means of production, by society (the state) according to the requirements of economic and social development in the form of predetermined economic plans or planning to coordinate social interest relations and allocate social and economic resources across society. "The planned distribution of working time in a society regulates the proper proportion of various labor functions to various needs."[1] From the 1950s to the 1970s, Chinese political and economic circles generally believed that the reason the planned economy was an economic operation system linked with the socialist mode of production was that the socialized development requirements of the socialist economy and the characteristics of social and economic life determined by the production relations of socialist public ownership made it possible to produce goods according to social production within the overall society. It was necessary and feasible to allocate social labor or economic resources consciously, uniformly, and systematically according to the law of balanced development. In the

---

1. Marx and Engels, *Complete Works of Marx and Engels,* vol. 23 (People's Publishing House, 1972), 96.

socialist mode of production, the public ownership of the means of production eliminated the contradiction between the socialization of production and private ownership of the means of production and eliminated the factors of exploitation and fundamental conflicts of interest in social and economic relations, interest relations, and distribution relations, and it ensured that the fundamental interests of workers were consistent. In a socialist economy, the consistency of the fundamental interests of workers and the development of the socialization of production connected social and economic activities into a whole, to a certain extent. The unity and integrity of the socialist economy, on the one hand, required unified planned management and regulation of social production, while also providing feasible conditions for society to manage and regulate the national economy in a unified and planned way. Therefore, the nature of socialist public ownership determined the characteristics of socialist social and economic interest relations, and then determined the specific forms of economic management and operation system suitable for this social interest relationship. At the micro level, the planned economic system meant that the production units, as part of the national economy, obeyed the state's regulation, guidance, and management, while at the macro level, the national economy operated in accordance with the unified plan reflecting the social will and the overall interests of the entire society, striving for balanced development.

The theoretical basis of the planned economy was the law of planned, proportional development of the national economy and the related categories of public ownership of the means of production and distribution according to work. Before the 1970s, Chinese political and economic circles had different opinions on the law of planned, proportional development of the national economy. Generally speaking, based on the logic of normative research, the economic conditions for planned, proportional development were socialized mass production and public ownership of the means of production. Because the socialist economy was socialized, mass production was carried out, the public ownership of the means of production was implemented, and planned, proportional development needed to be the unique economic law of socialism. There were also views on the separation of "planned" and "according to proportion," which held that "planned" was the subjective will of humans, not an objective economic law, while "proportionality" was a requirement of objective economic development and the economic law of large-scale socialized production. The superiority of the socialist system lay in consciously applying this law to guide economic development.[2] At that time, there were also some views on the relationship between the law of value and the law of planned proportionality. If the law of value and the law of planned, proportional development reflected the economic law of different social forms, they were contradictory. The law of planned, proportional development was in nature socialist and communist, while the law of value was by nature part of the commodity economy and capitalism. The socialist economy was dominated by the law of planned, proportional development, but not

---

2. Editorial Department of *Economic Research* and *Economic Trends*, *Debates on the Important Issues of Political Economics Since the Founding of the People's Republic of China (1949–1980)* (China Financial and Economic Publishing House, 1981), 110–113.

by the law of value. In a socialist society, the reason the law of value should be used was that state planning could not cover everything, while the law of value could only be used, but not function as the main basis for arranging the proportion of plans.[3] Regarding the relationship between the planned commodity economy and the law of value, there were also views that both could coexist under socialist conditions. When obeying the basic socialist economic law, these two economic laws acted on different aspects and different processes of social production. They restricted each other and reflected the characteristics of social production development from different aspects.[4] These views and opinions reflected the normative research method adopted for the political economics research at that time, which logically advanced from concept to concept, had dialectical characteristics of speculation, and gave the abstract conclusion of "what should be." This type of research method formed a kind of traditional acculturation, which affected the thinking mode and research practices of Chinese economic and ideological circles over a long period of time. In the 1950s, Chen Yun put forward the idea of "combining the main body and the supplementary mode" of the planned economy and market regulation from the perspective of national economic operations. In September 1956, Chen Yun proposed the idea of combining the planned economy with market regulation in his speech "New Problems After the Basic Completion of the Socialist Transformation." He proposed the mode of a "combination of subject and supplement," which was of operational significance in actual economic operations. At that time, Sun Yefang proposed that the law of planned, proportional development and the law of value were a unity of opposites. The planned, proportional development of the national economy needed to be based on the law of value. In discussing the law of planned, proportional development without the law of value, absolutizing planned, proportional development, especially if the proportion of departments was not regarded as the balance of social necessary labor among various production departments, which would violate the principle of equal value exchange. As a result, the tendency would be to go to the opposite side of the law of planned, proportional development.[5] Sun Yefang's discussion on the relationship between the law of planned proportion and the law of value had theoretical depth, given the historical conditions at that time.

Public ownership of the means of production was an important theoretical category and practical basis of the planned economy. When the People's Republic of China was founded in 1949, the new democratic economy was mainly composed of five economic components, the state-owned economy, the cooperative economy, the state-owned capitalist economy, the private capitalist economy, and the individual economy, with the state-owned economy taking the leading position. During the recovery period of the national economy from 1949 to 1952, the basic economic policy of "giving consideration to both public and private affairs, benefiting both

---

3. Yu Lin, "Commodities of Socialist Society," *New Construction*, no. 6 (1965); Xue Muqiao, "Further Discussion on Planned Economy and Value Law," *Planned Economy* (February 1957).

4. Editorial Department of *Economic Research* and *Economic Trends*, *Debates on the Important Issues of Political Economics Since the Founding of the People's Republic of China (1949–1980)* (China Financial and Economic Publishing House, 1981), 170.

5. Sun Yefang, *Some Theoretical Issues of Socialist Economy* (People's Publishing House, 1979), 12, 13, 331.

labor and capital, mutual assistance between urban and rural areas, and internal and external exchanges" was carried out. Under the leadership of the state-owned economy, all kinds of economic components had their own division of labor and cooperation. The Common Program of the Chinese People's Political Consultative Conference adopted on September 29, 1949, defined the status and role of various economic components in the national economy and established the basic policies of the Communist Party of China for the non-public sectors of the economy, such as the private sector and foreign capital. That is to say, it made full use of and gave full play to the positive role of private capital in the national economy and people's livelihood to promote the overall recovery and development of the national economy. At the same time, it was necessary to restrict the parts that were not conducive to the national economy and the people's livelihood, bring the non-public economy into the correct development track, and make all kinds of social and economic components work and cooperate under the leadership of the state-owned economy, so as to promote the development of the overall social economy.

From 1953, the policy on the non-public economy began to change. At that time, the general line and general task of the socialist transition period was put forward, noting that it was "to gradually realize the socialist industrialization of the country and gradually realize the socialist transformation of agriculture, handicraft industry, capitalist industry, and commerce" over a fairly long period of time.[6] The essence of the Party's general line in the transitional period was to make the socialist ownership of the means of production the only economic basis for the nation and society.[7] From 1953 to 1957, the composition of China's national economy became increasingly singular. After 1962, individual industries and other types of economic components in urban and rural areas disappeared from the statistical data, and a single public ownership structure (all the people and the collective) was formed. According to statistics from 1978, the total industrial output value of the entire country was 77.6% for the economy owned by all the people and 22.4% for the collective economy, and the figures for individual industry and other economic components were zero.[8] From the 1950s to the 1970s, decision-makers and theorists believed that the elimination of private ownership and the implementation of socialist public ownership would inevitably lead to the leapfrog development of social productive forces. Productive forces, relations of production, mode of production, and other categories were important concepts discussed and studied by political and economic circles at that time. It was a common understanding among economic and ideological circles, and the policy aimed to promote the development of productive forces by changing the relations of production.

China's policy and theory of socialist transformation was also affected by the industrial path, the mode of ownership, and the economic system of the Soviet Union. Mao Zedong pointed out, "The purpose of the socialist revolution is to liberate productive forces. Agriculture and the handicraft industry have changed from individual ownership to socialist collective ownership, and

---

6. Mao Zedong, *Collected Works of Mao Zedong*, vol. 6 (People's Publishing House, 1999), 61.

7. Mao Zedong, *Collected Works of Mao Zedong*, vol. 6 (People's Publishing House, 1999), 316.

8. Yang Yonghua, "Empirical Analysis and Theoretical Enlightenment on the Evolution of China's Ownership Structure in the Past 50 Years," *Journal of Tianjin Normal University*, no. 2 (2000).

private industry and commerce have changed from capitalist ownership to socialist ownership, which will inevitably liberate productive forces. In this way, the social conditions have been created for the great development of industrial and agricultural production."[9] In the propaganda from this period, the Central Committee of the Communist Party of China also emphasized that "only when the transition from private ownership of the means of production to socialist ownership has been completed will the situation be conducive to the rapid development of social productive forces and a technological revolution."[10]

The ownership structure was related to the economic operations system. The single public ownership structure determined that the allocation of resources was realized through centralized decision-making and planned allocation, and the economic system was shown to be a planned economy. The multiple ownership structure determined that the allocation of resources was realized through decentralized decision-making and market allocation, and the economic system was represented by the market economy.

Distribution according to work was also an important theoretical category related to the law of the planned, proportional development of the national economy. Distribution according to work was considered the principle of material benefit distribution under the condition of public ownership of the means of production. Under the condition of public ownership of the means of production, the only factor of production that people used to exchange the means of living was labor. It was generally believed that the principle of distribution according to work reflected the combination of public and personal interests among the working people, which was conducive to improving the workers' production enthusiasm and meeting the material interests of the working people. Therefore, it was an objective economic law of socialism. But there were some controversies and puzzles in the theory and operation of the category of distribution according to work. In theory, there were different opinions on distribution according to work and equalitarianism, the legal basis of distribution according to work (involving the individual ownership of labor force or part of labor individual ownership), distribution according to work and "bourgeois rights." In practice, the measurement of distribution according to work, distribution according to work and production efficiency, comparison of different types of labor of different natures, and the consideration relationship between distribution according to work and monetary wage all lacked specific standard scientific methods. Therefore, from the perspective of factor participation in distribution, distribution according to work was a realistic economic category, because in the planned economic system of public ownership of the means of production, the only exchange condition for workers to obtain the means of living was labor. However, from the perspective of economic theory, distribution according to work, as the objective economic law or theoretical basis of the socialist planned economy, had some disputes and contradictions at the level of both normative and empirical research.

---

9. Mao Zedong, *Collected Works of Mao Zedong*, vol. 7 (People's Publishing House, 1999), 1.

10. Party History Teaching and Research Office of the Party School of the CPC Central Committee, *Reference Materials for the History of the CPC (8)* (People's Publishing House, 1980), 45.

2. The Law of Value as the Theoretical Basis of Economic Research and Economic System Reform

The Third Plenary Session of the Eleventh Central Committee of the Communist Party of China re-established the ideological line of emancipating the mind and seeking truth from facts and opened the process of Reform and Opening Up. Ideological and theoretical circles broke through the theory of only production relations and established the historical materialist concept of determining the nature of the economic system, economic relations, and economic interests according to the development level of productive forces and the objective requirements of developing productive forces. Under the guidance of the spirit of the Third Plenary Session of the Eleventh Central Committee of the Communist Party of China and the ideological and theoretical guidance of the preliminary stage of socialism, the study of political economics made breakthroughs in a series of theoretical categories, especially in shifting the mainstream economic theory from the law of planned, proportional development to the law of value.

From the 1980s to the early 1990s, with the promotion of China's economic system reform from the "planned economy as the main task and market regulation as the supplement" to the "planned commodity economic system," the overall economic system gradually transformed from the law of planned, proportional development to the law of value. The socialist planned commodity economic system was based on commodity exchange and the value law. Planning was to be realized through the law of value, and the law of value was to be used to serve the planned economy. The socialist planned commodity economic system and operation mechanism were the combination of the planned economy and market regulation. The scope of action of plan and market covered society overall. In line with the practice of economic system reform, the main theoretical line of China's socialist political economics had also transformed from the law of planned, proportional development to the law of value. Starting from the theoretical category of the value law, the general law of the commodity economy and market regulation, it examines the relationship between planning and market in the socialist economy, as well as the relationship between socialist ownership, distribution, and economic operations.

From the perspective of the history of thought, there were outstanding research results in China's socialist political economics in the 1950s and the 1960s, which linked the socialist economy with commodity production and the law of value. However, from the 1950s to the 1970s, these ideas and views did not constitute the theoretical basis or mainstream views of China's socialist political economics. At that time, the mainstream was the Soviet Union's political economic model. The theoretical basis was the basic socialist economic law, that is, the law of planned, proportional development. Like that based on the normative study, this understanding also had some theoretical logic. From the perspective of abstract theoretical analysis, the planned economy was the characteristic of the socialist production mode and the embodiment of the socialist essential interest relationship on the level of economic operations. Although the routine of normative research had its own theoretical logic, the logical inference and speculative conclusion from concept to concept were separated from the real economy and had no explanatory function.

At that time, the mainstream view of political economics was divorced from the reality of its economic foundation. China's socialist mode of production was not established on the basis of the full development of the commodity economy, but on the basis of the natural economy and the small-scale production economy. This foundation of social productive forces determined that China's socialist mode of production was not a socialism with a highly developed socialized mass production, direct possession of the means of production, and the highly unified economic interests of all members of society as envisioned by classical Marxist writers. Therefore, China did not have a highly centralized, unified planned economic system as described by these writers. In addition to the subjective assumption of socialized mass production, there was another subjective assumption of political economics based on the law of planned, proportional development, that is, there was no fundamental difference or conflict of interests among the micro subjects of society, but a high degree of consistency of interests was maintained. However, in the real economy, the interest difference, interest conflict, and interest pursuit among micro subjects existed objectively. It was not practical to try to replace the pursuit of individual interests with the pursuit of overall unified social interests.

The theory of the preliminary stage of socialism clarified that China was in the developing stage of backward productive forces and an underdeveloped commodity economy. The basic task was to vigorously develop productive forces and realize the commercialization, socialization, and modernization of industrialization and production. The basic economic system must adapt to the basic national conditions, reform the planned economic system, and develop the commodity economy. In a general sense, the essence of the commodity economy was that independent commodity producers in the natural social division of labor system met their daily needs through the exchange of labor products. In this kind of exchange relation, the common rule was equivalent exchange. Equivalent exchange was the objective rule of market activities, which reflected the relationship between the economic interests of market subjects and the law of value. The law of value was the law that market supply and demand regulated the spontaneous equilibrium of social production. It was noted that "the law of value of commodities determines how much time society can spend in producing each special commodity in the total labor time it dominates."[11] If the value of all economic goods was abstracted as labor, the allocation of labor time determined the quantity and value of each special commodity. In the commodity economy, the law of value regulated the economic activities and economic operation of market subjects through market mechanisms (market price determined by the relationship between supply and demand). In the preliminary stage of socialism, in order to realize the commercialization, socialization, and modernization of industrialization and production, to develop the commodity economy, and to construct the planned commodity economic system and operation mechanism, political economics had to take the law of value as the basic theory, and the law of value and market regulation in the socialist planned commodity economy would inevitably become the mainstream viewpoint and main idea of political economics.

---

11. Marx and Engels, *Complete Works of Marx and Engels*, vol. 23 (People's Publishing House, 1972), 394.

In the 1980s and early 1990s, China's economic thought and socialist political economics gradually shifted to a theory based on the law of value, which was related to the transformation of the economic system from a planned economy to a planned commodity economy. In the process of reform and transformation, at the operational level, discerning how to combine the planned economy with market regulation and how to effectively regulate the national economy were challenges for economic management and theoretical research. There were two representative views on this issue. The first point of view was the "plate combination theory" and the "penetration combination theory." The "plate model" referred to market regulation that was "out of plan" in the original unified planned economic system. This had been the opinion since the 1950s. The "penetration model" advocated that the two plates of plan and market penetrated each other. The regulation of planning needed to consider the requirements of the law of value, while market regulation was to be guided and restricted by the macro plan. The second representative point of view was the "organic combination theory," which held that planning and market were not separately regulating the two parallel plates of different parts of the national economy, but were organically integrated to regulate the operations of the national economy at different levels. The plan mainly regulated the macro level, while the market mainly regulated the micro level. However, macroeconomic balance should be based on market supply and demand, and microeconomics should be guided by the plan. Others included the "general and special combination theory," the "basic and leading function combination theory," the "twice regulation theory," and the "three-dimensional cross network mode."[12] The discussion at that time can be summed up in two ways. The first was a discussion on how to combine the planned economy and market regulation in the plane space design, that is, how to combine the two in the plane planning of economic operation. The other was how to combine the planned economy with market regulation in three-dimensional space design, that is, to plan the "connection point" of the combination of the two at the level of economic operations, such as the planned economy governing the macro operation and the market regulating micro operations. These discussions were not lacking in insight, and sought to reflect the operability in the framework of the policy system at that time. However, the real economy showed that the "double track system" in economic management and operation led to economic phenomena such as the failure of the planning system, the failure of market regulation, a lack of control of the total amount, and the waste of resources. Moreover, exchanging "planned" and "out of plan" under the same market criterion would inevitably lead to the prevalence of "speculating" and "private profiteering," serious monopoly and market segmentation, and the coexistence of an overheated economy and low economic efficiency caused

---

12. Editorial Department of *Economic Research, Review and Prospect of China's Socialist Economic Theory* (China Economic Press, 1986); Wu Jinglian, "Discussion on the Relationship Between Planning and Market and the Direction of China's Economic System Reform," *Reform*, no. 1 (1991); Xiong Jun, "Comments on the Ten Outlooks of the Combination of the Planned Economy and Market Regulation," *Contemporary Finance and Economy*, no. 4 (1991); Yu Zuyao, "A Review of the Discussion on the Relationship Between Planning and Market in Recent Years," *Economic Trends*, no. 3 (1991); Shen Shanqing, "An Overview of Some Controversial Views Put Forward by Current Economic Theorists," *Social Science Review*, no. 4 (1991).

by repeated investment and construction. Therefore, in order to break through the theoretical and operational difficulties of the combination of the planned economy and market regulation, it was important to develop new theoretical ideas and the theoretical guidance of a new economic system reform. This theoretical consideration and guidance was summarized in the idea that the operation of the planned commodity economic system was based on the market mechanism.

The economic system was an economic operation and management system determined by a certain mode of social production, including a certain structure of production and interest relations and a certain mode of economic management and operations. The management and operation of the economic system was based on the corresponding economic mechanism. The economic mechanism was directly related to productive forces and social and economic interests. In the general sense, the process of social and economic movement was the process in which people used economic resources, through labor and exchange, to meet people's needs for different use values. In this process, in order to realize their special economic interests through labor and exchange activities, it was important to follow the laws or principles of economic activity. Therefore, economic interests constituted the basic motive or goal of economic behavior. Through people's pursuit of economic interests, all kinds of economic behaviors were linked, all kinds of economic activities were coordinated, and the way to promote the running of the social economy in a certain way was the economic mechanism. The economic mechanism was essentially a kind of interest incentive and restriction mechanism that was directly related to the people's pursuit of economic interests. As the operation mechanism of the commodity economy, the market mechanism was the concrete form of the function of the law of value. In the commodity economy, the interest difference among members of society determined the need for exchange and the coordination of various economic activities. This required the use of the law of value and the market mechanism through the stimulation and restriction of people's special economic interests to regulate their economic behavior, followed by regulation of social and economic operations. In a socialist commodity economy, economic operations needed to follow the objective requirements of the law of value, take value as the measurement scale, take equivalent exchange as the objective rule of economic activities, use a series of economic means and economic levers conforming to the law of value from the inside of the market process, and regulate the people's economic behavior through the stimulation and restriction of economic interests, and then regulate its social economic function. As a result, the operation of the socialist planned commodity economy was based on the market mechanism. The significance of this theoretical concept not only marked the transformation of the theoretical basis of political economics, but also prompted the evolution of China's economic system reform path to move toward a socialist market economy.

3. The Transformation of the Economic Thought Paradigm with the Close Combination of Economic Theory and the Real Economy

In the 1980s and early 1990s, the field of economic theory shifted from normative research on some broad concepts to the combination of classical theory and China's practice of Reform and

Opening Up to study a series of practical economic problems. The research content, research methods, theoretical framework, and other aspects began to shift from normative research to empirical research, which was more related to the real economy and had more applicability and explanatory power as a research paradigm transformation. During this period, there were two representative research fields, the relationship between public ownership and the commodity economy, which derived from the research on the reform of property rights and state-owned enterprises, and the distribution relationship in the socialist commodity economy, which led to a new study of labor value theory. These two research fields were interrelated in the reform of the socialist commodity economic system.

Because the law of value and the function of the market mechanism were connected to the micro basis of the commodity economy, economic theorists at that time were confused about the relationship between the market mechanism and public ownership, ownership of the means of production and the ownership and distribution of labor products. From the abstract level of simple commodity production, some theorists held that if the law of value and the natural law of market mechanism were recognized and each market subject was required to participate in market activities as an independent interest subject, then the public ownership of the means of production had to be changed, because only when the individual laborer owned both the means of production and labor products could there be independent interest subjects or market subjects in the full sense. Based on the established institutional conditions of public ownership, some theorists held that since the law of value and market mechanism were incompatible with public ownership, the role of the market mechanism in a socialist economy should be limited or not recognized, and they even questioned the concept of the socialist commodity economy.[13] At that time, the root of some differing opinions was similarly based on the basic categories of traditional socialist political economics as the relationship among independent interest subject, market mechanism, and ownership of means of production was discussed. However, this type of research method could not explain the actual needs of economic reform, nor could it provide theoretical support and thinking for economic reform. The study of economic theory had to proceed from the reality of economic reform and economic development, break through some traditional categories and viewpoints, and develop some new theoretical viewpoints in order to give the theory explanatory power.

By discussing the commodity economy not only in view of the ownership relationship, but also of the deeper social division of labor, it was possible to have a more realistic understanding of the socialist commodity economy. The independent interest subject was the abstract of simple commodity production, which referred to the commodity producer who produced independently with his own means of production to obtain labor products and exchange his labor products for his own production and living materials through market exchange. This concept had two meanings, the relationship between people's production activities and the ownership of means

---

13. Li Bin, "A Summary of the Symposium on the Combination of Socialist Public Ownership and the Commodity Economy," *Chinese Social Sciences*, no. 5 (1991).

of production and labor products, and the relationship between people's private and social labor. It was in this sense that the independent interest subject became the micro foundation of the commodity economy. The two meanings of the concept of independent interest subject were related to the contradictions caused by the social division of labor, which is the realistic basis of the commodity economy. There were two contradictions caused by the social division of labor. One was the contradiction between different kinds of specific labor, that is, if various use values did not contain useful labor of different qualities, they could not be used as commodities to oppose each other. The other was the contradiction of distribution relations caused by different forms of ownership of the means of production. The former stipulated the division of labor and the difference of the use value produced by the laborer, while the latter prescribed the laborer's production through different means of production and working conditions, and thus the distribution relations were determined. The social division of labor and the form of ownership were fundamentally determined by the development of social productive forces. In the primary stage of socialism in China, decided by the social division of labor, the laborer was subordinate to the social division system (i.e., the individual labor becomes a part of the social division system) and was relatively separated in property relations (i.e., the labors could not "jointly" own the means of production and labor products in a full sense, and the individual interests and "common" interests of the workers was not completely unified). Therefore, in a certain sense, the workers in the socialist economy became relatively independent interest subjects, and the law of value and market mechanism had to be linked with the personal economic interests of workers and play a role in order to regulate the operation of the social economy.

The discussion on the relationship between public ownership and the commodity economy led to the reform of state-owned property rights relations. A logical way of thinking about it was to seek to improve the micro basis of the operation of the socialist commodity economy, which meant that enterprises must become independent commodity producers with independent management, profits and losses, and development, and to make enterprises become independent commodity producers, it was necessary to give the property rights of enterprises a direct relationship with the operators and producers of enterprises, so that their economic interests and the enterprise's economic benefits had a direct relationship, making them bear the corresponding property rights responsibility for the effect of their own economic activities. Therefore, it was necessary to adjust the current property rights system and form a stable, effective property rights restriction relationship among the state, enterprises, and employees (including operators), so as to improve the operation efficiency of the socialist commodity economy. In the system reform and theoretical discussion of the socialist commodity economy, the reform of state-owned property rights system was carried out according to the idea of "separation of ownership and management rights." The theoretical significance of the separation of the two powers was to explain that the relationship between state-owned enterprises and the state (government) was the relationship between producers and operators and asset owners (representatives), and it was an economic contract relationship between different economic entities, rather than an administrative subordination relationship. The separation of the two powers was a development of the former "government enterprise integration" management system of state-owned enterprises. To a certain extent, it stimulated the enthusiasm of enterprise managers and producers and improved enterprise efficiency, but more importantly, it made the operation behavior and interest pursuit of state-owned enterprises approach the nature of a market subject in the commodity economic system to a certain extent, so as to ensure that the value law and market mechanism could play a regulating role in the commodity economy. The idea of separation of two powers was to apply the theory of "principal-agent" from Western economics, seeking to make management rights independent of ownership. But the principal-agent relationship in the modern enterprise system was different from the separation of two powers in the state-owned enterprise system. The key to the transformation of the management mechanism of state-owned enterprises was to make the enterprises become independent subjects of property rights. Being independent subjects of property rights meant that the ownership, management rights, and income rights of enterprise assets were unified, forming a complete property rights restriction. At that time, economic theorists generally believed that the ownership of assets and the ownership of legal persons of enterprises were two kinds of rights that could be separated from each other. The ownership of assets was embodied in the right of return on assets, while the ownership of legal persons was reflected in the right to operate assets. In fact, the ownership of assets and the ownership of legal persons were only different forms of the same right, not two separate rights. "Legal entity" was a concept corresponding to "natural person," which meant that the personality of an association was established in accordance with legal standards and was a concept of civil and commercial registration. The concept of "legal person ownership" was not accurate, let alone a right "separated" from the ownership of assets, which could be antagonistic toward and juxtaposed with the ownership of assets. In the modern enterprise system, the operator of an enterprise was the employer of capital who performed the management function, but did not have the right to operate. The management decision-making power of an enterprise (company) was controlled by the board of directors, because the asset management right was directly related to the asset ownership and income rights, and they belonged to the same property rights subject. In the reform of the socialist commodity economic system, although the management of state-owned assets and state-owned enterprises adopted the form of separation of two powers, the nature of the relationship between assets and property rights did not change. The defects of state-owned enterprises, such as insufficient vitality, weak property rights restrictions, and low efficiency, were not fundamentally eliminated, and new problems were introduced, such as "insider control" and short-term management behavior caused by the separation of powers. The reform of the state-owned property rights system and state-owned enterprises was a process closely related to the reform of the economic system. Economic theorists realized that in order to improve the socialist commodity economic system, a very important issue was straightening out the relationship between property rights and interests between the state and state-owned enterprises, to give the operators and producers of state-owned enterprises a certain relationship with the property rights of enterprises, give the relationship between state-owned asset managers and state-owned enterprise managers the nature of an economic contract, so that the benefits of business operations were directly related to the operators and producers. This kind of research was closely combined with the real economy, and it sought to produce operational ideas, which reflected the characteristics of the transformation of political economics in this period.

In connection with the practice of developing the socialist commodity economy, economic theorists carried out in-depth research on the interest relationship, distribution relationship, and distribution mode of the socialist commodity economy. An important aspect of this research field was to study the evolution of some categories and concepts of Marxist labor value theory in connection with the real economy, so as to make the theory more explanatory. In the study of the connotation evolution of "labor," it was recognized that the connotation of "productive labor" should be evolved from the production of material products to the use value of production. With the development of social demand, the use value takes the form of material and non-material ones. The use value of meeting non-material needs was the non-material form. As long as the use value produced by labor could meet the social needs, then this sort of labor created value. The labor value theory was an objective value theory. Objective value theory analyzed the origin of value creation from the supply side. However, it seemed to ignore the fact that supply and demand are inseparable, and without demand, there is no supply. In the period of the planned economy, social production was arranged from the perspective of supply, and the value production of the overall society was evaluated with the statistical index of "total output value of industry and agriculture," which made the production unable to meet social demand. In the study of value theory, even if the demand is abstracted when analyzing the source of value, then the evaluation result of supply should not fall on the material products or tangible products, but on the use value. The result of supply is not only the production of material products, but also the production of use value, because what meets the demand is not "products," but the use value of products. The use value is not always attached to the material (tangible) products, but also to the non-material (intangible) products. Labor creates wealth, the carrier of wealth is the use value, and the measurement scale of wealth is value. If restricted by the distinction between the material and non-material form of use value, excluding the labor of the tertiary industry from value creation will affect the measurement of social wealth and restrict the development of social demand.

This research on the evolution of the relationship between value creation and value distribution and between distribution according to work and the participation of production factors in distribution, to a certain extent, demonstrates that theories and concepts were innovated according to the development of the real economy. After Reform and Opening Up, the egalitarian distribution management system with administrative means as the main means in the planned economy period was gradually changed, and the market incentive and competition factors, especially the factors participating in the distribution, gradually became the basic adjustment mechanism of individual income distribution. After this change, the income sources of residents were diversified, and the income gap expanded. In connection with this economic reality, the study of distribution theory in political economics demonstrated an evolutionary process from a single, purely conceptual study of distribution according to work to the study of distribution according to work supplemented by other modes of distribution, and then to the combination of distribution according to work and distribution according to factors. According to Marxist economic theory, the basis of production factors participating in value distribution is not that they create value, but that they are the conditions for value creation. Value creation and value distribution are two separate issues. It is an essential problem that value comes from labor. The transformation of value into production price only involves value distribution, not value creation. Assuming that the value of the total social product consists of $C + V + M$, value distribution focuses on the compensation of C and the division of V and M, while value creation focuses on the source of value and the attribution of M. Marx's concept of social necessary labor time also includes production conditions. The socially necessary labor time, which determines the amount of commodity value, is "the labor time required to produce a certain use value under the normal production conditions of the existing society and under the average social proficiency and labor intensity." The "production conditions" here include "materialized labor" and production factors. Since production factors are the conditions of value production, they should participate in value distribution. But with the development of China's social economy, the scope of production factors also expanded. As new production factors, science and technology, business ability, knowledge, and information and innovation ability became the conditions of value production, and they also naturally became the basis of distribution. Factor owners participated in distribution by virtue of their possession of the production factors that participated in value production. This was the evolution form of distribution according to work in contemporary China's mode of production, which reflected the reality that distribution according to work was the main mode, while various distribution modes coexisted alongside it in the socialist commodity economy.

The operation mechanism of distribution according to work was that "equal work gets equal reward," which not only embodied the fair principle of taking labor time as a unified yardstick, but also embodied the efficiency principle of "more work, more pay." Fairness and efficiency is a classic proposition of income distribution. Efficiency is related to the "necessary condition" of economic growth and growth rate, while fairness is related to the "sufficient condition" that most people in society have the right to benefit from economic growth. Fairness and average are two different concepts. Average means that everyone gets equal income (average result), which is the physical quantity in distribution. It puts forward a hypothetical standard to compare with actual distribution. Fairness is the psychological quantity in distribution, which mainly investigates whether the rights in the distribution relationship are equal. Fairness emphasizes the equality of opportunity and right, but it allows for uneven results caused by the differences in ability, effort, and innovation ability. In this sense, there is a great consistency between fairness and efficiency. The distribution according to work in a socialist society is a natural privilege because of the acquiescence of different talents of individuals. The economic condition that connects the individual's talent with his economic interests is the social division of labor. In other words, as long as there is a social division of labor, different personal talents of workers, and thus different labor capacity, there is a kind of natural privilege. This kind of natural privilege will not lead to an average distribution result, but it is in line with the fair principle of distribution according to work. The distribution principle of giving priority to efficiency with due consideration to fairness not only opposes equalitarianism, but also pays attention to the expansion of the income gap.

Equalitarianism and a widening income gap are both manifestations of unfair distribution.

From the 1980s to the early 1990s, China's socialist political economics adapted to Reform and Opening Up and the requirements of economic system reform. Research on economic theory was closely combined with the operation of the real economy, paying more attention to and studying real economic problems and showing the transformation of the paradigm of economic research from normative research to empirical analysis.

6.2 The Research and Innovation of Marxist Economics and Socialist Economic Theory

1. An Extended Study of Traditional Theoretical Issues

From 1979 to 1992, the economic thought and practice of economic system reform propelled one another and developed together. The economic thought of this period had the significance of connecting the past and the future. It not only inherited some theoretical characteristics of the previous period, but also opened a new stage of economic prosperity and scientific development. In the study of Marxist economics and socialist economic theory in this period, the Soviet paradigm no longer constituted a development guide, but in studies of the classic theory of Marxism, it was combined with the practice of China's socialist economic development for new exploration and theoretical innovation. From the content of theoretical research, although there were still many discussions on principles, concepts, and definitions in this period, research on the real economy was expanding all the time. From the perspective of research methods, normative analysis remained the main method, but with the requirements of real economic research, the methods of empirical analysis and quantitative analysis were gradually adopted and given increasing attention. In terms of the academic atmosphere, the vague, metaphysical style was overcome, and a scientific, practical, objective attitude gradually developed. As a result, study of Marxist economics and socialist economic theory in China was more in line with real economic sciences. Economic and ideological circles extended the traditional theoretical categories such as the basic socialist economic law, the law of planned development of the national economy, distribution according to work, and the theory of labor value.

The basic economic laws of socialism were discussed from the 1950s to the 1960s, but the research and discussion in the 1980s put forward some new viewpoints from a new angle.

Primarily, some theorists raised the fundamental question of whether the basic economic law of socialism expressed by Stalin was valid, and there were two opinions on this matter in theoretical circle. The first held that there was no basic economic law in a socialist economy, pointing out that the theoretical premise of the basic economic law proposed by Stalin was wrong. At the same time, it held that the content of the basic economic law of socialism was unscientific. An important manifestation was that it emphasized the use of value to meet the needs and exclude value, which contradicted the need of the commodity economy produced for value. The second group held that Stalin's socialist basic economic law existed objectively, pointing out that since the public ownership economy occupied a dominant position in the national economy, the basic socialist economic law existed objectively.[14]

The content of the basic economic law of socialism was also discussed. With regard to the connotation of the basic socialist economic law, one view held that the basic socialist economic law included the purpose of production and the means to achieve it, while the other held that the basic socialist economic law only included the purpose of production, not the means to achieve it. There were three opinions on the expression of the basic socialist economic law. The first was that Stalin's expression of the basic socialist economic law was scientific, including not only the reasonable combination of science and technology and productivity, but also the idea of correctly handling the relations of production. The second was that Stalin's expression of the basic socialist economic law was too generalized and abstract. The third opinion was that Stalin's expression of the basic economic law of socialism had serious defects, in that it overlooked the fact that the all-round development of human beings was the ultimate goal of socialist production and did not propose that the way to realize the goal of socialist production was to improve economic efficiency.[15]

In addition, there was further development in the understanding of the basic economic law of socialism. The first view was that the law of value was the basic economic law of socialism, because in any society, as long as there was commodity production, the basic economic law of this society was the law of value. The second view was that the law of necessary value was the basic law of the socialist economy. The so-called necessary value referred to the value of new production after deducting the transfer value from the commodity value, which was equivalent to the V + M part of the commodity value equation. According to the third opinion, the law of distribution according to work was the basic economic law of socialism. Some also held that the relative independence of the interests of the state, enterprises, and workers was the basic law of the socialist economy.[16]

In the 1980s, economic circle studied the law of planned development of the national economy from three aspects. One was study of whether the law of planned development of the national economy existed. Some scholars held that the planned development law of the national economy did not exist, and the subjective plan could not play the role of an objective economic law. There were others who believed that the planned development of the national economy was an objective economic law. The law of planned, proportional development of the national economy based on the social division of labor existed in various social forms as a basic social law. However, the manifestation of this law in different social forms was not the same. Another point of view was

---

14. Editorial Department of *Economic Research, Contention on China's Socialist Economic Theory (1985–1989)* (China Financial and Economic Publishing House, 1991).

15. Editorial Department of *Economic Research, Debate on the Theoretical Issues of China's Socialist Economy (1985–1989)* (China Financial and Economic Publishing House, 1991).

16. Editorial Department of *Economic Research, Debate on the Theoretical Issues of China's Socialist Economy (1985–1989)* (China Financial and Economic Publishing House, 1991).

that the law of planned development of the national economy not only had objectivity, but was also a unique law of socialism. The second approach was to study the difference and connections between the law of planned development of the national economy and the law of value. One view was that the law of planned development of the national economy was not opposed to the law of value. The former was a form of action of the latter. Another view was that under the condition of a planned commodity economy, the law of planned development of the national economy and the law of value were neither mutually exclusive nor identical, and the functions of the two laws could not replace each other.[17]

In the 1980s, the research on distribution according to work was mainly carried out from two perspectives. One was the meaning of the law of distribution according to work, and the other was whether labor force was a commodity and its relationship with the law of distribution according to work. The discussion mainly focused on labor commodity. Under the premise that the labor force was a commodity, some people believed that distribution according to work was the distribution of labor value. Others disagreed with this idea.[18] Some theorists held to the idea of distribution according to work from the perspective of equal labor exchange under the condition of commodity production. Equal labor exchange, or the exchange of a certain amount of labor in one form with equal labor in another form, was proposed by Marx in the theory of distribution according to work. In Marx's theory, this type of labor was the direct socialized labor which had eliminated commodity production, that is, labor that did not need to go through a tortuous road to take the form of value. However, the reality of social practice had proven that commodity production existed in the historical stage of socialism. Therefore, the labor consumed by producers in the production of products was bound to show the value of these products, and the amount of labor calculated by labor time must be the value of these products. The exchange of equivalents was actually the exchange of goods according to their exchange value. Exchange according to value was the exchange according to the social necessary labor, which was the exchange of a certain amount of labor in one form for the same amount of labor in another form. Here, equal labor exchange had all the characteristics of general equivalent exchange through the market, so it can be said to be a "new type of equivalent exchange."[19]

The research on the theory of labor value in the 1980s mainly focused on the "monism of labor value" and the "pluralism of value determination." The basic theoretical problem was the understanding of the social necessary labor time discussed by Marx. According to the monism of labor value theory, it was not the two meanings of social necessary labor time that determined

17. Editorial Department of *Economic Research, Review and Prospect of China's Socialist Economic Theory* (China Economic Press, 1986); Zhang Xunhua, ed., *The Contending Department of Social Sciences: Volume of Socialist Economic Theory* (Shanghai People's Publishing House, 1991); *Dictionary of Economic Sciences* (Economic Science Press, 1987).

18. Economic Editorial Office of *China's Social Sciences, Economics Works* (1980) (Zhejiang People's Publishing House, 1981); Economic Editorial Office of *China's Social Sciences, Economics Works* (1981) (Zhejiang People's Publishing House, 1982); Economic Editorial Office of *China's Social Sciences, Economics Works* (1982) (Zhejiang People's Publishing House, 1983).

19. Lin Zili, *On the New Equivalent Exchange* (Economic Science Press, 1987).

commodity value, but only the first meaning of social necessary labor time that determined value.[20] The opposite view held that Marx discussed two kinds of social necessary labor time in *Das Kapital*. The socially necessary labor time given in the first volume of *Das Kapital* highlighted the average of the labor time and investigated the value determination of a single commodity, while the socially necessary labor time mentioned in the third volume of *Das Kapital* referred to the total social necessary labor time of a commodity and analyzed the relationship between the necessary labor time of the total commodity and social needs.[21] Other theorists put forward the idea of "new labor value theory monism." They held that the traditional labor value theory monism could no longer explain the value decision in real life. It was thus necessary to expand the extension of labor on the basis of the original labor value theory monism and add capital, land, and other non-labor production factors, as well as the interest relationship under the technological change, to create a realistic description of the value decision. In *Das Kapital*, introducing labor commodity indicated that the capitalist's surplus value came from the free possession of the value created by the surplus labor of workers.[22] The reinterpretation of Marx's labor value theory directly took technological change as the premise to discuss the interaction between technology and interest rather than the Marxist addition of technological change to analysis of the capitalist interest relations. Therefore, the logical negation of Marx's labor theory of value did not constitute a denial of Marxist economics, but a new interpretation of it.

The research on the history of political and economic theories was an important area of study during this period. The most representative work was Chen Daisun's *From the Classical Economic School to Marx: A Brief Introduction to the Development of Some Major Theories*.[23] This book systematically discussed the historical relationship between Marxist economic theory and the classical economics school, the science of Marx's critical inheritance of classical economic theory, and the process of establishing proletarian political economics. It expounded the emergence and development of the theories of value, surplus value, reproduction, and economic crisis from the classical economic school to Marx. In addition, Chen edited the textbook *History of Political and Economic Theories* (Volume 1 and Volume 2).

2. New Expression and Research on Traditional Theories and Concepts

Socialist ownership was a theoretical category that had been studied before, but studying the reform of socialist ownership from the purpose of adapting to the development of socialist

---

20. Hu Xiaofeng and Han Shuying, *An Outline of the Discussion on China's Socialist Economic Issues* (Jilin People's Publishing House, 1983); Editorial Department of *Economic Research*, *Review and Prospect of China's Socialist Economic Theory* (China Economic Press, 1986); Song Tao, *Exploration of Socialist Economic Theory* (Beijing University of Technology Press, 1994).

21. Pan Shi, "On the Relationship Between Two Kinds of Socially Necessary Labor Time," *Economic Research*, no. 8 (1990).

22. Gu Shutang and Liu Xin, "Monism of New Labor Value Theory," *Chinese Social Sciences*, no. 6 (1993).

23. Chen Daisun, *From Classical Economic School to Marx: A Brief Introduction to the Development of Some Major Theories* (The Commercial Press, 2014).

commodity economy brought a new perspective to the topic. The consensus in theoretical circles was that in order to establish the micro basis for the operation of the socialist commodity economy, ownership reform must be carried out.[24] In terms of the basic principles of ownership reform, some held that the reform of ownership should be based on the principle of meeting the requirements of productivity level and development of productivity, while others believed that the principle of ownership reform should be adhering to the dominant position of public ownership. A third view was that the ownership structure that was both controllable and efficient was preferable.[25] In the research and discussion of the reform of socialist public ownership, the idea of "separation of ownership and management rights" and the concept of property rights were put forward. The idea of "separation of two powers" was a valuable, innovative theoretical concept in the discussion of ownership reform, and it became the theoretical basis of the reform policy for a period of time. Its direct practical form was the implementation of the enterprise contract system. Although this idea had some defects in theory and practice, it was a theoretical innovation and had great practical significance.

In October 1984, the Decision of the Central Committee of the Communist Party of China on the Reform of the Economic System formally proposed that China's socialist economy be "a planned commodity economy on the basis of public ownership." Around that time, the debate on whether there was commodity production in the past socialist economy shifted to the research stage of how to correctly understand the socialist planned commodity economy and how to establish this new system and mechanism.

Based on the understanding of the basic characteristics of the socialist economy, some people held that the basic feature of the socialist economy was a commodity economy. The socialist commodity economy and planned economy were not parallel concepts operating at the same level. Commodity was a more basic objective existence, while planning was a form or means of economic management. The second point of view was that the socialist economy was a market economy. The commodity economy was a market economy, and the commodity economy was the essence of a market economy, while the market economy was the phenomenon of a commodity economy. The third view was that the basic feature of the socialist economy was a planned economy. A planned economy was not only the way and means of managing the national economy, but also the essential attribute and characteristic of the socialist economy and an important aspect of the socialist economic system and production relations.[26]

---

24. Editorial Department of *Economic Research*, *Debate on the Theoretical Issues of China's Socialist Economy (1985–1989)* (China Financial and Economic Publishing House, 1991); Li Zezhong, *The Theory of Socialist Economy in Contemporary China* (China Social Sciences Press, 1989).

25. Editorial Department of *Economic Research*, *Debate on the Theoretical Issues of China's Socialist Economy (1985–1989)* (China Financial and Economic Publishing House, 1991).

26. Editorial Department of *Economic Research*, *Review and Prospect of China's Socialist Economic Theory* (China Economic Press, 1986); Hu Xiaofeng and Han Shuying, *Outline of Discussion on China's Socialist Economic Issues* (Jilin People's Publishing House, 1983).

In the 1980s, the theoretical research on the reform of China's state-owned enterprises entered a new level. Its focus shifted to how to transform state-owned enterprises into independent commodity producers and operators, how to fundamentally improve the operating efficiency of state-owned enterprises, and how to make state-owned enterprises become legal persons with corresponding rights and obligations. In the research on the reform of state-owned enterprises, the main contents included the separation of ownership and management rights, the separation of ownership and property rights, and the reform of state-owned enterprises. In terms of reform mode, the paper put forward several ideas, including a contract management responsibility system, a shareholding system, an asset management responsibility system, a leasing system, and the formation of enterprise groups through horizontal alliances. Most of these theoretical ideas applied to reform practice, such as the contract and shareholding systems, which became the main forms of reform during that time. The practicality of the reform of state-owned enterprises further promoted the development of theoretical research and became a new growth point of economic development in the 1980s and into the 1990s.

In the 1950s and the 1960s, the problem of industrial structure existed in the theoretical form of the proportion of "agriculture, light industry, and heavy industry" and the comprehensive balance of the national economy. From the 1980s, the concept of "economic structure" and "industrial structure" was adopted, and industrial policies were formulated at the macro level. Industrial structure theory involved the growth stage of industrial structure, the rationalization of industrial structure, the coordination mechanism of industrial structure, the development mode of industrial structure, the performance and causes of the imbalance in the industrial structure in China, and the adjustment measures of the industrial structure. The theory of industrial policy involved the goal of industrial policy, the strategy of industrial development, the transformation of industrial structure, the research of international industrial policy, and other areas. In the late 1980s and early 1990s, there were several ideas on the choice of China's industrial policies. The first was industrial policy ideas based on agriculture, the second was industrial policy ideas dominated by heavy industry, and the third was industrial policy ideas focusing on the mechanical and electrical industries and tertiary industry.[27]

3. Focus on New Economic Issues

The socialist economic law system was a popular topic in the 1980s. It mainly introduced some new ideas and constructed a "law system" of "interconnection and interaction" through logical deduction on the basis of several major socialist laws summarized in the Soviet *Political Economics Textbook*. The research on this topic was a typical normative analysis in methodology, and the "law system" constructed by it had its own theoretical system, but it had little connection with the real economy. After the mid-1990s, research on this topic gradually became indifferent.

---

27. *A Dictionary of China's System Reform and Opening Up, Volume of Economic System Reform* (Sichuan Science and Technology Press, 1992).

In the discussion of the socialist economic law in the 1980s, theoretical circles highlighted the problem of studying the economic law system, which became a new theoretical hotspot for a period of time. At that time, it was generally believed that the relations of production were an organic whole, so the laws reflecting the development process of the relations of production could not be isolated and unrelated. Economic laws were interrelated and unified. They could not be separated and studied in isolation. As for the expression of the socialist economic law system, some theorists proposed that the economic law system was a scientific reflection of the overall economic laws that existed objectively in a certain social and economic form and which interrelated and intersected with each other. This included three ideas. The first was that production relations were an organic whole and objectively constituted a system. The second was that the essential connection among all levels, sides, and fields in the system of production relations was an objective economic law. As the production relations were an organic whole, the laws of the movement and development of the relations of production were interrelated and intersected, and there was a certain connection between them. On this basis, the whole of the economic law was formed. The third was that the economic law system was a scientific system, which was a scientific summary of the internal relationship of the objective economic laws. There were some people who advocated the study of the economic law system using the method of modern systems theory. The socialist economic law system could be expressed as an organic whole of various economic laws that governed the interaction and interdependence of the operation and development of the socialist economy. Others believed that the expression should highlight its objectivity, connection, and integrity. Therefore, the system of socialist economic law was the organic whole of the economic laws that socialist society controlled the development of social and economic movements, which existed objectively, depended on each other, and interacted with each other.[28]

Business cycle was another category in the theory of economic growth, but before the 1980s, there was no research on it in China. In the 1980s, with the fluctuation of China's macro-economic growth, more attention was given to the theory of business cycles, and research in this area was gradually launched.

Business cycle was generally considered to refer to the continuous occurrence of an economic upsurge and low tides in the process of economic development. Although the growth rate of gross social output value or national income was an important sign of economic upsurge and recession, the growth speed was not always completely consistent with economic fluctuations. Therefore, the business cycle should include the comprehensive performance of various economic phenomena, which referred to the business cycle business cycle of the overall national economy. As for the similarities and differences between the socialist business cycle and the capitalist business cycle, the majority view was that they were a kind of imbalance of economic aggregates and there was no substantial difference between them, though some held that there were differences between the

---

28. Zhongnan University of Finance and Economics, *A Dictionary of Economic Sciences* (Economic Science Press, 1987); Li Zezhong, *Contemporary Chinese Socialist Economic Theory* (China Social Sciences Press, 1989); Jiang Xuemo, *Socialist Political Economics* (Fudan University Publishing House, 1987); Yang Wenhan, *An Outline of the History of Socialist Economic Theory* (Shaanxi People's Publishing House, 1988).

two. The essential difference lay in that the socialist business cycle would not necessarily lead to a comprehensive economic crisis, because the new economic balance could be controlled by the state plan, rather than by market means such as economic crisis. Many scholars devoted themselves to the empirical analysis of China's business cycle fluctuations. They conducted extensive, in-depth studies on the classification of business cycles, the inspection indicators of business cycles, the time division of business cycles, the characteristics of business cycle fluctuations, and the causes of business cycle formation, and they proposed many counter cyclical policy suggestions.[29]

In China, inflation was an economic and theoretical hot spot formed in the late 1980s. Before that, due to the planned control of prices, inflation did not exist in China (aside from "hidden inflation" in the form of voucher supply). With the deepening of economic reform, especially price reforms, the relationship between price, money supply, and the total social supply and demand became increasingly close. Inflation then appeared in China's economy, and research on inflation began.

Regarding the causes of inflation, some scholars believed that inflation referred to the economic phenomenon of excessive money in circulation and viewed it as a phenomenon of currency devaluation caused by the amount of money issued exceeding the actual demand of commodity circulation. Therefore, it was understood in terms of the rapid growth of money supply that caused inflation. Some scholars identified causes from the perspective of supply and demand, believing that inflation was caused by insufficient supply or aggregate demand. Other scholars believed that the cause of inflation was the imbalance of industrial structure and the imperfection of the economic system.

Among some scholars, the attitude toward inflation was that moderate inflation was acceptable. As long as the monetary expansion did not cause hyperinflation, and as long as moderate inflation could achieve a higher economic growth rate, there was theoretically room for exploring inflation to promote economic development. The shortage of commodity supply in developing countries did not necessarily prove that resources had been fully utilized. Therefore, inflation could improve the resource allocation structure and efficiency under certain conditions, thus promoting economic growth. However, a considerable number of scholars believed that inflation was harmful, not beneficial, because inflation could produce very little forced savings in China, and compared with normal savings, the gains were not worth the losses. At the same time, inflation was not conducive to the use of idle resources, but would only make the inventory of goods and materials exceed the normal needs of enterprises, make the supply more tense, and encourage people to seize more scarce materials, so inflation policy should not be adopted rashly.

In discussing ways to control inflation, theorists put forward several suggestions. First was the theory of aggregate deflation, that is, the control of the further expansion of aggregate demand through monetary tightening. Another suggestion centered around the theory of structural

---

29. Jiang Xuemo, "Characteristics of Socialist Macroeconomics," *Humanities Journal*, no. 6 (1989); Chen Xin, "Economic System Reform and New Exploration of Socialist Macroeconomics," *Economic Research*, no. 11 (1990); Fan Gang, Zhang Shuguang and Yang Zhongwei, "Two Operating Mechanisms of Public Ownership Economy," *Economic Research*, no. 5 (1990).

adjustment, which created a structural basis for the balance of total supply and demand by promoting the optimization of industrial structure. A third suggestion involved promoting the reform theory, which held that double institutional friction was the institutional cause of China's inflation. In combination with the tightening policy, reform was to be further accelerated, especially in-depth reform of the enterprise and financial systems, and the institutional causes of inflation were to be fundamentally eliminated.

Macroeconomic regulation and management was a new topic in the study of Chinese economics at this time. From 1984 to 1985, when China's economy was overheated and there was serious inflation, macro-control became a hot topic in theoretical research and gradually extended to all major aspects and problems of macroeconomic management theory.[30]

In studying the causes of the macroeconomic imbalance, China's economic circles discussed the relationship between aggregate supply and aggregate demand. It was believed that the basic cause of macroeconomic imbalance lay in the expansion of aggregate demand, but there were also reasons for the imbalance of the aggregate supply structure. Some held that the overall lack of control was only a superficial phenomenon, and the underlying reason was structural imbalance. Regarding the ways and means of macroeconomic management, it was generally believed that a gradual change from direct control to indirect control was needed, which was an important step in China's economic theory research. The theory of overall balance of the national economy, which had always been applied in China, was based on the administrative distribution system of funds, materials, and products. It focused on the static observation of "long-term" and "short-term" in the national economy and regulated the macroeconomy by administrative means of setting up projects, allocating investment, and distributing materials, but it did not study the evolutionary mechanism from balance to imbalance and dynamic equilibrium as a process. Indirect macro-control was a process of realizing dynamic equilibrium by adjusting market and economic parameters. Therefore, the change from direct macro-control to indirect control promoted the exploration of new macroeconomic theories. The realization of indirect regulation and control required the following conditions: 1) to establish a sound market system, 2) to speed up enterprise reform and improve the micro basis of indirect regulation, and 3) to establish a macro-control system, including a financial control system, and distribution control system. The development trend of macroeconomic management theory was to use the principles, concepts, and analysis tools of Western macroeconomics to deepen research and gradually connect with the theoretical framework of mainstream Western economics. On this basis, many scholars believed that in order to analyze and judge China's macroeconomic situation promptly and accurately, it was necessary to establish a set of scientific theories and methods for socialist macroeconomics. In fact, by the end of the 1980s, several monographs on the theory of socialist macroeconomics had been published. Although these works lacked a common paradigm in research methods,

---

30. Zhang Xunhua, *The Socialist Contending Masters, Socialist Economic Theory* (Shanghai People's Publishing House, 1991); Editorial Department of *Economic Research, Review and Prospect of China's Socialist Economic Theory* (China Economic Press, 1986).

theoretical premise, and analytical framework, they were of certain academic value as an attempt to establish socialist macroeconomics.[31]

In the early 1980s, the concept of the ownership structure of the means of production was formed in China's economic circles, and it was advanced against the old system of single public ownership and single state ownership. This theory held that in a socialist society, various forms of ownership played a role in promoting the development of productive forces in different areas. The existence and development of non-socialist ownership was not only conducive to the development of productive forces, but also to the generation of a market competition environment and the sound development of a socialist public economy. The establishment of the concept of discussing the form of ownership from the standard of developing socialist productive forces indicated great progress in the theoretical study of Chinese ownership. Following this idea, it was important to recognize the diversity of the forms of socialist public ownership in theory and abandon the political and ideological standards to judge the difference between the forms of ownership, so as to open up ideas for exploring the diversification of forms of socialist ownership.

Because of the theoretical breakthrough in ownership structure, the reform of state ownership became a focus of theoretical research and reform practice. In the 1980s, the research on the state-owned system in China's economic circles entered the theoretical level of reforming the state-owned system through the decomposition and separation of multiple economic functions, including the separation of the functions of the state as ownership and as the manager of social life, the separation of state financial and investment functions, the separation of asset ownership and asset management, and the separation of asset management and enterprise management. At the end of the 1980s, economic circles raised the issue of property rights transactions, enterprise mergers, and reorganization, and they gave attention to the relationship between the reform of the property rights system and the transformation of industrial organization, the change of property rights structure in the formation and development of enterprise groups, and the development of market mechanisms.

The comparative study of the economic system, or comparative economics, was another new research field in China. This field developed gradually after the 1980s and reached a certain academic level. To a great extent, the methods of comparative study referred to foreign theories and models, which could be divided into three types. One was the comparison of decision-making power in the economic system. This method broke the economic system down into decision-making structure, information structure, and power structure and regarded economic operations as the process of making decisions on production, exchange, distribution, and consumption, and then compared the characteristics, advantages, and disadvantages of different economic systems

---

31. Refer to Chen Naisheng, "Operation and Mechanism Structure of Socialist Macro Economy," *Literature, History, Philosophy*, no. 1 (1991); Yang Jianbai, *On the Socialist Macroeconomy* (Dongbei University of Finance and Economics Press, 1990); Zhong Pengrong and Wu Tonghu, *On the Macro Economy* (Economic Science Press, 1990); Wu Shuqing and Hu Naiwu, *Macro-management of National Economy* (Peking University Press, 1993); Li Yining, *An Empirical Analysis of China's Macroeconomy* (Peking University Press, 1992); Liu Guoguang, *Stable Economic Growth in System Reform* (China Planning Economy Press, 1990).

in the aspects of decision-making, information, and power. The second was the comparative method of order theory. It divided the planning system into two basic forms, one with the central management organ as the undertaker of the plan, and the other with enterprise as the undertaker of the plan. The economic management of the former relied on central planning and did not have a commodity currency relationship, while the latter relied on the enterprise plan and had a commodity currency relationship. The third type of comparative study was the comparative method of transaction cost theory. In this method, transaction cost was regarded as the cost of system operations. By comparison, the efficiency of different economic systems could be measured. On the basis of the comparison of economic systems, comparative economic research was extended to the comparative study of economic development. Through the comparative study of different development modes of developed countries, moderately developed countries, and developing countries, efforts were made to find a reasonable model for China's industrialization development.[32]

In addition to the above, the new research issues after the beginning of Reform and Opening Up also included the socialist market system, the choice of economic reform path, quantitative economics, urban economics, consumption economics, property rights economics and other basic theoretical issues in economics. After 1979, the theoretical research of Marxist economics in China not only expanded in content and deepened in theory, but also had a free, relaxed research atmosphere, and there were many different views and opinions on the same issue. Scholars studied and spoke freely from different angles and methods, which promoted the prosperity and scientific nature of theoretical research.

4. Research on the Price Determination of the Socialist Commodity Economy and Marx's Value Theory

Price determination involves the setting of prices of commodities and factors of production, the distribution of income such as wages, interests and profits, and how the price mechanism regulates the rational allocation of social and economic resources. Therefore, it is an important topic both to economic theory and real life. According to the logical process of Marx's value theory, the discussion of price determination starts with value determination, and value determination is the core of Marx's value theory. For many years, there were numerous differences in the understanding of Marx's value determination principle, and the discussion focused on two issues.

The first was the understanding of social necessary labor time. Marx pointed out that the value of goods depends on the social necessary labor time involved. Social necessary labor time is defined in the first volume of *Das Kapital* as "the labor time needed to create a certain use value under the normal production conditions of the existing society, under the average labor

---

32. Virlyn W. Bruse, *The Operation of the Socialist Economy* (China Social Sciences Press, 1984); Ota Sik, "On the Socialist Economic Model," *Economic Research Materials*, no. S1 (1981); Rong Jingben et al., *Selected Works on Socialist Economic Model* (People's Publishing House, 1983).

proficiency and labor intensity of that society."[33] But in the third volume, Marx also pointed out that "only when all products are produced in the necessary proportion can they be sold. The quantitative limit of the share of social labor time that can be used in each special field of production is only a manifestation of the further development of the whole law of value, although the necessary labor time has another meaning here. In order to meet the needs of society, only so much labor time is necessary."[34] It was generally believed that Marx's discussion shows that there are two meanings of social necessary labor time, which have different relations with value determination, but these two meanings of social necessary labor time are simply Marx's different expressions of the same concept at different abstract levels. "The labor time required to produce a certain use value" put forward by Marx in the first volume of *Das Kapital* refers to the average labor time required by different commodity producers in the same department to produce the use value of a certain commodity. We read, "Here, a single commodity is taken as an average sample of the commodity. Therefore, commodities that contain equal amount of labor or can be produced in the same labor time have the same amount of value."[35] Apparently, these expositions of Marx explained that "the proportion of the value of a commodity to the value of any other commodity is the ratio of the necessary labor time for the production of the former to the necessary labor time for the production of the latter" on the assumption that exchange is established.[36] In other words, under fixed exchange conditions, social necessary labor time is the weighted average of individual labor time invested for the production of a certain use value. In this sense, Marx called this kind of labor time "social average labor time." When discussing the pure value entity, that is to say, when demonstrating the proposition that "as value, all commodities are only a certain amount of solidified labor time," it is absolutely necessary to abstract the exchange relationship, because only in this way can the "socially necessary labor time" have theoretical certainty. However, as long as the abstract form of value is left, Marx points out that "value is not determined by the labor time necessary for a producer to produce a certain amount of commodity or a commodity, but by the necessary labor time of society and the total amount of labor necessary to produce such a commodity on the market under the average social production conditions at that time."[37] That is to say, the socially necessary labor time is determined by two interrelated and interactive factors, the average social production conditions and the total amount of social labor necessary for a certain commodity to appear in the market. The social necessary labor time in an overall sense is the result of the interaction between production and exchange, and between labor and utility, and it is the reflection of their internal relationship. In theoretical research, for the sake of analysis, it is possible to abstract the exchange relationship temporarily, but the internal relationship between the two factors of social necessary labor time cannot be cut off or split into two. Otherwise, it will be too difficult to grasp the exact meaning of this concept.

---

33. Marx, *Das Kapital*, vol. 1 (People's Publishing House, 1972), 52.
34. Marx, *Das Kapital*, vol. 3 (People's Publishing House, 1972), 177.
35. Marx, *Das Kapital*, vol. 1 (People's Publishing House, 1972), 52–53.
36. Marx, *Das Kapital*, vol. 1 (People's Publishing House, 1972), 53.
37. Marx, *Das Kapital*, vol. 3 (People's Publishing House, 1972), 722.

The second issue was the question of which meaning of social necessary labor time determined value. Based on the above understanding of the two meanings of social necessary labor time, there were differences in theoretical circles over the issue of value determination. One view was that the value of a commodity is determined by the first meaning of social necessary labor time, while the second meaning of social necessary labor time does not determine the formation and the size of value, but only affects the realization of value. Another view was that the two meanings of social necessary labor time jointly determine the value of goods. In fact, if the two meanings of social necessary labor time are understood as different expressions of the same concept at different levels of abstraction, then there is no question of which kind of social necessary labor time determines the value. When discussing the value determination, it is important to take the social necessary labor time put forward by Marx in the third volume of *Das Kapital* as the standard concept, as it shows the internal relationship between value entity and value quantity, production and exchange, and labor consumption and social utility in value determination. It is a realistic form of social necessary labor time that can be verified. According to the concept of social necessary labor time in an overall sense, the labor time spent in the production of a certain commodity required by society according to a certain proportion of the total social labor not only affects the realization of the commodity value, but also directly determines the value of the commodity, because after introducing the exchange relationship variable, the individual labor time invested in a certain commodity is not transformed into value in the sense of average labor time of the total commodity quantity, but into value in the meaning of average labor time of the commodity quantity in line with social demand.

In the third volume of *Das Kapital*, Marx highlighted the general process of capitalist production, aiming to "show and explain various specific forms of the capital movement process as a whole." Since it was a "general survey," it was necessary to analyze the internal relations and interactions of various economic categories or economic variables in their specific forms. Therefore, Marx's value theory developed from abstract to a realistic form. There were two links in the evolution of Marx's value theory to reality. The first was from value to market value, and the second was from market value to price. They formed a value price theoretical system with strict logic and internal unity and explained how value, price determination principle, and price mechanism could spontaneously regulate production and circulation through the changes of market supply and demand, so as to make social reproduction possible.

In considering the transition from value to price, it is necessary to discuss the concept of market value. Marx noted, "Market value, on the one hand, should be regarded as the average value of the goods produced by a sector, and on the other hand, it should be regarded as the individual value of the commodity which constitutes a large number of the products in the sector under the average conditions of it."[38] Marx's concept of market value explains the relationship between the individual value of a certain kind of commodity and its social value, that is, how the various individual values of commodities in the same production department are averaged into a market

---

38. Marx, *Das Kapital*, vol. 3 (People's Publishing House, 1972), 199.

value. By comparing and analyzing the relationship between the quantity of goods produced by normal production conditions, worse production conditions and the best production conditions, Marx clarified the different provisions of market value under three different combinations.

Marx went on to point out that "the determination of the market value is realized through the competition between buyers in the actual market on the premise that the demand is just large enough to absorb all the commodities according to the value determined in this way. In the above-mentioned provisions on market value, we assume that the quantity of goods produced is constant and fixed, but that the proportion of each component of the total amount of production has changed under different conditions, and the market value of the same quantity of goods should be adjusted in different ways. Let's assume that the total is the normal supply, and we leave aside the possibility that a part of the goods produced will temporarily withdraw from the market. If the demand for this total amount is still ordinary demand, the commodity will be sold at its market value regardless of the situation."[39] Obviously, what Marx was analyzing here was the market value decision in abstract form, that is, the market value decision without change in supply and demand, just as he had neglected the change of exchange relationship when analyzing individual value decisions. When examining the market value decision, Marx put forward the hypothesis of supply and demand equilibrium completely for the need of analysis, because the actual internal law of capitalist production "can be realized only when supply and demand no longer work, that is, when they are consistent with each other."[40] However, if the equilibrium of supply and demand is the norm in theory, then the imbalance between supply and demand is the norm in reality. Therefore, "supply and demand will never be consistent in fact. If they are consistent, it is only an occasional phenomenon, so it is equal to zero in science, which can be regarded as something that has not happened."[41] Therefore, market value determination is not the actual form of value determination despite the change of supply and demand. It only shows how different producers in the same sector average the value of their commodities under the premise of a given demand. In order to make the market value decision evolve into the real value decision, it is necessary to introduce the factors of supply and demand changes. Once the supply and demand change factors are introduced, the market value determination analysis will be transferred to the market price determination analysis. Marx's price theory mainly studies the internal relationship between price determination and supply and demand changes based on the principle of labor value theory, and it offers a theoretical description of the price mechanism.

In the first level, Marx interpreted the market price as the value under the condition of supply and demand equilibrium. Marx said, "No matter how different the production conditions of different producers are, the market prices of all similar commodities are always the same. Market price is only the average amount of social labor necessary to supply a certain quantity of certain products to the market under average production conditions. The market price is calculated on the

---

39. Marx, *Das Kapital*, vol. 3 (People's Publishing House, 1972), 206–207.

40. Marx, *Das Kapital*, vol. 3 (People's Publishing House, 1972), 212.

41. Marx, *Das Kapital*, vol. 3 (People's Publishing House, 1972), 212.

basis of the total amount of the commodity. Within this range, the market price of a commodity is consistent with its value."[42] In other words, "if supply and demand are balanced, the market price of goods is equal to their natural price, that is, their value determined by the amount of labor necessary to produce them."[43] Marx's discussion shows that if supply and demand are balanced, then value, market value, and market price are basically consistent. They are a condensation of general human labor in pure form (abstract form). The profundity of Marx's price theory is that it excavates the final factors of price determination behind the relationship between market supply and demand.

In the second level, Marx introduced the factors of supply and demand in the analysis of price movement. Marx pointed out that once the factor of supply and demand change is introduced, such changes will have an effect on the determination of market value through price fluctuations. Marx notes, "If the demand is so strong that when the price is adjusted by the value of the goods produced under the worst conditions, the market value will be determined by the goods produced under the worst conditions... If the quantity of the goods produced is greater than that of this kind and a market can be found according to the medium market value, then the commodity produced under the best conditions will adjust the market value."[44] It is evident that in the case of extremely unbalanced supply and demand, the market value is regulated by the goods produced under the production conditions at one end. Some theorists believed that this was the result of the change of production conditions, and it did not show that social demand had a restrictive effect on the determination of value. A more accurate analysis is that the imbalance between supply and demand causes changes in price and market value in two ways. One is the result of changes in production conditions. For example, the supply of goods exceeds demand, and the price drops, prompting producers to improve technology and labor productivity, resulting in a significant proportion of goods produced under superior conditions, and the market value is regulated by such commodities. In this case, the market value is still consistent with the average value, and the value of the total commodity is equal to the sum of individual values. The other way is that in a certain period of time, there is no significant change in production conditions, mainly due to the abnormal imbalance between supply and demand, resulting in the market value shifting to inferior or superior production conditions. In this case, the market value is higher or lower than the average value, and the value of the total commodity is not equal to the sum of individual values. It is understood that Marx's discussion involves the latter situation.

Since the factors of supply and demand change have an effect on the determination of market value, and this effect is reflected by price fluctuation, price determination can be further examined based on the actual form of value determination. Marx pointed out that value is the basis of price, and price is the monetary expression of value. Price accords with value, which indicates that the exchange is carried out on the basis of equivalent value. It is only at this time that the social

---

42. Marx and Engels, *Complete Works of Marx and Engels*, vol. 2 (People's Publishing House, 2005), 177.
43. Marx and Engels, *Complete Works of Marx and Engels*, vol. 2 (People's Publishing House, 2005), 177.
44. Marx, *Das Kapital*, vol. 1 (People's Publishing House, 1972), 200.

necessary labor time determines value. That is to say, price determination is the actual form of value determination. First, price, as a form of value, is in accordance with the quantity of its object under the condition of balanced supply and demand. In other words, if supply and demand are balanced, then how much labor is condensed in a commodity and how the value of the commodity is determined is what determines its price. Second, if supply and demand are not balanced, prices will fluctuate with supply and demand. However, no matter what the commodity price is, what it represents is only the amount of commodity value recognized by society. In other words, how much of the labor is condensed in a commodity is recognized by society and converted into value, which is how its price determined. Therefore, the equivalent exchange required by the law of value requires that the price of a commodity should be equal to the value, that is, equal to the amount of social necessary labor contained in the commodity.

On the third level, Marx's price theory expounds the general mechanism between value, price, and supply and demand changes. As a practical form of value determination, price determination relates not only to the formation conditions of value, but also to the changes of market supply and demand. What it embodies is the internal relationship between production and exchange and between labor consumption and social utility. This relationship reflects a law, which states that to make the labor consumed in the production of a certain commodity have value, it must be connected with the utility and social demand. Engels pointed out that "[v]alue is the relations of production cost and utility. Value is used, first of all, to determine whether or not certain commodities ought to be produced; that is, whether or not the utility of such commodities covers their production costs. Only when this question has been answered can we speak of use value as a standard measurement for exchange. If the production costs of two commodities are equal, then their respective utilities would be the decisive factor in determining their relative value."[45] Utility here refers to the degree to which social needs are met. Therefore, "[f]or a commodity to be sold at its market-value, i.e., proportionally to the necessary social labour contained in it, the total quantity of social labour used in producing the total mass of this commodity must correspond to the quantity of the social want for it, i.e., the effective social want. Competition, the fluctuations of market-prices which correspond to the fluctuations of demand and supply, tend continually to reduce to this scale the total quantity of labour devoted to each kind of commodity."[46] This theory shows that in a commodity economy, equivalent exchange is an objective requirement of the law of value. In order to realize equivalent exchange, it is necessary to adjust the proportion of social labor input and the structure of economic resource allocation through the price mechanism. The adjustment function of the price mechanism reflects the inherent law between price determination and supply and demand changes.

In summary, Marx's labor theory of value is a complete system from value determination to price determination. In the study of value determination, Marx analyzed the final determinants of value with exquisite abstract force, while in the study of price movement, Marx scientifically

---

45. Marx and Engels, *Complete Works of Marx and Engels*, vol. 1 (People's Publishing House, 2005), 605.
46. Marx, *Das Kapital*, vol. 3 (People's Publishing House, 1972), 215.

analyzed the internal relations among value, price, and supply and demand, demonstrating the law of price determination and its regulating function on social economy. The focus of Marx's value theory is on the in-depth analysis of the social relations embodied in the value. Therefore, the logical starting point of this theory is the stipulation of value quality, not the quantitative relationship in price determination. However, through the analysis process from abstract to concrete, Marx demonstrated the theoretical and practical forms of value determination and expressed the relationship among value, price, and supply and demand in the same mechanism in theory, thus unifying the theory of value determination with the price movement in reality, and provided a theoretical basis for scientifically understanding the role of price determination and price mechanism.

It was important to understand Marx's value price determination principle correctly. With the deepening of economic system reform and the development of the socialist commodity economy, it was necessary to establish a price determination theory and related socialist microeconomics that could reflect the operation law of the modern commodity economy, scientifically explain the resource allocation mechanism in the socialist commodity economy, and describe the quantitative relationship between supply, demand, and price with empirical and quantitative methods. Therefore, it was necessary to overcome the traditional method of deducing the conclusion from the given premise and develop socialist political economics on the basis of a complete and accurate grasp of Marxist economic theory.

A correct understanding of Marx's value price determination principle was not only the need of the developing socialist political economics, but it also enabled China to scientifically analyze and evaluate Western economics, especially Marshall's equilibrium price theory, which was the basis of Western economics up to that point, and to use some reasonable theorems and methods for reference. From the disintegration of Ricardo school to Marshall, there were mainly two kinds of value theories in Western economics. One put emphasis on the supply side, typical of John Mueller's value theory of production costs, while the other leaned toward the demand side, represented by the marginalist theory of marginal utility value Marshall used the market equilibrium model to connect supply and demand to form an equilibrium price theory of market supply and demand. This theory examined not only the general relationship between supply and demand, but also the relationship between supply and price and between demand and price. Therefore, "equilibrium" referred not only to the balance between supply and demand, but also between supply and demand and price. When the supply and demand were in equilibrium, the output produced in unit time was the equilibrium quantity of the commodity, and the transaction price of the commodity was the equilibrium price, that is, the market price of the commodity. The outstanding contribution of Marshall's equilibrium price theory lay in the quantitative analysis of the relationship among demand, supply, and price movement, which was represented by geometric figures. He further used demand elasticity and supply elasticity to measure the response of demand and supply to price changes, so as to illustrate the regulatory role of price demand and supply. Marshall's price theory explained the internal relationship between price fluctuation and supply and demand quantitatively, making it possible to build a theoretical model of value reality movement based on the actual market and providing a methodological basis for explaining the price mechanism theory of resource allocation. However, the scientific nature of Marshall's equilibrium price theory was doubted or even denied in China's economic circles because its main analytical feature was the examination of the determination of commodity prices from the perspective of market supply and demand. Many people believed that Marx explained the relationship between supply and demand from the perspective of value, while Marshall explained value from the relationship between supply and demand, so Marshall's theory must be vulgar. In fact, this problem was actually the logical starting point or theoretical perspective of scientific research. As mentioned above, Marx mainly analyzed the exploitation relationship of capitalist surplus value in *Das Kapital*. Therefore, in analyzing value, the relationship between supply and demand and price fluctuation were abstracted in many places in order to reveal the essence of capitalist production relations in the pure form of value. However, Marshall did not study the essential characteristics of production relations, but the phenomenon forms of market relations. And he did not study the essential relations of value, but the phenomenon forms of value. From this logical starting point, Marshall did not focus on the abstract stipulation of value quality, but from the quantitative relationship between market supply and demand and price. If factors of supply and demand changes can be abstracted in the analysis of pure value entities, then when analysis is made of how the price mechanism regulates the distribution of social labor, focus can only be placed on the relationship between supply and demand in the market, because "the nature of commodity value... generally speaking, is in the form of market price, and further, it is expressed in the form of market price or market production price that plays a regulating role."[47] Therefore, in judging whether Marshall's theory was scientific or not, the key criterion was not to see whether it explained the relationship between supply and demand from the perspective of value or from the relationship between supply and demand, but to see how it analyzed the essential relationship between labor and utility in price determination. The fundamental defect of Marshall's theory of value lay in his failure to categorize the "production expense" and "production cost" in his production theory (i.e. supply theory) as part of the general human labor, but as the "negative utility" of human psychological motivation. However, as long as he did not go deep into the abstract level of value entity, he revealed some regular phenomena when describing the relationship between price determination and supply and demand changes.

6.3 The Influence of Western Economics on Chinese Economic Thought

1. On the Discipline Orientation of Economics

According to the theory of political economics in China since 1949, economics has been a social science which studied social economic relations and production relations. Western economists

---

47. Marx, *Das Kapital*, vol. 3 (People's Publishing House, 1972), 722.

regard economics as a "science" as precise as natural science, and they use "marginal analysis" and other tools to try to make quantitative analysis in every economic category. Of course, there are differences in the orientation of economics in Western economics. Many people hold that economics is a social science. However, the characteristics of Western economics in terms of research objects, research methods, and theoretical framework have deeply influenced Chinese economic circles. Some young and middle-aged economists have even put forward the idea that China has no economics at all, and that traditional political economics cannot be regarded as economics in the strictest sense. This view is certainly biased, but many scholars agree that China's economic theory research lacks an economic analysis framework and logical system based on the language, methods, and norms of modern economics. In the second half of the 1980s, Shanghai Sanlian Bookstore launched the Contemporary Economics Book Series, which included the *Contemporary Economics Library, Contemporary Economics Translation Library, Contemporary Economics New Knowledge Literature,* and *Contemporary Economics Teaching Reference Books.* The preface to this series states that it is committed to promoting the modernization and international standardization of domestic economics and seeks to gradually complete the transformation of Chinese economics from traditional to modern in terms of research scope, research content, research methods, and analytical techniques in a relatively short period of time. The "modern economics" mentioned here is Western economics. Because the development of Chinese economics is far behind that of the West, Western economics is "modern" by comparison. Since the mid-1980s, many academic papers published in some major economic journals in China have imitated the methods of Western economists in research methods and theoretical paradigms, established theoretical framework with several basic categories, and used some empirical analysis tools, including mathematical formulas, to "refine" the logical system and conclusion. Although up to the middle and late 1990s, the number of such papers still accounted for a small proportion of all economic research works, they did give people a sense of freshness and vitality, and they had a strong development momentum.

Economics is ultimately a social science. It cannot test its theory with "scientific methods" (controlled experiments) like the natural sciences. Economics studies human behavior. Everyone's preference and behavior can't always be the same, like the chemical elements in a test tube, and their utility can't be measured and compared absolutely by mathematical methods. It can be tested by statistical or other methods that the demand for a commodity will increase after its market price decreases, but it cannot be absolutely determined that the demand will increase by several percentage points. In Marshall's view, the "laws" described in economics can only be a kind of "trends," reflecting the general change in direction of economic activities, but they cannot say that it is absolutely certain. From the global perspective, the degree of mathematicalization of economics is already very high. According to statistics, 40% of the papers published in the *American Economic Review*, a renowned American magazine published in the 1990s, used relatively complicated mathematical contents.[48] The requirement of mathematics application is very strict. Mathematics requires a weaker hypothesis, stronger argument, and wider applicability. Under this kind of demand, economics hopes to likewise pursue stronger universality, accuracy, and brevity, but in the end, mathematics cannot replace economics, and mathematical principles cannot be widely applied to people's economic behavior. Economics always requires some basic assumptions, though they may be proved or falsified by experience and logic. Nobel Laureate in economics Ronald Coase has criticized the widespread use of mathematics in economics, believing that although mathematics makes economics precise and elegant, it also makes economics a theory that cannot be understood and used, and thus turns economic analysis into a game.

These comments are some extreme tendencies in the orientation of economics. However, for China's economic research, it seems that more emphasis should be placed on the transformation of analytical methods and theoretical paradigms. One of the biggest characteristics of economics that is different from other social sciences is its strong experimental nature. It is different from philosophy that can "create" causality completely by logical reasoning and deduce conclusions from concept to concept. Economics is directly produced in real economic life, and it should be able to withstand the test of real economic life. But the biggest defect of China's economic theory is that it is unable to explain real economic life. On the one hand, theory cannot explain the real economic relations in essence, and on the other, real economic activities in many places are not consistent with theory. The root cause of this phenomenon is that China's economic theory does not take real economic life as the starting point of analysis in many cases, but takes some vague concepts as the starting point. Therefore, the discussion of some problems has not yet reached a final conclusion, resulting in a series of "paradoxes" between theory and practice. To change this situation, it is necessary to learn from Western economics in the discipline orientation, theoretical paradigm, and analytical methods of economics and make a great change.

2. On the Category of Economics

The understanding of the subject category of economics in China's economic and ideological circles is no longer limited to the study of production relations stipulated by traditional political economics, but has been greatly expanded. Generally speaking, economic research can be divided into three parts, economic theory research, economic policy research, and economic application research. The characteristics and functions of these three parts are different, but there are also internal relations.[49]

Economic theory research includes pure theoretical research and realistic economic research. The former is the revision, improvement, and perfection of the economic theory system. It studies the original economic proposition or theorem in depth and establishes the economic

---

48. Xu Qingchun and Chen Zhang, "American Economic Society Director's Talk about the Mathematical-ization of Economic Theory," *Economics Trends*, no. 11 (1992).

49. Li Yi, "A Review of the Discussion on Some Issues of China's Economic Research," *Academic Trends*, no. 3 (1990).

theory system according to this proposition or theorem in a more systematic, perfect form. The latter is the theoretical research on the new problems in the actual operation of the economy, which explain the relevant economic phenomena on a theoretical level and develop new theories. The main function of economic theory research is to explain various economic phenomena with universal regularity and innovate the economic theory and economic analysis methods.

Economic policy research mainly refers to the study of social and economic public policy. It is characterized by the use of existing economic theory and analysis tools to formulate policy programs. Its main function is to put forward a variety of policy programs to solve the practical issues in social and economic activities and improve the operations of the social economy through the implementation of the program.

Economic applied research is commonly referred to as applied economics, including the specialized research of finance, trade, industry, agriculture, securities, investment, management, information, accounting, statistics, and other social and economic departments or branches of economics. Its main feature is the study of the operation law and professional theory of an economic department or a branch of discipline on the basis of basic economic theory, and its function is to provide operational planning and basic data.

In the late 1980s and early 1990s, the economic theory, economic policy, and economic application of China's economic research were basically formed, and economists basically determined their own position (of course, there were overlaps and changes in position). The classification and division of labor of this kind of economic research was consistent with the development trend of the world, and it was also a manifestation of the modernization of China's economic research.

3. An Analysis of the Trend of Integration Between Western Economics and Chinese Socialist Political Economics

Throughout the 1980s, China's socialist political economics and Western economics had their own development process and development cues, and the boundary was clear. Since the end of the 1980s, there had been a trend of integration between the two subject systems. This integration was not only manifested in the fact that some scholars engaged in the study of socialist political economics were involved in Western economics and that some scholars engaged in Western economic research were also interested in the construction of China's political economics, but it also showed that the concepts, categories, and methods of Western economics had found a foothold in the social political economics, and the principles and methods of Marxist economics were also used to examine and evaluate Western economic theories. In the discipline classification of China, as an independent secondary discipline under the first level discipline of theoretical economics, Western economics was incorporated into China's economics teaching system and postgraduate discipline training system.

Socialist political economics and Western economics are two theoretical systems. The basic category of the former is commodity, value, capital, and surplus value, while the latter is demand, supply, utility, and profit. There are great differences in the basic premises, basic methods, and basic content of the two systems, so it is impossible to completely integrate them into one. The current textbooks on political economics add the categories of equilibrium price, cost-benefit, and monopolistic competition into the "capitalist part," and the categories of consumption function, multiplier principle, and market equilibrium are added to the "socialist part." However, as long as it is based on the evolution of social production relations, rather than the actual social and economic operation as the starting point, then this theoretical system cannot be integrated with Western economics. Therefore, the integration of Western economics and Chinese socialist political economics refers to the intersection and absorption of the two systems in a number of categories, concepts, and methods, rather than a complete integration.

It is necessary to point out that there has always been a bias in the relationship between Western economics and China's socialist political economics. Many scholars rigidly mimic the principles of Western economics in theoretical research, believing that otherwise it is not enough to keep pace with international standards and modernize Chinese economics. Western economics is an economic theoretical system based on the capitalist market economic system. Many of its premises, assumptions, principles, and constraints are not applicable to China. If they are copied directly without regard to China's national conditions, it is difficult to draw scientific conclusions. For example, in the mid-1980s, some commentators copied Keynes's "prescription" for capitalist economic depression and underemployment, that is, the policy of stimulating effective demand to China. As a result, macroeconomic imbalance and serious inflation were caused. Another example is that some scholars, influenced by the "great advance" theory of Western development economics, advocated high accumulation and high growth. However, China's per capita share of resources was extremely low, and the shortage of resources was serious. It was unsustainable to rely on a large amount of investment to promote rapid economic growth, as the economic growth brought about by it could only be extensive and low-efficiency. In addition, in the research and application of new institutional economics and property rights economics, there was a tendency to ignore the established institutional conditions. All of these approaches suffered because they mechanically copied Western economics, which was unfavorable to the development of China's economic thought.

CHAPTER 7

The Theory of the Preliminary Stage of Socialism and the Planned Commodity Economy

7.1 The Meaning and Theoretical Characteristics of the Preliminary Stage of Socialism

1. The Basic Meaning of the Preliminary Stage of Socialism

In 1979, the fifth issue of *Economic Research* published Su Shaozhi and Feng Lanrui's article "The Stage of Social Development After the Proletariat Gains Power," which put forward the division of socialist development stages. The article advanced the view that China was still in the undeveloped socialist stage, though "it is absolutely possible to say that we are a socialist country. However, it cannot be said that we have established the first stage (socialist society) of the communist society envisaged by Marx and Lenin... We cannot think that our economic system is already developed or completely socialist."[1]

In June 1981, the Sixth Plenary Session of the Eleventh Central Committee of the Communist Party of China issued the Resolution on Some Historical Issues of the Party Since the Founding of the People's Republic of China. In September 1982, the report of the Twelfth National Congress of the Communist Party of China reiterated that China's socialist society was still in the preliminary, or primary, stage of development. In the Resolution on the Guidelines for the Construction of Socialist Spiritual Civilization in September 1986, the Sixth Plenary Session of the Twelfth Central

---

1. Su Shaozhi and Feng Lanrui, "The Stage of Social Development After the Proletariat Gains Power," *Economic Research*, no. 5 (1979).

Committee of the Communist Party of China (CPC) once again proposed that China was still in the preliminary stage of socialism. In November 1987, the report of the Thirteenth National Congress of the Communist Party of China systematically put forward and discussed in detail the theory, line, strategy, and basic policies of the primary stage of socialism in China, pointing out that China was in the preliminary stage of socialism. The preliminary stage of socialism did not refer to the initial stage that any country would go through when entering socialism, but to the inevitable stage of building socialism under the conditions of backward productivity and an underdeveloped commodity economy. In the 1950s, the socialist transformation of private ownership of the means of production in China was basically completed, and it took at least a hundred years for the socialist modernization to be basically realized, which were all part of the preliminary stage of socialism. This stage was not only different from the transitional period in which the socialist economic foundation had not been established, but was also different from the stage in which socialist modernization had been realized. At the time, the main contradiction in China was the contradiction between the people's growing material and cultural needs and the backward social productive forces. Class struggle would continue exist for a long time, to a certain extent, but it was no longer the main contradiction. The great significance of the theory of the preliminary stage of socialism lay in its new understanding and research on socialism from the perspective of China's national conditions. It not only laid a new theoretical foundation for the research and development of China's socialist economics, but also provided a scientific basis for the state to formulate correct lines, guidelines, and policies.

In October 1992, the report of the Fourteenth National Congress of the Communist Party of China expounded the theory of the preliminary stage of socialism as an important part of Deng Xiaoping Theory and emphasized once again that this stage of socialism was a historical stage of at least a hundred years. In September 1997, the Fifteenth National Congress of the Communist Party of China established the basic line and program for the preliminary stage of socialism, taking the theory as the basic component of Deng Xiaoping Theory and the theory of socialism with Chinese characteristics. It further stressed that China was now in and would be in the preliminary stage of socialism for a long time. The report of the Fifteenth National Congress of the Communist Party of China offered a comprehensive, systematic exposition of the basic characteristics of the preliminary stage of socialism in nine aspects, pointing out that "the preliminary stage of socialism is a historical stage of gradually eliminating underdevelopment and basically realizing socialist modernization. It is a historical stage for China to shift from an agricultural country with a large proportion of agricultural population, mainly relying on manual labor, to an industrialized country with a majority of non-agricultural population and modern agriculture and service industry. It is a historical stage to shift from the natural economy and semi-natural economy accounting for a large proportion of the overall economy to a higher degree of marketization of the economy. It is a historical stage to shift from a nation with a large proportion of the illiterate and semi-illiterate population and an underdeveloped science, technology, education, and culture to one with relatively advanced science and technology, education, and culture. It is also the stage in which the poverty-stricken population accounts for a large proportion and the people's living standards are relatively low, and gradually transformed into an overall relatively prosperous society. In this stage, the regional economy and culture are very unbalanced, and the gap is gradually narrowed through the development of the first and the second. It involves the establishment and improvement of a relatively mature and dynamic socialist market economic system, socialist democratic political system, and other aspects through reform and exploration. It is a historical stage in which the broad masses of the people firmly establish the common ideal of building socialism with Chinese characteristics, constantly strive for self-improvement, forge ahead with determination, work hard, and build a country with diligence and thrift, striving to build a spiritual civilization while building a material civilization. In this stage, the gap with the world's advanced level will gradually narrow and the great rejuvenation of the Chinese nation will be realized on the basis of socialism."[2] In November 2002, the Sixteenth National Congress of the Communist Party of China further enriched and developed the theory of the preliminary stage of socialism. It pointed out that China was in and would be in the primary stage of socialism for a long time. The prosperous society was still at a low-level, and China was an incomplete, unbalanced prosperous society. The contradiction between the people's growing material and cultural needs and the backward social production was still the main contradiction in China. In October 2005, the Fifth Plenary Session of the 16th Central Committee of the Communist Party of China pointed out that China must be soberly aware that it was in and would be in the primary stage for a long time, with underdeveloped productive forces and unbalanced development between urban and rural areas. The task of solving the problems of agriculture, rural areas, and farmers was quite arduous, the employment pressure was still great, and there were many contradictions in income distribution, with the problems of system and mechanism affecting development needed to be solved urgently, and it was more difficult to deal with the relationship of social interests. On October 15, 2007, the report of the Seventeenth National Congress of the Communist Party of China pointed out that China was still in the primary stage of socialism and would be in the primary stage of socialism for a long time. The characteristics of the current stage of China's development were the concrete manifestation of the basic national conditions of the preliminary stage of socialism in the new stage of the new century. In November 2012, the report of the Eighteenth National Congress of the Communist Party of China stressed that the primary stage of socialism was China's actual national condition and the general basis for building socialism with Chinese characteristics. In October 2017, the report of the Nineteenth National Congress of the Communist Party of China pointed out that China was and would still be in the primary stage of socialism for a long time, which was the basic national condition and the greatest reality.

---

2. Jiang Zemin, *Holding High the Great Banner of Deng Xiaoping Thought and Pushing the Cause of Building Socialism with Chinese Characteristics into the 21st Century: Report on the Fifteenth National Congress of the Communist Party of China* (People's Publishing House, 1997).

2. The Basic Characteristics and Tasks of the Preliminary Stage of Socialism

The basic economic characteristics of the preliminary stage of socialism are 1) the ownership of means of production should be the coexistence of various economic elements with public ownership as the main body, 2) distribution should be the coexistence of multiple distribution modes with distribution according to work as the main body, and 3) the commodity economy should be vigorously developed and some people encouraged to be the first to become prosperous through labor and legal management with the goal of common prosperity. The basic task of the primary stage of socialism was to vigorously develop productive forces and realize industrialization and commercialization and the socialization and modernization of production. The combination of the commercialization of production with the industrialization and socialization of production not only reflected the objective reality of the underdeveloped commodity economy in the preliminary stage of socialism, but also highlighted the task of establishing economic system reform based on the commodity economy.

The establishment of the primary stage of socialism in China was based on the law that the relations of production must be suitable for the development of productive forces. The theory of the primary stage of socialism was the starting point of socialism with Chinese characteristics. The Thirteenth National Congress of the Communist Party of China focused on the experience of socialist construction practice since Reform and Opening Up, systematically discussed the theory of the preliminary stage of socialism, clearly summarized and comprehensively elaborated the Party's basic line, put forward the strategy of economic construction and development, proposed the principles of economic and political system reform, and constructed the theoretical framework of socialism with Chinese characteristics. The theory of the primary stage of socialism was the development of the theory of scientific socialism and was of great significance to socialist thought and practice. Generally speaking, the preliminary stage of socialism in China was a stage of the gradual elimination of poverty and backwardness, in which an agricultural country based on manual labor, which accounted for the majority of agricultural population, was gradually transformed into a modern industrial country with a majority of non-agricultural population. It was a stage in which the natural economy and semi-natural economy accounted for a large proportion and became a highly developed commodity economy. It was a stage for establishing and developing a dynamic socialist economic, political, and cultural system in which all the people would rise up and work hard to realize the great rejuvenation of the Chinese nation. The basic national conditions in the primary stage of socialism were the cognitive and practical foundation for the construction and development of socialism with Chinese characteristics. The construction of socialism with Chinese characteristics needed to proceed from the reality of China's situation, and the key to this situation was that China was and would be in the primary stage of socialism for a long time. The report of the Fifteenth National Congress of the Communist Party of China made a more systematic exposition on the basic program, development process, main contradictions, and fundamental tasks of the preliminary stage of socialism.

3. An Innovation Combining Marxism with China's Reality

The theory of the primary stage of socialism was closely related to the theory and practice of socialism with Chinese characteristics, and it had a profound historical and theoretical inheritance relationship with the tradition of Marxism and scientific socialism. The theory of the primary stage of socialism was the cornerstone of Deng Xiaoping Theory and an important part of the theoretical system of socialism with Chinese characteristics. Deng Xiaoping pointed out that China firmly believed in Marxism, but Marxism must be combined with China's reality. Only Marxism combined with China's reality was the real Marxism China needed. Only by emancipating the mind, persisting in seeking truth from facts, proceeding from reality in everything, and integrating theory with practice could China's socialist modernization construction be carried out smoothly and the Party's theory of Marxism Leninism and Mao Zedong Thought develop smoothly. Emancipating the mind and seeking truth from facts meant that in socialist construction, it was necessary to proceed from China's national conditions, dare and be good at taking China's own road, and build socialism with Chinese characteristics. China was still in the primary stage of socialism, which was a scientific evaluation of China's basic national conditions.[3]

The conclusion of the preliminary stage of socialism included several points. First, China had entered a socialist society, and it was important to adhere to it, not leaving it. After the basic completion of socialist transformation, China would have the general characteristics of socialism. At present, China had established the socialist ownership relationship with the public ownership of the means of production as the main body and the socialist distribution system with distribution according to work as the main body, the foundation of socialist industrialization had been established, the national sovereignty of the working people as masters of the country had been consolidated, and the socialist spiritual civilization had been initially developed. Second, China's socialist society was still in its primary stage, and it was important to proceed from this reality and not go beyond this stage. Here, the "primary stage" emphasized China's historical position in the process of socialist development, that is, the "underdeveloped stage." The fundamental feature of the primary stage was underdevelopment. The fundamental reason was that China's socialist society was born out of a semi-colonial and semi-feudal society and did not fully develop the productive forces after the capitalist stage. It was important to face up to this stage and not go beyond it. The former indicated that the nature of China's society had the same nature as other stages of socialism, and the latter showed that the degree of development of socialism in China was different from the historical stage of modernization.

Marx and Engels founded the theory of scientific socialism. However, due to the limitation of historical conditions, they failed to make detailed plans for socialist practice. The victory of the Russian Socialist Revolution was the first development of the theory of scientific socialism. It not

---

3. Guiding Committee for Editing and Reviewing the National Cadre Training Materials, *Basic Issues of Deng Xiaoping Thought* (People's Publishing House, 2002).

only turned socialism from theory into reality, but also greatly promoted the understanding of socialism in practice. After that, Stalin adhered to and developed Lenin's theory that socialism could first be won and built in one country, put forward the principles of socialist industrialization and agricultural collectivization, comprehensively summarized the experience of socialist construction in the Soviet Union, and enriched and developed the theory of scientific socialism. After the founding of the People's Republic of China in 1949, the theory, line, and policy of socialist construction put forward and practiced by the Communist Party of China, as well as the various studies on socialism in China's theoretical circles, also promoted the development of scientific socialist theory.

After China's Reform and Opening Up, on the issue of the socialist development road, China adhered to its own road, did not regard books as dogma, and did not copy foreign models, but it took Marxism as the guide. It took practice as the only criterion for testing truth, emancipated the mind, sought truth from facts, and embarked from reality to build socialism with Chinese characteristics. The Thirteenth National Congress of the Communist Party of China focused on the experience of socialist construction practice since the beginning of Reform and Opening Up, systematically discussed the theory of the primary stage of socialism, clearly summarized and comprehensively elaborated the Party's basic line, put forward the strategy of economic construction and development and the principles of economic and political system reform, and constructed the theoretical framework of socialism with Chinese characteristics. The theory of the primary stage of socialism was the development of the theory of scientific socialism and was of great significance to socialist thought and practice.

7.2 Economic System Reform and the Development of the Theory of the Socialist Commodity Economy

1. Exploration on the Theory of the Socialist Commodity Economy

In April 1979, the Institute of Economics at the Chinese Academy of Social Sciences held a theoretical seminar on the role of the law of value in a socialist economy. At that time, many representatives believed that not only the means of living were commodities, but also the means of production, and not only the products exchanged between the two types of ownership were commodities, but also the products exchanged between enterprises under public ownership, and the law of value thus played an important role in the whole socialist economy. The discussion broke through the theoretical framework of the socialist political economics on the law of commodity production and value from the 1950s to the 1970s and began to integrate the socialist economy with the commodity economy and the law of value. After this, there were extensive discussions on the relationship between socialism and the commodity economy, between the planned economy and the commodity economy, and between planned regulation and market regulation. In November 1979, in a talk with American and Canadian scholars, Deng Xiaoping said, "It is certainly incorrect to say that the market economy exists only in a capitalist society and only in a capitalist market economy. Why can't socialism develop a market economy? This can't be said to be capitalism. We are mainly a planned economy with a market economy, but it is a socialist market economy. Although the method is basically similar to that of a capitalist society, there are also differences. It is the relationship between public ownership, of course, with collective ownership and with foreign capitalism. However, in the final analysis, it is socialism and a socialist society... This is how socialism uses this method to develop social productive forces. Taking this as a method will not affect socialism as a whole and will not mark a return to capitalism."[4] This thought played an important role in guiding and promoting the discussion of the socialist commodity economy at that time.

In the early 1980s, many theorists proposed the view of the socialist commodity economy, emphasizing that commodity production is the product of the development of human society to a certain historical stage. If the economic development of human society can be divided into three stages, the natural economy, the commodity economy, and the planned economy, then the world is still in the stage of the commodity economy. When capitalist ownership is abolished, the commodity economy can't be abolished at the same time. The commodity economy cannot be equated with capitalism, just as money cannot be equated with capital. Some theorists further analyzed that the opposite of the commodity economy is the natural economy, not the planned economy. The planned economy in modern China could only be established on the basis of the commodity economy. Without the exchange relationship, there would be no division of labor and cooperation among various economic units in modern China, and its entire society would not be able to form a whole, and there would be no plan to speak of. In 1982, some critics criticized the formulation of the "planned commodity economy," holding that the foothold of the socialist economy should be placed on the planned economy rather than on the commodity economy.[5]

In October 1984, the Third Plenary Session of the Twelfth Central Committee of the Communist Party of China adopted the Decision of the Central Committee of the Communist Party of China on the Reform of the Economic System. The Decision pointed out that in order to reform the planned economic system, it was necessary to first break through the traditional concept that opposed the planned economy with the commodity economy and clearly understand that the socialist planned economy must be consciously based on and apply the law of value, which was a planned commodity economy on the basis of public ownership. The full development of the commodity economy was an insurmountable stage of social and economic development and a necessary condition for the realization of China's economic modernization. Only by fully developing the commodity economy was it possible to really invigorate the economy, promote enterprises to improve their efficiency, operate flexibly, and flexibly adapt to the complex and

---

4. Deng Xiaoping, *Selected Works of Deng Xiaoping*, vol. 2 (People's Publishing House, 1994), 236.

5. Economic Editorial Office of *China's Social Sciences, Economic Anthologies (1980)* (Zhejiang People's Publishing House, 1981); Economic Editorial Office of *China's Social Sciences, Economic Anthologies (1981)* (Zhejiang People's Publishing House, 1982); Economic Editorial Office of *China's Social Sciences, Economic Anthologies (1982)* (Zhejiang People's Publishing House, 1983).

changeable social needs, which could not be achieved by simply relying on administrative means and mandatory plans. At the same time, it was important to see that even if it was a socialist commodity economy, its extensive development would produce some blindness. It was necessary to have planned guidance, regulation, and administrative management, which could be achieved under socialist conditions. Therefore, the implementation of the planned economy, the application of the law of value, and the development of the commodity economy were not mutually exclusive, but unified. It was wrong to set them against each other.[6]

The breakthrough of the Decision of the Central Committee of the Communist Party of China on the Reform of the Economic System in the theory of the socialist commodity economy was mainly manifested in several aspects. First, China had broken through the concept of opposing socialism and the commodity economy and realized that commodity was the basic feature of socialist relations of production, not a capitalist factor. As the basic law of the commodity economy, the regulation of value law ran through the movement process of the socialist economy, and the relationship between commodity and currency extended to the whole economic scope.

Second, the category of the socialist commodity economy did not refer to the existence of commodity production and exchange in a socialist economy, but should instead be understood as a form of socialist production, that is, the socialist economy was a planned commodity economy based on public ownership.

Third, it was important to realize that the full development of the commodity economy was an insurmountable stage of social development. It was impossible for socialist development to go beyond the commodity economy to prosperity. Developing the socialist commodity economy was the only path to socialist modernization.

In October 1987, the report of the Thirteenth National Congress of the Communist Party of China entitled "Along the Path of Socialism with Chinese Characteristics" pointed out that the "socialist economy is a planned commodity economy on the basis of public ownership," which is a scientific summary of the socialist economy made by the Party, a great development of Marxism, and the fundamental theoretical basis of China's economic system reform. The report of the Thirteenth National Congress of the Communist Party of China expounded the system and operation mechanism of the socialist planned commodity economy.

The system of the socialist planned commodity economy was to be the internal unity of planning and market. On this issue, it was necessary to clarify several basic concepts. First, the essential difference between the socialist commodity economy and the capitalist commodity economy lay in the difference of ownership basis. The socialist commodity economy established on the basis of public ownership provided the possibility of consciously maintaining the coordinated development of the national economy across society. The task was to make good use of the two forms and means of planned regulation and market regulation to turn this possibility into reality. The development of the socialist commodity economy was inseparable from the development

---

6. *The Decision of the Central Committee of the Communist Party of China on the Reform of the Economic System* (People's Publishing House, 1984).

and perfection of the market. The use of market regulation was by no means tantamount to capitalism. Second, planning must be based on commodity exchange and the law of value. The direct management mode based on mandatory planning could not meet the requirements of the development of the socialist commodity economy, and it could not equate planned regulation with mandatory planning. The scope of mandatory plans should be gradually reduced by signing order contracts between the state and enterprises or between enterprises in accordance with the principle of equivalent exchange. Generally speaking, the new economic operation mechanism should be a mechanism of "the state regulating the market and the market guiding enterprises." The state used economic means, legal means, and necessary administrative means to regulate the relationship between supply and demand in the market and create a suitable economic and social environment, so as to guide enterprises to make correct business decisions.[7]

2. Discussion on the Socialist Commodity Economy in Economic Circles

At the end of the 1970s and the beginning of the 1980s, the mainstream opinion in the field of economics held that China's socialist economy should be a planned commodity economy. As early as 1979, it was pointed out that "the commodity economy can be divided into the capitalist commodity economy and the socialist commodity economy." And, "if the objective planned characteristics of the socialist economy are included, we can also call the socialist economy a planned commodity economy."[8] Further, "the socialist economy is a planned commodity economy based on public ownership. This generalization is more in line with objective reality. This is because it can be distinguished from the capitalist anarchic commodity economy and the communist planned economy without commodities, which shows the transitional nature of this economy."[9] Ma Hong also pointed out clearly in his article "Several Issues on the Reform of the Economic System," published in 1981, "I think that at this stage, China is a planned commodity economy."[10] After the concept of the planned commodity economy was formally affirmed by the decision-makers, economists developed a full theoretical explanation of the planned commodity economy on the basis of original research.[11] Most scholars affirmed this idea. Yu Guangyuan believed that this important exposition affirmed that the socialist planned economy must be a planned commodity economy on the basis of public ownership, which was a breakthrough in

---

7. Zhao Ziyang, *Report on the Thirteenth National Congress of the Communist Party of China* (People's Publishing House, 1987).

8. Luo Gengmo, "On the Planned Economy, Market Economy and Others," *Economic Research*, no. 12 (1979).

9. Xie Youquan and Hu Peizhao, "Correct Understanding and Planned Utilization of the Law of Value Based on Reality," *Economic Research*, no. 12 (1979).

10. Ma Hong, "Several Issues on the Reform of the Economic Management System," *Economic Research*, no. 7 (1981).

11. Bai Yongxiu and Ma Xiaoyong, "A Review of Theoretical Research on China's Market Economy in the Past 60 Years Since the Founding of the People's Republic of China," *Guizhou Social Sciences*, no. 7 (2009).

Marxist political economics and conducive to the development of socialist productive forces.[12] Other representative views held that only by recognizing the property of the socialist economy as a commodity economy and consciously following and applying the role of the law of value could China really shift its economic work to the track of improving economic efficiency, strengthen the state's planning guidance for the overall national economy, and achieve greater macroeconomic benefits.[13] Since the commodity economy was the inherent essential connection of the socialist mode of production, it was not only a basic economic feature, but also an important economic feature, second only to the public ownership of the means of production.[14]

Some theorists regarded the socialist planned commodity economy as a "commodity economy with planned development," holding that the theory of the planned commodity economy clarified the characteristics of the socialist planned economy, thus drawing a clear line between the socialist planned economy and the communist planned economy and distinguishing the relationship between the socialist commodity economy and the capitalist commodity economy. The socialist commodity economy was a new type of commodity economy, and it was based on public ownership. The fundamental interests of commodity producers were consistent. The commodity production and circulation of the entire society were planned, not anarchic. The socialist economy was the unity of the planned economy and the commodity economy. On the one hand, it was a planned economy with commodity production and exchange, and on the other, it was a commodity economy with planned development.[15]

Some theorists put the "socialist planned commodity economy" on the commodity economy, pointing out that the full development of the commodity economy was a necessary condition for realizing China's economic modernization. The commodity economy could optimize the allocation of resources, improve economic efficiency, and promote the development of productive forces. Some views discussed the compatibility of public ownership and the commodity economy, pointing out that the commodity economy required enterprises to become independent commodity producers and operators, with complete independent management rights, which was the inherent requirement of the commodity economy. In a commodity economy, any form of ownership of the means of production, whether private ownership or public ownership, must meet the inherent requirement of the commodity economy. As a general economic form that could be used by private or public ownership, the commodity economy had no function of transforming any form of ownership, but could only be used as an economic operation form and as a shell of operation by any form of ownership. Therefore, making the public ownership better

---

12. Yu Guangyuan, "The Socialist Commodity Economic System as the Foundation and Center of the New Economic System," *Economic Research*, no. 1 (1988).

13. Ma Hong, "Re-examination of China's Commodity Economy Under the Socialist System," *Economic Research*, no. 12 (1984).

14. He Liancheng, "Further Discussion on the Socialist Commodity Economy," *Economic Research*, no. 5 (1985).

15. Shu Hualu, "The Socialist Economy Must Be a Planned Commodity Economy," *Hubei Social Sciences*, no. 12 (1989).

meet the inherent requirements of the commodity economy would not damage the nature of public ownership, but would instead enable public ownership to make full use of the commodity economy, form an organic and unified public ownership economic system, and promote the rapid development of social productive forces.[16]

Another point of view was that planning was not an essential attribute of the socialist economy. Like the market, planning was only an economic means. Therefore, reform should no longer be bound by the traditional concept that the planned economy was an essential attribute of socialism. Although the socialist economy was a planned commodity economy, to what extent it was planned depended on the degree of socialist mass production and the development of the commodity economy. The planned economy was just a summary of the product economy from the perspective of the economic operation mode, which was a derivative feature of the product economy. The practical meaning of the planned economy was more appropriately attributed to planned regulation, not to the economic system.[17]

It had become an irreversible objective trend for China's socialist economic reform to choose a market orientation and adhere to a combination with the market, because it adapted to the nature of contemporary socialized production and was the requirement of the development law of socialism itself. Socialism was a planned commodity economy established on the basis of public ownership, and market and market mechanism were the regulators of the rational allocation of resources inherent in the modern socialized commodity economy. The main drawback of the traditional planned system lay in its rejection and negation of the market and market mechanisms. Therefore, reform could only choose a market orientation. There was no other way. This market orientation referred to the objective mode of establishing the socialist commodity economic system proposed in the Decision of the Central Committee of the Communist Party of China on the Reform of the Economic System, as well as the three aspects of reforming the enterprise mechanism and establishing and perfecting the market system and the macro-control system dominated by indirect regulation.

The history and current situation of world economic development showed that planning and market were the common and complementary operation mechanisms of the modern socialized commodity economy, and they were the common regulators of realizing reasonable resource allocation beyond social system. Realizing the organic combination of plan and market or the integration of the planned market would contribute to coordinated, stable economic growth. The success of China's reform lay in adhering to a socialist market orientation.[18]

---

16. Yu Zuyao, "A Review of the Discussion on the Relationship Between Planning and the Market in Recent Years," *Economic Trends*, no. 3 (1991).

17. Fu Tingchen, "Is Planning the Essential Attribute of Socialism?" *Economic Trends*, no. 6 (1992); Wang Yiming and Liu Youyuan, "The Planned Economy is Not an Independent Economic System," *Reform Forum*, no. 4 (1991).

18. Wu Jinglian, "Discussion on the Relationship Between Planning and the Market and the Orientation of China's Economic System Reform," *Reform*, no. 1 (1991).

3. Theoretical Discussion on the Compatibility Between Socialist Public Ownership and the Commodity Economy

In the mid-1980s, theoretical circles began to discuss the inevitability of the existence of the socialist commodity economy, which mainly included several views.[19] The first view was that the main reason for the existence of the commodity economy under the socialist conditions was the existence of interest differences. In a socialist society, there were not only different forms of public ownership, but also various forms of ownership with public ownership as the main body, and they needed to establish economic relations with each other through commodity exchange. The differences and contradictions in their economic interests had to be adjusted according to the principle of the commodity economy of equivalent exchange, so there needed to be a commodity currency relationship. The second view held that the main reason for the existence of the commodity economy under socialist conditions lay in the different ownership of the means of production. In order to find the reasons for the existence of the commodity economy under socialist conditions, it was necessary to start from the ownership system. Enterprise ownership was a new form of public ownership. It was the transition form of ownership from class and group ownership to social possession, that is, from state ownership to free man association. It differed from collective ownership and was the reason for the existence of the commodity economy under socialist conditions. The third view held that the main reason for the existence of the commodity economy under socialist conditions lay in the individual ownership of the labor force. The fourth point of view held that the main reason for the existence of the commodity economy under socialist conditions lay in the coexistence of public ownership of the means of production and individual ownership of the labor force. The reason for the existence of the commodity economy under socialist conditions should be explained from the socialist combination of laborers and the means of production. The laborer who had personal ownership of the labor force and the means of production owned by the laborer were the two elements of socialist production. The fifth point of view was that the variation of the social nature of labor was the fundamental reason for the emergence and existence of commodities. As long as the variation of human labor existed, the commodity economy was an inevitable form of human labor exchange.

At the end of the 1980s, with the deepening of economic system reform, the compatibility of the commodity economy and public ownership gradually attracted the attention of theoretical circles, and this issue was widely discussed. Some scholars believed that workers were organized to work together in the enterprise. In recognizing the personal material interests of workers, it was impossible not to recognize the collective material interests of the workers who were united in the enterprise. This kind of material benefit difference caused by the means of making a living through labor was precisely the root of the existence of the socialist commodity economy. The fact that the commodity economy was rooted in the socialist public ownership economy

---

19. Han Zhiguo, "Commodity Economy: Exploration and Choice at a New Starting Point," *Chinese Social Sciences*, no. 6 (1986).

showed that public ownership and the commodity economy were compatible even with the deep interest relationship.[20] Some scholars pointed out that the reason for the incompatibility between the commodity economy and public ownership lay in the confusion of the conditions for the emergence and existence of the commodity economy. The condition for the existence of the commodity economy was that the social division of labor and the means of production belonged to the owners of different material interests. In a socialist society, owners with different material interests were independent commodity producers with different material interests. It was thus necessary and possible to develop the commodity economy on the basis of socialist public ownership.[21]

In May 1991, the National Theoretical Seminar on the Combination of Socialist Public Ownership and the Commodity Economy was held in Jinhua, Zhejiang Province. There were different views on the relationship between public ownership and the commodity economy. One view was that socialist public ownership and the commodity economy could be combined, but the socialist economy and the commodity economy could not be combined. Ownership and commodity exchange were both sides of the relations of production. Therefore, it was acceptable to combine socialist public ownership with the commodity economy. Socialism could contain the commodity economy, and even the socialist economy itself was a kind of commodity economy. However, the combination of the socialist economy and the commodity economy could not be accepted. The second view was that socialist public ownership was incompatible with the commodity economy in its essence. If public ownership was compatible with the commodity economy, logically speaking, it was only necessary to establish the commodity economy on the basis of the existing system. But in order for the reform of the form of public ownership to be compatible with the commodity economy, it would eventually be necessary to change public ownership. From this theoretical logical analysis, the emergence and full development of the commodity economy was bound to be related to private ownership. In the public ownership economy, the conditions for the full development of the commodity economy were not available, so property rights reform was needed, and property rights reform could not be carried out under the premise of public ownership. Therefore, the commodity economy and public ownership were incompatible in essence. Even if they were combined, it was only a superficial combination. The third view was that the socialist commodity economy was a "quasi commodity economy." The "quasi commodity economy" was subordinate to socialism and subject to public ownership. The meaning of the "quasi commodity economy" was that it could avoid all kinds of negative phenomena that may occur simply for the purpose of developing the commodity economy, and that it could correct the theoretical misunderstandings caused by the compatibility theory of public ownership and the commodity economy, as well as various far-fetched arguments that were difficult to justify. According to the logic of the "compatibility theory," it was only necessary

20. Gu Shutang and Chang Xiuze, "An Outline of the Socialist Commodity Economy," *Economic Research*, no. 6 (1990).

21. Bai Yongxiu, "The Theory and Practice of the Compatibility of Public Ownership and the Commodity Economy," *Economic System Reform*, no. 2 (1990).

to establish the commodity economy on the existing public ownership, which was obviously inconsistent with Marx's economic theory. The fourth point of view was that public ownership and the commodity economy could be adjusted and combined. There were contradictions between public ownership and the commodity economy, and only through mutual adjustment and combination could there be a way out. Public ownership and the commodity economy were not the same economic relations, as each had its own essential characteristics. The difference between the two was that between "equivalent labor exchange" embodied in the equality principle of public ownership and "equivalent value exchange" embodied in the commodity economy. At the current stage of the development of productive forces, the relatively sufficient "equal labor exchange" could only be realized in the different interest subjects of the public ownership economy, and the principle of equivalent exchange must be implemented throughout society. It was for this reason that the combination and conversion of "equal labor exchange" and "equivalent exchange" appeared. In economic operations, this combination had contradictions and friction. From this point of view, the combination of public ownership and the commodity economy could only be the combination of mutual adjustment, that is, public ownership should adapt to the development of the commodity economy and make full use of the law of value, and the commodity economy should adapt to the requirements of public ownership and adhere to the direction of common prosperity. However, it should be noted that in order to build socialism in a country with relatively backward productive forces, it was necessary to focus on how to adapt public ownership to the development of commodity economy. The key was to reform the traditional public ownership mode.[22]

7.3 Operational Mechanism of the Socialist Planned Commodity Economy

1. The Reform Policy and Operation Mode Based on Planning and Supplemented by the Market

In a speech on March 8, 1979, Chen Yun talked about planning and market issues. He pointed out that the drawback of the previous planning system was that there was only a plan in proportion, and there was no market regulation. Market regulation had involved little more than adjusting according to the law of value. Chen believed that the economy of the whole socialist period must have two parts: the planned economy part (the planned part according to the proportion) and the market regulation part (i.e. not making plans and allowing it to produce according to the changes of market supply and demand, that is, with the "blind" adjustment part). The first part was basic and necessary, and the second part was subordinate, secondary, and necessary. He pointed out

---

22. See Li Yiping and Zhang Wenduo, "A Summary of the Symposium on the Combination of Socialist Public Ownership and Commodity Economy," *Economic Trends* (1991); Zhong Shu, "A Summary of the National Symposium on the Combination of Socialist Public Ownership and the Commodity Economy," *The Party and Government Forum*, no. 7 (1991).

that in the future economic regulation and system reform, the proportion adjustment of the planned economy and market regulation would account for a large proportion.[23] Deng Xiaoping agreed with and supported Chen Yun's thinking. In his speech on January 16, 1980, he expounded on it, saying that in seeking a path of economic development in line with China's reality, "planned regulation and market regulation should be combined."[24]

In June 1981, the resolution of the Sixth Plenary Session of the Eleventh Central Committee of the Communist Party of China formally put forward that the planned economy must be implemented on the basis of public ownership, and at the same time, the auxiliary role of market regulation should be brought into play.

Since the beginning of 1982, the State Commission for Structural Reform and the Center of Economic Research under the State Council jointly organized and initiated a discussion on theoretical issues concerning economic restructuring. The focus was on the relationship between the planned economy and market regulation, because correctly handling the relationship between the two was the core issue of economic system reform.

During the discussion, it was generally believed that the characteristic of the socialist economy was planning, which was connected with commodity and market concerns. The two could be unified rather than diametrically opposed. Therefore, the reform of the economic system needed to adhere to the principle of giving priority to the planned economy supplemented by market regulation. The report of the Twelfth National Congress of the Communist Party of China made a brilliant exposition on this point, clearly pointing out that the planned economy should be implemented on the basis of socialist public ownership. At the same time, the production and circulation of some products were allowed not to be planned, but instead regulated by the market. This was a comprehensive summary of the discussion on the relationship between the planned economy and market regulation. The economic and ideological circles launched a discussion on this issue.

There were generally two types of opinions on how to describe the socialist economy scientifically. One was that the basic feature of the socialist economy was a planned economy, not a commodity economy. Some opinions were expressed as the "planned economy of commodity production and commodity exchange on the basis of public ownership of the means of production," while others focused on the "planned economy of a commodity nature" or the "planned economy of a combination of commodity and product type." Another view was that the socialist economy was a planned commodity economy. Some said that the socialist economy was both a planned economy and a commodity economy, and both were closely related to the basic characteristics of the socialist economy. Under socialist conditions, since there was commodity production and commodity exchange, there was a commodity economy.

In determining how to understand the essential characteristics of a planned economy, some

---

23. Literature Research Office of the CPC Central Committee, *Selected Important Documents Since the Third Plenary Session of the CPC Central Committee*, vol. 1 (People's Publishing House, 1982), 65.

24. Deng Xiaoping, *Selected Works of Deng Xiaoping*, vol. 2 (People's Publishing House, 1994), 247.

held that mandatory planning was an important feature of the planned economy and its basic form. Mandatory planning was a symbol of the socialist planned economy. Only by adhering to the mandatory planning could the state's ownership and right to use the means of production be unified, the leading position of the economy owned by all the people be strengthened, and the boundary between the socialist economy and the capitalist economy be drawn. Some held that the essential feature of a planned economy was to consciously realize the proportional development of the national economy through a pre-planned arrangement. The way to achieve proportional development was a matter of specific methods. According to practical experience, a variety of planning guidance methods could more effectively ensure the proportional development of the national economy and make the planned economy more perfect and effective than a single mandatory plan.

In discussing how to determine the scope and boundary of mandatory planning, guiding plans, and market regulation, there were generally three opinions on the scope of the mandatory plan. One was to divide it according to the enterprise. Large enterprises and enterprises owned by all the people issued mandatory plans. According to the second opinion, for important products related to the national economy and the people's livelihood, mandatory plans would be issued and allocated by the state. The third opinion was that the tasks should be divided according to their importance. In principle, the production of materials required by the state's key tasks, whether they were important products or general products and whether they were produced by large-scale enterprises or small and medium-sized enterprises, were to be arranged and distributed uniformly by the state. There were also different views on market regulation. Some held that products under planned management with economic leverage were regarded as market regulation, while others held that market regulation was limited to small commodities produced by small enterprises and individual workers, which were inconvenient for unified planned management, with small output value and greater variety.[25]

2. Target and Operation Mode of the Planned Commodity Economic System Reform

In October 1984, the Third Plenary Session of the Twelfth Central Committee of the Communist Party of China adopted the Decision of the Central Committee of the Communist Party of China on the Reform of the Economic System (hereinafter referred to as the Decision). The Decision clearly pointed out that the socialist planned economy must be intentionally based on and apply the law of value. It was a planned commodity economy on the basis of public ownership. On this basis, the Decision further clarified the direction of China's economic system reform, pointing out that in order to fundamentally change the economic system that constrained the development of productive forces, it was necessary to consciously sum up China's historical experience, carefully study the actual situation and development requirements of China's economy, and at the same time, absorb and learn from all the reflections of the world at that time, including developed

---

25. *China Economic Yearbook* (1983) (Economy and Management Publishing House, 1986).

capitalist countries. It was necessary to establish a socialist economic system full of vigor and vitality with Chinese characteristics and promote the development of social productive forces. This was the basic task of China's economic system reform.

With regard to the center of the system reform, the Decision pointed out that strengthening the vitality of enterprises, especially the vitality of large and medium-sized enterprises owned by the people, was the central link of the whole economic system reform focusing on cities. Around this central link, it was important to mainly solve two aspects of the relationship, that is, to establish the correct relationship between the state and enterprises owned by the people, expand the autonomy of enterprises, and establish the correct relationship between employees and enterprises to ensure the master status of workers in enterprises. The Decision also clearly pointed out that according to Marxist theory and socialist practice, ownership and management rights could be appropriately separated. The purpose of the "separation of two powers" was to make the enterprise truly become a relatively independent economic entity, become a socialist producer and operator with independent management and financing of profits and losses, have the ability of self-transformation and self-development, and become a legal entity with certain rights and obligations. With regard to the relationship between the planned economy and the commodity economy, the Decision held that it was necessary to first break through the traditional concept of opposing the planned economy and the commodity economy and clearly recognize that the socialist economy was a planned commodity economy based on public ownership. The implementation of the planned economy, the application of the law of value, and the development of the commodity economy were not mutually exclusive, but unified, and it was wrong to set them against each other.

The Decision summarized the basic points of China's planned economic system, noting that first, on the whole, China implemented a planned economy, not a market economy completely regulated by the market. In addition, production and exchange completely regulated by the market were mainly labor activities of some agricultural and sideline products, daily commodities, and service repair industries, which played an auxiliary role in the national economy. Further, the implementation of the planned economy did not mean that the mandatory plan was given priority, and both the mandatory plan and the guiding plan were the specific forms of the planned economy. Fourth, the guiding plan mainly relied on the use of economic leverage, and the mandatory plan must be implemented, while the economic law could not be neglected.

The theory of the planned commodity economy was a great transcendence of the traditional planned economy theory. It affirmed that the socialist economy was a commodity economy, and the commodity economy was regarded as an intrinsic attribute of socialism. In addition, it denied the traditional idea that mandatory planning was the fundamental feature of the socialist public ownership economy, which fundamentally shook the foundation of the socialist planned economy. Its shortcomings were that it recognized the commodity economy but not the market economy, and it regarded the market economy as a capitalist thing. Further, the development of the market system was only understood as the development of the commodity market, so the understanding of the market mechanism was relatively simple and one-sided.

In October 1987, the fourth part of the report of the Thirteenth National Congress of the Communist Party of China discussed in detail the reform of the economic system. The report pointed out that the system of the socialist planned commodity economy should be the internal unity of planning and market. On this issue, it was necessary to clarify several basic points. First, the essential difference between the socialist commodity economy and the capitalist commodity economy lay in the different ownership basis. Second, planning needed to be based on commodity exchange and the law of value. Third, the scope of action for the plan and the market covered the entire society. Generally speaking, the new economic operation mechanism should be the mechanism in which "the state regulates the market and the market guides the enterprises." The state used economic means, legal means, and necessary administrative means to regulate the relationship between market supply and demand and create a suitable economic and social environment, so as to guide enterprises to make correct business decisions. The report pointed out that the current task of deepening reform was to gradually establish the basic framework of a new planned commodity economy by carrying out the supporting reforms in planning, investment, finance, foreign trade, and other aspects of the central link of the transformation of the enterprise operation mechanism. The report of the Thirteenth National Congress of the Communist Party of China affirmed the inevitable economic phenomena, such as the market of the means of production, technology market, labor market, stock and bonds system, and so forth, along with the development of socialized mass production and the commodity economy, that were necessary for establishing the socialist market system, improving the macro-control system, and invigorating enterprises.

The reform mode of "the state regulating the market and the market guiding enterprises" was a major development of the theory of the planned commodity economy. First, it clearly pointed out for the first time that the difference between socialism and capitalism was not the difference between market and planning, but the difference of ownership and the difference between systems. Second, in this mode, the plan was based on the market mechanism. The indirect planning based on the system and the market mechanism were the basis of economic operations, which greatly improved the social status of the market. Finally, it clearly put forward the comprehensive nature of the socialist market system, which fundamentally broke through the traditional concepts of "limited commodity production" and "limited market regulation" in the long-standing socialist economy.

After the Thirteenth National Congress of the Communist Party of China put forward the reform mode of "the state regulating the market and the market guiding enterprise," theoretical circles mainly focused on the basis of the system of the state regulating the market and the market guiding the enterprise's economic operations, the relationship among the state, the market, and enterprise, and the relationship between planning and the market.

From the practice of economic system reform, by 1987, the scope of the state's mandatory plan and unified price gradually narrowed, the market for agricultural and sideline products and industrial consumer goods was basically formed, and the market for the means of production and the short-term capital market had seen a certain level of development. The number of industrial products under the direct management of the central government was reduced from more than 120 to 60, and the number of unified materials had been reduced from more than 180 to 22. In terms of the prices of various commodities, the proportion of state guided prices and market regulated prices had been implemented. Agricultural and sideline products accounted for 65%, industrial consumer goods accounted for 55%, and the means of production accounted for 40%.[26] The role of the law of value in linking production and demand and regulating the balance of supply and demand was strengthened.

7.4 Theoretical Exploration on the Combination of the Planned Economy and Market Regulation

1. The Connotation of the Combination of the Planned Economy and Market Regulation

In the late 1980s and early 1990s, the mainstream view of China's theoretical circles was that China's socialist economy was a planned commodity economy on the basis of public ownership. The main goal of China's economic system reform was to adapt to the development requirements of the planned commodity economy and construct an economic system and operational mechanism suitable for China's national conditions while combining the planned economy with market regulation. The discussion on this issue and the results it produced had certain innovative significance for the operation of the traditional socialist economy.

It was commonly believed that the planned economy was the basic economic system of socialism, and market regulation was the basic regulation form of the commodity economy. The combination of the planned economy and market regulation meant to introduce the market regulation mechanism into the planned economic system, giving full play to the regulatory role of market mechanisms so as to realize the planned economy more effectively. Its significance was that it reflected the characteristics of the socialist planned commodity economic system. Since the planned economy was the basic economic system of socialism, and the socialist economy of China was a planned commodity economy on the basis of public ownership, the economic operation mechanism of the combination of the planned economy and market regulation would naturally become the operation mechanism of the socialist economy. In addition, it reflected the characteristics of the new socialist economic operation mechanism. Due to the introduction of the market mechanism, the planned economy had changed from relying on mandatory planning to mainly using economic means. In order to realize the planned economy, planned regulation was to be in the leading position and provide guidance for market regulation. Many theorists made a distinction between the planned economy, the market economy, and planned regulation and market regulation. They believed that the market economy was an economic

---

26. Editorial Board of *China Economic Yearbook*, *China Economic Yearbook* (1988) (Economy and Management Publishing House, 1986), iii–3.

system based on private ownership of the means of production, and the economic operation was generally market-oriented and spontaneously regulated by the law of value. It reflected the essential characteristics of the capitalist economy. The planned economy and market economy were two fundamentally opposite economic systems and types of economic operations. They were not neutral economic categories. Planned regulation and market regulation were two main adjustment means adopted by the economic operation mechanism. Planned regulation referred to the behavior of macroeconomic management departments to regulate the economic operation through the formulation and implementation of the national economic plan according to the goal expected by the government. Market regulation referred to the spontaneous regulation of economic operation by the objective law of value under the condition of a commodity economy. Planned regulation and market regulation did not have obvious sociality or class nature, and they belonged to a neutral concept. They could combine with each other, coexist in the same social conditions, and play their respective functions.[27]

In 1989, when Deng Xiaoping reiterated the correctness of the basic point of Reform and Opening Up, he said, "We must continue to adhere to the combination of the planned economy and market regulation, which cannot be changed. In practical work, in the period of adjustment, we can strengthen or increase planning, and at another time we can adjust the market more flexibly. In the future, we will combine the planned economy with market regulation."[28]

After the Fourth Plenary Session of the Thirteenth Central Committee of the Communist Party of China, the term "combination of the planned economy and market regulation" was used in the reform of the economic system. In December 1990, the Seventh Plenary Session of the Thirteenth Central Committee of the Communist Party of China adopted the Proposal of the Central Committee of the CPC on the Formulation of the Ten-Year Plan for National Economic and Social Development and the Eighth Five-Year Plan.

In the reform of the economic system, the proposal pointed out that in accordance with the requirements of developing the socialist planned commodity economy and combining the planned economy with market regulation, it was necessary to further clarify and grasp the following points: 1) the planned economy can generally maintain proportional development of the national economy and rational allocation of resources, while market regulation can function as a mechanism for survival of the fittest and enhance economic development, and the combination of the two is to bring their advantages and strengths into full play so as to promote the sustained, stable, and coordinated development of the national economy; 2) the planned economy is not limited to the mandatory plan, and the guiding plan is also the specific form of the planned economy; 3) generally speaking, planning economy primarily regulates the overall quantity control, adjustments concerning economic structure and layout, and major economic activities related to the overall situation, which mainly play the role of planning, while the daily production

27. Xiong Jun, "Comments on the Ten Major Points of the Combination of the Planned Economy and Market Regulation," *Contemporary Finance and Economics*, no. 4 (1991).

28. Deng Xiaoping, *Selected Works of Deng Xiaoping*, vol. 3 (People's Publishing House, 1993), 306.

and operation of enterprises, general technical transformation, and small-scale construction and other economic activities are mainly regulated by the market; and 4) the main task of national economic management is to reasonably determine the planning macro-control objectives of national economic development, formulate correct industrial policies, effectively manage comprehensive balance, coordinate the major proportion relationship, and guide and adjust the economic operation by comprehensively supporting economic, legal, and administrative means.

The concept of "combining the planned economy with market regulation" was put forward against the backdrop of rectification and was related to the specific political and economic situation at that time. This formulation not only strengthened the function of national planned management and macro-control, but also had the intention of preventing privatization and unilaterally emphasizing the tendency of the market economy. However, there were different opinions on this formulation at that time. Some in theoretical circles held that the planned economy and market regulation were not at the same level. The conventional formulation was that the planned economy and the market economy were juxtaposed, belonging to the system level of the market economy, while planned regulation and market regulation were parallel, belonging to the level of economic operation mode and mechanism. However, the juxtaposition of the planned economy and market regulation implied that the socialist economic system was a planned economy, and it denied the market economy, which was a retrogression to the theory of the "planned commodity economy."

2. The Combination of the Planned Economy and Market Regulation

Regarding the way of the planned economy and market regulation, there were several representative views in the field of economic thought.

The theory of plate-style combination. At a conference in Wuxi in 1982, an argument was made that "planning should be combined with the market," that is, it should be a combination of plates. This argument divided the national economy into two major sectors, one regulated by planning and the other by the market. On the whole, the national economy was juxtaposed with a plate combination.[29] This view broke through the situation of the planned economy dominating the country and was the initial exploration of the combination of planning and the market. However, it still had traces of the old system. In fact, it still held that planning and the market were mutually exclusive and separated. This "plate theory" later developed into the "main and auxiliary theory," "cage bird theory," and "gradient combination theory."

Colloidal combination theory. This view was the opposite of the "plate theory," which held that the national economy could not be divided into two parts and that planned regulation and market regulation were integrated. In a unified body, the two interacted and influenced each other, forming a unified economic operation mechanism. The unity of planning and the market was

---

29. Editorial Department of *Economic Research, Review and Prospect of China's Socialist Economic Theory* (China Economic Press, 1986).

shown in their common direction of action, both of which reflected the requirements of objective economic laws. According to the current social needs, total social labor was to be allocated in proportion among the various departments of the national economy, so that social labor could be reasonably and effectively utilized. The scope of their functions was also the same, covering the entire national economy. But at the time, it was difficult to establish this kind of adjustment mechanism, because the current enterprise system, market system, and macro system were not perfect, making it difficult to completely integrate planning and the market.[30]

Penetration and organic combination. According to this view, the national economy was still divided into two parts. One was regulated by the plan and the other by the market. At the same time, each adjustment part had another adjustment factor, that is, the two cross parts were jointly regulated by the plan and the market. Under socialist conditions, there was no complete free market. The market itself was inherently planned, and the plan and the market were organically combined. Without the market, planned regulation would lose its dependence, and market regulation should also be guided and participated by the national plan. Therefore, planning was the guidance and the market was the foundation. The two were organically combined.[31]

There were many opinions and theories, but little practical significance, because the social economy was a whole entity with complex internal relations. From the perspective of two-dimensional space or three-dimensional space, any kind of economic regulation means covered the entire social economy. It was impossible to conceive of implementing one kind of adjustment means to a certain part or a certain level of a certain social economy at the same time point, while implementing another adjustment means for another part or another level, making them coexist peacefully and organically. The real economy demonstrated that the "double track system" in economic management and operation led to chaos in economic life, such as the failure of the planning system, the failure of market regulation, and the overall amount and the waste of resources spinning out of control. Moreover, the "planned" and "unplanned" blocks could not be exchanged under the same market criteria. Therefore, it was necessary to find a new way of thinking that combined with market-oriented thought.

3. Research on the Mode of the Combination of the Planned Economy and Market Regulation

This theoretical discussion showed that in the operation of the socialist commodity economy, planned regulation and market regulation could and should be combined. However, how to

---

30. Shen Shanqing, "An Overview of Some Controversial Viewpoints Proposed by the Current Economic Theorists," *Review of Social Sciences*, no. 4 (1991).

31. Yu Zuyao, "Review of the Discussion on the Relationship Between Planning and Market in Recent Years," *Economic Trends*, no. 3 (1991); Liu Shibai, "On the Combination of Planning and Market," *Economic Overview*, no. 5 (1991); Ma Hong, "On the Relationship Between Plan and Market," *Reform*, no. 1 (1991); Liu Suinian, "Further Discussion on the Combination of the Planned Economy and Market Regulation," *Research on Planned Economy*, no. 7 (1991).

combine the two, that is, how to achieve the organic unity of the regulatory role of the two in the economic operation according to the inherent relevance of the planned regulation and the market regulation, was still a problem that needed to be explained in connection with the real economy. At that time, it was generally accepted that the theoretical mode of the socialist planned commodity economy operation in China was that the state (plan) regulated the market, and the market (regulation) guided enterprises (economic subjects). This theoretical model was to be understood from several aspects.

Primarily, it was understood that in the planned commodity economy, the overall (macro) economic operation was mainly planned regulation. This was because planned regulation was an effective means of macroeconomic management. Marx pointed out, "It is only where production is under the actual, predetermining control of society that the latter establishes a relation between the volume of social labour-time applied in producing definite articles, and the volume of the social want to be satisfied by these articles."[32] Therefore, from the overall situation of social and economic development and the overall interests of society, planned regulation could uniformly and systematically distribute social labor across society to meet social needs. Second, in the socialist commodity economy, the fundamental consistency of workers' economic interests and the development of socialization of production linked social and economic activities into a relatively unified whole. The unity and integrity of socialist economy required, on the one hand, the planned management and regulation of social and economic activities on the macro level, and on the other, it provided feasible conditions for society to manage and regulate the national economy in a planned, unified way, so as to ensure the balanced development of the economy. Third, in socialist interest relations, there were also contradictions between individual interests, local interests, and overall interests, between short-term interests and long-term interests, and between micro and macro benefits. Therefore, it was necessary to scientifically plan and regulate various interest relations on a macro level, limit or avoid people's blindness in pursuing interests, and unify individual interests, local interests, and overall interests to the maximum extent through planning, so that the people's interest pursuits could be incorporated into a certain system of social norms and become the energy to promote economic development.

Secondly, in the socialist commodity economy, as a means of macroeconomic management, planned regulation could play an effective role through economic connection with the market. On the one hand, planning and the market were essentially an information exchange relationship. Planning was not a purely subjective product, and its objective basis was the market situation. Planning decisions were made according to the collection and judgment of market information. Market information determined the content of the plan, the stipulation of the plan index, and the feasibility of the plan target. Any economic plan that was divorced from the actual market would not work at all or would cause confusion in economic life. On the other hand, from the characteristics of the commodity economy, economic relations in the process of social production, the transformation of social material and energy, and various demands were realized in the

---

32. Marx and Engels, *Complete Works of Marx and Engels*, vol. 25 (People's Publishing House, 1975), 209.

form of market exchange in an indirect way. The essence of the market was the socio-economic connection based on the principle of equivalent exchange. In the market, economic entities only recognized the law of value and accepted the regulation of the market mechanism, which was directly related to their own economic interests. Therefore, in the socialist commodity economy, planned regulation could not ignore the law of value, but could only act on market activities on the basis of this law, nor could planned regulation replace the market mechanism, but could only regulate its economic behavior by stimulating and restricting the vital interests of economic subjects by market mechanisms. In other words, the market mechanism was the intermediary between planned regulation and the economic subject. Only through the transmission of the market mechanism in the market process could planned regulation have an effect on the behavior of the economic subject. As a general mechanism of the commodity economy's operation, the market mechanism was inseparable from the economic benefits of economic subjects. Otherwise, economic operations would deviate from the track of the law of value and lose vitality and efficiency.

Finally, this analysis of the internal relationship between planned regulation and market regulation determined the characteristics of the combination of planned regulation and market regulation, that is, the formulation and implementation of the plan should be based on the market and implemented through it, and the operation of the market should reflect the intention of the plan. In other words, the planned regulation of the socialist commodity economy was based on the macro level of economic operations, on the basis of fully understanding the planned development law of the socialist economy and the basic law of the commodity economy while consciously and effectively adjusting and correcting market activities with economic plans and economic means conforming to such objective laws, so as to improve the operation of the national economy.

The combination of the planned economy and market regulation was a principled formulation. In order to give this expression practical significance, it was necessary to solve two theoretical difficulties. First, what economic mechanism should the operation of the combination of planned economy and market regulation be based on? Second, how should the specific mode of the combination of planned economy and market regulation be decided? First of all, it was important to make clear the conceptual difference between the economic system and the economic mechanism. The economic system was a structural form of economic operations and the management system determined by a certain mode of social production. It included a certain structure of production relations and interest relations, a certain mode and method of economic management (including a series of laws, regulations, policies, and corresponding executive agencies), and the mechanism and process of economic system movement. A certain economic system was naturally closely related to a certain economic mechanism. However, as a mechanism process at the level of economic operations, the economic mechanism had a more direct relationship with the development of productive forces and social and economic interests, so it had greater tension than the economic system. For example, the market mechanism not only applied to the market economy system, but also played a role in the planned economic system.

In the discussion on China's economic system reform, an unsolved problem was whether the operation of the economic system combining the planned economy and market regulation was based on the planned mechanism or the market mechanism, or whether the two mechanisms worked at the same time. Logically speaking, the operation of any social economy could only be established on one economic mechanism in a certain period of time, and it was impossible for the two mechanisms to work at the same time. The operation of the socialist commodity economy was based on which kind of economic mechanism, and it was necessary to make an in-depth study of the relationship between social and economic interests.

In an abstract sense, the process of social and economic movement was that people used economic resources, through labor and exchange, to meet social needs for different use values. In this process, through some kind of interest restriction factor, people made the relationship between various resources, various production activities, and various production and needs more reasonable and coordinated in a special, efficient way to ensure the smooth progress of the production of the entire society and improved efficiency. This kind of benefit restriction factor that made the resource allocation tend to be reasonable and effective was one of the most basic socio-economic relations. It was an opportunity to connect people's production activities with the satisfaction of their material needs and coordinate people's interest relations. It showed that in order to realize their special economic interests through their own production activities, people must bring their own production activities in line with some objective natural laws. From the perspective of the individual, economic interests constituted the basic motivation or goal of economic behavior.

Through people's pursuit of economic interests, various economic behaviors could be related, various production activities could be coordinated, and the social production process could be started in a certain way, which was the economic operation mechanism. The economic operation mechanism was essentially a kind of interest incentive and restriction mechanism. It linked various economic behaviors through people's pursuit of economic interests, pushed the social economy to operate in a certain way, and objectively made the relationship between various economic activities tend to be reasonable and coordinated. Any economic mechanism had to be directly related to people's pursuit of economic interests; otherwise it was not an economic system. The market mechanism and planning mechanism were special forms of economic mechanisms. The reason they were different was not dependent on whether they were related to people's economic interests, but what kind of social and economic interests they were related to.

According to Marxist economics, in the socialist mode of production shared by the entire society, the means of rational allocation of social labor was the planned economy. The function mechanism of the planned economy was naturally the planning mechanism. The planning mechanism was also economic, that is, it required that people's pursuit of economic interests be taken as an opportunity to start and regulate economic operations. Taking the planning mechanism as the basic point of economic operation, one of the basic requirements was the high consistency of the economic interests of all members of society, that is, the individual interests of social members and the overall interests of society were unified at all levels, and there were basically no differences in interests among the members of society or between the members of society and the overall society. Therefore, society could make plans directly according to the requirements of the overall interests of society and manage and regulate economic operations accordingly. In this case, the planning mechanism had a direct, effective incentive and restrictive effect on the economic behavior of social members. Because the economic interests pursued by all members of society were consistent with the planned objectives, the planning mechanism was in line with the people's pursuit of interest. Starting from their own economic interests, the people needed to consciously follow the intention of the plan. In this way, all social and economic activities would be integrated into the planned track.

At the current stage of China's socialist development, it was obvious that such a high degree of unity of social interest relations did not exist. Since there was not a high degree of consistency in the interest relationship, the planning mechanism could not fit in with the special economic interests of social members, and it had no regulatory effect on the economic behavior of social members. For quite some time after the founding of the People's Republic of China, the planned economy it implemented was not based on an economic planning mechanism, but was basically carried out by administrative means, and the result was rigid and inefficient. Looking at several Five-Year Plans that were implemented, there was a large gap between the planned targets and the implementation results. As the operation mechanism of the commodity economy, the market mechanism was the realistic description of the function mechanism of the law of value. In the commodity economy, the interests of various members of society differed greatly, and the market mechanism was an economic mechanism that was consistent with the differences of social interest relations. As long as the social economy was a commodity economy, the economic interests of social members had to be relatively separated, which required the use of the law of value and market mechanisms to regulate people's economic behavior by stimulating and restricting their special economic interests, so as to regulate the social and economic operations. Therefore, the operation of the socialist commodity economy was based on the market mechanism.

7.5 Research on the Operation of the Socialist Commodity Economy

1. On the Relationship Between Public Ownership and the Market Mechanism

The law of value was the basic law of the commodity economy, and its regulating function on the social economy was realized through the market mechanism. The market mechanism was the function mechanism of the law of value regulating production and circulation in the market. As the sum of commodity exchange relations, the market was related not only to the formation conditions of value, but also to the changes of social supply and demand. What it reflected was the internal relationship between production and exchange, and between labor consumption and social utility. This relationship restricted the movements of production, exchange, distribution, and consumption in the commodity economy. This was the market mechanism, through which the law of value regulated the operation of the social economy.

As the operation mechanism of the commodity economy, the market mechanism was related to the micro foundation of the commodity economy. The micro foundation of the commodity economy operation was that every market participant must join the market activities as an independent interest subject (economic subject). The commodity economy, as a kind of social and economic form with the purpose of exchange directly in production, had certain objective stipulations, that is, people in a certain division of labor system could meet their own life needs through the exchange of their labor products. In this kind of exchange relationship, each market subject generally behaved as an independent and equal interest subject, and the common principle between them was equivalent exchange. Equivalent exchange was the objective norm of market activities, determining the size of people's economic activity and the degree of satisfaction of their economic interests. It fundamentally reflected the relationship between the value of commodities and the natural scale of social necessary labor time, which was regulated by the market mechanism. Therefore, the direct relationship between the market mechanism and the economic interests of market participants as independent interest subjects was the basic characteristic requirement of the operation of commodity economy. In other words, the regulatory role of the law of value and market mechanism on the operation of the social economy was reflected in the conscious activities of market subjects in pursuit of their own special economic interests. Taking abstract market activities as an example, all economic activities in the market were composed of two basic aspects, buying and selling, and the buyer and the seller represented different economic interests. Both sides pursued their own special economic interests and strove to obtain the maximum benefits with the minimum labor consumption. Therefore, the goal of producer behavior was profit maximization, and the goal of consumer behavior was to maximize utility. This kind of special interest-oriented trading behavior formed a mutual restriction and interaction market relationship and promoted the operation of the market. Therefore, the adjustment of market relations was caused by the adjustment of people's interest relations. People's pursuit of their own special economic interests was the driving force of market operations and created the opportunity for the market mechanism to regulate market activities. This analysis shows that in order to make the market mechanism work normally and to make the commodity economy operate normally, it was necessary to follow the objective requirements of the law of value, recognize that each market subject and every production body were independent interest subjects and that each of them directly accept the objective measure of social necessary labor time with their own labor or economic activity effect, and exchange labor according to the principle of equivalent value.

Because the function of the market mechanism needed to be connected with the micro foundation of the commodity economy, there were differences in the understanding of the relationship between the market mechanism and public ownership. One view was that the law of value and the natural law of the market mechanism required every laborer to participate in market activities as an independent interest subject. Therefore, it was necessary to change the public ownership of the means of production into private ownership, because only when the individual laborer owned both the ownership of the means of production and the ownership of labor products could he be regarded as an independent interest subject or become an independent commodity producer. Another view was that public ownership was practiced in socialism, which was an unchangeable premise. Since there was a contradiction between market mechanism and public ownership, the role of market mechanism in the socialist economy should be restricted or not recognized. The further development of this opinion was to question the concept of the socialist commodity economy. Although the conclusions of these two opinions were different, their cognitive roots were the same, that is, they absolutely linked the independent interest subject (economic subject) with private ownership, and both believed that market mechanism and public ownership were incompatible. In fact, connecting the concept of the independent interest subject with private ownership was based on a superficial understanding of the situation. The so-called independent interest subject was the abstract of the simple commodity economy, which meant that each commodity producer produced independently with their own means of production in order to obtain labor products and exchanged their own labor products for others' labor products that they needed through market exchange. Therefore, it had two interrelated meanings. One was the relationship between people's production activities and the ownership of the means of production and labor products, and the other was the relationship between people's private labor and social labor. It was in this sense that the independent interest subject became the micro foundation of the commodity economy. In other words, because the value of private labor products was closely related to the economic interests of commodity producers, the market mechanism could take this opportunity to regulate the economic behavior of commodity producers. The two meanings of the independent interest subject were related to the contradiction caused by the social division of labor, which was the realistic foundation of the commodity economy. Theoretical analysis indicated that the social division of labor had caused two contradictions from the beginning. First was the contradiction between various kinds of specific labor with different qualities, that is, "the labour spent upon them counts effectively, only in so far as it is spent in a form that is useful for others."[33] Second was the contradiction between different owners caused by the distribution of the means of production. Marx said, "The division of labour implies from the outset the division of the conditions of labour, of tools and materials, and thus the splitting-up of accumulated capital among different owners, and thus, also, the division between capital and labour, and the different forms of property itself."[34]

The contradiction between the two sides caused by the social division of labor was determined by the relationship between the two aspects contained in the social division of labor itself, that is, the relationship between labor division in the process of production and the relationship of property distribution in the process of distribution. The former stipulates the division of labor among different producers in terms of labor and the difference in the use values produced; the latter stipulates how different producers manufacture with different means of production and labor conditions as well as their possession of their own products. Therefore, the social division

33. Marx, *Das Kapital*, vol. 1 (People's Publishing House, 1975), 56.
34. Marx and Engels, *Selected Works of Marx and Engels*, vol. 1 (People's Publishing House, 1972), 73.

of labor and the ownership of the means of production were intrinsically linked. Marx and Engels stated, "The various stages of development in the division of labour are just so many different forms of ownership, i.e. the existing stage in the division of labour determines also the relations of individuals to one another with reference to the material, instrument, and product of labour."[35] The development of the social division of labor and ownership was fundamentally determined by the development of productive forces. The history of social development indicates that each different development stage of private ownership of the means of production adapted to the development of productivity and the social division of labor at that time. Similarly, the public ownership of the means of production was also a historical development process, which adapted to the different development levels of productivity and the social division of labor, and it had various forms of development. The highest form of public ownership was that the laborers who were members of the consortium directly combined with the ownership of the means of production and directly possessed the means of production and labor products. They were the real masters of the means of production and labor products, both in the personal sense and in the sense of the consortium. This form of public ownership was related to the high development of productive forces and the final demise of the old social division of labor. At this level of productivity development, China's public ownership took the form of state ownership. In this ownership relationship, determined by the social division of labor, laborers were not only relatively separated in labor (personal labor becoming a part of social division of labor system), but also relatively separated in property relations (workers could not "jointly" own the ownership of means of production and labor products in a complete sense, and the personal interests and "common" interests of workers was not yet completely unified). Therefore, in a certain sense, workers had become relatively independent interest subjects, and their special economic interests were the material motivation of their economic activities. The law of value and the market mechanism had to be linked with the personal economic interests of the workers.

Therefore, as the operation mechanism of the commodity economy, the basic function of the market mechanism was related to the realistic basis of the commodity economy. As long as the social economy was a commodity economy, the contradiction between the two sides caused by the social division of labor would inevitably separate the economic interests of workers, and the law of value and the market mechanism would inevitably regulate the economic behavior of workers by restricting and encouraging their economic interests, thus regulating the operation of the social economy.

2. On the Relationship Between Economic Interests and Property Rights

The essence of the ownership of the means of production was to determine people's economic interests in production. Any production process was the combination of human labor and the means of production to produce labor products. In this process, the relationship between the

---

35. Marx and Engels, *Selected Works of Marx and Engels*, vol. 1 (People's Publishing House, 1972), 26.

laborer and the ownership of the means of production determined the relationship between people and their own labor products, as well as the nature of people's production and interest relations. When analyzing the development of private ownership in *Das Kapital*, Marx pointed out that the mode of petty commodity production was based on the dispersion of land and other means of production, and that "it flourishes, it lets loose its whole energy, it attains its adequate classical form, only where the labourer is the private owner of his own means of labour set in action by himself: the peasant of the land which he cultivates, the artisan of the tool which he handles as a virtuoso."[36]

In other words, in the private ownership of petty commodities, workers produced their own labor products by virtue of their own means of production. The ownership of the means of production, the ownership of the labor force, and the ownership of labor products were unified among them. This kind of "[p]rivate property... where the means of labour and the external conditions of labour belong to private individuals"[37] was the necessary condition to develop social production and the free personality of laborers themselves. Of course, the mode of petty commodity production "excludes the concentration of these means of production, [and] also it excludes cooperation, division of labour within each separate process of production, the control over, and the productive application of the forces of Nature by society, and the free development of the social productive powers. It is compatible only with a system of production, and a society, moving within narrow and more or less primitive bounds... At a certain stage of development, it brings forth the material agencies for its own dissolution... Its annihilation, the transformation of the individualised and scattered means of production into socially concentrated ones, of the pigmy property of the many into the huge property of the few, the expropriation of the great mass of the people from the soil, from the means of subsistence, and from the means of labour, this fearful and painful expropriation of the mass of the people forms the prelude to the history of capital."[38] As a result, the private ownership of petty commodities was replaced by capitalist private ownership, which was based on exploiting others' free labor.

In capitalist private ownership, the laborer had neither the ownership of the means of production nor the ownership of the labor products, but only the ownership of the labor force. Although the capitalist owned the means of production, he did not participate in the production labor, so he could have the ownership of surplus labor products only by purchasing the labor force of the employed workers. Therefore, in this type of private ownership, the ownership of the means of production, the ownership of the labor force, and the ownership of labor products were not unified in both capitalists and employed workers. These three rights could only be unified under the medium of capital. This ownership relationship not only determined the exploitation relationship between capitalists and workers, but also produced an insurmountable contradiction, that is, the capitalists, as the owners of the means of production and labor products, had great

---

36. Marx, *Das Kapital*, vol. 1 (People's Publishing House, 1975), 830.

37. Marx, *Das Kapital*, vol. 1 (People's Publishing House, 1975), 831.

38. Marx, *Das Kapital*, vol. 1 (People's Publishing House, 1975), 830.

enthusiasm to expand reproduction under the drive of the law of surplus value, but the employed workers, as direct producers, did not have such motivation as their labor products and their financial gains were not directly linked, which inevitably hindered the development of productive forces.

Based on the above analysis of the evolution of private ownership, Marx said, "The capitalist mode of appropriation, the result of the capitalist mode of production, produces capitalist private property. This is the first negation of individual private property, as founded on the labour of the proprietor. But capitalist production begets, with the inexorability of a law of Nature, its own negation. It is the negation of negation. This does not re-establish private property for the producer, but gives him individual property based on the acquisition of the capitalist era: *i.e.*, on cooperation and the possession in common of the land and of the means of production."[39] That is to say, socialist public ownership was the negation of the negation of private ownership, meaning that it had changed the situation in which the ownership of the means of production in capitalist private ownership was owned by a few people, so that it was once again owned by the laborer. However, this kind of individual ownership was not a reaction to the private ownership of small commodities, but "the further socialisation of labour and further transformation of the land and other means of production into socially exploited and, therefore, common means of production."[40] This socialist public ownership referred to individual ownership based on the common possession of the means of production. In this kind of ownership relation, on the one hand, in order to meet the needs of the development of the socialization of production, the means of production were increasingly concentrated and were increasingly transformed into the social means of production, which could only be used together. On the other hand, each individual laborer was directly combined with the ownership of the means of production and the ownership of labor products. Marx and Engels stated that "in the appropriation by the proletarians, a mass of instruments of production must be made subject to each individual, and property to all."[41] Therefore, in socialist public ownership, the ownership of the means of production, the ownership of the labor force, and the ownership of labor products were unified in workers. It was precisely because socialist public ownership had solved the contradiction between socialization of production and private possession of the means of production and the separation of laborers from the ownership of means of production and labor products that the consistency of the fundamental interests of workers and of their pursuit of these interests with the development of production was determined. All these factors greatly improved the enthusiasm of workers in production and became a great driving force of economic development and social progress.

However, in view of China's actual situation, there were still many obstacles to overcome in order to make the economic interests of workers directly relate to their labor effects and to unify the ownership of the means of production, the labor force, and labor products, so as to stimulate

---

39. Marx, *Das Kapital*, vol. 1 (People's Publishing House, 1975), 832.
40. Marx, *Das Kapital*, vol. 1 (People's Publishing House, 1975), 831.
41. Marx and Engels, *Selected Works of Marx and Engels*, vol. 1 (People's Publishing House, 1972), 74–75.

the production enthusiasm of workers to the greatest extent. State ownership was a primary development form of public ownership and a transitional form of ownership. On the one hand, its transitional nature determined that the means of production was not owned by any private party, and on the other, it determined that the ownership of workers and means of production was not directly combined. Theoretically speaking, they only had the ownership of the means of production in the sense of "all," but in practice, such ownership had to be exercised through the intermediary of the state. Since the relationship between workers and the ownership of the means of production was not direct, the relationship between them and the ownership of labor products also needed to be indirect. In other words, the ownership of the means of production, the ownership of the labor force, and the ownership of labor products were not absolutely unified. One of the direct consequences of this process was that workers were incomplete in their identity as independent economic or interest subjects. Because the independent interest subject must be the unity of ownership of the means of production, labor ownership, and labor product ownership, their economic behavior was directly related to these three rights, and they were responsible for the effect of their economic behavior according to these rights. According to the theory of the commodity economy, every independent interest subject was a basic atom of the social economy and an independent market participant. The more complete their identity was, the higher the efficiency of their economic activities would be. If the economic activities of enterprises and individuals were not directly related to their economic interests, their activities would lack internal motivation, they would not be responsible for the benefits of their own economic activities, the market mechanism would not be able to play a normal role, and the overall economy would not be able to be brought into the orbit of the law of value. Therefore, in order to improve the operations of the socialist commodity economy, a key problem was to straighten out the relationship between property rights and interests and change the situation in which property rights were too abstract, making no one responsible, so that workers in the socialist commodity economy and enterprise property rights would have a certain direct contact, improving the micro basis of the operation of the socialist commodity economy.

In the 1980s and 1990s, the reform measures of property rights relations were mainly carried out along the idea of "separation of ownership and management rights." It was a big step forward over the previous period and could boost the producer's and operator's motivation and the enterprise's economic efficiency. However, "separation of two powers" was not the separation of property ownership itself, but only the separation of ownership and one of its functions. Some people compared the "separation of rights and powers" with Western enterprise legal entity system, but the two were not the same thing. The modern Western enterprise legal entity system was developed on the basis of the separation of original ownership or terminal ownership (shareholders) and corporate ownership (board of directors). The economic significance of original ownership lay in taking interest according to the shares, while the economic significance of the legal person's ownership lay in the operation of the enterprise's assets so as to increase the value of the assets. The responsibility and power of the legal entity's ownership was exercised and held responsible by the managers selected by the corporate ownership organization (board of directors), while the board of directors was elected from the shareholders according to the number of shares. In the series of shareholders, board of directors, and managers, the relationship of property rights was always clear (i.e., although the manager did not necessarily own equity, he was the personification of the board of directors and was fully responsible for the increase of enterprise assets). The separation of their functions was within the same subject of property rights. Their functions and powers had the attribute of property ownership and were directly related to ownership. Therefore, as an independent producer of commodities, corporate enterprises had all the legal operation rights, but also bore the responsibility of all property management. The meaning of "separation of two powers" in China meant that the state, as the representative of property ownership, handed over the management right of enterprise assets to the enterprise. That is to say, the operators and producers of enterprises had no direct relationship with the property rights of enterprises. They had no property basis for the operation rights of enterprises, that is, they were not derived from their ownership of enterprise assets, but delivered by the state as the representative of property ownership. The separation of ownership and management rights, which was not naturally developed from the same ownership subject, led to the several problems. First, the operators and producers of enterprises had no real ownership of enterprise assets, so they had no property restrictions or property capacity responsible for their own economic behavior (operation and production). This situation led to the softening of the property constraints of enterprises and the inertia of enterprises in operations, and the dependence on distribution cannot be eliminated. Second, the operators and producers of enterprises did not obtain personal income according to the economic principle of income distribution of property rights, but divided the profits according to the administrative contractual relationship with the state of the owner of property rights to obtain operating income and labor income. This type of behavior, which did not follow the law of benefit optimization, would inevitably lead to the gradual decrease of social accumulation proportion and the gradual increase of personal consumption proportion, which would eventually lead to the imbalance of social total supply and demand. Third, if an enterprise did not have ownership, it would not be an independent commodity producer. This made it difficult to form and perfect the market system, and it made it impossible for the state to regulate and control the behavior of enterprises with standardized economic means, thus resulting in disorder and low efficiency of social and economic operations.

In brief, in order to improve the micro basis of the operation of the socialist commodity economy, enterprises needed to become independent commodity producers with independent management, financing of profits and losses, and self-development. To make enterprises become independent commodity producers, it was necessary to make the property relations of enterprises clear, so that the operators and producers of enterprises could have a direct relationship with the property rights of enterprises and so that their economic interests and the operating efficiency of the industry was directly related to the value-added assets, which made them bear the corresponding property responsibility for the effect of their own economic activities.

3. On the Relationship Between Planned Regulation and Market Regulation

In the discussion of the macro operation of the socialist commodity economy, the relationship between planned regulation and market regulation was an important issue of concern in theoretical circles. The differences in various views mainly focused on one point: how to combine planned regulation with market regulation in the socialist commodity economy. In order to solve this problem, it was necessary to delve into analyzing the law of development of the modern commodity economy and the essential characteristics of the socialist mode of production.

The commodity economy was a historical development process related to the social division of labor. With the continuous development and deepening of productivity and the social division of labor, production was becoming increasingly socialized. On the one hand, the socialization of production made the social connection between producers more extensive and diversified, and on the other, it made production increasingly a matter of the overall society. Therefore, an objective requirement of the modern commodity economy, which was closely related to the high development of socialized mass production, was to allocate production factors and economic resources effectively within the social scope on the premise of the free and full flow of production factors and economic resources, so as to achieve balanced development of the social economy and optimization of benefits. Marx pointed out that "the amounts of products corresponding to the differing amounts of needs demand differing and quantitatively determined amounts of society's aggregate labour. It is self-evident that this necessity of the distribution of social labour in specific proportions is certainly not abolished by the specific form of social production; it can only change its form of manifestation."[42] The equilibrium relationship among demand, product, and total social labor was actually a problem of rational allocation of social labor and economic resources on a macro level. In a pure market economy, this problem was completely resolved through market regulation. However, on the one hand, the "perfect competitive market" was only a theoretical abstraction. Even in the capitalist world, market regulation had never been carried out in a complete sense, while on the other hand, as a general trend of economic development, the socialization of production conflicted with the dispersion, blindness, spontaneity, and space-time limitation of market regulation. According to the objective requirements of adapting economic operation to socialized mass production, it was necessary to correct the market mechanism on the whole so as to overcome the deviation, improve the operations, and orient the overall economic operations toward macro equilibrium. Therefore, since the 1930s, Western economics had abandoned Say's law that "supply will create demand by itself" and accepted the principle that effective demand determined the level of balanced income. It abandoned the classical definition of the economy tending to balance naturally by relying on the automatic regulation of the market mechanism and accepted the principle that the market mechanism was regulated by effective demand management, and then the operation of the social economy was adjusted. Generally speaking, this type of reform was in line with the requirements of the development of the modern

---

42. Marx and Engels, *Selected Works of Marx and Engels*, vol. 4 (People's Publishing House, 1972), 368.

commodity economy.

As a means of economic regulation and control, macroeconomic management was the internal requirement of social and economic development. The form of this means of economic control was related to a certain mode of social production. In the socialist mode of production, it was generally manifested as a planned economy. When it came to the concept of the planned economy, there were several issues that needed to be clarified. First of all, the planned economy referred to a kind of operation system, which was based on the public ownership of the means of production by the state in the form of planning and according to the requirements of objective economic laws, consciously and uniformly managing and regulating the operation of the social economy, rather than a form of the social economy. In other words, the concept of the planned economy was not corresponding to social economy forms such as the commodity economy or the product economy, but as the real embodiment of the law of planned, proportional development of the socialist economy on the basis of public ownership. The reason the planned economy was considered an economic system related to the socialist mode of production was that a series of requirements and characteristics of social and economic life determined by the degree of socialized development of the socialist economy and the production relations of socialist public ownership made it consciously uniform and planned in accordance with the law of balanced development of the social economy throughout society. It was necessary and possible to match social labor. Secondly, as an economic management and operation system, the development form of the planned economy was related to the development degree of the socialist production mode. In the exposition of classic Marxist writers, society distributed labor to various departments through a general plan including the production and circulation of the entire society and organized the production and distribution of society overall. All economic activities were carried out according to a predetermined plan, and society completely connected the balance of total supply and demand through the plan. The premise of this type of planned economy was the extremely high development of socialized mass production, the single, complete public ownership of the means of production by all of society, and the disappearance of the objective basis of the commodity economy. In a certain sense, planned regulation reflecting the planned development law of the social economy was consistent with market regulation, which reflected the requirements of the law of value. From the perspective of economic operations, both planned regulation and market regulation were the adjustment means for the optimal allocation of social labor. In the commodity economy, the law of value was the law of automatic equilibrium between supply and demand and social production. Clearly, "[m]agnitude of value expresses a relation of social production, it expresses the connexion that necessarily exists between a certain article and the portion of the total labour-time of society required to produce it."[43] The market mechanism was the adjustment mechanism which embodied and implemented this equilibrium law. The planned adjustment was to consciously allocate social labor to various departments of the national economy according to the objective proportion of social demand, so as to make the economy develop in a balanced way,

---

43. Marx and Engels, *Complete Works of Marx and Engels*, vol. 23 (People's Publishing House, 1975), 394.

because "[t]he planned distribution of labor time in society regulates the appropriate proportion of various labor functions to various needs."[44] Since the planned economy (planned regulation) and market economy (market regulation), as different systems of operation and management of the social economy, had the same goal and basic function in a certain sense, they also had the objective inevitability of combining in the socialist commodity economy. The socialist commodity economy was a commodity economy on the basis of public ownership. The operation of this social and economic body not only needed the joint adjustment of planning and market, but also provided feasible, realistic conditions for the effective combination of the two. Therefore, the term the "socialist planned commodity economy" was a scientific summary of the operational characteristics of the socialist commodity economy.

4. On the Specific Mode of the Combination of the Planned Economy and Market Regulation

The economic system was a structural form of economic operation and management system determined by a certain mode of production. It included the nature and structure of certain production relations and interest relations, the movement forms of social production at a certain stage of productivity development, and the economic management methods and means associated with it. The economic mechanism was the functional principle of the economic system, which explained the internal relations among the components of economic system and the mechanism and process of economic system movement.

A certain economic system was determined by a certain mode of social production. In other words, a certain economic system should not only reflect the essential characteristics of certain production relations, but also meet the development status and requirements of certain productive forces. According to this principle, the operation system of China's socialist commodity economy should reflect not only the essential characteristics of socialist production relations, but also the basic laws of commodity economy. The specific expression of this requirement is the combination of planned economy and market regulation.

The combination of the planned economy and market regulation was a principled formulation. In order to make this statement of practical significance, it was necessary to solve two theoretical difficulties. One was on what economic mechanism the joint operation of planned economy and market regulation is built. The other was how to combine the planned economy with market regulation.

The economic mechanism was essentially a mechanism of interest incentive and restriction. It linked all kinds of economic behaviors through people's pursuit of economic interests, pushed the social economy to operate in a certain way, and objectively made the relationship between various economic activities, various forms of production, and various needs tend to be harmonious and reasonable, so as to make the overall social and economic movement go smoothly and improve the efficiency of production activities. Any economic mechanism had to be directly related to

---

44. Marx and Engels, *Complete Works of Marx and Engels*, vol. 23 (People's Publishing House, 1975), 96.

people's pursuit of economic interests; otherwise it was not an economic mechanism. The market mechanism and planning mechanism were special forms of economic mechanisms. The reason they were different was not a question of whether they were related to people's economic interests, but what kind of social and economic interest relations they had with the people's economic interests.

The basic meaning of the combination of the planned economy and market regulation meant that the plan must be established on the basis of the law of value and connected with people's economic behavior through the market mechanism to regulate economic operations. The planned economy was a kind of economic management system in which subjective decision-making was connected with objective laws. In the socialist commodity economy, there were two objective requirements of an effective, scientific planned economy. On the one hand, the plan must correctly reflect the law of productivity development and social demand. Any plan divorced from the actual economic development and market demand would not work, or it would cause low efficiency of economic operations and a huge waste of economic resources. On the other hand, the plan must regulate the economic operation within the scope of law of value through the economic connection with the market. In the commodity economy, the people's economic connection in the production process, the general material exchange, and various demands were realized in the market exchange activities in a circuitous way in the form of value. In the socialist commodity economy, in order to effectively regulate economic operations, it was necessary to follow the objective requirements of the law of value, take the necessary social labor time as the natural yardstick of value, take the equivalent exchange as the objective norm of economic activities, and use a series of economic means and economic levers that conformed to the law from the market process through the special economic interests of the market subject. Incentives and restrictions were used to regulate their economic behavior and to regulate the operation of enterprises and even the operation of the overall economy. Otherwise, social and economic activities would have lost vitality and efficiency. However, in the 1980s, as economic system reform was in the early stage, the efficiency of planned regulation was greatly weakened, and market mechanism regulation was still in the preliminary reform test stage, both in concept and in actual economic operations. Therefore, there was a "double failure" problem of planning and market regulation in the operation of the national economy. According to statistics, in 1988, the total investment in fixed assets of society overall reached 431.4 billion yuan, exceeding the planned target of 100 billion yuan, of which 269.5 billion yuan was completed by units owned by the people. Among the investment amount of the units with public ownership, the investment within the budget was only 36 billion yuan.[45] This indicated that the efficiency of the planned system in the allocation of resources had been greatly weakened. From the perspective of industrial structure, China's economic development strategy once took agriculture, energy, raw material industry, transportation, and communication as strategic key industries. However, in the 1980s, these key strategic industries were still "bottleneck" industries in national economic

---

45. *China Economic Yearbook (1989)* (Economy and Management Publishing House), ii–1.

development, which seriously restricted the rapid economic growth. The main reason was that for a long period of time, social accumulation was scattered and the funds and resources controlled by the state were decreasing, which meant they could not meet the development needs of key industries. However, the regulatory effect of the market mechanism on resource allocation could not be brought into full play. Statistics showed that from 1978 to 1986, the proportion of capital construction investment in the national income decreased from 15% to 7.1%, while the fixed assets investment of the entire society continuously increased. In 1987, it was 17.3% lower than that in 1986. However, in 1987, local raised infrastructure investment exceeded the budget by 27%.[46] On the one hand, the proportion of key national construction investment was constantly decreasing, and on the other hand, local and enterprise independent financing capital construction investment was increasing, and most of these investments were invested in the general processing industry or even non-productive projects, which made the short-term shorter and the long-term longer, and it was difficult to rationalize the industrial structure and socio-economic structure. These phenomena seriously affected the sustained, stable, coordinated development of the national economy. One of the main reasons for these phenomena was the "double failure" of the planned management system and market regulation and the weakening of the macro-control ability of the economic system.

---

46. *China Economic Yearbook (1989)* (Economy and Management Publishing House), ii–4.

CHAPTER 8

Research on the Evolution of the Basic Socialist Economic System Theory and Important Related Theoretical Categories

8.1 The Reform Theory of the Basic Socialist Economic System

1. Political Economic Definition of the Basic Economic System

There has been an in-depth discussion on the economic system in the field of modern economics. Allan Gruchy stated that the "economic system is the complex of the development of organizations of various participants, and these participants are related to the allocation of scarce resources to meet individual and collective needs."[1] According to Lindbergh, an economic system is a set of mechanisms and organizations used to make decisions on production, input, and consumption in a certain region and to complete these decisions. Generally speaking, the economic system involves "decision-making organs and mechanisms for providing information, allocating resources, and coordinating economic decision-making; the definition of property ownership; the choice of incentives and orders between individuals and companies; and the relationship between decision makers (the relationship between the role of competition, the openness of the overall system, and the system of the outside world)."[2] North understood the economic system as rules, legal procedures, and moral norms, specifically the norms designed by humans and the constraints of human interaction, including formal constraints such as laws and regulations, as well as informal constraints such as moral and ethical norms, customs, and

---

1. Allan Gruchy, *Comparative Economic System* (China Social Sciences Press, 1985), 25.
2. He Zhengbin, *300 Years of Economics*, vol. II (Hunan Science and Technology Press, 2000), 918.

habits, and their enforcement mechanism. Marxism has always held that the economic system is the sum of production relations at a certain stage of human social development, and the sum of production relations of a certain society constitutes the economic system of that society. The economic system of a certain society is the economic foundation of the superstructure, which restricts the political and legal system and social ideology. Therefore, Marx studied the economic system from the category of "economic basis" and "production relations," and he held that the sum of the production relations constituting the economic basis is an organic whole composed of a certain form of ownership of the means of production, the exchange relations, and the distribution relations of products.

There are many economic systems in any social form. Each economic system is not abstract, but concrete. They are interrelated, and they restrict and interact with each other to form the social and economic system. The ownership relationship is the most basic production relationship in any society, and the sum of production relations constitutes the economic system. The whole content of production relations is the overall content of ownership form or property form. Therefore, ownership is the level of the basic economy within the economic system, and it has a decisive impact on other elements in the economic system and is the fundamental symbol by which to distinguish the nature of different social and economic systems. As a legal form of ownership, the property rights system is the manifestation of ownership on the level of economic operation, the behavior rights of economic subjects in economic activities under the established ownership form, the intermediate level connecting ownership and resource allocation mechanism, and the rules for handling the responsibilities, rights, and benefits of production relations. The mode of resource allocation is the realization of ownership in economic activities through the property rights system.

The basic economic system determines other specific systems and non-basic systems, which is of decisive significance to the formation of the economic system framework, other economic relations, and the superstructure. The decisive role of the basic economic system lies in its determination of various economic relations in the fields of production, exchange, distribution, and consumption. Each ownership relationship does not exist in isolation. It always plays a role in the links of production, exchange, distribution, and consumption, and it determines the nature, status, and role of specific economic relations in various links. The decisive role of the basic economic system is also reflected in its determination of the nature and development direction of society. The nature of a social form does not depend on how many forms of ownership or economic systems exist, but mainly on the ownership forms or economic systems that occupy the dominant position and play a dominant, decisive role. In a capitalist society, there are various forms of ownership, such as state ownership, individual ownership, and the cooperative ownership of workers. However, the dominant, decisive form of ownership is capitalist private ownership, so its social nature is capitalist. In socialist society, although there are the individual private economy and three capital enterprises, it is still the socialist public ownership that dominates and determines the dominant position. Therefore, the nature of society is socialist. The basic economic system not only has the function of determining social nature, but to a great extent also determines the direction of social development.

The important role of institutions in economic growth has been widely recognized in academic circles. The new institutional economics school emphasizes that the key to economic growth and development is institutional factors, and institutional framework restricts people's choice set. Institutions form a social incentive structure, so political and economic institutions are potential determinants of economic performance. An effective system that provides appropriate personal stimulation is the decisive factor to promote economic growth, among which property relations play the most important role. Without a change in technology, labor productivity can be improved and economic growth can be realized through institutional innovation. These rules not only create an incentive system to guide and determine economic activities, but also determine the basis of social welfare and income distribution, and as a result, the system structure determines the growth rate of an economic entity and its knowledge and technology outlet statically. Different institutional arrangements can not only affect or even change the role of various factors in economic growth, but also affect the actual benefits of economic growth. A good system can promote economic growth by improving the efficiency of the system, while a poor system can reduce the efficiency of the system.

The basic economic system includes two elements, one of which is the ownership and structure of society. It determines or affects other economic systems and determines the fundamental nature of society. The second element is the economic operation system. The ownership structure is related to the economic operation system. The allocation of resources under the public ownership structure is realized through centralized decision-making and planned allocation, and the economic operation system is represented by the planned economic system, while resource allocation under the multiple ownership structure is realized through decentralized decision-making and market regulation, and the economic operation system is represented as a market economic system based on the law of value and the market mechanism.

Since the founding of the People's Republic of China, a particular development path has been followed in the theoretical knowledge and policy decision-making of the basic economic system. This path began with single public ownership and a highly centralized planned economic system, moved to public ownership as the main body and non-public ownership as the supplement, with equal competition between public ownership and non-public ownership for common development, and then moved to unswervingly supporting the development of public ownership and non-public ownership and vigorously constructing the economic system of the combination of the mixed ownership economy and the planned market. The last stage involved public ownership as the main body in a multi-ownership economy developing together in a socialist market economy system.

Before the beginning of Reform and Opening Up, China implemented an ownership structure of single public ownership. After the completion of the socialist transformation in 1956, the socialist economic system based on single public ownership was established. The capitalist industrial and commercial economy has been transformed into a socialist state-owned economy, and the urban and rural individual commodity economy has been transformed into a collective economy. According to statistics, in 1978, the state-owned economy accounted for 56% of the national economy, the collective economy accounted for 43%, and the non-public economy accounted for only 1%.

The Third Plenary Session of the Eleventh Central Committee of the Communist Party of China re-established the ideological line of emancipating the mind and seeking truth from facts. The essence of socialism was to emancipate and develop productive forces, eliminate exploitation, eliminate polarization, and realize common prosperity. It formed the theory of the primary stage of socialism and provided theoretical support for the development of the diversified ownership economy. Theorists gradually obtained a series of new understandings on the issue of ownership components and forms under the socialist conditions. In terms of the selection criteria of ownership forms, they broke through the theory of strictly production relations and voluntarism and re-established the historical materialist view that ownership relations were determined by the development level of productive forces and the objective requirements of developing productive forces. In the understanding of ownership structure, many breakthroughs were made, and in the evaluation of ownership, it broke through the concept of "public ownership" and "private" and "non-public ownership" and established the idea that the non-public economy was an important part of the socialist market economy. In the existing form of public ownership, it broke through the simple form of state-owned or collective ownership, while in the leading role of the state-owned economy, it broke through the concept of only looking at the quantitative proportion and established the idea of emphasizing the control ability and the actual effect. In relation to the rights of public assets, it broke through the single right of possession that the more centralized the rights, the better, along with the separation of ownership and management rights. The practice of economic system reform and the theory of basic economic system reform enriched and creatively developed the Marxist theory of ownership, gradually eliminated the fetters of unreasonable ownership structure on productivity, formed a situation in which public ownership was the main body and various ownership economies developed together, and gradually established the basic economic system in the primary stage of socialism in theory. After the beginning of Reform and Opening Up, the transformation of the economic system and the adjustment of the ownership structure not only promoted the rapid development of China's economy, but also deepened the understanding of ownership theory. By summing up historical experience and applying the ideological line and scientific method of seeking truth from facts to the study of the ownership structure at the preliminary stage of socialism, it broke through the "doctrine of ownership" in traditional socialist political economics. In terms of the success or failure of the form of ownership, it took "three advantages" as the basic standard for judging and selecting, and it broke through the standard of purely basing evaluation on the degree of public ownership. In terms of the relationship between the public ownership economy and the non-public ownership economy, China completed the understanding from "opposition theory" to "beneficial supplement theory," and on to "common development theory," and then to adhering to an understanding based on the "two unshakables," thus forming the theory and policy of developing the diversified ownership economy under the premise of taking public ownership as the main body. From another point of view, the reform process of the basic economic system was also the process of the continuous development of the non-public economy. The development of the non-public economy played an irreplaceable role in the cultivation and growth of the market system and the formation of the market economy, and it also effectively promoted the reform of the public ownership economy.

2. The Evolution of Thought on the Reform of China's Basic Socialist Economic System

From the 1980s to the early part of the 21st century, the development of the basic economic system of socialism with Chinese characteristics can be divided into three stages, the first of which was from 1978 to 1991. This stage broke through the understanding that socialism could only be a single public ownership in theory, growing into a view of public ownership as the main body and the non-public economy as supplement. There was also a major breakthrough in the theory of public ownership property rights during this period, which greatly enriched the connotation of the basic economic system. In practice, the situation of public ownership dominating the country was dismantled. Rural areas implemented the separation of land ownership and management rights, and the household contract responsibility system was implemented. State owned enterprises carried out the reform of separation of ownership and management rights, and the coastal areas introduced foreign capital to develop China-foreign cooperation, joint ventures, and wholly foreign-owned enterprises. At the same time, the ownership structure was adjusted, and the proportion of the state-owned economy and the collective economy gradually declined.

The second stage was from 1992 to 2001. In theory, the development of the non-public economy as a "supplement" to public ownership and non-public ownership was an important part of the socialist market economy. It was proposed that a basic economic system with public ownership as the main body and various forms of ownership should develop together for a long time. The Fifteenth National Congress of the Communist Party of China determined the basic line and program for the primary stage of socialism. The main contradiction in the primary stage of socialism was the contradiction between the people's growing material and cultural needs and the backward social production, which ran through the whole process of the primary stage of socialism and all aspects of social life. The report of the Fifteenth National Congress of the Communist Party of China clearly pointed out that the construction of the socialist economy with Chinese characteristics was meant to develop the market economy under socialist conditions and constantly liberate and develop productive forces. It was a basic economic system in the primary stage of socialism in China that aimed to adhere to and improve the socialist public ownership as the main body and the common development of various ownership economies. The establishment of this system was determined by the nature of socialism and the national conditions at the primary stage.[3] The report of the Fifteenth National Congress of the Communist Party of China started

---

3. Jiang Zemin, *Holding High the Great Banner of Deng Xiaoping Theory and Pushing the Cause of Building Socialism with Chinese Characteristics into the 21st Century: Report on the Fifteenth National Congress of the Communist Party of China* (People's Publishing House, 1997).

from the basic national condition, which included the fact that China was in and would be in the primary stage of socialism for a long time. It raised the non-public economy from the "necessary and beneficial supplement" of the public economy to the status of an organic part of the basic socialist economic system and an important component of the socialist market economy, so that it could be integrated into the basic system, and it confirmed that this was true of the entire society The historical inevitability of the existence and development of the primary stage of socialism laid a foundation for the socialist economic theory to highly affirm the integration and common development of various ownership economies. After Deng Xiaoping's Southern Talks in 1992, the focus of the reform was on the transformation of the enterprise management mechanism and the establishment of the modern enterprise system, while also actively encouraging the development of the non-public ownership economy. At the same time, opening to the outside world presented a new pattern that was omni-directional, wide-ranging, and multi-level.

The third stage, beginning in 2002, was a stage in which the basic economic system was constantly improving.[4] The Sixteenth National Congress of the Communist Party of China set the goal of building an overall affluent society. In terms of economic construction and economic system reform, it was important to adhere to and improve the basic economic system with public ownership as the main body, with multiple ownership economies developing together. It was necessary to unswervingly consolidate and develop the public sector economy and persist in encouraging, supporting, and guiding the development of the non-public economy. In the process of adhering to public ownership as the main body, promoting the development of the non-public ownership economy, and unifying them in the process of socialist modernization construction, the two could not be placed in opposition. All kinds of ownership economy were to give full play to their respective advantages in market competition, promote each other, and develop together.[5] The Seventeenth National Congress of the Communist Party of China put forward the goal of building an overall prosperous society and the scientific outlook on development, as well as the improvement of the basic economic system and the modern market system. China committed to unswervingly consolidating and developing the public sector economy, encouraging, supporting, and guiding the development of the non-public sector of the economy, adhering to the principle of equal protection of property rights, and forming a new pattern of equal competition and mutual promotion of various ownership economies. On the basis of the modern property right system, it would develop a mixed ownership economy.[6] These important expositions established the guiding principles for further improving the basic economic system, which included adhering to

---

4. Comprehensive Economic Restructuring Department of the National Development and Reform Commission and the Economic System and Management Research Institute of the National Development and Reform Commission, *Thirty Years of Reform and Opening Up: From History to the Future* (People's Publishing House, 2008), 325.

5. Jiang Zemin, *Building a Well-off Society in an All-round Way and Creating a New Situation in the Cause of Socialism with Chinese Characteristics: Report on the National Congress* (People's Publishing House, 2002).

6. Hu Jintao, *Holding High the Great Banner of Socialism with Chinese Characteristics and Striving for the New Victory of Building a Moderately Prosperous Society in an All-round Way: Report on the Seventeenth National Congress of the Communist Party of China* (People's Publishing House, 2007).

the principle of equal protection of property rights, continuing to concentrate state-owned capital in important industries and key areas that could give full play to their own advantages, developing various forms of the collective and cooperative economies, developing the mixed ownership economy with the joint-stock system as the main form, and creating a good environment, strengthening policy guidance to encourage different ownership economies to compete equally, promoting each other, and developing together. Improving the basic economic system was the basis for completing the task of perfecting the socialist market economic system. The Eighteenth National Congress of the Communist Party of China put forward the goal of building an overall prosperous society and comprehensively deepening Reform and Opening Up. It was important to unswervingly consolidate and develop the public economy, implement various forms of public ownership, deepen the reform of state-owned enterprises, improve the management system of various state-owned assets, and constantly enhance the vitality, control, and influence of the state-owned economy. It was necessary to encourage, support, and guide the development of non-public sectors of the economy and ensure that all kinds of economies of ownership use production factors equally according to the law, participate fairly in market competition, and be equally protected by law.[7]

The Nineteenth National Congress of the Communist Party of China put forward the thought and basic strategy of socialism with Chinese characteristics in the new era and made it clear that the main social contradiction in the new era was the contradiction between the people's growing need for a better life and unbalanced, inadequate development. It was important to adhere to the new development concept, adhere to and improve China's basic socialist economic system and distribution system, unswervingly consolidate and develop the public sector economy, and unswervingly encourage, support, and guide the development of the non-public sector of the economy, so that the market could play a decisive role in the allocation of resources and the role of the government could be better played.[8]

From 1949 to 1978, China's basic economic system was characterized by single public ownership. During this period, a relatively complete, independent industrial system and a national economic system were established, and the economic level was significantly improved. However, it should be noted that taking the single public ownership and mandatory planned economy as the essential attributes of the socialist system as opposed to and mutually exclusive with the non-public ownership economy would lead to a socialist economic model known as the "shortage economy."[9] This sort of relations of production, which went beyond the stage of the

7. Hu Jintao, *Unswervingly Advancing Along the Road of Socialism with Chinese Characteristics and Striving to Build a Moderately Prosperous Society in an All-round Way: Report on the Eighteenth National Congress of the Communist Party of China* (People's Publishing House, 2012).

8. Xi Jinping, *Winning the Battle to Build a Well-off Society in an All-round Way to Win the Great Victory of Socialism with Chinese Characteristics in the New Era: Report on the Nineteenth National Congress of the Communist Party of China* (People's Publishing House, 2017).

9. Wei Xinghua and Hu Ruochi, "Theoretical Thinking on Upholding and Improving China's Basic Economic System," *Frontline*, no. 4 (2009).

development of productive forces and did not adapt to the development of productive forces, led to the stagnation of the development of productive forces, low efficiency of production, difficulties in the people's life, and an inability to embody the superiority of socialism.

After 1979, the economic system reform changed the subject and mechanism of resource allocation. The diversification of property rights system not only helped to improve the economic efficiency of the entire society, but also provided a good external environment for the establishment of the modern enterprise system. At the same time, great achievements were made in socialist ownership reform and structural adjustment. The commodity economy and the market economic system were based on the diversification of ownership structure. Therefore, without the transformation of ownership structure from public ownership to multiple ownership, and without the reform of the basic economic system, there would be no transformation from the planned economic system to the socialist planned commodity economy and the socialist market economic system.

With the deepening of the economic system reform, the continuous improvement of the basic socialist economic system became one of the important tasks for the improvement of the socialist economic system. The diversification of the forms of public ownership and the vigorous promotion of the development of non-public economy are important paths to better the basic economic system.

The form of ownership was relatively independent. A kind of ownership could have many forms of realization, and different types of ownership could also take the same form. Under the conditions of a market economy, owners could not only realize their own interests by controlling all the rights given by certain ownership system, but also realize their own interests through the division of rights and the paid transfer of some rights. In the form of realization of ownership, the owner controlled all the rights, which formed the capital organization form and the direct operation mode of operating assets of a sole proprietorship enterprise. When the owner transferred part of the rights, such as the management right, it formed a joint stock system and other forms of capital organization, along with the indirect operation mode of operating capital. In the primary stage of socialism in China, the level of social productive forces was low and development was unbalanced. At the same time, determined by the diverse levels of social productivity and the diversity of ownership structure, the forms for realization of public ownership could and should be diversified. The diversification of the forms of realization of public ownership was of great significance to comprehensive promoting of reform, improving the socialist market economic system, continuously consolidating and developing the public ownership economy, and improving the basic economic system. The Third Plenary Session of the Sixteenth CPC Central Committee adopted the Decision of the CPC Central Committee on Several Issues Concerning the Improvement of the Socialist Market Economic System. It was proposed that "we should adapt to the trend of the continuous development of economic marketization, further enhance the vitality of the public economy, vigorously develop the mixed ownership economy in which state-owned capital, collective capital, and non-public capital participate, and realize the diversification of investment subjects, so as to make shares more diversified and the share system become the main form of public ownership." The socialist basic economic system not only referred to a diversified ownership structure, but also included the mixed economic system and mixed asset organization form in the economic operation mechanism. The "mixed ownership economy" referred to a new property rights allocation structure and economic form established by diversified investment, mutual penetration, and integration of different property rights subjects in the same economic organization. In the primary stage of socialism in China, the mixed ownership economy referred to the combination of the public ownership economy and the non-public ownership economy. After the beginning of Reform and Opening Up, the development of the collective economy and the deepening of the reform of state-owned enterprises provided unprecedented opportunities for the development of the mixed ownership economy. The joint stock system, joint stock cooperation system, and joint stock economy developed rapidly. The joint stock system was an important organizational operation mode and realization form of mixed ownership. The stock system was the inevitable product of socialized mass production and the development of the market economy to a certain stage. It was an effective organizational form and operation mode for enterprises to win a competitive market advantage. Various ownership economies were organically combined through the joint stock system, which formed the property of enterprise legal entities. It could not only play out their respective advantages, but also gave full play to the overall function, which successfully realized the combination of public ownership and the market economy. To improve the socialist market economy, it was necessary to adhere to the dominant position of public ownership and give full play to the leading role of the state-owned economy. It was likewise necessary to adapt to the trend of economic socialization and marketization, actively implement the joint stock system, encourage cross shareholding and integration of all kinds of capital, and vigorously develop the mixed ownership economy with state-owned capital, collective capital, and non-public capital.

The non-public economy was an important part of the socialist market economy and played a positive role. The development of the non-public economy broke the pattern of the state-owned economy dominating the country and enhanced economic vitality. The development of the non-public economy diversified the main body of the market and formed a diversified competition pattern, which was conducive to saving social resources, improving economic efficiency, and building a perfect socialist market economic system. The development of the non-public economy promoted the reform of public enterprises, especially state-owned enterprises. The non-public ownership economy not only created pressure to speed up the reform and development of state-owned enterprises, but also established a "frame of reference" for the reform of state-owned enterprises, which was conducive to accelerating the reform process of state-owned enterprises. The development of the non-public economy was the necessary condition for the development of the mixed ownership economy, and it accelerated the development of China's national economy. The non-public economy played an irreplaceable role in many fields of the national economy. It not only provided a variety of products and services, but also provided many employment opportunities. With the advancement of the adjustment of the distribution of the state-owned economy, the promotion of the reform of the state-owned assets management system, the deepening of the reform of state-owned enterprises, the transition of the financial system to the public financial system, the expansion of opening up, and the continuous improvement of the socialist market economic system, the position of the non-public economy became increasingly important.

3. The Policy Thought on Ownership Structure Adjustment in the 1980s

The Third Plenary Session of the Eleventh Central Committee of the Communist Party of China affirmed that the members' private plots, family sideline work, and market trade were "necessary supplementary parts" of the socialist economy, and "no arbitrary interference" was allowed. On the basis of self-reliance, public enterprises were required to "actively develop economic cooperation based on equality and mutual benefit with all countries in the world."[10] In 1981, the Fourth Plenary Session of the Eleventh Central Committee of the Communist Party of China passed the Resolution on Several Historical Issues of the Party Since the Founding of the People's Republic of China, which clearly stated, "Our socialist system is still in the primary stage," and, "The reform and improvement of socialist relations of production must be adapted to the situation of productive forces and conducive to the development of production. The state owned and collective economies are the basic economic forms of our country, and the individual economy of laborers within a certain range is a necessary supplement to the public ownership economy. Specific management and distribution systems suitable for various economic components must be implemented." This resolution summarized the Party's new understanding of the form of ownership after the Third Plenary Session of the Eleventh Central Committee of the Communist Party of China in 1978 and formally put forward the argument that the individual economy was a necessary supplement to the public economy. In April 1982, the draft Amendment to the Constitution of the People's Republic of China, adopted at the 23rd Meeting of the Standing Committee of the Fifth National People's Congress, affirmed that public ownership was the foundation of the socialist economic system and that public ownership was the leading force in the national economy. At the same time, it put forward that "the individual economy of urban and rural workers within the scope of law is the supplement to the socialist public economy." And, "the state protects the legitimate rights and interests of the individual economy." The report of the Twelfth National Congress of the Communist Party of China in 1982 clearly put forward "the problem of upholding the leading position of the state-owned economy and developing various economic forms." In order to meet the urgent employment needs of a large number of educated youth after they returned to the city, under the support of the Party and the state policies and regulations, the individual economy in urban and rural areas in China gradually emerged and expanded, and a number of individual industrialists and businessmen emerged, which alleviated the labor and employment problems that had plagued China's economic life.

---

10. *Documents of the Third Plenary Session of the 11th Central Committee of the Communist Party of China* (People's Publishing House, 1978).

In 1982, the Twelfth National Congress of the Communist Party of China carried out a beneficial exploration on the formation of the basic socialist economic theory, noting that "over a long period of time, a variety of economic forms need to coexist." It went on to say that "in the countryside, the cooperative economy under collective ownership of the working people is the main economic form, and a considerable part of the industry and service industry in cities and towns should be organized by the collective," and "in both rural and urban areas, it is necessary to establish a cooperative economy under collective ownership of the working people." It was important at this stage to "encourage the proper development of the individual economy of workers within the scope prescribed by the state and under the administration of the industrial and commercial departments, as a necessary and beneficial supplement to the public economy."[11]

In 1984, the Third Plenary Session of the Twelfth Central Committee of the Communist Party of China adopted the Decision of the Central Committee of the Communist Party of China on the Reform of the Economic System, which clarified the necessity and urgency of accelerating the reform of the overall economic system focusing on cities and stipulated the direction, nature, tasks, and basic principles and policies of the reform. It was a programmatic document guiding China's economic system reform. It pointed out that China should "actively develop various economic forms and further expand economic and technological exchanges both at home and abroad." After analyzing the status and functions of the economy owned by all the people, the collective economy, and the individual economy, it also proposed that "on the basis of voluntariness and mutual benefit, flexible and diversified cooperative operation, and economic union among all the people, the collective economy and the individual economy should be widely developed. Some small enterprises owned by the people can also be rented or contracted out to the collective or individual workers for operation." The Decision further put forward that "using foreign capital to attract foreign investors to set up joint ventures, cooperative enterprises, and wholly-owned foreign enterprises in China is also a necessary and beneficial supplement to China's socialist economy." The decision-making with public ownership as the main body and various economic components coexisting began to take shape.

In 1987, the Thirteenth National Congress of the Communist Party of China first described the ownership structure in the primary stage of socialism as public ownership being the main body, with multiple forms of ownership coexisting. The report of the Thirteenth National Congress of the Communist Party of China pointed out that in order to speed up and deepen the reform, it was necessary to deepen the scientific understanding of the nature of China's economic system reform. The reforms that had already been carried out, including the development of the diversified ownership economy with public ownership as the main body, and even allowing the existence and development of private economy were determined by the actual situation of productive forces in the primary stage of socialism. Only in this way was it possible to promote the development of productive forces. The ownership structure in the primary stage of socialism

---

11. *Documents of the Third Plenary Session of the Twelfth Central Committee of the Communist Party of China* (People's Publishing House, 1984).

was to take public ownership as the main body. At that time, economic components other than public ownership had not developed very far, but they were still insufficient. It was important to continue to encourage the development of the urban-rural cooperative economy, individual economy, and private economy. The public ownership economy itself had many forms. In addition to public ownership and collective ownership, it was crucial to also develop public enterprises jointly owned by the people and collective ownership, as well as public enterprises in the form of mutual participation of various regions, departments, and enterprises. In different economic fields and regions, the proportion of various ownership economies should be allowed to vary.

On the 40th anniversary of the founding of the People's Republic of China in 1989, on behalf of the CPC Central Committee and the State Council, Jiang Zemin further discussed the proportion and status of various forms of ownership, saying, "We should continue to adhere to the principle of taking public ownership as the main body and developing various economic components and develop the individual economy, private economy, China-foreign joint ventures, cooperative enterprises, and foreign-funded enterprises as the beneficial and necessary supplementary role of the socialist economy." According to this speech, adhering to this policy aimed to better demonstrate the superiority of the socialist economy and promote the faster development of China's economy. It was absolutely not necessary to weaken or cancel the dominant position of the public ownership economy, let alone carry out economic "privatization." The speech also mentioned in particular that "the proportion and development fields of the non-public economy in China's national economy should be determined according to China's actual productivity level and objective needs, and its proportion should not be simply taken as a sign by which to measure the achievements of reform."[12]

With the improvement of the understanding of ownership and the theoretical breakthroughs, while actively promoting the reform and development of the public economy, especially the state-owned economy, it was necessary to vigorously develop the individual and non-public sectors of the economy, so that social productive forces could be liberated and developed. The proportion of the public sector of the economy declined, while that of the non-public sector increased. Within the public sector, the proportion of the state-owned economy had declined, while the proportion of the collective economy had increased. However, in the total economic volume, the public economy still occupied the dominant position, and individual industry in urban and rural areas and other economic types only accounted for a small proportion. In the period of the planned economy before Reform and Opening Up, the main body of investment in China was quite simple, with only the government serving as the main investor. After the launch of Reform and Opening Up, great changes took place in the investment structure, forming a structure in which various investors coexisted. In this process, the investment share of the state-owned investment units gradually decreased, while that of the non-state-owned investment units gradually increased. It is worth noting that the share of state-owned unit investment accounted for in the state budget

---

12. Jiang Zemin, *Speech at the General Meeting to Celebrate the 40th Anniversary of the Founding of the People's Republic of China* (People's Publishing House, 1989).

decreased rapidly after 1976, from 82% in 1975 to 59%, a decrease of 23 percentage points. It dropped to 40% in 1980 and 28% in 1982, 54% less than that in 1975. This situation continued, falling below 20% in 1987 and 9.7% in 1991 (see Table 8.1 and Table 8.2).[13]

TABLE 8.1 1978–1990 Changes in the Proportion of Various Economic Components in China's Total Industrial Output Value (%)

Year	State owned and state holding industry	Collective industry	Urban and rural individual industry	Other economic types
1978	77.63	22.37		
1980	75.97	23.54		
1985	64.86	32.08	1.8	1.2
1990	54.60	35.62	5.4	4.4

Data source: *China Statistical Yearbook*

TABLE 8.2 Proportion of Various Economic Components in Social Fixed Assets Investment (total investment = 100)

	State owned economic investment	Collective economic investment	Individual economic investment
Year 1980–1985	66.7	12.7	20.6
Year 1986–1990	64.8	13.4	21.8

Source: *China Statistical Abstract (1999)* (China Statistics Press, 1999), 42.

In December 1978, the Third Plenary Session of the Eleventh Central Committee of the Communist Party of China passed the Decision of the Central Committee of the Communist Party of China on Several Issues Related to Agricultural Development (Draft), which clearly pointed out that "the diversified operation of the commune is the socialist economy, while the members' private plots, family sideline business, and rural market trade are the legitimate supplements of the socialist economy. They must not be criticized and taken as capitalist economy. Members' private plots, family sidelines, and rural market trade are necessary supplements to the socialist economy and can not be criticized or labeled as the capitalist tail. On the contrary, while consolidating and developing the collective economy, we should encourage and assist farmers to run household sideline businesses, increase personal income, and invigorate the rural economy."[14] After that, the restrictions on the non-public economy were gradually relaxed and allowed to exist and develop.

---

13. Yang Yonghua, "Empirical Analysis and Theoretical Enlightenment of the Evolution of China's Ownership Structure in the Past 50 Years," *Tianjin Normal University Journal*, no. 2 (2000).

14. Decision of the CPC Central Committee on Several Issues Concerning Agricultural Development (Draft). Adopted in principle at the Third Plenary Session of the 11th CPC Central Committee on December 22, 1978. Issued by the Central Government, Issue 4, 1979.

While actively promoting the reform and development of the public economy, especially the state-owned economy, it was necessary to vigorously develop the non-public sectors of the economy, such as the individual and private sectors, so as to liberate and develop social productive forces.

On September 29, 1979, Ye Jianying pointed out in his National Day speech that "China is still a developing socialist country, the socialist system is not perfect, and its economy and culture are still underdeveloped... At present, the individual economy of urban and rural workers, which continues to exist within a limited scope, is the subsidiary and supplement of the socialist public economy."[15] Since 1981, various policies to encourage and support the individual economy had been introduced one after another. China's urban and rural individual economy developed rapidly, and the relevant policies and regulations became increasingly fleshed out. In July 1981, the State Council issued Some Policy Provisions on the Urban Non-agricultural Individual Economy. For the first time, the document comprehensively and systematically expounded China's individual economic policy and made clear, detailed provisions on the nature and business scope of the urban individual economy, as well as issuing guidelines on how to support and protect the development of the urban individual economy.

In summing up China's historical experience, the Third Plenary Session of the Eleventh Central Committee of the Communist Party of China made the major decision to open up to the outside world according to the favorable international conditions at that time. It stressed that the vision of economic work should be expanded from a domestic to an international scope, and foreign funds and technology should be fully utilized to accelerate socialist modernization. According to the needs of foreign capital utilization, the state formulated a series of regulations, policies, and measures. From the early 1980s, special economic zones were set up in coastal areas, and a number of coastal port cities were opened up, which initially improved the investment environment in China. By the end of 1985, there were 5,118 joint-venture, cooperative, and independent enterprises registered with the Chinese government by foreign businesspeople and Hong Kong and Macao businesspeople, with a total registered capital of 23.4 billion US dollars. The registered capital of the foreign side was 11.9 billion US dollars, accounting for 51.6% of the total capital. The total number of employees in these enterprises reached 367,000. Enterprises with foreign investment were distributed in 28 provinces, autonomous regions, and municipalities directly under the central government, excluding only the Tibet Autonomous Region. A total of 33 countries and regions came to China to invest. According to statistics at the end of July 1986, the Chinese government had approved a total of 6,814 contracts for foreign-funded enterprises. The amount of foreign investment agreed reached 18.1 billion US dollars, and the actual investment amount was about 6.7 billion US dollars.[16]

On January 22, 1987, the concept of "private enterprise" was used for the first time in the decision of the Political Bureau of the Central Committee of the Communist Party of China

---

15. *Selected Important Documents Since the Third Plenary Session of the CPC Central Committee* (People's Publishing House, 1982), 211.

16. Ji Chongwei, *The Course of China's Foreign Capital Utilization* (China Economic Press, 1999), 93–94.

to lead the in-depth rural reform. The decision pointed out that with the deepening of rural reform, both individual and private enterprises had developed to a certain extent, and "the rural economy will form a pattern dominated by public ownership and coexisting with various economic components and business forms."[17] On this basis, the central government formulated a sixteen character policy for the treatment of private enterprises, which stated China's intention "to allow the existence of private enterprises, strengthen management, promote advantages and suppress disadvantages, and gradually guide them." The Thirteenth National Congress of the Communist Party of China, held in October 1987, was of great significance in the history of China's non-public economic development in the new period. Based on an objective analysis of China's national conditions, the meeting clearly pointed out that China was at and would remain in the primary stage of socialism for a long time to come. The theory of the primary stage of socialism provided an important theoretical basis for the formation of China's private economic policy in the new period. The report of the Thirteenth National Congress of the Communist Party of China took as its premise the fact that China was still in the initial stage of socialism, and from this basic national condition, it determined that the fundamental task of the primary stage of socialism was to liberate and develop social productive forces. The report emphasized that "the reforms we have carried out, including the development of the diversified ownership economy with public ownership as the main body, and even allowing the existence and development of the private economy, are determined by the actual situation of productive forces in the primary stage of socialism. Only by doing so can we promote the development of productive forces."[18]

The report of the Thirteenth National Congress of the Communist Party of China also analyzed the significance of the development of the non-public economy, such as private and foreign capital for the liberation and development of social productive forces, clearly recognized the legal existence of the private economy, and expounded the status, nature, and positive role of the private economy. The report of the Thirteenth National Congress of the Communist Party of China preliminarily and systematically expounded the theory and policy of the development of the non-public ownership economy and pointed out that the ownership structure in the primary stage of socialism should take public ownership as the main body and develop a diversified ownership economy on this premise. It stated, "At present, economic components other than public ownership are developing, but are still not sufficient. We should continue to encourage the development of the urban-rural cooperative economy, individual economy, and the private economy... In different economic fields and regions, the proportion of different ownership economies should be allowed to vary."[19] The report also clearly pointed out that "the private economy is an economic component of employment labor relations. However, under socialist

---

17. *Selection of Important Documents Since the Twelfth National Congress of the Communist Party of China* (People's Publishing House, 1988), 1228.

18. Research Office of the CPC Central Committee, ed., *Selection of Important Documents Since the Thirteenth National Congress* (People's Publishing House, 1991), 25–26.

19. Research Office of the CPC Central Committee, *Selected Important Documents Since the Thirteenth National Congress* (People's Publishing House, 1991), 31–32.

conditions, it is bound to be associated with the dominant public ownership economy and greatly affected by the public ownership economy. Practice has proved that the development of the private economy to a certain extent is conducive to promoting production, invigorating the market, expanding employment, and better meeting the people's various living needs. It is a necessary and beneficial supplement to the public ownership economy."[20] This was the initial recognition of the status of private economy, that is, it was a "necessary and beneficial supplement" to the socialist public economy.

8.2 Theory on the Reform of State-owned Enterprises and the State-owned Property Rights System

1. Ownership Forms of State-owned Enterprises and State-owned Property Relations

In the early 1980s, Chinese enterprises could be divided into four categories according to the ownership of the means of production.

Enterprises wholly owned by the public. The means of production were owned by the public in such enterprises. This was one of the basic economic forms in China, occupying a leading position and playing a leading role in the overall national economy. These enterprises were directly operated and managed by the state, representing the interests of the people, and were also known as state-owned enterprises. According to the different subordinate relations of enterprises, they were divided into state-owned enterprises directly under the management of the central departments and local state-owned enterprises subordinate to the governments of provinces, cities, autonomous regions, and lower levels. The profits due from state-owned enterprises directly under the central government were turned over to the state finance, while the profits due from local state-owned enterprises were turned over to the local finance. In terms of industrial enterprises, in 1980, there were more than 80,000 enterprises owned by the public, of which 3% were enterprises directly under the central government and 97% were enterprises directly under the local government. The fixed assets of industrial enterprises owned by the people accounted for 90% of the total industrial fixed assets, the number of employees accounted for 69% of the total industrial number, and the output value accounted for 79% of the total industrial output value.[21]

Enterprises under collective ownership. This was another form of the socialist public ownership economy, in which the means of production and products were jointly owned by the workers within a certain collective scope, and their profits were controlled and used by the collective, except that they were turned over to a part of the state in the form of income tax. Collective owned enterprises were economic organizations with independent accounting and financing of

20. Research Office of the CPC Central Committee, *Selected Important Documents Since the Thirteenth National Congress* (People's Publishing House, 1991), 32.

21. Ma Hong, *Economic Events of Modern China* (China Social Sciences Press, 1982), 323.

profits and losses. They had greater independence and flexibility in operation and management. In terms of industrial enterprises, there were more than 290,000 collectively owned enterprises in 1980, accounting for more than 78% of all industrial enterprises.[22]

Joint ventures. These were mainly enterprises jointly operated by two or more units with different ownership systems by means of capital or machinery and equipment through agreement. There were more joint ventures between enterprises owned by the people and enterprises under collective ownership, and there were also a small number of China-foreign joint ventures.

In general, joint ventures between the people and the collective, as well as between the collective and the private, were carried out under the unified leadership and plan of the competent departments of the state. In terms of operation and management, they obeyed the policies and decrees of the state, turned in taxes and profits in accordance with the state regulations, and obtained their respective incomes according to the profit-sharing proportion negotiated at the time of establishment. Some of these joint ventures used and allocated raw materials, machinery, and equipment in a unified way, carried out joint operation and unified accounting, and finally shared the profits according to their respective investment proportion. Some of them jointly carried out production technology operation and management activities and independently calculated and accounted separately, distributing the profits and taxes respectively according to the provisions of different ownership forms.

A China-foreign joint venture was an enterprise jointly invested and established by Chinese and foreign companies, enterprises, or individuals in accordance with the principle of equality and mutual benefit. It was jointly managed by both sides and bore both profits and losses. All parties to the joint venture shared the profits, risks, and losses according to the proportion of the registered capital. Chinese laws protected the legitimate rights and interests of foreign joint ventures.

Individual industry and commerce. In the early days of the founding of the People's Republic of China, there were a large number of individual industries and businesses in China. In 1956, at the peak of socialist transformation, China basically realized cooperation and became a collective owned enterprise. After the Cultural Revolution, China summed up its positive and negative experiences. On the issue of ownership, it made clear that the state-owned economy and the collective economy were the basic economic forms in China, and the individual economy of workers in a certain range was a necessary supplement to the public ownership economy. The State encouraged the proper development of the individual economy of the working masses under the leadership and management of the public economy as an assistant and supplement to the state-owned and collective economy. Individual business operators were to abide by the laws and policies of the state and pay taxes to the state in accordance with regulations. By the end of 1980, there were about 700,000 to 800,000 individual businesses registered and issued business licenses by the administrative departments for industry and commerce.[23]

---

22. Ma Hong, *Economic Events of Modern China* (China Social Sciences Press, 1982), 323.
23. Ma Hong, *Economic Events of Modern China* (China Social Sciences Press, 1982), 323.

State owned enterprises were the basic units of the socialist economy. They carried out independent production and operation activities under the management of economic institutions of the central or local governments in accordance with the unified national plan.

The means of production of state-owned enterprises, including land, buildings, machinery, equipment, raw materials, etc., were owned by the state, the production and operation activities of state-owned enterprises were subject to the unified plan of the state, and the products were ordered by the state according to their different roles in the national economy or sold by the enterprises themselves according to relevant regulations. The profits of state-owned enterprises were left to enterprises in addition to regulations. Some were handed over to the state for unified control and centralized use. Employees of state-owned enterprises were recruited by the state according to the recruitment targets allocated by the state in a unified way or according to the recruitment targets allocated by the state according to the state plan. The wage standards and wage system of the staff and workers were uniformly prescribed by the state, and the main leaders of state-owned enterprises were appointed by the state.

The state guided the production and operation activities of enterprises through the plan and the technical and economic index system and evaluated the business achievements of enterprises. Enterprises were to complete the tasks of the state plan in an all-round way. If not, they bore the responsibility. During the First Five-Year Plan period, there were twelve mandatory indicators of state-owned enterprises, namely, total output value, output of main products, trial production of new types of products, important technical and economic quotas, cost reduction rate, cost reduction amount, total number of employees, number of workers arriving at the end of the year, total wages, average wages, labor productivity, and profits. In 1957, the industrial management system was reformed and power was decentralized. These twelve mandatory indicators were changed to four, the output of main products, the total number of employees, the total wages, and profits. The remaining eight items were changed to non-mandatory indicators, which were allowed to be modified according to the actual situation. In August 1960, with the beginning of the national economic adjustment, the indicators for assessing enterprises were added to six categories, namely, the output and specifications of main products, the output value of commodities and the completion of order contracts, the quality of products, the main technical and economic quotas (the consumption quota of main raw materials, the utilization rate of equipment and the quota of working hours), labor productivity (calculated by the total staff and by the production workers), and cost reduction rate (calculated by unit cost of main comparable products and by total cost). In addition to completing the above-mentioned six indicators, different enterprises could also add other assessment indicators according to the characteristics of the industry. During the Cultural Revolution, the overall economic management was seriously damaged, and some assessment indexes of the state for enterprises also lost their functions. In 1972, the Minutes of the National Planning Conference put forward seven indexes for assessing enterprises, including output, variety, quality, consumption, labor productivity, cost, and profit. In April 1975, the index of working capital occupation was added. In the Draft Decision of the Central Committee of the Communist Party of China on Several Issues Concerning the Acceleration of Industrial

Development (or, the Industrial 13 Articles) issued on April 20, 1978, the eight technical and economic indicators for assessing enterprises were formally determined as output, variety, quality, consumption, labor productivity, cost, profit, and occupation of working capital. In 1979, it was stipulated that only four indicators, output, quality, profit, and contract performance, should be assessed for pilot enterprises to expand enterprise autonomy. For enterprises with export tasks, performance rate and foreign exchange collection of export products were also assessed.

Generally speaking, for a relatively long period of time, in dealing with the relationship between the state and enterprises, state centralization exceeded the enterprise autonomy. Practice proved that this situation was not conducive to mobilizing the enthusiasm of enterprises and workers in production and hindering the improvement of economic effect. In October 1978, Sichuan Province first carried out a pilot project to expand enterprise autonomy in six enterprises, such as the Chongqing Iron and Steel Company. In April 1979, Sichuan Province expanded the pilot project to a hundred enterprises on the basis of summing up its experience. At the same time, Yunnan Province also began to carry out pilot projects in fifty enterprises.

In July 1979, the State Council issued five documents to reform the economic management system, including Several Provisions on Expanding the Autonomy of State-Owned Industrial Enterprises in Operation and Management. In response, all provinces, cities, and autonomous regions carried out pilot projects. By the end of 1980, there were more than six thousand enterprises in China, accounting for 16% of the total number of industrial enterprises within the state budget, output value accounting for about 60%, and profit accounting for about 70%. Among them, 191 enterprises carried out a pilot project of substituting tax for profit, independent accounting, and financing of profits and losses.[24]

In the pilot project of power expansion, the state gave enterprises several rights. The first was the right to draw up the production and sales plans of the enterprise according to the mandatory and guiding indicators issued by the state and market needs. When it was found that the planned indicators did not conform to the actual situation during the implementation of the plan, the enterprise could report to the department that issued the plan and put forward suggestions for revision. For the guiding plan, the enterprise had the right to make appropriate adjustments, supplements, and reports for department records.

They also had the right to sell a part of their own products within the scope prescribed by the state, including products divided according to regulations, products produced beyond planned production, products produced with main raw materials organized by themselves, new products produced for trial, products not purchased by material and commercial departments, and overstocked products. They had the right to withdraw and use the profit retained funds in accordance with the relevant provisions, and the right to apply for export of their own products, obtain and use their own share of foreign exchange in accordance with state regulations, and entrust relevant foreign trade companies to handle import business. They further had the right to employ workers according to the state's labor plan, record merit, reward and promote those

---

24. Ma Hong, *Economic Events of Modern China* (China Social Sciences Press, 1982), 330.

with outstanding achievements and outstanding contributions, and punish or even dismiss those who seriously violated the law and discipline or who refused to reform after repeated education. They had the right to decide their own organizational setup within the fixed number of personnel and to appoint or remove cadres below the middle level according to actual needs. And they had the right to refuse the social burden beyond the state's explicit provisions. According to state regulations, the social burdens that enterprises should bear were retirement wages of employees, subsidies for non-staple food, subsidies for one child, funds for enterprises to run nurseries, schools, and hospitals, and other similar items.

At the beginning of 1981, Shandong Province and other places implemented profit (loss) contracting for some enterprises on the basis of expanding enterprise autonomy. Subsequently, different contracting methods were implemented in all parts of the country. These measures, along with the relevant provisions in the pilot project of power expansion, were collectively referred to as the industrial economic responsibility system. By the end of August 1981, 65% of the state-owned enterprises at or above the county level had implemented the economic responsibility system, including more than 6,000 enterprises with expanded powers, 264 competent bureaus or companies contracted by industry, and 195 county economic committees contracted by regions. In terms of regions, nine provinces and municipalities, such as Shandong, Beijing, Tianjin, and Liaoning, had implemented more than 80%, while twelve provinces and autonomous regions, such as Hebei, Inner Mongolia, and Shanxi, had implemented 50 to 80%. In November 1981, the State Council approved and transmitted the Opinions on Several Issues Concerning the Implementation of the Economic Responsibility System for Industrial Production, issued by the Office of Structural Reform of the State Council and the State Economic and Trade Commission of the People's Republic of China, improving and further developing the industrial economic responsibility system.[25]

The implementation of the industrial economic responsibility system fixed the relationship between the state and enterprises with a set of laws and regulations. On the one hand, it made the economic responsibility of enterprises to the state clearer, and at the same time, it further implemented the independent rights of enterprises. However, the industrial economic responsibility system was implemented for some time, and many aspects still need to be further developed and improved. In particular, the form and reasonable boundary of profit distribution between the state and enterprises were still being explored. The common forms of profit distribution were as follows:

Profit retention. There were three kinds of retained profits, including full retained, excess retained, and base retained plus excess retained. Full retention meant that all profits were retained in a certain proportion. Excess retention meant that the profit in the plan was not retained, and the profit exceeding the plan was retained in a certain proportion. Base retained plus excess retained, that is, fixed profit (the amount of planned profit in the current year or the actual profit completed in the previous year) was taken as the base. The base part of the current year's profit was retained

---

25. Ma Hong, *Economic Events of Modern China* (China Social Sciences Press, 1982), 331.

at a lower proportion approved, and the excess part was retained at a higher proportion.

Contracted profit and loss. The profit-making enterprise implemented the profit contracting, that is to say, after the enterprise completed the task, the remaining part was left to the enterprise or divided between the state and the enterprise according to a certain proportion. If the task could not be completed, it was to be made up with the enterprise's own funds. The deficit enterprise implemented the deficit contracting, that is, the loss allowed by the enterprise in the current year was taken as the lump sum base and the deficit within this range could be compensated by state financing, while it was not compensated by state financing if it went beyond the range, and the remaining part after cutting the loss could be retained by the enterprise. The profit and loss contract included three forms of contracting based on enterprises, industries, and regions. If the contract was carried out based on industry and region, it could be adjusted among enterprises within the industry or region.

Full responsibility for its own profits and losses, or changing the profits turned in to payment of various taxes (fees). After the enterprises paid taxes (fees) to the state according to the regulations, the profits and losses were borne by the enterprises. In implementing this method, the tax (fee) system was not exactly the same in different places. For example, Shanghai implemented five taxes and two fees. The five taxes were value-added tax (taxed based on the balance of sales revenue minus the cost of raw materials, materials, fuel, etc.), differential income adjustment tax (the differential income of state-owned enterprises belongs to the state), vehicle and vessel license tax, real estate tax, and income tax, while the two fees include the fixed assets occupancy fee (calculated based on the net value) and the working capital occupation fee. Sichuan implemented three taxes, industrial and commercial consolidated tax, fixed assets occupancy tax (based on the original value), and income tax (one household rate, differential income in this tax adjustment). The tax rate on income tax was generally above 50%, and other tax (fee) rates were determined based on the situation.

After the implementation of the economic responsibility system, enterprises used the retained profits to establish production development funds, employee welfare funds, and employee incentive funds. The production development fund was mainly used for tapping the potential, innovation, and transformation of enterprises, and could also be used for expansion if conditions permitted. The staff welfare fund was mainly used for the construction of collective welfare facilities such as staff dormitories and other welfare undertakings such as medical subsidies and solving the living difficulties of employees. The incentive fund was used to reward employees' labor.

In China, the state mainly turned to comprehensive economic management departments (Economic and Planning Commission, etc.), professional management departments (departments of finance, taxation, banking, labor, materials, etc.), and competent departments of enterprises (companies, competent bureaus, and departments) to lead, manage, and supervise enterprises. The main methods included formulating economic plans for economic policies, issuing relevant instructions, decisions, and mandatory documents and requiring enterprises to implement them, inspecting and assessing the implementation, and investigating the responsibility of the relevant personnel if any violation was found. It included using economic levers, such as price, tax, and credit, to guide the production and operation activities of enterprises to conform to the overall national plan; giving preferential treatment to industries in urgent need of social development in terms of investment; stimulating production of products urgently needed by society through tax reduction, tax exemption, low interest loans, and appropriately raising product prices; restricting the production of products overstocked in society by restricting loans and reducing product prices; making market forecast, providing economic information, and guiding the production and development direction of enterprises; and, sending professionals to inspect and supervise the implementation of state policies and decrees. For example, the financial and taxation departments sent staff to the factory to inspect and supervise the implementation of financial discipline and the payment of tax and interest, while the bank sent credit officers to inspect and supervise the loan, repayment, use of funds and economic effects, and the economic management agencies sent quality supervisors to inspect and supervise the quality of products of enterprises. They then put forward suggestions on handling the problems found in the procuratorial work, so as to help enterprises improve in a timely way.[26]

2. Research on the Reform of "Separation of Two Powers" in the State-owned Property Right System

In October 1987, the report of the Thirteenth National Congress of the Communist Party of China stated that enterprises owned by the public would be invigorated according to the principle of separation of ownership and management rights. Separating ownership from management rights was an internal requirement for the establishment of a planned commodity economic system, as were giving management rights to the enterprise, straightening out the relationship among the owner, the operator, and the producer, protecting the legitimate rights and interests of the enterprise, and enabling the enterprise to operate independently and be responsible for its own profits and losses. The specific forms of the separation of ownership and management rights varied according to the nature of the industry, the scale of the enterprise, and the technical characteristics. No matter what kind of management responsibility system was implemented, it was important to use legal means to determine the responsibility and right relations between the state and enterprises and between enterprise owners and enterprise managers in the form of a contract. At the time, the various forms of management responsibility systems, such as contracting and leasing, were a beneficial exploration of the separation of the two powers, which needed to be continuously reformed and improved through practice.[27]

After the policy idea of "separation of two powers" of state-owned property rights was put forward, economic and ideological circles began to discuss the concept. The general discussion

---

26. Ma Hong, *Economic Events of Modern China* (China Social Sciences Press, 1982), 332–333.

27. Zhao Ziyang, *Marching Along the Path of Socialism with Chinese Characteristics: Report on the Thirteenth National Congress of the CPC* (People's Publishing House, 1987).

addressed various specific operation modes and efficiency on the premise of affirming the separation of the two powers, but there were also different opinions based on the perspective of property rights theory. Some theorists held that the right of management was always attached to ownership. The ownership of enterprises included the possession, use, income, and disposal of the means of production. Without these, the right of management would become a meaningless category. Without the ownership of the means of production, it was impossible for an enterprise to have complete management rights, and without complete management rights, an enterprise could not become a commodity producer with independent management and financing of profits and losses. Therefore, according to the viewpoint of "separation of two powers," it was only a kind of unrealistic fantasy that aimed to retain the state's ownership of the means of production and let enterprises become commodity producers with independent management and financing of profits and losses.[28] Some people held that if the two powers in state-owned enterprises were completely separated, the state's status as the owner of the state would be cancelled, and the state's macro-control over the economy would be out of order because of the loss of the right to manage the micro basis. Therefore, in the full combination of the four rights of ownership, right of use, right of possession, and right of domination, ownership should belong to the state, the right of use should be completely left to the enterprise, and the right of possession and control should be separated between the state and the enterprise.[29] At the end of the 1980s, the mainstream view of economic and ideological circles involved discussion of various paths and modes of the reform of state-owned enterprises under the policy framework of "separation of two powers," such as enterprise ownership, virtual private ownership, divided production management system, stock production sharing system, risk responsibility system, and contract management responsibility system.[30]

In the 1980s, China's state-owned property rights system and state-owned enterprise reform measures were mainly carried out according to the idea of "separation of ownership and management rights." The theoretical significance of the separation of the two powers lay in that the relationship between the enterprise and the state was that between the producer and the owner of the property, an economic contract relationship between different economic parties, rather than an administrative subordination relationship. Therefore, the separation of the two powers was a great development on the original basis, which could stimulate the enthusiasm of operators and producers to a certain extent and improve the vitality and efficiency of enterprises. However, the separation of two powers at that time was not the separation of property ownership itself, but only the separation of ownership and one of its functions. On this basis, a sound enterprise management mechanism conforming to the operation law of the commodity economy could not be developed.

Looking at the reform practice in the 1980s, the reform of state-owned enterprises generally

---

28. Han Zhiguo, "Questioning the Separation of Two Powers," *Economic Weekly* (August 20, 1987).

29. Jiang Xuemo, "Some Opinions on China's Socialist Ownership Reform," *Economic Trends*, no. 2 (1986).

30. Editorial Department of *Economic Research, Debates on the Theoretical Issues of China's Socialist Economy (1985–1989)* (China Financial and Economic Publishing House, 1991), 108–113.

experienced three processes, from the expansion of enterprises' power, the two-step "profit to tax," to the "separation of two powers." The main purpose was to improve the production enthusiasm and business interests of enterprises by means of interest incentives. But this kind of reform was only superficial and could not form a management mechanism with both internal incentives and external restrictions inside the enterprise, nor could it construct an enterprise as the main body of the market. Therefore, the enterprise reform needed to develop to a deeper level, advance to the core of a property rights relationship, and form an enterprise operation mechanism in line with the basic law of the commodity economy on the basis of the relationship between the economic interests of enterprise operators and producers and the relationship between property rights, so as to improve the micro basis of the operation of the socialist commodity economy.

3. Discussion on the Reform of the State-owned Property Right System and Individual Ownership of the Laborer

In the 1980s, in the discussion of the reform of state-owned enterprises and state-owned property rights system, in order to solve the problem of the connection between the employees of state-owned enterprises and the property rights of the enterprises, China's economic and ideological circles studied Marx's theory of "re-establishing individual ownership," put forward the topic of the individual ownership of workers, and produced various views.[31]

Marx put forward the theory of "re-establishing individual ownership" in the study of the primitive accumulation of capital. The primitive accumulation of capital was the starting point of the capitalist mode of production. The primitive accumulation of capital was the separation of the laborer and the means of production. Marx notes, "The capitalist system presupposes the complete separation of the labourers from all property in the means by which they can realize their labour. As soon as capitalist production is once on its own legs, it not only maintains this separation, but reproduces it on a continually extending scale... The so-called primitive accumulation, therefore, is nothing else than the historical process of divorcing the producer from the means of production."[32] Primitive accumulation was a process in which "two very different commodity owners" were antagonistic to each other, and thus connected. On the one hand, they were the owners of money, the means of production, and the means of living. Although they had ownership of the means of production, they needed to buy other people's labor force to increase their total value. On the other hand, they were free laborers who were involved in direct production. However, they were the direct producers separated from the means of production. They had lost the means of production, leaving only their own labor force and becoming the sellers of their labor. Therefore, the primitive accumulation of capital only meant the deprivation of direct producers, that is, the disintegration of private ownership based on their own labor.

---

31. Editorial Department of *Economic Research*, *Debate on the Theoretical Issues of China's Socialist Economy (1985–1989)* (China's Financial and Economic Publishing House, 1991), 107–109.

32. Marx, *Das Kapital*, vol. 1 (People's Publishing House, 1975), 783.

The essence of the ownership of the means of production reflected the people's economic interests in production. Any social production was a process in which workers combined with the means of production to produce labor products. In this process, the relationship between the people and the ownership of the means of production determined the relationship between people and labor products, and the nature of the people's relations of production and economic interests. The nature of private ownership of small-scale production was that these private owners were laborers, and the private right of laborers to their means of production was the basis of small-scale production. In the private ownership of small-scale production, laborers produced their own labor products with their own means of production and through their own labor. The ownership of the means of production, the ownership of labor force, and the ownership of labor products were unified. Their economic behavior was directly driven by their economic interests, and their economic interests were directly related to the ownership of the means of production and labor products. At a certain stage of the development of social productive forces, the private ownership of small production was a necessary condition for the development of social production and the free individuality of the laborers themselves.

The nature of capitalist private ownership was that the direct producer did not possess the ownership of the means of production, while the owner of the means of production was an indirect producer. In this kind of private ownership, the ownership of the means of production, the ownership of labor force, and the ownership of labor products were not unified in both capitalists and producers. As a direct producer, laborers did not own the ownership of the means of production, and thus did not own the ownership of labor products, while as the owner of the means of production, capitalists did not have the ownership of labor force, but must acquire the ownership of labor force and realize the ownership of surplus labor products through the purchase of labor force. Therefore, in this kind of private ownership, the unity of ownership of the means of production, ownership of labor force, and ownership of labor products were destroyed. These three rights could only be unified under the media of capital. The internal law of capital movement was the law of surplus value.

The production of the means of production was the concentrated embodiment of production relations, and its evolution was related to the development of productive forces. Historically, private ownership of the means of production experienced different stages of development, such as private ownership of small production and private ownership of capitalism. Private ownership of small production was only compatible with the narrow natural boundaries of production and society. When it developed to a certain extent, it created the material means to eliminate itself. Therefore, private ownership based on the combination of independent workers and their working conditions was replaced by the capitalist private ownership with exploitative relations but free labor. However, with the development of productivity and capitalist mode of production, the forms of cooperation in the expanding labor process were constantly developing, and the means of production were increasingly transformed into means of production that could only be used together.

Marx summed up this evolution of private ownership as follows, "The capitalist mode of appropriation, the result of the capitalist mode of production, produces capitalist private property. This is the first negation of individual private property, as founded on the labor of the proprietor. But capitalist production begets, with the inexorability of a law of Nature, its own negation. It is the negation of negation. This does not re-establish private property for the producer, but gives him individual property based on the acquisition of the capitalist era: *i.e.*, on co-operation and the possession in common of the land and of the means of production."[33] An accurate understanding of this passage is the key to grasping Marx's thought of "re-establishing individual ownership." I believe that in understanding Marx's exposition, there are three points that require attention.

First, Marx always came from the perspective of the relationship between workers and the means of production. The basis of private ownership of small-scale production was the private right of laborers to the means of production, while the basis of capitalist private ownership was that workers were deprived of the ownership of the means of production and became free workers "separated from the means of production" and "re-established" personal ownership, as a negation of the negation of capitalist private ownership, which meant that workers regained the means of production. Ownership meant that the laborer and his working conditions were combined directly. Therefore, Marx's "individual ownership" did not refer to the form of ownership, but to the nature of ownership, that is, the relationship between direct producers and the ownership of the means of production.

Second, Marx consistently analyzed the evolution of ownership with the development of productive forces as a guide. The development of social productive forces created the material conditions for the elimination of private ownership of small-scale production. The further development of productive forces, the continuous improvement of the degree of socialization of production, and the concentration of the means of production also created the material conditions for the elimination of capitalist private ownership. Therefore, the reestablishment of individual ownership was a "double negation" of capitalist private ownership, that is, it was not a simple response to the private ownership of small production. They were two modes of production based on different productive forces. Private ownership of small-scale production was based on the decentralization of land and other means of production, while the reestablishment of individual ownership was based on the further socialization of labor and the further transformation of land and other means of production into public means of production.

Third, due to the great improvement of the socialization of production, all means of production, as the means of production of combined social labor, were increasingly transformed into common, social, or public means of production. Therefore, the ownership of the means of production that adapted to the development of productive forces could only be based on the common possession of the means of production. In other words, the re-established individual ownership was individual ownership based on the common possession of the means of production. In this kind of ownership relations, on the one hand, because labor was no longer a scattered

---

33. Marx, *Das Kapital*, vol. 1 (People's Publishing House, 1975), 832.

labor, but social labor, and because the means of production were increasingly concentrated and increasingly transformed into social means of production that could only be used together, the possession of the means of production could only be "shared" by the entire society, and no one could carry out private possession of social means of production or exploit others. In this sense, this kind of possession of the means of production could be called "public ownership." On the other hand, every individual laborer was directly combined with the ownership of the means of production and the ownership of labor products. In other words, "under the proletarian system of possession, many means of production should be controlled by each individual, while property is subject to the control of all individuals."[34] Therefore, the ownership of the means of production, the ownership of labor force, and the ownership of labor products were unified again. According to Marx's analytical logic, if the ownership of the laborer and his working conditions were separated, the result of this process would be that the means of production and means of living of society would be transformed into capital, and the direct producers would be transformed into wage workers. Therefore, the direct combination of the direct producer and the ownership of the means of production on the basis of joint possession of the means of production is the essence of "individual ownership." Of course, how to combine the ownership of the means of production with the direct producers on the basis of the common possession of the means of production in the whole society was a technical problem that Marx did not discuss.

According to the above analysis, "individual ownership" included two meanings. First, it was based on the common possession of the means of production by society, so it was public ownership. Second, the ownership of the individual laborer and the means of production was directly combined, so it was also "individual ownership." Generally speaking, socialist public ownership should include these two meanings, because socialist public ownership solved the contradiction between the socialization of production and private possession of the means of production and the separation of laborer's ownership of the means of production and ownership of labor products. It thus determined the consistency of the fundamental interests of workers and their pursuit of interests with economic growth, which greatly improved the enthusiasm of workers in production, making it a great driving force for the development of productive forces.

Marx's argument was related to his overall conception of future society, including the further improvement of social productivity on the basis of the achievements in the capitalist era, the disappearance of the commodity economy, the direct combination of laborers as a member of the consortium, and the ownership of the means of production. Whether in the sense of a consortium or in the personal sense of members of the consortium, labor force had a close relationship with the ownership of the means of production. The producers were the real masters of the means of production and labor products. If it was not related to these conditions, it was meaningless to discuss "re-establishing individual ownership." Moreover, as a theoretical conception, "individual ownership" had corresponding theoretical value, but it would not have practical value in China at the end of the 20th century, nor could it become a theoretical model for China's economic reform.

---

34. Marx and Engels, *Selected Works of Marx and Engels*, vol. 1 (People's Publishing House, 1972), 74–75.

8.3 The Reform of State-owned Enterprises and the Theoretical Research on the Shareholding System

1. On the Theory of the Joint Stock System and the Reform of State-owned Enterprises

In October 1987, the report of the Thirteenth National Congress of the Communist Party of China pointed out that the joint stock system, which appeared in the reform and included state-owned shares, shares held by departments, regions, enterprises, and individuals, was a kind of organization mode of socialist enterprise property that could be continued for trial implementation. The property rights of some small enterprises owned by all the people could be transferred to collectives or individuals with compensation.[35] In the discussion of the stock system in theoretical circles, a representative point of view held that the stock system was a new form of socialist public ownership. It embodied the essential characteristics of the public economy that the laborer group was the master of the means of production. The shareholding system of enterprises was the expansion of the public economy, not the weakening of it. The stock system was a good form of socialist public ownership.[36] Another representative point of view was that the nature of the joint stock system was private ownership, which could not be taken as the direction of state-owned enterprise reform. Although the joint-stock-system partly resolved the contradiction between private capital ownership and socialized mass production, socialist public ownership itself was a complete sublation of the capitalist mode of production. The ability to concentrate capital far exceeded the level that capitalism could achieve, and it was more likely that the best entrepreneurs would be chosen for management. Therefore, the joint stock system aiming at capital concentration and high-quality management was of little practical significance to the enterprises owned by the public. The short-term behavior of enterprises in the reform was not the inevitable result of public ownership. If the stock system was used to correct it, it would have strengthened unreasonable behavior.[37] Some also held that the joint-stock system produced in the process of China's reform was a mixed ownership economy. Among them, a large portion of the joint stock economy controlled by the public sector was regarded as a form of public ownership.[38]

On the basis of in-depth study, some scholars suggested that the essence of the stock system was private ownership. The stock system had both positive and negative effects. The reform of China's state-owned enterprises could take advantage of the joint stock system, but it had to adopt its advantages and prevent its disadvantages. As for the ownership nature of the joint stock

---

35. Zhao Ziyang, *Marching Along the Path of Socialism with Chinese Characteristics: Report on the Thirteenth National Congress of the CPC* (People's Publishing House, 1987).

36. Li Yining, "The Conception of Ownership Reform in China," *People's Daily*, September 26, 1986; Huang Fanzhang, "Joint Stock System: A Good Form of Socialist Public Ownership," *Economic Research*, no. 4 (1989).

37. Fan Maofa et al., "The Stock System is Not the Reform Direction for Publicly Owned Enterprises," *Economic Research*, no. 1 (1986); Wu Shuqing, "Joint Stock System is Not the Reform Direction of Large and Medium-sized State-owned Enterprises," *People's Daily*, March 16, 1987.

38. Zhang Zhuoyuan et al., *An Outline of the History of New China's Economics (1949–2011)*. China (Social Sciences Press, 2012), 245.

system, the viewpoint quoted Marx's relevant exposition in *Das Kapital,* which stated that due to the emergence of the joint-stock company system, "Transformation of the actually functioning capitalist into a mere manager, administrator of other people's capital, and of the owner of capital into a mere owner, a mere money-capitalist... this function in the person of the manager is divorced from ownership of capital... In stock companies the function is divorced from capital ownership... This result of the ultimate development of capitalist production is... a self-dissolving contradiction... It reproduces a new financial aristocracy, a new variety of parasites in the shape of promoters, speculators and simply nominal directors; a whole system of swindling and cheating by means of corporation promotion, stock issuance, and stock speculation. It is private production without the control of private property... [s]ince property here exists in the form of stock... but the conversion to the form of stock still remains ensnared in the trammels of capitalism."[39]

This discussion shows that, firstly, the shareholding system was the most favorable and necessary condition for the development of private capital and enterprises into the "socialized mode of production." From this point of view, in a socialist society, in order to effectively attract social idle funds, it was possible and necessary to adopt the stock system. Second, after all, the stock system was still "confined within the limits of capitalism," and the stock form was just a private "ownership certificate to obtain future surplus value." Therefore, under socialist conditions, if the joint-stock system was carried out without restriction, socialist public ownership would be sublated. Because the stock system itself was the most typical and developed private capitalist form, it was impossible to transform into a more perfect public ownership. If its prevalence was not enough to transform the current public ownership into private ownership, it would at least affect the consolidation of the existing public ownership. As for the consequences of speculation and fraud in the stock market, it was important to seriously consider them.[40]

As far as the socialist economic system and the reform of state-owned enterprises are concerned, there were several advantages to using the joint-stock system. First, the joint-stock system was the most effective way to raise large-scale socialized production and circulation funds. Second, the joint-stock system had a strong vitality to meet the needs of the market. Third, the share-holding system could effectively share risks. Fourth, the joint-stock system opened up the use of funds for public and private funding institutions' investment opportunities. It was also important to prevent and limit the disadvantages of the joint stock system. First was the contradiction between the nature of the private ownership of the joint stock system and socialist public ownership. If the enterprises owned by the people were changed into joint stock enterprises with individual shares, it would be a denial of socialist public ownership. Second, the prosperity of the joint stock system would inevitably lead to speculation. Third, the joint stock system would lead to monopolies. Fourth, the joint stock system would be implemented for a long time, but

---

39. Marx and Engels, *Complete Works of Marx and Engels*, vol. 25 (People's Publishing House, 1975), 493–497.

40. Hu Jichuang, "Socialism and Shareholding System," *Academic Monthly*, no. 8 (1987).

there would be a "profiteer" class. Through the analysis of the advantages and disadvantages of the stock system, it was clear that it would not be easy to completely reconcile with the socialist system, but in order to meet the needs of the primary stage of socialism in China, the only option was to adopt the most favorable key advantages and prevent the disadvantages. In other words, if the adoption of the joint-stock system did not pose a threat to socialist public ownership, it was conducive to raising large-scale operating funds and was adaptable to the needs of the market, which had great practical significance and made up for the two shortcomings at the current stage. The use of stock management to further improve work efficiency and invigorate the national economy had greater practical significance.[41]

2. An Analysis of the Ownership Attributes of the Shareholding System Reform of China's State-owned Enterprises in the 1980s

A common view in theoretical circles was that the stock system did not have the property of private ownership. In fact, fundamentally speaking, the joint stock system was a kind of property rights form and operation mode which grew from the basis of private ownership and was connected with large scale socialized production. As a form of property rights, share capital was a kind of joint social capital created by the credit system. As a mode of operation, a joint stock company was a typical form of separation of capital ownership and capital function. From the perspective of ownership, the ownership nature of a joint stock company depended on who controlled the company. If it was controlled by individuals, it was naturally private ownership, while if it was state-owned, it was state property. It was evident that there is a premise to say that shareholding did not have the property of private ownership. Historically, the stock system naturally had the characteristics of private ownership. Only when it was carried out under the premise of non-private ownership could it have different ownership attributes. According to the trial implementation of China's joint stock system, the state's Pilot Measures for Joint Stock Enterprises stipulated that the equity structure of joint stock enterprises must take public ownership (state shares) as the main body. The Opinions on the Joint Stock Limited Company Standard issued by the State Restructuring Commission stipulated that the shares held by a natural entity (excluding foreign shares) should not exceed five thousandths of the total shares of the company. Taking Shanghai as an example, in the first half of 1992, twenty state-owned large and medium-sized industrial enterprises were restructured into joint stock companies. The capital composition of these enterprises generally accounted for 60% to 70% of the total national shares. From the perspective of capital structure, the ownership nature of these joint-stock companies was naturally state-owned. In addition, in the capital structure of Shanghai's joint-stock companies, legal entity shares generally accounted for 20 to 30% of their total shares. These legal entities were basically state-owned enterprises and institutions. If the capital they used to purchase shares was state-owned assets, then the ultimate ownership of these shares was also owned by the state. If this part of corporate shares

---

41. Hu Jichuang, "Socialism and Shareholding System," *Academic Monthly*, no. 8 (1987).

was included, then the share of public ownership in the joint-stock companies would be even greater. Moreover, according to the regulations of Shanghai Securities Regulatory Commission, all enterprises and institutions could not sell legal entity shares to individuals without the approval of the Commission, nor could they subscribe for legal person shares in the form of individual fund-raising by employees. This limited the loss of corporate shares to individuals and ensured the public ownership of corporate shares.

This analysis shows that in the 1980s, China's joint stock economy was basically carried out within the scope of state ownership. Within this scope, the composition of share capital was unlikely to produce a sufficient number of secondary property rights, and its ownership was public. This was the theoretical premise of studying China's stock economy.

However, in the discussion on the stock economy in China at that time, some viewpoints were contrary to this premise and to the actual situation. In terms of methodology, some expositors designed various schemes or methods for the individualization of property rights from the perspective of the combination of the individual laborer and the ownership of assets, and they regarded the shareholding system as the main choice for the individualization of property rights and the main idea for the transformation of the enterprise management mechanism. It was not accurate to regard the stock system as a property system that combined individual workers and property rights.

Marx offered a detailed theoretical exposition of the joint stock economy in *Das Kapital*. He pointed out that the joint stock company made "the actually functioning capitalist into a mere manager, administrator of other people's capital, and of the owner of capital into a mere owner, a mere money-capitalist. Even if the dividends which they receive include the interest and the profit of enterprise, *i.e.*, the total profit (for the salary of the manager is, or should be, simply the wage of a specific type of skilled labour, whose price is regulated in the labour-market like that of any other labour), this total profit is henceforth received only in the form of interest, *i.e.*, as mere compensation for owning capital that now is entirely divorced from the function in the actual process of reproduction, just as this function in the person of the manager is divorced from ownership of capital. Profit thus appears (no longer only that portion of it, the interest, which derives its justification from the profit of the borrower) as a mere appropriation of the surplus-labour of others, arising from the conversion of means of production into capital, *i.e.*, from their alienation vis-à-vis the actual producer, from their antithesis as another's property to every individual actually at work in production, from manager down to the last day-labourer. In stock companies the function is divorced from capital ownership, hence also labour is entirely divorced from ownership of means of production and surplus-labour."[42] Based on this argument, we come to several conclusions.

First, the separation of capital ownership and capital function in the capitalist stock system does not mean the separation of capital ownership, possession, control, and use rights, but refers to the separation of production labor management and enterprise assets operation. This capital function

---

42. Marx, *Das Kapital*, vol. 3 (People's Publishing House, 1975), 493–494.

is separated from capital ownership. The function of capital is to bring profit, that is to consume means of production and labor force in the process of production, and produce labor products containing surplus value. In the real economy, the function of capital is to operate the enterprise assets according to the principle of profit maximization. The separation of capital function and capital ownership means that the capital owner no longer performs the function of capital, but it is performed by managers instead. As the executor of the function of capital ownership in the process of reproduction, the manager is the employer of capital just like the worker. The difference is that the worker pays for the labor, and the manager pays for the management ability, which is what Marx called "management labor." He states, "Generally speaking, there is a trend in the stock enterprises which develop with the credit industry, that is, making the management labor as a function more separated from the ownership of one's own capital or borrowed capital."[43] In the modern enterprise system, both managers and workers are the employers of capital. How then can they have the right to possess, control, and use that capital? In China's state-owned property rights system, the actual owner of state-owned enterprise assets is the state. If we say that the employees of state-owned enterprises are not the owners, they can own the right of possession, control, use, and corresponding right of income of the enterprise assets, which is the alienation of the state-owned system, and it does not make logical sense. The result of the practice is that there is no property standard and property restriction in the enterprise behavior, the income of state-owned assets is lost, and the problem of operating efficiency is not fundamentally resolved.

The essence of the problem is not whether employees can own the shares of the company. In fact, China has long issued internal shares in state-owned enterprises in the reform of the shareholding system of state-owned enterprises, and employees of joint-stock companies in Western capitalist countries can also own their own shares. However, once the employees own the stock of the enterprise, is it directly related to the property rights of the enterprise? Can a reasonable, effective enterprise management mechanism be formed on this basis? Further theoretical analysis is needed. Stock capital is a kind of joint capital created by the credit system. Nominally, each shareholder is associated with this joint capital. Because of the relationship between dividend income and capital appreciation, shareholders naturally care about the business activities of the enterprises they participate in. However, for the general shareholder, he is only the owner of the stock he owns, and only owns the ownership of the capital value of this certain amount of stock. Generally speaking, stock is regarded as the ownership certificate of share capital, which is not accurate in theory.

Stock is a kind of fictitious capital, which is only the certificate of ownership of the capital value it represents, or the ownership certificate of the corresponding part of the surplus value realized by the actual investment capital, but which has no direct relationship with the real capital. From the investment point of view, the shareholder uses his currency to buy stocks, that is, to convert his monetary capital into some kind of financial assets (interest bearing capital). He is directly concerned about the income that the monetary capital can bring. Once the company's

---

43. Marx, *Das Kapital*, vol. 3 (People's Publishing House, 1975), 436.

poor operation affects the shareholders' income, he can sell the stock at any time and convert its monetary capital into other financial assets with greater expected return (from the trial implementation of the joint stock system, the purchase of stocks is not invested in enterprises, but in securities. The purpose of shareholders' investment is mostly short term stock price income rather than long term dividend income. The purpose of this investment is basically determined by the limited shares held by the general shareholders and the small interest in dividends). From the distribution point of view, the joint stock system is distributed according to capital, and the investors receive the dividend corresponding to the number of shares. For the general shareholders and employees with small share participation, this distribution mechanism basically does not have the effect of stimulating the enthusiasm of employees. In the joint stock economy, it is the major shareholders who control the stock capital entity (real capital) that has direct and fixed connection with the ownership of the stock capital entity. In other words, in order to have a direct relationship with the property rights of a joint stock enterprise, the number of stocks must be controlled to achieve the control of real capital. Therefore, if the state-owned enterprise is transformed into a joint stock company, if it is controlled by the state and the employees, as general shareholders, do not have direct contact with the ownership of enterprise assets, then it is difficult to form an incentive and restriction mechanism on the basis of the combination of direct producers and enterprise property rights by taking the opportunity of employee participation. Some points of view proposed that the enterprise legal entity controls this to ensure that a kind of enterprise legal entity resides in the legal representative. However, the final ownership of corporate ownership (terminal ownership) is bound to be specific to individuals or countries, because corporate ownership is only the determination of de facto ownership. A legal entity means that the personality of the association exists according to the law. As the subject of property right, a legal entity has an independent personality and capacity of civil liability. An enterprise is the capital entity of various production factors, and it is a production organization, so it is impossible to become a subject of ownership.

According to this analysis, as an effective form of fund-raising, joint stock production can widely absorb social capital, expand the economic strength and production scale of state-owned enterprises, enable a certain amount of state-owned assets to absorb and control a larger amount of social capital, increase social accumulation, and promote faster economic growth. As a scientific form of operations, the separation of ownership and capital functions, as well as the corresponding principles, regulations, and mechanisms, are conducive to improving the level of operation and management of enterprises, hardening the external constraints of enterprises and improving the competitive consciousness of enterprises, and ultimately improving the operating efficiency of enterprises. As a modern form of property rights, the nature of stock ownership is determined by the shareholders. Under a state holding, this form of property rights is also conducive to straightening out the relationship between property rights and corresponding interests within a certain range, to the separation of government from enterprises, and to the circulation, reorganization, and effective allocation of production factors. Therefore, the joint stock system can be an important direction of state-owned enterprise system reform.

The Third Plenary Session of the Eleventh Central Committee of the Communist Party of China re-established the ideological line of emancipating the mind and seeking truth from facts and opened the process of Reform and Opening Up. Ideological and theoretical circles broke through the theory of production relations-alone and established the historical materialist concept of determining the nature of the economic system, economic relations, and economic interests according to the development level of productive forces and the objective requirements of developing productive forces. Under the guidance of the spirit of the Third Plenary Session of the Eleventh Central Committee of the Communist Party of China and the ideological and theoretical guidance of the primary stage of socialism, the study of political economics made breakthroughs in a series of theoretical categories, especially in putting the economic system, economic operations, and economic activities on the basis of the law of value, primarily through realizing the transformation of the mainstream theory of political economy from the law of planned, proportional development to the law of value.

From the 1980s to the early 1990s, with the promotion of China's economic system reform from the "planned economy as the main task and market regulation as the supplement" to a "planned commodity economic system," the whole economic system gradually transformed from the planned and proportional development law to the law of value. The socialist planned commodity economic system was based on commodity exchange and value regulation. On the basis of law, planning was also to be realized through the law of value, and the law of value was to be used to serve the planned economy. The socialist planned commodity economic system and operation mechanism were the combination of the planned economy and market regulation, and the scope of action of plan and market covered society as a whole. In line with the practice of economic system reform, the theoretical main line of China's socialist political economics also transformed from the law of planned, proportional development to the law of value. Starting from the theoretical category of the law of value, the general law of the commodity economy and market regulation, the subject of study was the relationship between plan and market in the socialist economy, as well as the relationship between socialist ownership, distribution, and economic operations.

CHAPTER 9

The Evolution of the Economic Development Strategy

9.1 The Transformation of the Guiding Ideology for Economic Development and the Formation of the New Economic Development Strategy

1. The Transformation of the Guiding Ideology for Economic Development in the Late 1970s and Early 1980s

After the economic construction from the 1950s to the 1970s, the defects of China's economic development strategy were widely recognized. Finding ways to explore and formulate new, more scientific economic construction guidelines, policies, and measures according to China's low per capita income, lack of social funds, and low economic efficiency became the main agenda for China's economic development strategy transformation.

From the Third Plenary Session of the Eleventh Central Committee of the Communist Party of China in December 1978 to the ten principles for future economic construction elaborated at the fourth session of the Fifth National People's Congress in November 1981, according to the spirit of the Third Plenary Session of the Eleventh Central Committee of the Communist Party of China, a new economic development strategy was put forward at the Twelfth National Congress of the Communist Party of China in September 1982. The development strategy characterized by one-sided pursuit of high-speed economic growth was updated into a more practical, scientific development strategy centered on improving economic benefits which was in line with the national conditions and national strength.

On March 14, 1979, Chen Yun and Li Xiannian wrote to the Central Committee of the Communist Party of China and put forward some suggestions for the future financial and economic work of the state. The first was a commitment to move forward steadily, no longer tossing about. It was necessary to avoid repetition and a large saddle shape in the development trend. In the long run, the fastest speed for the national economy to develop in proportion was the preferred approach. At the time, there was no comprehensive balance in the national economy, and the imbalance was quite serious. It would thus take two or three years to adjust the imbalance in various aspects.

In addition, the index of steel must be reliable. The development direction of steel should not only emphasize quantity but also quality. The speed of steel development should take into account the proportion of the development of all walks of life.

Further, to borrow foreign debt, it was necessary to fully consider the nation's ability to repay the principal and interest, and also consider the capacity of domestic investment.[1]

In April 1979, the CPC Central Committee held a working conference to discuss economic issues. The meeting comprehensively analyzed the current situation of China's economic construction and decided to focus on the adjustment of the national economy in three years. It formally put forward the policy of "adjustment, reform, rectification, and improvement" of the national economy. The meeting pointed out that economic construction must be suitable for China's national conditions and conform to economic and natural laws. It was necessary to act according to the country's ability, moving forward step by step and paying attention to actual results so that the development of production could be closely combined with the improvement of people's living standards. It was important to actively carry out economic exchanges and cooperation with foreign countries on the basis of independence and self-reliance and proceed according to a Chinese approach to the path to modernization.

Based on the situation at that time, the change of the guiding ideology of economic development first concentrated on the understanding that economic development must be carried out according to the nation's ability and in line with the national conditions, national strength, and the objective economic law. Deng Xiaoping pointed out, "According to our experience, we should not go too fast or too hurry. In the past, we went too fast and made some mistakes, which we now call 'leftist.' As a result, the speed of economic development has slowed. To develop the economy now, we still have to rely on the principle of self-reliance and act according to our ability."[2] The *People's Daily* published two editorials, on April 7 and June 9, 1980, entitled "The Guiding Ideology of Acting According to One's Ability is Very Important" and "Acting According to One's Ability is an Important Policy for Capital Construction." The editorials mainly discussed the notion that the speed of economic construction should adapt to national strength and point out that acting according to one's ability is acting according to the objective law of economic

---

1. *Selected Important Documents Since the Third Plenary Session of the CPC Central Committee*, vol. 1 (People's Publishing House, 1982), 69.

2. Deng Xiaoping, *Selected Works of Deng Xiaoping*, vol. 2 (People's Publishing House, 1983), 361–362.

development. Over the previous thirty years, China's economic construction had experienced two big ups and downs, and the loss and waste were staggering. The fundamental reason was that China had not done what it could. The editorial went on to say that whether economic development and capital construction were carried out according to China's ability or not was actually a matter of what path the nation should take to develop its economy, that is, the policy of economic construction.

In November 1981, the government work report entitled "The Current Economic Situation and the Guidelines for Future Economic Construction" was delivered at the fourth session of the Fifth National People's Congress. On the basis of summing up the experience of the People's Republic of China over the previous 32 years, especially the experience accumulated since the Third Plenary Session of the Eleventh Central Committee of the Communist Party of China, it was proposed that China should effectively change the long-term "leftist" thinking. A set of old practices, starting from the actual situation of China, would take a new road with more practical speed, better economic benefits, and more tangible benefits for the people. The core of the new way was to "do everything possible to improve the economic benefits of production, construction, circulation, and other fields." Centering on this core, the report put forward ten principles for future economic construction:

1) Rely on science and policies to accelerate the development of agriculture.
2) Put the development of the consumer goods industry in a key position and further adjust the service direction of heavy industry.
3) Improve the efficiency of energy utilization and strengthen the construction of the energy and transportation industries.
4) Technological transformation should be carried out systematically and emphatically to give full play to the role of existing enterprises.
5) Carry out the comprehensive rectification and necessary reorganization of enterprises in groups.
6) Pay attention to the way to generate, gather, and use capital to increase and save construction funds.
7) Adhere to the policy of opening up to the outside world and enhance China's ability to rely on itself.
8) Actively and steadily reform the economic system and fully and effectively mobilize the enthusiasm of all sectors.
9) Raise the scientific and cultural level of all workers.
10) Proceed from the idea of "everything for the people" and make overall arrangements for production, construction, and the people's life.[3]

---

3. Zhao Ziyang, *The Current Economic Situation and the Policy for Future Economic Construction* (People's Publishing House, 1981).

This was the first time in the guiding ideology of China's economic construction that China focused on improving economic benefits. These ten new guidelines for the development of the national economy with the improvement of economic efficiency as the core marked an important change in China's economic development from the traditional guiding ideology of one-sided pursuit of the growth rate to the new guiding ideology of pursuing economic benefits, and it laid the foundation for the formation of China's new economic development strategy.

2. The New Economic Development Strategy Takes Shape

In September 1982, the Twelfth CPC National Congress was held. Deng Xiaoping pointed out in his opening speech that China's modernization drive must proceed from its actual situation, which was the basic starting point for the nation to formulate economic development strategies and various policies and measures. Generally speaking, the basic national conditions of China were 1) the socialist system had been established, but was still not perfect, 2) it had laid a substantial material foundation, but this foundation was still very thin, 3) it had a long cultural tradition, but the culture, science, and technology were still quite backward, 4) the population was large and the labor resources were sufficient, but the consumption was large and the social and economic burden was heavy, and 5) the land was large and the natural resources were rich, but the available land, especially cultivated land, was scarce, many resources were poorly developed and utilized, and the natural conditions and economic development in various regions were extremely unbalanced. These were the characteristics of China's national conditions, which formed the special conditions and contradictions of China's modernization. Among these characteristics, the two most important were the weak foundation and the large population and scarcity of cultivated land. These two important characteristics formed a series of unique contradictions. According to the objective analysis of China's national conditions, Deng Xiaoping stressed that China should overcome the "leftist" errors in its economic construction strategy and formulate an economic development strategy based on its own national conditions and objective economic laws, so that the nation's economy could gradually achieve coordinated development and stable growth, achieving a virtuous cycle, so that the investment would be relatively small, the accumulation appropriate, and the economic benefits relatively good, allowing the people to thrive. This was a new mode of economic development in which the advantages of the socialist system could be brought into full play.

At the Twelfth National Congress of the Communist Party of China, Hu Yaobang delivered a report entitled "Comprehensively Creating a New Situation for Socialist Modernization Construction," which put forward strategic objectives, points, and steps, along with a series of important principles for China's economic construction by the end of the 20th century. The strategic goal put forward in the report stated that from 1981 to the end of the 20th century, the general goal of China's economic construction was to quadruple the annual total output value of industry and agriculture in China, from 710 billion yuan in 1980 to 2.8 trillion yuan in 2000. If this goal could be achieved, China's total national income and the output of major industrial and agricultural products would be in the global forefront, the modernization process of the whole national economy would make greater progress, the income of both urban and rural dwellers would be doubled, and people's material and cultural life could reach an affluent level.[4] In order to achieve this strategic goal, over the next twenty years, it was crucial to firmly grasp the basic links of agriculture, energy and transportation, education, and science and make them the strategic focus of economic development.

In order to achieve this strategic goal, the strategy steps should be divided into two steps. In the first ten years, from 1981 to 1990, China should lay a good foundation, accumulate strength, and create the necessary conditions. From 1991 to 2000, it was important to strive to enter a new period of economic revitalization.

The strategic objectives, strategic priorities, and strategic steps of China's economic construction by the end of the 20th century put forward by the Twelfth National Congress of the Communist Party of China constituted a comprehensive, systematic long-term development strategy for China's socialist construction in a new historical period, and it was also the first time that the term "economic development strategy" was explicitly used in Chinese policy. It marked a new stage in the development of the guiding ideology and theory of China's economic strategy. Compared with the traditional strategy, this approach pointed to great changes in economic development goals, development priorities, and reproduction mode. In terms of development goals, the new strategy not only took the quantitative growth of output value as the goal, but also took improving economic efficiency as the prerequisite for the growth of output value and formulated an appropriate economic growth rate on the basis of an objective understanding of national conditions and national strength. The development focus of the new strategy did not emphasize the development of heavy industry in a one-sided approach like the traditional strategy had, but paid attention to the coordinated and balanced development of economic structure, taking agriculture, energy, transportation, and other basic industries as well as science and technology as strategic priorities. In terms of the mode of reproduction, the new strategy did not mainly rely on large amounts of financial and material resources to build new projects and expand the extension of reproduction, but mainly relied on technological progress and the improvement of labor productivity to expand reproduction.

When analyzing the capitalist expansion of reproduction, Marx pointed out, "One might answer the question by pointing out that the constantly expanding production expands annually for two reasons: firstly because the capital invested in production is continually growing; secondly because the capital is constantly used more productively; in the course of reproduction and

---

4. Deng Xiaoping put forward the original idea of the strategic objectives formulated by the Twelfth National Congress of the Communist Party of China. In December 1979, Deng held talks with visiting Japanese Prime Minister Masayoshi Ohira, pointing out that China's GDP should quadruple by the end of the 20th century, so that the GNP would reach 100 billion US dollars. If the population at that time increased to about 1.2 billion US dollars, the per capita GNP would reach 800 US dollars, so that the people's lives would reach an affluent level. On this basis, it would develop for another thirty to fifty years, striving to close the gap with developed countries.

accumulation, small improvements are continuously building up, which eventually alter the whole level of production. There is a piling up of improvements, a cumulative development of productive powers."[5] He continued, "This part of the value of the fixed capital transformed into money may serve to extend the business or to make improvements in the machinery which will increase the efficiency of the latter. Thus reproduction takes place in larger or smaller periods of time, and this is, from the standpoint of society, reproduction on an enlarged scale—extensive if the means of production is extended; intensive if the means of production is made more effective. This reproduction on an extended scale does not result from accumulation—transformation of surplus-value into capital—but from the reconversion of the value which has branched off, detached itself in the form of money from the body of the fixed capital into new additional or at least more effective fixed capital of the same kind."[6] This discussion shows that there were two forms of expansion of reproduction. One was extension expansion reproduction, which mainly depended on increasing accumulation and investment to expand production scale, and the other was connotation expansion reproduction, which mainly relied on technical reform and renovation of original fixed capital to expand production scale.

The world economy shows that the inevitable trend is that the development of productivity and science and technology changes the mode of social production from extension to connotation. Among the fixed assets investment in the United States, the proportion used for the renovation of existing enterprises averaged 55% from 1947 to 1950, and 77% from 1971 to 1978. In the industrial capital construction investment of the Soviet Union, 51% was used for the technological transformation of existing enterprises in 1959, and this figure increased to 70% in 1979.[7] At the beginning of socialist industrialization in the early days after the founding of the People's Republic of China, due to the extremely weak material and technical foundation of industry, especially heavy industry, it was necessary to concentrate on the construction and expansion of the heavy industry sector for a certain period of time. After a long period of construction, and after a certain material and technical foundation had been established, economic construction gradually shifted from mainly external expansion and reproduction to mainly internal expansion and reproduction. This was not only in accordance with the general law of productivity development, but was also determined by China's national conditions. China had a large population, a weak foundation, a low accumulation capacity, and a shortage of capital and foreign exchange, which determined that its development should be based on the progress of production technology, the improvement of the quality of production factors, and the improvement of social and economic benefits, so that limited investment could promote higher economic growth. Some people calculated that, according to the main financial indicators of industrial enterprises owned by the people, the output value realized by the original value of fixed assets per 100 yuan was 101.16 yuan in 1980 and 95.71

---

5. Marx and Engels, *Complete Works of Marx and Engels*, vol. 26, bk. 2 (People's Publishing House, 1972), 598.

6. Marx and Engels, *Complete Works of Marx and Engels*, vol. 24 (People's Publishing House, 1973), 192.

7. Liu Hong and Wei Liqun, *China's National Conditions and Economic and Social Development Strategy* (Red Flag Press, 1982), 85.

yuan in 1981. That is to say, an increase of 1 yuan of industrial output value required investment of 1 yuan of industrial fixed assets. Considering the industrial distribution of output value growth, the total agricultural output value could not be quadrupled in twenty years. In order to achieve the goal of quadrupling the total industrial and agricultural output value, industrial output value should be more than quadrupled. For example, the industrial output value increased from 497.4 billion yuan in 1980 to 2,362.5 billion yuan in 2000, with a net increase of 1,865.1 billion yuan, which required a corresponding increase of 1,865.1 billion yuan in fixed assets investment. Along with the investment in transportation and other non-productive infrastructure, this would still require about 4 trillion yuan to quadruple. In the first half of the 1980s, the state's fiscal revenue was no more than 110 billion yuan per year, and the extra budgetary funds were only 170 billion yuan, while the investment in capital construction was about 50–80 billion yuan, which could not meet such a huge investment demand even if it was increased each year.[8] The problem of funding was very pressing. On the one hand, the national foundation was weak, and on the other, economic efficiency was too low. As far as capital construction was concerned, 1 yuan of capital construction investment could only form 0.7–0.8 yuan of fixed assets, while in state-owned industrial enterprises, 1 yuan of fixed assets could only achieve output value of 0.96 yuan. If China remained at its current levels of technology and economic benefits, the output value would quadruple and the investment would need to quadruple. Moreover, with fixed assets, China could not enter the production process, and it would need to put in working capital. At the time, the working capital occupied by state-owned industrial enterprises was equal to more than one quarter of the fixed assets, and the nation's fiscal revenue was only a little more than 100 billion yuan a year. If China insisted on increasing investment in fixed assets, consumption funds would be compressed, which could lead to an imbalance of proportion and economic chaos. The way out was to improve management and adopt advanced technology to increase economic benefits. Future economic construction would require abandoning the old road of external expansion and reproduction to mainly internal expansion and reproduction.[9]

A comprehensive approach to the fundamental point of this transformation of China's new economic development strategy relative to the traditional development strategy was to take the improvement of economic efficiency as the premise of economic growth and expansion of reproduction, which was an important development in the understanding of economic growth theory. In the first thirty years of socialist construction, there was a big gap between the growth of China's national income and the total output value of industry and agriculture. The growth of output value was fast, while the growth of national wealth was slow. The fundamental reason lay in the low labor productivity and poor social and economic benefits. In his *Theory of Surplus Value*, Marx quoted Ricardo, saying, "real wealth consists in producing the greatest possible amount of values in use having the least possible [exchange-]value." And Marx later states in the

---

8. Dai Yuanchen, "Investment Structure Strategy," in *On Economic Structure* (China Social Sciences Press, 1984).

9. *China Economic Yearbook (1983)* (Economy and Management Publishing House, 1983).

same passage, "In Ricardo's work the contradiction between riches and value later appears in the form that the net product should be as large as possible in relation to the gross product."[10] In *Das Kapital*, Marx further noted that "the greatness of a man's or a nation's wealth should be measured, not by the absolute quantity produced, but by the relative magnitude of the surplus-produce."[11] Therefore, in order to make economic growth meaningful, it was important not pursue the growth of output value, but the growth of national income. The fundamental way to make the national income increase rapidly was to improve economic efficiency, because the essence of economic benefit was the rate of surplus products. The better the economic efficiency, the more output driven by a certain input, the higher the rate of surplus products, the faster the growth of national income, and the greater the national wealth. Therefore, further understanding of the essence of economic growth could be regarded as the most valuable part of the new development strategy.

3. Practice of New Economic Development Strategy

In December 1982, the fifth session of the Fifth National People's Congress adopted the Sixth Five-Year Plan for National Economic and Social Development of the People's Republic of China (1981–1985). The Sixth Five-Year Plan was a relatively complete economic plan following the First Five-Year Plan. Its basic task was to continue to implement the principles of adjustment, reform, rectification, and improvement, further solve various problems that hindered economic development left over from the past, and achieve a decisive victory in realizing the fundamental improvement of the financial and economic situation. It also laid a solid foundation and created better conditions for national economic and social progress during the Seventh Five-Year Plan period. During the Sixth Five-Year Plan period, the gross output value of industry and agriculture was planned to increase by 21.7%, with an average annual increase of 4%, and great effort was put forth to reach 5% in implementation, which was the so-called "four guarantees for five." The total investment in fixed assets was planned to be 360 billion yuan, of which 230 billion yuan was used for capital construction. Urban and rural residents planned to increase 22% according to the average consumption level of the population, with an average annual increase 4.1%. During this period, China aimed to maintain a basic balance between the state's fiscal and credit revenues and expenditures and a basic stability of prices.

During the implementation of the Sixth Five-Year Plan, from the fourth quarter of 1984, bank credit was out of control, the scale of capital construction was over expanded, and the means of production were in short supply. At the same time, the excessive bonus paid by employees stimulated the rise of consumption demand. The excessive expansion of social aggregate demand promoted a great increase of foreign trade import and a super accelerated growth of production. In the first quarter of 1985, industrial production increased by 18% over the same period of the

---

10. Marx and Engels, *Complete Works of Marx and Engels*, vol. 26, bk. 3 (People's Publishing House, 1975), 281–282.

11. Marx and Engels, *Complete Works of Marx and Engels*, vol. 23 (People's Publishing House, 1975), 257.

previous year, which was much higher than the five year average. However, the total social supply still could not meet the expansion of the total social demand, which eventually led to serious inflation.

In September 1985, Deng Xiaoping delivered a speech on the proposal of the CPC Central Committee on formulating the Seventh Five-Year Plan for National Economic and Social Development at the National Congress of the Communist Party of China. He pointed out that during the period of the Seventh Five-Year Plan, the annual growth rate of the gross industrial and agricultural output value was set at about 7%, which was not low. If the speed was too high, there would be many problems, and this would have a negative impact on the reform and social atmosphere. It was better to be prudent, controlling the scale of investment in fixed assets and not expanding infrastructure. China must first do a good job in management and quality, stressing economic and social benefits in general. Only in this way could the speed of reform be ideal.[12]

In April 1986, the fourth session of the Sixth National People's Congress discussed and adopted the Seventh Five-Year Plan for National Economic and Social Development of the People's Republic of China (1986–1990). The Seventh Five-Year Plan was a concrete embodiment of the economic development strategy of the Twelfth National Congress of the Communist Party of China. In terms of main construction policies, the Seventh Five-Year Plan stipulated:

- We should adhere to the basic balance between total social demand and total supply to ensure the stable growth of the national economy.
- We should attach great importance to the improvement of economic benefits, especially the quality of products, and correctly handle the relationship between quality and quantity and between efficiency and speed.
- We should strictly control the investment structure of fixed assets to improve the investment efficiency.
- We should put scientific and technological progress and intellectual development in an important strategic position to better develop science and education.
- We should focus on enhancing the ability of exports to earn foreign exchange and promote the further development of foreign economic trade and technological exchanges.
- We should take into account production, construction, and living consumption, arrange people's consumption level, and adjust consumption structure according to China's national conditions and national strength.

The Seventh Five-Year Plan emphasized that the determining factor for whether China's economic development strategy could be transferred from the old model to the new model, and whether China's economic development could embark on the track of a virtuous circle, lay in whether it could persist in putting the improvement of efficiency and quality as its first priority and make practical advancements. During the period of the Seventh Five-Year Plan, it

---

12. *China Economic Yearbook (1986)* (Economy and Management Publishing House, 1986), i–24.

was important to more consciously adhere to the principle of putting quality and efficiency first, increase quantity on the basis of improving quality and efficiency, and seek an appropriate growth rate, so that all economic work could be further transferred to the track of taking improving economic benefits as the center.

The Seventh Five-Year Plan stipulated that during the period of the plan, the total output value of industry and agriculture in China would increase by 6.7% on average, of which the total output value of agriculture would increase by 4% (including the village run industries by 6%), the total industrial output value by 7.5% (excluding the village run industries by 7%), and the average annual growth rate of the gross national product was 7.5%. This economic growth rate was lower than that actually achieved during the Sixth Five-Year Plan period, which was basically stable and had room for improvement. It is worth pointing out that the comprehensive index of the economic growth rate in the Seventh Five-Year Plan continued to use the index of gross industrial and agricultural output value and adopted the index of gross national product for the first time. This was an improvement in China's economic planning and statistics.

According to the Seventh Five-Year Plan, the total investment in capital construction of units owned by the people was 500 billion yuan, of which 245 billion yuan was invested in the state budget, 54 billion yuan was bank loans, 93.7 billion yuan was independently raised investment, 46.5 billion yuan was utilized foreign capital, and 60.8 billion yuan was invested in other fields. With the investment in renovation and transformation, the investment in fixed assets of units owned by the people was equivalent to 20.1% of the total national income in the same period, and the accumulation rate was 30%.[13] These two indicators were not low. If China could effectively improve its economic efficiency, the economy would have greater development in the following five years.

9.2 The Steady Improvement of the New Economic Development Strategy

1. Economic Development Thought Based on National Conditions

The Thirteenth CPC National Congress was held in October 1987. The report of the Thirteenth National Congress of the Communist Party of China, entitled "Marching Along the Socialist Road with Chinese Characteristics," comprehensively and systematically put forward the economic development strategy that would extend to the end of the 20th century, a strategy based on the theory of the primary stage of socialism.

The report pointed out that building socialism in an underdeveloped Asian country such as China was a new topic in the history of Marxist development. It was necessary to proceed from the national conditions, combine the basic principles of Marxism with China's reality, and open up a

---

13. *Seventh Five-Year Plan for National Economic and Social Development of the People's Republic of China (1986–1990)* (People's Publishing House, 1986).

socialist road with Chinese characteristics in practice. A clear understanding of the basic national conditions and a correct understanding of the current historical stage of socialism in China were the primary issues in building socialism with Chinese characteristics and the fundamental basis for formulating and implementing correct lines and policies. The report clearly stated that China was in the preliminary stage of socialism. That is to say, on the one hand, it had established a socialist system, but on the other hand, with a large population and a weak foundation, the per capita GDP still ranked behind many other parts of the world. The prominent contradiction was that, a population of more than 800 million out of the total 1 billion in rural areas, still depended on hand-made tools for their living and some modern industries coexisted with a large number of industries that were decades or even hundreds of years behind modern development. At the same time, some economically developed areas coexisted with the vast number of underdeveloped and poverty-stricken areas, and a small amount of science and technology on par with the world's advanced levels existed within the general situation in which the level of science and technology were not high, and illiteracy and semi-illiteracy still accounted for nearly a quarter of the population. The backwardness of productive forces determined that in terms of relations of production, the degree of socialization of production necessary for the development of social public ownership was still very low, the commodity economy and the domestic market were very underdeveloped, the natural economy and semi-natural economy accounted for a considerable proportion, and the socialist economic system was not mature and was still imperfect. In terms of superstructure, a series of economic and cultural conditions necessary for building a highly socialist democratic politics were not sufficient. The forces of feudalism, decadent capitalist ideas, and small-scale production habits still had a wide influence in society and often invaded Party cadres and state civil servants. This showed that China was still in the primary stage of socialism.

According to these characteristics of China's historical stage at that time, the report pointed out that the primary stage of China's socialism was a stage of gradually eliminating poverty and backwardness, and as an agricultural country based on manual labor, which accounted for the majority of agricultural population, it was gradually transformed into a modern industrial country with a majority of non-agricultural population. It was a stage that moved from a natural economy with a large proportion of semi-natural economy into a business economy with a highly developed product economy, establishing and developing a dynamic socialist economic, political, and cultural system through reform and exploration, and enabling the national rejuvenation of the Chinese nation.

The discussion on the primary stage of socialism was a process of deepening the understanding of China's national conditions. This theory had a formulative process. In the Resolution on Some Historical Issues of the Party Since the Founding of the People's Republic of China, the Sixth Plenary Session of the Eleventh Central Committee of the Communist Party of China put forward for the first time that "our socialist system is still in the primary stage." The Sixth Plenary Session of the Twelfth Central Committee of the Communist Party of China reiterated in the Resolution on the Guidelines for the Construction of Socialist Spiritual Civilization that "China is still in the primary stage of socialism." From that time, the discussion on the theory of the primary stage of socialism was gradually carried out in theoretical circles, reaching a peak around the time of the Thirteenth National Congress of the Communist Party of China. The report of the Thirteenth National Congress put forward a systematic theory of the primary stage of socialism, which expounded on the theory of scientific socialism, the theory of socialist economy, the strategy of socialist economic development, and economic reform development in great depth.

According to this understanding and analysis of China's national conditions, the report of the Thirteenth National Congress of the Communist Party of China pointed out that in the primary stage of socialism, the historical task to be resolved in developing social productive forces was to realize the industrialization, commercialization, socialization, and modernization of production. China's economic construction shouldered the dual task of not only promoting the industrial revolution, but also catching up with the world's new technological revolution. To accomplish this task, it was necessary go through long-term, step-by-step, phased efforts. After the Third Plenary Session of the Eleventh Central Committee of the Communist Party of China, China's strategic plan for economic construction was generally divided into three steps. The first was to double the GNP of 1980 and solve the problem of food and clothing for the people. This task was basically completed. Second, by the end of the 20th century, China's gross national product (GNP) was to be doubled and people's living standards reach a well-off level. Third, by the middle of the 21st century, the per capita GNP was to reach the level of moderately developed countries, the people's lives be relatively rich, and modernization be basically realized. And then, on that basis, China would continue to progress. At that time, though, the most important thing was to take the second step, as China would make great progress in its modernization drive after realizing the second task. Social and economic benefits, labor productivity, and product quality would be significantly improved. The gross national product (GNP) and the output of major industrial and agricultural products would increase by a large margin, and the per capita GNP would rise significantly. In terms of technology, the main industrial fields would be close to the level of developed countries in the 1970s or early 1980s, and the technical level of agricultural and other industrial sectors would be greatly improved. Junior high school education would be popularized in towns and most rural areas, and senior high school and vocational and technical education equivalent to senior high school would be basically popularized in big cities. The people would be able to live a relatively comfortable life. The key to achieving the goal of the second step was to solve the contradiction in which the efficiency of economic activities was too low. Only by effectively improving economic benefits and striving for progress every year could China gradually alleviate the contradictions of its large population, relatively insufficient resources, and serious shortage of funds, and thus ensure the sustained development of the national economy at a higher speed. It was thus necessary to unswervingly implement the strategy of focusing on efficiency and improving quality, coordinated development, and stable growth.[14]

---

14. Zhao Ziyang, *Advancing Along the Socialist Path with Chinese Characteristics: Report on the Thirteenth National Congress of the Communist Party of China* (People's Publishing House, 1987).

2. The Core Theme and Path of the New Economic Development Strategy

The report of the Thirteenth National Congress of the Communist Party of China pointed out that in the primary stage of socialism, the historical task to be resolved in developing productive forces was to realize the industrialization, commercialization, socialization, and modernization of production. This was a deepening understanding of industrialization and modernization. At the beginning of the founding of the People's Republic of China, China put forward the task of national industrialization. At that time, it was generally believed that the main sign of industrialization was that the industrial output value exceeded the agricultural output value, accounting for the main share of the total industrial and agricultural output value (60 to 70%). Judging by this standard, it was naturally understood that the goal of industrialization was achieved, so China put forward the goal of modernization. Now, it seemed that after more than thirty years of construction, China had indeed made great achievements, establishing an independent and relatively complete industrial and national economic system, and seeing the industrial output value exceed the agricultural output value. However, as pointed out in the report of the Thirteenth National Congress of the Communist Party of China, China's economy was characterized by a serious "dual economy," and on the whole, it had not realized industrialization. To realize industrialization, not only should the industrial output value exceed the agricultural output value, but the whole economic structure and industrial structure should also be changed qualitatively, from a majority agricultural population to a majority non-agricultural industry population. This transformation was based on the substantial increase of overall social productivity, especially agricultural production capacity. Overall social production was based on the material and technological foundation of large machines, and the average GNP reached a high level. By this standard, China's industrialization task was far from complete. However, in the 1980s and 1990s, China was faced with the severe challenge of the vigorous development of the world's new technological revolution. In order to shorten the economic and technological gap with developed countries, China had to devote itself to this development trend. At this stage, China's economic construction was faced with dual tasks. On the one hand, it needed to focus on promoting the traditional industrial revolution characterized by large machine production and electrification, that is, to realize industrialization, while on the other hand, it needed to invest in the world's new technological revolution marked by high technologies such as microelectronics technology, information technology, bioengineering, and new material technology, so as to promote the modernization of economic technology. China's industrialization continued in the international environment in the second half of the 20th century, so it was necessary to transform and develop traditional industries with advanced technology. However, China's modernization started on the basis of a backward economy and technology, so it had to first promote the realization of industrialization. These were the new characteristics of China's industrialization process in the new situation.

Based on a more objective, more profound understanding of China's national conditions, this strategy put forward more practical steps and long-term development goals. In terms of development goals, a popular formulation since the 1960s was that by the end of the 20th century, China's economy would be in the forefront of the world. The Sixth Plenary Session of the Eleventh Central Committee of the Communist Party of China held in 1981 comprehensively summarized the historical experience since the founding of the People's Republic of China, analyzed and criticized the "leftist" mistakes of the past, and proposed that China's socialist modernization must proceed from the national conditions, act according to the nation's ability, and realize the goal of modernization one step at a time. In 1982, the Twelfth National Congress of the Communist Party of China formulated the strategic goal of China's economic construction up to the end of the 20th century via a two-step strategic step. In terms of strategic objectives, the Twelfth National Congress of the Communist Party of China proposed that by the year 2000, it would be in the forefront of the world in terms of total national income and the output of major industrial and agricultural products. The strategy put forward by the Thirteenth National Congress of the Communist Party of China provided more specific, practical targets for the goals to be achieved at the end of the 20th century, and the strategic steps were divided into three steps, with planning that extended to the middle of the 21st century. By the middle of the 21st century, when the third step of this strategy was completed, China's per capita GDP would reach the level of moderately developed countries and basically realize modernization. The strategy formulated by the Thirteenth National Congress of the Communist Party of China was to plan economic development from a deeper level of understanding and a longer time span, which further embodied the guiding ideology of realizing modernization according to the appropriate steps and proceeding from the national conditions. In terms of strategic objectives, it was not only limited to gross industrial and agricultural production and gross national product, but also highlighted the per capita gross national product, which made the strategic objectives more practical.

3. Performance Target of the New Economic Development Strategy

The new strategy inherited and developed the strategy formulated by the Twelfth National Congress of the Communist Party of China, emphasizing the pursuit of coordinated economic development and stable growth on the premise of improving economic benefits. In the mode of economic development, it was necessary to shift from extensive management (mainly relying on increasing capital and labor input to achieve economic growth in quantity) to intensive management (mainly promoting the improvement of economic quality and quantity on the basis of improving efficiency). For China, population pressure and shortage of funds and resources were the two major constraints on economic development. The fundamental way to break through these two constraints was to improve economic efficiency. Large population needs not be doomed to fall behind. Japan, South Korea, and other countries and regions had a high population density, but their economic benefits were high and the per capita national income level was likewise high, so their economic growth was very fast. The amount of resources was not the decisive factor of economic development. In fact, in many countries and regions with poor resources, economic development happened very rapidly. Therefore, to improve the overall level of quality and quantity of a country's economic development, the key was to have higher economic benefits. After the Third Plenary Session of the Eleventh Central Committee of the Communist Party of China, China gradually changed its earlier development strategy of unilaterally pursuing output value and output growth, and it began to turn to the strategy of taking improving economic benefits as the center and ensuring long-term, stable growth of the national economy. But on the whole, the traditional thought of ignoring efficiency and pursuing speed unilaterally continued to have a considerable impact on economic development, and the situation of poor economic benefits had not fundamentally changed. According to the statistics of the World Bank, in the late 1980s, the average fixed assets occupied by Chinese industrial workers was 40% higher than that of low-income countries, but the net output value was only 17% more. In the manufacturing industry, the average fixed assets occupied by Chinese workers was four times higher than that of low-income countries, close to the level of middle-income countries, while the net output was only 50% higher than that of general low-income countries and less than half that of middle-income countries.[15] The development strategy formulated by the Thirteenth National Congress of the Communist Party of China clearly recognized this point and further took improving economic efficiency as the central link of China's economic development. The report of the Thirteenth National Congress of the Communist Party of China put forward that the development of science and technology and education should be put in the primary position in the development strategy, so that economic construction could be transferred to the track of relying on scientific and technological progress and improving the quality of workers. This was a far-sighted decision. China's backward economic development and low efficiency of economic activities were, in the final analysis, due to backward science and technology, backward management, and the poor cultural and technical quality of workers. The report of the Thirteenth National Congress of the Communist Party of China pointed out that modern science and technology and modern management were the decisive factors for improving economic efficiency and the main pillars for China's economy to move toward a new stage of growth. It was important to be soberly aware that there was no way out for backward technology, backward management, and economic development by consuming large amounts of resources. In March 1988, the government work report of the first session of the Seventh National People's Congress also pointed out that in order to achieve a substantial increase in economic benefits and gradually shift from extensive management to intensive management, it was necessary to vigorously promote scientific and technological progress and constantly strengthen scientific management. Otherwise, the economic and technological gap between China and developed countries would be further widened, and China would not have its due position in the world.[16] This discussion shows that the progress of science and technology and the improvement of the management level would fundamentally determine the process of China's industrialization and modernization, and it was a major event related to the revitalization of the nation. Improving economic efficiency on

---

15. General Office of the Publicity Department of the CPC Central Committee, ed., *Guidance Materials for the Study of the Documents of the Thirteenth National Congress of the CPC* (internal materials), 118.

16. *China Economic Yearbook (1988)*. Economy and Management Publishing House, 1988. p. ii–2.

the basis of scientific and technological progress and scientific management was the only path to China's economic development.

The formation and improvement process of China's economic development strategy in the 1980s show that the basic guiding ideology of this development strategy was to transfer the economy to the track of sustainable, stable, and coordinated development centered on improving economic benefits. From the Third Plenary Session of the Eleventh Central Committee of the Communist Party of China to the Fifth Plenary Session of the Thirteenth Central Committee of the Communist Party of China, this guiding ideology was basically embodied in the strategic principles, strategic objectives, and strategic deployment of economic development. The analysis shows that this guiding ideology was in line with the national conditions and the law of productivity development, so it was scientific. As for the fact that the development and operation of the real economy were not consistent with the requirements of the economic development strategy, and even deviated greatly, there were various reasons, among which the main factor was the economic system. As long as the development strategy was truly implemented in various forms of economic work and the actual economic operation was consistent with the principles and requirements of the economic development strategy, then China's economic development would become a whole new scene.

9.3 Comments on the New Strategic Thought on Economic Development

1. Theoretical Analysis of Capital Accumulation, Technological Progress, and Economic Growth

In the theories of economic growth and economic development in the 1950s and the 1960s, a widely accepted view was "capital fundamentalism," which regarded capital accumulation as the only determinant of economic growth. This view held that economic growth was mainly driven by investment growth, while capital shortage was the main restrictive factor of economic growth. The Harrod-Domar model was the first to offer a systematic theoretical exposition of "capital fundamentalism." On the basis of the Keynes system, Harrod's growth theory developed the short-term comparative static equilibrium analysis adopted by Keynes into long-term dynamic equilibrium analysis. In Keynes's income analysis, only the income changes caused by investment changes were examined, and the impact of income changes on the next round of investment was not examined. Moreover, the goal was only to stimulate the increase of demand by investment so as to achieve the current equilibrium between aggregate demand and aggregate supply. There was no change in aggregate supply and new equilibrium. Therefore, it was a static, short-term equilibrium analysis. By contrast, Harrod held that the double growth of national income caused by the increase of investment could achieve a full employment balance in this period. However, the increase of investment not only stimulated the aggregate demand and caused the income to increase exponentially (multiplier principle), but also stimulated the aggregate supply, causing the growth of production capacity. The additional production capacity brought about the more rapid growth of income in the next period, and more income would be converted into more additional investment (acceleration principle), which was progressive. As a result, the national income of the current period would not be sufficient to provide full employment in the next period, and the total supply and demand could not be balanced. In order to achieve full employment, the investment in the current period must be greater than that in the previous period, so that the investment could adapt to the balanced growth of the national income. The intention of Harrod's model was to explain the conditions needed for stable economic growth and the causes of fluctuations, as well as how to adjust the economy to achieve long-term balanced growth. The model was widely used in economic growth research in developed and developing countries as a useful analytical tool to observe the relationship between economic growth and capital accumulation.

This discussion shows that from classical economics to the mid-20th century, the theory of economic growth regarded capital accumulation as an important factor in determining economic growth. In order to give the national economy a certain level of growth, it was necessary to maintain a certain accumulation rate. Foreign research showed that in the fifteen years before 1975, the increase of physical capital investment alone accounted for about 50% of the total income growth of nine developed countries. According to the study of middle-income countries such as South Korea, the Philippines, and Mexico, the contribution of the growth of physical capital stock to income growth was about 1/4 to 1/3, while it was as high as 1/2 in poorer countries.[17] Therefore, the effect of capital accumulation on economic growth could not be underestimated, especially in the countries whose economic growth was in the primary stage. However, if the accumulation rate was regarded as the only important cause of economic growth, it was difficult to pass the test in theory or practice. From the perspective of China's situation, after 1949, the accumulation rate was generally above 30%, and the investment rate was basically close to 20%, which was higher than the level of 10% to 12% required by Rostow's economic "take-off." But China's economic growth (the growth of the national income) was still not fast, and the economy had not taken off. Facts showed that studying economic growth only from the perspective of capital accumulation was not sufficiently comprehensive in theory. In Western economics, technological progress was defined as the upward movement of the production function curve, that is, under a certain combination of production factors input, technological innovation that could increase output was called technological progress. From the perspective of the impact of technological progress on economic growth, it could be divided into three categories: capital saving technological progress, labor saving technological progress, and neutral technological progress between the two. The distinction between these 3 types of technological progress is generally based on the presence or absence of changes in the income distribution ratio. If capital is K and labor is N, the profit rate and the real wage rate are r, w, respectively, the distribution rate of capital and labor is πk, πn, and $\pi k + \pi n = 1$, then the income distribution ratio of capital and labor is:

$$\frac{\pi k}{\pi n} = \frac{rK}{wN}$$

---

17. Malcolm Gillis et al., *Development Economics* (Economic Science Press, 1989), 341.

The above formula shows that if technological progress makes the capital / labor ratio K/N and the product of profit rate and real wage rate ratio r/w are unchanged, the capital and labor income distribution ratio $\pi k/\pi n$ also remains unchanged. Hicks first called this kind of technological progress neutral technological progress, or what is called Hicks Neutrality.

This situation in which the income distribution ratio remains unchanged can also be examined from another perspective. As long as the capital distribution rate πk remains unchanged, the income distribution ratio $\pi k/\pi n$ will also remain unchanged. If rK is used to represent capital allocation, the ratio of capital allocation rate to income is:

$$\pi k = \frac{rK}{Y}$$

Obviously, if technological progress keeps the profit rate r and capital coefficient K/Y unchanged, then the technological progress is also neutral, which is demonstrated by Harrod, or what is called Harrod Neutrality. In the process of technological progress, as long as the labor distribution rate remains unchanged, this income distribution ratio will remain unchanged. The labor distribution is wN, and the ratio of labor distribution rate in income is as follows:

$$\pi n = \frac{wN}{Y}$$

Clearly, if technological progress keeps the real wage rate w and labor productivity N/Y unchanged, then technological progress is also neutral, which is proposed by Solow, called Solow Neutrality.

According to Harrod's neutral technological progress, although technological progress improves capital productivity, it also increases capital input, that is, it increases the capital / labor ratio. Therefore, the income (profit) of capital remains unchanged, and the impact of technological progress on capital growth is neutral. At the same time, although technological progress can promote the growth of labor force, it also "reduces the most appropriate labor."[18] Therefore, the wage income is relatively constant, and the impact of technological progress on the growth of the labor force is also neutral. Since Harrod's concept of "neutral technology" holds that the influence of technological progress on capital growth and labor growth is neutral, that is, it does not change the capital output ratio, an important assumption of Harrod's economic growth model is that the production technology and capital output ratio remain unchanged (another assumption is that the propensity to consume and the propensity to save remain unchanged). Based on this premise, Harrod mainly analyzes the decisive role of capital accumulation for economic growth.

In the second half of the 1950s, American economists Solow, Swann, and Mead put forward a new theory and model of economic growth. They criticized some defects in the Harrod-Domar model, gave up the unreasonable assumption of a constant capital coefficient, and established a production function with a variable capital coefficient. Their models are basically the same.

---

18. Harrod, *Dynamic Economics* (The Commercial Press, 1981), 30.

They all take the perfect competition market economy as the object. Any disequilibrium can tend to equilibrium through the automatic adjustment of price. Therefore, their theory is called the neoclassical growth model. Among them, the Solow model is the most representative. He states, "The modern industrial economy grows steadily in the form of capital intensity in the sense of per capita capital of workers, while productivity continues to rise."[19] Therefore, to establish the model of stable economic growth, it is necessary to consider the two factors of technological progress and increasing returns to scale. But in the real economy, technological progress is the more important. "Given the capital stock, there is a lasting relationship between employment and output, and the assumption of constant returns to scale transforms this into a long-term relationship between employment and output calculated by the average unit capital. According to this inference, whenever the capital output ratio is constant, the capital labor ratio will also remain unchanged. The introduction of technological progress will change this situation so that, over time, both capital and output can increase faster than employment. Continuous innovation can avoid diminishing returns. Otherwise, this effect will bring any such growth process to a standstill."[20]

Solow's total production function is $Q = F(K, L, t)$, where Q represents output, K and L represent capital input and labor input respectively, and t represents time variable. Solow said the factor t was added to the total production function to take into account technological changes. The so-called technological change is to express any form of change in the production function. With the acceleration and deceleration of the economy, the improvement of labor education, and so on, all the factors that change the production function will appear in the form of "technological change." If the change of production function makes the marginal substitution rate between labor and capital unchanged, but simply increases or decreases the output achieved by the given input, then this change is called neutral technological change. In this case, the production function will take a special form: $Q = A(t)f(K, L)$. The multiplier factor $A(t)$ is used to measure the cumulative effect of long-term technological changes. The simplified Solow-Mead model with technological changes is as follows:

$$\frac{\Delta Q}{Q} = a(\frac{\Delta K}{K}) + b(\frac{\Delta L}{L}) + \frac{\Delta T}{T}$$

where $\frac{\Delta T}{T}$ is the rate of technological progress. The model shows that the rate of economic growth depends on the growth rate of capital and labor, the elasticity of output and relative income share of capital and labor, and the time varying technological change (technological progress rate).

The neoclassical economic growth model has two important implications for the analysis of economic growth in developing countries. First, it assumes that the factors of production (capital and labor) are mutually replaceable. Therefore, the capital output ratio can be changed

---

19. Solow, *Economic Growth Theory: An Interpretation* (Shanghai Sanlian Bookstore, 1989), 36.
20. Solow, *Economic Growth Theory: An Interpretation* (Shanghai Sanlian Bookstore, 1989), 36.

by adjusting the capital labor ratio, thus increasing the adjustability of the economic growth rate and overcoming the problem in the Harrod-Domar model in which the growth rate has only one unique value, that is, the "knife-edge." In addition, it breaks through the long-term dominant view that capital accumulation is the only decisive factor of economic growth in the theory of economic growth. It puts forward for the first time the view that "technological progress makes the most important contribution to economic growth" and opens up a new analysis model for the economic growth and development of developing countries.

The model has inspired comprehensive analysis of the factors of economic growth. Since then, some economists have devoted themselves to the empirical analysis of economic growth factors, studying various factors affecting economic growth and measuring the role of these factors in economic growth, in order to identify modes of economic growth under various conditions. In 1971, Kendrick analyzed the private economic growth of the United States from 1948 to 1966, and calculated that the economic growth rate during this period was 4%, of which 1.5% was attributed to the increase of factor input and 2.5% to the increase of factor productivity.[21] In Kendrick's definition, "factor productivity" mainly includes technological progress, the diffusion of technological innovation, the improvement of resource allocation, and economies of scale. Therefore, his research shows that the improvement of factor productivity plays an increasingly important role in modern economic growth. The improvement of factor productivity mainly comes from technological progress, so technological progress plays a decisive role in current economic growth. In addition, Kuznets and Denison's studies also show that the growth of factor productivity based on technological progress plays an increasingly important role in economic growth. According to the Research Report of Japan's Economic Planning Agency, about 60% of Japan's economic growth from 1982 to 1986 was contributed by technological progress.[22]

However, technological progress must have corresponding conditions to promote economic growth. Research shows that the contribution of technological progress to economic growth in developed countries is greater than that in developing countries. In the 1970s, some Western economists used the methods of Solow and Dennison to analyze the economic growth factors of developing countries and calculated the contribution of various input factors to economic growth. The conclusion of this study was that the contribution of capital investment growth to economic growth in developing countries is greater than that in developed countries, while the contribution of improving resource allocation efficiency to economic growth in developed countries is greater than that in developing countries. In other words, for developing countries, the improvement of resource allocation efficiency characterized by technological progress has a relatively small role in promoting economic growth, while the increase of capital investment is the most important source of economic growth. In his book *Economic Progress and Policies in Developing Countries,* published in 1970, Angus Maddison examined the economic growth of 22 developing countries and regions from 1950 to 1965. The results indicated that the average

21. Tan Chongtai, *Development Economics* (Shanghai People's Publishing House, 1989), 94.

22. Zhang Jinrui, *Technological Progress and Economic Development* (China Renmin University Press, 1990), 2.

economic growth rate of these countries and regions was 5.55%, in which the average growth rate of human resources was 1.94%, and the contribution to economic growth was 35%. The average growth rate of capital was 3.06%, accounting for 55% of economic growth. The average growth rate of resource allocation efficiency was 0.55%, and the contribution to economic growth accounted for 10%.[23] This research pointed to three problems. First, the contribution of technological progress to economic growth is affected by the stage of economic growth. Second, "advanced technology is the source of allowing economic growth, but it only provides a potential possibility, which is a necessary condition, not a sufficient condition."[24] Advanced technology must be combined with material capital, human capital, market conditions, system conditions, and ideology to form a sufficient condition for economic growth. Third, in developing countries, the contribution of technological progress to economic growth has great potential. However, to give full play to this potential, it is necessary to take the corresponding capital investment as the condition. Because the progress of technology and the application of advanced technology in production are also driven by capital investment, capital accumulation is still the first and most sustained driving force of economic growth in developing countries.

This analysis shows that the emphasis on technological progress in the economic development strategy is certainly a kind of development in theory, but in order to put the economic growth on the track of technological progress, it was necessary for China to carry out various effective reforms, especially to maintain a certain accumulation rate, so as to meet these conditions.

2. The Significance of the Neoclassical Growth Model to the Evolution of China's Development Strategy

The neoclassical economic growth model had two important implications for the economic growth analysis of developing countries. First it assumed that the factors of production (capital and labor) are mutually replaceable. Therefore, the capital output ratio can be changed by adjusting the capital labor ratio, so that the capital output ratio can be changed. Thus, the adjustment of the economic growth rate is increased, and the problem that the growth rate has only one unique value (i.e., the "knife-edge" problem[25]) in the Harrod-Domar model is overcome.

In addition, it broke through the long-term dominant view that capital accumulation is the only decisive factor of economic growth in the theory of economic growth, and it put forward

---

23. Tan Chongtai, *Development Economics* (Shanghai People's Publishing House, 1989), 141.

24. Kuznets, "Modern Economic Growth: Discovery and Reflection," in *Selected Papers on Modern Foreign Economics*, vol. 2 (The Commercial Press, 1981), 21.

25. The Harrod-Domar model assumes that technology is neutral and capital output ratio is constant, and the capital labor ratio is constant, which negates the substitutability of production factors, and growth depends on the saving rate. When the savings rate is fixed, the guaranteed growth rate GW has only one unique value. If the growth rate determined in this way is not equal to the natural growth rate GN (GW ≠ GN), then the economy cannot have steady growth, and it is very difficult for the two to be consistent. Solow called the narrow growth path prescribed by this model the "edge," while Harrod-Domar model's equilibrium was called "equilibrium on the knife-edge."

for the first time the view that technological progress makes the most important contribution to economic growth, thus forming a severe challenge to the "capital fundamentalism" which was so widespread after the Second World War. This opened up a new mode of analysis for the economic growth and development of developing countries.

The model inspired scholars to make a comprehensive analysis of the factors of economic growth. After that time, some economists devoted themselves to the empirical analysis of economic growth factors, studying various factors affecting economic growth and measuring the role of these factors in economic growth, in order to find a mode of economic growth for various conditions. These empirical analyses verified from different perspectives Solow's theory that technological progress is an important factor of economic growth.

Of course, theoretically speaking, the neoclassical economic growth model also has defects. In this model, long-term productivity growth was attributed to exogenous technological progress, while the factors that promote the efficiency of the economic system were neglected. Beginning in the 1980s, Western economists discussed the factors that determine economic growth within the economic system, publishing many research results, which formed a new idea in the theory of economic growth, the endogenous economic growth theory. One of the main ideas of the endogenous economic growth theory is that an economic system can achieve sustained growth through internal forces. Paul Romer, an American economist, completed his doctoral thesis entitled *Dynamic Competitive Equilibrium with External Things: Increasing Revenue and Endless Growth* in 1983. In 1990, he published two papers, "Endogenous Technological Change" (*Journal of Political Economics*, 1990) and "Is Nonconvexity Essential to Understanding Growth?" (*American Economic Review*, 1990). In these works, Romer put forward a new theory about economic growth. He overthrew the traditional view of the neoclassical school which held that only two factors of production (capital and labor) were to be considered. He believed that there are four factors of production, capital, unskilled labor, human capital (measured by the number of years of education), and new ideas (measured by the number of patents). In addition, the British economist Morris Scott, the American economist Robert Paul, and some other Western economists put forward a new view of economic growth from this perspective. Their theories mainly analyzed and demonstrated several problems. First, it was necessary to identify which factors constituted the internal forces of economic growth. Second, it analyzed the process and mechanism of these forces to promote economic growth. Third, it was important to discover the motive force and condition of this mechanism. The theory of endogenous economic growth listed the factors influencing economic growth, such as human capital, economic externality of technology, learning effect, knowledge accumulation, and specialized economy from technological progress, and it demonstrated the influence of the efficiency of economic organization on economic growth and opened up a broader path for the research and practice of economic growth.

The emphasis on technological progress in the economic development strategy was certainly a kind of theoretical development, but in order to make economic growth truly move onto a track based on technological progress, it was necessary to carry out various effective reforms, and especially to maintain a certain accumulation rate, so as to meet these conditions. After

Reform and Opening Up, due to the changes in the distribution pattern of the national income, government savings tended to decline, while residents' savings began to increase rapidly from the extremely low levels in the period of the planned economy. According to research data, by 1995, China's household savings had reached 70% of domestic savings, and more than 25% of the GDP.[26] Since the total social savings was equal to the total social investment, the high savings rate of Chinese residents supported capital accumulation and economic growth.

9.4 Comparative Analysis of China's Economic Growth Ideas in the 1980s

1. Introducing Foreign Capital to Promote Economic Growth

In the real economy, economic growth is the function of capital, labor, natural resources, and other input factors and technological progress. Assuming that technological progress is established, economic growth depends on these three input factors. In China's situation, labor resources were rich, so as long as the proportion of skilled labor in the total labor was increased, labor supply would not become a constraint on economic growth. Although natural resources were relatively poor, as long as China could speed up the introduction of technology and equipment for in-depth development and through trade channels, it would not become a constraint on economic development. Therefore, the key to economic development lay in capital investment. China's capital investment was restricted by the level of national economic development, and it could not be matched with other input factors to achieve more rapid, reasonable economic growth. One way to make up for the "capital gap" was to introduce foreign capital through various channels.

In Western development economics, the relatively systematic, influential theory of introducing foreign capital to support the ideal economic growth rate was the "two gap model" proposed by Chenery and Strauss in 1966.[27] This theory pointed out that the necessary condition for economic growth in developing countries was the expansion of investment. The expansion of investment was constrained by three factors: capital absorption capacity, the level of savings, and the amount of foreign exchange. If there was a saving gap, the required investment level could not be reached, and if there was a foreign exchange gap which could not meet the import needs of machinery and equipment, the ideal growth rate would not be achieved. The solution was to introduce foreign capital to make up for the two gaps. The "two gap model" emphasized the important role of utilizing foreign resources to promote economic growth. Utilizing foreign capital could increase export capacity, thus directly promoting economic growth, while utilizing foreign capital could increase investment rate and accelerate economic growth through investment multiplier.

---

26. Barry Norton, *China's Economy: Transformation and Growth* (Shanghai People's Publishing House, 2010), 386.

27. Chenery and Strauss, "Foreign Aid and Economic Development," *American Economic Review* (August 1966).

However, this analysis is only theoretical abstraction. In the real economy, assuming that there is no obstacle to the inflow of foreign capital, three problems should be considered in the introduction of foreign capital: the scale of foreign debt, the efficiency of foreign debt investment, and the structure of foreign debt.

(1) Debt Ratio, Debt Borrowing Ratio, Debt Repayment Ratio and Moderate Scale of Foreign Debt
Internationally, there are three main indicators involved in investigating the scale of a country's foreign debt: debt ratio (debt ratio = total debt / GDP), debt borrowing ratio (debt borrowing ratio = balance of foreign debt / foreign exchange income from export and labor services), and debt repayment ratio (debt repayment ratio = debt service amount / foreign exchange income of export and labor services). Generally speaking, the debt ratio is 20%, the debt borrowing ratio is 100% to 150%, and the debt repayment rate is about 20%. Within these indicators, the scale of foreign debt can be considered moderate and safe, but if it exceeds these values, it will exceed the warning line, which will have adverse effects on economic growth. China's debt ratio was lower than 6% before 1985, and 9% in 1988, while the average debt ratio of developing countries was 35.4% in 1986. According to the data released by the State Administration of Foreign Exchange, in 1990, China's foreign debt balance was 52.55 billion US dollars, the debt borrowing ratio was 89.3%, and the debt repayment rate was 8.5%.[28] These three values were all lower than the internationally recognized warning level, indicating that the scale of China's foreign investment introduction was not large.

However, these numerical indicators are only a reference value and do not absolutely determine the scale of a country's external debt. If the foreign debt utilization efficiency, export exchange ability, and domestic capital matching capacity are higher, the debt repayment ratio and debt ratio can be improved. For instance, the debt repayment rate of South Korea was higher than 25%, but there was no debt repayment difficulty. If these capabilities are low, the debt ratio, debt borrowing ratio, and debt repayment ratio should not be increased. Theoretically speaking, the appropriate scale of foreign debt can be defined as the inflow of foreign capital when the marginal income of foreign capital equals its marginal cost. If we assume that the marginal cost of foreign capital is fixed (in the short run, the change of the inflow of foreign capital will not have a great impact on the interest rate change of the international capital market), then the appropriate scale of foreign debt depends on the size of the marginal income of foreign debt. The larger the marginal income of foreign debt is, the stronger the solvency is, and the lower the debt repayment rate is, the higher the debt ratio and the larger the scale of foreign capital inflow can be. The size of the marginal income of foreign debt generally depends on two factors: the efficiency of foreign debt investment and the supply capacity of matching production factors of debtor countries. The matching production factors of foreign debt inflow include domestic capital matching, labor quality, foreign exchange management ability, information dissemination ability, economic system efficiency, and some basic industries, infrastructure, and other production factors. Their

---

28. *Economy Daily*, September 3, 1991.

supply status also determines the marginal income of foreign debt. From the perspective of capital matching, in the 1980s, China needed about 5 yuan of matching funds to borrow 1 US dollar of foreign loans. During the period of the Seventh Five-Year Plan, China borrowed foreign loans equivalent to 10% of the fixed assets investment of enterprises owned by the people in the same period. Domestic supporting funds were in short supply, and the progress of some projects was affected due to the lack of supporting funds. Other matching factors of production, such as high-quality labor, management, and infrastructure, were also in short supply in China and could not be changed in the short term. Therefore, the shortage of matching factors of production made the marginal income of foreign debt begin to decline earlier, which became a constraint factor in the expansion of foreign debt.

(2) Investment Benefit and Scale of Foreign Debt

In the eleven years from 1979 to 1990, China used more than US$50 billion of foreign debt to build a number of large-scale energy, transportation, and infrastructure projects, promoted the technological transformation of tens of thousands of old enterprises, introduced a large number of advanced technology and management experience, increased the supply of many short-term products, improved the quality and grade of products, and replaced the earlier ones. Some imports and exports were expanded, and good economic benefits were achieved. However, from the input-output ratio of foreign debt, the situation was not optimistic. According to statistics, in 1985, China's national income increased by 1% for every additional US$3 billion in foreign debt. According to this input-output ratio, China's national income increase by external debt in the 1980s was 3.3%, only 0.33% per year on average. Some developing countries adopted the strategy of relying on foreign debt to develop their own economy and achieved success. However, China had a large population, and its domestic production capacity, technical level, and overall economic benefits were relatively backward, making it difficult to achieve long-term economic growth by introducing foreign capital on a large scale.

(3) Composition and Scale of Foreign Debt

The composition of China's foreign debt was mainly divided into three parts: loans from foreign governments, international financial institutions, and international commercial loans (including issuing bonds abroad); absorbing foreign direct investment; and importing various equipment and means of production from foreign countries through processing with supplied materials and compensation trade, which were to be paid back by the export of enterprise products or industrial fees. Among these three parts, the first and second were the main ones. At the end of June 1988, China's foreign debt balance was 35 billion US dollars, including 10 billion US dollars of long-term low interest loans provided by governments and international financial institutions, and 12.1 billion US dollars of foreign capital absorbed through foreign investment.[29]

Foreign direct investment (FDI) was an effective means of utilizing foreign capital. Its main

---

29. *China Economic Yearbook (1989)* (Economy and Management Publishing House, 1989), ii–48.

advantage was that the interests of debtor countries and foreign investors were equally involved, which could stimulate foreign investors to give attention to investment income, so as to improve production capacity and increase income. However, foreign direct investment was not easy to control in the direction of investment. From the perspective of China's foreign investment structure, medium and long-term loans from international organizations and foreign governments were basically invested in agriculture, basic industry, infrastructure, education, and science, and the use was basically reasonable. However, FDI was concentrated in the production of consumer goods for a long time, such as cosmetics, food processing, textile and other sectors, as well as hotels, restaurants, and other tertiary industries. According to international experience, foreign investment in basic industries was conducive to the economic strength of debtor countries and the overall development of the national economy. However, if the debtor countries could not effectively control the direction of foreign investment, the increase of the share of foreign direct investment would conflict with its industrial policy, which was not conducive to the rational development of the industrial structure of debtor countries. This analysis proceeded from the foreign direct investment direction to the foreign debt scale stipulation limit.

Loans from international financial organizations, foreign government loans, and international commercial loans were also the main channels for China to introduce foreign capital. From the perspective of China's situation, commercial loans accounted for 50% of the total foreign debt in 1985 and 60% in 1991, exceeding the average level of 50% of the total debt of developing countries. The interest rate of commercial loans was high, and it was a floating rate. It was thus easy for China to be affected by the fluctuation of the international capital market. Moreover, the repayment period was relatively short, generally about five years, and the longest was no more than ten years. Therefore, the cost of loans was relatively high and the risk was high. The debt crisis in developing countries was mainly caused by commercial loans, which meant that China's international commercial loans should not be increased on a large scale. International financial organizations and foreign government loans generally had a long term, low interest rate, so they were good channels to introduce foreign capital. However, these loans had certain restrictions on the investment direction and were greatly affected by the international and domestic political situation, so it was not easy to control the import scale. This analysis proceeded from the international loan source aspect to the foreign debt scale stipulation limit.

In short, introducing foreign debt to make up for part of the domestic capital gap and promote economic growth was an important foundational policy, and it needed to be implemented over a long period of time. However, due to China's national conditions, the scale of foreign debt introduction was restricted by various conditions and factors, so China could not rely on large-scale introduction of foreign debt to promote long-term economic growth.

2. Relying on High Domestic Accumulation to Promote Economic Growth

There were two different views on China's accumulation rate and investment scale in economic and ideological circles. One was that China's investment scale was in a vicious expansion in the

1980s, which caused inflation and economic chaos due to investment expansion and economic overheating. The other was that China's actual accumulation rate was not high, and investment was not inflation but serious shortage, and it even affected the normal development of the economy. This view held that if there was no ability to reduce the demand for new investment in the growth of national income through improving economic efficiency, economic growth could only be maintained by increasing investment. This view also held that, since developing countries were hindered by the "late development effect," even under the optimal growth hypothesis, the growth gap of per capita income between developing countries and developed countries would be further widened rather than narrowed over a long period of time. Therefore, developing countries should have a greater sense of urgency when it came to rapid economic growth.

One of the main theoretical assumptions of the idea of high accumulation and high investment was the principle of "investment multiplier." By using the investment multiplier principle to analyze the relationship between investment and national income growth, the following conclusions were reached:

When the marginal propensity to consume is a certain value ($0 < cy < 1$), the absolute amount of the national income will increase by multiples of investment increment according to consumption tendency.

Under the given social production technology level and investment efficiency, the growth of the national income mainly depends on the growth of investment.

When the absolute amount of investment growth remains unchanged, the growth rate of the national income shows a downward trend.

Another main theoretical assumption of the idea of high accumulation and high investment was that China's current accumulation rate was overestimated. If Japan's "investment rate" was adjusted to China's accumulation rate of comparable caliber, the annual average accumulation rate of Japan during the period of rapid economic growth from 1956 to 1970 was as high as 40.3%, while that of China in the same period was only 26.8%, and the average annual accumulation rate of Japan from 1952 to 1976 was 36.8%, higher than that of China's 27.2%. The accumulation rate of China, which was generally considered to be high in the 1980s, was also lower than that of Japan.[30] According to this idea, the level of accumulation indicated the strength of a country's economic development. On the premise of ensuring that people's consumption level increased year by year with economic growth, the accumulation level should be as high as possible, which was conducive to the rapid growth of the national economy.

The idea of high accumulation and high investment was insightful in the analysis of the relationship between investment growth and national income growth. For developing countries still in the process of industrialization, maintaining a certain level of accumulation rate and investment rate was a necessary condition for economic growth. Based on the sample survey of eighty developing countries, the world bank comprehensively showed that developing countries with a high economic growth rate in 1965 to 1987 were corresponding to their high savings rate,

---

30. Guo Shuqing et al., "The Accumulation Level of China in Recent Years," *Economic Research*, no. 1 (1990).

while those with a low economic growth rate were corresponding to their low savings rate.[31]

As for the over-estimation of accumulation rate, the main reason was rightfully the statistical caliber. However, no matter how the accumulation rate was counted, it always corresponded to the consumption rate. The increase of the accumulation rate meant the decrease of the consumption rate. Therefore, from a social point of view, the limit of the accumulation rate was the "social discount rate" acceptable to the public (social discount rate refers to the different importance given by society to the net income and consumption in different periods, and the social discount rate acceptable to the public refers to the greatest present consumption sacrifice that the public is willing to make for the development of national economy and more income and consumption in the future). If this limit were exceeded, the normal consumption demand of the public could not be met, or the current consumption level of the public tended to decline, it would inhibit the enthusiasm of workers in production, and it would affect social stability, and ultimately affect economic growth. From the perspective of China's situation, on the one hand, it was necessary to scientifically determine a suitable accumulation rate, so as to make the accumulation scale reach the highest level on the premise of ensuring that the people's living standards were improved each year. On the other hand, China had a large population, low per capita income, and low living standard. These factors fundamentally limited the substantial growth of the accumulation scale. Even if the accumulation rate was high, the total amount and per capita accumulation would not be greatly improved. It thus seemed that the condition of high accumulation and high investment was difficult to overcome.

3. Improving Economic Efficiency and Promoting Economic Growth

This analysis shows that the contradiction between capital supply and economic growth could not be fundamentally solved by introducing foreign debt and increasing the accumulation rate. Therefore, many in economic circles were of the opinion that, in order to promote faster economic growth, the more reasonable path was to strive to improve economic efficiency, increase the contribution share of technological progress to economic growth, and achieve the maximum output benefit under the premise of certain investment with limited funds support of a higher economic growth rate, on the basis of China's national conditions and national strength with low per capita resources, low per capita income, lack of funds and low efficiency. The basis and connotation of improving economic benefits was technological progress. This train of thought theoretically involved the relationship between technological progress and economic growth. Western economic growth theory combined technological progress with economic growth and defined technological progress as the upward shift of the production function curve, that is, under a certain combination of production factors input, technological innovation that could

---

31. World Bank, *World Development Report in 1989* (China Financial and Economic Publishing House, 1989), 26.

increase output was called technological progress. American economist Solow proposed that in the long run, it was not the increase of capital investment and labor input, but technological progress that was the most fundamental determinant of economic growth. The Solow model inspired people to comprehensively analyze the factors of economic growth. Many economists studied and measured various factors that affected economic growth and the size of these factors in economic growth, so as to explore the modes of economic growth under various conditions. These empirical analyses verified Solow's theory that technological progress was an important factor in economic growth.

Beginning in the 1980s, the basic guiding ideology of China's overall economic development strategy has been to turn the economy to the track of sustainable, stable, coordinated development centered on improving economic benefits. After the Third Plenary Session of the Eleventh Central Committee of the Communist Party of China, this guiding ideology was basically embodied in the strategic principles, strategic objectives, and strategic deployment of economic development. It should be noted that this kind of strategic design conformed to the objective law of economic growth, and also adapted to the characteristics and requirements of China's economic growth stage. However, according to the actual situation in the 1980s, there were many obstacles in the implementation of China's economic development strategy focusing on improving economic efficiency, so that the principles and requirements of the real economy and the development strategy were not completely consistent. For example, the economic development strategy repeatedly stressed the need to maintain stable economic growth on the premise of improving economic benefits, so as to turn the economy into an effective development track based on technological progress. However, from the 1980s, China's economy had an extensive growth situation of high input, low output, high cost, and low benefit, and some major macroeconomic benefit indicators had even shown a downward trend. For example, China's economic development strategy repeatedly emphasized the overall balance and structural coordination of national economic development and formulated corresponding industrial policies. From the 1980s, the imbalance of China's economic aggregate led to serious inflation, and the structural imbalance led to the increasingly serious restriction of industrial "bottlenecks" on economic development. The underlying reason for these contradictions and difficulties lay not in the guiding ideology, but in the incompatibility between the economic system and the economic development strategy.

This situation can be explained from at least two perspectives. First, the decentralization of national income weakened the state's ability of macro-control and led to the diversification of investment subjects, out of control total investment, and an imbalance of investment structure. Since the 1980s, China had been excessively inclined to individuals in the distribution of national income and to local governments in national revenue, resulting in the dispersion of financial and material resources. From 1984 to 1988, the average annual growth of the national income was 19.5%, while the average annual growth of total wages of employees was 19.7%, and the purchasing power of social groups increased by 20.6% on average from 1983 to 1988. At the same time, the proportion of national fiscal revenue in the national income decreased from 31.9% in 1979 to

18.8% in 1989, while in national fiscal revenue, the proportion of central fiscal revenue decreased from 57.6% in 1981 to 45.2% in 1989.[32] The dispersion of national income distribution pattern led to the dispersion of investment. Statistics show that the investment inflation in 1985 was basically not a "state behavior." Of the 274.5 billion yuan of fixed asset investment completed by society overall in 1985, only over 90 billion yuan was directly controlled by the state, accounting for only a little more than one third. However, the investment by local bodies and enterprises with extra budget funds and collective and individual investment accounted for nearly two thirds. Of the 16.5 billion yuan investment completed by the units under the ownership of the people, only 50% of the total investment was directly controlled by the state.[33] In 1990, the state directly controlled only 35 billion yuan of investment in the budget, and the state could control only 80 billion yuan, accounting for 20% of the total social fixed assets investment of more than 400 billion yuan.[34]

The diversification of investment subject and the decentralization of investment decision aggravated the contradiction of industrial structure imbalance. On the one hand, driven by local interests, all regions and departments set up various processing industries with high prices and high profits, in pursuit of a complete processing industry system. The convergence of the regional processing industry not only caused the development of basic industry to lag behind, but also led to the processing industry being unable to form a scale economy, and a large amount of the production capacity was idle, resulting in huge amounts of waste. On the other hand, with the continuous growth of fixed asset investment in society overall, due to the decrease of funds and resources held by the state, it could not meet the needs of the development of strategic key industries. The decentralization of the national income also reduced the national financial resources, making the country lack the corresponding economic strength and economic means to regulate and control social and economic operations, leading to the failure of the macro-economic management system, reducing the efficiency of the whole social economic resource allocation, and also reducing the social accumulation capacity.

Second, on the premise of public ownership, the property rights relationship and operation mechanism of state-owned enterprises were not rationalized and perfected, resulting in the problems of insufficient vitality, softening constraints, and low efficiency of state-owned enterprises. From China's situation, the improvement of the vitality and efficiency of state-owned enterprises was the fundamental guarantee and concrete embodiment of the improvement of social and economic benefits. If the enterprise reform did not make substantial progress and the enterprise did not become an independent commodity producer, on the one hand, it made it difficult to form and perfect the market system, and on the other hand, the state could not regulate enterprise behavior with standardized economic means, thus causing disorder and low efficiency of social and economic operations.

---

32. *China Economic Yearbook (1989)* (Economy and Management Publishing House, 1989), 37.

33. *China Economic Yearbook (1986)* (Economy and Management Publishing House, 1986), ii–10.

34. *Guidance Materials for Studying the Spirit of the Seventh Plenary Session of the Thirteenth CPC Central Committee* (People's Publishing House, 1991), 212.

This analysis shows that to really lead China's economy onto the track of benefit oriented growth, it was necessary to not only formulate the "software" of scientific economic development strategy, but also to establish a sound, efficient economic management and operation system, the "hardware," so as to make the economy develop healthily and smoothly.

According to the situation of the economic system in the 1980s, the reform of macro management system needed to be based on the law of productivity development in a specific stage of economic growth, and appropriate forms and means of economic management needed to be selected. World economic history shows that both developed and developing countries have to go through a stage of strengthening state intervention in the process of industrialization. From the actual situation in China, in order to realize industrialization and modernization, it was necessary to maintain a rapid economic growth rate on the premise of improving economic benefits. Rapid economic growth objectively needed the corresponding growth of accumulation and investment. Therefore, on the one hand, the state needed to master and regulate part of social accumulation to ensure the centralized use and effective allocation of funds and resources, and on the other hand, it needed to strengthen the macro management of the economy to control the total scale and growth rate of the national economy and coordinate the relationship between economic growth and social development.

In the reform of the micro operation mechanism, it was important to create an incentive and restriction mechanism based on the relationship between the economic interests of the microeconomic subjects and the existing property rights relations according to the characteristics of the property rights relationship of China's state ownership, so as to fundamentally solve the problem of economic vitality and efficiency. China needed to straighten out the relationship of economic interests and define the rights and obligations of enterprises with the laws and rules of the commodity economy, so as to improve labor productivity and economic efficiency and promote effective economic growth.

CHAPTER 10

Changes in the Introduction of Western Economics

10.1 The Introduction of Western Economics in the 1980s

1. Changes in the Evaluation of and Reference to Western Economics

From the 1950s to the 1970s, the introduction of Western economics into China's economic circles was small, selective, and critical. In the 1980s, in order to meet the needs of Reform and Opening Up and economic development, classical and neoclassical Western economic theories were introduced more frequently and studied to provide theoretical support for some new economic policies. During this period, the attitude of China's economic and ideological circles toward Western economics changed from strictly criticism to a combination of criticism and reference applications. The influence of Western economic theories and methods also became a symbol of the transformation and development of China's economic thought.

There was a process of development in the evaluation of Western economic theory. From the founding of the People's Republic of China in 1949 to the end of the 1970s, Chinese academic circles basically held a critical attitude toward Western economic theories, and their evaluation was mostly negative. In the early 1980s, this situation changed from total negation to criticism, reference, and utilization. At the Second Annual National Meeting of the Society for the Study of Foreign Economic Theory, Chen Daisun, chairman of the society, pointed out that contemporary Western economics was the product of the Western capitalist system. The economic system of these countries was fundamentally different from China's socialist economic system. Therefore, as a system, modern Western economics could not be the guiding theory for the development of China's national economy. But this did not mean that there was no place for it as a reference, and there was room for utilization of Western economics. In some main aspects, modern Western economics was useful for promoting the modernization of China's economic construction. This evaluation was approved by most scholars and was representative of that time.

Beginning in the mid-1980s, with the deepening of China's market-oriented reform and the spread of Western academic culture, some young and middle-aged scholars basically accepted Western economics. They believed that the Chinese socialist economics based on Marxist principles was too abstract and vague to explain the real economy and solve various contradictions in the economic process. However, the empirical analysis and concept category of Western economics could at least explain the real economy and explain the motivation and purpose of people's economic behavior. Western economics had a strict definition and standard for the research object and preconditions, and it had logically established a complete theoretical framework. With the deepening of commercialization and marketization of China's economy, the applicability of Western economics became increasingly important. This view was once very popular.

By the end of 1980s and the beginning of 1990s, many young and middle-aged scholars, some of whom had returned from studying abroad, raised objections to the overall acceptance of Western economics. Based on a more comprehensive and accurate study of Western economics, they pointed out that it was not a perfect system, but had many defects, and even some of its most basic assumptions were unreasonable. Due to the limitations of the theoretical premise of Western economics, there would be many fallacies and specious conclusions when the entire theoretical framework was used to analyze China's economy. Therefore, they were committed to "reforming" and innovating Western economics from the perspective of preconditions, analytical methods, and theoretical framework, so as to make their theories more tensive and be able to explain China's own economic reality.

As for how to learn from Western economics, Chen Daisun held that China should not only recognize that in the development of foreign economics in recent years, there had been some aspects worthy of reference, such as reasoning analysis, measurement technology, and management means, but also that it should not blindly praise them and or copy them wholesale. From the essence of the overall system, the mode of economic development in capitalist countries could not become the economic model of China, and modern bourgeois economic theory could not become the guiding ideology for developing China's national economy.[1]

The representative point of view was that China must have a scientific attitude toward modern Western economics. It could not deny its usefulness because of its class nature and limitations, and it could not deny its class nature and limitations because of its usefulness as a reference. It was important to have a clear understanding of the overall modern Western economic system, but it

---

1. Chen Daisun, "Research on Modern Western Economics and China's Socialist Economic Modernization," *Journal of Beijing University (Philosophy and Social Issue)*, no. 3 (1983).

was also important to make concrete analysis of specific problems. At the same time, it should also be pointed out that boldly drawing on some principles of modern Western economics did not mean copying the system wholesale. Different countries had different national conditions and different economic conditions, and even if some principles of modern Western economics had an application value, they can only be used as a reference.[2]

2. The Stages of the Introduction and Research of Western Economics

In the first half of 1980s, the introduction and research of Western economics mainly focused on classical and neoclassical economic theories, and most important were the introduction and research of some important works of the post-Keynesian mainstream school. For example, American economist Samuelson's *Economics,* the representative work of contemporary post-Keynesian mainstream school, was very popular in China. Most colleges and universities took it as the designated reference book for economics majors. Others such as Gardner Ackley's *Macroeconomics*, Thomas Delberg and Duncan McDougall's *Macroeconomics*, Brian Morgan's *Monetarism and Keynesian School*, Lawrence Klein's *Keynesian Revolution*, John Hicks's *Keynesian Crisis*, Joan Robinson's *An Introduction to Modern Economics,* and J. Harvey's *Modern Economics* were the main works of post-Keynesian mainstream schools. During this period, Chinese economists' research on Western economic theory also focused on classical economics and Keynesian economics. There were three reasons why Keynesian economics was very popular in China. First of all, when China's economic reform was gradually unfolding and deepening, there was a collision between the growth of new economic factors and the old system, which led to macroeconomic chaos, while the traditional planned control system basically failed. Modern Western macroeconomics with Keynesian theory as the core filled the gap in China's economic theory, making observations and offering analysis for Chinese economists. The operation of the national economy under unplanned regulation provided a theoretical tool. Further, in the 1980s, both academia and government departments adopted an attitude of urgency toward accelerating economic growth and catching up with the pace of world development. In Keynesian theory, the model of insufficient stimulation of effective demand to generate national income growth, investment multiplier, and other analysis tools catered to this mentality, in a certain sense. Finally, Keynesian economics was a revolution of the laissez faire tradition of classical economics. It held that market power alone could not lead to macro aggregate balance and advocated that the government should intervene in the economy. This policy proposition was easily accepted in China's special economic environment. Because of these three factors, the introduction, research and application of Western macroeconomics with Keynesian theory as the core came at the right time for China.

During this period, some other non-mainstream theories, such as monetary school and supply-side school, were translated and studied. However, as the renaissance of traditional economic

---

2. Hu Daiguang, "Several Issues on Drawing upon Western Economics," *Chinese Social Sciences*, no. 5 (1990).

liberalism, their theories and policy propositions were not suitable for China, whose reform goal was a planned commodity economy. At the same time, many scholars believed that the theories of these schools were relatively poor and their policies were relatively flat, so they could not replace the Keynesian school. Of course, some thought that these theories made up for the shortcomings of Keynesian theory and could be incorporated into mainstream Western economics.

In the second half of the 1980s, the introduction and research of Western economics changed to the theory of economic growth and development economics. At the same time, the introduction and research of economic management and enterprise management theory also became a focus. In terms of economic growth theory and development economics, the translated and published works in this period include Domar's *Economic Growth Theory*, Kuznets' *Modern Economic Growth*, Rostow's *Economics from Takeoff to Sustained Growth*, Solow's *Economic Growth Theory: An Interpretation*, Harrod's *Dynamic Economics*, Gillis et al.'s *Development Economics*, Kindleberger et al.'s *Development Economics*, Chenery et al.'s *Comparative Study of Industrialization and Economic Growth*, and Schultz's *Transformation of Traditional Agriculture*. Domestic scholars' research on economic growth and economic development was also carried out on a large scale.

There were methodological reasons for the popularity of Western economic growth theory and development economics in China. From the characteristics of economic development, the theoretical core of neoclassical economics or Keynesian economics was the operation of market price mechanism. For developing countries, many concepts and categories of this theory were not applicable due to the underdeveloped commodity economy, the underdeveloped market system, and the imperfect price system. Neoclassical economics regarded economic change as marginal and incremental adjustment, while developing countries needed large-scale economic change and structural improvement. Based on the conditions of developed countries, Keynesian economics attributed the business cycle to insufficient effective demand and excessive savings. The main causes of poverty and unemployment in developing countries were insufficient savings, capital shortage, and insufficient supply. Therefore, the theory of economic growth and development economics, with their theoretical characteristics more suitable for the economic situation of developing countries, as well as the characteristics of strong positivity and comparative analysis in analytical methods, had a wider impact on the development of China's macroeconomic theory. In addition, economic growth theory and development economics believed that in developing countries, industrialization was basically initiated by the government, coupled with the low degree of marketization and socialization of the economy and the slow accumulation of modern factors. Therefore, in order to achieve rapid economic growth and realize industrialization, it was necessary to go through a stage of strengthening state intervention. This policy proposition was also in line with China's economic situation.

By the end of 1980s and the beginning of 1990s, the characteristics of the introduction and research of Western economics had changed again, with the focus shifting to the introduction and research of new Western institutional economics and property rights economics. The works of such economists as Coase, Demsetz, Alchia, North, Davis, Buchanan, Williamson, Knight,

Zhang Wuchang, and Kurt were translated into Chinese in large quantities. It can be said that there was a "property rights fever" in China's economic circles, and the ideas and methods of new institutional economics or property rights economics had a broad influence.

From the perspective of methodology, there were some specific reasons why the institutional analysis of property rights economics had such great repercussions and received such great attention in the field of Chinese economics. Classical and neoclassical Western economics generally regarded economic growth as a function of capital investment and technological progress. In this type of model, the property rights system and the economic system were regarded as an established factor or exogenous variable. Property rights economics held that the innovation of system had great influence on economic development. Modern society relied on the property rights mechanism or property rights system, which could provide some effective incentives or constraints to reduce waste, so that scarce resources could be optimally allocated. Property rights economics believed that institutional change (rather than technological change) was the more essential source of income growth, and it introduced institutional change as an endogenous variable into the analytical framework of modern economics. This theory had important significance for China's economic research. In China, due to the leapfrog development of economic history and the historical dislocation of the economic system, the institutional conditions of economic development were quite different from those of developed Western countries. The industrialization and modernization of developed Western countries and the development and maturity of the market economy system and enterprise system were mutually complementary and reinforcing. The development of productive forces and the reform of the system were basically mutually adaptive and gradual, and there was no great leap forward or big dislocation. In the history of China, there had never been a unified, complete market system, as well as the corresponding property rights system and enterprise system. In addition, the long-term implementation of the administrative planned economic system led economic development to suffer from serious institutional obstacles. In this context, the process of China's economic development was not only manifested in the total growth and structural transformation, but also in the institutional reform and innovation. Its essence lay in changing the system and behavior mode which was not suitable or was even hindering the development of productive forces, and in promoting the progress and modernization of social economy. It was precisely because the characteristics of China's economic growth and institutional change were consistent with the theoretical logic and analytical methods of property rights economics that the theory and methods of property rights economics were very popular in China and were on the rise.

Property rights economics took transaction costs as the basic analysis tool and revised and supplemented traditional microeconomics, which was regarded as another "revolution" of Western economics. The economics of property rights in Western countries also rose from the 1920s and 1930s, and gradually matured in the 1960s and 1970s, making it the frontier discipline of economics. The research and application of this theory in China's economic circles not only had innovative significance in theory and analytical methods, but also shortened the distance between China's economic research and the development of world economics, indicating that

China's introduction, research, and application of Western economics had basically been in line with the development of world economics.

3. An Overview of the Research Results of Western Economics

Throughout the 1980s, the research on Western economic theory in Chinese economic circles gradually began, and much was achieved in the late 1980s and early 1990s.

In the first half of 1980s, in order to give the theorists a basic understanding of Western economic theory, in addition to the translated works, some relevant popular books were published, such as *Lectures on Foreign Economics* (a series of four volumes) compiled by the Foreign Economic Theory Research Association, briefly introducing Western classical economics and its main academic schools from the perspective of theoretical history. This played an important role in popularizing Western economic theories. Other publications in this field included *Evaluation of Foreign Economics*, compiled by the Department of Economics of Peking University, *Foreign Economists on the Economy of China and Developing Countries*, compiled by the Editorial Department of *Economic Research*, *A Summary of Modern Foreign Economic Theories* by Chen Daisun, *An Introduction to Contemporary Bourgeois Economics* by Yin Bocheng and Shi Shijun, *History of Economic Theories*, edited by Lu Wenzhang and Li Zongzheng, *History of Economic Theories* by Wu Feidan, *Main Contemporary Western Economic Thought* by Fu Yincai, *Economists of Nobel Prize Winners*, compiled by the Editorial Department of *World Economy*, *Main Schools of Contemporary Bourgeois Economics*, edited by Hu Daiguang and Li Yining, *Review of Western Economic Thought*, compiled by The Commercial Press, *Selected Papers on Modern Foreign Economics*, compiled by The Commercial Press and Foreign Economic Theories Research Association, *Lectures on Modern Foreign Economic Thought*, by Hu Daiguang et al., *Selected Works of Bourgeois Classical Political Economics*, edited by Wang Yanan, and other works.

At that time, there were also a few textbooks of Western economics compiled by Chinese scholars, such as *Contemporary Western Economic Theories*, edited by Liu Diyuan and Tan Chongtai, *Macroeconomics and Microeconomics*, co-edited by Zhang Peigang and Li Yining, *Concise Western Economics*, by Li Yining, *An Introduction to Western Economics*, by Liang Xiaomin, *Invisible Hands: Microeconomics*, compiled by Yang Junchang, and *Basic Modern Western Economic Theories*, by Fu Yincai.

During this period, special research on Western economics included *Main Schools of Contemporary Bourgeois Economics*, co-authored by Hu Daiguang and Li Yining, *A History of Value Theory*, edited by He Liancheng, *Growth Economics*, edited by Song Chengxian and Fan Jiaxiang, *The Supply-side School*, by Zhang Jialin, *Galbraith*, by Fu Yincai, *Critique of Keynesian Effective Demand Principles and Employment Multiplies Theory*, by Fan Hong, *Keynesianism*, by Yang Xuezhang, *Ricardo's Economic Theory*, by Chen Dongye, *Milton Friedman and His Monetarism*, by Hu Daiguang, *Review of Western Welfare Economics*, by Li Yining et al., *Consumption Economics*, compiled by Li Yining, *Economic Theoretical System of Adam Smith*, by Chen Dongye et al., *Economic Theory of the Physiocratic School*, by Zhang Renjia, *History of Political Economics*, by

Chen Daisun, and *Classical Bourgeois Political Economics*, by Ding Bing, among others.

In the second half of the 1980s, the number of research works on Western economics increased sharply, especially the proportion of textbooks. Examples included *Basic Contemporary Western Economic Theories*, translated and compiled by Hu Jichuang, *The Concise Course of Bourgeois Political Economics*, edited by Wu Kuigang and Li Ke, *Keynesian Revolution: Macroeconomics*, compiled by Yang Junchang, *Fifteen Lectures on Modern Western Economic Theories*, compiled by Tao Dayong et al., *The Concise Course of Contemporary Western Economic Theories*, compiled by East China Normal University, *Popular Microeconomics*, compiled by Huang Zhixian et al., *Fundamentals of Contemporary Western Economics*, edited by Fang Junxiong, et al., *Contemporary Western Economics*, compiled by Yang Deming, *Principles of Contemporary Western Economics*, compiled by Song Zexing, *Principles of Contemporary Western Economics*, compiled by Gao Hongding and others, *Compendium of Contemporary Western Economics*, compiled by Luo Jieli, *Macroeconomics*, compiled by Zhao Chongling and Jiang Ziqiang, *Microeconomics*, compiled by Zhou Shouxuan, *Microeconomic Analysis*, compiled by Xiao Jingru and Zhu Zhongming, *An Introduction to Western Pricing Science*, compiled by Leng Shouyi, *Principles of Contemporary Western Economics*, compiled by Luo Jieli, *An Introduction to Western Economics*, compiled by Li Keshan, *Microeconomics and Macroeconomics*, compiled by Jia Zhiyong and others, *Modern Western Economics*, compiled by Song Chengxian, *Microeconomics*, compiled by Bai Baoli and Gong Yixin, *A Concise Course of Contemporary Western Economic Theory*, compiled by Wu Xianzhong et al., *Principles of Contemporary Western Economics*, compiled by Ding Bing, *Modern Economics*, by Gao Hongye and Wu Yifeng, *Contemporary Western Economics* (Volume 1 and Volume 2), by Luo Zhiru, Fan Jiaxiang, Li Yining, and Hu Daiguang, *Popular Macroeconomics*, compiled by Huang Haichao, *Western Microeconomics*, by Lan Yuping, *Dictionary of Contemporary Western Economics*, compiled by Wang Shenzhi, *Dictionary of Western Economic Thought*, compiled by Yu Junwen, *A Textbook of Modern Western Economics*, compiled by Zhang Yunling, *Principles of Contemporary Western Economics*, compiled by Liu Houjun, *A New Version of Western Economics*, compiled by Zheng Tianlun, *A Course of Contemporary Western Economics*, compiled by Ding Liangcheng and Zhang Jian, *Exercises and Solutions of Principles of Modern Western Economics*, compiled by Li Chong, *A Course of History of Economic Theories*, compiled by Fang Chonggui and Yin Bocheng, *Modern Western Economics*, compiled by Xiang Baohua and Zhou Wenqian, *An Introduction to Modern Western Economics*, compiled by Li Yining and Qin Wanshun, *Macroeconomic Management*, compiled by Hou Ronghua, *Modern Western Economics*, by Li Yiyuan, *An Introduction to Western Economics*, by Liang Xiaomin, and *Exercises and Solutions of Modern Western Economics*, compiled by Niu Baode.

The works on the history of economic theory included *Western Economic Theory Since 1870*, by Hu Jichuang, *The History of Modern Western Political Economics*, compiled by Feng Yiming, *The History of Economic Theory*, compiled by Wu Zhongguan, *Marginalism in Economics*, by Yan Zhijie, *Contemporary Western Economic Theory and Its Main Schools*, compiled by Fan Yijun and Wang Xiaobin, *A Compendium of the History of Bourgeois Political Economy*, compiled by Zhan Junzhong, *The Thought and Schools of Contemporary Economic Theories*, compiled by Wu

Chengnian, *The Emergence and Development of Micro- and Macroeconomics*, by Zhang Peigang and Li Yining, *The Review of Contemporary Economic Theories*, compiled by Nie Xibin and Hu Xining, and *The Development History of Modern Western Economic Theories*, compiled by Zhu Tongshu.

Special research works on Western economists and their theories included *David Ricardo*, by Chen Qiren, *Adam Smith and the Wealth of Nations*, by Wan Qiao and Wu Yuhui, *A Study on the Nature and Causes of National Wealth*, by Chai Yongyuan, *Friedman and Modern Monetarism*, compiled by Liu Diyuan and Chen Duanji, *Malthus*, compiled by Fan Jinchun and Wu Jianming, *John S. Mueller and His Principles of Political Economics*, by Ji Tao, *Keynes Theory and China's Economy*, by Lin Yizhi, *On Reagan Economics*, by Yang Lujun, *Contemporary Western International Economic Thought*, by Zhu Tigang, *Contemporary Western Economics and Financial Theories*, by Gao Ronggui and Zhang Xiaofeng, *Normative Economics and Social Choice*, by Sun Laixiang, *Bohm-Bawerk*, compiled by Xiao Bucai, *Freiburg School of Economics*, by Zuo Dapei, *The Re-revolution of Keynesian Revolution*, by Xue Jinjun, *The Review of Keynesian Employment Theory*, by Liu Diyuan, *The Depression Fate: On Keynesian Theory*, by Ren Dingqiu, *A Review of Western Economic Thought*, compiled by The Commercial Press, and *An Evaluation of Modern Western Economic Thought*, compiled by Liu Dajun.

Other works included *Development Economics*, by Tan Chongtai, *Macro Control Theory*, compiled by Wen Qian, *Development Economics: Theory, Policy, and Practice*, compiled by Wan Xiaoguang, *An Introduction to Comparative Economics*, by Jiang Zehong, *Development Economics*, by Tao Wenda, *An Introduction to Western Development Economics*, compiled by Yang Jingnian, *Specialized Frontier Topics of Modern Economics*, compiled by Tang Min and Mao Yushi, *An Introduction to Key Western Economic Works*, compiled by Si Zhengjia, *Contemporary International Economic Relations*, by Zhou Qizhi and Jiang Shengfu, and others.

These statistics generally reflect China's academic achievements in Western economic theory research in the 1980s. Of course, these works and textbooks were different in academic level and their grasp of Western economics, especially for the theoretical research of some frontier disciplines and sub-disciplines. But with such a quantitative basis, the research level of Western economic theory was later further improved and developed.

10.2 The Methodological Influence of Western Economics

1. The Influence of Empirical Research Methods

Generally speaking, Marxist economics or socialist economics was inclined to normative research, while Western economics tended to empirical research. With their different research methods, economics could be divided into normative economics and empirical economics.

Normative economics was based on a certain value judgment, put forward some standards as the yardstick for analyzing problems, established the premise of economic theory as the basis for formulating economic policies, and studied how to meet these standards. It had two characteristics. The first was that it did not consider how the economic system actually operates, but was concerned with how it should operate, that is, to answer the question of "what should be." The second was that the content of the study was not objective, and the conclusions could not pass the test. Empirical economics attempted to transcend or exclude all value judgments, only considering the laws of establishing the relationship between economic things, and under the influence of these laws, analyzing and predicting the effect of people's economic behavior. Empirical economics also had two characteristics. The first was that it only expressed and analyzed the existing situation, but did not suggest how to change it, that is, it mainly answered the question of "what it is." The second was that its research content was objective, and whether its conclusions were correct could be tested by empirical facts. In terms of analytic methods, the differences between the two were that normative economics was mainly qualitative analysis, emphasizing logical reasoning, while empirical economics was mainly quantitative analysis, processing statistical data and falsifying hypotheses.

Empirical research constituted the basic content of economics and was also a basic method of economics. Western economics believed that in order to make economics a real science, it was necessary to abandon the problem of value judgments and make economic analysis empirical. Admittedly, classical Western economics also had a tradition of normative research, and some disciplines such as welfare economics were normative economics, but the main body of Western economics was empirical.

The empirical research methods of Western economics had a great influence on Chinese economists, especially on young and middle-aged scholars. They believed that economics, as an empirical science, assumed that individual preferences were given in advance. That is to say, economists were not interested in what kind of value preference and moral standards the analysis object had. They merely studied people's economic behavior and its consequences under the given value standard conditions. In this sense, as a discipline, economics had the characteristics of "moral neutrality."

Economic and ideological circles also had different opinions on these views. Some scholars believed that whether economists talked about morality or not, in the final analysis, depended on whether economics should explore the moral standards of economic behavior and whether to explore the value scale of the advantages and disadvantages of economic activities and economic system. The Western institutionalism school emphasized the status and role of spiritual factors and moral values in economic research and advocated that economics should explore the ethical value and moral norms of economic behavior. At the time, some "anomie" in China's ethics and morality was an inevitable turbulence in the transition from a non-commodity society to a market economy. Economists had much to do in this regard.[3]

---

3. Chen Zhang, Chen Guodong, and Liu Xiahui, *Western Economic Theory and Empirical Methodology* (Peking University Press, 1993); Li Yi, "A Review of the Discussion on Some Issues of China's Economic Research," *Academic Trends*, no. 3 (1990); Tang Jie, "Reform of Economic Research Methods and Progress in Economics," *Nankai Economic Research*, no. 2 (1992).

Chinese economics had a profound tradition of normative analysis (in fact, Marxist economics is not absolute normative analysis, and Marx's investigation and analysis of division of labor, production, exchange, market, profit, interest and other categories are empirical), which meant that economics was unable to explain the real economy to a large extent, and there would never be a similar conclusion in the discussion of many issues. Therefore, the introduction of the empirical method in economic research was not only an important methodological problem, but also determined the social value of economics. Of course, China could not go to the other extreme and abandon normative analysis completely. Even Western economics was not absolutely empirical. With the re-emergence of welfare economics integrating into microeconomics and institutional analysis, empirical analysis and normative analysis trended toward integration in Western economics. However, in China, where normative analysis was well established, it was necessary to emphasize empirical analysis. The training of empirical methods was not an overnight process. Even those economists who advocated positivism still wrote articles with a strong normative touch. There was thus still a long way to go for China's economics to be truly based on empirical evidence.

2. Influence of Structural Analysis Methods

In the second half of the 1980s, China's economic theorists conducted in-depth discussions on the evaluation of the macroeconomic situation and strategic choices. This was a period of great development in China's macroeconomic theory. Various discussions were not limited to the analysis and judgment of economic phenomena, but also went deeper into the differences between diverse economic analysis methods and theories. As industrial structure was an important macroeconomic problem, with the development of the understanding of industrial structure theory, different opinions were expressed on the analysis methods of the macro-economy in economic circles. Generally speaking, one school advocated total amount analysis and the other advocated structural analysis.

The significance of structural analysis in methodology lay in examining the process of social and economic development from the perspective of "economic integrity," which took the internal structural change of economic process as the standard for dividing the stages of economic development, noting that the qualitative change in the process of economic development was realized through structural transformation. Scholars who advocated structural analysis believed that although the contradiction of China's macro-economic imbalance directly showed that the total demand was greater than the total supply, the macro-control policy to restrain the aggregate demand had not fundamentally solved the contradiction between the aggregate supply and demand and the structural contradiction. Obviously, the prominent contradiction of China's macro-economy could not be explained simply by the concept of total amount. The main contradiction of China's macro-economy was that the structure of production and the structure of demand were not compatible. Therefore, strengthening the structural analysis in theory and carrying out structural adjustment in practice could solve the main contradictions in China's macro-economy. Some scholars held that the total growth depended on the structural state to a certain extent, and the long-term aggregate growth depended on the transformation of industrial structure. If the total amount increased to a certain extent, it would inevitably lead to the orderly change and transformation of the structure, and the faster the total growth, the higher the structural transformation. The contradiction between aggregate and structure in China's economic development manifested itself in the contradiction between aggregate growth and structural hyperstability. The root cause lay in the lack of self-organization function and self-regulation mechanism of industrial structure in economic operation. At the same time, in theory and practice, there was a tendency to attach importance to aggregate growth and neglect structural transformation, which was derived from the traditional system and traditional development strategy.[4]

Structuralism was an analytical method adopted by Western economic growth theory and development economics, and also a theoretical system with great influence in modern economics. The characteristic of this method was to analyze the economic development from the perspective of economic integrity and structural decomposition. Advocates of the field believed that in developing countries, the economic structure was inflexible, the relative change of price had little effect on resource reallocation, and the movement of supply and demand to the equilibrium point could not be carried out automatically, so that the market could not be closed and the gap could not be filled. It was thus not a balanced system, but a persistent disequilibrium in the economies of developing countries. The main source of this imbalance was the structural difference between departments. Therefore, it was necessary to deconstruct the economy into several components and analyze the process of economic development from the perspective of structural connection.[5]

From the mid-1980s, China's economic structural adjustment and macroeconomic analysis methods shifted toward structuralism. Many economists accepted that the characteristics of economic growth stage were the different development heights of industrial structure and the structural benefits associated with it. In the economic development strategy formulated by the Thirteenth National Congress of the Communist Party of China and the industrial policies put forward in the Seventh Five-Year Plan, China not only paid attention to the quantity balance of industrial structure, but also paid attention to the role of industrial structure transformation in promoting economic growth, which reflected the theoretical touch of structuralism. It should be said that this change was in line with the development trend of world economic theory, and

---

4. Zhang Delin, "Exploration and Contention of Aggregate Analysis, Structural Analysis, and Institutional Analysis," *Economic Trends*, no. 6 (1990); Liu Xiaoxuan, "On the Basic Categories and Basic Relations of Macroeconomic Analysis," *Economic Research*, no. 5 (1988); Hu Jichuang, *An Analysis of Differences in Economic Theories* (Fudan University Press, 1991).

5. Zhang Delin, "Exploration and Contention of Aggregate Analysis, Structural Analysis, and Institutional Analysis," *Economic Trends*, no. 6 (1990); Zhang Weiying, "Aggregate Analysis, Structural Analysis, and Budget," *Economic Research*, no. 8 (1987).

it basically adapted to the characteristics of China's economic growth stage. From the current situation of China's economic development, in the process of industrialization, it was an objective requirement of China's economic growth to reform the development mode with the growth rate of total output value as the strategic goal, and the theoretical thinking and development mode related to the total growth and structural transformation, which also indicated the great development in the theoretical analysis method of China's macroeconomy at that time.

3. The Influence of Institutional Analysis Method

The new Western institutional economics and institutional analysis methods exerted a broad influence on China's economic and ideological circles beginning in the late 1980s. In the discussion on macroeconomic theories and methods in the late 1980s, one view in the field of economic thought suggested that economic analysis must be based on an established economic system. The economic analysis of Western economics was based on a mature market economic system. But in China, what economic analysis faced was an economic system with a short history and an immature, transitional nature. When applying the method of studying a relatively mature and stable economic system to study of an immature, unstable economic system, it was important to pay attention to several issues. First, the existing economic system was not a perfect economic system, and further, the existing economic structure was an economic structure in the process of continuous evolution. In addition, many aspects of the operation mechanism in the existing economy were only of temporary significance. Some scholars further put forward that the certainty of the aggregate relationship could only be established when the organizational system was homogeneous and stable. However, in China, with the coexistence of the planned economy system and the market economy system, the formation of the aggregate relationship was affected by different operating mechanisms and organizational behavior patterns of heterogeneous organizational structures. Under the condition of a homogeneous organizational structure, the theory of total causality had lost its ability to explain and predict. Therefore, in China's macroeconomic analysis, it was imperative that the analytical framework of Western economics not simply be followed, but that it should proceed from the particularity of economic reality and analyze the organizational structure so as to correctly identify a new causal relationship.[6]

Since the middle of the 20th century, the economists of the new institutional economics school in the West had provided a theoretical framework to analyze the system after painstaking research work. By incorporating institutions into the constraint framework of the neoclassical model, the relationship between institutional restriction and individual choice was established, thus achieving the integration of institutional approach and neoclassical economic theory. North, an American economist, reexamined European economic history from the perspective of institutional change,

---

6. Zhang Delin, "Exploration and Contention of Aggregate Analysis, Structural Analysis, and Institutional Analysis," *Economic Trends*, no. 6 (1990).

and he believed that efficient economic organizations were the key to economic growth, and the development of efficient economic organizations in Western Europe was the reason for the rise of the Western world. The emergence of efficient organizations needed to make arrangements and establish property rights in order to create an incentive effect on people's economic activities. According to the comparison of transaction costs, private benefits were close to social benefits, and social welfare tended to be at a maximum. If a society did not achieve economic growth, it was because that society had not provided incentives for economic innovation activities, that is to say, there was no institutional guarantee for the rewards or benefits that the actors of innovation activities should receive.[7]

Henry Lepage, an American economist, observed that the property rights movement in economics had four pillars, which included the concept of transaction costs, property rights economics, comparative economic organization research, and institutional analysis.[8] In fact, both in methodology and in theoretical basis, the four pillars overlapped and were difficult to distinguish. For example, using the concept of transaction costs and the theory of property rights, it was possible to effectively explain the alternation of various forms of economic organization in history (for example, enterprises replace the market), and the change of economic organizational forms would lead to the changes of institutions in the economic sense, such as the rules, procedures, and ethical behavior norms (i.e., the property right structure caused by the company system and management system changes). According to this logic, the established system could also affect or even determine the size of transaction costs. As North noted, institutional theory focused on the role of institutions in determining transaction costs, and the goal of institutional economics was to study how people made decisions in the real world and how these decisions changed the world in the context of institutional evolution.[9]

Institutional analysis and new institutional economics had more unique significance to China's economic reality than neoclassical economics. There were many "paradoxes" in the analysis of China's economy with neoclassical economics, because it was difficult for China's economy to meet the institutional conditions on which neoclassical economics were based. New institutional economics took transaction as the analysis unit, transaction costs as the main analysis tool, property rights as the core of resource allocation, and the economic system as an important variable of economic growth, and the size of transaction costs was related to the efficiency of economic system operation. All of these held greater enlightenment value for China's economic research and economic development.

---

7. Hodgson, *Manifesto of Modern Institutionalism Economics* (Peking University Press, 1993).

8. Henri Lepage, *American Neo-liberal Economics* (Peking University Press, 1985), 9–15.

9. North, *Structure and Change in Economic History* (Shanghai Sanlian Bookstore, 1994).

10.3 Comments on the Methods and Theories of Western Economics

1. A Review of Structural Analysis Methods in Western Economics

American economists Kindleberger and Herrick put forward the neo-classical approach and radicalism, or the neo-Marxist and structuralist approach.[10] Structuralism was a kind of theoretical thinking and analysis method with great influence at that time. Its theoretical feature was to analyze economic development from the perspective of economic integrity and structural decomposition. From there, the origin of classical economics could be traced back to the Western classical economics. Francois Quesnay published the *Economic Table* in 1758. The analysis feature of the *Economic Table* was that a capitalist society was divided into three basic classes (the productive class, the unproductive class, and the landowner class) and two major production sectors (agriculture and industry). The national income (the agricultural products produced in a year) was taken as the starting point of the production cycle, and the activity relationship between the basic elements of the capitalist economy was described through the form of circulation. According to Quesnay's schema, a quantitative model could be established to represent the overall relationship of economic activities. This was the earliest basis for quantitative analysis of economic structure. On the basis of dividing capitalist society into three classes (workers, capitalists, and landlords) and dividing national income into three kinds of income (wages, profits, and land rent), Adam Smith offered a detailed analysis of the relationship among diverse variables in the economic system. His value theory, division of labor theory, and exchange theory all reflected the theory of economic integrity analysis.

When examining the reproduction of total social capital, Marx divided social production into two categories: production of the means of production and production of the means of consumption according to the physical form and final use of total social products. The two categories theory had an important impact on Leontief's input-output analysis method.

In 1874, Leon Walras, the founder of the Lausanne school, published *The Foundation of Pure Political Economics* and established the theoretical system of general equilibrium. The characteristic of Walras's general equilibrium analysis stated that from the premise that the supply, demand, and price of various commodities in the market influenced and depended on each other, price was determined according to the condition in which the supply and demand of each commodity reached the equilibrium state at the same time. Walras's model based on his general equilibrium theory included a set of simultaneous equations to reflect the equilibrium relationship between economic behaviors in a fully competitive market, in which each equation determined a price. The basic elements in the equation were the production sector and the consumer, whose quantitative relationship was determined by the "production coefficient," while the production coefficient was determined by the technical relationship. They could measure the quantity of elements required for each final product in a production unit. In this way, the Walras system could determine all the

---

10. Kindleberger and Herrick, *Economic Development* (Shanghai Translation Publishing House, 1986), 210.

prices: the prices of the services produced, the prices of the products produced, and the prices of the final products. As the competition among the owners formed an automatic adjustment force, the relationship between prices could always be in equilibrium, so as to achieve production equilibrium. The Walras model sought to explain the relationship between production sectors and the competitive demand of each sector for production factors. His production equilibrium equation and its general equilibrium method had a great influence on the later economic structure theory.

In the 1930s, the Keynesian Revolution took place in Western economics. After the classical school, the thought of economic integrity analysis (macro analysis) began to revive. In this period, Wassily Leontief made an important contribution to the theory of economic structure. According to the view of economic integrity and general equilibrium theory, he founded the input-output theory (for which he won the Nobel Prize in economics in 1973). Leontief's input-output analysis divided all kinds of economic activities in a society into several "production" sectors, such as agriculture, industry, construction, transportation and service, and "final demand" sectors on the basis of Walras' general equilibrium theory. According to these sectors, specific factual data was collected and sorted out to reflect the actual relationship between departments. Because the overall economic activity was divided into limited sectors, it was easy to deal with the statistics, which solved the defects of the Walras model, such as its diverse formulas and difficulties in practical application. As a result, the general equilibrium theory was developed through practical application.

(1) The Development of Structuralism

The real development of economic structure theory came in the middle of the 20th century. The evolution process of this theory can be explained by two concepts: dual economy and demand complementarity among departments in the process of economic development (represented by balanced growth and unbalanced growth theory).

William Arthur Lewis was one of the founders of economic structure theory after the Second World War. His outstanding contribution lay in the fact that the existence of a large number of surplus labor force in developing countries not only did not affect the economic development, but was also the driving force for the economic development of these countries. According to this theory, the economic structure of developing countries was composed of the modern capitalist industrial sector and the traditional agricultural sector. The former was a department where capitalists used capital and employed workers to produce for profit (similar to Smith's "productive labor," that is, the labor of employed workers who exchange capital with capital and produce profits for capitalists). The latter was a department that did not use or rarely used capital. The per capita output of the traditional sector was much lower than that of the modern sector, but there was a large number of surplus labor. At the same time, in the traditional sector, production was only for self-sufficiency, and there was little or no commercial agricultural activity. Profits and prices had no stimulating effect on it. According to the theory of diminishing marginal productivity, the marginal productivity of the agricultural labor force must be very low, and some of the marginal productivity of the labor force would even drop to zero. Under such conditions, the income level of agricultural workers was very low and could only maintain a minimum living standard. Lewis pointed out that it was this kind of living income that determined the wage limit of the modern industrial sector, which enabled that sector to obtain the labor force needed for industrialization from the traditional agricultural sector. Capitalists only needed to pay low wages to these laborers that were compatible with the living standards of the traditional agricultural sector, so as to obtain greater profits. They would accumulate more and more profits to update technology, hire more workers and expand reproduction. In this way, when the surplus labor force no longer existed, the dual structure disappeared, and economic development reached a new stage. The Lewis model emphasized the structural difference between the modern sector and the traditional sector. Compared with the total development model, it was closer to the reality of developing countries and opened up a new way to analyze the economy of those countries. Ranis and John C. H. Fei were the heirs to Lewis. They published the *Theory of Economic Development* for the first time and put forward the Ranis-Fei model, which developed Lewis's model in some aspects, which was later called the Lewis-Fei-Ranis model. The theory of the dual economic structure was an important theoretical contribution to the division of the two major production sectors of the national economy and the analysis of the industrialization of rural surplus labor force.

Another important concept of economic structure theory was demand complementarity among departments. The theory of this concept was the theory of balanced growth and unbalanced growth. The idea of balanced growth was put forward by Knox, and then gradually formed the system theory represented by Nurkse and Paul Rosenstein Rodan. According to this theory, due to the "indivisibility" in the economy of developing countries, a small amount of investment could not solve the problem at a fundamental level. It was necessary to invest capital in various industrial sectors (especially in infrastructure construction) in an all-round, large-scale way. Through the "great promotion" of this kind of investment, it was possible to break through the stagnation and poverty of the economy and promote industry overall, thus achieving industrialization.

In view of this theory, Hirschman and Singer put forward the idea and theory of unbalanced growth. Hirschman pointed out that he was in agreement with the balanced growth theorists on the importance of technological complementarity among various industries at different stages of production. But he believed that in the economy, the complementary relationship between some industries was stronger than that among other industries. Therefore, the purpose of development policy should not be to promote all aspects at the same time, but to select and focus on those "strategic sectors" or "leading sectors" that could be expected to have the strongest chain effect of interdependence. He believed that these leading sectors could be found where a series of input-output relations were most closely expressed. Economic development followed the growth of the leading sector to drive the growth of other sectors, and the growth of one enterprise or factory led to the growth of another enterprise or factory. Hirschman further analyzed the economic relations between departments and proposed the definitions of the backward chain effect and forward linkage effect. The backward chain effect, also known as "raw material supply, extended demand," referred to the increase of investment in other industries caused by the demand for production input by a department or an industry. The forward chain effect, also known as "product utilization," referred to the production of a sector or an industry that could "trigger the attempt to use its products as raw materials for some new production." The greater the chain effect of the industrial sector, the greater the role of promoting the process of economic development. Hirschman pointed out that it was impossible for underdeveloped countries to provide capital, technology, and management personnel to run a large number of new enterprises at once. Therefore, developing countries should invest their limited factors of production into the leading industries with the strongest driving force.

Although the views of balanced growth theory and unbalanced growth theory were different, their economic structure analysis methods were consistent. The theoretical center of the theory emphasized the relationship between the structure of various sectors in the economy, so it was important to give full attention to the related role of the development of different industrial sectors in determining the economic development strategy.

The further development of economic structure theory was to link economic growth with structural transformation, that is, to study the process of economic development from the perspective of structural transformation. After the 1970s, some economists conducted in-depth research on the internal relationship between economic development and structural transformation on the basis of empirical processing of a large amount of statistical data. Kuznets first proposed the structural transformation factor of economic growth, and he won the Nobel Prize in economics in 1971 for his outstanding research achievements in this field. Kuznets's creative contribution lay in the discovery of historical data of various countries and a thorough study of the relationship between the changes of industrial structure and per capita income and economic growth in various countries through the modern economic statistics system. He dealt with structural transformation as a whole rather than as a group of separate phenomena. Relying on the extensive national income accounting of developing countries, he established the statistical basis for long-term growth research, which also made it possible to analyze cross-sector and cross-border and compare the development results of developed countries in a historical time series. Kuznets also divided the national economy into three parts, agriculture, industry, and service industry, which provided the basis for further research on the normative model. Through empirical and comparative analysis, Kuznets identified six characteristics of modern economic growth and pointed out that among these characteristics, the most important was the high growth rate of economic aggregate and the high change rate of economic structure. Following this, many economists conducted a large amount of empirical analysis on the relationship between the two basic characteristics. The book *Development Patterns (1950–1970)*, jointly published by Chenery and Syrquin in 1975, absorbed the research results of Kuznets and Clark and used a large amount of statistical data to analyze and compare the transformation process of economic structure of 101 countries (regions) from 1950 to 1970. The development model of standard structure was established, which was an inevitable change of the economic structure with the development of economy. According to the conclusion of the standard structure, 75 to 80% of the total structural changes occurred in the per capita GNP 100–1,000 US dollar development range, in which the most important accumulation process and resource allocation process would have profound, significant changes. According to Rostow's stage theory of economic growth, modern economic growth was essentially a process of departments, which were rooted in the accumulation and diffusion of production functions provided by modern technology. These changes in technology and organization could only be studied from a sectoral perspective. Rostow demonstrated his view mainly from the perspective of innovation and leading sectors. He pointed out that 1) the absorption of new technology is a process of a department, technological innovation is specific, and it is always associated with economic problems in a particular sector, 2) the introduction of new and important technology or innovations into a certain sector is a complex process related to the operation of other sectors and the whole economy, and 3) economic growth is the result of the replacement of the leading departments in turn. Therefore, "the complete sequence of growth is no longer just a movement of the total amount, but a succession of high tides in a series of departments and a sequence related to the leading departments in turn, which also marks the course of modern economic history."[11]

After the study of these economists, it was generally recognized that there was a close relationship between the transformation of economic structure and economic growth. This relationship not only indicated that the economic structure of different income levels was different, but also that the transformation of economic structure could accelerate economic growth. It was in this sense that "structural transformation" had become a specific concept, defined as an economic development process associated with economic growth. Chenery pointed out that "a common, narrow definition of structural transformation category should include the accumulation of material and human capital and the transformation of the composition of demand, production, trade, and employment, which are generally regarded as the economic connotation of transformation. Closely related to this are social and economic processes such as urbanization, population change, and income distribution change. These processes go beyond the main stage of structural transformation and are considered the outer phenomenon below the main trunk of structural transformation."[12] In another book, he further explained, "The concept of structural change can be used to link research on various aspects of development issues, including agricultural structural change, industrialization, demographic change, and urbanization. Each concept describes one or more aspects of the whole structural transformation process. Therefore, the theoretical analysis of structural change is characterized by the relationship between growth and structural change."[13]

---

11. Rostow, "Preface and Postscript," in *Economics from Takeoff to Sustainable Growth* (Sichuan People's Publishing House, 1988), 7.

12. Chenery, "Structural Transformation: An Empirical Research Procedure of Economic Development," in *A New Pattern of Development Economics: Progress and Prospect* (Economic Science Press, 1987), 13–14.

13. Chenery, *A Comparative Study of Industrialization and Economic Growth* (Sanlian Bookstore, 1989), 19.

(2) An Analysis of Structuralism

Structuralism theory was an influential thought and method of economic development. According to the characteristics of economic development, the theoretical core of neoclassical economics or Keynesian economics was the operation of the market price mechanism, but the commodity economy of developing countries was not developed, the market system was not developed, and the price mechanism was not perfect, so some concepts and categories were not applicable. Neoclassical economics regarded economic change as marginal, incremental adjustment, while developing countries needed large-scale economic change and structural improvement. Based on the conditions of developed countries, Keynesian economics attributed the business cycle to insufficient effective demand and excessive savings, while the main causes of poverty and unemployment in developing countries were insufficient savings, capital shortage, and insufficient supply. Structuralism theory was thus more suitable for the economic status of developing countries. Further, its strong positivism and comparative analysis in the analysis method had been tested by economic history and the real economy to a large extent, and it had a wider impact on China's economic development and structural adjustment thought. Under the influence of this method, the basic idea of structural analysis in China's economic circles was that economic structure was a comprehensive system, including industrial structure, regional structure, investment structure, demand structure, trade structure, and ownership structure. In the process of industrialization, the basis (or core) of economic structure was industrial structure. Because the essence of industrial structure was productivity structure, it had more direct significance for reflecting the qualitative change of productivity development in the process of industrialization.

Industrial structure included two aspects. First, it referred to the proportion of production among industries, which mainly involved the horizontal equilibrium of structure, such as the balance between primary, secondary, and tertiary industries, the balance between production of the means of production and production of the means of consumption, the balance between basic industry and the processing and manufacturing industry, and similar issues. Second, it referred to the connection between industries, mainly involving the vertical transformation of structural height and structural efficiency. Obviously, the proportion relationship between industries constituted the quantitative aspect of industrial structure, while the connection mode between industries constituted the qualitative aspect of industrial structure. Over a prolonged period, discussion on the road of industrialization and economic structure in China mainly involved the quantity of industrial structure, and the related macroeconomic analysis method was inclined to the total amount analysis. However, the essence of the economic growth process was the qualitative aspect of the industrial structure (of course, there was an internal relationship between quality and quantity). Therefore, it was necessary not only to examine and analyze the economic growth and industrialization process from the perspective of industrial structure and structural efficiency, but also from the perspective of industrial structure height and structural efficiency. According to the theory of economic structure, there was a direct positive correlation between structural transformation and economic growth. It was the different development heights of industrial structure and the structural benefits that determined the stage characteristics of economic growth.

Structural height referred to the stage or level of a country's industrial structure in the historical and logical sequence evolution process of economic development. In this historical and logical sequence, the evolution of industrial structure mainly included three aspects. 1) In the entire industrial structure, the dominant proportion of primary industry gradually evolved to the dominant proportion of secondary and tertiary industry. 2) The change of the above industrial structure caused the change of the utilization and dependence of social production on various economic resources, and this change showed that the industrial structure gradually changed from labor-intensive industry to capital intensive and technology intensive industry. 3) The evolution of industrial structure was reflected in the change of industrial structure, that is, the processing degree of industrial production was deepening, and the dependence of industrial growth on raw materials was declining. This change was that in the industrial structure, the dominant proportion of manufacturing primary products was gradually changing to that of manufacturing intermediate products and final products. The structural benefit referred to the effect of the height of industrial structure and its changes on the growth of national income.

According to the Petty-Clark Law, the evolution of industrial structure was an orderly process determined by the law of productivity development. William Petty first found that the difference in per capita national income was due to the different industrial structure. He compared the income of British farmers with that of seafarers, and he found that the per capita income of different industries was different, with the income of seafarers being four times that of farmers. He also found that the per capita national income of Holland was higher than that of other European countries. Through the above investigation, Petty concluded that compared with that of agriculture, the revenue of industry is higher, and that of commerce is the highest of the three.[14] In the language of modern economics, that is, in agriculture, industry, commerce, and other industries, the added value of per capita labor productivity was increasing. This was known as the Petty Law. The economic significance of this discovery was that it established the basic idea that the improvement of labor productivity and the transformation from low productivity industry to high productivity industry could promote economic growth. In 1940, Colin Clark sorted out the long-term statistical data of more than forty countries in his book *Conditions of Economic Progress* and rediscovered the Petty Law. Through international comparison, Clark deduced three stages of economic development in various countries. The first was low development of the economy and society. At this stage, agriculture was the main source of people's income, and due to the low per capita income of agriculture (the Petty Law), the per capita national income of low development society was less. The second was that with the development of the economy, the proportion of manufacturing industry had increased. As the per capita income of manufacturing industry was higher than that of agriculture, the per capita national income of the entire society

---

14. William Petty, *Political Arithmetic* (The Commercial Press, 1978), 19–20.

increased. Finally, with the further development of the economy, tertiary industry, especially the service industry, developed rapidly. As the per capita income of commercial service industry was higher than that of agriculture and industry, the growth of per capita national income of the overall society was further accelerated.

The findings of Petty and Clark's derivation are called the Petty-Clark Law. The significance of this rule is that the increase of per capita national income is explained by the changes of industrial labor productivity and industrial structure, and the regularity between per capita national income (economic growth) and industrial structure transformation is revealed. World economic history suggests that the development of industrial structure is a progressive process from a low level to a high level. In this process, the proportion of the first industry is very large at the beginning, and then gradually decreases. The proportion of secondary and tertiary industries is small at first, and then increases. In the stage of industrialization, the proportion of secondary industry increases rapidly and exceeds primary industry to occupy the dominant position of social production. After reaching a certain height, it begins to slowly decline. At the same time, the proportion of tertiary industry rises rapidly, gradually replacing the dominant position of secondary industry. From the internal structure of the industry, in the process of industrialization, the proportion of light industry is larger, and then the proportion of heavy industry gradually exceeds that of light industry. The evolution of industrial structure is the natural result of the development of productive forces.

Generally speaking, the theory of economic structuralism is in line with the characteristics of large machine production mode. Marx said that "modern industry never regards the existing form of a certain production process as the final form. Therefore, the technological basis of modern industry is revolutionary, while the technological basis of all previous modes of production is essentially conservative. Modern industry, through machines, chemical processes, and other methods, causes the social integration of workers' functions and labor processes to constantly change with the technological basis of production. In this way, it has also continuously revolutionized the division of labor across society, constantly transferring a large number of capital and workers from one production sector to another. Thus the nature of big industry determines the transformation of labor, the change of functions, and the overall mobility of workers."[15] Beginning in the mid-1980s, China's economic structural adjustment theory and macroeconomic analysis method shifted to structural theory. In the economic development strategy formulated by the Thirteenth National Congress of the Communist Party of China and the industrial policies proposed in the Seventh Five-Year Plan, both the quantity balance of industrial structure and the promotion of economic growth by industrial structural transformation were given attention, which reflected the theoretical side of structuralism. It should be said that this transformation was in line with the development trend of world economic theory, and was also basically adapted to the characteristics of China's economic growth stage. From the current situation of China's economic development, in the process of industrialization, it was the objective requirement of

---

15. Marx, *Das Kapital*, vol. 1 (People's Publishing House, 1972), 533–534.

China's economic growth that there be a change in the development mode which only took the growth rate of total output value as the strategic goal, adopting instead the theoretical thinking and development mode that was related to the total growth and structural transformation, which also explained the great development of China's theory in this respect.

2. Comments on the Value Determination of Equilibrium Price Theory in Western Economics

The analysis of the internal relations among demand, supply, and price in Marshall's equilibrium price theory formed the theoretical basis for micro analysis of Western economics. In the tradition of Western economics, natural price, determined by production cost and relative to market price, was always equal to value. So Marshall's equilibrium price also referred to value, and his equilibrium price theory was his theory of value. Chinese academic circles basically held negative views of Marshall's equilibrium price theory. Against the backdrop of the reform practice and theoretical discussion of the combination of China's socialist commodity economy, planned economy, and market regulation in the 1980s, according to the principles of Marxist economics, I offer here an objective evaluation of Marshall's value theory from the perspective of the development and evolution of Western value theory, which is of great significance for the accurate understanding of the equilibrium price theory at the level of market operation.

(1) The Logical Starting Point of Marshall's Value Theory

Marshall's theory of value (the theory of equilibrium price) is characterized by examination of the determination of commodity price (value) from the perspective of market supply and demand. Many theorists believe that Marx explained the relationship between supply and demand from the perspective of value, while Marshall explained value from the relationship between supply and demand, so his theory must be vulgar. In fact, this is a logical starting point or theoretical perspective of scientific research. The key point of Marx's value theory lies in the in-depth analysis of social relations embodied in value, so the logical starting point of this theory is the stipulation of value quality, not the quantitative relationship in the movement of real value price. In *Das Kapital*, Marx demonstrates that the value entity is the abstract human labor condensed in the commodity body, explains that the amount of value depends on the time of social necessary labor, and reveals that the essence of value is not matter, but production relations. In the process of this analysis, Marx abstracts the changes of supply and demand and price fluctuation on many occasions in order to reveal the essence of capitalist production relations in the pure form of value. By contrast, Marshall's theory of value does not study the essential characteristics of production relations, but the phenomenon forms of market relations, and it does not study the essential provisions of value, but the phenomenon forms of value. Therefore, from the logical starting point, Marshall does not focus on the abstract value entity, but on the realistic relationship between market supply and demand and value price movement. It can be seen that Marshall's theoretical perspective is determined by the research goal of Western economics. Starting from the premise of scarcity of resources, Western economics focuses on how to make full, effective use of limited resources in economic activities, so as to better satisfy people's needs and carry out economic analysis to solve the problems of what to produce, how much to produce, when to produce, and for whom to produce. These problems reflect the relationship among production, distribution, exchange, and consumption, which is to further say, the relationship between supply and demand. Under the conditions of the commodity economy, the relationship between supply and demand of a variety of goods and services is shown by price. Therefore, the problem of price mechanism, that is, the internal relationship between price movement and market supply and demand, naturally becomes the logical starting point of economic analysis in Western economics. If the change of market supply and demand can be abstracted from the analysis of pure value entity, then when analyzing the method of price mechanism regulating the allocation of economic resources, focus is solely on the internal relationship between market supply and demand and price movement, because "the nature of commodity value… generally speaking, is expressed in the form of market price or market production price."[16] The characteristic of Marx's value theory lies in digging out the final determinant of value from the market supply-demand relationship, and unifying the labor value theory principle with the real value price movement in theory, which is the essence of Marx's value theory. Therefore, to judge whether Marshall's theory is scientific or not, the key is not to see whether it explains the relationship between supply and demand from the perspective of value or from the relationship between supply and demand, but to see how it analyzes the essential relationship between market supply and demand and price movement, and how to treat the essential relationship between labor and utility in value determination. Admittedly, from the perspective of political economics, Marshall's theory does not involve the value judgment of production relations, so it lacks theoretical tension and logical depth. But if it does not go deep into the level of value entity, this theory can reveal some regularity in describing the relationship between real price movement and market supply and demand changes and the general mechanism of market mechanism, and then it can have scientific value in a certain sense.

(2) Analysis of Supply and Demand in Marshall's Value Theory
There are two main characteristics of Marshall's demand theory: one is to transform demand into demand price; the other is to put forward the concept of demand elasticity. Marshall thought that demand is the satisfaction of people's desire, and desire is satisfied by the utility of goods. Since utility is human's subjective feeling, it cannot be measured directly, so it can only be measured indirectly through the external phenomenon it produces. This external phenomenon refers to the amount of money consumers are willing to pay for a certain amount of goods, that is, the demand price. The demand price is determined by the marginal utility of a certain quantity of goods to the buyer. According to Gossen's law, as marginal utility decreases, so does the marginal demand price. According to the law of diminishing marginal demand price, Marshall lists a demand table, and thus obtains a universal law of demand: the quantity of demand increases

---

16. Marx, *Das Kapital*, vol. 3 (People's Publishing House, 1972), 722.

with the decrease of price and decreases with the increase of price. Since the increase or decrease of demand caused by price fluctuation is determined by the nature of different commodities and the situation of consumers, Marshall further proposed the concept of "demand elasticity," which is used to measure the ratio of increase or decrease of demand caused by a certain proportion of price rise or fall, that is to measure the response of demand to price changes. Marshall's theory transforms demand into demand price and puts forward the concept of demand elasticity, which makes it possible to conduct quantitative analysis on the relationship between demand and price.

Similar to transforming demand into demand price, Marshall also transforms supply into supply price. Supply price refers to the price that must be paid for the efforts and sacrifices needed to produce goods. In this sense, Marshall's concept of "supply" is not only a certain amount of goods in the market or which can be provided to the market, but it also reflects the relationship between production costs and prices. Marshall studied production cost from the perspective of monetary cost and real cost. Real cost refers to the "efforts and sacrifices" to produce a certain amount of goods, while monetary cost refers to the total amount of money that must be paid for these efforts and sacrifices. Money cost can also be called production cost, that is, the supply price of goods.

It is evident from this that Marshall's supply and demand is not simply the quantity of goods that the seller is willing to sell and the buyer is willing to buy. He interprets "supply" as the quantity of goods that producers are willing and able to provide at a certain price, while "demand" refers to the quantity of goods that consumers are willing and able to buy at a certain price, that is to say, supply (quantity) and demand (quantity) are regarded as functions of price. Therefore, his supply-demand relationship not only represents the general market exchange relationship, but also reflects the interaction among the production field, circulation field, and price (value) determination.

(3) Analysis of the Relationship Between Utility and Cost in Marshall's Value Theory

There are two kinds of value theories in Western economics. One is to seek the cause of value from the exchange ratio of two kinds of commodities, such as the theory of supply and demand, the theory of partial equilibrium, and the theory of general equilibrium. In discussing the theory of supply and demand value, which regards the equilibrium ratio or equilibrium price formed by exchange as value, Marx once asked, "Why does the market price just represent such a monetary amount, but not another currency amount? Clearly, the actual internal law of capitalist production cannot be explained by the interaction between supply and demand."[17] The other type involves exploring the source of value from the property itself, such as labor value theory, various utility theory, and production cost theory. The value theory of production cost in this kind of theory is nothing more than the value or price of the production factors that participate in the production

---

17. Marx and Engels, *Complete Works of Marx and Engels*, vol. 25 (People's Publishing House, 1975), 211–212.

of a product to determine its value. If this theory is to be established, it is necessary to affirm the definite value of various factors of production. However, in exploring how the value of various factors of production is determined, it is necessary to also identify the value of various other factors of production that participate in the production of these elements, and with the circular arguments, the problem remained unresolved. Therefore, only from the two aspects of labor and utility can the origin of the value of wealth and goods be explored.

The labor value theory of classical Western economics is analyzed along this line of thought. However, it is difficult to explore the causes of value from the two aspects of labor and utility, namely, how to analyze the relationship between the two in the formation of value and express their respective roles in the same mechanism. Classical economics did not solve this problem. In analyzing the origin of value, attention was only given to labor, while utility was ignored as a natural prerequisite. After the disintegration of the Ricardo school, the value theory of Western economics mainly had two types of biases. One was inheriting the production cost theory in the classical labor value theory, which focused on the supply side, such as John Mill's production cost value theory, and the other was inheriting the early utility theory, which focused on the utility aspect, represented by the marginal utility value theory. The former mainly sought the decisive factors of value from the production field, while the latter mainly sought the causes of value from the circulation field. This continued into the Marshall era. Marshall combined the production cost (supply) and utility (demand) with the function of market equilibrium to form an equilibrium value theory of market supply and demand. On the basis of examining the relationship between supply and demand and between supply and demand and price (value), this theory held that when supply and demand were in equilibrium, the output produced in unit time was the equilibrium quantity of the commodity, and the transaction price of the commodity was the equilibrium price, that is, the market value of the commodity. Some scholars criticized Marshall's equilibrium price theory as the determinism of supply and demand, which was not comprehensive. Since Marshall's concept of supply was related to the cost of production, according to the concept of classical axiology, production cost was nothing more than a derivative form of labor consumption, so the relationship between Marshall's supply and demand was actually the relationship between utility and labor consumption. Marx and Engels offered incisive exposition on the relationship between utility (social demand) and production cost (labor consumption) in value determination. In the history of economic theory, Engels first proposed the relationship between production cost and utility. In his *Critique Outline of Political Economics* (1844), Engels criticized classical British economics and the one-sided views of Say and Malthus. Classical economics emphasized that the cost of production represented real value. Say and others asserted that the real value depended on the effectiveness of the goods to be measured. Engels pointed out, "The value of goods contains two elements, both sides of the dispute insist on separating these two elements, but as we can see, both sides have no result. Value is the relationship between production cost and utility. First of all, value is used to solve the problem of whether certain goods should be produced, that is, whether the utility of the goods can compensate for the production costs. Only after this problem is solved can we talk about the problem of using value to exchange. If the production costs of two goods are equal, then utility is the decisive factor in determining their comparative value."[18] For a long time, there was a view in Chinese economic circles that Engels' principle that "value is the relationship between production cost and utility" was wrong. It was pointed out that the entity (abstract labor) that formed value had nothing to do with utility. A more accurate understanding is that from the abstract level of value entity, it is general human labor that forms value entity, rather than utility (the use value of social needs). But this abstract analysis is based on the premise that general human labor is condensed in products with certain use value. If labor consumption does not form social use value, then this type of labor will not form value. From the development of classical Western value theory, one of the reasons Ricardo's labor value theory was more advanced than Smith's labor value theory was that Ricardo disagreed with Smith's view that useless goods could have exchange value, recognizing that use value was the material premise of exchange value, and that things without utility would not have exchange value.

Theoretical research shows that the social evaluation of value quantification is a dual process. On the one hand, different labor costs must be averaged into standard labor costs, while on the other hand, the social measurement standards of this standard labor consumption are determined by the labor time necessary to produce a certain commodity in the market under the social average production conditions. Marx clearly pointed out in *Das Kapital* that "the nature of the value of commodities asserts itself, its determination not by the labour-time necessary in the case of any individual producer for the production of a certain quantity of commodities, or of some individual commodity, but by the socially necessary labour-time; that is, by the labour-time, required for the production of the socially necessary total quantity of commodity varieties on the market under the existing average conditions of social production."[19] Marx also said, "The market price expresses only the *average amount of social labour* necessary, under the average conditions of production, to supply the market with a certain mass of a certain article. It is calculated upon the whole lot of a commodity of a certain description."[20]

According to Marx and Engels, the process of value determination is as follows:

- Labor input (labor time) = commodity value
- The social general contract (equalization) of input labor amount = social necessary labor time (the social measurement standard of value quantity, i.e. the equivalent basis of exchange of two commodities)

The dual process of social commensuration of input labor amount:

---

18. Marx and Engels, *Complete Works of Marx and Engels*, vol. 1 (People's Publishing House, 1974), 605.
19. Marx, *Das Kapital*, vol. 3 (People's Publishing House, 1972), 722.
20. Marx and Engels, *Selected Works of Marx and Engels*, vol. 2 (People's Publishing House, 2012), 177.

- The average of labor time in the same production department, that is, the average of production conditions in the same commodity production department.
- The average of the labor time for producing a certain kind of commodity in the overall society, that is, whether the labor time consumed in the production of this kind of commodity is consistent with the total amount of labor time necessary for society. In other words, whether society is prepared to exchange other goods with the same amount of labor.

In brief, if labor intends to form value, it must be connected with utility, that is, social demand. Moving beyond the abstract concept to understand the problem from the internal logical relationship between value and use value, there is no doubt about Engels' argument.

According to this analysis, it is possible to make pertinent comments on Marshall's analysis of the relationship between cost and utility. In Marshall's view, cost and utility are two forces that jointly determine price or value, but the effect of the two on the equilibrium price is affected by time. Marshall divided time into three kinds: extremely short or instantaneous time, short-term, and long-term. Associated with this, equilibrium can also be divided into temporary equilibrium, short-term equilibrium, and long-term equilibrium. Marshall believed that in the short run, it was generally the utility (demand) that acted on the equilibrium price. Because the so-called "short-term" meant that the production technology conditions remained unchanged, the equilibrium price at this time generally depended on the actual inventory. But even in the short term, production costs also played an invisible role, because in the case of market demand changes, producers could change the production volume by changing working hours or machine utilization rate to meet market demand, so production volume could still be changed under the same production technology. The change of production quantity naturally drove short-term supply prices to be consistent with normal prices (i.e. value) reflected by the real production cost. In the long run, all kinds of production equipment could be fully adjusted with the change of demand, so the production volume could also be increased or decreased freely. At this time, the price of goods was almost completely determined by the production cost, and demand could only determine the quantity of transactions. In the long-term equilibrium, the price represented by the intersection of demand curve and supply curve was normal price or normal value. It meant that the demand price reflected by the marginal utility of consumption was exactly the same as the supply price reflected by the producer's real production cost after adjusting production. At this time, the quantity of equilibrium price directly depended on the consumption of unit cost under the condition of average normal supply.

There were some reasonable factors in Marshall's analysis of the relationship between supply (cost) and demand (utility) and the formation of equilibrium price. First of all, Marshall's analysis system focused on the supply based on the cost of production, which was an important symbol of his continuation of the value theory of classical British economics. It was more rational than the marginal utility value theory which focused only on marginal utility. In addition, Marshall's theory of supply and demand also gave attention to the role of demand (utility). Even in the long-term equilibrium, the determination of equilibrium point was the result of supply and demand. Due to the interaction between supply and demand, once the market equilibrium was reached, if the market price deviated from the equilibrium price, it would automatically restore the equilibrium point and continue to maintain the equilibrium. This analysis overcame the bias of the classical production cost theory to a certain extent. Further, Marshall's analysis explained quantitatively the internal relationship between production cost, utility, and value determination, and he expressed this relationship in the same mechanism, making it possible to build a theoretical model of value price movement based on the real market and providing a methodological basis for theoretically explaining the resource allocation mechanism of a price centered market mechanism. In fact, the fundamental defect of Marshall's value theory lay not in his analysis of the relationship between demand, supply, and value determination, but in his subjective psychological feelings such as "negative utility" and "forbearance." As mentioned above, Marshall's real production cost included labor and capital. According to the principle that "capital is accumulated labor," it is clear that Marshall put the production cost on labor. But the labor Marshall referred to was not all kinds of work which the laborer was engaged in objectively (i.e. the consumption of laborer's labor force), but the effort and sacrifice that the laborer suffered subjectively in the labor, that is, the "negative utility" of labor, as Jevons calls it. This method of transforming labor into subjective feeling was the connection between Marshall and the marginal utility theory of subjectivism, which also showed that Marshall did not understand the duality of labor producing goods, so he could not scientifically solve the fundamental problem of the essence and substance of value.

PART 3

The Transformation of Mainstream Economic Thought in the People's Republic of China (1990s–2010s)

CHAPTER 11

The Emergence and Development of the Theory of the Socialist Market Economy

11.1 Research on Deng Xiaoping's Theory of Economic System Reform

1. Definition of the Nature of Socialism and the Reform of the Economic System

The combination of the market economy with the basic socialist system to establish a socialist market economic system was an innovative concept in Deng Xiaoping's theoretical system, and it set the goal for the reform of China's overall economic system. In October 1992, the report of the Fourteenth National Congress of the Communist Party of China established the goal of economic system reform, which was to establish and improve the socialist market economic system by adhering to public ownership and distribution according to work as the main body and other economic components and distribution methods as supplements. The establishment of the socialist market economy theory and reform goal was a new starting point for the development of China's economic thought in the 1990s. In November 1993, the Third Plenary Session of the Fourteenth Central Committee of the Communist Party of China adopted the Decision of the Central Committee of the Communist Party of China on Several Issues Concerning the Establishment of a Socialist Market Economic System, which made specific arrangements for the establishment of a socialist market economic system.

In Deng Xiaoping's theory on building socialism with Chinese characteristics, socialist economic system reform thought was an important, creative part of the theory, and it had far-reaching guiding significance in the process of China's economic system reform. The main function of the economic system was to solve the problems of the micro efficiency and macro equilibrium of economic operations through a corresponding decision-making, management, and regulation system, so as to realize the effective allocation of economic resources and the balanced, stable, sustainable growth of the social economy. As a kind of institutional factor, the pattern and content of the economic system were related to certain social production and interest relations. However, fundamentally speaking, the development type and stage of the economic system were determined by productivity and the socio-economic development level. After the founding of the People's Republic of China, there was an ongoing tendency to emphasize the nature of production relations in the understanding of the essence of socialism and the socialist economic system, which seriously affected the scientific nature of ideological understanding and the performance of economic development. On the basis of summing up the historical lessons of China's socialist construction, Deng Xiaoping properly defined the essence of socialism according to the principle of scientific socialism and pointed out that the nature of socialism was to liberate, develop, and eliminate exploitation and polarization for ultimate common prosperity.[21] He said that China's previous understanding of what socialism and Marxism was not entirely clear. Marxism attached great importance to the development of productive forces. As a result, the most fundamental task at the socialist stage was to develop productive forces, and the superiority of socialism was reflected in its higher, faster development of productivity than capitalism.[22] Beginning in the late 1970s, Deng Xiaoping consistently emphasized in a series of expositions that the basic principle of Marxism was the development of productive forces and that the essence, advantage, and future of socialism required the vigorous development of those forces. He also established the basic line of centering on economic construction.

Since China regarded the emancipation and development of productive forces as the criterion for judging the nature of socialism, its understanding of the nature of the economic system and the orientation of reform also underwent revolutionary changes. Deng Xiaoping pointed out that there were two fundamental defects in the previous economic system. One was that the guiding ideology was divorced from the core of developing productive forces, and the other was that in operation, power was too centralized and administrative impact was too strong to manage the economy through economic means. Therefore, in order to liberate and develop productive forces, it was necessary to reform the traditional economic system. In December 1978, Deng Xiaoping pointed out at the Central Working Conference that "at present, the power of China's economic management system is too centralized, and it should be decentralized, systematically and dramatically. Otherwise, it will not foster the full enthusiasm of the state, local governments, enterprises, and individual workers, nor will it be conducive to the implementation of modern economic management and the improvement of labor productivity."[23] After Deng Xiaoping's speech, the Third Plenary Session of the Eleventh Central Committee of the Communist Party of China was held and a decision on the reform of the economic system was made. While there

21. Deng Xiaoping, *Selected Works of Deng Xiaoping*, vol. 3 (People's Publishing House, 1993), 373.

22. Deng Xiaoping, *Selected Works of Deng Xiaoping*, vol. 3 (People's Publishing House, 1993), 63.

23. State Commission for Structural Reform, *Ten Years of China's Economic System Reform* (Economy and Management Publishing House, Reform Press, 1988), 11.

was no complete, specific reform plan at that time, Deng Xiaoping's speech and the Third Plenary Session of the Eleventh Central Committee made it clear that the purpose of China's economic system reform was to develop productive forces, and he stressed that the nation should act according to economic laws. This opened up a proper path for the scientific exploration and the bold practice of economic system reform and facilitated the vigorous development of the reform wave.

On November 26, 1979, Deng Xiaoping, then Vice Premier of the State Council, met in Beijing with Frank Gibney, Vice Chairman of the editorial board of the *Encyclopedia Britannica*, and Lin Daguang, Director of the Institute of East Asian Studies at McGill University in Canada. During the conversation, when Gibney asked whether it was possible to develop some form of market economy within the scope of China's socialist system at some time in the future, Deng Xiaoping replied that it was certainly incorrect to say that the market economy was limited to a capitalist society and the capitalist market economy and that the market economy should not be viewed as something of capitalism, but rather as something that existed as early as in the feudal society, which meant that socialism could develop a market economy as well.[24] On October 23, 1985, when meeting a delegation of American entrepreneurs in Beijing, Deng further expounded on the issue of the socialist market economy, stating that there was no fundamental contradiction between socialism and the market, that the question was what approach would be more conducive to the development of social productive forces, and that China should combine the planned economy with the market economy to further liberate productive forces and accelerate their development.[25] The theoretical significance of Deng Xiaoping's two talks lay in the fact that it shook the traditional notion that the market economy naturally belonged to the category of the basic system of a capitalist society, thus theoretically, conceptually, and politically opening up the way for socialist countries' market-oriented reform. This clearly put forward the idea that the fundamental criterion for judging the merits and demerits of an economic system was to see whether it was conducive to social production, thus setting a scientific, Marxist guiding ideology for the practice of China's economic system reform.

Based on this analysis, the theoretical connotation of Deng Xiaoping's economic system reform thought lay in its deep understanding and creative development of the scientific socialist principle and the productivity standard of historical materialism. The standard of productivity was the basic viewpoint of historical materialism, and the evolution theory of the social form of Marxism was based on the development of productive forces. According to the expositions of Marx and Engels, a socialist society was based on the high development of capitalism, and it was more progressive than the capitalist society and had a higher level of productivity development. Deng Xiaoping accurately grasped the principle of scientific socialism, put it in the context of the experience and lessons of socialist practice in China and the world, precisely pointed out that the basic principle of Marxism and the essence and fundamental task of socialism were to

---

24. Deng Xiaoping, *Selected Works of Deng Xiaoping*, vol. 2 (People's Publishing House, 1994), 236.
25. Deng Xiaoping, *Selected Works of Deng Xiaoping*, vol. 3 (People's Publishing House, 1993), 148.

develop productive forces, and noted that poverty was not part of socialism, but that socialism was instead expected to eradicate poverty. If China did not develop productive forces and improve the people's living standards, it could not claim to be in line with the requirements of socialism. Only by developing social productive forces could it truly present the superiority of the socialist system in practice. To develop productive forces, it could not judge socialist economic relations and the economic system with the abstract principles and utopian models of some metaphysical theories. It was important to abandon the traditional economic system which had proven to be rigid, inefficient, and unfavorable to the development of productive forces. It was necessary to reform the economic system according to the specific economic development situation and the requirements of productivity development to adapt it to and promote the development of social productive forces. It was precisely because of this profound theoretical connotation that Deng Xiaoping's economic system reform theory became a scientific guiding principle leading China's economic system reform practice to break the shackles of various ideas and concepts and embark on a path of socialist market-oriented reform with Chinese characteristics and achieve great things.

The breakthrough of China's economic system reform was its infiltration of market adjustment factors into the unified planned economic system. Throughout the 1980s, the theoretical core of economic system reform was the relationship and combination of planning and the market. In 1979, when meeting Gibney and visitors from other countries, Deng Xiaoping remarked that China practiced mainly a planned economy with a part that was a market economy. In 1985, when meeting a delegation of American entrepreneurs, Deng said, "In the past, we implemented the planned economy, which was certainly a good practice. However, years of experience have shown that practicing this alone will restrain the development of productive forces. We must combine the planned economy with the market economy to further liberate and accelerate the development of productive forces."[26] After this, Deng restated on various occasions that China needed to continue to adhere to the combination of the planned economy and market regulation, which could not be changed. The difference between capitalism and socialism was not that between planning and market. Socialism also had market regulation and capitalism had planned controls. Planning and market were both simply economic means.

In June 1981, the Sixth Plenary Session of the Eleventh Central Committee of the Communist Party of China pointed out that the planned economy should be implemented on the basis of public ownership, with market regulation playing the auxiliary role, and the reform mode of "the planned economy as the main factor and market regulation as the auxiliary" was officially launched. In October 1984, the Third Plenary Session of the Twelfth Central Committee of the Communist Party of China adopted the Decision of the Central Committee of the Communist Party of China on the Reform of Economic System, which put forward the important theory that the socialist economy was a planned commodity economy on the basis of public ownership. In October 1987, the report of the Thirteenth National Congress of the Communist Party of China

---

26. *People's Daily*, October 2, 1985.

pointed out that the system of the socialist planned commodity economy should be an internal unified system of planning and market, and it designed the system reform mode of "the state regulating the market and the market guiding the enterprise." In December 1990, the Seventh Plenary Session of the Thirteenth Central Committee of the Communist Party of China adopted the Proposal of the Central Committee of the Communist Party of China on the Formulation of the Ten-Year Plan for National Economic and Social Development and the Eighth Five-Year Plan. The Proposal pointed out that the basic direction of deepening the reform of economic system was to establish an economic operation mechanism combining a planned economy with market regulation. Therefore, throughout the 1980s, China's economic system reform basically followed Deng Xiaoping's design and was carried out around the combination of planning and the market. It aimed to establish an economic operation and management system that not only embodied the essential characteristics of the socialist mode of production but also conformed to the basic laws of the commodity economy. Deng Xiaoping's reform design for the combination of planning and the market proved to be effective in practice. Theoretically, the idea mainly involved several key contributions, which will be examined below.

(1) A Correct Understanding of the Theory and Practice of the Planned Economy

From 1926, when the Soviet Union issued its first Five-Year Plan, until the 1980s, the planned economy had a history of more than 60 years in socialist countries. China implemented the planned economy from the 1950s to the 1970s. Theoretically speaking, the planned economy was a kind of economic management and operation system based on the public ownership of means of production according to the objective economic law and social demand in the form of a predetermined economic plan aiming to coordinate social interest relations, allocate social economic resources, and organize social production activities. Practice showed that the planned economy had the advantages of unified allocation of resources, centralized use of productive forces, a guarantee of fair social distribution, and reasonable coordination of social interest relations. The reason China's socialist construction could achieve certain development in a relatively short period was related to the long-term implementation of the planned economy. However, many setbacks in China's economic construction, the low efficiency of economic activities, and the huge waste of economic resources were also directly related to the planned economy. This was because for a long time, the understanding and implementation of the planned economy was divorced from actual economic development. People only realized that the planned economy was related to the socialist economy, but they did not further realize that the planned economy was related to a certain social and economic development. Marx's economic operation mode in which production was controlled by social reality was based on the extinction of the commodity economy. Since the commodity economic foundation no longer existed, it was possible to directly calculate the social needs and the labor time of producing various products to meet this need and to directly distribute social labor according to the proportion without the aid of value or exchange value. However, China was a society that did not have a fully developed commodity economy. Its productivity was relatively backward, and its degree of socialization of production was relatively low. Therefore, China did not have the conditions for implementing a highly centralized, unified planned economy. One of the important reasons China's economic development suffered many setbacks in the 1950s to 1970s was that the economic system had not adapted to the actual productive forces, with the mistakes made in planning and decision-making and the non-economy of the means of implementing the plan also playing a part. Deng Xiaoping was keenly aware of the contradiction between the traditional planned economic system and the development of productive forces, and he pointed out that the economic system should be tied to the commodity economy and the law of value, and that planning and the market should be combined. This idea was in line with China's economic reality and the requirements of the development of productive forces.

(2) On the Economic Rationality of the Combination of Planning and Market

Theoretically speaking, planning and the market could not be integrated. The planned economy in the pure sense included all economic activities of the entire society, and the pure market economy was dominated by market supply and demand and the price mechanism. If market regulation was allowed in the planned system, it was not a perfect planned economy, and if planning intervened in the market, it was not a perfect market economy. However, the discussion of the relationship between planning and the market was not confined to theoretical abstraction. Just as there had never been a pure monopoly or complete competition, there had also never been a complete planned economy or a complete market economy in real economic terms. The macro intervention system of Western market economy countries played an important role in ensuring economic stability and sustainable growth. Strengthening national macro-control was regarded as a major change in the capitalist mode of production. In Eastern Europe, some former socialist countries carried out the practice of combining planning with the market. For example, Hungary had long carried out the economic management system mode of "combining planning and the market," and Yugoslavia's autonomous planned management system was basically a system model based on the market mechanism and characterized by value management. Therefore, from a global point of view, the combination of planning and the market had long been a practice. These situations reflected the objective requirements of socialized mass production for economic management and operations. In the 1980s, China's economic system reform centered on the combination of planning and the market conformed to this global development trend. Further analysis shows that this kind of reform was determined by China's current economic situation. The socialist market economy not only reflected the essential characteristics of the socialist mode of production, but also conformed to the basic laws of the market economy. The specific manifestation of this requirement was the combination of planning and the market. Planning and the market were both ways or forms of economic resource allocation. They had certain compatibility and complementarity at the level of economic operations, and their effective combination was an important guarantee for the coordinated, stable, sustainable development of the national economy.

The theory of the socialist market economy came into being at the end of the 1970s. In early 1979, some views on this theory were expressed. That same year, when meeting visitors from other countries, Deng Xiaoping issued a statement on the relationship between the market economy and socialism, and he further expressed this idea in 1985. In October 1987, the Thirteenth National Congress of the Communist Party of China established the reform goal of "the socialist planned commodity economic system," pointing out that the operation of this system should be the internal unity of planning and the market, and that "the scope of action of planning and the market covers all of society." This was a great development in the understanding and practice of the relationship between planning and the market and between socialism and the market economy. After the Thirteenth National Congress of the Communist Party of China, discussion on the socialist market economy was prevalent in theoretical circles. Some scholars clearly put forward that China should adopt the formulation of the market economy to highlight the operation mechanism and resource allocation characteristics of the commodity economy. However, at the end of the 1980s, the economic reform turned into the period of governance and rectification, and the discussion on "marketization" was less active due to the lack of a corresponding political and economic environment.

In October 1990, the State Economic Restructuring Commission organized the compilation of Foreign Debates and Practices on the Issue of Planning and the Market and Comments on the Relationship between China's Planning and the Market, which was submitted to Jiang Zemin, General Secretary of the CPC Central Committee, and Li Peng, Premier of the State Council, as reference materials. The report introduced the great debate on the mode of resource allocation in Western economic circles in the 1930s. The party represented by Fred M. Taylor, President of the American Economic Association, supported the idea of central planning and allocation of resources put forward by Italian economist Vilfredo Pareto in the early 20th century, while Friedrich Hayek, the leader of the Austrian school of economics, believed that the planned economy was not feasible in practice. This required listing millions of equations on the basis of millions of data points. By the time the equations were solved, the information on which they were based was outdated. Drawing on the opinions of the experts in other countries, the report believed that it was feasible to link up the planning mechanism with the market mechanism on the premise of a clear definition, and it was also reasonable from the perspective of the internal requirements and objective trends of economic development. The main purpose of the report was to clarify that the planned economy and the market economy were only two different means of resource allocation. The debate took place before the emergence of socialism, so there was no inevitable social attribute. The report was affirmed by the main leaders of the Central Committee at that time and provided a reference for top-level decision-making at that time.[27]

In the spring of 1992, Deng Xiaoping toured the South and delivered a series of talks. One of the most important ideas he expressed was the relationship between socialism and the market economy. He said that emphasizing planning or the market was not an essential difference between

---

27. *China Newsweek*, no. 32 (2012). In 1992, the report's author Jiang Chunze published the report in the second issue of *Reform* with the title of "Historical Background and Contemporary Practice of the Debate Between Planning and Market in the World."

socialism and capitalism. The planned economy was not equal to socialism, and capitalism also had plans, while the market economy was not equal to capitalism, and socialism also had a market. Planning and the market were both economic means.[28] After the publication of Deng Xiaoping's speech made during his visits to the southern region, the "socialist market economy" became a hot topic in the field of economic theory. In addition, after thirteen years of reform, the factors of the market economy were greatly developed. The concepts of commodity and the market, opening and competition, incentive and efficiency, and democracy and the legal system had been formed in Chinese society. Market oriented reform had penetrated into the economic life of the entire society and become an irresistible, irreversible historical trend. The establishment of the goal of the socialist market economic reform had mature conditions in which to expand.

In October 1992, the Fourteenth CPC National Congress was held. Jiang Zemin pointed out in the report to the Fourteenth National Congress of the Communist Party of China that the goal of the reform of the economic system was to establish and improve the socialist market economic system on the basis of adhering to public ownership and distribution according to work as the main body and other economic components and distribution methods as supplements. On October 18, the resolution of the Fourteenth National Congress of the Communist Party of China made it clear that "the goal of China's economic system reform is to establish a socialist market economic system," marking the formal establishment of the reform goal of the socialist market economy throughout the party.

The establishment of the socialist market economic thought and reform goal indicated that China's reform had entered a new stage. The reform was bound to greatly promote the development of productive forces and take the opportunity of connecting with international standards to make China a mainstream in world development. In theory, the socialist market economy was a kind of historical institutional innovation. It was not only a transition in the level of economic operation, but also a profound change in production relations, concept forms, and even the property rights system. In order to make this historical system innovation successful, it was important to have an accurate understanding of some problems in theory, which put forward new requirements for the development of socialist political economics.

Throughout the reform of China's economic system in the late 20th century, from "the planned economy as the main factor with market regulation as the supplement" to "the combination of the planned economy and market regulation," and finally to "the socialist market economy," there was a clear market-oriented reform track. This reform process was the realistic embodiment of Deng Xiaoping's economic system reform thought and reflected its theoretical guiding significance and practical function. New Western institutional economics regarded institutional factors as important endogenous variables affecting resource allocation and economic performance, which was particularly important for China. Due to the leapfrog development of economic history and the historical dislocation of the economic system, the foundation of China's economic development was quite different from that developed of Western countries. The industrialization of developed

---

28. Deng Xiaoping, *Selected Works of Deng Xiaoping*, vol. 3 (People's Publishing House, 1993), 373.

countries occurred on the basis of the market economy system. Therefore, their industrialization appeared as economic growth marked by gross growth and structural transformation. However, China had never formed a unified, perfect market system, and the social economy had not been able to realize marketization. In addition to the long-term implementation of the administrative planned economy, its economic development was subject to serious institutional obstacles. In this context, China's industrialization process was not only manifested in total growth and structural transformation, but also in system reform and innovation. Compared with the adjustment of marginal increment, it was more important to improve the conditions of institutional supply for economic development. This was a remarkable feature of the economic development of China and other late developing industrialized countries. In the late 20th century, the ideological and practical development of China's economic system reform showed people's understanding and evolution of these characteristics and demonstrated that with the promotion of system reform and the deepening of economic marketization, China's economy had entered a period of accelerated growth. It was true that the establishment of the socialist market economic system would be a difficult, long-term process due to the contradictions involving a series of systems, concepts, and interests, but this was certainly the trend of social development, and it fundamentally determined whether China's economy could achieve modernization.

2. The Response of Theorists to Deng Xiaoping's Southern Talks

The publication of Deng Xiaoping's Southern Talks invited broad reactions in the field of economic theory. Shanghai *Wenhui Daily* published a commentator's article on the establishment of the socialist market economy on July 15, 1992, pointing out that Deng Xiaoping had held many discussions on the relationship between planning and the market and stressed the need to attach importance to and make use of the market economy. The Southern Talks fundamentally denied the traditional idea that planning and the market were the essential attributes of socialism and capitalism. Deng Xiaoping's views not only enriched and developed the theory of building socialism with Chinese characteristics, but were also a powerful spiritual force for further emancipating cadres and the masses.

Under the traditional system, the planned economy had been regarded as the only way to realize socialism, which was the most basic, most essential feature of socialism, while ignoring the various drawbacks of the economic system which completely depended on planned instructions. After putting forward "market orientation" in the reform, the negative effects brought about by the spontaneity of the market were often all that were observed, while the positive role of the market in stimulating enterprise competition and promoting economic development went unnoticed. In particular, the fact that the market was also a way of allocating resources and its promoting role in optimizing the allocation of resources were ignored. Obviously, this was a one-sided understanding.

Many facts indicated that the market was an effective way to allocate resources and provide incentives. It allocated scarce resources to the links that could create the best benefits through competition and price leverage and brought pressure and motivation to enterprises. Moreover, the response of the market to various signals was also sensitive and rapid. The information structure under the traditional system was a vertical structure from top to bottom or from bottom to top. The administrative organs gave orders to the enterprises, and the enterprises reported the production situation to the administrative organs and put forward various requirements. This type of information transmission came at a high cost and was often untrue. The information structure in the market economy was horizontal. The information transmission between enterprises was carried out through the price mechanism. Price fluctuation was the indicator of production activities and purchase and sales activities. Enterprises could produce based on social requirements. The key reason market coordination resource allocation was more effective was that the market connected the information system with the incentive system. In the case of clear property rights, each independent participant of the social economy, be it a natural or legal entity, would balance their own interests, enter into contracts with each other, and coordinate their actions, so as to make the most effective use of resources and maximize social utility. It was because of these advantages that people in socialist countries increasingly recognized the positive role of the market in economic development. The previous one-sided understanding and prejudice of the market was gradually abandoned.[29]

Many theorists discussed the deepening of China's economic reform and economic theory from the perspective of eliminating the shackles of defining its nature in terms of "capitalism" or "socialism." Some pointed out that the issue of "capitalism" or "socialism" in Reform and Opening Up puzzled China's thinking, fettered its hands and feet, and restricted it in speeding up the pace of Reform and Opening Up. With a reform measure, it was important not judge in terms of whether its nature was "capitalist" or "socialist," focusing instead on whether it was conducive to the development of social productive forces and to the enhancement of China's overall national strength and the improvement of people's living standards. Those who advocated discussing the nature of the reform being "socialist" or "capitalist" were actually skeptical, dissatisfied, or even opposed to Reform and Opening Up.[30]

Some scholars questioned the qualitative standard of the social system. They thought that the qualitative standard of the social system was to decide on the nature of the social system being "socialist" or "capitalist." If it was "capitalist," it was not feasible, even if it could promote the development of productive forces. For example, the problems of planning and the market were originally the forms and methods used to adjust the allocation of resources, without the attributes of the social system. In insisting on defining planning as socialist and the market as capitalist, China could not establish a planned commodity economic system. For example, the introduction of foreign capital and the establishment of foreign-funded enterprises had the attribute of the social system, but all of them promoted the development of productivity, enhanced China's

---

29. Commentator in *Wenhui Daily*, "Establishing Socialist Market Economy," *Wenhui Daily*, July 15, 1992.

30. Lin Ling et al., "On the Issue of 'Capitalism' or 'Socialism' in the Reform and Opening Up," *Reform*, no. 4 (1992).

economic strength, and improved the people's living standards. Although these reforms were categorized as "capitalist," they were desirable. Throughout the reform, most of the measures did not have the attributes of the social system, so it was very reasonable for Deng Xiaoping to disapprove of the categorization of social systems as "socialism" and "capitalism."[31]

Theorists also put forward new opinions on the debate on the reform of market orientation. Many scholars pointed out that since the traditional system excluded the market and market mechanisms and restricted the development of productive forces, the reform aimed to give full play to the role of market mechanism, expand the scope and proportion of market regulation, activate the national economy with the help of market forces, and liberate productive forces and develop productive forces. At the same time, in order to invigorate the overall national economy and ensure its stable, coordinated, efficient development, the reform of market orientation in socialist countries needed to be combined with planning guidance and macro-control. In short, market-oriented reform required a real revolution in the traditional planning system and work. With the proposition of the theory of the socialist market economy and the completion of China's economic system reform, the goal of China's economic system reform was finally clear. Only by affirming that the socialist economy was also a kind of market economy could China's economy completely escape its isolation, be open to the outside world in every aspect, and participate in international competition.[32]

Some held that the debate over the issue of the market economy was essentially a dispute between persisting in reforming the old system and maintaining it. The market economy was the market-oriented economy, or relying on the market-oriented economy to allocate resources. This kind of economy itself did not have the attribute of "capitalism" or "socialism." It was based on public ownership and carried out under socialist conditions, which was the socialist market economy. When combined with capitalism based on private ownership, it was a capitalist market economy. The relationship between the market economy and the socialist market economy was that between the general and the specific. Since China was engaged in the socialist market economy, the general practice of the market economy could be boldly adopted. It was important not to understand that the general way of adopting the market economy was to engage in capitalism. If the reform did not take the market economy as the goal, it could only be a repair of the old system.[33]

Some said that the essence of a socialist country's reform was to replace the planned economy with the market economy. Those who opposed the establishment of the market economy as the goal of China's reform put forward some objections, mainly 1) it was a universally accepted rule that the planned economy was equal to socialism, and the market economy was equal to

31. Fang Sheng, "On the Issue of 'Capitalism' or 'Socialism,'" in *Cross-century Choice* (Shanghai People's Publishing House, 1992).

32. Dong Fuzhi, "On the Debate in Reform and Opening Up," *Reform*, no. 3 (1992).

33. Zhang Zhuoyuan, "Trilogy of China's Economic Reform Theory: Commodity Economy Theory, Market Orientation Theory, and Market Economy Theory," in *Cross-century Choice* (Shanghai People's Publishing House, 1992).

capitalism, 2) the implementation of the market economy meant that the economy was dominated by blind market forces, leading to "anarchy of production," and 3) the law of value would lead to polarization between the rich and the poor. None of those statements were correct, and they were denied or revised in practice, and new concepts were accepted in their place. However, it was merely the common prejudice of "dogmatic socialists" and "dogmatic anti-socialists" that "the market economy equals capitalism and the planned economy equals socialism." The difference between the socialist and the capitalist market economy lay in the difference of ownership basis. Further, the planned allocation of resources could not guarantee economic development without crisis. In contrast, with the improved market supplemented with planned guidance, China could reduce economic fluctuation and avoid serious crisis. And finally, the law of value would lead to an income gap between people with different resource endowments, but provided that China paid attention to the equality of initial distribution, adopted progressive income tax, high estate tax, and other tax measures, and took welfare measures for the low-income class, polarization could be prevented.[34]

3. The Establishment of the Target Model of Economic System Reform

What kind of target model China's economic system reform would set was a major issue concerning the overall situation of socialist modernization construction. The key to this issue was to correctly understand and deal with the relationship between planning and the market. The Twelfth National Congress of the Communist Party of China (CPC) proposed that the planned economy should be given priority, supplemented by market regulation. The Third Plenary Session of the Twelfth CPC Central Committee pointed out that commodity economy was an insurmountable stage in the development of the socialist economy, and China's socialist economy was a planned commodity economy based on public ownership. The Thirteenth CPC National Congress proposed that the system of the socialist planned commodity economy should be the internal unity of planning and the market. After the Fourth Plenary Session of the Thirteenth CPC Central Committee, it was proposed that an economic system and operation mechanism that combined the planned economy with market regulation be established to adapt to the development of the planned commodity economy. In particular, Deng Xiaoping's key speech at the beginning of 1992 further pointed out that the planned economy was not equal to socialism, as capitalism also had plans, and that market economy was not equal to capitalism, as socialism also had a market. He noted that planning and the market were both economic means, and that an emphasis on planning or the market was not the essential difference between socialism and capitalism. This conclusion fundamentally lifted the ideological shackles of taking the planned economy and the market economy as the category of the basic social system and made a major breakthrough in China's understanding of the relationship between planning and the market. China carried out

---

34. Xiao Liang, "Market Economy: The Best Choice for Reform," in *Cross-century Choice* (Shanghai People's Publishing House, 1992).

extensive, in-depth studies on the relationship between socialism and the market economy and the direction and goal of socialist economic system reform, and it put forward a positive point of view.[35] Practice proved that if China's economy was to optimize its structure, improve its efficiency, accelerate its development, and participate in international competition, it should continue to strengthen the role of the market mechanism. In line with the development of practice and the deepening of understanding, the Fourteenth National Congress of the Communist Party of China clearly pointed out that the goal of China's economic system reform was to establish a socialist market economic system, so as to further liberate and develop productive forces.

The report of the Fourteenth National Congress of the Communist Party of China pointed out that the socialist market economic system was combined with the basic socialist system. In the ownership structure, public ownership, including the economy owned by the people and collective ownership, was the main body, supplemented by the individual economy, private economy, and foreign capital economy. A variety of economic components could develop together for a long period. Different economic components could also voluntarily carry out various forms of joint operations. State owned enterprises, collective enterprises, and other enterprises entered the market, with state-owned enterprises playing the leading role through competition on an equal footing. In the distribution system, distribution according to work was the main body, and other distribution methods were complementary, giving consideration to efficiency and fairness. The use of various regulatory means, including the market, could not only encourage the advance, enhance efficiency, and reasonably widen the income gap, but could also prevent polarization and gradually realize common prosperity. In terms of macro-control, socialist countries can combine the people's current interests with long-term interests, local interests, and overall interests and make better use of the advantages of planning and the market. National planning was one of the key means of macro-control. In order to update the concept of planning and improve the planning method, the key point was to reasonably determine the strategic objectives of national economic and social development, effectively manage economic development predictions, total control, major structure, and productivity layout planning, concentrate necessary financial and material resources for key construction, and make integrated use of economic leverage to promote better, faster economic development.

In September 1997, the report of the Fifteenth National Congress of the Communist Party of China stated that the construction of the socialist economy with Chinese characteristics aimed to develop the market economy under socialist conditions and constantly liberate and develop

35. Xue Muqiao, "On Socialist Market Economy," in *Famous Scholars on Socialist Market Economy* (People's Publishing House, 1992); Dong Fuzhi, "On Market and Socialist Market Economy," *Famous Scholars on Socialist Market Economy* (People's Publishing House, 1992); Wu Jinglian, "Some Thoughts on Socialist Market Economy," *China's Industrial Economy Research*, no. 6 (1992); Wu Jinglian, "On the Establishment of the Term 'Socialist Market Economy,'" *Finance and Trade Economy*, no. 7 (1992); Wang Shu, "Socialist Economic Reform Should Be Market-oriented," *Reform Overview*, no. 3 (1992); Yu Zuyao, "On Economic Marketization and Modernization," *Finance and Trade Economy*, no. 8 (1992); Yu Guangyuan, "Modern Market Economy Is the Key," *Methods*, no. 6 (1992).

productive forces. It was necessary to adhere to and improve the basic economic system with socialist public ownership as the main body and the common development of various ownership economies. It was likewise important to adhere to and improve the socialist market economic system so that the market could play a fundamental role in resource allocation under the state's macro-control, and to adhere to and improve the various distribution methods with distribution according to work as the main body, allowing some regions and some people to become wealthy first and propel the rest forward. China needed to adhere to and improve opening up and actively participate in international economic cooperation and competition to ensure the sustained, rapid, and healthy development of the national economy and allow the people to share the fruits of economic prosperity.

11.2 Discussions on the Theory of the Socialist Market Economy

1. The Market Economy, the Commodity Economy, and the Planned Economy

In 1992 and the years following, research on the socialist market economy in China's economic and ideological circles boomed, creating a scene of theoretical research and reform practice that constituted an important stage in the expansion of research and the transformation of an academic style of modern, contemporary economic thought in China.

In the field of comprehensive economic thought historiography, there were several understandings. As an economic category, the market economy could not be equated with the commodity exchange of commodity producers, nor could it be equated with the commodity economy. The market economy was a category of dynamic development and a process of adapting to the development of contemporary social productive forces. The connotation of the market economy included two aspects: the marketization of the economy and the modernization of the market. Economic marketization meant that the market covered the entire national economy, and the guiding role of the market mechanism pervaded microeconomics and the macroeconomy. Market modernization referred to the modernization, scientization, and standardization of market organization, operation planning, operation subject, management method, operation means, and market facilities. Economic marketization and market modernization were interrelated, restricted, and inseparable from each other. The market economy, or the market-oriented economy, reflected a kind of economic operation pattern based on and dominated by market regulation. The essence of the market economy was to allocate the resources and productivity of the entire society through the laws of supply and demand and value. The market economy was a kind of economic management system or economic regulation mode, and there was no inevitable connection between the market economy and ownership of the means of production and the economic system. The market economy was an economic form that included commodity production, commodity exchange, and currency circulation for the purpose of direct exchange. Regardless of the difference between capitalism and socialism, the market economy could be defined as the whole of interrelated production departments in a given political geographical region, which emphasized the market as an important feature. When referring to the national economy, it was a generalization of the social economy at the national level, which was manifested in the combination of the market, government, and other non-market parts within the scope of a country to form a specific sum of various parts of the national economy. In theory, the market economy was a form of self-realization of the commodity economy. In practice, the market economy was a means of resource allocation.[36]

Because Chinese economists were used to the concept of the commodity economy in Marx's *Das Kapital*, it was necessary to analyze the relationship between the market economy and the commodity economy when studying the concept of the market economy. In the discussion on the relationship between the market economy and the commodity economy, it was generally believed that there were differences and connections between the market and commodity economies. First of all, the market and commodity economies were closely linked. The market economy was categorized as a commodity economy, and the commodity economy was the basis of the market economy. The commodity economy, from the most abstract level, was the exchange economy formed on the basis of the social division of labor. The understanding of commodity and the commodity economy began with commodity exchange. Without exchange, commodity and the commodity economy were out of the question, and the sum of exchange relations was the market. In Marxist economics, the market had always been linked with the commodity economy. If the market economy was separated from the commodity economy, it was necessary to deny the commodity economy itself. Logically speaking, since the market was categorized as a commodity economy and the performance of the social division of labor, then the market economy was naturally categorized as a commodity economy and the performance of the social division of labor. Therefore, the market and commodity economies were inseparable. Some scholars further distinguished the commodity economy from the market economy, pointing out that "the commodity economy" was a concept drawn from a Russian word commonly used in Soviet works. Since China's socialist political economics was mainly introduced from the Soviet Union, "the commodity economy" had also become a commonly used phrase in China. "The market economy" was a popular word in the early 20th century, and its popularity was related to the deepening of economic research. Neoclassical economics, developed at the end of the 19th century and the beginning of the 20th century, had grasped the core problem of the operation of the economic system—the allocation of scarce resources. It analyzed how the market economy

---

36. Liu Shibai, "On Socialist Market Economy," *Economist*, no. 5 (1992); Wang Jue, "Some Understanding of Market Economy," *Yangcheng Evening News*, November 11, 1992; He Liancheng, "Theoretical Thinking on Market Economy," *Guangming Daily*, August 1, 1992; Wu Jinglian, "Only the Realization of Market-oriented Reform can Revitalize China," *Hebei Daily*, September 23, 1992; Tong Dalin, "Speeding up the Pace of the Modern Market Economy," *Modernization*, no. 7 (1992); Liu Guoguang, "Building a Socialist Market Economy," *China Business Daily*, June 6, 1992; Yu Guangyuan, "Building a Socialist Market Economy," *Economic Reference Daily*, July 19, 1992; Zhang Chaozun, et al., "On the Socialist Market Economy," *Chinese Social Sciences*, no. 4 (1992); Fan Hengshan, "On the Construction of a Socialist Market Economic System," *Guangming Daily*, August 8, 1992.

could realize the effective allocation of resources through the formation mechanism of balanced prices and the sensitive response of enterprises to price signals. Since all developed commodity economies allocated resources through the market mechanism, the economic forms of "the monetary economy" and "the commodity economy" were called "the market economy" according to their resource allocation mode.[37]

In the first half of the 1990s, some theorists examined the correspondence between the market economy and the planned economy and discussed the relationship between the two economic systems from the aspects of economic operations, resource allocation, and macro regulation. Some thought that developing the socialist market economy did not mean rejecting the planned economy, but instead provided a new objective basis and conditions for the accurate, scientific implementation of the planned economy. It was necessary to adhere to planned regulation, organically combine planned regulation and market regulation, and give full play to the advantages of the two kinds of regulation, so as to promote the rapid development of the national economy. The market economy and the planned economy had a unified objective basis, evident in the fact that 1) the market economy under the condition of socialized mass production also required the implementation of planning, 2) the market and planned economies could be unified with the market as the joint part, with the market economy taking the market as the economic environment and forming the operation order by the market regulation mechanism, while the planned economy would not only take the change of market supply and demand as the planning basis, but also take the market as the intermediary, and 3) the market economy and planned economies could progress toward the same goal. The goal of market economy aimed to maximize profits, while the goal of planned economy was to exchange more products with less investment and maximize added value.[38]

2. The Characteristics of Socialist Market Economy System

In the ideological and theoretical environment of the early 1990s, linking the market economy with the economic system and even the social system was still a common practice. It was believed

---

37. Xiao Liang, "On the Problems of the Socialist Market Economy," in *Theory and Practice of Socialist Market Economy* (China Financial and Economic Publishing House, 1992); Xiao Zhuoji, "Adhering to the Market Economy and the Developing Market Economy," in *Theory and Practice of Socialist Market Economy* (China Financial and Economic Publishing House, 1992); Liu Guoguang, "Several Issues on the Theory of the Socialist Market Economy," *Economic Research*, no. 7 (1992); Wang Jianyou, "A Summary of the National Symposium on Socialist Market Economy Theory," *Economics Trends*, no. 3 (1994); He Liancheng, "A Brief Discussion on China's Socialist Market Economy," *Humanities*, no. 6 (1992); Zhang Shuguang, *China's Economics* (Shanghai People's Publishing House, 1995); Research Group of Macroeconomic Research Institute of State Planning Commission, "Basic Connotation and Main Characteristics of the Socialist Market Economy," *Macroeconomic Research*, no. 12 (1998).

38. Xiao Liang, "China's Economic Research in 1993: Hot Issues, Debates, and Progress," in *China Economic Science Yearbook* (1994) (China Statistics Press, 1994); Xiao Yu, "A Summary of the Symposium on the Operation Law of the Socialist Market Economy," *Economics Trends*, no. 11 (1995); Sheng Hong, *China's Economics* (Shanghai People's Publishing House, 1996).

that the market economy was a conventional concept, and it entailed not only the method of resource allocation, but also an economic system. The reform of China's economic system could not copy Western market economies, and the economic theory guiding the reform of the socialist economic system should not apply the category of the market economy, which had a specific meaning. Western economic works, important literature, news media, and political figures generally connected the market economy with private ownership and even capitalism. In the history of economic thought, the term "market economy" had been put forward and popularized as a concept opposite to socialism or the planned economy. In some former socialist developed countries, there were leaders who adhered to Marxism and socialism who opposed the implementation of the market economy, while the West encouraged and supported socialist countries to carry out the market economy in their peaceful evolution. Some former socialist countries that turned to the market economy eventually deviated from socialism, and their social economy tended to deteriorate.[39]

Around 1992, most economists had accepted and adopted the concept of the socialist market economy. Different analysis of the view that market economy was equivalent to capitalism were proposed, and it was generally held that some Western scholars in fact equated the market economy with capitalism. Some Western documents regarded countries with central planning as socialist countries and countries with a market economy as capitalist countries, in terms of economic classification. However, allowing research to proceed from the concept and act according to the Western definition was not a correct approach. Because the concept was still developing, the content could be changed. For example, in the beginning, China regarded commodity, currency, capital profit, and capital appreciation as the exclusive property of capitalism, but they were now being used to serve socialism. In the early 1980s, some scholars did not allow the use of the concept of the commodity economy, but it had now become an important category in the socialist part of political economics. What's more, Western scholars did not all regard the planned economy and the market economy as institutional concepts, with some understanding them as a mode of resource allocation instead.[40]

---

39. *Heilongjiang Daily* Publishing, *Famous Economists on Socialist Market Economy* (Heilongjiang Education Press, 1992); Jiang Xuemo, "Several Controversial Theoretical Issues in the Socialist Market Economy," *Social Science Front*, no. 1 (1994); Wei Xinghua, "Response to 'Discussion on Planning and the Market as a Mode of Resource Allocation,'" *Chinese Social Sciences*, no. 3 (1992); Yue Fubin, "Understanding of the Commodity Economy, the Market Economy, and the Planned Economy," *Economic Research Reference*, no. 84 (1992); Hong Yinxing, "Theory of the Modern Market Economy and Construction of the Socialist Market Economic System," *Economy Review*, no. 6 (1998).

40. Ri Shan, *Distinguished Scholars of the Socialist Market* (People's Publishing House, 1992); Wu Jinglian, *The Road to Market Economy* (Beijing University of Technology Press, 1992); Yu Guangyuan, *Theory and Practice of Socialist Market Economy* (China Finance and Economics Press, 1992); He Liancheng, *The Theory and Practice of China's Market Economy* (Northwest University Press, 1992); Wang Qinggong and Fan Yuejin, "On the Meaning, Basic Characteristics, and Functions of the Market Economy," *Journal of Liaocheng Normal University* (Social Science Edition), no. 3 (1993); Zhang Wenmin et al., *The Great Debate on China's Economy* (Economy and Management Publishing House, 1996).

By the end of the 1990s, scholars who had insisted on the basic attribute of the market economy as a social and economic system had changed their views. The key was to change the definition of the market economy. Traditionally, there were several definitions of the market economy in China, which included 1) abandoning the planned economy and completely implementing the market economy to engage in capitalism, 2) the notion that the market economy was an economy based on private ownership and spontaneously regulated by the market, which was also the general formulation of Western countries, and 3) the idea that in the public ownership economy, the market's self-adjustment completely without planning was an auxiliary part complementary to the market economy. According to these definitions, a logical conclusion was that the market economy was a capitalist economic system. However, with the deepening of theoretical research and the promotion of market-oriented reform, especially after the Fifteenth CPC National Congress, the public's thinking underwent profound changes. By the end of the 1990s, theoretical circles had generally accepted the view that the market economy and capitalism were separate and defined as a mode of resource allocation. Scholars who insisted that the market economy referred to the social system also agreed that the socialist market economy implemented in China was different from the traditional definition. It referred to the market economy under socialist conditions, that is, the market economy combined with the socialist system. The purpose of implementing this system was to allocate resources effectively and develop productivity better and faster.[41]

This issue was a theoretical conundrum. In fact, the relationship between socialist public ownership and the commodity economy had not been fundamentally resolved, and in practice, the reform raised the issue of the relationship between socialist public ownership and the market economy. The essence of the two problems was the same, and different opinions were put forward by theoretical circles. Based on the discussion and research at that time, the general opinion was that according to the most essential interest relationship, public ownership was a non-commodity relationship, which was in contradiction with the market economy. It was mainly manifested in the contradiction between the equal amount of labor exchange on the basis of public ownership and the equivalent exchange relationship under market conditions, but it did not deny that the two could be combined in the operation of the socialist economy. It was necessary to establish the equivalent exchange relationship between enterprises by pushing enterprises to the market, and to extract the differential income of some enterprises through the intermediary of a national income distribution policy, so as to ensure the realization of an equal labor exchange relationship. On the premise of recognizing public ownership, by defining the property right boundary of

41. Wang Jianyou, "A Summary of the National Symposium on the Socialist Market Economic Theory," *Economics Trends*, no. 3 (1994); Chen Zongsheng et al., *Research on the Marketization Process of China's Economic System* (Shanghai People's Publishing House, 1999); Li Tieying, "The Formation and Major Breakthrough of the Socialist Market Economy Theory," *Economic Research*, no. 3 (1999); Lin Yifu, "A Review of China's Economic Research in 1999," *Economic Research*, no. 11 (2000); Wu Shuqing, "The New Definition of the Socialist Market Economy at the Fourteenth CPC Conference Is of Great Significance," *Observer*, no. 42 (1999); Tang Zaixin, "On the Distribution Mode of the Socialist Market Economy," *Economist*, no. 2 (1997).

public ownership, that is, on the premise that state-owned assets were exercised by the state on behalf of all the people in the country, the ultimate ownership of state-owned assets was separated from that of a legal entity, and the right of asset management and supervision was separated from the right of operation, so that enterprises could directly possess and use these assets for production and operation and obtain corresponding income. Some doubted whether a market economy could be established on the basis of public ownership. They believed that single public ownership excluded the market, and it was impossible to develop a real market relationship on the basis of single public ownership, let alone establish a market economy.[42]

3. The Law of Operation and the Basic Framework of the Socialist Market Economy

In May 1995, the Chinese Society for the Systematic Study of Socialist Economic Laws conducted a seminar in Yinchuan to discuss the law of socialist social and economic operations, focusing on the relationship between the general laws of the market economy and the special laws of socialism. One approach involved understanding the system and characteristics of the socialist market economy from the perspective of combining general laws with special laws. To establish the socialist market economy was to combine the general laws of the market economy with the special laws of socialism. Deng Xiaoping's notion of "emancipation of productive forces, development of productive forces, elimination of exploitation, elimination of polarization, and ultimately achieving common prosperity" was proposed as a generalization of the basic socialist economic law, because these thoughts expounded on the task, purpose, and means of socialism. Some commentators concluded that both the capitalist market economy and the socialist market economy were market economies transformed by the basic economic system, and the market economy adapted to the requirements of the basic economic system. The essence of this type of transformation and deformation was the combination of the general interest relationship reflected in the market economy and special interest relationship reflecting the essence of the system. Only when the two kinds of interests were combined could the market economy play its proper role in resource allocation.[43]

---

42. Zhao Erlie, "Establishing a New Market Economic System with Public Ownership as the Main Body," *Finance and Trade Economy*, no. 8 (1992); Xiang Huaicheng et al., *China's Market Economy and Macro-control* (China Financial and Economic Publishing House, 1993); Wei Xinghua, "Review and Analysis of Economic Theory and Practice Development in the Past 20 Years of Reform," *Economics Trends*, no. 12 (1998); Research Group of the Macroeconomic Research Institute of State Planning Commission, "Basic Connotation and Main Characteristics of the Socialist Market Economy," *Macro-economy*, no. 12 (1998); Liao Yuanhe, "The Relationship Between the Public Ownership System and the Market Economy," *Journal of the Graduate School of the Chinese Academy of Social Sciences*, no. 3 (1993); Wei Jie and Zhang Yu, "The Market Economy and Public Ownership Reform," *Economic Research*, no. 3 (1993); Fan Gang, "On the Development of the Market Economy and the Reform of Property Rights Relations," *Reform*, no. 1 (1993); Liu Chunxu, "A Preliminary Analysis of Property Rights in the Public Ownership Economy." *Journal of Peking University (Philosophy and Social Edition)*, no. 4 (1993).

43. Xiao Yu, "A Summary of the Symposium on the Operation Law of the Socialist Market Economy," *Economics Trends*, no. 11 (1995).

It is worth pointing out that the research on the system of the socialist economic law shifted from the previous study on the system of the basic socialist economic law to the study of the relationship between the law of the market economy and the basic law of socialism, attempting to explain the similarities between the market economy and socialism from the perspective of the economic law. The effect of this kind of research was mainly seen in the aspect of ideology, in that it helped to popularize the concept of the market economy.

The discussion on the basic framework of the socialist market economic system was relatively broad, moving from the level of economic operations, from the level of production relations and ownership, and from the level of the social system, which also reflected the lack of paradigm agreement and "academic community" norms in China's economic thought and theoretical research. The general understanding discussed at that time held that the main frame of the socialist market economy involved the ownership structure and modern enterprise system, price formation mechanism and the market system, government function and the macro-control system, and the income distribution system and the social security system. Determined by this main frame, the direction of China's economic system reform was to establish an ownership structure suitable for the socialist market economy, a modern enterprise system adapted to the socialist market economy, a price system and a market system adapted to the socialist market economy, a macro-control system adapted to the socialist market economy, and a socialist market-oriented system. The establishment of the social security system aimed to adapt to the socialist market economy, while the establishment of a complete legal system aimed to adapt to the socialist market economy. There were three basic structures of China's market economy. First, based on the system of independent enterprises, enterprises were independent entities (natural persons and legal entities) that operated independently and were responsible for their own profits and losses, and they competed equally in the market. Second, competitive markets were not only the places where they acted, but also their means of contact, and the price formed by competition was the basic parameter of this economic system. Third, as the representative of society, the government regulated market activities by means of economic, legal, administrative, and even moral means.[44]

11.3 The Development of the Theory of the Socialist Market Economy: Perfecting the Socialist Market Economic System

At the beginning of the 21st century, with the advancement of economic system reform, the theory of the socialist market economy was developing rapidly, mainly manifested in the combination

---

44. Wang Shiyuan, "The Basic Framework of Establishing the Socialist Market Economic System," *Party Building,* no. 12 (1993); Dai Yuanchen, "Macro-management in Socialist Market Economy," in *China Economic Science Yearbook (1993)* (China Statistics Press, 1993); Xiao Liang, "China Economics Research in 1993: Hot Spots, Debates, and Progress," in *China Economic Science Yearbook (1994)* (China Statistics Press, 1994); He Lüye and Cui Jianhua, *Modern Market Economy* (Economic Science Press, 1997); Yu Tongshen, "In-depth Analysis of China's Economic Marketization Process," *Economic Research,* no. 4 (2000).

with the requirements of China's economic growth and economic and social practice. There was, however, some repetition of concept discrimination as well.

1. Perfecting the Reform Thought of the Socialist Market Economic System

(1) The Decision of the CPC Central Committee on Several Issues Concerning the Improvement of the Socialist Market Economic System

In October 2003, the Third Plenary Session of the Sixteenth CPC Central Committee passed the Decision of the CPC Central Committee on Several Issues Concerning the Improvement of the Socialist Market Economic System, which pointed out the importance and urgency of deepening the reform of the economic system. Since the Third Plenary Session of the Eleventh Central Committee of the Communist Party of China launched Reform and Opening Up, the Fourteenth National Congress of the Communist Party of China had set the goal of socialist market economic system reform, and the Third Plenary Session of the Fourteenth Central Committee made relevant decisions, allowing China's economic system reform to make great progress in both theory and practice. The socialist market economic system was formulated, the basic economic system with public ownership as the main body and the common development of various ownership economies was established, and the pattern of all-round, wide-ranging, and multi-level opening up had basically taken shape. The continuous deepening of reform had greatly promoted the improvement of social productivity, comprehensive national strength, and the people's living standards, and it helped China withstand the severe tests of international economic and financial turmoil, serious domestic natural disasters, and major epidemics. At the same time, there were also some problems in the development, such as an unreasonable economic structure, unsound distribution relations, slow growth of farmers' income, prominent employment contradictions, increasing pressure on resources and the environment, and weak overall economic competitiveness. The key reasons were that China was in the primary stage of socialism, the economic system was not perfect, and the development of productive forces was still facing many institutional obstacles. In order to adapt to the international environment of economic globalization and accelerated scientific and technological progress and to the new situation of building a moderately prosperous society in all aspects, it was necessary to accelerate reform, further emancipate and develop productive forces, and inject a powerful impetus into economic development and all-round social progress.

The Decision defined the objectives and tasks of improving the socialist market economic system. In accordance with the requirements of balancing urban and rural development, regional development, socio-economic development, harmonious development between man and nature, domestic development, and opening to the outside world, it was important to give greater play to the fundamental role of the market in the allocation of resources, enhance the vitality and competitiveness of enterprises, improve the national macro-control system, and improve the government's social management and public service functions, so as to provide a strong institutional guarantee for the construction of a moderately prosperous society in all aspects.

The main tasks were to improve the basic economic system with public ownership as the main body and the common development of various ownership economies, to establish a system conducive to gradually changing the dual economic structure of urban and rural areas, to form a mechanism to promote the coordinated development of the regional economy, to build a unified, modern open market system with orderly competition, to improve the macro-control system, administrative system, and economic legal system, to improve the economic and legal system, to improve the employment, income distribution, and social security systems, and to establish mechanisms to promote the sustainable development of the economy and society.

With regard to upholding and improving the basic economic system, the Decision called for further consolidation and development of the public sector of the economy and the encouragement, support, and guidance of the development of the non-public sector of the economy. Various effective forms of public ownership were to be carried out. It was important to adhere to the dominant position of public ownership and give full play to the leading role of the state-owned economy, and to actively promote various forms of effective realization of public ownership and accelerate the adjustment of the layout and structure of the state-owned economy. It was necessary to adapt to the trend of economic marketization, further enhance the vitality of the public ownership economy, vigorously develop the mixed ownership economy with the participation of state-owned capital, collective capital, and non-public capital, realize the diversification of investment subjects, and make the joint-stock system the main form of public ownership.

China aimed to vigorously develop and actively guide the non-public sector of the economy. The private and non-public economy were important forces to promote the development of China's social productive forces. It was important to clear up and revise laws, regulations, and policies that restricted the development of the non-public sector of the economy and eliminate institutional barriers. China aimed to relax market access and allow non-public capital to enter infrastructure, public utilities, and other industries and fields not prohibited by laws and regulations. Non-public enterprises enjoyed the same treatment as other enterprises in investment and financing, taxation, land use, and foreign trade. It was important for China to support the development of non-public small and medium-sized enterprises and encourage them to become both stronger and bigger. Non-public enterprises were to operate according to the law, pay taxes according to regulations, and protect the legitimate rights and interests of employees. It was necessary to improve the service and supervision of non-public enterprises.

China aimed to establish and improve its modern property rights system. Property rights were the core and main substance of ownership, including property rights, creditor's rights, equity, and intellectual property rights. The establishment of a modern property rights system with clear ownership, clear rights and responsibilities, strict protections, and smooth circulation would be conducive to maintaining public property rights and consolidating the dominant position of the public economy. It was similarly conducive to protecting private property rights and promoting the development of the non-public ownership economy, to the flow and restructuring of various types of capital and the development of a mixed ownership economy, and to enhancing the entrepreneurship and innovation of enterprises and the public to form a good credit foundation and market order. This was the internal requirement of perfecting the basic economic system and the important foundation of constructing the modern enterprise system. It was important to protect all kinds of property rights in accordance with the law, improve the trading rules and regulatory system of property rights, promote the orderly circulation of property rights, and guarantee the equal legal status and development rights of all market entities.

(2) The Strategic Decision of the Seventeenth National Congress of the Communist Party of China on Improving the Socialist Market Economic System and Promoting Sound Rapid Social and Economic Development

In October 2007, the report of the Seventeenth National Congress of the Communist Party of China proposed that the socialist market economic system should be improved in the practice of deepening reform. Combined with the social and economic situation at that time, the important strategic nodes for improving the socialist market economic system were as follows:

Adhering to the "Two Unswerving Principles." In order to improve the basic socialist economic system, it was necessary to unswervingly consolidate and develop the public sector of the economy, give full play to the leading role of the state-owned economy, and unswervingly encourage, support, and guide the development of the non-public sectors such as the individual and private sectors, so that they could promote and develop together in the process of socialist modernization. To this end, China needed to deepen the reform of state-owned enterprises, further explore various effective forms of public ownership, especially state-owned ownership, and vigorously promote the innovation of the enterprise system, technology, and management. Except for a very small number of enterprises that were to be wholly owned by the state, China needed to actively promote the joint-stock system and develop a mixed ownership economy. The main body of investment was to be diversified, with the key enterprises controlled by the state. In accordance with the requirements of the modern enterprise system, large and medium-sized state-owned enterprises continued to implement standardized public ownership reform and improve the corporate governance structure. China promoted the reform of monopoly industries and actively introduced competition mechanisms. Through market and policy guidance, it was important to develop large companies and enterprise groups with international competitiveness. China aimed to further liberalize and invigorate small and medium-sized state-owned enterprises, and to deepen the reform of collective enterprises and continue to support and help the development of various forms of collective economy. It further committed to give full play to the important role of non-public sectors of the economy, such as the individual and private sectors, in promoting economic growth, expanding employment, and invigorating the market. It also relaxed market access for domestic private capital and took measures in investment and financing, taxation, land use, and foreign trade to achieve fair competition. Supervision and management according to law were strengthened and the healthy development of the non-public sector of the economy promoted. It was also important to improve the legal system for protecting private property.

Improving the income distribution system and standardizing the income distribution order. The distribution system was related to the improvement of people's living standards, the enhancement of people's enthusiasm for labor, and the development of the national economy. At that time, given the actual situation in China, the disparity of income distribution had become a problem that could not be ignored. For example, in the mid-1980s, the income gap between urban and rural residents in China was 1.8:1, and it was 3.2:1 in 2003. Taking into account other factors, the actual gap had expanded to the range of 5:1 to 6:1. In addition, the mechanism of production factors participating in the distribution was not perfect, the distribution order was not standardized, and the supervision and control system of income distribution was not perfect. Therefore, it was necessary to improve the income distribution system and standardize the income distribution order. The distribution system in which distribution according to work was the main body and various modes of distribution coexisted needed to be adhered to. On the basis of economic development, it was necessary to pay more attention to social equity, strive to improve the income level of the low-income group, gradually expand the proportion of the middle-income group, effectively regulate excessive income, resolutely ban illegal income, and promote common prosperity.

Improving the social security system to ensure the basic livelihood of the masses. In order to adapt to the aging population, urbanization and diversification of employment modes, China needed to gradually establish a social security system covering urban and rural residents, which was connected with social insurance, social assistance, social welfare, and charity. It needed to raise social security funds through multiple channels, strengthen fund supervision, ensure that the social insurance funds were collected and paid as a whole, steadily consolidate individual accounts, actively promote provincial coordination, and implement the basic pension system as part of the national overall planning when conditions permitted. It aimed to accelerate the reform of the old-age insurance system in government organs and institutions and to steadily establish a rural minimum living security system and explore the establishment of various forms of rural endowment insurance system where conditions permitted.

Coordinating the interests of all parties and properly handling social contradictions. To adapt to the changes of China's social structure and interest pattern, it was necessary to form a scientific, effective interest coordination mechanism, a demand expression mechanism, a contradiction mediation mechanism, and rights and interests protection mechanism. It was necessary to adhere to improving people's living standards as the joint part for correctly handling the relationship between reform, development and stability, correctly grasping the relationship between the fundamental interests of the overwhelming majority of the people, the common interests of the masses at this stage, and the special interests of different groups, and making overall plans for the interests of the masses in all aspects.

2. Academic Discussions on Bettering the Socialist Market Economic System

At the beginning of the 21st century, China's economic and ideological circles generally believed that although China's economic reform and development had made great advancements, the task of economic system reform had not been completed, and there were still many institutional obstacles in economic development, which were mainly manifested in the separation of urban and rural systems, the imperfection of the property rights system, the unfinished task of establishing a modern enterprise system by state-owned enterprises and the adjustment of state-owned economic layout, the underdevelopment of capital and other factor markets, the chaotic market order, the transformation of government functions that were not in place, the weak functions of social management and public services, and the imperfections in the systems of science and technology, education, culture, health, and social security. In order to improve the socialist market economic system, economic and ideological circles carried out extensive discussions in an effort to improve the socialist market economic system.

Many experts believed that the main reason for the contradictions and problems in China's economic system lay in the lack of coordination between the basic socialist system and the market economy. Therefore, the key to improving the socialist market economic system was to continue to explore the effective means of combining the basic socialist system with the market economy. Only by solving this problem could the development of the socialist market economy be guaranteed. Some believed that according to the practical experience of China, the means of combining the basic socialist system with the market economic system were to establish a basic economic system with public ownership as the main body and various ownership economies developing together, to adjust the layout of the state-owned economy and establish a modern enterprise system, to establish a distribution according to work as the main body and allow various distribution modes to coexist and work effectively, to establish a multi-level social security system to ensure the basic survival and living needs of social members, improve a unified, open, competitive, and orderly modern market system, reform the government management system, correctly handle the relationship between opening up, independence, and self-reliance, and safeguard national economic security. These approaches to creating an effective combination of the basic socialist system and the market economy were the key link to improving the socialist market economic system. Some viewpoints generalized that the most essential feature of the socialist market economic system was the combination of the basic socialist system and the market economy. From the perspective of the economic system, the basic socialist system was no longer public ownership dominating the country, but "the basic economic system with public ownership as the main body and multiple ownership economies developing together." In this basic system, the core part was "taking public ownership as the main body," and the biggest difficulty in combining the basic socialist system with the market economy lay in the combination of the public ownership economy and the market economy as the economic subject. In order to realize this combination, it was necessary to establish the microeconomic foundation needed for the market economy on the basis of the public ownership economy, which was a historical pioneering work not seen before, and was also the "joining point" between the basic socialist economic system and the market economy. China's reform practice discovered this "joining point," that is, through the reform of state-owned enterprises, the state-owned enterprises should be built into producers and operators. The path was "the clear property rights, clear responsibilities, clear separation between government and enterprises, and management science," and the important form of public ownership.[45]

With the promotion of reform practice and the deepening of theoretical research, economic theorists put forward some innovative views on improving the socialist market economic system. To improve the socialist market economy, it was crucial to study and implement five aspects of system innovation. First, in view of the incompatibility between the market mechanism and the traditional public ownership mode, great effort needed to be made to innovate the specific forms of public ownership. By looking for the specific forms of public ownership that could adapt to the market mechanism, it was possible to enhance the endogenous development ability of the public ownership economy and form economic development under the market system, the growth of the public ownership economy, and the enhancement of the control and influence. Second, with building a strong macro-control mechanism being the goal, it was important to strengthen and improve the macro-control system and improve its effectiveness. The third step was to take economic, administrative, social, moral, and other institutional arrangements to form the economic freedom under the institutional constraints. Fourth, it was important to strengthen income regulation, improve the socialist distribution relations and guarantee the fairness of distribution. Fifth, it was necessary to vigorously build a developed and efficient public goods production and supply system to improve people's livelihood and social welfare. Academic circles analyzed the compatibility of a harmonious society and a modern market economy. In order to allocate resources effectively, the construction of a harmonious society had to be achieved through the establishment of a modern market economic system. A relatively perfect market economic system could fully meet the characteristics of a harmonious society. The primary feature of a harmonious society was democracy and the rule of law, and the essence of a modern market economy was the rule of law. One of the basic characteristics of the modern market economic system that was different from the traditional market economy system was that it was based on the rule of law, i.e., governing the nation with the rule of law. The primary function of the rule of law was to restrict the government's arbitrary intervention in economic activities, which was the fundamental difference between "the rule of law" and "the legal system." The rule of law meant that law enforcers were also bound by the law. The second function of the rule of law was to restrain the behavior of economic entities, and the guarantee of the rule of law was democracy. Therefore, democracy and the rule of law were the foundation and institutional guarantee of a harmonious society, and also the fundamental institutional basis for the establishment of a modern market economic system. A market economy would fill society with vitality and enable the economy to

---

45. Institute of Economics and Resource Management, Beijing Normal University, *China's Market Economy Development Report* (University of International Business and Economics Press, 2003); Wu Jinglian, "Economists, Economics, and China's Reform," *Economic Research*, no. 2 (2004); Liu Shijin, "The Goal of Improving the Socialist Market Economic System and the Key Points of the Recent Reform," *Economics Trends*, no. 2 (2004); Wei Liqun, "Actively Promoting Various Effective Forms of Public Ownership," *Macroeconomic Management*, no. 12 (2003); Liu Shibai, "The Great Strategic Decision to Change China's Destiny: On the Reform of Building the Socialist Market Economy in China," *Economist*, no. 4 (2008).

see effective growth. The combination of the modern market system and the role of government could also solve the problem of fairness and justice. The market system could also address the issues of honesty, social order, and harmony between man and nature. Therefore, the construction of a harmonious society was completely consistent with the modern market economic system. In order to build a harmonious society and the long-term stability of the country, it was necessary to further improve the modern market system.[46]

At the beginning of the 21st century, in the discussion of perfecting the socialist market economic system, there were also disputes about the direction of China's economic system reform, such as whether it were "left-leaning" or "right-leaning," the nature of "capitalism" or "socialism," and "socialist orientation" or "market orientation." It was generally believed that there were three major debates on the reform in economic and ideological circles. The first was in 1980–1984, the second was in 1989–1992, and the third began around 2005 and continued until 2009. The topics of these debates were roughly the same, that is, "planning or market," "capitalism or socialism," and "fairness or efficiency." As mentioned above, the discussion on the guiding position of Marxist economics was basically dominated by mainstream views, and there were few corresponding views directly arguing against them. But the lack of direct debate did not mean that those views did not exist. Those theorists studied economic issues according to their own views, published works, and gave lectures. Some targeted works were published during this time.

"What Is the Correct Direction of China's Reform?" published in the 6th issue of *Economic Trends* in 2006, pointed out that the essence of the debate was not whether to adhere to the reform, but which reform direction to adhere to. Was it adherence to the reform direction of socialist self-improvement, or to leading China to the direction of capitalist reform under the banner of supporting Reform and Opening Up? Was it adherence to the basic socialist economic system, that is, public ownership as the main body and multiple ownership developing together, or should China adopt the reform direction of capitalist privatization? Was it adherence to the socialist market economy as the goal, or taking the capitalist market economy as the goal or the reform direction called "market-oriented reform"? On the whole, China's reform adhered to the socialist direction. However, to be specific, the direction of reform was disrupted in many important aspects, such as the issue of public ownership as the main body and the issue of social equity in distribution. The central government put forward the scientific outlook on development and the construction of a harmonious society, trying to eliminate those interferences, but the trend was not completely reversed. This type of interference in the correct direction of reform, that is, the socialist direction, was there to stay. It was natural and absolutely necessary for the masses and scholars to reflect on it and put forward suggestions for improvement. It was improper to categorize it as an opposition to the reform. On major issues concerning the fate of the country

---

46. Wu Jinglian, "Economists, Economics, and China's Reform," *Economic Research*, no. 2 (2004); Zhang Zhuoyuan, Li Yining, Su Xing, Chen Xiwen, and Liu Shijin, "China's Economic Reform and Development in the New Century," *Economic Research*, no. 12 (2002); Huang Fanzhang. "Thirty Years of Institutional and Theoretical Innovation: On the Establishment of Transition Economics and Socialist Market Economics with Chinese Characteristics," *Economist*, no. 6 (2008).

and the people, advocating the "non-ideological" and "non-politicization" could only deceive those who had no common knowledge of Marxism.[47]

The publication of this article ignited a discussion among economic theorists on whether the nature of the market economy was "capitalist" or "socialist." Unlike the discussions in the late 1980s and early 1990s, its focus was centered on economic liberalism. Some economists believed that there was a new liberal view of the market economy and reform which advocated privatization, liberalization, and globalization. The market economy was not to be overgeneralized as "capitalist" or "socialist." Instead, in the framework of different countries, social systems, and political systems, the market economy may have different characteristics, either "capitalist" or "socialist." It was important not to confuse the nature of the two types of the market economy and negate the basic characteristics of the socialist market economy. The link between socialism and the market economy was not private ownership, but socialization, that is, the combination of socialized productive forces and socialized production relations.[48]

In the discussion about the market economy being "capitalist" or "socialist," some viewpoints re-emphasized the necessity of planned regulation and control, holding that the market played a fundamental role in the allocation of resources under the premise of the state's macro-control, and it played a fundamental role in the allocation of resources. Not all resources were completely allocated by the market, and some key resources should be allocated by the state. Therefore, it was important to emphasize the guiding role of planning and regulation. In addition to policy-oriented provisions, this sort of plan also had necessary indicators, projects, and mandatory tasks to be completed. Therefore, mandatory plans could not be completely ruled out. The report of the Seventeenth National Congress of the Communist Party of China pointed out the importance of giving full play to the guiding role of national development planning, regulation, and industrial policies in macro-control, along with the comprehensive use of fiscal and monetary policies to improve the level of macro-control. This was a reaffirmation that national planning, like fiscal and monetary policy, was an important means of macro-control, in which national planning and industrial policy played a guiding role in the development of the national economy.

Some scholars commented that the debate about the planned economy and the market economy, ranging from whether socialism allowed for the existence of the commodity economy to whether to give priority to planned or market regulation, and finally to the debate on whether reform orientation was a planned or a market economy. All of these questions centered on the main idea of whether or not to change the planned economy. Once the main line changed, some would view this as a departure from the general direction of socialism. The socialist standard that

---

47. Liu Guoguang, "What Is the Correct Direction of China's Reform? On a Market-oriented Reform," *Economic Trends*, no. 6 (2006).

48. Wang Zhongbao, "Public Ownership Is the Economic Basis for Sustainable Scientific Development," *Marxism Research*, no. 2 (2008); Wei Xinghua, "Thirty Years of Reform and Opening Up, Practice, and Theory Should be Summarized," *Theory World Trends* (December 10, 2008); Huang Taiyan and Dai Muzhen, "Ranking and Analysis of China's Economic Research Hotspots in 2007," *Economic Trends*, no. 2 (2008).

these people adhered to was nothing more than the traditional Soviet socialist model, which had proven to be a failure after seventy years of practice. By contrast, China's thirty year reform line had proven to be in line with reality and had kept pace with the times. It had not deviated from socialism, but was building a socialist society with Chinese characteristics based on China's actual situation.[49]

At the end of the 20th century and the beginning of the 21st century, China's economic and ideological circles generally referred to the economic system reform as "marketized reform" or "market-oriented reform." In a general context, this statement would not cause ambiguity, but in a special context, such as in the discussion of "capitalism or socialism," it was regarded as having an ideological bent. Liu Guoguang pointed out that it was problematic to generalize the direction of the reform with marketization. Instead, it was important to establish a socialist market economy, not a general market economy. China's socialist market economy was a market economy under the basic socialist economic system, not a market economy under the capitalist system.[50] China's reform of socialist self-improvement aimed at the establishment of the socialist market economy and was definitely not a simple "market-oriented reform." Where did the documents of the central government mention that China should implement a "market-oriented reform"? When it came to Reform and Opening Up, it was always linked with adhering to the Four Cardinal Principles, the modifier "socialist" was always added before "market economy," and the term "socialism" always emphasized "public ownership as the main body." Those who advocated the slogan of market-oriented reform, almost without exception, did not mention these keywords. Some people wanted to leave everything in economic life to the market and "marketize," pushing social life, cultural life, and national political life to "marketization," excluding the plan from the socialist market economy and all economic and social fields, regarding it as a forbidden zone, and ultimately abandoning it. This was not only due to the naivety of being superstitious about the market, but also had ulterior motives behind it.[51]

Some people thought that "marketization" and the "socialist market economy" were not the same, and that their connotations and denotations were not the same. Even the description of marketization as a market process could not cover the whole of the general market economy. Only emphasizing "marketization" was bound to fall into "pan-marketization," "absolute marketization," and "market fundamentalism." China's reform was the "self-improvement" of socialism. It was impossible to separate the market economy from socialism, nor could the basic economic system be blurred or changed. Some commentators pointed out that the goal of China's economic system reform was to establish a socialist market economy. Therefore, it could said that the goal of economic system reform was a market-oriented process. However, the question that remained was whether the socialist market economy meant that all aspects of social reproduction

---

49. Gu Shutang, "Debate and Analysis on Economic System Reform," *Economic Trends*, no. 2 (2008).

50. Liu Guoguang, "Understanding of Some Economic Issues Discussed in the Report of the Seventeenth CPC National Congress," *Economics Trends*, no. 1 (2008).

51. Liu Guoguang, "What is the Correct Direction for China's Reform?" *Economics Trends*, no. 6 (2006).

such as production, circulation, distribution, and consumption, should be addressed through and decided by the market. Even in the most developed market economies, the process of social reproduction would not be completely market-oriented. Therefore, although China regarded the socialist market economy as the target mode of economic system reform, it did not mean complete marketization.[52]

Some commentators did not agree with the statement that "reform deviates from the socialist direction." They thought that due to the lack of experience in Reform and Opening Up, there were some mistakes in some specific policies and measures which needed to be seriously improved in the process of reform, but the direction of reform was not involved at all. If there were problems in the direction, how could the productive forces develop so rapidly in practice, so that China's national strength could be so greatly enhanced and people's living standards be improved so quickly? Some people even thought that the reform had embarked on the path of bourgeois liberalization under the guidance of neo-liberalism, which was not tenable. It was important not to regard some reform measures of keeping pace with the times and developing Marxism as heresy, or even misinterpret them as neo-liberalism in the way of dogmatism. It was likewise important not to regard the traditional socialist system which hindered the development of productive forces as a standard that should remain unchanged forever. In the process of reform, there were many differences and debates, which were mainly the result of the long-term public education in an ideology based on the Soviet model of the economic system. With such indoctrination, the traditional socialist economic system model was deeply rooted in many people's minds. Once this mode was changed, it would naturally cause widespread antipathy. But with practice and discussion, especially after studying the report of the Seventeenth National Congress of the Communist Party of China, it was possible to come to a correct understanding.[53]

3. On Perfecting the Socialist Market Economy, Freeing the Market Economy, and State Intervention

By the early 1990s, China's market-oriented reform had been going on for nearly twenty years. The establishment of the goal of the socialist market economic reform and the reform practice created huge social wealth in China in just twenty years, and the total economic volume and

---

52. Yang Chengxun, "Accurately Grasping the Essence of Socialist Market Economic Reform," *Economics Trends*, no. 5 (2006); Ni Ying and Li Yan, "Summary of the Fifteenth Annual Meeting and Theoretical Seminar of China Economic Law Research Association," *Economics Trends*, no. 6 (2006); Lei Yun, "Interpretation of the Correct Direction of Our Reform and Opening Up," *Journal of the Party School of Ningbo Municipal Committee of the CPC*, no. 2 (2009); Zhang Yu. "Financial Crisis, New Liberalism, and China's Choice," *Economics Trends*, no. 4 (2009); Liu Yingqiu, "Theoretical Reflection on the International Financial Crisis and New Liberalism," *Economics Trends*, no. 4 (2009); Yang Xinming and Lu Menglong, "A Review of Political Economics Research in 2009," *Economics Trends*, no. 4 (2010).

53. Gu Shutang, "Debate and Analysis on Economic System Reform," *Economics Trends*, no. 2 (2008).

comprehensive national strength had been promoted to a pivotal position in the world. However, with the development of the economy and the increase of social wealth, some contradictions related to wealth distribution, fairness, and justice had become more complex and acute, which led to the development of certain ideas in economic ideological circles. From the perspective of economics, the main line of academic discussion in this field centered on the debate between the free market economy and the market economy with state intervention.

From the 1980s to the beginning of the 21st century, the policy path of China's economic system reform had the characteristics of state intervention and regulation. The Seventeenth National Congress of the Communist Party of China summed up the experience of China's Reform and Opening Up. In terms of economic system reform and economic construction, it was necessary to combine the basic socialist system with the development of the market economy, give full play to the advantages of the socialist system and the effectiveness of market allocation of resources, make economic activities follow the requirements of the law of value, liberate and develop social productive forces, enhance the comprehensive national strength, and improve the overall national strength and people's living standards. At the level of economic activities, adhering to the basic socialist system was mainly reflected in two aspects. One was to emphasize and continuously optimize macro-control and not adopt the theory and policy of a *laissez faire* market economy. The other was to emphasize the combination of improving efficiency and promoting social equity, which not only attached importance to enhancing social vitality and promoting economic development, but also to the foundation of economic development through the realization of social equity to promote social harmony. It also required that focus be put on the development of social undertakings, improvements made to the income distribution system to protect and improve people's livelihood, and the common prosperity of the entire society be realized. Therefore, from the top-level design of system reform and social transformation and development, adhering to the political premise of the socialist system determined that China's socialist market economy could not be a free market economy model. This "perfection" also referred to the more effective and complete agreement between the basic social system of socialism and the market economy. It was in this sense that the establishment and improvement of the socialist market economic system was not only a historical contribution to Marxism and socialism, but also a major innovation in the overall civilization of human society.

In the field of international economics, the argument between the Keynesian school and the theory of spontaneous order and the *laissez faire* policy of neo-liberalism lasted for a prolonged period. Although the theories and policies of neo-liberalism were adopted by the UK, the US, and other major capitalist countries since the 1970s, the global financial crisis in 2008 prompted Western economists to reexamine and debate *laissez faire* theories and policies. Some scholars sought theoretical support from Western classical economics to analyze whether the logic of the market economy naturally contained the value of order and equilibrium, and whether government intervention was one of the social conditions for the orderly operation of the market economy. When European countries were trapped in the debt crisis arising from the financial crisis, they tried to cut down public expenditure to achieve fiscal balance. The large-scale civil protest that resulted demonstrated that people were still pursuing an economic operation goal of ensuring the balance of social welfare. China's discussions and policy thought on improving the socialist market economy were also related to this evolution in international economic thought.

The theoretical system of socialism with Chinese characteristics included Deng Xiaoping Theory, the important thought of the Three Represents, and the scientific outlook on development. The main line of this theoretical system was to liberate and develop productive forces. The development of productive forces was the final decisive force for the development of human society, and socialist modernization was to be based on developed productive forces. The main contradiction in the primary stage of socialism was always the contradiction between the people's growing material and cultural needs and the backward social production. The liberation and development of productive forces was always the central task of the construction of socialism with Chinese characteristics. Only with the development of productive forces and the enhancement of economic strength and the comprehensive national strength could people's lives be continuously improved, the country enjoy long-term stability, and a solid material foundation be laid for promoting the all-round development of human lives. Only then could China take a more prominent position in the international structure.

The gradual formation and improvement of the theoretical system of socialism with Chinese characteristics was also the process of the establishment and improvement of China's socialist market economic system. The Fourteenth National Congress of the Communist Party of China clearly put forward the reform goal of establishing the socialist market economic system. The Third Plenary Session of the Fourteenth Central Committee of the Communist Party of China issued the Decision of the CPC Central Committee on Several Issues Concerning the Establishment of the Socialist Market Economic System, and the Third Plenary Session of the Sixteenth Central Committee of the Communist Party of China issued the Decision of the CPC Central Committee on Several Issues Concerning the Improvement of the Socialist Market Economic System, coinciding with the reform of China's economic system. The theory, policy, and practice of socialism with Chinese characteristics were consistent with the main line and connotation of the theoretical system of socialism with Chinese characteristics. The reform of the economic system greatly promoted the liberation and development of social productive forces, and China's comprehensive national strength and people's living standards improved significantly. However, during this period of economic development, there were also some problems, such as unreasonable economic structures, unsound distribution relations, slow growth of farmers' income, prominent employment contradictions, increasing pressure on resources and environment, and weak overall economic competitiveness. The only way to solve these problems was to speed up the reform, further liberate and develop productive forces, adhere to the reform direction of the socialist market economy, inject a strong impetus into economic development and social progress, and provide strong social security for building an overall moderately prosperous society.

11.4 The Development of Socialist Market Economic Thought: Accelerating the Improvement of the Socialist Market Economic System

1. Speeding Up the Reform of the Socialist Market Economy

In November 2012, the report of the Eighteenth CPC National Congress proposed a comprehensive deepening of reform, accelerated improvement of the socialist market economic system, and the transformation of the mode of economic development. It was necessary to adapt to the new changes in the domestic and international economic situation, accelerate the formation of a new mode of economic development, shift the foothold of promoting development to improving quality and efficiency, strive to stimulate new vitality in the development of various market entities, strengthen the new driving force for innovation-driven development, strive to build a new system for modern industrial development, and cultivate new advantages for open economic development, so as to make economic development more dependent on domestic demand, especially consumption demand, on the modern service industry and strategic emerging industries, on resource conservation and the circular economy, and on coordinated interaction between urban and rural regional development, continuously enhancing the long-term development potential. Deepening reform was the key to accelerating the transformation of the mode of economic development. The central issue of the economic system reform was to handle the relationship between the government and the market. It was important to give greater respect to the market law and give full play to the role of the government.[54] The report of the Eighteenth National Congress of the Communist Party of China proposed that the core point of comprehensively deepening the reform of the economic system was to increasingly respect the market law and to give better play to the role of both the government and the market in the allocation of resources. It was necessary to improve the functions of economic regulation and market supervision, further reduce and adjust industry approval items, and reduce government intervention in microeconomic activities.[55]

In November 2013, the Third Plenary Session of the Eighteenth CPC Central Committee adopted the Decision of the CPC Central Committee on Several Major Issues Concerning Comprehensive Deepening of the Reform. The overall goal of comprehensive deepening of the reform was to improve and develop the socialist system with Chinese characteristics and promote the modernization of the national governance system and governance capacity. It was necessary to give increased attention to the steadiness, integrity, and coordination of reform, accelerate the

---

54. Hu Jintao, *Unswervingly Advancing Along the Road of Socialism with Chinese Characteristics and Striving for Building a Moderately Prosperous Society in All Aspects: Report on the Eighteenth National Congress of the Communist Party of China* (People's Publishing House, 2012).

55. Liu He, "Comprehensively Deepening the Reform of the Economic System and Accelerating the Formation of a New Mode of Economic Development," in *Guidebook of the Report of the Eighteenth National Congress of the Communist Party of China* (People's Publishing House, 2012), 117–118.

development of the socialist market economy, democratic politics, advanced culture, harmonious society, and ecological civilization, release the vitality of all labor, knowledge, technology, management, and capital in competition, and allow all sources of social wealth to flow at full strength, so that the development achievements would more fairly benefit all the people. Economic system reform was the key point of deepening the reform in all aspects. The core issue was to handle the relationship between the government and the market, so that the market could play a decisive role in the allocation of resources and give better play to the role of the government. The market's determination of the allocation of resources was a general law of the market economy. To improve the socialist market economic system, it was necessary to follow this law and strive to resolve the problems of the imperfect market system, excessive government intervention, and inadequate supervision. It was important to actively and steadily promote market-oriented reform in both breadth and depth, greatly reduce the direct allocation of resources by the government, and promote the allocation of resources in accordance with market rules, market prices, and market competition to maximize gains and efficiency. The main responsibilities and functions of the government were to maintain macroeconomic stability, strengthen and optimize public services, ensure fair competition, strengthen market supervision, maintain market order, promote sustainable development, increase common prosperity, and make up for market failures.[56]

The Third Plenary Session of the Eighteenth Central Committee of the Communist Party of China (CPC) made decisions on the overall goal, key points, and core issues of comprehensive deepening of the reform to implement the strategic plan of the deepened reform. The overall goal was to improve and develop the socialist system with Chinese characteristics and promote the modernization of the national governance system and governance capacity. This was the first time that the modernization of the national governance system and governance capacity was raised to the height of improving and developing the socialist system with Chinese characteristics. The key point of deepening the reform in every aspect was the reform of the economic system. The key issue of the reform of the economic system was the proper handling of the relationship between the government and the market, so that the market could play a decisive role in the allocation of resources and give fuller play to the role of the government. The decision of the Third Plenary Session of the Eighteenth CPC Central Committee furthered the report of the Eighteenth CPC National Congress, which stated that "the core issue of economic system reform is to handle the relationship between the government and the market, to pay more attention to the market law, and to give better play to the role of the government." It clearly put forward that the way to deal with the relationship between the government and the market was to make the market play a decisive role in the allocation of resources and give better play to the government, to promote market-oriented reform in breadth and depth, and to define the boundary between "the decisive role of the market in resource allocation" and "better playing the role of the government." The Decision of the Third Plenary Session of the Eighteenth Central Committee of the Communist

---

56. *Decision of the CPC Central Committee on Several Major Issues Concerning Comprehensive Deepening of the Reform* (People's Publishing House, 2013), 3–6.

Party of China strategically and operationally pushed the reform of China's economic system and the construction of the socialist market economic system into an overall deepening stage.

In October 2017, the report of the Nineteenth National Congress of the Communist Party of China announced that socialism with Chinese characteristics had entered a new era, indicating a new historical direction for China's development. The main social contradiction in China had been transformed into that between the people's growing need for a better life and the unbalanced, inadequate development. It was necessary to adhere to comprehensive deepening of the reform and the new development concept and to accelerate the improvement of the socialist market economic system. The economic system reform needed to focus on improving the property rights system and the market-oriented allocation of factors, so as to realize effective incentives of property rights, flexible price response, fair and orderly competition, and survival of the fittest enterprises.[57]

The report of the Nineteenth National Congress of the Communist Party of China connected comprehensive deepening of the reform, implementing the new development concept, and building a modern economic system. In order to build a modern economic system, it was necessary to focus on building a system with an effective market mechanism, dynamic micro subjects, and moderate macro-control. In 2017, China's market entities reached 90 million, including about 30 million enterprises. In addition, there were bout 200 million family-run farmers and urban non-industrial and commercial entrepreneurs, forming an important micro basis for economic development. At the same time, the mode of macro-control had been constantly innovated. To build a modern economic system, it was important to adhere to the direction of socialist market economic reform, make the market play a decisive role in the allocation of resources, give better play to the role of the government, adhere to the principle of streamlining administration and decentralization, combine decentralization with governance, optimize services, improve the basic economic system, the modern market system, and the macro-control system, and fully mobilize the initiative, proactiveness, and creativity of all market subjects to make decisions and operate independently. Governments at all levels were urged to perform their due responsibilities in economic regulation, market supervision, public service, and social management.[58]

2. Academic Discussion on Speeding Up the Perfection of the Socialist Market Economic System

The Third Plenary Session of the Eighteenth Central Committee of the Communist Party of China proposed that the key to comprehensive deepening of the reform was economic system reform, and the core of economic system reform was straightening out the relationship between

---

57. Xi Jinping, *Winning the Victory in Building a Moderately Prosperous Society in All Respects and Socialism with Chinese Characteristics in the New Era: Report on the Nineteenth National Congress of the Communist Party of China* (People's Publishing House, 2017).

58. Ning Jizhe, "Building a Modern Economic System," in *Guidebook of the Report of the Nineteenth CPC National Congress* (People's Publishing House, 2017), 175–177.

the government and the market, so that the market could play a decisive role in the allocation of resources. Some theorists used the neoclassical growth model to demonstrate the productivity and competition effects of deregulation on China's economic growth. Using the micro data of industrial enterprises from 1998 to 2007, the researchers found that the deregulation of upstream enterprises could explain the rise of 40% of China's economic growth rate, and that nearly 80% of the contribution came from the improvement of productivity of downstream industries, that is, the decrease of input cost caused by the competition effect. The rent-seeking activities that resulted from government regulation made enterprise growth more dependent on traditional factors rather than on innovation, which would eventually erode the basis of the long-term growth of these enterprises.

Because the core mechanism was for private enterprises to break through the threshold of market access through political connections, the key to promoting the transformation of China's economic development power lay in deepening industry access and factor market reform.[59] Some scholars interpreted that the primary highlight of the Decision of the Third Plenary Session of the Eighteenth CPC Central Committee was the use of the expression "the market plays a decisive role in resource allocation" to replace "the market plays a fundamental role in resource allocation," which had been in use for 21 years. The only difference was replacing the word "fundamental" with "decisive," but the meaning was very different. A decisive role could more accurately and clearly express the dominant role of the market mechanism on resource allocation, and it better reflected the inherent requirements of the basic law of the market economy, that is, the law of value. The market played a decisive role in the allocation of resources, which mainly pointed to three steps. The first step was to address the problem of excessive government intervention in the allocation of resources. The second was to address the market environment issue of an unsound market system and the real formation of fair competition. And the final step was to address the discriminatory regulations on the non-public economy, including the elimination of various hidden barriers. The highlights of the Decision of the Third Plenary Session of the Eighteenth Central Committee of the Communist Party of China also included the transformation of state-owned assets supervision institutions from a focus on enterprise management to capital management, proposing that the mixed ownership economy was an important realization of the basic economic system and that accelerating the improvement of modern market system could help better play the decisive role of the market in the allocation of resources.[60] Some scholars regarded the reform of resource allocation as a breakthrough in the theory of the socialist market economy. The market played a decisive role in resource allocation and the government played its role better, which was a new breakthrough in resource allocation theory. It meant that the market was no longer under the control of the government, but independently played a decisive role,

---

59. Fan Liangcong and Zhou Minghai, "The Path of the Socialist Market Economy with Chinese Characteristics: A Summary of the Theoretical Seminar on Commemorating the 40th Anniversary of Reform and Opening Up," *Economic Research*, no. 8 (2018).

60. Zhang Zhuoyuan, "A Review of China's Market-oriented Economic Reform in the Past Forty Years," *Economic and Management Research*, no. 3 (2018).

returning to the original meaning of the market economy. Another part of the new definition of the socialist market economy was giving better play to the role of the government, which was an organic whole with the market determining the allocation of resources. The relationship between the government and the market was not one of ebb and flow, but of playing a role at various levels.[61] Some people believed that "implementing the new development concept and building a modern economic system" put forward by the Nineteenth National Congress of the Communist Party of China was an important proposition of China's economic construction. Using the phrase "modern economic system" to refer to the socialist market economic system not only showed the modernization process of China's economic system reform, but also avoided falling into the discourse trap of "the socialist market economy being no market economy" set by Western countries. To grasp the socialist market economy from the perspective of the modern economic system avoided, to a certain extent, the rhetorical dispute. The "modernization" spoken of here meant that the socialist market economy was different not only from the traditional planned economic system, but also from the Western market economic system in that it was a realization of the combination of public ownership and the market economy in economic practice.[62]

The Eighteenth National Congress of the Communist Party of China proposed comprehensive deepening of the reform and acceleration of the improvement of the socialist market economic system. The Third Plenary Session of the Eighteenth Central Committee of the Communist Party of China outlined a road map for comprehensively deepening the reform. The focus was on the reform of the economic system, and the central issue was to properly handle the relationship between the government and the market, so that the market could play a decisive role in the allocation of resources and give fuller play to the role of the government.

As a result, the path of economic system reform after the Eighteenth CPC National Congress in November 2012 was clear, which was also in line with the system and mechanism characteristics of the market economy. The central issue of the economy was resource allocation. The efficiency of resource allocation determined the efficiency of economic activities and operations, the quality of economic development, and the growth of social welfare. At the level of resource allocation, the common ground of the market economic system enabled the market to play a decisive role in resource allocation and better play the role of government. Therefore, the central issues of the economic system reform put forward in the Decision of the Third Plenary Session of the Eighteenth Central Committee of the Communist Party of China conformed to the general provisions of the market economy and were the key link in accelerating the improvement of the socialist market economic system. The advantages of the market economy in regulating economic operations, optimizing the allocation of resources, and improving the efficiency of economic activities had been confirmed by the development of the world economy, but the market mechanism also had its limitations. There would inevitably be "market failures" in the

---

61. Hong Yinxing, "Major Breakthroughs in the Logic of Economic Reform and Political Economics in the Past Forty Years," *Economist*, no. 12 (2018).

62. Zhou Wen and Bao Weijie, "Further Discussion on the Socialist Market Economic System with Chinese Characteristics," *Economist*, no. 3 (2019).

economy, so it was important to implement scientific and effective macro-control. The market economy and government intervention complemented each other. The economic, scientific, and effective government intervention were important guarantees for the healthy operation of the market economy. Meanwhile, the perfection of the market system, the standardization of market transactions, and the development of the market economic system were the basis for improving the efficiency of government intervention. In the reform of the socialist market economic system, to develop the market economy, it was necessary to reduce administrative intervention to the economy. However, the undeveloped market economy made the government's economic intervention ineffective, forcing the government to resort to administrative means, and thus hindering the natural formation and development of the market system. Therefore, to discuss the market economy, it was necessary to study the objectives, means, and effects of government intervention under the conditions of undeveloped markets in theory, system, and operation, so as to realize the basic, decisive role of the market in the allocation of resources and give fuller play to the role of the government.

3. Accelerating the Improvement of Socialist Market Economic System and the Transformation of Government Functions

The Decision of the Third Plenary Session of the Eighteenth Central Committee of the Communist Party of China gave fuller play to the role of the government and connected with the transformation of government functions. The transformation of government functions aimed to substantially reduce the direct allocation of resources by the government. The main responsibilities and functions of the government were to maintain macroeconomic stability, strengthen and optimize public services, ensure fair competition, strengthen market supervision, maintain market order, promote sustainable development and common prosperity, and make up for market failures.[63]

The marginal equilibrium point of the government function transformation was to define the optimal boundary between government and market. In the market economy, the theoretical premise of government intervention in the economy was the existence of market failure, that is, the price mechanism was distorted or ineffective in some fields. There were four kinds of market failure: monopoly, information asymmetry, externality, and demand for public goods. The purpose of government intervention was to make up for the market defects and improve the market mechanism, rather than replace the market. The optimal boundary between government and market was based on the comparison of transaction cost. If the transaction cost of the market mechanism was lower than that of government intervention, the market was relatively effective, while if the transaction cost of the market mechanism was higher than that of government intervention, government intervention was relatively effective. Government and the market

---

63. *Decision of the CPC Central Committee on Several Major Issues Concerning Comprehensive Deepening of the Reform* (People's Publishing House, 2013), 6.

were not exclusive. Sometimes the cost of government intervention was lower and the efficiency was higher if the government used market-oriented regulation methods, tools, and means. For example, in order to solve the external problem of environmental pollution, in the 1970s, the Environmental Protection Agency of the United States first adopted an emission trading policy, combining government intervention with market trading (price mechanism), which reduced transaction costs and improved intervention efficiency.

In the real economic environment, the optimal boundary between government and market was dynamic, and there was no unified equilibrium solution. Different countries had different national conditions and development status, stages, requirements, and characteristics, so the marginal equilibrium point of government and market was different. Therefore, the transformation of government functions needed to adapt to the development of economy and market in order to promote economic development. China was in a special period at that time, still in the process of industrialization, and it was facing and actively integrating into the tide of economic globalization. It was important to not only cultivate the market and develop industries according to the law of industrialization development, but also to follow the behavior standards and common rules of globalization and internationalization to obtain the opening dividend. This kind of double coordinate friction and collision made the determination of the reasonable boundary between the government and the market more complex and special, and it put forward higher reform requirements for the transformation of government functions.

In terms of operation, the transformation of government functions had three dimensions. The first was the concept level, the second was the technical path level, and the third was the executive level.

Concept dimension referred to improved transparency. At the time, the management mode of international high standard investment rules was "pre-access national treatment + negative list." The idea of this management mode was to enhance the transparency of the administrative management system, that is, to be open and transparent in the aspects of competition neutrality principle, non-discriminatory expropriation compensation, free investment transfer policy, intellectual property protection, trade dispute settlement procedure, and other areas and to be open and transparent in fields that did not allow foreign investment or have restrictions. Therefore, the change from the examination and approval system to the implementation of the record system was only a superficial operational change. The core idea was to enhance the transparency of administrative management, which was a fundamental reform for China's administrative management system.

The technical path dimension of government function transformation was to reduce the government's excessive intervention in the market and economic activities and to strengthen the government's public management (including the supply of public goods). In a field where the market mechanism could play an effective role, the government needed to reduce or cancel regulation and intervention and play the basic role of the market in the allocation of resources, so as to make the economy more dynamic and efficient. In the field of public management, the government needed to further strengthen its functions, provide reliable system guarantees for market operation and social order, build favorable economic environment for enterprises, and provide an effective legal basis for economic and social activities.

The executive dimension of the transformation of government functions was to promote the process supervision from prior approval to in-process and after the event, which involved not only the administrative ability, but also the administrative style of diligence or laziness. It was necessary to establish a service mode of acceptance, comprehensive approval, and efficient operation, a comprehensive evaluation mechanism of industry information tracking, supervision, and collection, and a centralized and unified market supervision and law enforcement system. At the same time, the administrative supervision system also faced new business and industry, which brought about the transformation of the administrative management mode and the expansion of its content, which had high requirements for administrative management ability and required comprehensive improvement of the theoretical basis, knowledge preparation, system design, and talent reserve. In addition, in order to ensure the effectiveness of the process supervision during and after the event, it was necessary to set up a supervision mechanism to restrain the lazy behavior of administrative omission and truly establish a simplified, efficient administrative management mechanism.

CHAPTER 12

The Reform of the Socialist Market Economic System and the Classification of Research Directions in Economic Theory

12.1 Research on the Micro Basis of the Socialist Market Economy (Manufacturer Behavior)

1. A Study on the Evolution of State-owned Enterprise Reform Policy in the Socialist Market Economy

On October 12, 1992, the report of the Fourteenth National Congress of the Communist Party of China, entitled "Accelerating Reform, Opening Up, and Modernization and Striving for Greater Victory in the Cause of Socialism with Chinese Characteristics," officially established that the goal of China's economic system reform was to establish a socialist market economic system, which was conducive to further liberating and developing productive forces. The first important link in establishing such a system was to transform the management mechanism of state-owned enterprises, especially large and medium enterprises, to push them into the market, enhance their vitality, and improve their quality. This was the central link in the establishment of the socialist market economic system and the key to consolidating the socialist system so as to give full play to the superiority of socialism. By straightening out the relationship between property rights, separating the government from the enterprise, and implementing the autonomy of enterprises, enterprises could truly become legal entities and the main body of market competition with independent operations, self-sufficiency, self-development, and self-restraint, and they could bear the responsibility of maintaining and increasing the value of state-owned assets.[64] On November 14, 1993, the Third Plenary Session of the Fourteenth Central Committee of the Communist Party of China adopted the Decision of the Central Committee of the Communist Party of China on Several Issues Concerning the Establishment of a Socialist Market Economic System, which proposed that the mode of state-owned enterprise reform should be the establishment of a modern enterprise system. The modern enterprise system with public ownership as the main body was the foundation of the socialist market economy. Over the previous decade, the state had taken measures such as expanding the autonomy of state-owned enterprises and reforming their management methods, which laid a preliminary foundation for enterprises to enter the market. The establishment of the modern enterprise system was an inevitable requirement for the development of socialized mass production and the market economy, and it set the direction for the reform of state-owned enterprises in China. Its basic characteristics were first, that the ownership of state-owned assets in an enterprise belonged to the state and the enterprise had all the legal entity property rights formed by the investment of investors including the state, making it a legal entity with civil rights and civil liabilities. Second, the enterprise, with all its legal entity properties, operated independently according to the law, was responsible for its own profits and losses, paid taxes in accordance with regulations, and bore the responsibility for maintaining and increasing the value of assets to investors. Third, investors enjoyed the rights and interests of owners according to the amount of capital invested in the enterprise, i.e., the rights to benefit from assets, the right to make major decisions, and the right to choose managers. When an enterprise went bankrupt, the investor was only responsible for the debt of the enterprise based on the amount of capital invested. Fourth, enterprises organized production and operations according to market demand with the purpose of improving labor productivity and economic benefits, and the government did not directly intervene in the production and operations of enterprises. If an enterprise survived as the fittest in the market competition and lost money over a long period, it would go bankrupt, according to the law. The fifth characteristic was the establishment of a scientific enterprise leadership and organizational management system, the adjustment of the relationship among owners, managers, and employees, and the formation of a business mechanism combining incentive and restraint. All enterprises were to make efforts in this direction. Modern enterprises could have a variety of organizational forms according to the composition of property. The implementation of the company system in state-owned enterprises was a beneficial exploration for establishing a modern enterprise system. A standard company could effectively realize the separation of investor's ownership and the enterprise's property rights as a legal entity, which was conducive to the separation of government and enterprise, the transformation of the operation mechanism, the enterprise's dependence on administrative

---

64. Jiang Zemin, *Accelerating Reform, Opening Up, and Modernization and Striving for Greater Victory in the Cause of Socialism with Chinese Characteristics: Report on the Fourteenth National Congress of the Communist Party of China* (People's Publishing House, 1992).

organs, and the state's unlimited responsibility for the enterprise. It was also conducive to raising funds and dispersing risks.[65]

The modern enterprise system to be established in China was a new enterprise system which adapted to the requirements of the socialist market economy, and it took the standardized, perfected enterprise legal entity system as the main body and the limited liability system as the core. Its basic characteristics included the separation of responsibilities between government and enterprise, a clear relationship of property rights, the ownership of state-owned assets in enterprises belonging to the state, and enterprises having the property rights of legal entities and being independent legal entities that operated independently and were responsible for their own profits and losses. Enterprises enjoyed civil rights and bore civil liabilities according to the law, with all the corporate properties formed by investors including the state, and they bore civil liabilities and the responsibility of value-added assets maintenance for investors. The investor was to enjoy the rights and interests of the asset owner according to the amount of capital invested in the enterprise and bear limited liability, while the enterprise was to organize production and operation according to the market demand, with the purpose of improving labor productivity and economic benefits, and the government would not directly intervene in the production and operations of the enterprise. The enterprise was to formulate the articles of association, establish a scientific, standardized leadership and organizational management system, and adjust the relationship among the owner, the manager, the staff, and the workers to form a management mechanism for the combination of encouragement and restraint. The enterprise operated according to law, paid taxes according to regulations, accepted the government's supervision, and adapted to national macro-control. Obviously, this view generalized the modern enterprise system as a system including the property system (or property rights system), the responsibility system, the organization system, and the management system.[66]

On September 12, 1997, the report of the Fifteenth National Congress of the Communist Party of China stressed that accelerating the reform of state-owned enterprises and further clarifying that the establishment of the modern enterprise system was the direction of the state-owned enterprise reform. In accordance with the requirements of "clear property rights, clear rights and responsibilities, separation of government and enterprise, and scientific management," it was important to carry out standardized corporate reform of large and medium-sized state-owned enterprises, allowing enterprises to become legal entities and competitive subjects that adapted to the market, and to further clarify the rights and responsibilities of the state and enterprises. The state enjoyed owner's rights and interests according to the amount of capital invested in the enterprise and undertook limited liability for the debts of the enterprise, while the enterprise

65. *Decision of the Central Committee of the Communist Party of China on Several Issues Concerning the Establishment of a Socialist Market Economic System* (People's Publishing House, 1993).

66. Modern Enterprise System Research Group of the State Economic and Trade Commission, "Establishing a Modern Enterprise System Compatible with the Socialist Market Economic System," *People's Daily*, December 21, 1993.

operated independently according to the law and was responsible for its own profits and losses. The government could not directly intervene in the business activities of enterprises, and enterprises could not be free from the restraint of the owners nor damage the owners' rights and interests. In order to be effective in the whole state-owned economy, it was necessary to carry out strategic reorganization of state-owned enterprises in accordance with the principle of grasping large ones and invigorating small ones, and to strive to establish a modern enterprise system for most of the large and medium-sized key state-owned enterprises by the end of the 20th century.[67]

In November 2002, the report of the Sixteenth National Congress of the Communist Party of China put forward the goal of building a well-off society in all aspects and improving the socialist market economic system. It was necessary to deepen the reform of state-owned enterprises, further explore various forms of effective realization of public ownership, especially state-owned ownership, and vigorously promote innovation in the system, technology, and management of enterprises. In addition to a very small number of enterprises that were to be wholly owned by the state, it was necessary to actively promote the joint-stock system and develop a mixed ownership economy. The main body of investment was to be diversified and important enterprises were to be controlled by the state. According to the requirements of the modern enterprise system, large and medium state-owned enterprises continued to carry out standardized corporate reform and improve the corporate governance structure. The reform of monopoly industries was promoted and competition mechanisms actively introduced. Through the guidance of market and policy, it was important to develop large companies and enterprise groups with international competitiveness, and to further liberalize and invigorate small and medium enterprises.[68]

On October 14, 2003, the Third Plenary Session of the Sixteenth Central Committee of the Communist Party of China adopted the Decision of the Central Committee of the Communist Party of China on Several Issues Concerning the Improvement of the Socialist Market Economic System. With regard to the establishment and improvement of the management and supervision system of state-owned assets, the Decision separated the public management functions of the government and the functions of the investors of state-owned assets. The state-owned assets management institutions performed the functions of investors in accordance with the law for the state-owned capital authorized to be supervised, safeguarded the rights and interests of the owners and of enterprises as market subjects, and urged enterprises to maintain and increase the value of state-owned assets and prevent loss.[69] The function of the state-owned assets investor of the government was reassigned to a specially established state-owned assets management organization (State-owned Assets Management Committee). The State-owned

---

67. Jiang Zemin, *Holding High the Great Banner of Deng Xiaoping Theory and Pushing the Cause of Building Socialism with Chinese Characteristics into the 21st Century: Report on the Fifteenth National Congress of the Communist Party of China* (People's Publishing House, 1997).

68. Jiang Zemin, *Building an Affluent Society in All Aspects and Creating a New Situation in the Cause of Socialism with Chinese Characteristics: Report on the National Congress* (People's Publishing House, 2002).

69. *Decision of the Central Committee of the Communist Party of China on Several Issues Concerning the Improvement of the Socialist Market Economic System* (People's Publishing House, 1993).

Assets Management Committee was authorized by law to supervise state-owned capital and perform the investor's duties and to authorize the state-owned enterprises to operate. This system improved the separation of ownership of assets and property rights of legal entities, and it further straightened out the relationship between the property rights of state-owned assets. For state-owned enterprises, it was crucial to improve the governance structure. According to the requirements of the modern enterprise system, it was necessary to standardize the rights and responsibilities of the board of shareholders, board of directors, board of supervisors, and managers and to improve the appointment system of enterprise leaders. The reform of monopoly industries was accelerated and improved. For monopoly industries, market access was to be relaxed and a competition mechanism was to be introduced. Qualified enterprises were to actively promote the diversification of investors.[70]

In October 2007, the report of the Seventeenth National Congress of the Communist Party of China proposed the deepening of the reform of the shareholding system of state-owned enterprises, improvement of the modern enterprise system, optimization of the layout and structure of the state-owned economy, and enhancement of the vitality, control, and influence of the state-owned economy. The reform of monopoly industries was deepened, competition mechanisms introduced, and government and social supervision strengthened. The government was to speed up the construction of a budget system for the operation of state-owned capital and improve the management system and system of all kinds of state-owned assets.[71]

In November 2012, the report of the Eighteenth National Congress of the Communist Party of China proposed comprehensively deepening the reform of the economic system. It was important to deepen the reform of state-owned enterprises, improve the management system of all kinds of state-owned assets, promote more investment of state-owned assets in important industries and key fields related to national security and the lifeline of the national economy, and constantly enhance the vitality, control, and efficiency of the state-owned economy.[72]

On November 12, 2013, the Third Plenary Session of the Eighteenth CPC Central Committee adopted the Decision of the CPC Central Committee on Several Major Issues Concerning Comprehensive Deepening of the Reform. The overall goal of comprehensive deepening of the reform was to improve and develop the socialist system with Chinese characteristics and promote the modernization of the national governance system and capacity. It was important to adhere to and improve the basic economic system, give full play to the leading role of the state-owned economy, and promote state-owned enterprises to improve the modern enterprise system. State

---

70. *Decision of the Central Committee of the Communist Party of China on Several Issues Concerning the Improvement of the Socialist Market Economic System* (People's Publishing House, 1993).

71. Hu Jintao, *Holding High the Great Banner of Socialism with Chinese Characteristics and Striving for the New Victory of Building a Moderately Prosperous Society in All Aspects: Report on the Seventeenth National Congress of the Communist Party of China* (People's Publishing House, 2007).

72. Hu Jintao, *Unswervingly Advancing Along the Road of Socialism with Chinese Characteristics and Striving for Building a Moderately Prosperous Society in All Aspects: Report on the Eighteenth National Congress of the Communist Party of China* (People's Publishing House, 2012).

owned enterprises, owned by all the people, were an important force in promoting national modernization and safeguarding the common interests of the people. As a whole, state-owned enterprises were integrated with the market economy, so they were to adapt to the new situation of marketization and internationalization and further deepen the reform of state-owned enterprises by focusing on standardizing business decision-making, maintaining and increasing the value of assets, participating fairly in competition, improving enterprise efficiency, enhancing enterprise vitality, and undertaking social responsibility. It was important to accurately define the functions of different state-owned enterprises. State-owned capital aimed to increase its investment in public welfare enterprises and make greater contributions to the provision of public services. It was thus necessary to improve the corporate governance structure with coordinated operations and effective checks and balances.[73]

In October 2017, the report of the Nineteenth National Congress of the Communist Party of China proposed the acceleration of the improvement of the socialist market economic system from the perspective of implementing the new development concept and building a modern economic system. It was necessary to improve the management system of all kinds of state-owned assets, reform the authorized operations system of state-owned capital, speed up the optimization of the state-owned economic layout, structural adjustment, and strategic restructuring, promote the maintenance and appreciation of state-owned assets, promote state-owned capital to become bigger, better, and stronger, and effectively prevent the loss of state-owned assets. It was necessary to deepen the reform of state-owned enterprises, develop a mixed ownership economy, and cultivate world-class enterprises with global competitiveness.[74]

By the first decade of the 21st century, after long-term reform, state-owned enterprises were integrated with the market economy. However, some major aspects of deepening the reform of state-owned enterprises were still needed, including standardizing business decision-making, maintaining and increasing the value of state-owned assets, and improving the vitality, efficiency, and market competitiveness of state-owned enterprises. However, more emphasis was placed on the social responsibility of state-owned enterprises in providing public services to make greater contributions in terms of services. At the same time, it was to be connected with the development of the mixed ownership economy and cultivating world-class enterprises with global resource allocation ability and competitiveness in the open economic environment.[75]

---

73. *Decision of the CPC Central Committee on Several Major Issues Concerning Comprehensive Deepening of the Reform* (People's Publishing House, 2013).

74. Xi Jinping, *Winning the Victory in Building a Moderately Prosperous Society in All Respects and Socialism with Chinese Characteristics in the New Era: Report on the Nineteenth National Congress* (People's Publishing House, 2017).

75. *Decision of the CPC Central Committee on Several Major Issues Concerning Comprehensive Deepening of the Reform* (adopted at the Third Plenary Session of the Eighteenth Conference of the Central Committee on January 12, 2013); Xi Jinping, *Winning the Victory in Building a Moderately Prosperous Society in All Respects and Socialism with Chinese Characteristics in the New Era: Report on the Nineteenth National Congress* (People's Publishing House, 2017).

2. Analysis of Property Rights of the Enterprise Legal Entity in the Reform of State-owned Enterprises

For some time, the reform of China's state-owned enterprises had been evolving alongside the idea of establishing a modern enterprise system. The organizational form of the modern enterprise system was basically a company system, and the capital form of the enterprise was basically a share-holding system. An idea of property right reform was the separation of ownership and management right, and the concept of "legal entity property rights" was created as the legal basis for the separation of the two rights. According to the academic point of view and policy implication, the ownership of assets and the property rights of legal entities were two kinds of rights that could be distributed. The ownership of assets was embodied in the right of return on assets, while the property rights of legal entities were embodied in the right to operate assets. The ownership of state-owned assets in an enterprise belonged to the state. The enterprise owned all the property rights of a legal entity formed by the investment of investors including state-owned assets, and it became a legal entity with civil rights and civil liabilities. An enterprise was to operate independently with all its legal entity property and be responsible for its own profits and losses.

According to international civil law, only joint stock limited companies and limited liability companies qualified as enterprise legal entities. Because there were many investors in a joint-stock company or a limited company, it was necessary to establish the company's status as a legal entity and make it a legal subject separated from the investor (natural person). However, the concept of a corporate legal entity did not lead to the concept of "corporate property rights." Looking at the laws of various countries all around the world, no reference to "corporate property rights" or "corporate ownership" could be found. In the common law system, property rights could be divided into legal property rights and equity interests. Whoever had the legal property rights, no matter what kind of property, was the owner and had the right to dispose of the property. The person who enjoyed equitable rights and interests was a beneficiary and had a claim on the use of property. The division of these two kinds of rights and interests was the basis of the trust property system of the common law system. Both movable and immovable property could be an established trust. In the system of trust property, the property could be transferred to the trustee for the benefit of others (the beneficiary), and the trustee would manage the property and pay part or all of the trust property or its income to the beneficiary according to the agreement. In the trust property system, the trustee became the legal owner of the trust property. The beneficiary had an equitable interest in the property. When the trustee failed to perform his obligations, the beneficiary had the right to sue. However, the trustee was not a legal entity, and the legal property rights and interests were not "legal entity property rights." This property trust system was obviously not the same thing as the practice of the state owning the property rights of assets and enterprises owning the property rights of legal entities. It was stipulated in the corporate law of various countries that the legal representative of a joint-stock company was the board of directors. Because the board of directors was the substitute or permanent organization of the general meeting of shareholders (according to the provisions of American corporate law, the general meeting of shareholders had two organizations, the general meeting of shareholders and the board of directors), which specifically represented stock rights and implemented management rights and had the obligation and ability to bear the legal responsibility, making it the legal representative of the company. In other words, capital ownership and legal representative were the same subject of property rights, and the qualification of a legal representative was based on capital ownership, which was the standardization of property rights. If the capital ownership and the legal representative were separated into two property rights subjects, then the rights and responsibilities of the legal representative had no property basis, and the property rights were not standardized. (The legal representatives of many enterprises in China were managers, factory directors, or chairmen of the board of directors, which was contrary to international practice and did not make logical sense. If the legal representative could be a natural person, why should the legal entity status of an enterprise be established? In a joint stock company, the chairman of the board was only the legal representative, not the legal entity. If the company property right were further divided into asset ownership and legal entity property right, the property right would become less standardized.)

In order to further explain this problem, it is necessary to clarify theoretically the property rights relationship between shareholders and a corporate legal entity in a joint-stock economy. One main conclusion drawn from the viewpoint of the "property rights of an enterprise legal entity" is that the investor of the joint stock company has the ownership of its invested capital, and all the capital invested by the investor forms the property of the company legal entity. After the formation of the corporate property, it is separated from the investor and becomes an independent "legal entity property right," which belongs to the enterprise legal entity. It is true that once the investor invests in the joint-stock company, its equity can only be transferred, but not withdrawn. Relative to the change of shareholders, the company is independent. However, further analysis is needed on the property rights relationship between shareholders and a legal entity. A legal entity is a legal concept and a civil subject with an independent legal personality. From the perspective of a corporate legal entity, company property should be recognized as a unified whole in law to form the property basis of an independent legal personality. However, the independence of the company property in law does not mean that the property ownership is separated from the investor and forms a legal entity property right. There is only one ownership of the company's property, which undoubtedly belongs to the investors. When any civil action occurs, the company's legal entity, as an independent civil subject, is liable for all its property. However, this kind of liability of the company legal entity is based on the limited liability of the shareholder, that is, the limited liability of the shareholder is the source of the liability of the legal entity of the company. Just as the ownership of the capital of the shareholder is the source and ownership of the property right of the company, it cannot arbitrarily separate the property right from the shareholder. In addition, the phrase "corporate property rights" owned by the enterprise legal entity is a kind of ambiguous statement. What exactly does "enterprise legal entity" mean here? If it refers to the enterprise itself, that is to say, as a collection of various production factors, the enterprise has the ownership of these input factors, which is not logical. If it refers to the operators and producers of enterprises, it does not make sense. The operators and producers get the corresponding remuneration because they are employed by the capital owners. On what basis do they have the property rights of an enterprise legal entity? It is also unreasonable to refer to the board of directors of a company. The board of directors exercises the management right on behalf of the capital ownership. The power of the board of directors is entrusted by shareholders, not given by law. According to the regulation of property rights, the power source of a company can only be one, that is, the management right comes from the ownership. If there are two parallel sources of power, the management right does not come from the capital ownership, but from the "corporate property rights," then the property rights are not standardized.

During this period, scholars used the empirical method to study the dual efficiency loss of state-owned enterprises. The public property right of state-owned enterprises determined that there were double losses of production efficiency and innovation efficiency in state-owned enterprises. Through the design of supervision and incentive mechanism, the reform of state-owned enterprises realized the matching of residual claim rights and residual control rights in production to a certain extent, thus improving the production efficiency of state-owned enterprises. However, due to the special nature of innovation, which was different from general production, the existing state-owned enterprise reform measures could not match the residual claim right and the residual control right in the innovation, so it could not improve the innovation efficiency of state-owned enterprises.[76]

3. Profit Maximization, Pareto Optimality, and the Basic Micro Property Rights Paradigm of the Market Economy

The purpose of establishing and improving the socialist market economy was to improve the efficiency of resource allocation and economic activities, to develop productivity better, and to meet the needs of social welfare growth. Before the Keynesian revolution, mainstream Western economics was basically microeconomics, and its main task was to study efficiency. According to the efficiency standard of economics, under the condition of the established property rights paradigm, the profit (income) maximization goal and the resource allocation optimization goal (Pareto optimality) of market entities needed to be unified. This was a theoretical criterion that needed to be established in the reform of the socialist market economic system, and it was also a basic topic in the theoretical study of economic thought related to the reform of the socialist market economy.

In a neoclassical framework, profit maximization was a basic hypothesis set by economics in analyzing the behavior of firms, which meant that the criterion of firms' behavior was to maximize profits. This chapter builds a simple model of the firm's profit and constructs a reasonable hypothesis

---

76. Wu Yanbing, "Research on the Dual Efficiency Loss of State Owned Enterprises," *Economic Research*, no. 3 (2012).

of the maximum output. The profit maximization hypothesis was not able to completely explain firms' behavior. For example, in general competitive equilibrium, firms with increasing returns to scale pursued the marginal cost pricing principle (efficiency requires that the price equals to the marginal cost), rather than profit maximization. But in the long run, the firm's decision-making behavior was closer to profit maximization. Therefore, profit maximization seemed to be the most reasonable starting point for the analysis of firms' behavior, and it was only in some cases that this assumption needed to be relaxed.

The significance of profit maximization as the purpose of manufacturer's production was not only at the level of instrumental rationality, but also involved the deeper social production purpose and the growth of national wealth. In the modern economy, enterprise production was the source of social wealth growth, and the level of enterprise production efficiency determined the quality and speed of a country's national economic growth. Only when every enterprise pursued profit maximization could economic resources be effectively utilized and social needs be better met. Therefore, under normal market conditions, the more profit maximization an enterprise pursued, the more conducive it would be to the development of the national economy and the improvement of social welfare.

If profit maximization was the efficiency standard of production, then the efficiency standard of resource allocation was Pareto optimality. In fact, the efficiency standard or definition of efficiency in neoclassical economics was Pareto optimality or Pareto efficiency. Pareto optimality was not only an abstract criterion of efficiency, but also a proof of the idea of free competition in classical economics since Adam Smith. Kenneth J. Arrow and Gerard Debreu later proved two theorems of new welfare economics. First, under the neoclassical hypothesis, competitive equilibrium was Pareto efficiency. Second, assuming that returns to scale were not increasing, then any Pareto efficient resource allocation could be decentralized into a competitive equilibrium.[77] Economist and statistician Francis Ysidro Edgeworth used Edgeworth's box to test the Pareto optimality of exchange. In the Edgeworth box diagram, the so-called "contract curve" was formed by connecting the tangent points of each indifference curve between the trading parties. The transaction point of both parties needed to be on the contract line, and only the transaction point on the contract line could satisfy the Pareto optimality condition. Using the Edgeworth box diagram, it was proved that the Pareto optimality was developed under the classical assumption of perfect competition market (though there may have been other ways to achieve the Pareto optimality). Under the classical assumptions of no externalities, increasing returns, and perfect competition, free trade would move the transaction point to a point on the contract line and achieve Pareto exchange optimization.

The analysis of Pareto optimality through free trade was basically an explanation of wealth growth caused by the market economy. The reason the market economy was more efficient was that it was a free trade economic relationship based on free property rights. It realized the

77. K. J. Arrow, "Uncertainty and the Welfare Economics of Medical Care," *American Economics Review* (1963), 53; G. Debreu, *The Theory of Value* (Wiley, 1959).

transaction through individual's free choice and ensured that the benefit effect and damage effect of the transaction were directly borne by the transaction parties under the premise of clearly defined property rights. According to the comparison of cost and benefit and the principle of utility (profit) maximization, the parties to a transaction judged whether a transaction was beneficial or harmful to them and made a choice whether to conclude the transaction. When a large number of transactions were completed under such circumstances, the allocation of resources throughout society would tend to be optimized, and social welfare would increase. This analysis indicated that under the assumption of a classical perfect competition market, profit maximization was related to Pareto optimality, and Pareto optimality was achieved through the maximization of trading parties. The consistency between the maximization of individual interests and the maximization of social interests (Pareto optimality) in a perfect competitive market was precisely the belief advocated by classical economics.

In the classical perfect competitive market hypothesis and Coase's "zero transaction cost" world, the restriction on the behavior of the parties to the transaction came from the pursuit of maximization by the trading party. In other words, free exchange based on self-interest motivation itself was an effective incentive constraint mechanism. A deal would not be concluded unless both sides benefit. Pareto optimality was achieved when the interests of all parties in the transaction reached the maximum trading point.

From the perspective of methodology, classical economics discussed the efficiency of resource allocation under the premise of established system. If the classical institutional hypothesis was relaxed, then the institution was not the premise of discussing efficiency, but the content of efficiency. Based on the proposition that "transaction cost is positive" (relaxing the hypothesis of "zero transaction cost"), modern property economics studied what kind of institutional arrangement (incentive constraint mechanism) could eliminate externalities to the greatest extent and unify the pursuit of personal interests with the growth of social welfare. As an economic relationship, property rights were related to transaction. If there was no transaction, there were no property rights. In other words, "In Robinson's world, property rights do not work." The development of property rights was related to the development of transaction, and the development of transaction was related to the development of division of labor and of resource scarcity. It was in this sense that property rights were brought into the economic framework as an analysis element. Although the concept of "property rights" was not clearly given in classical economics, the mechanism of mutual checks and balances of private property rights had revealed the objective law of property rights in the market economy. In modern society, property rights were the norm of people's property rights, that is, the restriction of an individual's pursuit of private interests. The essence of property rights was an exclusive right. In a system of exclusive rights, each person's rights were not only effectively restricted by the rights of others, but also effectively prevented the infringement of others' rights.

The exclusiveness of property rights determined its relativity. In a transaction, the exclusive property rights of each party restricted the other's damage to their own rights. Therefore, property rights were relative rather than absolute for each party in the transaction. The absolute ownership of property (ownership) in the legal sense and the relativity of property rights in the economic sense were not at the same level. Ownership emphasized the relatively static and one-way domination of rights from the perspective of the relationship between people and property, while property rights emphasized the relatively dynamic and two-way restriction of rights from the perspective of transaction contracts. The absoluteness of ownership determined the exclusiveness of property rights, but when exclusive property rights entered into transactions, rights became relative. The exclusiveness and relativity of property rights indicated the institutional value of property rights. If property rights were not relative, that is, they were not restricted and regulated, then there was no right to speak of. Determined by the nature of property rights, the subject of property rights had two behavioral characteristics. One was the incentive and right to pursue their own interests maximization, and the other was restriction by the rights of other property rights subjects. Under the rule of pursuing the maximization of one's own interests and being restricted by the rights of others, the maximization of micro individual interests tended to be consistent with the maximization of social interests.

Therefore, in the reform of the socialist market economic system, it was imperative that the modern property rights system with clear ownership, clear rights and responsibilities, strict protections, and smooth circulation be improved.[78] This was the micro basis that allowed the market economy to reach the goal of efficiency. The reform of state-owned enterprises had always been one of the main elements of China's economic system reform. In fact, the reform of the urban economic system started from the reform of state-owned enterprises. In the process of establishing a perfect socialist market economic system, the reform of state-owned enterprises ran through the entire reform process. After years of reform, the market-oriented character of state-owned enterprises gradually formed, which was in line with the market economy. However, due to the nature of property rights, state-owned enterprises still needed to deepen the reform in the areas of flexible adaptation to market changes, standardization of business decision-making, preservation and appreciation of assets, fair participation in competition, improvement of enterprise efficiency, and enhancement of enterprise vitality. In the research on how to promote the market-oriented reform of state-owned enterprises, there were basically two ideas. One was that the key link of state-owned enterprise reform was to build a fair competition market environment, and in this market environment, state-owned enterprises needed to consciously carry out market-oriented reform in order to survive and develop. The other was that the core problem of state-owned enterprise reform was enterprises, the reform of internal governance structure, and the formation of an incentive restraint mechanism. In fact, the cultivation of the market environment and the adjustment of governance structure were originally two interrelated aspects in the reform process, and the reform of these two aspects needed to be carried out simultaneously.

An operational plan for the reform of state-owned enterprises involved establishing a modern enterprise system, improving the corporate governance structure of modern enterprises

---

78. *Decision of the CPC Central Committee on Several Major Issues of Comprehensive Deepening of Reform* (People's Publishing House, 2013), 8.

(companies), and establishing a long-term incentive restraint mechanism. In both incentive effect and constraint effect, it was important to have a perfect market system and market environment as conditions, including a product market, a factor market, and an operator market. Only in a perfect competitive market could the prices of products and elements be reasonable, the evaluation indexes be objective, and the incentive constraint effect be strengthened. For example, from the perspective of constraints, the constraints on managers mainly came from two aspects. One was the competition between agents, and the other was market pricing. Under the condition of agent competition, the entrusted talents could restrain the agent by choosing, and then reduce the cost of controlling the agent's behavior. Market pricing referred to the market pricing of products and stocks. Generally speaking, the stock market price, product price, quality, and market share were the objective criteria reflecting the business performance of an enterprise, and therefore were also the evaluation index of the operator's ability. Especially for joint-stock companies, the stock market price basically reflected the behavior of shareholders to choose operators by "voting with their feet," acting as powerful constraints on the operators. Therefore, if there were no perfect market system, even if the enterprise system and governance structure were very modern and standardized, it would not help.

Aside from that, the formation of the market environment of fair competition depended on whether the behavior of market participants conformed to the characteristics of micro subject of market economy. In the market economy, transactions were actually the result of the free choice of the parties to each transaction. In order to realize free trade, there needed to be many traders in the economic sphere, and transactions needed to be carried out equally among the transaction subjects with clear property rights. According to the comparison of cost and benefit and the principle of maximum utility, the transaction subject judged the transaction that realized the allocation of resources and determined whether it was beneficial and whether to trade. Therefore, the so-called optimal allocation of resources was a process in which market entrants benefited from free trade. In this process, property rights were to be clearly defined. The clear definition of property rights guaranteed the rational incentive and effective restraint of the parties to the transaction, so the transaction cost was low, the externality was small, and the efficiency was high.

From the perspective of China's situation, market-oriented reform was the creation of a new system and the transformation of the old system. These two aspects were inseparable. While creating a competitive market environment, if corresponding changes were not made to the original property rights relations and enterprise system, then market information such as price and interest rate would not have an effect on the enterprise behavior. Similarly, while transforming the state-owned enterprises according to the requirements of the modern enterprise system, if there were no corresponding market system, then the internal governance structure of modern enterprises would also be difficult to build. Thus, these opinions needed to coexist and complement each other.

In the theoretical framework of the integration of neoclassical economics and new institutional economics, these ideas could be communicated. In order to improve the efficiency, it was important to carry out free market transaction, and to carry out the free market transaction, it was necessary to have the economic relationships and institutional guarantees of the modern property rights system and fair trade, which could be integrated into a theoretical framework. In the practice of reform, the deepening of the market and the reform of the economic organization and system were a mutually related and natural development process. The enterprise system or governance structure in Western countries had evolved with the development of the market economy. If there were no corresponding economic market-oriented basis, thousands of state-owned enterprises would be transformed into "modern enterprises" by the government's instruction. This was a behavior of an "artificial economy," which would not have great practical effect. On the other hand, with the development of China's market economy, the normal growth of the market economy would be disturbed if there were no flexibility in system supply and no corresponding enterprise reform and innovation. Therefore, China's enterprise reform needed to be a dynamic process, that is, on the basis of vigorously promoting the market construction, the guarantee of system reform had to be given in law and policy, so that the ownership structure, property rights structure, and enterprise system could be adjusted and reformed in a timely manner, making it consistent with the development degree and characteristics of economic marketization.

4. Agency Cost and Profit Maximizations: An Analysis of Manufacturer Behavior Variation

(1) Enterprise Income Tax and Manufacturer Behavior

Profit (π) is the difference between total revenue (TR) and total cost (TC).

$$\pi = TR - TC$$

According to the profit maximization hypothesis of neoclassical economics, the rational behavior of a manufacturer is to choose a production (Q) that maximizes π. From the point of view of marginal analysis, the output with the largest profit should be that it can no longer increase π by changing Q. To express this concept in terms of calculus, the first order differential of π to Q should be equal to zero.

$$\frac{\mathrm{d}\pi}{\mathrm{d}Q} = 0 = \frac{\mathrm{d}TR}{\mathrm{d}Q} - \frac{\mathrm{d}TC}{\mathrm{d}Q}$$

The differential of Q to TR and TC is the slope of the TR curve and the TC curve, namely marginal revenue (MR) and marginal cost (MC). Therefore, the condition of profit maximization is the slope of the TR curve and the TC curve, or $MR = MC$.

From the total analysis, the larger the difference between TR and TC, the greater the profit. The difference between TR and TC can be increased by increasing TR or decreasing TC. In the perfect competition market, the manufacturer has no power to control the price and can only accept the fixed price. Therefore, manufacturers have to reduce TC to increase profits.

This is the profit maximization behavior analysis of the manufacturer without considering tax factors. If tax factors are introduced, this analysis will change.

Generally speaking, tax is an exogenous variable for the production process, which cannot be controlled by manufacturers. Although tax is not included in production cost in financial accounting, it is a part of investment cost in economic analysis. Both income tax or turnover tax have to affect the income or profit of the manufacturer, so they are the cost factors that manufacturers should consider when making investment decisions.

Enterprise income tax is a tax on profits which is directly borne by the manufacturer, that is, the manufacturer cannot transfer the tax burden by raising the product price. But manufacturers can reduce the revenue loss caused by taxation by adjusting the relationship between cost and profit. When introducing an enterprise income tax, the balance of $TR-TC$ is not the profit income of the manufacturer, and only the profit after tax deduction (after tax profit) is the disposable income of the manufacturer. With a fixed tax rate, the larger the total profit, the more disposable income the manufacturer will lose. Therefore, assuming that the firm's behavior is rational, it will not pursue profit maximization, but pursue the maximization of disposable income.

If the manufacturer pursues the maximization of disposable income, then the profit maximization hypothesis should be revised. According to neoclassical economics, when there is a fixed price, manufacturers always try to reduce the total cost in order to maximize profits. However, if income tax is introduced, a part of non-cost expenditure or assets will be included in the cost. To a certain extent, the cost will be increased, the profit before tax will be reduced, and the disposable income (including after tax profit and the part of non-cost expenditure or assets included in cost) will be increased. For example, manufacturers can accelerate the depreciation and share part of their assets into the cost. They can buy high-end cars, modern communication equipment, and luxury office supplies, and these expenses can be included in improving personal utility into the cost. They can also pay in-kind bonuses to improve their consumption level in the name of business negotiation and business travel, and this part of expenditure can be included in the cost. The indifference curve can be used to analyze the variation of firm behavior after income tax. See Figure 12-1.

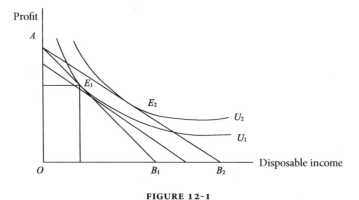

FIGURE 12-1

In Figure 12-1, the vertical axis represents profit and the horizontal axis represents the firm's disposable income. AB_1 and AB_2 are the firm's income constraint lines. U_1 and U_2 are the indifference curves of manufacturers. Assuming that the preference of the firm and the income are fixed, the influence of the introduction of income tax on the firm's behavior is investigated.

If income tax is not taken into account, the profits of the manufacturer are regarded as disposable income. If a manufacturer wants to increase one unit's disposable income, it should reduce one unit's profit, and vice versa. Therefore, the absolute value of the slope of the income constraint line AB_1 is equal to 1, and the indifference curve U_1 is tangent to point E_1. Point E_1 is the maximum utility point that the manufacturer can reach under the constraint of AB_1 curve.

If the income tax factor is introduced, assuming that the tax rate is t, $0 < t < 1$, the after tax profit is $\pi - \pi \cdot t$. At this time, if the manufacturer wants to increase one unit of disposable income, the profit and loss that the manufacturer has to bear is $1 - 1 \cdot t$. In other words, for a firm, the cost of a unit of disposable income is $1 - 1 \cdot t$ profits, and $1 - 1 \cdot t < 1$. If the cost of replacing profit by disposable income is regarded as the price of disposable income, and the cost of replacing disposable income with profit is regarded as the price of profit, then the cost of replacing profit with disposable income is reduced, which means that the price of the disposable income is reduced. When the profit price remains unchanged and the price of disposable income decreases, the firm's income constraint line will change (price effect), and the income constraint line will shift from AB_1 to AB_2. AB_2 is tangent to point E_2 with the higher indifference curve U_2. Since the utility represented by U_2 is greater than that of U_1, the manufacturer achieves greater utility at E_2 than at E_1.

Theoretically speaking, if there is no financial accounting system control, the manufacturer will pursue disposable income infinitely and transfer all the profits to the cost (the profit is zero). Because the enterprise income tax is to tax profits, it does not change the marginal cost of the manufacturer. When the price of the product is fixed, the behavior of transferring part of the profit into the cost to maximize the disposable income does not affect the equilibrium output of the manufacturer. But in the long run, the decline of profit rates will weaken the accumulation ability of enterprises, which will affect the expansion of reproduction capacity and development potential of enterprises.

(2) Agent Behavior and Agency Cost: Deviation from Profit Maximization

This analysis demonstrates that in the relationship of $\pi = TR - TC$, if the price is fixed, any decrease of profit is an increase of total cost. As long as the loss of profit reduction is not fully borne by the enterprise owner (for example, existing corporate income tax), the enterprise owner will not have 100% incentive to reduce costs. Therefore, after the introduction of tax factors, the value of enterprises will be less than that of enterprises without tax factors. The essential reason for this difference lies in the fact that the owner of the enterprise cannot obtain all the surplus (profit).

According to M. Jensen and W. Meckling, the enterprise value when the operator is the complete owner of the enterprise is greater than the enterprise value when the operator is not the complete owner of the enterprise, and the difference between the two is the "agency cost."[79] Based on this definition, the essential source of agency cost is the separation of enterprise operator and residual claim. According to the earlier analysis, even if the operator is the owner of the enterprise, with the introduction of an income tax, the enterprise value he pursues is different from the profit maximization hypothesis of neoclassical economics. In other words, only the utility of the external owner of the enterprise is the profit function or stock value. Once the owner becomes the operator, some other variables will enter his utility function, and his behavior will deviate from the goal of profit maximization.[80] There are differences in the degree between owner operator deviation from profit maximization and non-owner operator deviation from profit maximization, but the essential reason is the same, with both occurring due to different degrees of separation from residual claim rights (unable to obtain all surplus).

Based on the logic of this analysis, assuming that the enterprise operator and the residual claim are completely separated, then he will infinitely deviate from the goal of profit maximization. After A. Berle and G. Means put forward the proposition of "separation of ownership and control" in the 1930s, economists developed the principal-agent theory on the condition of asymmetric information. The core of this theory is to design a mechanism based on the assumption of asymmetric information, so that the agent can maximize the utility of the principal on the condition of maximizing his own utility. The negotiation of a principal-agent contract is a game problem, because the contract should be accepted by both parties. The final contract is called an "equilibrium contract," which should meet the following conditions:

- Incentive compatibility constraint. An agent chooses his behavior in a way that maximizes his utility.
- Participation constraint. An agent gains a utility no less than a certain reservation value.
- The optimal equilibrium of the principal's utility. Using any other contract (including the principal's own operation) cannot improve the principal's utility.

An equilibrium contract is a kind of Nash equilibrium. At the equilibrium point, if the other party does not change its decision, neither party can improve its utility by changing its own decision and behavior.

Based on the assumption of asymmetric information, agents have an information advantage. Therefore, the equilibrium contract mainly serves to form incentives and constraints on agents. Because of the information asymmetry, the agent will present a "moral hazard." In order to prevent the moral hazard of the agent, the principal needs to control the process of contract execution and

---

79. M. Jensen and W. Meckling, "Theory of the Firm: Managerial Behaviour, Agency Costs, and Capital Structure," *Journal of Financial Economics* (1976): 3.

80. M. Jensen and W. Meckling, "Theory of the Firm: Managerial Behaviour, Agency Costs, and Capital Structure," *Journal of Financial Economics* (1976): 3.

supervise the agent's performance behavior. The cost caused by this is called "supervision cost." If the supervision cost is too high to observe the performance of the agent, the principal will agree to let the agent participate in the residual sharing, so as to increase the opportunity cost of the agent's moral hazard. The negotiation cost, the supervision cost, and the residual share of the agent constitute the "agency cost" borne by the principal. As long as agency costs occur, the strict assumption of profit maximization in neoclassical economics is relaxed, and the utility of the principal cannot reach the profit maximization in the classical sense, but can only be sub-optimal. However, if the agency cost exceeds the benefits brought by the principal-agent contract, even the suboptimal goal cannot be achieved. In this case, the principal will withdraw from the contract.

(3) Contract Selection Under Agency Cost Constraints: Profit Suboptimal Model

Agency cost is a special form of transaction cost. The introduction of agency cost relaxes the classical assumption that the transaction cost is zero. With agency cost, the choice of contract becomes an important variable that affects the operation performance.

The essence of contract selection is an issue of mechanism design, which is a special incomplete information game. The principal selection mechanism, rather than using a given mechanism, is a basic feature of mechanism design.[81]

Zhang Wuchang further studied the form of tenancy contracts in agriculture. In his view, if the transaction cost is zero, under the constraints of private property rights (property rights are exclusive and transferable), different contractual arrangements will produce the same efficiency of resource allocation. If the assumption of zero transaction cost is relaxed, the choice of different contract arrangements depends on the comparison of transaction cost, risk aversion cost, and income.[82] According to Zhang's research, the choice of contract is determined by the weighting of the benefits from risk diversification and the transaction costs associated with different contract forms. If only the transaction costs are compared, the sharing contract will not be more advantageous than the quota contract and the wage contract, but the sharing contract has the function of dispersing risk, that is, the change of income is shared by both parties. If the higher transaction costs can at least be compensated by the benefits of risk diversification, the sharing contract will be more advantageous than the quota or wage contract.

The most interesting thing about Zhang's research on contract form is that under the assumption of positive transaction costs, the choice of contract arrangement itself becomes one of the factors in maximizing the resource value of participating contracts. Admittedly, Zhang failed to fully develop this thought in his research, but it gave his theory the color of new institutional economics. The essence of new institutional economics was to take institutional factors (organization, contract, property rights) as established or exogenous traditional analysis methods and demonstrate that institutional change would not only affect the use of resources, but also be a

---

81. Zhang Weiying, *Game Theory and Information Economics* (Shanghai Sanlian Bookstore, 1996).

82. Zhang Wuchang, "Private Property Rights and Shared Tenancy," *Political Economics*, no. 76 (1968); Chapter 4 of *On Shared Tenancy* (University of Chicago Press, 1976).

resource use activity, and then introduce institutional change as an endogenous variable into the framework of economic analysis.

If other variables affecting the choice of principal-agent contract are assumed to be fixed, then the choice of contract is only constrained by agency cost. From the perspective of cost comparison, agency cost is the best operating cost that asset owners should pay for the property right structure chosen according to the principle of minimum cost. In other words, in the case of the agency relationship, the cost of the owner's own operation should be greater than the agency cost, so he will transfer the management right and become the external owner. Therefore, under the condition of principal-agent relationship, the owner and the management are separated and become the external owner. As an external owner, the utility function of the principal conforms to the classic principle of profit maximization. He tends to pursue the maximization of profit or enterprise value more than when he is in charge of his own business. Even the enterprise income tax does not affect him. But once the principal-agent relationship occurs, there will be agency costs. Under the constraint of agency costs, the result of the execution of an equilibrium contract is not profit maximization, but profit suboptimization.

As mentioned above, the agency cost borne by the principal can be divided into three parts: the negotiation cost of the balanced contract, the profit share of the agent, and the supervision fee for the agent's behavior. If the negotiation cost is regarded as fixed, the client can control the other two parts of the cost. Moreover, these two parts of cost are interchangeable. The greater the profit share of the agent, the smaller the moral hazard motivation and the lower the supervision cost. In an extreme case, if the agent fully enjoys the surplus, the supervision fee is zero. By contrast, if the agent's behavior of executing the contract is completely controlled, he cannot share the profits. However, both are paradoxes of the principal-agent relationship. The agent should be allowed to fully enjoy the surplus, that is, the principal transfers the residual claim to the agent, which can reduce the supervision cost to zero, but the agent often does not have the property and risk bearing capacity of a residual claim. The agent should then be allowed to get a fixed salary, that is to say, not to share the surplus. Although this avoids the surplus loss, the supervision cost will be too high to bear (in fact, if we assume asymmetric information, "complete supervision" cannot be realized).

Under the constraint of agency cost, the choice of equilibrium contract can be considered from several aspects. The first is the degree of specificity of the resources involved in the contract. E. Williamson put forward the theory of asset specificity to explain enterprise scale expansion (vertical integration). But what needs analysis here is the degree of specificity of the resources involved in the contract and the choice of equilibrium contract. If the principal's resource in the contract is monetary capital and the agent's resource in the contract is operational capability, then the operational capability is a kind of asset with a high degree of specificity (if the operating capacity is subdivided by industry, the degree of specificity is higher). Due to the different degree of asset specificity of participating contracts, the principal and agent have different preferences for the duration and continuity of contracts. The principal prefers to choose a short-term contract in order to terminate the principal-agent relationship conveniently and with low cost. Agents prefer to choose long-term contracts. In order to control the agent's behavior more effectively, the discontinuous contract can be designed, which cannot only satisfy the agent's preference for a long-term contract, but also make it restricted by a termination contract.

The second aspect is the size of the "moral hazard." Holmstrom's Impossibility Theorem expresses the common nature of moral hazard. According to B. Holmstrom's research, in a team production whose output depends on the joint efforts of many people, it can be proved that if the budget is balanced, it is impossible to design a wage compensation mechanism that only depends on the observable total output, so as to form a Nash equilibrium that maximizes the sum of the total team members' utility. According to any kind of wage compensation contract, everyone has the motivation of "free riding."[83] The reason "moral hazard" cannot be contained is that the cost of supervision is too high. If the productivity of each member in the production team can be accurately decomposed, measured, and linked with the reward, then the Holmstrom Impossibility Theorem cannot be proved. When the cost of supervision is very high, the principal cannot control the agent's behavior of executing the contract (that is, the principal can't observe the agent's effort level), so he can only deduce the agent's optimal strategy under the assumption of moral hazard, and the resulting contract is inefficient. When the agent's behavior cannot be observed and controlled, assuming that the agent is risk-averse, optimal risk sharing (the agent does not bear any risk) will conflict with the incentive constraint, and the optimal contract cannot be realized. But if the agent is allowed to share the risk, that is, the income of the agent is related to the profit, the best contract design is to make the profit sharing rate of the agent equal to its marginal productivity, so as to optimize the principal's interests under the constraint of agency costs. How to determine the optimal profit sharing rate in technology remains an unsolved problem in economic theory. Holmstrom pointed out that the optimal profit sharing rate should be based on "sufficient statistics" which can reflect the agent's private information. It is true that if the agent's private information can be fully reflected, the determination of the optimal profit sharing rate is technically feasible. But this seems to return to a more basic question, that is, under the assumption of asymmetric information, can the "sufficient statistics" of an agent's private information be realized? Therefore, the determination technology of the optimal profit sharing rate requires the further development of information economics.

The third aspect is the attitude toward risk. In modern stock companies, the risk preference of shareholders and managers is asymmetric. Due to the decentralization of residual claims, the risks of shareholders (clients) are also dispersed. However, because the assets and interests of the operator (agent) are more related to the contract, the variance of income[84] is larger and the degree of risk is higher. Therefore, generally speaking, shareholders hold a risk-neutral attitude, while

---

83. B. Holmstrom, "Moral Hazard in Teams," *Bell Journal of Economics,* no. 13 (1982); H. Varian, *Microeconomics: A Modern Perspective* (Shanghai Sanlian Bookstore, 1994).

84. The variance or standard deviation σ of the return of an investment project is the average of the sum of squares of the deviation between the possible return value *ri* and the mathematical expectation value *E(r)*, which reflects the average difference of various possible income values of investment projects. The greater the variance of return, the greater the risk of the investment project; otherwise, the risk is smaller.

managers hold a risk-averse attitude.

Assuming that the performance of the agent cannot be directly observed (asymmetric information, high cost of supervision), and assuming that the agent is risk averse, it can be proved that the optimal contract requires the agent to share part of the risk. In the principal-agent model, the agent bears the risk, that is, the agent shares the surplus, so the principal should choose a contract that satisfies the agent's participation constraint and incentive compatibility to maximize his expected utility function. In this contract, the agent's income is a constant (minimum retention value) multiplied by a random variable (residual share rate), and the risk shared by the agent is the product of the variance of the random variable and the square of the constant. Because the agent is risk averse, the incentive effect of the agent sharing the surplus should be greater than the risk cost, which is to say that the agent requires risk compensation. Generally speaking, the greater the variance of risk aversion and income, the higher the agency cost.

The fourth aspect is asset maintenance costs. The cost of asset maintenance involves the arrangement of asset ownership in the principal-agent relationship. If the ownership of the assets owned by the client is fixed, the level of the asset maintenance cost will affect the client's choice of the fixed amount contract or the sharing contract. If the cost of maintaining the assets is low, the principal may borrow, lease, or contract the assets to the agent and charge a fixed amount of interest or rent according to a fixed amount contract. If the cost of asset maintenance is high, a quota contract is not desirable, because the agent will not maintain the asset to maximize his own income, but will also make use of it.[85] Therefore, in order to reduce the cost of asset maintenance, the principal will choose to let the agent bear part of the asset risk. There are two operation methods. One involves transferring part of the asset ownership to the agent, and the other allows the agent to bear part of the asset maintenance cost. In the former, the agent should share the corresponding share of the surplus, while in the latter, the agent should share the corresponding share of the asset income. In essence, both are divided contracts.

Asset maintenance cost is a kind of risk cost, which cannot be included in the strict sense of agency cost. However, the decomposition of risk cost between principal and agent will cause the change of agency cost, so the choice of contract is still based on the comparison of agency cost and income. From the principal's point of view, if the cost of asset maintenance is low and the cost of risk is low, he can choose the contract form with lower agency cost (such as quota contract). If the cost of asset maintenance is high, the risk cost is also high. In order to transfer part of the risk to the agent, he should choose the contract form with higher agency cost (such as sharing contract). The principle is that the profit brought by risk transfer should be able to compensate for the rise in agency costs.

---

85. This may be one of the reasons the contract system in China's rural areas is "effective immediately at the contract," but such is not satisfactory in urban industrial enterprises. Land is an asset with low maintenance cost, so it is suitable for such a contract. The maintenance cost of physical assets in industrial enterprises is high. If the agent takes short-term action, the principal will lose substantial assets. If the asset loss approaches or exceeds the principal's income, the contract is not quite efficient.

This analysis has been carried out within the framework of a standard market economy system. The core of this system is the exclusiveness and transferability of property rights. Under this institutional condition, the variation of firm's behavior (deviation from profit maximization) is analyzed, relaxing some classical assumptions, but if the basic institutional framework conditions are not established, such as different property rights arrangements, then the analysis will be more complex. In different property rights arrangement and legal system, the incentive restraint mechanism is different, leading to different behavior of both manufacturer and contract.

5. Principal Agent Theory and the Path of Deepening the Reform of State-owned Enterprises

Being owned by the people, state-owned enterprises were an important force in promoting national modernization and safeguarding the common interests of the people. However, in accelerating the reform of the socialist market economic system, state-owned enterprises needed to adapt to the new situation of marketization and internationalization and improve the corporate governance structure with coordinated operations and effective checks and balances.[86] The nature of state-owned enterprises owned by all the people necessitated the principal-agent theory as the theoretical basis of their governance structure. In a principal-agent framework, the so-called "agency problem" referred to the need for the principal to design a contract or mechanism which could provide some incentives and constraints to the agent, so that the agent could maximize the utility of the principal under the condition of maximizing his own utility. The agency problem would lead to the "agency cost," that is, the cost of implementing and supervising the principal-agent contract or mechanism. The agency cost was accompanied by the separation of ownership and management rights. The essence of the agency cost was that the owner (client) tried to control the expenses of management rights when ownership and management rights were separated. The "separation of the ownership and management rights" was not a legal procedure, but a business procedure, a cost comparison, and a choice of governance structure. In the case of the principal-agent relationship, the cost of the owner's own operation needed to be greater than the agency cost, which meant that the owner transferred the management right and became the external owner, especially in the system of state-owned enterprises owned by all the people.

If other variables affecting the choice of the principal-agent contract were assumed to be fixed, then the choice of contract was only constrained by the agency cost. The size of the agency cost was related to the degree of separation of the ownership and management rights, and the degree of separation of the ownership and management rights was related to the degree of decentralization of the property rights. The more decentralized the property rights were, the greater the degree of separation between the ownership and management rights was, and the greater the supervision costs and possible residual losses of the client. In addition, the more levels and scope of the principal-agent, the higher the cost of negotiation and supervision. If the agency

---

86. *Decision of the CPC Central Committee on Several Major Issues Concerning Comprehensive Deepening of the Reform* (People's Publishing House, 2013), 9–10.

cost exceeded a certain limit, the principal would weaken the supervision, thus leading to the problem of "insider control." Determined by the basic economic system of socialism with Chinese characteristics, state-owned enterprises were owned by all the people. In the system of state-owned property rights, all citizens were the subject of state-owned property rights. However, it was quite expensive for all citizens to implement the responsibility of the property rights subject together, making it impossible in practice. Therefore, it was necessary for the government to exercise the main responsibility of property rights on behalf of all citizens. Thus, in the state-owned property rights system, there was a principal-agent relationship between all citizens and the government. However, this could lead to issues in the relationship among the government, the state-owned assets units, and the managers of state-owned enterprises, meaning that the principal-agent relationship of the state-owned assets of the entire society was large-scale and multi-leveled, and the games and contracts were numerous and dynamic. The principal-agent relationship of the entire society led to a high agency cost. More importantly, the large-scale and multi-leveled principal-agent relationship weakened the restriction of property rights. In the layered principal-agent relationship, it was increasingly difficult for state-owned property rights to form an incentive constraint mechanism for the behavior of principals at all levels, and the principals were decreasingly characterized by the behavior of the property subject (representative). As the ultimate owner of state-owned assets and state-owned enterprises, the cost of full, effective supervision of agents was very high. Theoretically, it was difficult to restrain the opportunistic behavior of agents. Therefore, an important task of comprehensively deepening the reform and accelerating the improvement of the socialist market economic system was to improve the management system of all kinds of state-owned assets, reform the authorized operation system of state-owned capital, accelerate the optimization of the layout, structural adjustment, and strategic restructuring of the state-owned economy, so as to maintain and increase the value of state-owned assets, promote the state-owned capital to become stronger, better, and bigger, and effectively prevent the loss of state-owned assets.[87]

There were three ways to deepen the reform of state-owned assets and state-owned enterprise system. The first involved developing a mixed ownership economy in which state-owned capital, collective capital, and non-public capital were cross shareholding and integrated. It was necessary to allow more the state-owned economy and other ownership economies to develop into a mixed ownership economy. A mixed ownership economy was an important realization form of the basic economic system. Non-state-owned capital was allowed to participate in state-owned capital investment projects. This was not only conducive to enlarging the function of state-owned capital and maintaining and increasing its value, but was also conducive to the mutual restriction, mutual promotion, and common development of various ownership capital rights. The mechanism of property rights separation, interest coordination, and win-win cooperation formed by mixed

---

87. Xi Jinping, *Winning the Victory in Building a Moderately Prosperous Society in All Respects and Socialism with Chinese Characteristics in the New Era: Report on the Nineteenth National Congress of the Communist Party of China* (People's Publishing House, 2017).

ownership was suitable to the characteristics of a market economy, and also conducive to the improvement of state-owned assets operation efficiency.

Second, it was important to improve the management system of state-owned assets, strengthen the supervision of state-owned assets, and reform the authorized operation system of state-owned capital. In terms of operation, a number of state-owned capital operating companies were to be established to support the reorganization of qualified state-owned enterprises into state-owned capital holding companies.

The third way was to improve the modern enterprise system of the state-owned enterprises. As a whole, state-owned enterprises had been integrated with the market economy. They thus needed to adapt to the new situation of marketization and internationalization and further deepen the reform of state-owned enterprises. It was necessary to define the functions of different state-owned enterprises accurately, and the natural monopoly industries in which state-owned capital continued to control and operate were to implement the reform with the separation of government and enterprise and the separation of government and capital, franchising, and government supervision. It was important to improve the corporate governance structure with coordinated operations and effective checks and balances. It was necessary to establish a professional manager system, promote the tenure system of managers and contractual management, and give fuller play to the role of entrepreneurs.

Three important steps were to form an enterprise property right structure with clear ownership, clear rights and responsibilities, incentive compatibility, and interest balance from the perspective of property rights; to strengthen supervision and effectively prevent the loss of state-owned assets; and to form a modern corporate governance structure and a flexible, efficient market-oriented operation mechanism. According to the data, by the end of 2016, the total assets of state-owned enterprises (excluding financial and cultural state-owned enterprises) reached 1,549 trillion yuan, an increase of 73.1% over the end of 2012, and 82 state-owned enterprises entered the Fortune Global 500.[88] However, after forty years of reform, there were still some problems in state-owned enterprises, such as the imperfect system and mechanism, the unreasonable layout structure, the imbalance of the vitality and efficiency of operation and management.

According to the analysis of the principal-agent theory and the research on the path of deepening the reform of state-owned enterprises, there were several choices for the principal-agent mode of state-owned enterprises. The first was the state-owned mode. The first mock exam was applicable to large scale basic industries, which were necessary for national security and national economic security. SASAC directly authorized the operation, but effectively controlled the enterprise management rights. In personnel rights, the state-owned assets management department directly appointed the enterprise leadership, and the enterprise leadership was directly responsible to the state-owned assets management department. The operational decision-making powers included the government's investment decision-making, financing mode and quantity, main business direction, medium and long-term development strategy, and enterprise change.

---

88. Xiao Yaqing, "Deepening the Reform of State-owned Enterprises," *People's Daily*, December 13, 2017.

Another consideration was the main financial indicators, which the government issued to the enterprises. These included output value, sales volume, profit rate, depreciation rate, and profit distribution principle. These indicators were to become the business objectives of enterprises. Due to the administrative monopoly nature of state-owned enterprises, the government was to directly control them, so their operational autonomy was relatively limited. Because the government and the enterprise directly constituted a principal-agent relationship, the level was simple and the monitoring was direct, keeping the agency cost low. However, the number of such enterprises needed to be limited in order to prevent disruption of the economic order, which would lead to the agency cost rising sharply, resulting in low efficiency.

The second was the enterprise group model of mixed ownership. The term "enterprise group" was first used in Japan in the middle of the 20th century to refer to an enterprise cluster with great strength as the core, capital connection as the main link, and products, technology, supply and marketing, processing, and other relations as the auxiliary link. Through holding shares and purchasing assets, contracts, and other forms, the enterprise group closely connected many enterprises and institutions to coordinate their actions. Competitive industries with economies of scale, such as the metallurgical industry, mining industry, chemical industry, manufacturing industry, construction industry, and other similar sectors were considered suitable for the establishment of such groups. The development of enterprise groups in these industries met the needs of China's economic growth stage and industrial structure adjustment. At the time, China needed to develop capital technology intensive industries with economies of scale in terms of industrial structure. These industries had a large scale and a long industrial chain, which had a strong driving effect on the national economy. Therefore, if the requirements of economic growth and industrial development in the form of enterprise organization were adopted, it would play a powerful role in promoting the national economy. In the principal-agent relationship, the government directly authorized the operation of the core enterprises in the enterprise group. The government (the state-owned assets management department) directly granted the management and management rights of the Chinese owned assets of the enterprise group to the core enterprises. The core enterprise, as the agent, managed the state-owned assets in the enterprise group (including the core enterprise itself), and it was responsible for maintaining and increasing the value of the state-owned assets it ran. The government had two functions, social and economic management and ownership management of state-owned assets. Through the formulation and implementation of relevant laws and regulations, industrial policies, and macroeconomic policies, it guided and standardized the development of enterprise groups. In addition, it exercised the function of the owner, supervised the implementation of the principal-agent contract, and conducted external audits on the financial affairs of the enterprise group. The essence of the government's exercise of the owner's function was to establish an effective restraint mechanism between the ownership and management rights, so as to protect the rights and interests of the owners of state-owned assets from infringement and effective growth.

The third was that the mode of a state-owned capital operation company could also be called a holding company mode. The government supported the reorganization of state-owned enterprises into state-owned capital investment companies, and it granted the management and management rights of state-owned assets to the investment companies as economic entities. Investment companies used the mode of asset management to manage the state-owned enterprises. Through a variety of asset restructuring forms, China invested in important industries and key fields related to national security and the lifeline of the national economy, as well as important forward-looking strategic industries, so as to realize the value appreciation and quality improvement of state-owned assets. The state-owned capital investment company was a kind of high-level management mode of state-owned assets. By granting asset management rights to superior enterprises, they were able to carry out asset management according to market economic rules as suited the needs of their own development and industrial structure transformation. It allowed for the promotion of stock reorganization and optimal allocation of state-owned assets while realizing its own scale expansion and pursuing scale economic benefits to provide public services for economic development, ecological protection, scientific and technological progress, and national security.

12.2 Research on the Socialist Market Economy and the Role of the Government

1. On the Policy Evolution of Establishing and Perfecting the Socialist Market Economic System and the Role of the Government

In October 1992, the report of the Fourteenth National Congress of the Communist Party of China described the relationship between the market and the state macro-control as follows: "The socialist market economic system we want to establish includes making the market play a fundamental role in the allocation of resources under the macro-control of socialist countries and making economic activities follow the requirements of the law of value and adapting to the changes in the relationship between supply and demand. It also aims to see that the market has its own weaknesses and negative sides, which requires strengthening and improving the state's macro-control over the economy."

An important link in establishing the socialist market economy system was to accelerate the transformation of government functions. The fundamental way to make this change was to separate government from enterprise. The main functions of the government were overall planning, mastering policies, guiding information, organizing and coordinating, and providing services, inspection, and supervision. It was necessary to further reform the management systems of planning, investment, finance, and various specialized departments, strengthen auditing and economic supervision, and improve the scientific macro management system and methods.[89] In

---

89. Jiang Zemin, *Accelerating Reform, Opening Up, and Modernization and Striving for Greater Victory in the Cause of Socialism with Chinese Characteristics: Report on the Fourteenth National Congress of the Communist Party of China* (People's Publishing House, 1992).

terms of macro-control, it was important to give fuller play to the strengths of both planning and the market. National planning was one of the important means of macro-control. Planning was still the main means of resource allocation at the macro level. The key to updating the concept of planning and improving the planning method was to reasonably determine the strategic objectives of national economic and social development, make effective economic development predictions, effectively implement total amount control, major structure, and productivity layout planning, concentrate necessary financial and material resources for key construction, and comprehensively use economic leveraging to promote better, faster economic development.

On November 14, 1993, the Third Plenary Session of the Fourteenth Central Committee of the Communist Party of China adopted the Decision of the Central Committee of the Communist Party of China on Several Issues Concerning the Establishment of a Socialist Market Economic System, which made it clear that the establishment of a socialist market economic system involved making the market play a fundamental role in the allocation of resources under the state's macro-control. The Decision put forward the system reform requirements of changing government functions and establishing and improving the macro-control system. The transformation of government functions mainly meant that the government used economic means, legal means, and necessary administrative means to manage the national economy, and it did not directly interfere with the production and operation activities of enterprises. The functions of the government in managing the economy were mainly to formulate and carry out macro-control policies, do well in infrastructure construction, and create a good environment for economic development. In the meantime, it was necessary to cultivate a market system, supervise market operations, maintain equal competition, adjust social distribution, organize social security, control population growth, protect natural resources and the ecological environment, manage state-owned assets, and supervise state-owned asset operations, so as to realize the national economic and social development goals.[90] The transformation of government functions basically meant that the government did not directly intervene in the production and operation of enterprises, but managed the national economy from the macro level. It also defined the main functions of the government in managing the economy as formulating and implementing macro-control policies, effectively managing infrastructure construction, and creating a good economic development environment. The main tasks of macro-control were to maintain the basic balance of the total economic volume, promote the optimization of the economic structure, guide the sustained, rapid, healthy development of the national economy, and promote all-round social progress. Macroeconomic regulation and control mainly adopted economic measures, establishing a mechanism of mutual coordination and restriction among planning, finance, and financial administration, and strengthening the comprehensive coordination of economic operations.[91] According to this approach to policy, macro-control covered total balance, structural optimization, economic growth, and social

---

90. *Decision of the Central Committee of the Communist Party of China on Several Issues Concerning the Establishment of a Socialist Market Economic System* (People's Publishing House, 1993).

91. *Decision of the Central Committee of the Communist Party of China on Several Issues Concerning the Establishment of a Socialist Market Economic System* (People's Publishing House, 1993).

progress, and there was still a certain trace of "the combination of the planned economy and market regulation."

In December 1990, the Seventh Plenary Session of the Thirteenth Central Committee of the Communist Party of China adopted the Proposal of the Central Committee of the Communist Party of China on the Formulation of the Ten-Year Plan for National Economic and Social Development and the Eighth Five-Year Plan, which put forward the major economic activities related to the overall situation, such as total amount control, economic structure, and economic layout adjustment, as well as major economic activities related to the overall situation, mainly playing the role of planning. In addition, the daily production and operation of enterprises and general technical transformation, small-scale construction, and other economic activities were mainly regulated by the market. The main task of national economic management was to reasonably determine the planning and macro-control objectives of national economic development, formulate correct industrial policies, effectively manage comprehensive balance, coordinate major proportion relations, and guide and adjust economic operation by comprehensively supporting economic, legal, and administrative means.[92] The main tasks of the plan for national economic management stipulated here were not different from the main responsibilities of the government in economic management and the economic fields covered by macro-control as defined in the Decision of the Third Plenary Session of the Fourteenth CPC Central Committee, except that the concept of "macro-control" was not used in 1990. The concept of macro-control put forward in the Decision of the Third Plenary Session of the Fourteenth CPC Central Committee was of great significance in the reform of China's socialist market economy system. This was because the concept of the macro-economy in modern economics had been clearly adopted at the level of national policy, and that the methods or tools of macro-control were planning, finance, and financial administration. It was necessary to establish the coordination among planning, finance, and financial administration to strengthen the comprehensive coordination of economic operations. The plan put forward the objectives and tasks of national economic and social development, as well as the necessary supporting economic policies. The central bank took stabilizing the currency value as the primary goal, along with adjusting the total amount of money supply and maintaining the balance of international payments. The fiscal department used budget and tax means to focus on regulating the basic balance between the total social demand and supply and to facilitate the coordinated national economic and social development in line with industrial policies.[93] The monetary policy, the fiscal policy, the total amount of money supply, the total social demand, and the aggregate supply were all basic elements of macroeconomics.

In September 1997, the Fifteenth National Congress of the Communist Party of China put forward the basic line and program for the primary stage of socialism. Based on its unified

---

92. *The Proposal of the Central Committee of the Communist Party of China on the Formulation of the Ten-Year Plan for National Economic and Social Development and the Eighth Five-Year Plan* (People's Publishing House, 1990).

93. *Decision of the Central Committee of the Communist Party of China on Several Issues Concerning the Establishment of a Socialist Market Economic System* (People's Publishing House, 1993).

understanding and accurate grasp of the basic national conditions in this stage, the construction of the socialist economy with Chinese characteristics aimed to develop the market economy under socialist conditions and constantly liberate and develop productive forces. In accordance with the requirements of the socialist market economy, it was necessary to transform the functions of the government and realize the separation of government and enterprise. The main task of macro-control was to maintain the balance of the total economic volume, curb inflation, promote the optimization of the major economic structure, and achieve stable economic growth. Macro control mainly relied on economic and legal means. It was necessary to deepen the reform of the financial planning systems and improve the means of macro-control and the coordination mechanism.[94]

In November 2002, the report of the Sixteenth National Congress of the Communist Party of China proposed the continuous improvement of the socialist market economic system, adherence to the reform direction of the socialist market economy, expanded application of the basic role of the market in resource allocation under the state's macro-control, and improvement of the unified, open, competitive, and orderly modern market system. It was necessary to improve the government's functions of economic regulation, market supervision, social management, and public service and reduce and standardize administrative examination and approval. It was important to take promoting economic growth, increasing employment, stabilizing prices, and maintaining the balance of payments as the main objectives of macro-control.[95] In order to improve the socialist market economic system, the Report of the Sixteenth National Congress of the Communist Party of China emphasized giving fuller play to the basic role of the market in the allocation of resources, and it defined the functions of the government as economic regulation, market supervision, social management, and public service. It defined the main objectives of macro-control as promoting economic growth, increasing employment, stabilizing prices, and maintaining the balance of international payments. The policy evolution demonstrated the accurate grasp of government functions and macro-control under the conditions of an open market economy, especially the definition of social management and public service as government functions, as well as the requirements of modern development of the administrative management and governance systems.

On October 14, 2003, the Third Plenary Session of the Sixteenth Central Committee of the Communist Party of China adopted the Decision of the Central Committee of the Communist Party of China on Several Issues Concerning the Improvement of the Socialist Market Economic System. The goal of perfecting the socialist market economic system was to give full play to the basic role of the market in the allocation of resources, enhance the vitality and competitiveness of enterprises, improve the national macro-control system and the government, and improve social

---

94. Jiang Zemin, *Holding High the Great Banner of Deng Xiaoping Theory and Pushing the Cause of Building Socialism with Chinese Characteristics into the 21st Century: Report on the Fifteenth National Congress of the Communist Party of China* (People's Publishing House, 1997).

95. Jiang Zemin, *Building a Well-off Society in All Aspects and Creating a New Situation in the Cause of Socialism with Chinese Characteristics: Report on the National Congress* (People's Publishing House, 2002).

management and public service functions in accordance with the requirements of balancing urban and rural development, regional development, economic and social development, harmonious development between humans and nature, and domestic development and opening up, thus providing a strong institutional guarantee for building a moderately prosperous society in all aspects. The main tasks were 1) to improve the basic economic system with public ownership as the main body and the common development of various ownership economies, 2) to establish a system conducive to gradually changing the urban-rural dual economic structure, 3) to form a mechanism to promote regional coordinated development, 4) to build a unified, open, and competitive modern market system, 5) to improve the macro-control system, administrative system, and economic legal system, 6) to improve the system of employment, income distribution, and social security, and 7) to establish mechanisms to promote sustainable socio-economic development. It was thus necessary to improve the national macro-control system and accelerate the transformation of government functions. China aimed to further improve the macro-control system in which the state plans, fiscal policies, and monetary policies cooperated with each other. The macro-control objectives and general requirements specified in the state plan were the main basis for formulating fiscal and monetary policies. Fiscal policy was meant to play an important role in promoting economic growth, optimizing structure, and regulating income, and in improving the effective implementation of fiscal policy. Monetary policy was meant to play an important role in maintaining the stability of currency value and total balance, improve the transmission mechanism of monetary policy, and change the economic management function of the government. It was important to deepen the reform of the administrative examination and approval system and effectively transfer the government's economic management function to that of serving the main market players and creating a good development environment. It was necessary to improve the scientific, democratic, and standardized decision-making procedures for major economic and social issues of the government, make full use of social intellectual resources and modern information technology, and enhance transparency and public participation.[96] The Third Plenary Session of the Fourteenth Central Committee of the Communist Party of China put forward reform requirements for changing government functions. The report of the Fifteenth National Congress of the Communist Party of China proposed changes to the functions of the government and separating government from enterprise. The report of the Sixteenth National Congress of the Communist Party of China regarded "reducing and standardizing administrative examination and approval" as an important element of transforming government functions, and it connected the transformation of government functions with administrative examination and approval, that is, the allocation of resources by administrative means. The Third Plenary Session of the Sixteenth CPC Central Committee called for the deepening of the reform of the administrative examination and approval system. After that, the reform of administrative examination and

---

96. *Decision of the Central Committee of the Communist Party of China on Several Issues Concerning the Establishment of a Socialist Market Economic System* (People's Publishing House, 2003).

approval system was linked with the reform of the modern commercial system, the reform of the supervision system was undertaken during and after the event, and the reform of administrative management system of "decentralization, strengthening management, and optimizing service" became the main reform path for the transformation of government functions. The only way to improve the socialist market economic system was to give full play to the basic role of the market in the allocation of resources and make the market play a decisive role in the allocation of resources.

The first major task in the economic work in 2005 put forward by the Central Economic Work Conference the previous year aimed to continue to strengthen and improve macro-control to ensure rapid, steady economic development. The concept of the "economic cycle" was used for the first time in the 2003 Central Economic Work Conference and the judgment of the economic operation situation in which "China's economic development is in the rising stage of the economic cycle," making it clear that the central government had considered the macro-control issues within the framework of the economic cycle and economic growth stage, and the goal was to try to alleviate the cycle of economic ups and downs to maintain the stable, sustained growth of the national economy.

The theoretical basis of the government's economic regulation was the existence of market failure. It was generally believed that there were more defects in the market of developing countries, such as the low level of market development, the lack of effective competition, the existence of a large number of externalities, barriers to the supply of public goods, distortion of the price system, and other similar issues. Fixing these market defects depended on the intervention of the government. China was a developing country and its economy was in the process of transformation. After more than twenty years of market-oriented reform, China's social and economic market factors had been greatly enhanced, and the market-oriented trend of economic development had been established. However, China's transition from a planned economy to a socialist market economy had not been going on long, and the maturity of market system still needed a prolonged historical stage. The micro basis and institutional conditions of resource allocation by price mechanism still needed to be further improved. This being the case, in order to avoid severe shocks in the process of economic and social transformation, maintain rapid, stable economic growth, and implement favorable guidance for economic development, it was necessary for the government to strengthen and improve macro-control, coordinate domestic and international economic and interest relations, and guide the overall economic and social development with a scientific outlook on development.

When emphasizing the importance of the government's macro-control, it was likewise important to attach great emphasis on the understanding of the relationship between strengthening macro-control and playing the role of the market mechanism, pay attention to the use of economic and legal means, and give play to the basic role of the market in allocating resources. Economic growth and market development were a dynamic process. One of the major purposes of macro-control was to make up for market defects and promote market development, that is, to establish a system to support the market and promote the effective operation of the market. The basis and situation of China's economic development made it necessary to not only play the role of macro-control, but also pay attention to the economic and market characteristics of the regulation methods, tools, and means, which was conducive to the growth of the market economic system. The economic and market-oriented nature of regulation means, tools, and methods aimed to make the regulation intention affect the expectation and behavior of economic entities through the transmission of economic parameters (variables affecting the price system), and then affect economic operations. The core problem here was that each economic subject needed to make decisions freely according to the judgment of the relationship between the parameter changes and their own economic interests, and the free decision-making of the economic subjects on the basis of their own interests was the fundamental mechanism of the micro basis of the market economy. In the market economy, it was the price mechanism that determined and regulated the allocation of resources. As the price level changed, the relative prices of various products and services also changed. If the economic entities were independent property rights and interest subjects, they could freely choose (make decisions) and be responsible for the financial results of their economic decisions, then the relative price changes could play a regulatory role in their behavior, and subsequently play a regulatory role in the allocation of resources. Macroeconomic regulation and control needed to pay more attention to the use of economic and legal means, which was conducive to the strengthening of the macro-control effect and the growth of the market economic system.

Primarily, the policy objectives were to be continuous and stable, so as to maintain the expected stability and rapid, steady economic growth. Secondly, it was important to pay attention to the use of economic means and economic leverage to improve the effectiveness of economic policies. Finally, it was necessary to emphasize the "neutral" feature of fiscal monetary policy and dilute its color as a tool of policy intention. The financial monetary policy of the nature of market economy had its independent principle, with the independent principle of fiscal policy being to maintain budget balance, while the independent principle of monetary policy was to maintain the stability of currency value. For a long time, China had been accustomed to using fiscal monetary policy as a tool to implement the intention of macro-control policy, while ignoring its independent economic policy function. It was also an important performance of the market-oriented operation of macro-control to let the fiscal policy fade out of the swing of policy expansion and contraction, return to the track of "discretionary choice," and make the financial variable become the signal of market-oriented parameter adjustment. From the perspective of monetary policy, reducing the policy control on the scale and structure of credit was an urgent task, alongside the need to use more standard monetary policy tools to act on the intermediate target interest rate and influence people's economic behavior and economic operations through the change of interest rate. Interest rate was a kind of price index, which affected both the supply and demand of money. The use of interest rate levers to regulate the economy could balance the total supply and demand, and it was bound to be related to the deepening of financial reform and the marketization of interest rate, which was conducive to the development of China's market economy.

At the present stage of China's economic and social development, both the strengthening and improvement of macro-control and the growth of the market economic system needed to focus on promoting economic system reform. In addition, if China hoped to make more use of economic and market-oriented means to implement macro-control, it needed to promote the reform of economic system, including the reform of enterprise system, financial system, investment system, and administrative management system, along with the construction of the social credit and economic legal systems. By deepening the reform, the institutional guarantee of comprehensive, coordinated, and sustainable development could be established and guaranteed, and the social democracy of the system of market economy could be improved.

The US subprime mortgage crisis, which began in July 2007, triggered the global financial crisis and the sovereign debt crisis of European countries, seriously affecting the world economy. From the second half of 2008, in order to cope with the international financial crisis, China's macro-control policies took maintaining rapid, stable economic development as the primary task, focusing on maintaining growth, expanding domestic demand as the fundamental way to maintain growth, accelerating the transformation of development mode and structural adjustment as the main direction of maintaining growth, deepening the reform and improvement of key areas and key links and increasing the level of opening to the outside world as a powerful driving force for growth, and improving people's livelihood as both the starting point and end point of maintaining growth. That is to say, the major issues of China's economic and social development, such as expanding domestic demand, changing the mode of development, adjusting the economic structure, deepening reform, raising the level of opening up, and improving people's livelihood, were all related to the steady, rapid economic growth. The solution of these major problems was complementary to the steady, rapid economic growth. This guiding ideology conformed to the law of economic growth and industrial development, and it was the practical verification of Deng Xiaoping's "development as the absolute principle."

The maximization of output value (rapid economic growth) was a normal development process in a specific period of industrial development. The total output value had internal relations with industrial structure and economic structure (Kuznets theory). Industrialization brought about the increase of per capita income, and the increase of income led to the change of the quantity and structure of consumption demand, which promoted the upgrading of industrial structure and the transformation of economic structure. Therefore, the evolution of industrial structure from labor-intensive and capital intensive to technology intensive, along with the transformation of development mode from relying mainly on investment to relying on technological progress, was basically the natural process of economic development and the process of industrialization and the increase of per capita income. Compared with small and medium-sized countries in the world, the process of industrialization in China was longer and more complicated. China needed to maintain a relatively fast economic growth rate over a long historical period and have a process of accumulation and expansion of economic aggregate, which was an insurmountable development stage of China's industrialization. Therefore, the government's macro-control function needed to maintain stable economic growth (including currency stability) and realize full employment, so as to meet the requirements of China's economic growth stage and the changes in the world economic situation.

The moderately loose macroeconomic policy of "maintaining growth" implemented in the second half of 2008 allowed China's economy to take the lead in achieving a stable recovery in the world, while the economic stimulus policy also caused investment overheating, overcapacity of some industrial products, and strengthening inflation expectations. After 2010, the Central Bank raised the reserve ratio three times, implemented open market operations to recover the currency, and took the lead in launching the policy of stimulating the world economy, ensuring the "soft landing" and stable growth of the macro-economy. From 2009, the research on China's macroeconomic policy mainly focused on the moderation, effectiveness, and exit arrangement of its macroeconomic policy. As for the timing of the exit of the loose monetary policy, academic circles held that it was timely and flexible, which was deduced from three aspects. The first was domestic economic fundamentals, mainly inflation factors and expected changes. The second involved changes in asset prices, private investment, and unemployment rate. And the third included international economic situation, world economic recovery, and global monetary policy coordination factors. The idea of the "wide fiscal and tight currency" regulation after 2010 played a two-way regulatory role in consolidating the stabilization and recovery of the domestic economy. The moderately loose fiscal policy was able to make up for the credit gap caused by the tight monetary policy, and the tight monetary policy hedged liquidity, reduced the bubble in the economy, and paved the way for the withdrawal of the loose fiscal policy.[97] From 2008 to 2010, timely adjustments were made to China's macro-control policies according to the changes in the domestic and foreign economic situation, reflecting the gradual improvement of the socialist market economic system and the gradual maturity of the macro-control system. Admittedly, with the deepening of the reform of the economic system and the increasingly complex economic relations domestically and internationally, China's fiscal policy, monetary policy, and exchange rate policy were also more complex, which required the adaptive development of macro-control theory and policy ideas to ensure the stable, effective, sustainable growth of the national economy.

In October 2007, the report of the Seventeenth National Congress of the Communist Party of China proposed that in order to promote the sound, rapid development of the national economy, it was necessary to deepen the reform of the fiscal, taxation, and financial systems, improve the macro-control system, and improve the national planning system. It was important to give full play to the guiding role of national development planning, along with planning and industrial

---

97. Liu Lanbiao, Zhang Jingjia, and Cao Yuantao, "A Review of Recent Macroeconomic Policy Research," *Economics Trends*, no. 6 (2010); Ba Shusong, "Timely Withdrawal of China's Moderately Loose Monetary Policy from the Perspective of Monetary Policy Rules," *Journal of Central University of Finance and Economics*, no. 10 (2009); Luo Yunfeng, "The Effectiveness of China's Fiscal Policy: The Adjustment and Application of the Mundell-Fleming Model in China," *Shanghai Economic Research*, no. 1 (2010); Wu Yanyan, "On Several Issues of Current Macro-control," *Finance and Trade Research*, no. 2 (2010); Zhang Yan, "Oozing-out Effect of China's Fiscal Policy," *Financial Research*, no. 1 (2010).

policies in macro-control, and comprehensively use fiscal and monetary policies to improve the level of macro-control.[98]

2. Research on the Policy Evolution of the Comprehensive Deepening of the Reform and the Government's Role

In November 2012, the report of the Eighteenth National Congress of the Communist Party of China proposed comprehensive deepening of the reform of the economic system. It was clear that the core issue of the economic system reform was to deal with the relationship between the government and the market. It was important to pay more attention to market laws and give better play to the role of the government. It was necessary to deepen the reform of the administrative examination and approval system, continue to streamline administration and delegate powers, and promote the transformation of government functions to creating a good development environment, providing high-quality public services, and safeguarding social equity and justice.[99] The report of the Eighteenth National Congress of the Communist Party of China clearly defined handling the relationship between the government and the market as the core issue of the economic system reform, made it clear that deepening the reform of administrative examination and approval was one of the main tasks for promoting the reform of the political system, and clearly defined the transformation of government functions for social management and public services, which reflected the reform requirements for accelerating the improvement of the socialist market economic system and for playing, to a greater extent and across a broader range, the basic role of the market in allocating resources.

On November 12, 2013, the Third Plenary Session of the Eighteenth CPC Central Committee adopted the Decision of the CPC Central Committee on Several Major Issues Concerning Comprehensive Deepening of the Reform, which marked the first expression of the idea that the market played a fundamental role in the allocation of resources, just as it played a decisive role in the allocation of resources in structural reform. It emphasized that economic system reform was the key to comprehensive deepening of the reform. The core issue was to properly handle the relationship between the government and the market, make the market play a decisive role in the allocation of resources, and give fuller play to the role of the government. Efforts needed to be made to solve the problems of the imperfect market system, excessive government intervention, and inadequate supervision. It was necessary to actively and steadily promote market-oriented reform in both breadth and depth, greatly reduce the direct allocation of resources by the

---

98. Hu Jintao, *Holding High the Great Banner of Socialism with Chinese Characteristics and Striving for the New Victory in Building a Moderately Prosperous Society in All Aspects: Report on the Seventeenth National Congress of the Communist Party of China* (People's Publishing House, 2007).

99. Hu Jintao, *Unswervingly Advancing Along the Road of Socialism with Chinese Characteristics and Striving for Building a Moderately Prosperous Society in All Aspects: Report on the Eighteenth National Congress of the Communist Party of China* (People's Publishing House, 2012).

government, and promote the allocation of resources in accordance with market rules, market prices, and market competition to maximize efficiency. The main functions of the government were to maintain macroeconomic stability, strengthen and optimize public services, ensure fair competition, strengthen market supervision, maintain market order, promote sustainable development, promote common prosperity, and make up for market failures.[100] The Decision of the Third Plenary Session of the Eighteenth Central Committee of the Communist Party of China (CPC) set as an internal requirement that full play must be given to the advantages of the socialist market economy as scientific macro-control and effective government governance. The main tasks of macro-control were to maintain the balance of economic aggregate, promote the coordination of major economic structures and the optimization of productivity distribution, slow down the impact of economic cycle fluctuations, guard against regional and systemic risks, stabilize market expectations, and achieve sustained, healthy economic development. The macro-control system was guided by the national development strategy and rules, with fiscal policy and monetary policy as the main means. It was important to fully and correctly perform government functions, further streamline administration and decentralization, deepen the reform of the administrative examination and approval system, minimize the central government's management of micro affairs, cancel the examination and approval of all economic activities that could be effectively regulated by the market mechanism, and standardize the management and improve the efficiency of the reserved administrative examination and approval items. The government needed to strengthen the formulation and implementation of development strategies, plans, policies, and standards, strengthen the supervision of market activities, and strengthen the provision of various public services.[101] The Decision of the Third Plenary Session of the Eighteenth Central Committee of the Communist Party of China (CPC) extended macro-control to six aspects: total amount, structure, region, economic cycle, risk prevention, and economic development. It further defined government functions as economic and social levels. The economic level was mainly macro-control and market supervision, while the social level was mainly public service and promoting sustainable development, environmental protection, and promoting common prosperity. This was the requirement of economic and social development and a new challenge faced by deepening reform in every aspect.

In October 2017, the report of the Nineteenth National Congress of the Communist Party of China announced that after long-term effort, socialism with Chinese characteristics had entered a new era, which was the new historical orientation of China's development. In order to implement the new development concept and build a modern economic system, it was necessary to accelerate the improvement of the socialist market economic system. The reform of the economic system needed to focus on the improvement of the property rights system and the market-oriented allocation of various factors. It was important to deepen the reform of the commercial system

---

100. *Decision of the CPC Central Committee on Several Major Issues Concerning Comprehensive Deepening of the Reform* (People's Publishing House, 2013).

101. *Decision of the CPC Central Committee on Several Major Issues Concerning Comprehensive Deepening of the Reform* (People's Publishing House, 2013).

and improve the market supervision system, and also to innovate and improve macro-control, give full play to the strategic guiding role of the national development plan, and improve the coordination mechanism of financial, monetary, industrial, and regional economic policies.[102] According to the report of the Nineteenth National Congress of the Communist Party of China, the overall goal of comprehensively deepening the reform was to improve and develop the socialist system with Chinese characteristics and promote the modernization of the national governance system and governance capacity. In order to build a modern economic system, it was necessary to strive to build an economic system with an effective market mechanism, dynamic micro subjects, and moderate macro-control. In terms of government functions and macroeconomic regulation and control reform, the reform of the administrative system needed to be deepened, the mode of administration innovated, the credibility and executive power of the government enhanced, a government under the rule of law and a service-oriented government constructed, and the modernization of the governance system and governance capacity promoted.

On February 28, 2018, the Third Plenary Session of the Nineteenth CPC Central Committee adopted the Decision of the CPC Central Committee on Deepening the Reform of the Party and State Institutions. With regard to optimizing the establishment of government institutions and the allocation of functions, the decision emphasized that the transformation of government functions was an important task in deepening the reform of party and state institutions. It was important to resolutely break away from the institutional defects that restricted the decisive role of the market in the allocation of resources and give better play to the role of the government. It was similarly crucial to focus on promoting high-quality development, building a modern economic system, strengthening and improving the government's functions of economic regulation, market supervision, social management, public service, and ecological environment protection, adjusting and optimizing government functions, comprehensively improving government efficiency, and building a service-oriented government to meet the expectation of the people.[103] In operation, the key was to reasonably allocate the functions of macro management departments. It was important to scientifically set up the responsibilities and authorities of macro management departments, strengthen the functions of formulating the national development strategy and unified planning system, and give fuller play to the guiding role of national strategy and planning. It was important to improve the macro-control system, innovate the regulatory methods, and build a mechanism for policy and work coordination in development planning, finance, and financial administration. Further streamlining needed to be done in administration and decentralization of powers. It was necessary to reduce the efficiency of the government's examination and approval of all kinds of affairs and to stimulate the efficiency of market management. Improvements needed to be made to the market supervision and law enforcement systems. Reform needed to be implemented in

---

102. Xi Jinping, *Winning the Victory in Building a Moderately Prosperous Society in All Respects and Socialism with Chinese Characteristics in the New Era: Report on the Nineteenth National Congress of the CPC* (People's Publishing House, 2017).

103. *Decision of the CPC Central Committee on Deepening the Reform of the Party and State Institutions* (People's Publishing House, 2018).

the management system of natural resources and the ecological environment. Improvements were needed in the public service management system. It was important to strengthen supervision during and after the event, transfer more administrative resources to strengthen this supervision, improve administrative efficiency, and form a high-efficiency organization system from the top to the bottom.[104] The Decision of the Third Plenary Session of the Nineteenth Central Committee of the Communist Party of China clearly defined the functions of the government from the perspective of the reform of state institutions, and it clearly defined the functions, responsibilities, and powers of the macro management departments, making the reform of "better playing the role of the government" more practical.

3. Discussion on the Relationship Between Government and Market in the Process of Socialist Market Economic Reform

It was generally believed that there were market defects in developing countries, such as low market development, lack of effective competition, high cost of information, barriers to the supply of public goods, price distortions, and other factors which required government intervention to make up for the losses they incurred. Chinese economists generally believed that in the process of China's transition from a planned economy to a socialist market economy, the development of the market system needed a long historical stage, and the micro basis and institutional conditions for the allocation of resources by price mechanism needed to be gradually improved. In order to avoid major shocks in the process of economic and social transformation, maintain stable and rapid economic growth, and implement favorable guidance for economic and social development, the government needed to strengthen and improve macro-control and better play its role.

The report of the Eighteenth National Congress of the Communist Party of China put forward that the core issue of economic system reform was to deal with the relationship between the government and the market. It was important to give greater respect to the market law and give fuller play to the role of the government. The function of government was discussed in the field of economic theory. Some scholars believed that the government's function of intervening in the economy should be limited. It was important to strengthen the market-oriented government, and the government needed to transition from an all-powerful government to a limited government, from a controlling government to a regulatory government, from a development-oriented government to a service-oriented government, and from a rule-of-man government to a rule-of-law government.[105] Some believed that the size of the Chinese government had no significant impact on economic growth. After China entered the ranks of middle-income countries, the continuous expansion of government scale had a significant negative impact on growth. Moreover,

---

104. *Decision of the CPC Central Committee on Deepening the Reform of the Party and State Institutions* (People's Publishing House, 2018).

105. Hu Jiayong et al., "How to Further Promote Reform from the Perspective of Political Economics: Summary of the Fifteenth Annual Meeting of China Political Economics Forum," *Economics Trends*, no. 10 (2013).

the more underdeveloped the economy was, the greater the damage of government scale was to economic growth. The government needed to reduce the scale, control the economy, and increase economic freedom. Accelerating the market-oriented reform was thus the key to promoting the long-term development of China's economy.[106]

Some scholars observed that replacing the "basic role" with the "decisive role" of the market in resource allocation further emphasized the role of the market in resource allocation, further promoted market-oriented reform in breadth and depth, and sought to solve the problems of excessive direct allocation of resources by the government, excessive intervention in micro economic activities, excessive examination and approval of micro economic activities, and inadequate market supervision by the government. There were some problems, such as the formation and improvement of fair competition environment; the government's public service and social management not being in place or being absent, and being sorely lacking in its ability to meet society's needs; and the government failing to break various forms of administrative monopolies in accordance with the law, and even adopting some discriminatory policies to hinder the development of the non-public economy. This required the government to transform, withdraw from the offside field, fill in and effectively manage the work of the original vacancy, and realize the transformation of government functions.[107] Regarding how to correctly understand the role of the government, it was argued that the role of the government in the market economy was mainly reflected in the protection of property rights, the protection of fair competition, the provision of public services, the strengthening of social governance, the promotion of sustainable development, and macro-control. The purpose of the government playing these roles was to create an environment and provide services for the market to play a better role, rather than to replace the role of the market. The government needed to return from offside and misplaced areas and make up for the vacancy. This was exactly the problem to be solved in the transformation of government functions.[108] Some pointed out that an important sign of better playing the role of the government would be that the government itself should abide by the market order. The government's function mechanism was to be connected with the market mechanism, and the government's allocation of public resources needed to be combined with the market's allocation of market resources.[109] Some scholars pointed out that China's transition from a planned economy to a market economy had not yet been fully realized. The strong intervention in and control of the government and the state-owned economy in the overall economy and society hindered the market from playing a fundamental role in resource allocation. The strengthening of state power's intervention in and

---

106. Lai Xiaoqiong and Li Feilong, "Comprehensive Deepening of Reform and Promoting New Development of China's Economic Theory: Summary of the Seventh Annual Meeting of China Political Economics Forum," *Economics Trends*, no. 2 (2014).

107. Zhang Zhuoyuan, "What Issues Need Serious Study in the Decision?" *Economic Research*, no. 1 (2014).

108. Liu Shijin, "Implementing the Decisive Role of the Market in Resource Allocation," *Economic Research*, no. 1 (2014).

109. Hong Yinxing, "On the Role of Government After the Market Plays a Decisive Role in Resource Allocation," *Economic Research*, no. 1 (2014).

control of economic activities strengthened the institutional basis of rent-seeking activities and widened the gap between the rich and the poor.[110]

In the discussion on the functions and role of the government, some scholars did not agree that the achievements of Reform and Opening Up should be fully attributed to the progress of marketization. They believed that the root causes of social contradictions such as excessive government intervention, insufficient marketization, and polarization were mainly due to excessive government power and excessive corruption. The next step of reform was to weaken the government's management and intervention in the economy. The viewpoint that marketization was the panacea to the problem was neo-liberalism and market fundamentalism.[111] There were also views on the combination of the "effective market" and "promising government." For countries in transition, a promising government was particularly important. In the 1970s and 1980s, neo-liberalism prevailed, emphasizing the market, ignoring the role of the government, and pursuing privatization, liberalization, and marketization. As a result, the economy of countries carrying out the Washington consensus advocated by neo-liberalism generally collapsed and stagnated, and the crisis continued. Over the same period, a few economies were successful. They had a common feature, which was that there were both "effective market" and "promising government" in economic development and transformation.

It was important to eliminate the interference and distortion of the market and allow the resources to be allocated by the market. In this process, the government needed to play a role in protecting property rights, maintaining macro stability, overcoming market failure, and promoting the structural changes of technology, industry, and systems.[112] From the perspective of criticizing the "pan-market trend of thought," some theorists put forward the idea that the state's management and regulation of economic affairs was denounced as a sort of planned economy. The root of the pan-market trend of thought mainly came from the Western Neo-liberal economic school. The economic theory of socialism with Chinese characteristics not only respected the market law, but also gave full play to the regulatory role and function of the government, which was the development of Marxist economic theory.[113]

Some literature used empirical research methods to analyze the impact of government intervention on the market exit of manufacturing enterprises. The conclusion showed that the stricter the regulation of labor mobility, the greater the probability of enterprises' market exit; the higher the degree of regional financial repression, the greater the risk of enterprises' exit from the market; the higher the intensity of government subsidies, the higher the risk of enterprises' market exit; and the longer the proportion of the person in charge of enterprises dealing with

---

110. Wu Jinglian, "Formulating an Action Plan for Comprehensive Reform," *China Reform*, no. 8 (2013).

111. Liu Guoguang, "Further Discussion on the Direction of China's Economic System Reform," *Economist Weekly*, September 19, 2013.

112. Lin Yifu, "Effective Market Also Needs Government," *Economist Weekly*, December 7, 2013.

113. Zhou Xinjun, "The Pioneer of Pan-market Criticism," *Economist Weekly*, November 23, 2013.

the government, the greater the risk of enterprises' market exit.[114] Some scholars discussed the difference between the planned economy and the market economy against the backdrop of the Internet and big data technology. They held that the essence of the difference was whether the resources were allocated by administrative power or by the market subject's independent choice and judgment under the control of the law of value. The Internet and big data could make the plan more scientific, but it could not solve the most important problem of creativity and the enthusiasm of the people in this era. Only when the Internet and big data were combined with the market could they have the greatest effect.[115] Some commentators demonstrated the role of the government from the macro-control system. They believed that compared with Western macro-control, China's macro-control theory system was more complete and the policy toolbox was more robust. China's current macro-control system was based on the aggregate supply and demand model and could be divided into three parts: demand management, supply management, and market environment management. Demand management mainly included Keynes' demand management, demand-oriented innovation, and demand side reform; supply management mainly included factor price policy, financial policy, supply-oriented innovation, and supply side reform; and market environment management policy mainly included "market environment reform and market environment fine adjustment policy based on the established system."[116]

There were three kinds of research methods in the field of economic thought. One was policy interpretation, another was normative research, and the third was empirical research on a certain topic. The views of the discussion within these fields were different and even conflicting, but they were all based on the understanding and vision of China's socialist market economic system reform, with a strong color of localization. From the perspective of economic theory, the theoretical basis of governmental regulation and intervention on economic activities was the existence of market failure. According to the standard economic understanding, market failure meant that when the actual economic environment could not meet the conditions of the first theorem of welfare economics (i.e., the complete competitive market model of microeconomics), the market was inefficient in resource allocation, that is, "market failure." The typical performance of market failure was externality. In reality, the causes of market failure included monopolies, incomplete information, and public goods. Neoclassical economics tried to make up for market failure through economic tools and methods such as taxation, subsidy, and property rights arrangements to reduce transaction costs. There were also theories that explored some non-market alternatives, such as the mechanism design theory. If government elements were introduced, it was necessary to establish the concept that the purpose of government intervention was to make up for market defects (such as limiting monopolies, reducing information costs, or improving the flexibility

114. Wang Mingyi and Shi Lijing, "Path Analysis of the Impact of Government Intervention in the Market Exit of Chinese Manufacturing Enterprises," *Economics Trends*, no. 6 (2018).

115. Gao Shangquan, "Review and Reflection on China's Reform and Opening Up in the Past 40 Years," *Xinhua Digest*, no. 9 (2018).

116. Su Jian and Chen Yang, "Macro Control Policy System with Chinese Characteristics and Its Application," *Economist*, no. 6 (2019).

of institutional supply to reduce transaction costs), so as to make the market mechanism more perfect rather than to replace the market. The system of government intervention in the economy was considered to be the general institutional characteristics of late industrialized countries, which had the effect of starting industrialization and promoting the process of industrialization. However, empirical facts showed that the return of this system was increasing at the beginning, but with the development of economy, the cost rose, efficiency declined, and returns decreased, which hindered economic development. The optimal boundary between government and the market was based on the comparison of transaction costs. If the transaction cost of the market mechanism was lower than that of government intervention, the market was relatively effective. If the transaction cost of the market mechanism was higher than that of government intervention, government intervention was relatively effective.

4. The Development of the Socialist Market Economy and the Evolution of Macro Policy Tools

In the framework of macroeconomics, fiscal policy and monetary policy are the two main macro policy tools for government intervention. The government uses fiscal and monetary policies to control the relationship among inflation, employment, and economic growth, and also to deal with the changes of business cycle. In the process of the establishment and improvement of China's socialist market economy system, with the development of the market economy, especially the change of capital formation conditions, these macro-control tools also had an evolution process. Capital formation referred to the conversion of savings into actual investment. From the perspective of statistics, capital formation could be regarded as total investment, while from the perspective of macroeconomic analysis, capital formation referred to the process of converting savings into investment, or the mechanism linking savings and investment. The change of capital formation conditions changed the capital formation mode accordingly, and then changed the adjustment mechanism and effect of monetary policy. In China's planned economy period and the early stage of Reform and Opening Up (1950s–1980s), the feature of capital formation was that the government was not only the main body of savings, but also the main body of investment, mainly through the form of financial allocation. The function of the bank was basically the channel of money input and withdrawal and the tool of financial overdraft. The economy associated with this "financial leading" investment system had the characteristics of a "shortage economy." In this kind of economic system, investment was a function of money increment. The government's macro-control means was to control the amount of new money and credit according to the economic plan. The investment demand had stable, sufficient elasticity to the money supply. Beginning in the mid-1990s, with the deepening of economic system reform and economic development, China's capital formation conditions also changed. The change of the distribution pattern of national income diversified the main body of savings, and the savings of enterprises and residents became the main part of national savings. The reform of the investment and ownership systems diversified the investors. The government was no longer the only investor, and the share of government investment in the total investment of society overall tended to decline. In the composition of capital sources of fixed assets investment in the entire society, state budget funds decreased from 28.1% in 1981 to 6.4% in 2000, the share of domestic loans increased from 12.7% to 20.3%, the share of foreign capital utilization increased from 3.8% to 5.1%, and the share of self-financing and other funds increased from 55.4% to 68.2%.[117] By 2016, based on the actual investment in fixed assets of 61.69335 trillion yuan, the share of national budget funds was 5.87%, the share of domestic loans was 10.89%, the share of foreign capital utilization was 0.37%, the share of self-raised funds was 67.08%, and the share of other funds was 15.79%.[118] At the same time, the reform of the financial system gradually transformed finances into public finances, state-owned specialized banks transformed into commercial banks, and the independence of the Central Bank gradually increased. In particular, the national economy transformed from a "seller's market" with a shortage of supply to a "buyer's market" with excess supply. Market demand became the main factor affecting economic operations.

The change of the economic system led to the transformation of China's capital formation mode from a fiscal type to a financial type. In order to adapt to the changes of capital formation conditions, the monetary policy adjustment mechanism of the People's Bank of China also changed. From January 1, 1998, the People's Bank of China cancelled the loan limit control of state-owned commercial banks and gradually implemented an indirect control system based on the risk management of asset liability ratio management. On March 21, 1998, the People's Bank of China began to reform the deposit reserve system. These two reforms gave China's monetary policy the significance of a market economy, demonstrating that the essence of the change of the intermediate variable of monetary policy from credit scale limit to monetary supply was to control the supply of basic money instead of directly controlling the quantity of credit money created by commercial banks. The central bank used monetary policy tools to inject basic money into the economy, which was converted into the reserves of commercial banks. The commercial bank system determined the total amount of monetary supply in a certain period through the monetary multiplier effect. Monetary supply corresponded to monetary demand, so the central bank's control of basic monetary supply would definitely affect the movement of monetary demand cash flow. This type of monetary policy adjustment mechanism was adapted to the change of capital formation conditions.

In the stage of comprehensively deepening the reform, China needed to improve the macro-control system guided by the national development strategy and planning, with fiscal policy and monetary policy as the main means, strengthen the coordination of fiscal policy and monetary policy with industry, price, and other policy means, and improve the level of discretion. In order to improve the macro-control system, it was necessary to improve the financial market system, especially accelerating the marketization of interest rates. An effective and liquid financial market promoted the transaction of assets and the creation of new assets. An effective financial market allocated savings to more efficient industries, resulting in higher capital intensity and higher

---

117. National Bureau of Statistics, *China Statistical Yearbook (2001)* (China Statistics Press, 2001), 159.
118. National Bureau of Statistics, *China Statistical Yearbook (2017)* (China Statistics Press, 2017), 294.

output and consumption levels. Effective capital market and market-oriented interest rate also made monetary policy more effective. In financial markets, interest rate was the price of credit. With the assumption of credit risk, market equilibrium interest rates reflected the borrowing behavior of all economic units based on the combination of production opportunities and utility preference. If the established assumption of credit risk was relaxed and it was assumed that the net wealth and income were fixed, the economic unit determined the holding amount of money, financial assets, and physical assets and the issuance of liabilities and consumption according to the principle of maximizing the total utility, so as to achieve a reasonable combination of assets, liabilities, and consumption. In a state of equilibrium, the marginal utility brought about by holding various assets was the same, the equilibrium interest rate was determined, the financial market was cleared, and the savings in the economy were allocated effectively.

Fiscal policy was a kind of policy tool to adjust and control the economy through government expenditure, tax, and other variables. The change of government expenditure on goods and services could affect the total demand, and then affect the level of short-term national output. Such changes of tax would change the disposable income and consumption level of residents, the after tax income, and investment demand of enterprises, and then affect the total demand and the level of national output. Fiscal policy was believed to have more structural regulation effect. In the market economy, fiscal policy and monetary policy needed to be effectively coordinated and selected according to circumstances, so as to achieve better control effect. For example, in order to maintain a certain market tightening pressure to promote the optimization of resource allocation and industrial structure adjustment, China needed to implement a moderately tight monetary policy, but in order to reduce unemployment pressure and economic downward risk, it could also implement moderate expansion or positive fiscal policy. If the government expenditure was appropriately increased for the construction of infrastructure and public services, it could not only solve the adverse impact of the insufficient supply of infrastructure and public goods on economic development and social life, but also effectively create employment opportunities and improve the level of national output and income.

12.3 Studies on the Socialist Market Economy and Growth Transformation (Development Strategy)

1. Research on the Development Strategy of Pursuing Stable, Sustained Growth of the National Economy with Improving Economic Benefits as the Core

The period from the Third Plenary Session of the Eleventh Central Committee of the Communist Party of China in December 1978, to the new economic development strategy put forward in the report of the Twelfth National Congress of the Communist Party of China in September 1982, and then to the elaboration of the economic development strategy in the 1990s in the report of the Fourteenth National Congress of the Communist Party of China in October 1992, marked a transition in China's economic development strategy, changing the one-sided pursuit in the period of the planned economy. The development idea characterized by high-speed economic growth formulated a more scientific development strategy centered on improving economic benefits in line with the national conditions and national strength and with the stage of economic growth.

The Twelfth CPC National Congress was held in September 1982. In his opening speech, Deng Xiaoping pointed out that China's modernization drive should proceed from the actual situation in China, which was the basic starting point for the nation to formulate economic development strategies and various policies and measures. It was necessary to overcome the leftist errors in the economic construction strategy and formulate an economic development strategy based on China's national conditions and objective economic laws, so that China's economy could gradually achieve coordinated development and stable growth, forming a virtuous cycle. China needed to find a path with less investment, appropriate accumulation, better economic benefits, more tangible benefits for the people, and comparative advantages of the socialist system to give full play to the new approach to economic development.[119] The report of the Twelfth National Congress of the Communist Party of China put forward the strategic objectives, strategic points, strategic steps and important principles of China's economic construction by the end of the 20th century. From 1981 to the end of the 20th century, the general goal of China's economic construction was to quadruple the total annual output value of the country's industry and agriculture from 710 billion yuan in 1980 to 2.8 trillion yuan in 2000, on the premise of continuously improving economic benefits. If this goal was achieved, China's total national income and the output of major industrial and agricultural products would be among the best in the world. Greater progress would be made in the modernization process of the entire national economy, the income of urban and rural people would be doubled, and people's material and cultural life could reach an affluent level. In order to achieve this strategic goal, the most important thing was to solve the problems of agriculture, energy, transportation, education, science, and technology. Over the next twenty years, it was important to firmly grasp the basic links of agriculture, energy and transportation, education, and science and technology, making them the strategic focus of economic development. In order to achieve this goal in twenty years, two steps needed to be taken in strategic deployment. The first ten years would mainly be used to lay a good foundation, accumulate strength, and create conditions. The next ten years would enter a new period of economic revitalization. The report emphasized that during the period of the Sixth Five-Year Plan from 1981 to 1985, it was necessary to continue to unswervingly implement the policy of adjustment, reform, rectification, and improvement, practice a strict economy, oppose waste, and shift all economic work onto the track of focusing on improving economic efficiency. In all economic work, China had to continue to implement the ten principles of economic development approved by the Fourth Session of the Fifth National People's Congress. It was important to pay special attention to settling several important issues: 1) concentrating funds for key construction and continuing to improve people's

---

119. Deng Xiaoping, *Selected Works of Deng Xiaoping*, vol. 2 (People's Publishing House, 1983).

living standards, 2) maintaining the leading position of the state-owned economy and developing various economic forms, 3) the correct implementation of the principle of giving priority to the planned economy supplemented by market regulation, and 4) adhering to self-reliance and expanding economic and technological exchanges with other countries.[120]

The strategic objectives, priorities, and steps of China's economic construction by the end of the 20th century put forward by the Twelfth National Congress of the Communist Party of China was a comprehensive, systematic, medium and long-term development strategy for China's socialist construction in a new historical period, and it was the first time that the term "economic development strategy" was explicitly used. Compared with the economic development policy in the period of the planned economy, this development strategy changed greatly in its economic development goal, development focus, and production mode. In terms of development goals, it no longer took the quantitative growth of output value as the goal, but the improvement of economic efficiency as the prerequisite for the growth of output value, and on the basis of objective understanding of national conditions and national strength, it formulated an appropriate economic growth rate. In terms of development priorities, it no longer placed one-sided emphasis on the development of heavy industry, but on the coordinated, balanced development of economic structure, with agriculture, energy, transportation, and other basic industries as well as science and technology as strategic priorities. In terms of reproduction mode, it no longer relied mainly on a large amount of financial and material resources for construction and extension expansion, but mainly relied on technological progress and improving labor productivity to expand the connotation of production. To sum up, the economic development strategy put forward by the Twelfth National Congress of the Communist Party of China took the improvement of economic efficiency as the premise of economic growth and expansion of production and emphasized that all economic work should be transferred onto the track of improving economic efficiency, which was an important transformation of modern economic growth and economic development strategy.

In October 1987, the report of the Thirteenth National Congress of the Communist Party of China systematically expounded the theory of the primary stage of socialism. In the primary stage of socialism, the historical task to be solved in developing social productive forces was to realize the industrialization, commercialization, socialization, and modernization of production. The third part of the report of the Thirteenth National Congress of the Communist Party of China expounded on the economic development strategy of focusing on efficiency and improving quality, coordinated development, and stable growth. After the Third Plenary Session of the Eleventh Central Committee of the Communist Party of China, China's strategic plan for economic construction was generally divided into three steps. The first step was to double the GNP in 1990 over that of 1980, so as to solve the problem of food and clothing for the people. This task was basically realized. Second, by the end of the 20th century, China's gross national product

---

120. Hu Yaobang, *Comprehensively Creating a New Situation in Socialist Modernization Construction: Report on the Twelfth National Congress of the Communist Party of China* (People's Publishing House, 1982).

(GNP) was to be doubled and people's living standards were to reach an affluent level. Third, by the middle of the 21st century, the per capita GNP was to reach the level of moderately developed countries, the people's lives were to be relatively prosperous, and modernization was to be basically realized. And then, on that basis, China aimed to move on. At the time, the most important thing was to take the second step. China aimed to make great progress in its modernization drive after realizing the second task. There were many favorable conditions for achieving the goal of the second step, as well as many difficulties and contradictions. The focus of the contradiction was the low efficiency of economic activities. It was thus necessary to unswervingly implement the strategy of focusing on efficiency and improving quality, coordinated development, and stable growth. The basic requirements of this strategy were to strive to improve the quality of products, stress the marketability of products, reduce material consumption and labor consumption, realize the rational allocation of production factors, and improve the efficiency of capital and resource utilization. In the final analysis, it was necessary to gradually shift from extensive operations to intensive operations. According to the basic requirements of the development strategy, it was important to focus on solving three important problems. The first was to put the development of science and technology and education in the primary position and put economic construction onto the track of relying on scientific and technological progress and improving the quality of workers. The second was to maintain a basic balance between total social supply and demand and rationally adjust and transform the industrial structure. The third was to further expand the breadth and depth of opening up and constantly develop economic and technological exchanges and cooperation with foreign countries.[121]

The period from the Twelfth National Congress of the Communist Party of China in 1982 to the Thirteenth National Congress of the Communist Party of China in 1987 was basically the span of the Sixth Five-Year Plan for National Economic and Social Development (1981–1985). The Sixth Five-Year Plan was a relatively complete and well executed economic plan following the First Five-Year Plan. Its basic task was to continue to implement the policy of adjustment, reform, rectification, and improvement, to further solve various problems that hindered economic development lingering from the past, to achieve a decisive victory in realizing the fundamental improvement of the financial and economic situation, and to lay a better foundation for the national economic and social development during the Seventh Five-Year Plan period and create better conditions. However, during the period of the Sixth Five-Year Plan, bank credit was out of control, the scale of capital construction was over expanded, consumption demand rose sharply, and total social demand expanded, leading to serious inflation. In April 1986, the Fourth Session of the Sixth National People's Congress adopted the Seventh Five-Year Plan for the National Economic and Social Development of the People's Republic of China (1986–1990). The Seventh Five-Year Plan was the embodiment of the practical economic development strategy of the Twelfth National Congress of the Communist Party of China. It highlighted the basic

---

121. Zhao Ziyang, *Advancing Along the Socialist Road with Chinese Characteristics: Report on the Thirteenth National Congress of the Communist Party of China* (People's Publishing House, 1987).

balance between total social supply and demand, the steady growth of the national economy, and the correct handling of the relationship between quality and quantity and between efficiency and speed. The comprehensive index of the economic growth rate in the Seventh Five-Year Plan not only continued to use the index of gross industrial and agricultural output value, but also adopted the index of gross national product (GNP) for the first time.[122] This was an important reform in China's economic planning and statistics.

Against this background of economic development, the economic development strategy put forward by the Thirteenth National Congress of the Communist Party of China continued the core idea of focusing on efficiency and improving quality, coordinated development, and stable growth, and it advanced a new viewpoint of reducing material and labor consumption and realizing reasonable allocation of production factors, that is, from the perspective of reducing production costs, optimizing resource allocation, focusing on efficiency, and improving quality. The economic development strategy put forward by the Thirteenth National Congress of the Communist Party of China also prioritized the development of science and technology and education, emphasizing that modern science and technology and modern management were the decisive factors in improving economic efficiency and the main pillar for China's economy to move toward a new stage of growth. It was necessary to shift economic construction onto the track of relying on scientific and technological progress and improving the quality of workers, so that the development strategy would move from the level of improving social and economic benefits to the level of transferring economic growth to the level of technological progress and the improvement of the quality of production factors, which conformed to the general law of modern economic growth. The economic development strategy determined by the Thirteenth National Congress of the Communist Party of China was characterized by openness. Further expanding the breadth and depth of opening up and continuously developing economic and technological exchanges and cooperation with foreign countries were listed as one of the three important issues that needed to be resolved in the economic development strategy. It was proposed that economic and technological cooperation and trade exchanges with other countries be further expanded, including those with developed and developing countries, so as to create better conditions for accelerating China's scientific and technological progress and improving its economic benefits.

2. Research on the Development Strategy of Promoting Rapid Economic Growth on the Basis of Improving Quality, Optimizing Structure, and Increasing Efficiency

In October 1992, the report of the Fourteenth National Congress of the Communist Party of China systematically expounded the theory of building socialism with Chinese characteristics, including the development path, stage, fundamental task, development power, external conditions, political guarantees, and strategic steps of socialist construction. It clearly pointed out that the goal of

---

122. *The Seventh Five-Year Plan for National Economic and Social Development of the People's Republic of China (1986–1990)* (People's Publishing House, 1986).

China's economic system reform was to establish a socialist market economic system, so as to further liberate and develop productive forces. On the strategy of economic development, the report of the Fourteenth National Congress of the Communist Party of China put forward the strategic thought of rapid growth. The report pointed out that the essence of current international competition was a contest of comprehensive national strength based on economic and scientific and technological strength. Many countries in the world, especially countries and regions around China, were accelerating their development. If China's economic development was slow, the consolidation of the socialist system and the long-term stability of the country would encounter great difficulties. Therefore, whether China's economy could accelerate development was not only a major economic question, but also a major political issue. In the 1990s, the growth rate of China's economy was originally set at an average annual growth rate of 6% of the GNP. Now, judging from the development of the international and domestic situation, it could be faster. According to preliminary estimates, it was possible to increase it by 8% to 9%, and China needed to move toward this goal. By the end of the 20th century, the overall quality and comprehensive national strength of China's national economy would reach a new level. The gross national product (GNP) would exceed the expectation of quadrupling the original figure of 1980, and the people's concerns would move from securing food and shelter to those of an affluent society. China needed to seize the favorable opportunity and accelerate development. Those who had the conditions to accelerate their development would move faster. As long as the measures taken were of high quality and good efficiency and adapted to the changes of market demand at home and abroad, it was important to encourage development. The report emphasized that China needed to proceed from reality, pay attention to what it could do according to its ability, and effectively manage comprehensive balance. In discussing the acceleration of development, it was important not to rush into mass action and tend toward the old thinking of neglecting efficiency, pursuing output value unilaterally, competing for competition, blindly embarking on new projects, and blindly expanding the scale of infrastructure construction. Instead, it was necessary to find a way to develop the national economy with higher speed and better benefits.[123]

In September 1997, the report of the Fifteenth National Congress of the Communist Party of China expounded the historical position and guiding significance of Deng Xiaoping Theory. It systematically expounded the basic line and program of the primary stage of socialism. The main social contradiction in the primary stage of socialism was the contradiction between the people's growing material and cultural needs and the backward social production, which ran through the whole process of the primary stage of socialism in China and all aspects of social life. The report put forward the goal of economic and social development by the middle of the 21st century. In the first decade, the gross national product (GNP) would be doubled compared with that of 2000, so that the people's life would be more affluent and a relatively perfect socialist market economic

---

123. Jiang Zemin, *Accelerating Reform, Opening Up, and Modernization and Striving for Greater Victory in the Cause of Socialism with Chinese Characteristics: Report on the Fourteenth National Congress of the Communist Party of China* (People's Publishing House, 1992).

system would be formed. After another ten years of efforts, the national economy would be further developed and various systems would be improved. By the middle of the 21st century, the 100th year of the founding the People's Republic of China, it would basically realize modernization and become a prosperous, strong, democratic, and civilized socialist country. It was important to actively promote the fundamental transformation of the economic system and the mode of economic growth, so as to lay a solid foundation for basically realizing modernization by the middle of the 21st century. In this period, rapid, healthy development of the national economy was a major issue to be resolved in order to establish a relatively perfect socialist market economic system and maintain the growth. It was important to find a path of economic coordinated development with a faster speed, better benefits, and continuous improvement of overall quality.[124]

In November 2002, the report of the Sixteenth CPC National Congress put forward the goal of building an overall affluent society. After realizing the first and second goals of the three-step strategy of modernization, the people's life would generally reach a well-off level. However, it would still need a long period of concerted struggle to consolidate and improve the affluent level that had been achieved. The contradiction between people's growing material and cultural needs and backward social production was still the main contradiction in Chinese society. For the first twenty years of the 21st century, it was important to concentrate efforts on building an affluent society of a higher level that benefited more than one billion people through a comprehensive approach. This was a necessary stage of development to achieve the third step in the strategic goal of modernization. The goal of building an overall affluent society on the basis of optimizing the structure and improving efficiency involved quadrupling the GDP of 2000 by 2020 and significantly enhancing the comprehensive national strength and international competitiveness. In order to achieve this goal, the main tasks of economic construction and reform in the first twenty years of the 21st century were to improve the socialist market economic system, promote the strategic adjustment of economic structure, basically realize industrialization, vigorously promote informatization, accelerate modernization, maintain the sustained, rapid, and healthy development of the national economy, and constantly improve the people's living standards. In the first ten years of the 21st century, it was important to comprehensively complete the Tenth Five-Year Plan and the goals set in 2010, so as to raise the total economic output, comprehensive national strength, and people's living standards to a higher level and lay a good foundation for greater development in the following ten years.[125]

From the 1990s to the beginning of the 21st century, under the guidance of the development strategy of rapid economic growth, China's economy achieved rapid growth. This was especially true from 2003 to 2007, when China's economy achieved double-digit growth for five consecutive

124. Jiang Zemin, *Holding High the Great Banner of Deng Xiaoping Theory and Pushing the Cause of Building Socialism with Chinese Characteristics into the 21st Century: Report on the Fifteenth National Congress of the Communist Party of China* (People's Publishing House, 1997).

125. Jiang Zemin, *Building a Well-off Society in All Aspects and Creating a New Situation in the Cause of Socialism with Chinese Characteristics: Report on the National Congress* (People's Publishing House, 2002).

years, and from 2000 to 2010, when the average growth rate of China's GDP was 10.36%.[126] From the perspective of the strategic development framework, rapid growth was necessary to the struggle for faster development on the basis of improving quality, optimizing structure and enhancing efficiency, and taking a path of national economic development with higher speed and better efficiency. The report of the Fifteenth National Congress of the Communist Party of China clearly pointed out that it was necessary to fundamentally change the mode of economic growth and take the path of coordinated economic development with greater speed, better efficiency, and continuous improvement of the overall quality. The report of the Sixteenth National Congress of the Communist Party of China linked industrialization, informatization, and modernization, and it pointed out that informatization was the inevitable choice for China to accelerate industrialization and modernization. It was important to persist in using information technology to drive industrialization and using industrialization to promote informatization. China needed to find a new mode of industrialization with a highly scientific and technological base, good economic benefits, low resource consumption, and less environmental pollution, all while giving full play to human resource advantages. In order to take the path of new industrialization, it was necessary to give full play to the important role of science and technology as the first productive force, pay attention to relying on scientific and technological progress and improving the quality of workers, and improve the quality and efficiency of economic growth. At the same time, it was important to promote the optimization and upgrading of the industrial structure, and to form an industrial pattern with high-tech industry as the guide, basic industry and manufacturing industry as the support, and the service industry developing in all aspects.[127] These strategic ideas and industrial policies provided theoretical elements for the new development strategy of the development of science and technology and overall high-quality development.

Some studies pointed out that at the beginning of the 21st century, the actual level of China's per capita GDP exceeded 1,000 US dollars. Based on Rostow's theory of economic development stage, China's urban economy had entered the stage of mass consumption of economic development. While the rural economy was still in the transition period from takeoff to maturity, it was important to make the economic development strategy of income a priority. If the income constraint hindered the improvement of consumption level and led to insufficient domestic consumption, various contradictions accumulated in the initial stage of development would intensify and affect the growth of the national economy.[128]

---

126. Official Website of National Bureau of Statistics, www.stats.gov.cn.

127. Jiang Zemin, *Building a Well-off Society in All Aspects and Creating a New Situation in the Cause of Socialism with Chinese Characteristics: Report on the National Congress* (People's Publishing House, 2002).

128. Fan Conglai et al., *Income Priority Growth: Aggregate and Structure* (Economic Science Press, 2016), 35–36.

3. Research on the New Strategy of Scientific Development and Shifting from Rapid Growth to High Quality Development

In October 2007, the report of the Seventeenth National Congress of the Communist Party of China pointed out that the most remarkable achievement in the new period was rapid development. China aimed to implement the three-step strategy of modernization and promote China's sustained, rapid development at a speed that had rarely been seen in the world. At the same time, it analyzed the difficulties and problems in that development, including the high cost of resources and the environment of economic growth, the urban-rural imbalance, and regional and socio-economic development. In order to address the remaining difficulties and problems in the process of development, it was important to thoroughly implement the scientific outlook on development. Entering a new stage in the new century, China presented a series of new characteristics, especially the lack of fundamental change in the long-term structural contradictions and extensive growth mode. These facts indicated that China's basic national conditions, which were still in and would remain in the primary stage of socialism for a long time, had not changed, and the contradiction between the people's growing material and cultural needs and the backward social production had not changed. It was important for China to base its approach on the reality of the primary stage of socialism, scientifically analyze the new opportunities and challenges of its full participation in economic globalization, fully understand the new situation and new tasks of the in-depth development of industrialization, informatization, urbanization, marketization, and internationalization, deeply grasp the new issues and new contradictions in its development, and take a more conscious path toward scientific development. In the scientific concept of development, the key idea was development, the core was people-oriented, the basic requirement was comprehensiveness, coordination, and sustainability, and the fundamental method was overall consideration. According to the requirements of the scientific outlook on development, the development goal of building a moderately prosperous society in all aspects by 2020 had been optimized. On the basis of optimizing the structure, improving efficiency, reducing consumption, and protecting the environment, the per capita GDP needed to be quadrupled by 2020 compared with 2000. The development path involved accelerating the transformation of the economic development mode and promoting the optimization and upgrading of the industrial structure. It was necessary to adhere to the policy of expanding domestic demand, especially consumption demand, and promoting the transformation of economic growth from mainly relying on investment and export to relying on coordinated promotion of consumption, investment, and export; from mainly relying on secondary industry to relying on the coordinated driving of primary, secondary, and tertiary industries; and from mainly relying on increasing the consumption of material resources to relying mainly on scientific and technological progress, improving the quality of workers, and management innovation and transformation.[129]

---

129. Hu Jintao, *Holding High the Great Banner of Socialism with Chinese Characteristics and Striving for the New Victory in Building a Moderately Prosperous Society in All Aspects: Report on the Seventeenth National Congress of the Communist Party of China* (People's Publishing House, 2007).

In November 2012, the report of the Eighteenth National Congress of the Communist Party of China pointed out that comprehensive coordination and sustainability was to be taken as the basic requirement for the in-depth implementation of the scientific outlook on development, and the overall layout of economic, political, cultural, social, and ecological civilization construction was to be fully implemented, so as to coordinate all aspects of modernization and promote production relations and productivity. The superstructure needed to be coordinated with the economic base, and the road of civilized development with production development, a rich life, and a good ecology should be constantly explored. The report of the Eighteenth National Congress linked building a moderately prosperous society in all aspects with comprehensively deepening Reform and Opening Up. In order to realize the grand goal of building a prosperous society in all aspects by 2020, it was necessary to take scientific development as the theme, accelerate the transformation of the economic development mode as the main line, and shift the foothold of promoting development to improving quality and efficiency. The main direction of accelerating the transformation of the mode of economic development was to promote the strategic adjustment of economic structure. It was necessary to focus on improving the demand structure, optimizing the industrial structure, promoting regional coordinated development, and promoting urbanization, and to strive to solve the major structural problems that restricted sustained, healthy economic development. It was necessary to firmly grasp the basic strategic point of expanding domestic demand, accelerate the establishment of a long-term mechanism for expanding consumer demand, release residents' consumption potential, maintain a reasonable growth of investment, and expand the scale of the domestic market. It was necessary to firmly grasp the solid foundation for the development of the real economy, implement policies and measures that were more conducive to the development of the real economy, strengthen the demand orientation, promote the healthy development of strategic emerging industries and advanced manufacturing industries, accelerate the transformation and upgrading of traditional industries, promote the development and growth of the service industry, especially the modern service industry, and reasonably lay out and construct infrastructure and basic industries. At the same time, scientific and technological innovation was to be placed at the core of the overall national development, and the innovation driven development strategy needed to be implemented.[130] The report of the Eighteenth National Congress of the Communist Party of China continued the scientific outlook on development put forward by the Seventeenth National Congress of the Communist Party of China, and it combined the scientific outlook on development with the "five in one" overall layout of building socialism with Chinese characteristics, so as to make the development more comprehensive and more coordinated in all aspects of modernization, and to strive for comprehensive, coordinated, and sustainable development. In terms of operation, the expansion of domestic demand was taken as the basic strategic point for the strategic adjustment of the economic structure, the development of the real economy was the solid foundation for

---

130. Hu Jintao, *Unswervingly Advancing Along the Road of Socialism with Chinese Characteristics and Striving for Building a Moderately Prosperous Society in All Aspects: Report on the Eighteenth National Congress of the Communist Party of China* (People's Publishing House, 2012).

the strategic adjustment of the economic structure, and scientific and technological innovation was taken as the strategic support for improving social productivity and comprehensive national strength, so as to realize the transformation of the mode of economic development.

In order to implement the strategic plan of the Eighteenth CPC National Congress for the comprehensive deepening of the reform, the Third Plenary Session of the Eighteenth CPC Central Committee adopted Decision of the CPC Central Committee on Several Major Issues Concerning Comprehensive Deepening of the Reform on November 12, 2013. The Decision took accelerating the transformation of economic development mode as one of the main components of deepening the reform of the economic system. Therefore, in terms of accelerating the transformation of government functions, it was necessary to improve the evaluation system of development achievements, correct the bias of evaluating political achievements only by the speed of economic growth, increase the weight of indicators such as resource consumption, environmental damage, ecological benefits, overcapacity, scientific and technological innovation, production safety, and new creditor's rights, and pay more attention to labor and employment, residents' income, social security, and people's health.[131] Improving the evaluation system of development achievements from the perspective of political performance evaluation would effectively speed up the transformation of the economic development mode.

In October 2017, the report of the Nineteenth National Congress of the Communist Party of China announced that socialism with Chinese characteristics had entered a new era and formed the thought of socialism with Chinese characteristics in a new era. On the basis of building an affluent society in all aspects, it was necessary to take two steps to build a prosperous, strong, democratic, civilized, harmonious, and beautiful modern socialist nation in the middle of the 21st century. The contradiction between the people's growing needs for a better life and unbalanced, inadequate development needed to adhere to the people-centered development thought and constantly promote people's all-round development and common prosperity for all the people. Further, it needed to make clear that the overall layout of the cause of socialism with Chinese characteristics was "five in one," and the strategic layout was the "four comprehensives" (in all aspects, building a moderately prosperous society, deepening reform, promoting the rule of law, and governing the Party strictly). It was likewise important to emphasize confidence in the nation itself and its theory, institutions, and culture. The overall goal of the comprehensive deepening of the reform was to improve and develop the socialist system with Chinese characteristics and modernize the national governance system and capabilities. In the process of economic and social development, it was necessary to adhere to the concept of new development, in an effort to implement the thought of socialism with Chinese characteristics in the new era. Development was the basis and key to solve all of China's problems. Development was to involve scientific development and unswervingly implement the development concept of innovation, coordination, greenness, openness, and sharing. In terms of strategic development objectives, the report of the Nineteenth

---

131. *Decision of the CPC Central Committee on Several Major Issues Concerning the Comprehensive Deepening of the Reform* (People's Publishing House, 2013).

National Congress of the Communist Party of China likewise emphasized the development goals of "two centenaries." On the basis of the people's prosperity as a whole, by the time the party was a century old, it would have a prosperous society with a more developed economy, more sound democracy, more advanced science and education, more prosperous culture, more harmonious society, and a more prosperous life for the people. China would struggle for another thirty years, and by the time the People's Republic of China was a hundred years old, it would have basically realized modernization and turned itself into a modern socialist nation.[132]

In order to implement the new development concept, it was necessary to build a modern economic system. According to the report of the Nineteenth National Congress of the Communist Party of China, China's economy had changed from a stage of high-speed growth to a stage of high-quality development, and it was in the critical period of transforming the mode of development, optimizing the economic structure, and transforming the driving force of growth. It was important to adhere to the principle of quality and efficiency first, take the supply side structural reform as the main line, promote the quality, efficiency, and power changes of economic development, improve the total factor productivity, focus on accelerating the construction of an industrial system with coordinated development of the real economy, scientific and technological innovation, modern finance, and human resources, and strive to build an effective market mechanism, dynamic micro subjects, and macro-control. China's economic system had continuously enhanced China's economic innovation and competitiveness. The construction of a modern economic system included six aspects. The first was the deepening of the structural reform of the supply side. It was important to put the focus of economic development on the real economy, take improving the quality of the supply system as the main direction, and significantly enhance the quality advantage of China's economy. The second aspect was accelerating the construction of an innovative nation. Innovation was the primary power leading development and the strategic support for building a modern economic system. The third involved implementing the strategy of rural revitalization. The fourth focused on implementing the strategy of regional coordinated development. The fifth aspect was accelerating the improvement of the socialist market economic system. And the sixth was promoting the formation of a new pattern of comprehensive opening up and accelerating the cultivation of new advantages in international economic cooperation and competition.[133]

The theory of socialism with Chinese characteristics in the new era created a new positioning for the main social contradictions in the new era. The Sixth Plenary Session of the Eleventh Central Committee of the Communist Party of China said of the main social contradictions that "the main contradiction in our society is the contradiction between the people's growing material and cultural needs and the backward social production." The orientation of this major

---

132. Xi Jinping, *Winning the Victory and Building a Moderately Prosperous Society in All Respects and Socialism with Chinese Characteristics in the New Era: Report on the Nineteenth National Congress of the Communist Party China* (People's Publishing House, 2017).

133. Xi Jinping, *Winning the Victory of Building a Moderately Prosperous in All Aspects and Socialism with Chinese Characteristics in the New Era: Report at the Nineteenth National Congress of the Communist Party of China* (People's Publishing House, 2017).

social contradiction had guided China's Reform and Opening Up for nearly forty years. Over the previous four decades, great progress had been made in China's socialist modernization drive. According to the historical orientation of socialism with Chinese characteristics entering a new era, the Nineteenth National Congress of the Communist Party of China proposed that the main social contradictions in China had been transformed into the contradiction between the people's growing needs for a better life and unbalanced, inadequate development. The people's growing need for a better life put forward new requirements for development. Development needed to be balanced and sufficient, and it needed to be scientific development. The development concept of innovation, coordination, greenness, openness, and sharing was to be implemented. The new development concept enriched the connotation of scientific development and paid greater attention to comprehensive, coordinated, sustainable development, including all important aspects of economic and social modernization. The vehicle for carrying out the new development concept was the modern economic system. Building a modern economic system would transform China from a high-speed growth stage to a high-quality development stage and realize the development mode of optimizing the economic structure and transforming the growth momentum. The construction of the modern economic system included six aspects, with the main line being the supply side structural reform. The important measures for deepening the supply side structural reform included adhering to capacity, inventory, and leverage, reducing costs, making up for weaknesses, optimizing the allocation of stock resources, expanding high-quality incremental supply, and realizing the dynamic balance of supply and demand. Since the beginning of Reform and Opening Up, China's economic development strategy had always focused on the coordinated, balanced development of economic and industrial structure. However, the report of the Nineteenth National Congress of the Communist Party of China accurately defined structural adjustment and reform as supply side structural reform, and as the main line of implementing the new development concept and building a modern economic system, which adapted to China's development status and transformation development requirements. Some studies showed that after nearly forty years of Reform and Opening Up, in general, China's social productivity had improved significantly, the production capacity of its supply system was very strong, and the production capacity of more than 220 major industrial and agricultural products ranked first in the world. However, most of China's production capacity could only meet the demand of the middle and low-end, low-quality, and low-price, and with a large amount of excess capacity in the production capacity. The supply structure did not adapt to the new changes in demand, and the effective supply was seriously insufficient. Key core technologies had long been dependent on imports. Some important raw materials, key parts, high-end equipment, and high-quality agricultural products relied on imports. The supply of various industries in the service trade could not meet the needs of residents. These were the most prominent structural imbalance contradictions faced by China's economy.[134] In order to solve such development contradictions,

---

134. *Guidebook of the Report of the Nineteenth National Congress of the Communist Party of China* (People's Publishing House, 2017), 189.

it was necessary to promote the structural reform of the supply side, focus on the real economy, and take improving the quality of the supply system as the main direction of attack, so as to significantly enhance the quality advantage of China's economy.

4. Analysis of Industry Hollowing Out and Economic Deleveraging

The report of the Nineteenth National Congress of the Communist Party of China pointed out that in order to build a modern economic system, it was necessary to focus on the real economy, accelerate the construction of a manufacturing power, accelerate the development of the advanced manufacturing industry, and accelerate the development of the modern service industry. This was an important strategic concept. Since the first decade of the 21st century, the market demand of traditional industries in China's real economy had been saturated, the profit margin was low, and the investment risk was high, but the progress of industrial structural upgrading and development transformation was not fast. In this economic situation, the risk of economic hollowing increased due to the "shift from the actual to the virtual" of financial leverage.

Industry hollowing referred to the economic phenomenon in which the life cycle of the existing industry or product of a country or region entered a recession period, or in which the production cost rose, while the new industry failed to grow fully, resulting in the shrinkage of the economic pillar and economic growth point, which in turn led to the decline of the economic growth rate. If there were no effective innovation mechanism and favorable investment conditions, the new industry could not develop rapidly and the industrial structure could not be transformed and upgraded smoothly, which would bring a risk of economic recession.

Industrial hollowing was often associated with economic virtualization. When the investment conditions worsened and the industrial structural transformation was not smooth, the demand for industrial investment would decline. At this time, the savings rate was higher than the investment rate, and a large amount of funds were stranded in the financial system, becoming "interest-generating capital" and investments in financial asset transactions in order to pursue profits. This situation led to the shrinking of the real economy and the expansion of the speculative economy, and the demand for speculation led to a bubble economy, which made the financial system and even the whole economic system much riskier. From the perspective of China's situation, the change in economic situation altered the investment mode. The general processing industry and the energy and raw material industry had an overcapacity, and the industrial capacity utilization rate was less than 70%. Some key industries, such as the electronic information products manufacturing industry, automobile manufacturing industry, petrochemical and fine chemical industry manufacturing industry, high-quality steel manufacturing industry, and other similar fields, tended to decline in industrial added value and return on investment. The average annual return on net assets of the manufacturing industry was basically around 6%. Industrial transformation and upgrading was not smooth. The lack of independent innovation ability of enterprises caused by various factors became the main obstacle to industrial transformation and upgrading. New industries could not fully develop to form industrial scale. This situation in the industrial industry made the investment risk higher, the rate of return on investment low, and the conditions for obtaining capital investment poor. There were not only the reasons for industrial transformation, but also for the efficiency of the financial market (i.e., the lack of tools and products for venture capital and equity financing).

According to the current situation in China's economy, there were two ways to achieve economic deleveraging—the financial side and the industrial side. The short-term expedient measures included "debt to equity swap," the transfer of high-risk liabilities to off balance sheet, the divestiture of non-performing assets, and debt rollover or debt write down of local financing platforms, which would not fundamentally improve the quality of the balance sheet. In order to achieve economic deleveraging, it was necessary to improve the efficiency of the financial market, strengthen financial supervision, and prevent systemic financial risks. The path to industrial end economic deleveraging was to deepen supply side structural reform, improve the market exit mechanism, optimize resource allocation, and support industrial transformation and upgrading. The fundamental solution was to adjust the economic structure through deepening reform, improve the efficiency of resource allocation, and realize economic "rebalancing."[135]

Generally, efficient financial markets allocate savings to more efficient industries, which can lead to greater capital formation and higher output levels. But China's financial market, especially the capital market, was still underdeveloped and the system was not perfect, resulting in narrow financing channels, poor capital flow and allocation, imbalance in the relative proportion of indirect financing and direct financing, and highly concentrated risks in the banking system. On the operational level, it was important to construct a multi-level capital market system and develop a variety of over-the-counter trading markets, such as the property rights trading market, over-the-counter trading (OTC) system, and private equity investment (PE) market, so as to provide a trading platform for equity capital, strengthen capital liquidity, and broaden direct financing channels.

Effective financial supervision was not only an important guarantee for the opening and innovation in the financial field, but also the basic condition for economic deleveraging. After the global financial crisis in 2007 to 2009, there were two changes in financial supervision globally. One approach was to pay more attention to macroprudential policy and macroprudential management, and the other was to transform from a single prudential financial regulation to a "double peak framework" of prudential and behavioral supervision.

Generally, countries make macro prudential management a priority, sometimes prioritizing it over micro prudential management. Unlike macro policy's (fiscal monetary policy) correspondence to aggregate economy, microprudential management corresponds to individual behavior of enterprises, and macroprudential policy and management correspond to the whole financial system, which is the intermediate link between macro policy and microprudential. The main

---

135. According to the data of Listed Companies in Shanghai and Shenzhen, the asset liability ratio of listed companies was 59.38% in the middle of 2017, decreased slightly to 59.08% at the end of 2017, and increased again to 59.82% in the first half of 2018. See *21st Century Business Herald*, August 31, 2018.

objective of a macroprudential policy is counter cyclical, that is, to use counter cyclical strategies, such as limiting the maximum leverage ratio, limiting the rate of leverage accumulation, and so on, to prevent the expansion of financial bubbles and maintain financial stability. Beginning in 2009, the People's Bank of China studied and gradually implemented macroprudential management. From 2016, the dynamic adjustment of differential reserves and the management mechanism of consensual loans was upgraded to "macroprudential assessment system" (MPA). In 2015, Shanghai's pilot Free Trade Zone also launched implementation rules for macroprudential management of overseas financing and cross-border capital flow of FT account sub-accounting business.

Secondly, countries attach importance to and develop the supervision of financial behavior and implement overall process supervision of financial behavior with strict preventive supervision standards, intervening early in financial behaviors that violate regulations or which may cause risks to financial consumers. At present, the international high standard financial regulatory framework includes prudential management (macro and micro), behavioral regulation, and capital flow management (CFM) for cross-border capital flow. China's behavior supervision remains in the research stage today. It is important to establish a behavior supervision system independent of the prudential management system as soon as possible and implement discretionary capital flow management. An effective financial supervision system is the infrastructure condition for financial deepening, which makes the financial system healthier and the financial market more effective.

Overcapacity is the norm in a market economy. In the case of overcapacity, market regulation means are bankruptcy, merger, and reorganization, along with adjusting the investment expectation and investment structure according to the changes in market demand. With this mechanism, due to market competitiveness, enterprises will undergo technological innovation, and their profit model and industrial structure will be adjusted. But there is a system issue in this process, that is, the rights and responsibilities among investment decision-making, investment behavior, and investment effect are balanced, and there are no non-economic barriers to market clearing. When the investment behavior is basically not regulated by the market mechanism and the rights and responsibilities of investment are unbalanced, this type of distortion hinders the regulation of the market mechanism and makes it difficult to realize structural adjustment and development transformation. Therefore, through the deepening of the reform, it is imperative that China make the market play a decisive role in the allocation of resources and use the market mechanism to force the adjustment of industrial structure and the transformation of development mode. In order to truly implement the transformation of government functions, the government must play a better role in providing public goods and management services and maintaining market order, so as to provide a good business environment for the normal operation of the market economy.

In the framework of an open economy, another market-oriented method of addressing overcapacity is industrial transfer. International industrial transfer aims not only to digest the excess productivity, but also to digest the pressure of rising costs and seek a more effective combination of production factors. Globally, there are two trends in industrial transfer, especially in manufacturing industry transfer. The first is that some labor-intensive processing and manufacturing industries which occupy a large amount of land resources are transferred to low-cost countries and regions. The second is that developed countries and some moderately developed countries attract high-end manufacturing industry to return and transfer by virtue of their complete market system, industrial system, supply chain system, and higher labor productivity. Manufacturing is currently the backbone of China's national economy. Thus, the transformation and upgrading of the manufacturing industry and the development and transformation of the entire economy cannot be realized. The value added features of the manufacturing industry tend to decline, which makes the national economy lack structure. Regarding the increase in the proportion of tertiary industry or service industry as the performance of industrial structure adjustment reflects a view that is not comprehensive, and the extreme result will hollow the national economy. The transfer of the manufacturing industry should learn from the experience of developed economies such as those of the United States, Europe, and Japan. These do not focus on the transfer of the entire industrial chain, but the transfer of some links of the industrial chain, while still occupying the high end. China's manufacturing industry should develop toward the high end in terms of standards, technology, quality, and brand, and it must develop intelligent manufacturing technology to improve labor productivity and reduce production costs. At the same time, China must also rely on the relatively complete industrial system and the small and medium-sized enterprise groups with strong supporting ability to continue to attract the transfer of global middle and high-end manufacturing industry, and it must promote the development of the manufacturing industry toward the high-end through the allocation of global elements and the construction of the industrial chain. This is also an important aspect of supply side structural reform.

CHAPTER 13

Research on the Transformation of the Socialist Market Economy and Socialist Political Economics

13.1 The Paradigm Transformation of Political Economics Against the Backdrop of Market-Oriented Reform

1. Analysis of the Current Situation of Political Economics

In the 1990s, the distance between traditional socialist political economics and the actual economic reform and development expanded constantly, and it lacked explanatory and predictive power for the real economy. As a result, the research object, theoretical framework, and analytical methods of socialist political economics were discussed again in economic circles. The starting point of this discussion did not aim to revise and expand the socialist political economics system as it did in the 1980s, but to reflect on its paradigm, framework, and methods more generally and to try to reconstruct socialist political economics with Chinese characteristics on the basis of this criticism.

Many people believed that political economics, as a basic discipline, faced great challenges. Many current political economics theories and factors were patched together: Marxism, Western economics, and China's practical problems. Some practical and operational knowledge also impacted the theoretical system of political economics. There were contradictions between ideology and theory and between theory and practice in the discipline of political economics, especially the contradiction between labor value theory, ownership theory, and the real economy. If these contradictions were not solved, it would be difficult for political economics to become a complete, systematic discipline. Some people analyzed the main defects of "traditional" political economics (referring to the economic theories represented by various versions of socialist political economics textbooks introduced and rearranged from the Soviet Union since 1950), holding that traditional political economics was the theoretical reflection of the planned economic system, and that its focus of discussion was economic relations in the planned economy. In the actual conditions of socialist market economic system reform, this theory would conflict with the economic reality, and it would be contrary to the reform goal. Traditional political economics was composed of three parts: public ownership, the three laws, and the commodity economy. In the area of public ownership, it mainly explained the formation, nature, function, superiority, and form of public ownership, while the three laws included the basic socialist economic law, the law of distribution according to work, and the law of planned and proportional development. Strictly speaking, this part of the analysis of the commodity economy was an introduction to the socialist part of the reform, which was undoubtedly education, and it represented great progress in the material content. However, in the practical arrangement, it was put in the theoretical framework of the planned economy for elaboration. Too much of the discussion centered on the particularity of the commodity economy in the socialist system, while less analysis was made of the connotation and function of its important market mechanism. In fact, it served the planned economy. Such a system structure and arrangement could only cover and explain the real content of the socialist economy with great difficulty, and to a large extent, it was contrary to the actual situation. In terms of analysis and research methods, almost all the original textbooks included too much normative analysis, qualitative analysis, and abstract analysis, and too little empirical analysis, quantitative analysis, and specific analysis. Naturally, it was impossible for political economics not to involve the value judgment of economic problems, and normative analysis was also essential. But too much normative analysis in the traditional textbooks of that time caused the common problem of political economics largely becoming overly concerned with the interpretation and demonstration of theory and policy. It divorced the content of economics from reality and lacked operability, which resulted in the disjunction of theoretical discussion and the real economy. The standard premise related to the textbook was far from the actual situation, and with this standard premise, the theory obtained with the help of logical reasoning inevitably struggled to play a guiding role in practice.[1]

Some theorists focused on the methodological defects of socialist political economics, first addressing the tendency of one-sided use of abstract law. Marx's scientific abstract method moved from concrete to abstract, and then back to concrete. If this research process from

1. Xu Lei and Sun Changyou, "The New Development of Contemporary Socialist Political Economics," *Economy and Management*, no. 3 (1993); Liu Yongjie, "The Times Require the Reform of Socialist Political Economics," *Journal of Hebei University of Economics and Trade*, no. 3 (1993); Fang Yue and Ma Qixiang, "A New Understanding of the Six Viewpoints of Traditional Political Economics," *Journal of Zhongnan University Finance and Economics*, no. 5 (1994); Jiang Yumin, "Rethinking the Problems of the Socialist Political Economic System," *Finance and Trade Research*, no. 6 (1994); Yang Jiazhi, "The Theoretical Framework of the Socialist Part of Political Economics Should Be Reconstructed," *Hubei Social Sciences*, no. 1 (1995).

concrete to abstract was abandoned, then the only path left was to use abstract categories to deduce a conclusion and carry out so-called normative analysis. It was impossible to construct a category that conformed to the objective facts and integrated theory with practice. The second area of focus was the tendency to belittle empirical evidence. There were misunderstandings and deviations in the understanding and application of the empirical analysis method. It was believed that the empirical method meant conducting actual investigation and research, generating case studies, and adding several mathematical formulas. It was difficult to grasp, master, and apply the empirical analysis method from the perspective of scientific methodology and philosophy, and it was difficult to eliminate the accumulated habit of normative analysis. The third area was the tendency to reject the use of mathematical tools. This was mainly caused by the defects of knowledge structure and mathematical training of this generation of economists. Obviously, this view was based on the methodology of Western economics to refer to the evaluation of socialist political economics, but the comments were reasonable. Some economists were not even concerned with any methodology at all, simply talking in any way they liked. For example, in 1994, it was proposed that the relationship between public ownership and the market economy was one of a unity of opposites, with both unity and contradiction. It could not generally be said whether the combination of public ownership and the market economy was possible or not. If contradictions were properly handled, they could be combined. Otherwise, they could not. It was no wonder that "socialist political economics" was in crisis if this was what passed for economics studies.[2]

Some scholars believed that the task and purpose of studying socialist economic problems and Marxist economics studies of capitalist economic problems were not exactly the same. Marxist study of capitalist economic problems aimed to expose its contradictions and reveal its development law, while the study of socialist economic problems aimed to serve the socialist construction and reform, which could not only study the relations of production, but also the allocation of resources. Therefore, the research object of political economics could be defined as economic interests. Resource allocation was economic benefit, and production relations were also economic benefit. In this way, it was possible to unify the research objects of Western economics, Marxist political economics, and socialist political economics through the same concept. Some scholars pointed out that there were three basic defects in the traditional study of political economics. The first was that it failed to see through the full process of investigation of social and economic development from the origin of human society, instead being limited to the study of

---

2. Qiao Jianmin, "Some Thoughts on the Defects of Socialist Political Economics," *Northern Forum*, no. 3 (1993); Fan Gang, *Comparison and Synthesis of Three Modern Economic Theory Systems* (Shanghai People's Publishing House and Shanghai Sanlian Bookstore, 1995); Zou Xiangdong, "On the Problems Existing in the Socialist Part of Political Economics Textbooks," *Journal of Qiqiha'er Normal University (Philosophy and Social Edition)*, no. 6 (1995); Zhang Pinxiu, "On the System of Socialist Political Economics," *Finance and Trade Research*, no. 3 (1996); Chen Lin, "Poverty in Political Economics," *Shanghai Economic Research*, no. 8 (1996); Xiao Liang, "Thinking in Confusion," *Shanghai Economic Research*, no. 8 (1996); Jin Xiaoyu, "Comparison of Two Theoretical Analysis Methods of Market Economy," *Journal of Nanjing University (Philosophy and Social Edition)*, no. 2 (1995).

modern social and economic conditions, which resulted in a lack of comprehensive understanding on key issues. The second defect was its failure to study the relationship between man and nature as the starting point, focusing instead only on the research on the relationship between humans and nature and thus being limited in the relationship between people, which made the theoretical framework of the discipline lacking in profound explanatory power. The third was that it failed to focus on the essence of economic life, being largely limited to the analysis of economic forms, which resulted in the separation of theory and practice. Some believed that the research object of China's political economics should be decided by China's national conditions. China's most basic national conditions were that it was a large developing country, and it was in a period of economic restructuring. Therefore, it was important to take the transformation of economic system and economic development as the main thrust of political economics research. Other opinions held that political economics should mainly study three aspects: 1) the relationship and function between production relations and productivity, 2) the relationship between the existing economic operations under certain system conditions, including macro-control, the role of the state, and resource allocation, and 3) the content of development economics, including how the dual economic structure became a modern economy with sustainable development. Other views held that the fundamental purpose of the discipline construction of socialist political economics was to serve socialist construction. The fundamental task of socialism was to develop productive forces. Therefore, socialist political economics should take the effective allocation of resources as the research object, and the study of production relations should be subject to and serve the purpose of effective allocation of resources. Others proposed that the research object of Chinese's economics was market relations in the primary stage of socialism. The study of this sort of market economic relations included not only the study of the economic system, but also the study of economic operations. The research object of Marxist political economics was the relations of production, which was characterized by the study of production from the perspective of class relations, that is, the relationship between the capitalist class and the working class in production. Like Marxist political economics, the research object of socialist market economics was also to be determined according to practical requirements depending on the contemporary historical conditions, but not by subjective will. The fundamental task of socialism was to develop productive forces, which was the historical condition of socialist market economics. Therefore, the study of economics needed to focus on how to develop the economy.[3]

After the mid-1990s, there were two main opinions on the research objects of political economics or economics in China. One was that economics was a science concerned with resource

---

3. Wang Jue and Wei Min, "A New Theory on the Nature and Characteristics of the Socialist Economy," *Reform*, no. 6 (1993); Wang Hongyuan, "Common Prosperity: The Research Object of Socialist Political Economics," *Contemporary Finance and Economics*, no. 12 (1995); Li Yiping, "The Current State and Revolution of China's Theoretical Economics," *Economics Trends*, no. 11 (1996); Gong Xikui, "Qualitative Research of Economics Is Still Necessary," *Shanxi Development Guide* (July 9, 1996); Jiang Xuemo, "Several Issues on Socialist Political Economics," *Economist*, no. 2 (1997).

allocation, and the other was that the research object of political economics or economics was the mode of production or production relations. The study of the mode of production also included the study of resource allocation, but resource allocation was subordinate to production mode. Economics mainly studied the mode of production and the relations of production corresponding to the mode of production.

From a broader historical background of economic thought, these distinctions differences between Marxist economics and Western economics were matters of their research objects. In the preface of the first German edition of *Das Kapital*, Marx pointed out that what the book studied was the capitalist mode of production and its corresponding relations of production and exchange. According to Marx's definition, socialist political economics aimed to study the socialist mode of production and its corresponding relations of production and exchange. Therefore, the research object of political economics or economics was the mode of production in each stage of historical development in human society and the production relations or economic relations corresponding to the production mode. On the issue of the research object of economics, the fundamental difference between Marxist economics and Western economics lay not in whether to study resources, but in 1) whether to study the mode of production, 2) whether to study the production relations corresponding to the mode of production, and 3) whether to distinguish the general resource allocation of abstract production from that of a specific mode of production and to study the resource allocation of a specific mode of production. There were both connections and fundamental differences between the resource allocation of the research object of Western economics and the mode of production in the sense of resource allocation of Marxist capital. Although both emphasized that the laborer and the means of production should be reasonably allocated within the social production units, Western economics emphasized the generality of resource allocation, which was an abstract category of pure productivity mainly dependent on the technical level of a society. Marx emphasized that the specific social and historical nature of resource allocation was a social and historical category mainly dependent on the dominant ownership form of a society. Therefore, different societies had different methods of resource allocation. Because the research object of Western mainstream economics was limited to the allocation of resources in the sense of technology, the result was that the economic relations formed in social and economic activities were eliminated from economics, thus greatly reducing the research scope of economics as a human science. Further, the research object was simplified and idealized. Taking neoclassical economics as an example, the basic content of the theory was the maximum-minimum theory under the basic assumption of rational economic man. Finally, there was nothing to be done about the characteristics and evolution of social economic system. Because Western mainstream economics not only confined the research object of economics to resource allocation but also narrows down the extension of resource allocation and only studies resource allocation in the technical sense, it was necessary to study resource allocation on the assumption that the system remained unchanged. Therefore, the new institutional economists, represented by Coase and North, introduce institutional variables into economic research to make up for the defects of mainstream economics. Some held that the basic theory of Western mainstream economics was in a profound paradigm crisis because the research object of Western mainstream economics was limited to narrow resource allocation.[4]

2. Opinions on the Reform of Socialist Political Economics

Some scholars pointed out that there were two defects in the existing textbooks on political economics. The first was the lack of an internal logical system. The textbooks on political economics were generally divided into the capitalist and socialist parts. The capitalist part was divided into pre-monopoly capitalism and monopoly capitalism. The different parts were obviously lacking an internal logical consistency. The pre-monopoly capitalism part was basically an abbreviation of Marx's *Das Kapital.* The monopoly capitalism part had gradually broken through Lenin's framework and ideas in *On Imperialism,* but there were many narratives with a weak theoretical nature, and the research on internal regularity was insufficient. The socialist part was mostly compiled according to the practice of China's economic system reform, especially according to the spirit of the central documents from various periods. There was thus no consistency in the basic concepts, basic analysis framework, and conclusions. The second defect was that it lacked basic stability and relative independence in scientific development. This defect was obviously reflected in the socialist part of political economics, which was a type of "policy hermeneutics" and "policy propaganda," to a certain extent, and altered with the changes of central documents and government policies. Almost every time the Central Committee held an important meeting on economic work, the textbook of political economics had to be revised as soon as possible. It was constantly amended and adapted, and often demolished and supplemented again, indicating that it was attached to the political situation and changed with the political climate. These were the two most fundamental defects of the existing textbooks. Without addressing these two fundamental problems, it was impossible to produce a political economics textbook with inherent logic unity, relative stability, and independence. Some thought that there were many theoretical errors in the textbook system of socialist political economics, and there was no logical connection in its structure. It was only a compilation of economic laws, economic categories, and economic relations among various departments. Another point of view noted that the current theoretical system of political economics in China was still based on the combination of the "capitalist part" and the "socialist part." The relationship between the two parts was totally antagonistic, which

---

4. Wang Xinxin, "A Comparative Analysis of the Research Objects of Political Economics," *Jiangsu Social Sciences*, no. 3 (1996); Wu Yifeng, "On the Research Object of Political Economics or Economics," *Chinese Social Sciences*, no. 2 (1997); Wei Xinghua, "Lessons and Thoughts Caused by the Explorative and Tortuous Nature of Socialist Economic Theory," *Economic Longitude*, no. 6 (1997); Jiang Xuemo, "Socialist Economic Relations as the Research Object of Political Economics," *Economic Review*, no. 1 (1998); Huang Guitian, "Summary of the 12th National Symposium on Socialist Economic Theory and Practice in Colleges and Universities," *Economics Trends*, no. 12 (1998).

could not result in a reasonable disciplinary system. To construct a new textbook system of political economics, it was first necessary to re-establish the research object, which needed to be adapted to the new discipline system and not be limited to the analysis of socialist production relations, but should instead be studied from the perspective of economic system, micro and macro-economic operations, economic growth, and economic development. In addition, it was necessary to enrich the research methods of political economics. The principle of the interaction between productivity and production relations, economic base, and superstructure was still the theoretical guidance of political economics research, but it was important to learn from descriptive and universal principles and methods in Western economics and combine qualitative analysis with quantitative analysis, normative analysis with empirical analysis, and abstract analysis with concrete analysis to achieve the unity of scientificity and practicality. The third was to establish the scientific starting point of the new discipline system. Because the general knowledge of economics had the generality beyond the limits of social system, it was applicable to all countries with a market economy. It was thus important to first introduce the general knowledge of economics when establishing a new discipline system. Then, a new discipline system of political economics should be established in combination with China's national conditions.[5]

There were generally two approaches to the reform of socialist political economics. One was to mend the original framework and add the relevant content from the socialist market economy, and the other was to abandon the original framework and establish a new analytical concept and system structure. Some scholars pointed out that the first method, as a path of transition, was not appropriate for that stage, because the conditions for establishing a completely new socialist political economics were not mature enough. However, from the development point of view, this method had no way out. Incorporating the new theory reflecting the actual situation into the framework formed under the condition of the planned system would certainly restrain the development of the theory. Therefore, in order to establish a socialist political economics which met the practical requirements and could guide the reform practice, it was necessary to break the original framework and establish a new system structure and analysis framework, because with the gradual establishment of the socialist market economic system, the micro main body behavior of the market and the macro government behavior had gradually undergone one great changes. Therefore, the economic law based on the micro and macro main body behavior rules also under went fundamental changes. The law of the market economy was certainly different from the law of the planned economy, and the economic relationship was also different. Traditional socialist political economics took the economic relations and laws under the conditions of the planned

---

5. Meng Zhaoyuan, "Two Issues on the Construction of Socialist Economics with Chinese Characteristics," *Economic Overview*, no. 12 (1994); Shi Wenwen, "Review and Prospect of the Establishment of a New System of Socialist Political Economics," *Tibet Party School*, no. 1 (1996); Zhang Shuguang, "A Tentative Discussion on the Content, Nature, and Function of Economics," *Social Science Front*, no. 4 (1996); Wang Shouchun, "Review and Enlightenment of Socialist Political Economics," *Economist*, no. 5 (1998); Wei Dazhi, "A Glimpse of the Current Situation in China's Economic Circles," *Economist*, no. 5 (1998).

economy as the research object, which meant that the political economics which took the socialist market economic law as the research object naturally needed to establish a new framework.

Some held that China was still in the primary stage of socialism, the socialist economy itself was still very underdeveloped, various economic contradictions and laws had not been fully demonstrated, and it was impossible for immature economic relations to form a completely scientific economic system. Instead of relying on previous hypotheses and logical reasoning to deduce the system, it was thus better to observe the actual situation and summarize the characteristics of various realistic socialist economic models. Some commentators emphasized that socialist political economics and bourgeois political economics were fundamentally opposites in terms of their systems. The system of socialist political economics could only reflect the theory and viewpoint of socialist economies, and it was also a reflection of socialist practice. On the basis of the traditional socialist political economic system, socialist political economics should be compiled based on an outline of the Decision of the CPC Central Committee on Economic System Reform. Some scholars also pointed out that the establishment of socialist political economics might be a long process, which could only be carried out systematically with the development and transformation of the larger society. It was important to accumulate existing research materials and conduct in-depth, systematic, steady research.[6]

Generally speaking, the guiding ideology of socialist political economic reform was Marxist economics, not Western economics. Because socialism was a social system that constantly promoted the development of productive forces, created higher labor productivity, and realized the common prosperity and all-round development of the entire society, only by using Marxist economics to guide the reform and development of socialism was it possible to realize the goal of socialism. On the issue of not involving the fundamental social system, many studies of Western economics were worth affirming. Some theoretical achievements had revealed the basic laws of the market economy and its operation, which were of great significance to the socialist economy. Some scholars further analyzed and pointed out that the most important reason Western economics could not be used as the guiding ideology of socialist political economic reform lay in the different national conditions, mainly in different social systems and different stages of social and economic development. The differences between Western economics and China's economics inevitably resulted in broad differences between them, which involved research topics, methodologies and basic theories. However, it was also pointed out that the guidance of Marxist economics

6. Gu Shutang and Liu Zhanjun, "Reconstruction of China's Theoretical Economics Facing the 21st Century," in *Where Does China's Economics Go* (Economic Science Press, 1997); Liu Wei, "China's Economics Should Face the Reality of Reform and Development," in *Where Does China's Economics Go* (Economic Science Press, 1997); Li Guangxin, "On Socialist Politics Some Views on the Innovation of Governance Economics," *Journal of Qinghai University for Nationalities (Social Science Edition)*, no. 4 (1997); Wei Xinghua, "Where is China's Economics Going?" *Economic Review*, no. 2 (1998); Zhong Peihua, "A Summary of the Symposium on the Discipline Construction of Political Economics," *Economics Trends*, no. 2 (1998); Gu Shutang, "My Views on Political Economics (Especially the Socialist Part)," *Economics Trends*, no. 11 (2010).

could not be dogmatic. The research object of Marxist economics was the mode of production and the production relations of free capitalism, and its abstract method was its scientific nature, though this was conditional and relative. If these general conditions were ignored, they would be regarded as general conditions. As far as the research topic was concerned, the task of Marxist economics was to reveal the movement law of capitalist mode of production, and its main subject was the transformation of production relations, not the construction of a socialist economy. As far as the basic theory was concerned, the theory of labor value was the basic principle of Marxist economics, but this principle was conditional and limited. If it were generalized and absolute, it would lead to deviation in understanding and practice. Some critics believed that Deng Xiaoping Theory should be taken as the guiding ideology for the reconstruction of socialist political economics. Deng Xiaoping Theory was contemporary Marxism, and his economic theory was a new development of economic science. It provided a scientific methodology and a series of basic principles for the reconstruction of socialist political economics, which contained important theoretical innovations. The main content of Deng Xiaoping's economic theory involved five aspects.

1) The theory of national conditions (the primary stage of socialism). This was the starting point and premise to correctly understanding the extreme importance, connotation, and method of national conditions. The core substance was to determine the basic national conditions of China at present and in the future, that is, the meaning of the "primary stage of socialism" and its differences and relations with other stages.

2) The essence of socialism (what is socialism?).

3) The theory of Reform and Opening Up (that is, how to understand the goal, motive force, object, nature, arduous, long-term nature, risk, cost, etc.) and the theory of the socialist market economic system. The theoretical breakthrough was the historical status, achievements, fundamental defects, and drawbacks of a highly centralized planned economic system, allowing socialism to engage in the market economy. The relationship between the characteristics of the modern market economy and macro-control, how to transform from a planned system to a market economic system, and theoretical achievements of Western economics of the economic system, were all concerns as well.

4) Economic development. Science and technology were the first productive forces, followed by Reform and Opening Up and special economic zones. The key points driving the overall situation, the three-step theory, and giving consideration to reform, development, and stability were all highlighted. Agriculture was the foundation, and sustainable development, the combination of speed and efficiency, and the transformation of the economic growth mode were key concerns. Learning from the scientific achievements of Western development economics was prioritized.

5) The history of the theory and practice of socialist reform. This focused on the history of utopian socialism before Marx, Marx's classical scientific socialism theory and practice,

Soviet socialist theory and practice, and Mao Zedong's socialist theory and practice.[7]

3. Discussion on the "Paradigm" of Political Economics

The concept of paradigm was first proposed by Thomas Kuhn, a contemporary American philosopher of science, in his *Structure of Scientific Revolutions* (1962). He pointed out that a paradigm is a method of observing the world and practicing science and a synthesis of beliefs, value standards, technical means, and other concerns that are mastered by general researchers in specific disciplines. Kuhn believed that in a certain period of the development of a science, a "community of science" often forms. The scientific community is made up of practical workers with expertise who have received the same education, absorbed the same technical literature, and obtained the same discipline training. The "paradigm" is what the members of the scientific community share. The contents of the paradigm include common basic theories, basic viewpoints, and basic methods, which provide scientists with a common theoretical model and framework for solving problems, a common psychological belief, and a natural view that guided and connected the theoretical system and psychological cognition. It is this three-part paradigm, as the entity of scientific activities, that becomes the basis for further activities in a certain period of time. Therefore, the development of science is not only a movement of theoretical systems, but also a movement of paradigm including the natural view, theoretical system, and psychological cognition. In Kuhn's work, the significance of paradigm in methodology referred to a set of conceptual systems, basic theorems, and analytical methods accepted and used by a group of scientists in a certain discipline and used as a common tool for ideological exchange. The concept of paradigm in economics was transplanted from the theory of the philosophy of science, but it retained the basic meaning of the paradigm concept as used in analyzing scientific development.[8]

In the historical logic of economic development, the concept of the "paradigm" of scientific development was used to define economics as an integral part of scientific knowledge, that is, to

---

7. Gu Haibing, "A Review of the Status, Methods, and Future Development of Economics," *Learning*, no. 11 (1995); Wu Xinmu, "The Historical Mission of Marxist Economics in the 21st Century," *Economics Trends*, no. 7 (1996); Lin Yi, "What Should Chinese Economists Do," *Financial Science*, no. 1 (1996); Xu Yonglu, "A Preliminary Study on the Methodology of China's Theoretical Economics," *Social Sciences*, no. 9 (1996); Hu Yongyong, "Traditional Socialist Political Economics Should Be Reformed," *Economics Trends*, no. 2 (1998); Wang Zeke, "Political Economics: Respect for Practice and Science," *Reform*, no. 5 (1998); Yuan Wenping, "Creating a New Socialist Political Economics," *Financial Science*, no. 1 (1998); Zeng Kanglin, "How to See the Crisis of China's Economics," *Economist*, no. 3 (1998); Wu Dong, Wang Li, and Wang Li, "Thoughts on Upholding and Developing Marxist Economics," *Economics Trends*, no. 2 (1998); Huang Guitian, "The Premise of Economic Theory Synthesis," *Economics Trends*, no. 2 (1998); Yang Jiyong and Xiong Xiaoqi, "The Development Trend of the Political Economics System in the New Century," *Economics Trends*, no. 3 (1999); Yan Zhijie, "On the Significance of Political Economic Reform," *Economics Trends*, no. 4 (1999).

8. T. S. Kuhn, *Structure of Scientific Revolution* (Shanghai Science Press, 1980); Mark Blaug, *Economic Methodology* (Peking University Press, 1990); Lloyd Reynolds, *Three Worlds of Economics* (The Commercial Press, 1990).

incorporate the historical development of economics into the historical development of scientific thought. After Reform and Opening Up began, China's economic theorists realized that there were serious defects in the original "socialist political economics" paradigm, and new theories needed to be adapted to the new practice, which the original paradigm did not or could not provide. So scholars began to think about how to develop a new theoretical paradigm. During this period, there were generally three theoretical propositions or theoretical tendencies.

The first was original "Soviet paradigm," in which the main problem was that it did not correctly reflect the "original intention" of Marxist classical writers, instead adding many incorrect views originated by Stalin. Therefore, in the view of some scholars, the way to transform the original paradigm was to "return to Marx" and reinterpret the basic theoretical issues with Marxist classical theory. Over a long period of time, a large number of papers thus devoted their efforts to citing the classics of Marx and Engels' economic works, attempting to criticize the "Soviet paradigm" with classic Marxist economics.

The second main problem of the original "Soviet paradigm" was dogmatism, in that it was too rigid to adhere to the ready-made formula and "formulation" of classical writers without innovation and development, thus making the theory rigid and incapable of reflecting the changed situation. According to this idea, what needed to be done was to add some "innovative" elements that could reflect the development of practice into the original paradigm, so as to transform and update the original paradigm in this way and adapt to the new needs.

These two tendencies had one thing in common, that is, they held that the original paradigm was basically available, but there were some minor or serious defects, so it needed to be modified or supplemented. This view was the "mainstream" in academic circles for a long time, and it was the view held by most in economic circles. This also reflected an ongoing basic situation in the field of China's economics, which was that most people still clung to the original paradigm in terms of knowledge structure, and what people were familiar with, mastered, and used were still the concepts and methods of the original paradigm. This being the case, although most scholars recognized the defects of the original paradigm, it was impossible for the majority to abandon the original paradigm and immediately implement a "scientific revolution" in the sense of methodology. This also indicated that over a prolonged period, China's economic theory had not gone beyond the framework of the original paradigm.

At the same time, among a small number of young scholars who had studied and accepted Western economics, another trend emerged, which was that of seeing the original theoretical paradigm as basically "outdated" and no longer able to address the actual economic situation. Therefore, a new paradigm needed to be adopted, which involved a set of new concepts, terms, and analytical methods, along with various theories and methods of modern economics which had been developed by humans for more than a hundred years to analyze real economic problems. One of the important reasons was that people did not know much about or have a good grasp of modern economics. Even more, they were unable to apply the theories and methods of modern economics to analyze China's practical problems and come up with feasible countermeasures and suggestions. Therefore, over a long period of time, this kind of theoretical view was not widely supported or discussed.[9]

There were mainly five opinions on the theoretical defects of the "Soviet paradigm."

1) *The defects of the research object.* According to the definitions provided by Soviet textbooks, the so-called "relations of production" referred to the ownership of the means of production and the relationship between the people and their distribution in the production process formed on this basis. This definition of "production relations" was the research object of political economics, which excluded the relationship between people and things and exchange relations in the process of production. Determined by this "research object," the "Soviet paradigm" political economics had no practical value in the real economic life, could not solve real economic problems, could not demonstrate the commodity currency relationship in the socialist economy, and could not meet the actual needs of economic development and growth.

2) *The defects of ownership theory.* An important feature of the "Soviet paradigm" in the theory of ownership was the recognition that ownership played an important role in the overall relationship of production and was the basic factor in economic relations. But this theory was only applicable to the analysis of the capitalist economy, not to the analysis of the socialist economy, because the root cause of all the defects of capitalism lay in the ownership system, and if there were any problem in the socialist economy, it was caused by reasons other than ownership, and it was necessary to seek to solve all economic problems under the premise of established ownership. Another characteristic of the "Soviet paradigm" in the ownership problem was the assumption that there was no conflict of interest and no opportunistic behavior such as a "moral hazard." This was not in line with real economic relations.

3) *The defects of value theory.* Value theory was one of the most basic principles in any economic theory. On this issue, the fundamental defect of the "Soviet paradigm" was that it ignored and rejected some important scientific research results of the development of modern economic theory for many years, so it was increasingly divorced from reality and unable to explain the real economy.

4) *Defects in the purpose of production.* Under the conditions of the socialist planned economy, the real meaning of the proposition of "production purpose" lay in what was the "objective function" taken by state planners when arranging social production. Under the conditions of the market economy, the objective function of individual economic behavior was "individual utility," and the goal of enterprise was profit. In the theoretical model of neoclassical economics, the objective function of a "social planner" was "social

9. Fan Gang, "Rethinking the Modernization and Sinicization of Economic Science," *China Book Review*, no. 5 (1995); Fan Gang, "Critique of the Soviet Paradigm," *Economic Research*, no. 10 (1995); Zhang Shuguang, "On the Basic Premise and Hypothesis of Economics," *Social Science Front*, no. 5 (1995); Ding Wenfeng, "Is Economics a Discipline of Science," *Contemporary Economic Science*, no. 3 (1996).

welfare," which was a kind of "social preference" composed of numerous individual utility functions. In the socialist political economics of the "Soviet paradigm," in fact, it was theoretically inferred from the premise of "public ownership" and the "fundamental interest consistency" between people that socialism should take "the needs of society overall as the goal of arranging social and economic activities in a planned way," because the starting point was that "fundamental interests are consistent." This theory assumed, first of all, that in the socialist economy, there were no significant differences in the "preferences" (goals or target systems) between individuals and enterprises or between local governments. Therefore, the common goal of the "entire society" could be constructed without any difficulty. Secondly, planners (or governments or countries) did not have special goals and preferences (including the "time preference" for determining the relationship between accumulation and consumption), and they should thus naturally aim at the needs of "everyone."

5) *Defect in ideological method.* As far as the ideological method was concerned, the theoretical problem of "production purpose" and the "basic economic law" in the "Soviet paradigm" lay not only in simply denying the interest contradiction of public ownership, but also in proving as "law" everything that "should be" or "is intended to be." Under the guidance of this "paradigm," people took the "basic economic law" as the core and put forward the "socialist economic law system" composed of dozens of "laws," including the law of continuous improvement of labor productivity, the law of distribution according to work, the law of increasing consumption, and the law based on agriculture. In fact, the process of increasing the number of "laws" in the "system" was actually a process of further exposing the "vulgarity" of the "Soviet paradigm." However, many found that there were numerous things in the economic system that "shouldn't" happen according to the theoretical paradigm, but the process of further emphasizing how it "should" conform to the theory had not really changed the basic mode of thinking.[10]

Other views held among economic and ideological circles included the notion that the Soviet paradigm was not equal to Marxist economics, or the "Marxist paradigm," nor could it explain China's real economy. Therefore, it was necessary to abandon this paradigm and reconstruct a new paradigm of political economics to meet China's needs. In considering how to construct a new paradigm, the representative opinion was that the paradigm of Western economics provided an economic category system composed of demand, supply, and utility, so the formation of China's economic paradigm should be dominated by Western economics. However, it was important to also consider the Western economic paradigm in light of China's social and economic reality and Marx's holistic approach, absorb its reasonable core, sublate its irrationality, and adjust it to suit

---

10. Fan Gang, *Comparison and Synthesis of Three Modern Economic Theory Systems* (Shanghai People's Publishing House, Shanghai Sanlian Bookstore, 1995). Fan Gang, "Critique of the Soviet Paradigm," *Economic Research*, no. 10 (1995).

China's reality. The formation of China's economic paradigm should be based on China's social and economic reality, led by Marxism and its methodology, guided by the paradigm of Western economics, and considered comprehensively. At the same time, it should absorb the scientific achievements of other economic schools to form a new concept and category system, ultimately forming the concept or category system that China's economic paradigm should have.[11]

Different opinions were also put forward in the field of economic thought on the criticism of the "Soviet paradigm." The "new comprehensive paradigm of Marxism" attempted to "integrate" Marxist and Western economics in the research object and value theory of political economics to construct a new paradigm. In terms of research objects, this "new paradigm" held that socio-economic relations were, on the one hand, the relationship between people and things, and on the other hand, the relationship between people. Marxist economics focused on the relationship between people, while Western economics focused on the relationship between people and things. These were different views of the same object, both of which were scientific and one-sided. Therefore, the integration of the two needed to be realized.

Critical opinion held that the difference between Marxist economics and bourgeois economics lay not in their research object materials, but in their differences in standpoint, viewpoint, and method. On the basis of critically inheriting the scientific achievements of classical bourgeois political economics, Marx founded proletarian political economics and comprehensively expounded the law of the emergence, development, and the inevitable extinction of capitalist production relations. In fact, Marxist political economics was not just revolutionary and critical, and not constructive or resource allocation, as some viewpoints said, and Western economics did not only study the relationship between people and things, but also had a distinct class nature.

In the theory of value, the "new paradigm" held that one of Marx's contributions to the development of economics was its ability to clearly distinguish value and use value from the value concept of classical economics, and then to clearly explain value with labor and define the usefulness of things useful to people as use value. At the same time, exchange value was understood as "the contradictory unity of value and use value." Some later Marxist economists only paid attention to Marx's theory of labor value, while ignoring his theory of exchange value. As a result, the labor theory of value could not successfully introduce demand and absorb the achievements of modern economics. Therefore, it was necessary to integrate the theory of labor value with the theory of marginal utility value, so that the theory of labor value could escape this predicament.

Critical opinion held that Marx's concept of objective use value could not be interpreted as the concept of the utility of subjective axiology. There was no "exchange value theory" in Marx's

---

11. Jin Chengxiao, "The Debate Between Two 'Paradigms' and the Construction of China's Economics," *Shanghai Economic Research*, no. 10 (1995); Meng Zhaoyuan, "A Preliminary Discussion on the Methodology of Social Economics with Chinese Characteristics," *Journal of Liaoning Normal University (Social Science Edition)*, no. 5 (1996); Zhou Xiaoliang, "Constructing China's Economics with Chinese Characteristics in a Comprehensive Way," *Economist*, no. 6 (1997); Lu Genxin, "Basic Ideas for the Development of China's Theoretical Economics," *Financial Research*, no. 7 (1999).

theory of labor value. Labor value theory and marginal utility value theory could not be brought into a theoretical system.[12]

Some commentators pointed out that the basic theory of Western economics was in a profound paradigm crisis, that is, members of the scientific community were no longer willing to accept a set of assumptions and theorems based on it because of the increasing number of abnormal phenomena. For example, Western economics found that increasingly, "preference order" could not be expressed by utility function. The preference order which could not be expressed by utility function could not be maximized, which would bring great confusion to the so-called "basic theory" that "behavioral rationality" was equal to "utility maximization." For example, some research results suggested that the restrictions on the individual demand function (such as continuity, zero order homogeneity, etc.) did not restrict the total demand function, which meant that the "general equilibrium" theory had no "micro basis." This research result caused many economists to no longer engage in the invalid research of "general equilibrium" theory. Additionally, Western economists proved that even under the assumption that the transaction cost was zero, the Coase Theorem is not tenable. If it was to be true, a strong restriction should be added, which was that the order of human preference was "parallel preference." This proof caused many to think that the Coase Theorem was at best meaningless tautology. Theorists held that the paradigm crisis of Western economics indicated that there was no universal or universally accepted "basic theory" of economics. Therefore, Chinese scholars should not only stay at the level of "application" and "basic theory," but also bravely undertake the task of creating "basic theory." As long as they faced major new problems in the actual situation (i.e. the "abnormal" phenomenon in the classic "paradigm"), it was possible to overcome the paradigm crisis of Western economics on the basis of Chinese practice and make a global contribution to the basic theory of economics.[13]

In the discussion of "paradigm," some scholars proposed their views from the perspective of economic development and paradigm transformation. The logical basis of economic paradigm was an axiomatic norm of normative economic issues. Therefore, in terms of logical characteristics, the essence of conventional economic development was the gradual expansion and application of logical space and thinking methods of an economic paradigm. As a stable development period of knowledge form, conventional economics constituted the expansion of the economics research field and the accumulation growth of knowledge content. The emergence of a new economic paradigm was like the discovery of a rich mineral deposit, while the

12. Ding Baojun, "Critique of the Soviet Paradigm," *Contemporary Economic Research*, no. 4 (1996); Ouyang Wenhe and Zhou Chengming, "Research Trends of Chinese Economics in 1997," *Financial Research*, no. 3 (1998); Cheng Enfu and Qi Xinyu, "Some Issues in the Reconstruction of China's Economics," *Financial Research*, no. 7 (1999); Chen Chengming, "Transformation and Development of China's Economics," *Financial Research*, no. 7 (1999); Chen Tong and Bao Buyun, "Basic Issues of Theoretical Economics Methodology," *Economics Trends*, no. 3 (1999).

13. Cui Zhiyuan, "Paradigm Crisis of Western Economic Theory: A Discussion with Mr. Fan Gang," *China Book Review*, no. 9 (1995).

development of conventional economics was like the development and utilization of this mineral deposit. With the continuation of the conventional economic process, the unused logical space of the original paradigm became smaller, and the scope for researchers to adjust their own views became narrower. Therefore, in the later stage of the development of conventional economics, there were usually two possible situations. One was that the explanatory power and forecasting ability of the traditional economic analysis theory to the actual economy were declining and becoming increasingly irrelevant. Traditional economists' painstaking repair and interpretation could not constitute a real improvement, and theoretical failures occurred frequently and accumulated constantly. In addition, due to the drastic reform of the real economic process, new problems and new situations emerged and accumulated outside the logic space or explanatory ability of the original paradigm. When people began to attribute the repeated failure of theory and problem-solving to the economic paradigm itself, rather than reviewing their ability to use the paradigm, the development of conventional economics came to an end and the economic ideological revolution of paradigm transformation was coming. At this time, the problem of normative economics moved from behind the scenes to the front of the stage, and discussion, criticism, and qualitative and normative academic debate replaced the usual economic analysis to address difficult problems. Many competing normative theories and factions began to emerge. The challenge faced by economics was not the elaboration and development of a paradigm or theory, but the choice between various competing theories and viewpoints. The old paradigm was gradually abandoned, and the new paradigm had not yet formed. This was the replacement of the old and new paradigms, the interruption of the process of economic knowledge accumulation, and the creation of economic ideas, marking a transition stage in the rise of the new process.[14]

13.2 Research and Discussion on "China's Economics"

1. On the Construction of "China's Economics"

There were different opinions on "China's economics" in the field of economic theory. Some scholars believed that the term "China's economics" referred to *China's* economics, that is, the economics based on China's social and economic reality. To be more exact, it was based on the social and economic reality of contemporary China or China since 1949, which was different from the "Western" economics based on the social and economic reality of Western countries. It also referred to China's economics, which was the same as the "economics" of Western economics,

---

14. Jin Chengxiao, "The Debate Between Two 'Paradigms' and the Construction of China's Economics," *Shanghai Economic Research*, no. 10 (1995); Lu Jialiu, "Paradigm and Paradigm Shifts in Economics," *Jianghai Journal*, no. 2 (1996); Song Donglin, "Looking at the Development of Economics from the Perspective of Paradigm Crisis," *Contemporary Economic Research*, no. 2 (1997); Li Wenpu, "On Two Theoretical Logical Premises of Economic Analysis," *Economist*, no. 4 (1998); Guo Yi, "Paradigm Synthesis and Chinese Construction of Economics," *Journal of Shanxi University of Finance and Economics*, no. 3 (1998).

because both were "economics," or "theoretical economics." It was true that due to the difference between having "China" and the "West" as an actual background, their theoretical idea were not the same. Therefore, "China's economics" was the theoretical economics or political economics based on the actual background of the contemporary Chinese social economy, because it provided the most fundamental theoretical basis for the decision-making of the entire social economy in China. Some critics believed that China's economics could be divided into narrow and broad senses. In the narrow sense, China's economics referred to China's economics as a science, that is, Chinese economic discipline. In the broad sense, China's economics referred to China's economic research, which was the organic unity and general name of Chinese economic disciplines, Chinese economists, Chinese economic schools, and Chinese economic tools and methods.

Other scholars believed that under the guidance of Marxism, Mao Zedong Thought, and Deng Xiaoping Theory, and with the practice of China's Reform and Opening Up and the construction of socialism as the source, the emerging Chinese economics scientifically reflected and revealed the laws of socialist construction in contemporary China, absorbed the positive elements of Western economics, and inherited the excellent economic heritage of Chinese history. This new economics with Chinese theoretical characteristics, style, and spirit was a new development of Marxist economics.

There were also quite a few scholars who did not think there was such a thing as "China's economics." They often used terms such as "sinicization of economics," "localization of economics," and the "Chinese school of economics" in their writings. They questioned whether China's economics were even different from Western economics, saying it was similar to the question of whether China wanted to build a building with Westerners or start a new one. The answer was clear: economists all over the world should be building the same building. New classics, new definitions, and new theories would appear in China's economic research, but this was only a contribution to the common building of economics, which was the "Chinese school of economics."

Some scholars cited Kuhn's view, looking at "China's economics" from the perspective of a paradigm. They believed that to establish "China's economics" as an economic revolution, it was important to be able to put forward a brand new theory in the field of China's economic life. This theory was composed of a set of categories, concepts, laws, and methods which was recognized by academic circles and could stand up in practice and offer a new explanation based on the test of history. Some people further believed that a paradigm was "a theoretical understanding of practical activities." The innovation of economic theory (covering the emergence of "China's economics") included the innovation of category, analysis method, and theoretical system. The ancient and long-standing traditional culture and the current system gave the Chinese people their own understanding of their economic activities. Foreign culture needed to be combined with the reality of their own country to form their own category, thought, and theory, so as to have "China's economics." Some theorists advanced the proposition of the "localization of economics." This localization meant that Chinese economists should first understand all types of phenomena in economic life and make clear what were the main economic, political, and social variables behind the complicated social and economic phenomena, and then construct a simple logical system to explain the causal relationship between these important variables. Thus, understanding the economic phenomena to be explained was the first step in the theoretical innovation of economic science. As for the economic phenomena that happened in a society, only economists who lived in that society could understand it clearly. For those economists who were not involved in it, they could only scratch the surface. It was important to note that any influential economic theory was first and foremost a localized one.[15]

Academic circles generally held that the cultural tradition and theoretical source of "China's economics" had four aspects: traditional Chinese economic thought, Marxist economics, Western economics, and Chinese economic activities.

The first focused on traditional Chinese economic thought. It was believed that traditional Chinese economic thought was deeply rooted in China's soil and had a profound impact on the people's way of thinking and the government's decision-making. If China's economics did not integrate with traditional Chinese economic thought and inherit its useful parts, the resulting economics would be like water without source or a tree without roots for China, and it would not be the desired Chinese economics. The basic spirit of economics involved "saving, mutual benefit, and balance." In the past, economics had only paid attention to competition and regarded the pursuit of maximization as the spirit of economics. This was a wrong understanding. The pursuit of maximization was only a basic assumption of personality, which could not be regarded as the spirit of economics. Under this assumption, economics had the higher pursuit of "saving, mutual benefit, and balance." Therefore, it was necessary to seek the philosophical basis from traditional Chinese culture and create an economics with cooperation as the main line. Some people believed that "China's economics" referred to an economics with Chinese cultural characteristics and universal significance. Traditional Chinese culture, especially Confucian culture, emphasized factors such as "harmony," "cooperation," and the pursuit of human unity. It was important to take "cooperation" as the main line to provide a basic methodology for economics and a cultural basis for economic revolution. On this basis, Chinese economics could be created.

---

15. Tan Minxian, "Multiple Relations and the Rational Exploration of China's Economics," *Contemporary Economic Science*, no. 6 (1994); Fan Gang, *A Political and Economic Analysis of Gradual Reform* (Shanghai Far East Publishing House, 1996); Chen Caihong, "China's Economics and Chinese Economists," *Research on Financial Issues*, no. 6 (1996); Lin Jue, "A Summary of the Symposium on the Development of China's Economics," *Social Sciences*, no. 2 (1996); Jin Haiping, "Establishing China's Own Economics," *Academic Monthly*, no. 1 (1997); Liu Shibai, "Some Issues in the Construction of China's Economics," *Economist*, no. 3 (1997); Gu Shutang and Liu Zhanjun, "The Reconstruction of China's Theoretical Economics in the 21st Century," *Academic Quarterly*, no. 2 (1997); Sheng Hong, "Is There a Chinese School of Economics?" *Southern Weekend*, October 10, 1997; Liu Jianhua and Gao Xiaohong, "On the Issues of the Sinicization of Economics," *Changbai Academic Journal*, no. 3 (1997); Chen Zongsheng, Xu Feng, and Liu Shuxiang, "Possible Future Development of China's Economic Direction," *Economics Trends*, no. 7 (1997); He Liancheng and Ding Wenfeng, "Where China's Economics Is Going?" *Economics Trends*, no. 2 (1997); Fan Bingsi and Hu Xiaojing, "China's Economics in the Period of Reform," *Economist*, no. 3 (1997); Jian Xinhua; "What Theoretical Economics China Needs at the Present Stage," *Finance and Economics Science*, no. 2 (1998); Liu Shen, "Some Thoughts on the Reconstruction of China's Economics," *Financial Research*, no. 7 (1999).

The second view, the one held by most people, stated that China's economics were rooted in Marxist political economics. The core and backbone of China's economics were theoretical and political economics. It was self-evident that political economics was the main theoretical source of China's economics, because it aimed to reveal the essential connection between social and economic activities, and it was the theoretical basis for analyzing and revealing diversified social economic activities and multi-level economic relations. Therefore, to establish China's economics, it was important to first focus on the innovation of political economics and seek to re-examine and scientifically discuss the basic principles of economics under the new historical conditions of building a socialist market economy, so as to write better, more applicable monographs on political economics.

The third view was that Western economics was the main source of China's economics. From the perspective of China's development trend, as long as the market-oriented reform did not reverse, some basic theories and analytical methods of Western economics would inevitably be integrated into China's socialist economics. Together, they formed a new theoretical framework and a new mainstream economics. In other words, Western economics and Chinese socialist economics were the theoretical sources of China's economics. This view discussed the influence of Western economics on China's economics from three aspects: the point of view, neoclassicism, and the new Keynesianism introduced in the first half of the 1980s to economic growth theory and development economics introduced in the second half of the 1980s, and then to new institutional economics and property rights economics in the 1990s. In terms of the perspective of its methodology, the empirical analysis method, structural analysis method, and institutional analysis method of Western economics offered great enlightenment for China's economic research. From the perspective of discipline construction, Western economics had reference significance for the academic orientation, discipline category, and integration of China's economics.

The fourth view was that the first three "roots" were mainly discussed from the perspective of the history of thought, and it was more appropriate to call them the theoretical origin of China's economics. The real "root" of China's economics actually referred to the objective basis for its survival and development. Therefore, this "root" was not traditional Chinese economic thought, Western economics, or Marxist economics, but only Chinese economic activities. There were three reasons. The first was that it was consistent with the general principles of epistemology. After all, the establishment and development of China's economics was not the history of economic thought, but the knowledge of China's reform and development. The second was to prevent the reverence for the ancient from misleading the establishment and development of China's economics. The third was to restore the true nature of the relationship between the theory and practice of China's economics, so as to ensure the healthy development of China's economics.

Some pointed out that it was necessary to firmly establish the concept of the root of China's economics. From the treasure house of the history of China's economic thought, the history of Marxist economic thought, and the history of foreign economic thought, it was important to calmly think, analyze, and compare, and to absorb nourishment, which was formed by many factors, such as China's social and economic structure, the Chinese people's way of thinking, psychological structure, geographical environment, cultural customs, and outstanding traditions. It was important to absorb and learn from all the outstanding achievements of human civilization and construct China's economics based on Chinese culture. Only by establishing the concept of the root of China's economics could the nation find a breakthrough in theory and methodology on the path of constructing China's economics, making it possible to reflect on some major basic theoretical issues in a deeper way.[16]

The discussion on the construction of "China's economics" mainly included the following ideas:

1) The path of constructing "China's economics." There were three kinds of representative exploration opinions on the path to constructing China's economics in the field of economics. First, based on a Chinese cultural foundation, it was necessary to absorb the advantages of Western civilization, constructing economics with Chinese cultural characteristics and trying to find the root of China's economics. Second, through the research path of localization of modern economics, it was important to gradually realize the organic combination of internationalization and localization of Chinese economic research, trying to construct China's institutional economics with the theme of China's institutional change through case studies. Third, it was important to try to build a new system of China's economics within the framework of political economics by learning from the scientific research methods of modern Western economics and through the integration and improvement of its methods. This generalization, to a certain extent, reflected the exploration and effort made by economic circles in the construction of China's economic path. Although it had shown distinctive characteristics of individuality, it could only gradually formulate through future exploration. Based on a certain research path, it could absorb and learn from the theoretical achievements formed by other research paths, and then on the basis of long-term exploration, create a path and framework for China's economics that would truly reflect the characteristics of Chinese culture and reveal the direction of its future development.

2) The research object and content of "China's economics." Generally speaking, the research object of China's economics was political economics. To establish China's economics, it was necessary to first focus on the innovation of political economics, which required great effort to study economic theory, especially the theory of the socialist market economy. This research would form the main content of China's economics. Broadening of the research field of economics was advocated and five contents of China's economic research were

---

16. Lin Yixiang, "The Root of China's Economics" *Shanghai Securities Journal* (February 4, 1996); Liu Guibin, "The Root of China's Economics," *Shanxi Development Guide* (August 6, 1996); Zhu Leyao, "The Necessity and Direction of Economics Becoming China's Science," *Research on Financial Issues*, no. 10 (1996); Ye Tan, "Looking for the Root of China's Economics," *Chinese Social Sciences*, no. 4 (1998).

proposed, including serving the liberation and development of productive forces, the main realistic mission of China's economics; the improvement of production relations, the main research topic of China's economics; the optimization of economic structure, the key task of China's economic research; and the research of economic operation mechanism, the main content of China's economics and the innovation of production organization form. Other scholars believed that the socialist part and the capitalist part of political economics should have a unified research object—production relations and its development law—so as to maintain the unity of the research objects of political economics. Socialist theoretical economics consisted of three parts: productivity economics, socialist political economics, and socialist micro and macroeconomics. Another view was that China's economics should develop Marxism, especially in economic management and operation. Although the main purpose of Marxist political economics was to seek the movement law of the occurrence, development, and extinction of capitalism and the study needed to involve the management and operation of the capitalist market economy. The operation of the socialist market economy was bound to involve the management of the role of the law of value and its specific operation. In the construction of China's economics, it was thus important to focus on the development of Marxism in management and operation. Marx talked about the management and operation of the market economy, such as the stock system, exchange, virtual capital, organic composition of capital, separation of ownership and management power, productive labor, and non-productive labor, but it had not been fully recognized by theoretical circles. It was an important task for Chinese economics to study these scattered concepts, principles, and arguments in a standardized, systematic way.

3) The academic standard of "China's economics." Some scholars pointed out that theoretical economics should follow the norms of academic research in the process of innovation. In essence, theory should be a very strict logic system, seeking to discover the causal relationship of several variables through logical reasoning. Therefore, the innovation of economic theory should first comply with the requirements of formal logic. It was true that theory was not a logical game, but an attempt to explain social phenomena. Therefore, the various inferences of a theory should be consistent with the social phenomena it explained. The debate on economics also needed to abide by the relevant norms. Since theory was a set of logical systems to explain social phenomena, the debate on theory should meet two conditions: first, determining whether there was a problem in the logic system of the theory and whether the causality and inference were rigorous, and second, determining whether the theory was consistent with the phenomenon it analyzed. If these two conditions were satisfied, then the economic theory was not falsified and could be provisionally accepted. In order to oppose it, it was necessary to collect more social phenomena to prove the deficiency of the theory and its inference. At the time, this standard had not been widely observed. For example, some people discussed problems

using one set of theories and logic systems, while others used another set of logic systems, making it impossible to point out whether the logic had problems and whether the theory was consistent with reality. As a result, there was little progress in theory.[17]

2. On Methodology of "China's Economics"

In 1938, Liu Jie'ao published his *Economic Methodology* as part of the *College Series*, which was presided over by Cai Yuanpei, Ma Yinchu, Hu Shi, Feng Youlan, Li Siguang, and others. The book pointed out that "the development of science lies in the study of pure theory of a kind of object. Since people in China today advocate material interests and despise theory, it is enough to hinder the future of development and cause China's economics to stop forever in the realm of 'comprehensive economic knowledge.'" It went on "China's current lack of methodological research has led our economics studies astray, so the author would like our people to fill in the gaps. It is necessary to understand the importance of research methodology, and then to lay a solid foundation for the independent development of theoretical economics in China with three and five years, or eight and ten years."[18] From the 1950s to the 1970s, economic methodology basically became a forbidden area for theoretical research. It was not until 1988, more than ten years after the beginning of Reform and Opening Up, that *The Evolution of Basic Theories of Contemporary Western Economics: Methodology and Micro Theory* (by Yang Deming) and *The History of Methodology of Political Economics* (by Liu Yongji) were published, realizing Liu Jie'ao's vision of half a century earlier.

After the beginning of Reform and Opening Up, some scholars paid attention to and explored economics methodologies from different perspectives. In March 1985, Cui Changjie wrote an article entitled "Suggesting the Establishment of Economic Research," and in July 1987, Lü Yimin published the article "The Need for an Economic Science," putting forward the relevant content of the discipline. In August 1991, Liao Shixiang edited and published *Economic Methodology*, and in 1992, Liu Yongji published *Methodology of Political Economics*. In addition, in 1990, Peking University Press published two translated works, *Economic Methodology* by Mark Blaug and *Why Is Economics Not Yet a Science*, edited by A. S. Eichner. In May 1994, *Economic Sciences*, edited by Huang He, was published by China Financial and Economic Publishing House. In February 1995,

---

17. Li Huai and Gao Liangmou, "The Path and Value Orientation of China's Economics in the 21st Century," *Economics Trends*, no. 3 (1997); Hong Yuanpeng and Yu Fuhai, "The Development and Innovation of Economics," *Economics Trends*, no. 3 (1997); Xu Lei, "Some Thoughts on the Modernization of China's Economics," *Shandong Social Sciences*, no. 2 (1997); Chen Shuxiang, "Reflections on the Construction of 'China's Mainstream Economics'," *Economic Review*, no. 2 (1997); Gu Jie and Li Zhiqiang, "Theoretical Dilemma and Reconstruction of China's Economics, *Economist*, no. 1 (1997); Gao Hongsheng, "Some Thoughts on How to Develop Economics," *Theoretical Front of Colleges*, no. 2 (1997); Gu Shutang and Gu Jie, "Theoretical Innovation and Development of China's Economics," *Economic Review*, no. 2 (1998); Shen Liren, "Reflections on How to Develop China's Economics in the 21st Century," *Economist*, no. 2 (1998).

18. Liu Jie'ao, *Economic Methodology* (The Commercial Press, 1937).

An Overview of Economic Methods, edited by Chen Xian, was published by China Economics Press. These works undoubtedly played an important role in promoting China's research into economic methodologies.

However, the status of economic methodologies was far from the requirements of economic development and research. As an independent branch of the economic theory system, economic methodology had not been fully recognized in China. Even the authoritative *Encyclopedia of China (Economics)* explained in its entry for "economic methodology" that "it refers to the theories of various methods adopted by Western economic circles in the study of economic theories and problems," reflecting the low level of China's economic methodology research.

Some theorists studied the basic assumptions of Chinese economics. To set up a hypothesis is to limit and abstract the scope of the selected research problem. Because things are generally connected, any kind of economic phenomenon is affected by various factors. If the scope is not limited, it will be impossible to grasp the key points, and the essence of things will not be recognized. Sometimes, due to the limitations of research methods and conditions, it is only possible to exclude complex situations and limit the problems to a relatively simple range. It is true that according to the needs and convenience of any research, the scope of the limit can on occasion be gradually expanded, that is, the hypothesis can be relaxed. A reasonable premise for a hypothesis should conform to the phenomenon as much as possible. However, it should be made clear that in fact, any assumption cannot fully conform to the reality, because the hypothesis itself is a reconstruction of reality. Reasonable premises mean that the assumed object still retains its essential characteristics in the natural state, and these essential characteristics are more obvious and general. The premise of any theory is a set of assumptions, so there can be no logical contradiction between the assumptions. The presupposition should make the logical deduction operable and reach a definite conclusion. Otherwise, no matter how good the hypothesis is, it will be meaningless.

This idea emphasized that the establishment of a presupposition in the research process was of great significance to the development of "China's economics." The clear hypothesis not only repelled the unnecessary dispute of concepts, but also avoided misunderstandings of theory. There were many hypotheses put forward by economic and ideological circles. Representative theories included the hypothesis of institutional change. This hypothesis meant that China's economy was in the process of changing from one economic system to another, which was the most basic operating feature of China's economy for a long period of time. Because it was easy to observe, it was also discussed more often in academic circles. Some scholars even equated China's economics with China's transitional economics or its institutional economics. No matter how different the expression was, in terms of the construction or innovation of China's economics, the affirmation of the overall characteristics of institutional change and the theoretical representation of the process of institutional change would undoubtedly become the basic theory among them. The development of this theory would determine the development and innovation of many other specific theoretical analysis methods and conclusions and determine the fundamental features of China's economics in the future, just as the core theory of neoclassical economics was the description of the operation law of the market economy on the premise of a mature market economic system.

The second was the incomplete information hypothesis. Incomplete information not only referred to incomplete information in the absolute sense—that is, due to the limitation of cognitive ability, people's understanding of economic things had produced varying degrees of "uncertainty"—but also referred to the "relative" sense of incomplete information—that is, the real economy itself could not produce enough information and effectively allocate it, and its outstanding performance was the wide range of different economic subjects, resulting in asymmetry. Therefore, China's economics needed to take it as a basic assumption and further study the particularity of its manifestation and possible research fields after it was combined with other basic assumptions of China's economic operation.

The third was the cultural hypothesis of Confucianism. This mainly referred to the unique historical and cultural impact on economic operations, and this influence was more profound, more extensive, and more complex than other assumptions. In a sense, the unique historical and cultural background was perhaps the most fundamental reason for the uniqueness or individuality of China's economics.[19]

Regarding the research norms of "China's economics," the general opinion was that it was necessary to take China's socialist market economy and modernization construction as the starting point, take Marxist economic methodology as the guidance, and correctly treat and actively learn from Western scientific philosophy theory and economic methodology. Scientific abstraction was based on China's reality. It was important that China's special economic contradictions be taken as the research foothold, the phenomenal materials that could reflect China's special economic contradictions be taken onboard, and the phenomenal materials be compared and classified according to abstract thinking methods to allow for induction and analysis, concepts defined through synthesis, and the movement of concepts discussed thoroughly. The unity of logic and history was not only the basic principle of economic research, but also the necessary condition for establishing Chinese theoretical economics. Therefore, it was important to fully understand the close relationship between China's economic history, the history of China's economic thought, and Chinese theoretical economics to avoid duplication of "imitative deductive" economics. The purpose of statistical testing was to determine whether a theoretical hypothesis could stand the test of empirical data. Based on the test results, it was possible to draw conclusions and put forward policy suggestions in line with the conclusions.

Economic research needed to shift from normative research focusing on "what should be" to empirical research focusing on "what is." The past socialist political economics had become empty sermons and rigid dogma as a result of its neglect of the research on the reality of the

---

19. Ding Wenfeng, "Reflection on the Methodology of China's Economics," *Economist*, no. 3 (1997); Yu Zhongying, "An Introduction to China's Economic Research Outline," *World Economic Journal*, no. 2 (1998); Chen Bogeng, "Innovation of Contemporary China's Economics," *Jianghai Journal*, no. 1 (1998); Lu Xinbo, The Premise and Hypothesis of Some Basic Issues in China's Economics," *Economist*, no. 3 (1998).

socialist economy. Since the beginning of Reform and Opening Up, this situation had greatly improved, but it still could not eliminate the status of policy hermeneutics. There were many reasons for the serious lag of China's economic theory relative to its economic reality, among which the important point was that economic theory had not completely realized the separation of value judgment and fact judgment. Empirical testing was to be regarded as the standard and basis for judging a theory. For a long time, Marx and Engels' works had been used to explain and demonstrate economic problems in China's economic circles. Although some brilliant expositions in Marx's and Engels' works had explanatory power for many economic problems at the time, this was different from taking predecessors' works as the standard of evaluation theory, and it led to a strange phenomenon in theoretical circles, in which both sides of the debate quoted the classic works of Marx and Engels to illustrate the correctness of their opposing theories, and each thought their own way was correct. Economics had not yet formed a generally accepted standard for evaluating theory, and few people were committed to evaluating theory with empirical data. China's economics was still in a pre-scientific state. Changing this situation depended on a change in the people's concept and the introduction and wide adoption of econometrics and other technical means.[20]

3. Comment on "China's Economics"

(1) Defining "China's Economics"

After the mid-1990s, with the deepening of China's economic market-oriented reform, China's economic theory research gradually become mature and rational. During this period, some economists proposed fundamental problems concerning the development of economic theory from a new perspective, such as the modernization of China's economics, the root search of China's economics, the Chinese school of economics, and the transitional economics of China. In the discussion of these problems, economic circles highlighted the proposition of "China's economics." In the 1980s, "China's economics" was a conventional term, mainly referring to China's socialist political economics. However, in the 1950s, 1960s, and early 1980s, China's socialist political economics basically followed the Soviet paradigm, while after that, it mainly used classical Marxist theory and some theories and methods drawn from Western economics to revise the Soviet paradigm, which was not an independent form of economics. By the 1990s, the proposition of "China's economics" had new meaning. There were different opinions on

---

20. Zhang Chenshu, "Experimental Methods of Economics," *World Economy*, no. 3 (1996); Xie Deren, "Are Empirical Economics and Normative Economics Mutually Exclusive?" *Economist*, no. 4 (1997); Jia Chunxin and Wang Tingting, "Poverty of Economic Imagination," *Economist*, no. 2 (1998); Zhang Yufei, "Building China's Economic System Cannot Be Hasty if It Is to Be Successful," *Economics*, no. 5 (1998); Zhao Xuebin and Wu Xuezhen, *Socialist Market Economics* (China University of Mining and Technology Press, 1998); Yang Chunxue, "Three Debates and Reflections on 'Economic Man,'" *Economics Trends*, no. 5 (1997); Lin Yi, "Two Issues that Demand Attention in the Construction of China's Economics," *Financial Science*, no. 2 (1998); Zhang Xu, "China's Economics: History, Theory, and Practice," *Economist*, no. 3 (1998); Liu Runkui, "Perspective on Difficulties in Establishing China's Economics," *Economics Trends*, no. 3 (1999).

how to understand "China's economics." Some scholars believed that "China's economics" was based on the integration of classical economics, modern economics, Marxist economics, and Chinese traditional economic thought. It was an economic system with both independent cultural value and "practical value." Some scholars pointed out that "China's economics" was a theoretical framework of the socialist market economy based on the reality of China's economic development at the primary stage of socialism and that it integrated the beneficial elements of Marxist economics, development economics, and transitional economics. In analyzing these viewpoints, some commentators put forward amendments, pointing out that it was important not to mix several theoretical systems with differing fundamental paradigms to form a "hodgepodge" theoretical system. Instead, what was needed was a foundation of Marxist economics, the most scientific basic paradigm that could best meet the requirements of the socialist market economy, as the basis and main body to absorb the excellent achievements of Western economics. Some scholars interpreted "China's economics" from the perspective of transitional economics, arguing that "China's economics" was to be regarded as an important part of modern economics, a cognitive tool for Chinese scholars to interpret China's transition from a centrally planned economy to a market economy in the common context of modern economics, starting from the realistic basis of China's economy. In addition, there were other understandings, such as regarding "China's economics" as an economics that specialized in studying China's economic problems, economics undertaken by Chinese people, or economics of Chinese schools.

In fact, it was difficult to understand "China's economics" as a theoretical system. There were basically two guidelines to the development of theoretical economics in China: the study and research of Marxist economics and the introduction, research, and application of modern Western economics. These two development guidelines met and merged, forming a mainstream trend of integration. However, Marxist and Western economics were two theoretical paradigms. There were great differences in their basic category system, theoretical framework, research object, research method, and basic content. In China in the 1990s, although the two theoretical systems met and merged, they were not integrated into the same framework. Beyond these two theoretical systems, there was no third systematic economics with independent theoretical paradigm and analytical framework in China. If "China's economics" was understood as an economics specialized in the study of China's economic problems, then what kind of economics was the study of foreign economies by Chinese economists? And did foreign economists study China's economy as "China's economics"? If the economic research carried out by Chinese economists was called "China's economics," then was the research done by those Chinese scholars who had obtained green cards abroad counted as "China's economics"? In short, no matter which angle it was examined from, there were obstacles to understanding "China's economics."

(2) Analysis of "China's Economics"

To construct an independent form of economics, it was necessary to have a unique theoretical paradigm and framework. The biggest difference between economics and other social sciences lay in its strong experimental nature. Economics was directly produced in real economic life, and its assumptions and concepts had to be able to withstand the test of real economic life. The economic activities and economic behaviors of human society were broadly applicable, so economics had a certain universality about it, making it difficult to develop a new paradigm and framework. But this was not to say that the creation of "China's economics" was totally impossible. With diligent study, it was possible to finally form such a theoretical system, that is, on the basis of public ownership as the main body, it was possible to put forward some basic hypotheses of human nature and human behavior with an axiomatic nature on the basis of public ownership. Under these assumptions, it was possible to carry out empirical analysis on the economic activities of a socialist society and people's economic behaviors, and to develop a set of corresponding concepts and categories, and in this theoretical framework, the interest relationship of people in the public ownership economy and the behavior mechanism generated for the pursuit of interests could be explained, making it possible to then explain the relationship between this behavior mechanism, resource allocation, and income distribution. This would be a great contribution to human civilization. At the time, many people advocated "China's economics," indicating that they already had a sense of this aspect, which was welcome in any case. Western economics had also gone through hundreds of years of development and the efforts of several generations before taking its current form. Unless the capitalist market economy lasted forever, Western economics would eventually encounter a paradigm crisis and need to make fundamental changes.

In addition, "China's economics" had the connotation of a specific form of thinking and cultural tradition. In the discussion on the proposition of "China's economics," an important approach was to attach importance to the study of the history of economic theories and trace back the cultural characteristics and humanistic implications of Chinese economic thought. This phenomenon was linked to the vigorous rise of academic history research in China since the 1990s. The rise of the study of academic history was not only due to the cultural introspection at the end of the century, but more importantly, it demonstrated the mature trend of Chinese philosophy and social sciences research, and it reflected the serious thinking of Chinese intellectuals on academic value and academic essence, as well as rational exploration of academic humanities and cultural tradition. From the perspective of economics, some scholars investigated the characteristic thought of China's economic theory against the background of Chinese ideological and cultural tradition, and they explored its historical and cultural traditions. Some examined the historical blending of Chinese and Western academic cultures from the perspective of the history of world economic theories, trying to prove the due position of ancient Chinese economic thought in the history of world economic theories. Other scholars were committed to correcting the biased "scientism" of economics so that it could return to the classical academic norms of the "humanities," which aimed to promote economics from empiricism and instrumental rationality to "ideology," the logical form of scientific rationality, which could at least include the humanities. The publicity of academic history research further indicated that China's academic research had gradually come in line with global academic standards, subject classification, knowledge system, academic language, analytical methods, and other academic standards and expression. It expressed the requirements of the times to further strengthen academic exchanges between China and foreign countries and allowed for China's academic integration in the world. If "China's economics" was regarded as an academic discipline with a Chinese thought pattern and cultural tradition, it seemed easier to understand. This academic genre paid attention to synthesis, its humanistic implication, and its normative nature. Learning from the characteristics of Western academic disciplines, which focused on analysis, scientism, and positivism, it was possible to realize a great economic revolution.

(3) Analysis of the Academic Form of "China's Economics"

The discussion on "China's economics" inevitably involved the prevailing attitude toward Western economics. In the second half of the 1990s, there was a great debate on Western economics in China. In view of the attitude of many young and middle-aged economists toward Western economics, such as "affirming" and "copying" Western economics, some middle-aged and older economists, especially those specializing in the history of foreign economic theories and the teaching and research of Western economics, criticized the class justification of Western economics and the defects of some hypotheses, categories, and theories by means of class analysis from the viewpoint and standpoint of defending Marxist economics. They pointed out that duplicating Western economics could not solve China's economic problems, nor could China's economic development follow the path of Western economics. Instead, it was necessary to adhere to Marxism and develop socialist political economics. The opposite view was that the theory and methods of traditional socialist political economics were powerless to explain real economic operations, and the "law" revealed by them was not very relevant to social and economic activities. The development of China's economics needed to shift from the revision of the system to its criticism and reconstruction. They advocated using the basic assumptions, theoretical framework, and research methods of Western economics to construct China's economics, and even opposed the formulation of "China's economics" and "Western economics." Regardless of whether the views and conclusions of both sides were correct, it was a normal phenomenon and a manifestation of the prosperity of academic freedom. The complexity of the problem lay in the fact that the two schools' theories might never come to a conclusion by using different theoretical frameworks and academic languages based on different value judgments, and even ideological and social system preferences. The attitude toward Western economics was a problem arising from the collision between Chinese and Western cultures.

One of the main sticking points was the concept of "Eurocentrism" in the social sciences. Due to the European conquest of the entire world in modern times, the concept of "Eurocentrism" was formed in terms of ideology, culture, and thought. This idea was especially true in economics, because economics was not a science of pure thinking, but had a strong experimental nature and was considered to be more widely applicable. However, with the progress of society, the progress of academic research, and the deepening of cultural understanding, the Western world had changed its narrow, arrogant concept of "Eurocentrism" and begun to treat other civilizations with a fairer, more objective attitude. However, many scholars in China still regarded Western learning as a standard or classic form, and they used it as a reference to judge and criticize Chinese scholarship, showing the supposed superiority of "Westernization." This was actually a superficial mentality. Due to the different natural environment, the different ways of obtaining the basic means of living, and the different social structure, from the perspective of genealogy, each nation or civilization had different basic concerns, and their thought patterns were different. Because of the differing fundamental problems involved, the background knowledge and thought patterns were different. As long as there was an independent form of civilization, there would be an independent form of thought and an independent form of learning. It was true that there were some basic elements in different forms of civilization: the law of sameness and difference and the law of correlation in thinking, ontology, the scarcity and choice of resources in economics, and so on. Scientific research aimed to reveal the stimulation or influence of different natural and cultural environments on these elements, which led to different thought patterns and academic disciplines. These basic elements constituted the basis for the exchange and dialogue among different civilizations and cultures, and also provided a path for the pursuit of universality of science. To carry out communication and dialogue, it was necessary to have a general framework for thinking and a standard discourse system, which was a technical means and a tool for cultural and academic exchanges. Chinese scholars might be relatively backward in mastering such means or tools, but this should not lead to an inferiority complex in Chinese culture and scholarship. In a sense, the reason China couldn't communicate with others on equal footing was that Chinese scholars were backward in mastering the technical means of communication, not because of the backwardness of Chinese culture and academics. Moreover, the purpose of communication and dialogue was to absorb and complement each other, not to entirely depend on each other. Blindly depending on oneself not only meant despising oneself, but also letting others look down on oneself. In short, the introduction, research, and application of Western economics was essentially an academic exchange. Western economics could provide a general analytical framework and a normative discourse system (for example, the most basic market model and the successful use of mathematical language), but it could not sink China's academic tradition, nor could it completely change China's thought patterns and academic style. In the United States and the United Kingdom, there might be no significant differences in academic traditions, thinking habits, and academic disciplines in economic research, because they were both part of Western civilization. However, China belonged to a different form of civilization from the US and UK, so it was difficult to eliminate the above differences (even for Japan, which claimed to "leave Asia and enter Europe," its corporate form and corporate economics were not completely consistent with those of the West). As long as economics had not become a pure natural science, this difference would exist. Differences did not hinder communication, as long as one mastered the technical means of communication, but the purpose of communication was to develop oneself rather than to rely on others. The universality of science was a kind of tolerance, which naturally excluded geographical, racial, and cultural intolerance. This was the wisdom of science.

13.3 An Analysis of the Theoretical Dimensions of the Socialist Market Economy

1. The Relationship Among the Market Economy, Resource Allocation, the Commodity Economy, and the Property Rights System

From the 1980s to the early 1990s, in the discussion on the socialist planned commodity economy, China's political and economic circles generally believed that the market economy was not a neutral system category, but that it reflected the essential characteristics of the capitalist economy. Market regulation and the market mechanism were neutral concepts related to the law of value which could play a role in the socialist economy, but from the 1950s to the 1980s, discussion and research on the law of value and market regulation in China's socialist political and economic circles constituted the early ideological resources for the socialist market economy. In the 1980s, economic theorists also put forward an argument for market-oriented reform. Some scholars believed that the market economy was an organic system mainly composed of independent operators, self-financing enterprises, the competitive market system, and the macro management system mainly regulated by the market. As a system, these three aspects were interrelated and inseparable. Only when these three pillars were established could the economic system work effectively. Therefore, economic reform needed to be carried out simultaneously in these three interrelated aspects.[21] After Deng Xiaoping's Southern Talks in 1992, the discussion on the socialist market economy in economic circles upsurged, gradually deepening with the advancement of the reform process of the socialist market economy system. After the reform goal of the socialist market economy system was put forward, socialist political economics continued the discussion from several important theoretical dimensions and saw new development in economic theory.

(1) The Relationship Between the Market Economy and Resource Allocation

In the reform of China's economic system that began in the 1980s, from the combination of the planned economy and market regulation to the socialist planned commodity economy, and then on to the socialist market economy, one of the main lines was the optimization of the allocation of resources. In the 1980s, economic system reform mainly emphasized the regulation of the law of value and the market mechanism. By the early 1990s, the main line of resource allocation optimization was clearer. In October 1992, the report of the Fourteenth National Congress of the Communist Party of China suggested that the goal of economic system reform was to establish and improve the socialist market economic system. The purpose was to make the market play a fundamental role in the allocation of resources under the macro-control of socialist countries and to allocate resources to the links with better benefits. At the end of 1980s, some economists concerned about reform pointed out that the fundamental feature of the planned economy system was to allocate resources through administrative means and mandatory plans. If China

---

21. Wu Jinglian, Zhou Xiaochuan et al., *The Overall Design of China's Economic Reform* (China Prospect Press, 1990).

did not change the resource allocation mode of the planned economic system, it would not be able to achieve a fundamental change in the economic operations of the state by "decentralization of power and profit" and the "double track system." The only form of resource allocation that could replace administrative orders was to base on the market mechanism. It was important to overcome the defects of the order-based economy in the information and incentive mechanisms to create the most effective allocation and utilization of economic resources.[22]

As far as China's socialist political economy was concerned, the transformation that saw the main research object or research content turn to resource allocation was a key development. From the perspective of research object, political economics could be divided into normative economics and empirical economics. Normative economics mainly studied the social and production relations between people in social and economic activities, as well as the interest relations and distribution relations determined by them, while empirical economics mainly studied the quantity and technology relations in social and economic activities, that is, how to improve efficiency and meet social needs under the constraints of resources and technology (production possibility curve). These two research objects or methods were not absolutely separated, but intersected, because economics, as a social science that studied human economic activities, needed to consider many aspects of human social and economic activities, especially empirical research, which would inevitably involve people's relations of production, exchange, and distribution in economic activities. However, the main method and research object of socialist political economics in China from the 1950s to 1970s were normative economics. Since the 1980s, greater attention was given to the combination of theoretical research and the real economy, with a transformation trend from normative to empirical economics. This transformation was a requirement of economic theory development in the practice of economic system reform. In fact, resource allocation and efficiency analysis had always been a central topic in economics. The general process of economic activities was the production of goods and services through exchange to meet the basic needs and development of human society. Economic empirical research aimed to improve the efficiency of resource allocation and meet the needs of human society to a greater extent under the assumption of a scarcity of resources. Efficiency analysis formed the basis of microeconomics, because the main idea of effective resource allocation could be expressed in the simplest form of a linear production activity analysis model. But at the level of economic system analysis, effective resource allocation needed to be related to the acquisition, processing, and transmission of knowledge and information, because information and knowledge about demand, resources, and technology played an important role in coordinating economic activities. Hayek believed that the function of the market and price mechanism was to exchange information among various economic actors, with the purpose of coordinating economic activities.[23] The market mechanism was the coordination mechanism of economic activities with the lowest cost and the highest efficiency.

---

22. Wu Jinglian, *A Coursebook of Contemporary China's Economic Reform* (Shanghai Far East Publishing House, 2010), 68.

23. F. Hayek, "The Use of Knowledge in Society," *American Economic Review*, no. 35 (1945), 519–53.

Even so, Hayek and neo-liberal economic thought had an impact on China's economic reform and political economics transformation from a planned economy to a market economy. At that time, some critics demonstrated the effectiveness and rationality of the resource allocation mode based on the market mechanism from the defects of the information and incentive mechanisms of the planned economy.[24]

The significance of political economics regarding resource allocation as the main research object also lay in the transformation of methods and theoretical forms. The definition of "economic science" in Western economics usually referred to the empirical economics of resource allocation optimization. British economist Lionel Robbins successfully defined economics as "the science that regards human behavior as the relationship between purpose and resources with multiple uses." The research object of economic science was not all human economic activity, but one aspect of human economic activity, i.e., the shortage of economic resources, or the idea that the demand of individuals and society was infinite, while the supply of resources to meet these needs was limited.[25] Although Robbins's view that economic science should be different from the discussion of economic issues involving value judgment was criticized (because value judgment is expressed in the form of "good" or "bad" evaluation, involving the utility comparison between individuals), his definition of "economic science" still widely affected economists' understanding of the nature of economic discipline. China's socialist political economics took the allocation of resources as the main research object, which needed to be a demonstration of the transformation from normative economics to empirical economics.

(2) The Relationship Between the Market Economy and the Commodity Economy

In the process of economic system reform from the planned commodity economy to the socialist market economy, economic theorists discussed the relationship between the market economy and the commodity economy. Generally speaking, the terms market economy and commodity economy were regarded as synonyms, and their connotations were basically the same, with the market economy generally understood to be a commodity economy with a certain degree of socialization that made it an advanced form of the commodity economy. There were also views that held that the commodity economy and the market economy could not be equated. Under the condition of China's planned economy, there was a commodity economy and a market, though it was not the market that regulated the economy, but the national plan. The historical process of theory and practice of China's economic development moved from the development and transformation of the socialist commodity economy to a socialist market economy.[26] The two concepts were discussed by economic theorists not only because of the need to interpret the

---

24. Wu Jinglian, Zhou Xiaochuan et al., *The Overall Design of China's Economic Reform* (China Prospect Press, 1990).

25. Lionel Charles Robbins, *An Essay on the Nature and Significance of Economics Science* (London: Macmillan, 1932).

26. Wei Xinghua, "Research on the Economic Theoretical System of Socialism with Chinese Characteristics," *Economics Trends*, no. 5 (2011).

process of economic system reform, but also because the two concepts of the commodity economy and the market economy were of special significance in the discourse on China's socialist political economics, the theoretical function of which lay in revealing the essential characteristics of the relationship between commodity production and commodity exchange. Political economics needed to address these two terms within the framework of Marxist economic theory, so as to provide a theoretical basis for economic system reform.

The two concepts of the commodity economy and the market economy had an internal logical connection. The essential meaning of the commodity economy was that in the natural social division of labor system, independent commodity producers met the needs for their livelihood through the exchange of labor products. The objective law of commodity exchange was equivalent exchange, that is, the value of the exchanged goods should be equal. The objective yardstick to measure whether the value of various commodities was equal was social necessary labor time. The essential connotation of social necessary labor time was the balance of supply and demand. The essence of the market was the relationship between use value and exchange value, between commodity and currency, between buyer and seller, and between production and consumption. Therefore, the commodity economy and the market economy were different abstract expressions of the social economic form of production with the purpose of exchange: the concept of the commodity economy was the overall abstract expression of economic phenomena such as commodity production, commodity exchange, value relationship, and monetary relationship, which focused on the analysis of the qualitative stipulation of commodity production and the exchange relationship. The concept of the market economy was a general abstract expression of the relationship of commodity exchange and value on the operational level, with a focus on the analysis of the quantitative relationship in the movement of commodity production and exchange. Therefore, the concepts of the commodity economy and the market economy are intrinsically linked. If there is commodity, there will be a market, and if there is commodity exchange, there will be a market operation. The market economy is the performance of the real operation of the commodity economy. Theoretically, the two concepts are different on the abstract level. Emphasis on the analysis of the economy from the perspective of resource allocation or the market-oriented nature of economic system reform allows for use of the concept of the market economy.

(3) The Relationship Between the Market Economy and the Property Rights System
In the discussion of the socialist commodity economy, the reform of the ownership and property rights system was a part of economic theory. In the system of socialist political economics, the relationship between the market economy and the property rights system seemed to be a theoretical difficulty. Many viewpoints did not discuss this issue positively, but merely mentioned that the market economy was not categorized as "capitalist." It was true that the market economy may not be categorized as "capitalist," but economic theories discussed it under the institutional conditions of free property rights. The market economy was logically and practically related to the property rights system with a separation of property rights and independent property rights.

In order to discuss the market economy and property rights system under the condition of public ownership, especially under the condition that state ownership was the main body and the number of state-owned enterprises was huge, several problems needed to be solved in both theory and practice. The first was the subject of the market. The main body of the market was the subject of interest, that is, the subject of property rights. The significance of market subject as the subject of property rights lay in that both sides of the transaction should have clear, exclusive, and freely transferable property rights to the goods they exchanged. Otherwise, the exchange would be difficult or even impossible. In the market economy, the property rights boundaries of all parties in the transaction needed to be clear, so as to have clear rights and clear constraints. The market operated in this pursuit of their own rights and were constrained by the rights of others. However, in the state-owned economic system, from the overall sense of the state-owned economy, the boundary of property rights was clear, but from the perspective of a single state-owned asset unit, because its terminal ownership lay outside any individual, belonging instead to the state, it was impossible for the state-owned units with assets to have a clear definition of property rights, and they did not have complete property rights. The state-owned assets units were not the subject of property rights in the complete sense, and their rights and constraints were not complete, so their transaction behavior conformed to the market rules only with great difficulty. The weakness of market competition consciousness, the softening of the property restraint mechanism, the difficulty of curbing short-term behavior, and the low efficiency of production and operation were the common problems of state-owned enterprises in Western countries. How to make the state-owned property rights system adapt to the requirements of the market economy and transform state-owned enterprises into real market subjects was a problem to be solved through theory.

The second subject of interest was the market system. The core principle of the market system was to carry out fair trade and fair competition on the basis of protecting free property rights, so as to make the market run in an orderly way. Modern property rights economics held that the essence of exchange was not the exchange of goods and services, but the exchange of rights. Therefore, the core of the market system focused on how to define property rights, how to exchange them, and under what conditions. The operation basis of the market system was the system of free property rights, which determined individual's freedom of behavior in pursuit of private interests and limited one's right to infringe on others' rights in pursuit of private interests. It was on this basis that equivalent exchange took place. In the state-owned system, the subject of property rights of state-owned assets was not an individual, but the state, making it difficult to guarantee the property rights of state-owned assets. In order to protect state-owned assets from being damaged through market activities, it was necessary to have a complete set of sound, effective state-owned assets management laws and regulations, along with a large number of competent state-owned asset managers with a strong sense of responsibility, which was quite costly. But failing at this would make it difficult to effectively curb the behavior of damaging the public and benefiting the private in the market. The social cost of market transactions would also be very high, and it would not be able to operate normally, which would eventually cause great damage to both state-owned assets and society.

The final subject was market efficiency. Once property rights were clearly defined, all parties to the transaction would strive to reduce transaction costs, so that resources could flow to the most efficient level and achieve the Pareto optimality of resource allocation. According to this theory, transaction cost was inversely proportional to market efficiency. The reason the market economy was highly efficient lay in the reduction of transaction costs and the full, effective use of scarce resources due to the definition of property rights. But in the public ownership category, property rights were not easily defined clearly and they were not exclusive. Therefore, the restrictive factors that promoted the reduction of transaction costs did not exist, and resources were inevitably wasted. The purpose of establishing a market economy was to utilize its high efficiency in resource allocation. However, if the property rights system did not match the market mechanism, the property rights were not easily defined and the obstacles of high transaction costs were not solved, and as a result, the advantages of the market economy in resource allocation would not be fully realized.

The concepts of ownership, the state-owned system, and the basic economic system had always been a sensitive topic in the field of political economics after China's Reform and Opening Up policy began. After the reform strategy of establishing and improving the socialist market economic system was determined and implemented, the interpretation of "public ownership as the main body," the adjustment of the state-owned economy layout, and the test of various forms of public ownership all aimed at making the operation and management of state-owned enterprises conform to the market economy.

The basis of the socialist market economic system was the basic economic system of socialism with Chinese characteristics, that is, public ownership was the main body and various ownership economies developed together. Both the public and non-public economies were important components of the socialist market economy and the important foundation of China's economic and social development. In order to make the public and market economies fit together, it was necessary to innovate in the composition and realization form of the public ownership economy. In the composition of the public ownership economy, it was clear that it included not only the state-owned and collective economies, but also state-owned and collective components in a mixed ownership economy. A mixed ownership economy was an important realization form of the basic economic system. In terms of the realization forms of the public ownership economy, it was clear that the realization forms of public ownership should be diversified. All the operation modes and organizational forms reflecting the law of social production could be used. Effort needed to be made to test which realization forms of public ownership that could greatly promote the development of productive forces. Property rights were the core of ownership. Improving the modern property rights system with clear ownership, clear rights and responsibilities, strict protection, and smooth circulation was the basis for the operation of the socialist market economy. In the process of establishing and perfecting the socialist market economic system, the theory of property rights had become an enduring research field of political economics. The reform of the socialist market economy system was not only a transition of economic operations, but also a profound change of property rights and production relations. In seeking to perfect the historical system innovation of socialist market economy, a key problem was to reform the state-owned property rights system under the premise of public ownership as the main body. Theoretical research combined with this reform practice constituted the main aspect of the transformation of socialist political economics.

The market economy was an economic system which was connected with socialized mass production and the value relationship. Its operation mechanism was a market mechanism. A market mechanism was an economic mechanism related to the difference of social interests. It was an opportunity to connect people's economic behavior with the satisfaction of their material needs and to coordinate people's interest and behavior relationships. It demonstrated that in order to realize their special economic interests through their own economic behaviors, people needed to make their economic behaviors follow some objective laws. It linked all kinds of economic behaviors through people's pursuit of economic interests, moved the social economy to operate in a certain way, and objectively created the relationship between various economic activities, while production and demand tended to be harmonious and reasonable, so as to improve the orderliness of the entire social economy and the efficiency of production activities.

The incentive effect and the restrictive effect of the market mechanism were related to property rights. Property rights referred to the mutual recognition behavior standard caused by people's use of the things they owned. It focused on the behavior relationship between property owners. The arrangement of property rights determined the code of conduct of each person corresponding to the object, or defined the cost of not complying with the code of conduct. The relationship of property rights in market transactions could be described as first requiring that both parties to the transaction had exclusive ownership, free transfer rights, and exclusive rights of income for the commodities they exchanged, or the exchange could not be carried out. Second, both parties of the transaction should carry out equivalent exchange according to the value of their own commodities, or the exchange would not be completed. Therefore, in the market economy, property rights were used to define how people benefited, how they might be damaged, and how to compensate between them. The core of the market system was the definition of property rights, and fair trade and fair competition were carried out on the basis of protecting free property rights.

In short, the market economy was essentially an economic system composed of many independent stakeholders, with clear definition of property rights and free and fair trade. The function of the market economy system was to allow the parties to the transaction to judge whether a transaction to realize the allocation of resources was beneficial, unprofitable, or harmful to each according to the comparison of cost and benefit and the principle of maximizing interests through the corresponding definition of property rights and institutional arrangements. When a large number of resource allocation transactions were carried out in this situation, it would improve the resource allocation of the overall society and lead to the growth of social wealth. In the existing state-owned property rights system, due to the large-scale and multi-level principal-agent relationship, large-scale and repeated game and contract, the transaction cost was very high, resulting in low efficiency of resource allocation. At the same time, the agent's economic behavior easily deviated from the goal of maximizing return on assets, which caused a large number of state-owned assets to become "common property" to be eroded. Therefore, as a non-exclusive property rights arrangement, the state-owned property rights system was in contradiction with the natural characteristics of the market economy. At the same time, it was necessary to reform the property rights system of state-owned assets and adapt it to the property rights system of the market.

2. Property Rights as the Core Rights of the Modern Market Economic System

The Decision of the Central Committee of the Communist Party of China on Several Issues Concerning the Improvement of the Socialist Market Economic System adopted by the Third Plenary Session of the Sixteenth Central Committee of the Communist Party of China listed the improvement of the basic economic system with public ownership as the main body and the common development of various ownership economies as the primary task to improve the socialist market economic system. In order to improve this basic economic system, it was necessary to establish and improve the modern property rights system with clear ownership, clear rights and responsibilities, strict protection, and smooth circulation. The modern property rights system was helpful in protecting public and private property rights. All kinds of property rights needed to be protected according to law, and the equal legal status and development rights of all market subjects were to be guaranteed.[27] In the documents of the CPC Central Committee, the property rights and the property rights system were elaborated in depth, indicating that China's economic system reform had been promoted to the core level of property rights system reform.

In economic theory, property rights are the legal definition of an economic subject's rights in connection to the property. A market economy is an economic system in which economic subjects with different interest orientations conduct free and fair trade under the condition of clearly defined property rights. In a market economy, property rights are used to define how people benefit, how they are damaged, and how they may be compensated. According to modern property rights theory, the essence of property rights is an exclusive right. In the exclusive rights system, the rights limitations of each economic subject are clear. Economic entities have the right to pursue their own interests, but they are constrained by the rights of others, that is, people's behavior cannot damage the rights of others. Under a system which allows for the pursuit the maximum of one's own interests restricted by the rights of others, economic activities tend to be orderly and efficient. Modern society provides strong support for economic growth by relying on an effective property rights system. Paul Samuelson, a renowned American economist, predicted in the 1950s that the region with the fastest economic development would be South America, because South America was rich in resources and highly educated, but he was wrong. In the second half of the 20th century, the fastest growing economies were in Europe and the Pacific. Although the resources in Europe and the Pacific region were relatively poor, due to the reasonable

---

27. *Decision of the CPC Central Committee on Several Issues Concerning the Improvement of the Socialist Market Economic System* (People's Publishing House, 2005).

property rights system, there was rapid economic growth in these areas. Samuelson believed that the conditions on which his original expectation was based were not the most basic thing in the economic system, and the property rights system was the basic element of the economic system. Property rights determined the incentive mechanism and people's behavior, so they played an important role in economic efficiency.

The reason the property rights system was the basic element of an economic system was that it affected or determined the efficiency of resource allocation and the economic system in several ways. First, if property rights were clearly defined, then the benefit and damage effects of the transaction would affect the transaction parties to a greater extent, that is, the transaction parties were fully responsible for the results of their own behavior, reducing the externality of transactions and improving the level of social welfare. For example, the protection of the patent law concentrated the benefits of innovation on the inventors, thus giving effective incentives to innovation and making it conducive to social progress. Second, the modern property rights system was the foundation of the social credit system. Clearly defined and protected property rights reduced uncertainty in economic activities and clarified the interest expectations and legal responsibilities of economic parties. Transactions in the modern market economy were essentially based on credit, such as contract, creditor's rights and debt, guarantee, insurance, bill, and other similar areas. If credit was lacking, the risk of market transactions would increase and fraud and dishonesty would rise, resulting in rising transaction costs, a disorderly market, and a decline of economic efficiency. Therefore, the market economy was a credit economy, and the perfection of the credit system depended on the property right system. If the property rights were not clearly defined and lacked protection and the rights, responsibilities, and obligations of the transaction subject were not regulated by the legal system, there would be no security in the transaction, and the operation efficiency of the economy would be greatly affected. Third, the modern property rights system guaranteed an economic relationship of free choice and fair trade. The clear definition of property rights ensured that the beneficial and damage effects of the transaction were borne directly by the transaction parties, which determined that the transaction parties had the right of free trade. According to the comparison of costs and benefits, the parties to a transaction judged whether a transaction was favorable, unprofitable, or harmful, and then made a choice whether or not to trade. When a large number of transactions were carried out under such conditions, the allocation of resources across society would be optimized and social welfare would increase. Therefore, the optimization of resource allocation was a process in which trading subjects benefited or avoided damage through free trade. In this process, property rights were to be clearly defined. The clear definition of property rights ensured the parties' free choice, income incentive, and damage restraint, so that resources could be allocated for more efficient use.

The Decision of the Third Plenary Session of the Sixteenth CPC Central Committee pointed out that property rights were the core and main content of ownership. The modern property rights system was an internal requirement for perfecting the basic economic system of public ownership as the main body and the common development of a varied ownership economy, and it was an important foundation for the construction of the modern enterprise system.[28] This explanation showed an accurate grasp of the characteristics of the modern market economy system. According to modern economic theory, the market was not a "natural order," but a system. An institutional market was a kind of trading procedure and rule, which provided standards for trading behavior. The core foundation of the institutional market was the property rights system. In the market economy, people's economic behavior and even overall social economic operations were defined and regulated by property rights. The "social contract" generated on this basis had economic and legal characteristics. Therefore, when discussing economic development, it was important to not only analyze resource constraints, but also institutional constraints. In other words, institutions and resources were both scarce. When institutional supply was short, economic development and social progress would be restricted. Under some conditions, institutional constraints were more critical than resource constraints, which could be illustrated by the development of both the world economy and China's own economy. From China's situation, the construction and improvement of the socialist market economic system were the basic institutional conditions for further liberating and developing productive forces and building a prosperous society in all aspects. Deepening the reform of the economic system would enhance the flexibility of the system supply, and making timely adjustments and changes in the ownership structure, property relations, and property rights system, made them conform to the development degree and development requirements of the socialist market economy.

3. On the Socialist Market Economy and the Reform of the Ownership Structure

The theory of ownership was a difficult point in the study of China's economic theory. The difficulty lay not in the topic itself, but the constraints of ideology and political principles. Ownership in China was not a simple economic issue, but a political issue closely related to the socialist system. After the beginning of China's Reform and Opening Up, ownership was a key issue from the perspectives of both economic theory research and economic system reform. China's economic system reform and economic theory research sought to bypass ownership, the most typical example being the theoretical thinking and reform practice of "separation of two powers," followed by efforts to build a socialist market economic system on the basis of public ownership. The main purpose of the long-standing discussion on "re-establishing individual ownership" in theoretical circles sought to find a theoretical basis for the ownership reform from the Marxist classics. At the same time, in economic theory, the most difficult thing was not only to clarify the theoretical logic of market-oriented reform and improvement of economic efficiency, but also to avoid touching the "forbidden zone" of ownership issues. Therefore, theoretical circles spent a good deal of energy and ink on these topics.

---

28. *Decision of the CPC Central Committee on Several Issues Concerning the Improvement of the Socialist Market Economic System* (People's Publishing House, 2005).

With the development of the theory of socialism with Chinese characteristics and the socialist market economy, the concept of ownership in theoretical circles changed significantly. An important point was to realize that ownership was only a means and could not be fixed as an end. In the final analysis, the reason socialism adhered to the dominant position of public ownership and distribution according to work was to liberate and develop productive forces, eliminate exploitation, and realize common prosperity.[29] As an essential characteristics of the socialist economy, public ownership and distribution according to work were secondary to Deng Xiaoping's essence of reflecting the fundamental task and internal purpose of socialism, and could even be said to be only means determined by the fundamental purpose and task. The aim was not ownership, but the common prosperity proposed by Deng Xiaoping. Ownership was a means to develop productivity, not an end. In this case, there was a problem of choice, reform, and innovation in ownership, which needed to be brought into line with the development of productive forces. Ownership was an integral part of the relations of production, which was restricted by and served productive forces. In other words, the development of productive forces was the end and a certain form of ownership was the means. Ownership was a means, not an end, which required China to adjust the ownership structure according to the needs of the development of productive forces. In the social and economic structure, the proportion of public ownership was neither better nor the same. It needed to be adjusted in accordance with the principle conducive to the development of productive forces. In order to adjust the form of public ownership, in addition to the current state ownership and collective ownership, new forms of public ownership, such as stock ownership, community ownership, and cooperative ownership, needed to be created according to the requirements of the market economy, so as to adjust the departmental structure and scale structure of public ownership and improve the quality of public ownership.[30]

Many in the field of economic thought held that state ownership and the market economy could be conditionally compatible. The condition for the compatibility of the two was to break the exclusive ownership of overall society, make many social enterprises become real independent market competition subjects with property, and make the market mechanism play a fundamental role in the allocation of resources. In order to organically combine state ownership with the market economy, the first step was to implement the mutual penetration of various economic elements, and the second was to reform the state-owned economy, so that state-owned enterprises could become independent commodity producers and operators. State ownership and the market economy could be organically combined, that is, the main body of market transactions had independent, exclusive, and transferable property rights, and it did not change the form of public ownership of the means of production. The reform of China's rural property rights system did not

29. Qiu Shi, "On the Opposition and Unity of Socialism and Capitalism," *Financial Research*, no. 9 (1992); Zhou Shulian, "Ownership Is an Economic Means," *Economic and Social System Comparison*, no. 5 (1993).

30. Wang Yu, "Reconstruction of Different Property Right Subjects Outside the State-Owned Economy," *Reform*, no. 3 (1993); Guo Xiaolu, "Theoretical Basis of China's Ownership Reform," *Jianghan Forum*, no. 10 (1994); Lu Zhongyuan, "Ownership, Market, and Efficiency," *Reform*, no. 4 (1993); Guo Zhenying, "On China's Ownership Structure," *China Social Sciences*, no. 2 (1992).

change the state-owned nature of land and other properties. It only gave farmers the full right to operate freely and changed the surplus labor achievements from exclusive ownership of property owners to sharing with property operators, so that farmers could conduct market transactions as commodity owners. The basic experience was that even if there was only one subject of property ownership, as long as the property management and use rights were decentralized and belonged to different property users, the labor products also belonged to different property operators. The property owners could obtain fixed property income only by virtue of ownership, which could promote the development of the market economy. State ownership was a form of ownership that adapted to modern mass production, and its specific form could be constantly changed according to the requirements of the market economy. There were two ways to combine state ownership with the market economy. One was to actively develop various forms of ownership to realize the diversification of the property rights structure. The other was to reform the management system of state-owned enterprises and establish a property rights form that met the requirements of the market economy.[31]

Ownership structure was a subject that could be deepened by the research of ownership theory, and it was a breakthrough for the integration of ownership reform and the market economy. It generally held that in the ownership structure, the dominant position of public ownership needed to be consolidated, with public ownership (including the economy owned by all the people and collective ownership) as the main body, the individual economy, private economy, and foreign-funded economy as the supplements, and a variety of economic components developing together over a long period. The ownership structure with public ownership as the main body and various economic components coexisting had to include the dominant position of public ownership in the national economy, maintained nationwide, and not excluding the possibility that public ownership may play a dominant role in some fields and in some places. Considering the imbalance of the development of productive forces, the proportion of different forms of ownership could be different in different fields and different regions. Therefore, in the overall ownership system across the country, there could be different ownership systems in different regions and different economic fields throughout the national economy. The dominant position of public ownership did not require the state-owned economy to occupy the dominant position in the national economy, but included the state-owned economy and the public sector economy, including the collective economy and other public sectors, in the dominant position. The coexistence of various economic components included not only different forms of public economy such as state-owned

---

31. Liao Yuanhe, "The Relationship Between the Public Property Rights System and the Market Economy," *Journal of Graduate School of Chinese Academy of Social Sciences*, no. 3 (1993); Wei Jie and Zhang Yu, "The Market Economy and Public Ownership System Reform," *Economic Research*, no. 3 (1993); Liu Xirong and Gu Peidong, "Rethinking the Reform of Socialist Ownership," *Economic Theory and Management*, no. 3 (1993); Wei Jie, "The Basic Idea of Compatibility Between Public Ownership and the Market Economy," *Social Science Front*, no. 5 (1993); Wang Zongkeng, "The Reform of State-Owned Property Relations and the Transformation of the Enterprise Management Mechanism," *Journal of Fuzhou University (Philosophy and Social Edition)*, no. 3 (1993); Liu Chunxu, "Property Rights in a Public Ownership Economy: Preliminary Analysis," *Journal of Beijing University (Philosophy and Social Edition)*, no. 4 (1993).

economy and the collective economy, but also different forms of the non-public economy, such as the individual economy, the private economy, and state capitalism. It was a combination of the public and non-public economy.[32]

Some scholars sought to interpret mixed ownership in relation to basic ownership. Basic ownership, such as state ownership, capitalist ownership, and individual ownership, were primary ownership, while mixed ownership referred to the combination of the original ownership, which was secondary. For example, the combination of individual ownership was a cooperative system, and the joint-stock system was also a form of mixed ownership. Because mixed ownership could complement the advantages of each and meet the needs of the market economy, it had a bright future in China. It was important to distinguish the two concepts of dominant ownership and subject ownership. In China, the dominant ownership was state ownership, but mixed ownership could become a large number of subjective ownerships. The mixed ownership structure was not only the objective requirement and inevitable trend of the development of the modern market economy, but also demonstrated great vitality and superiority, which offered broad prospects for development.[33]

Some theorists developed a mathematical model to compare the social surplus of mixed ownership and complete private ownership and drew a conclusion that when ownership and management rights were separated, and the two enterprises were in a Cournot type competition (monopoly competition), and the social surplus under mixed ownership was greater than that under complete private ownership. Under the condition that the ownership and management rights of one enterprise were not separated and the two enterprises were in a Cournot type competition relationship, the social surplus under a mixed ownership structure was inevitably greater than that under complete private ownership.[34]

The report of the Fifteenth National Congress of the Communist Party of China pointed out that public ownership as the main body and the common development of various ownership economies was a basic economic system in the primary stage of socialism in China. The establishment of this system was determined by the nature of socialism and the national conditions at the primary stage. Primarily, China was a socialist country and needed to adhere to public ownership as the foundation of the socialist economic system, and it was in the primary stage of socialism and needed to develop a varied ownership economy with public ownership as the main body. In addition, all forms of ownership in line with the "three advantages" could and should be used to serve socialism.

32. Wang Yu, "Reconstruction of Different Property Rights Subjects Outside the State-Owned Economy," *Reform*, no. 3 (1993); Shen Jianming and Liu Yaling, "Some Ideas on the Relationship Between Property Rights of State-Owned Enterprises," *Economist*, no. 2 (1993); Fan Gang, "On the Reform of the Relationship Between the Development of the Market Economy and Property Rights," *Reform*, no. 1 (1993); Zhou Shulian, "Several Issues on Property Rights of State-Owned Enterprises," *China Industrial Economy Research*, no. 7 (1993).

33. Xiao Liang, "Mixed Ownership: A Form of Ownership with Great Development Prospect," *Party School Forum*, no. 11 (1993); Mao Tianqi, "Straightening Out the Relationship Between Property Rights and a Developing Mixed Economy," in *China Economic Science Yearbook* (China Statistics Press, 1994).

34. Zhu Dongping, "On the Economic Rationality of Mixed Ownership," *Economic Research*, no. 5 (1994).

In March 1999, Article 16 of the Amendment to the Constitution, passed at the Second Session of the Ninth National People's Congress, amended what was stated in Article 11 of the Constitution, that "the individual economy of urban and rural workers within the scope prescribed by law is a supplement to the socialist public economy. The state protects the legitimate rights and interests of the individual economy." And, "the state guides, helps, and supervises the individual economy through administrative management," and, "the state allows the private economy to exist and develop within the limits prescribed by law. The private economy is the supplement of socialist public ownership economy. The state protects the legitimate rights and interests of the private economy and guides, supervises, and administers the private economy." The revisions stated, "The non-public economy, such as the individual and private economies within the scope prescribed by law, is an important part of the socialist market economy," and "the state protects the legitimate rights and interests of the individual economy and the private economy. The state guides, supervises, and administers the individual and private economies."

Based on the actual situation in the primary stage of socialism, the report of the Fifteenth National Congress of the Communist Party of China made a major breakthrough in ownership theory and enriched and developed Marxist theory. Theoretical circles subsequently summarized the breakthrough of the Fifteenth CPC National Congress in the theory of socialist ownership from several aspects.

The breakthrough of the theoretical problems of ownership was mainly manifested in two aspects. One was the theoretical transformation from the single public ownership theory to one with public ownership as the main body and the common development of various ownership economies, forming the ownership structure theory. The other was the separation of the ownership from the realization form, forming the theory of the realization form of public ownership.

It was pointed out that taking public ownership as the main body and the common development of various ownership economies was a basic economic system in the primary stage of socialism in China. The previous formulation was "with public ownership as the main body, a variety of economic elements develop together." Although it was only a difference of a few words, it reflected a great ideological liberation and theoretical breakthrough. The new formulation of the Fifteenth National Congress of the Communist Party of China led the non-public economy into the system from "outside the system," which greatly expanded and enriched the connotation of the basic socialist economic system and was conducive to continued adjustment and improvement of the ownership structure and further liberation and development of productive forces.

According to the basic national conditions of China's primary stage of socialism, it was important to comprehensively understand and scientifically define the meaning of the public ownership economy. The public ownership economy was not only to be understood as the state-owned economy and collective economy in the traditional sense of single ownership, nor could it be understood as taking the state-owned economy as the main body. The status and function of different forms of the public ownership economy could not be evaluated by the level of public ownership. Since the beginning of Reform and Opening Up, the form of mixed ownership had developed rapidly, and the share of the public ownership economy in the mixed ownership economy was constantly increasing, and some had taken a controlling position. Therefore, the present public ownership economy needed to include the state-owned and collective components in the form of the mixed ownership economy.

The embodiment of the dominant position of public ownership was made clear, that is, public assets occupied the dominant position in the total social assets, and the state-owned economy controlled the lifeline of the national economy and played a leading role in economic development, which was in terms of the entire country. Some localities and some industries could be different, and the dominance of public assets required not only the advantages of quantity, but also the improvement of quality.

It was clear that the leading role of the state-owned economy was mainly reflected in the control power, which was conducive to strategically adjusting the layout of the state-owned economy, ensuring the key points, and enhancing its control and competitiveness. It was pointed out that the realization forms of public ownership could and should be diversified. The same nature of ownership could have multiple forms of realization, and different natures of ownership could also adopt the same form of realization. The joint stock system, the company system, contracting, leasing, trusteeship, mergers, acquisitions, and sales were all forms of realization. Private ownership could be adopted, and public ownership could also be adopted. The theory of diversified forms of public ownership was conducive to people's bold use of all business and organizational forms reflecting the law of social production, and it was conducive to people's efforts to find a realization form of public ownership that could greatly promote the development of productive forces.

It also put forward a clear standard for choosing the realization form of public ownership. The traditional view held that the realization form of public ownership needed to be purely socialist in nature. Ownership by all the people was superior to collective ownership, and collective ownership was superior to the individual and private economies of a non-public ownership nature. This was the starting point of the once emerged "transition in poverty" and "shared ownership." As a matter of fact, ownership by all the people and collective ownership were both forms of realization of public ownership and were of a socialist nature. It was impossible to measure who was superior to the other in terms of nature, but only in terms of social and economic benefits and the degree of promoting the development of productive forces.

The legal status of the non-public economy was effectively established. Previously, the non-public sectors of the economy, such as the individual and private sectors, were always limited to the status of "supplement." Now, they had become "an important part of the socialist market economy." It was important to continue to encourage and guide the non-public economy into healthy development. This was not only conducive to meeting people's diversified needs, increasing employment, and cultivating new economic growth points, so as to promote the development of the national economy; it was also conducive to the state improving the property legal system, protecting the legitimate rights and interests of various enterprises and fair competition, and supervising and managing them.

The nature of the stock system was clearly defined and it was stated that the stock system could be used in socialism. In the reform of the previous twenty years, the joint stock system was arguably the most controversial and most frequently "labeled," with comments such as "the joint stock system is a disguised private ownership" and "the joint stock system is a potential private ownership" often passed. The report of the Fifteenth National Congress of the Communist Party of China stipulated that the joint stock system was a form of capital organization of modern enterprises. It was conducive to the separation of ownership and management rights and to improving the operational efficiency of enterprise capital, and both capitalism and socialism could use it. It could not be generally stated whether the shareholding system was public or private. The key lay in who held the controlling shares. State and collective holding shares had an obvious public nature, which was conducive to expanding the scope of public capital's domination and enhancing the main role of public ownership.

It was proposed that China should focus on the development of capital and other factors of the production market and that the marketization process of the national economy be accelerated, various markets developed, focus placed on the development of capital, labor, technology, and other factors of production market, and the price formation mechanism of production factors improved.[35]

The Third Plenary Session of the Sixteenth Central Committee of the Communist Party of China adopted the Decision of the Central Committee of the Communist Party of China on Several Issues Concerning the Improvement of the Socialist Market Economic System, which proposed the further consolidation and development of the public economy and the encouragement, support, and guidance of the development of the non-public economy. It was important to adhere to the dominant position of public ownership and give full play to the leading role of the state-owned

---

35. Lü Zheng, "On the Realization Form of Public Ownership," *China Social Sciences*, no. 6 (1997); Su Xing, "The Socialist Market Economy with Public Ownership as the Main Body," *China Social Sciences*, no. 6 (1997); Dong Fuzhi, "The Joint Stock System is a Kind of Public Ownership," *China Opening-up Guide*, no. 9 (1997); Xia Zhenkun, "Public Ownership Discussion on the Form of Realization," *Theory Monthly*, no. 10 (1997); Chen Xiaolin, "Eight Breakthroughs in Ownership Theory at the Fifteenth National Congress of the Communist Party of China," *Economics Trends*, no. 12 (1997); Chen Zheng, "New Breakthroughs in Ownership Theory," *Economics Trends*, no. 12 (1997); Xiao Liang, "The Joint Stock System, Cooperative System, and Joint Stock Cooperative System: On the Realization Form of China's Public Ownership," *China Reform Daily*, August 14, 1997; Li Guangyuan, "Individual Workers and the Realization Form of Socialist Public Ownership," *Management World*, no. 1 (1998); Xiao Liang, "Some Theoretical Issues of Ownership Reform," *Economics Trends*, no. 1 (1998); Zhou Jiwang, "Correct Understanding of the Great Development of Ownership Theory in the Fifteenth CPC National Congress," *Journal of Huazhong University of Science and Technology (Philosophy and Social Edition)*, no. 2 (1998); Li Fengsheng, "The Connotation of the Realization Form of Public Ownership," *Economist*, no. 2 (1998); Wu Xuangong, "On the Realization Form and Diversification of Public Ownership," *China Economic Issues*, no. 3 (1998); Wang Yu, "A Precise Definition of Socialist Public Ownership," *Contemporary Finance and Economics*, no. 10 (1998); Du Ying, "The Realization Form of Public Ownership Depends on the Nature of Productivity and Development Requirements," *Journal of Hebei University of Economic and Trade*, no. 12 (1998).

economy. It was necessary to actively promote various forms of effective realization of public ownership and accelerate the adjustment of the layout and structure of the state-owned economy, and also necessary to adapt to the trend of market-oriented development, further enhance the vitality of the public ownership economy, vigorously develop the mixed ownership economy with the participation of state-owned capital, collective capital, and non-public capital, realize the diversification of investment subjects, and make the joint stock system the main realization form of public ownership. Large companies and enterprise groups needed to be developed with international competitiveness. China needed to continue to open up and invigorate small and medium-sized state-owned enterprises, focus on clarifying property rights, deepen the reform of collective enterprises, and develop various forms of the collective economy.

The aim was to vigorously develop and actively guide the non-public sector of the economy. The private and non-public economies were an important force for promoting the development of China's social productive forces. It was necessary to clear up and revise laws, regulations, and policies that restricted the development of the non-public sector of the economy and eliminate institutional barriers. Market access needed to be relaxed and non-public capital allowed to enter infrastructure, public utilities, and other industries and fields not prohibited by laws and regulations. Non-public enterprises enjoyed the same treatment as other enterprises in investment and financing, taxation, land use, and foreign trade.

China aimed to establish and improve the modern property rights system. Property rights were the core and main content of ownership, including property rights, creditor's rights, equity, and intellectual property rights. The establishment of a modern property rights system with clear ownership, clear rights and responsibilities, strict protection, and smooth circulation was conducive to maintaining common property rights and consolidating the dominant position of the public economy. It was also conducive to protecting private property and promoting the development of the non-public ownership economy, to the flow and restructuring of various types of capital and promoting the development of mixed ownership economy, and to the enhancement of entrepreneurship and innovation of enterprises and the public to form a good credit foundation and market order. This was the internal requirement for perfecting the basic economic system and the foundation for constructing the modern enterprise system. It was important to protect all kinds of property rights in accordance with the law, improve the trading rules and regulatory system of property rights, promote the orderly circulation of property rights, and guarantee the equal legal status and development rights of all market entities.

According to the report of the Seventeenth National Congress of the Communist Party of China, it was necessary to correctly handle the relationship between adhering to public ownership as the main body and promoting the development of the non-public economy, unswervingly consolidate and develop the public sector economy, give full play to the leading role of the state-owned economy, and unswervingly encourage, support, and guide the development of the individual and non-public sectors of the economy, so that they could promote and share in the process of socialist modernization with development. Therefore, it was necessary to give full play to the important role of non-public sectors, such as the individual and private sectors, in promoting economic growth, expanding employment, and invigorating the market. Market access was to be relaxed for domestic private capital and measures taken in investment and financing, taxation, land use, and foreign trade to achieve fair competition. It was important to strengthen supervision and management according to law and promote the healthy development of the non-public sector of the economy, while improving the legal system for protecting private property.[36]

The Third Plenary Session of the Sixteenth Central Committee of the Communist Party of China proposed that the joint stock system be made the main realization form of public ownership. How to understand the joint stock system and the relationship between the joint stock system and the public ownership became a key issue in economic and ideological circles as a result.

Some scholars put forward the concept of "new public ownership" enterprises. There were four forms of "new public ownership" enterprises. The first was the new state ownership after restructuring, the second was the joint stock enterprises controlled or shared by the state, that is, the mixed ownership enterprises, and the third was public holding enterprises without state investment, which could be divided into public direct holding shares and public indirect holding shares. The fourth was public welfare fund ownership enterprises.[37] Some scholars held that the view that the joint stock system was equivalent to public ownership "violates not only the basic principles of Marxism, but also the relevant resolutions of the party since the Fifteenth National Congress of the Communist Party of China, and does not conform to the contemporary situation."[38] It was pointed out that under the condition of socialist market economy, whether an economy was public or private needed to be distinguished carefully. It was important to undertake a comprehensive investigation of enterprises from the perspective of production relations system, so as to open up the phenomenon and grasp the essence. It was not right to regard public ownership or the establishment of the corporate governance structure required by the modern enterprise system as the main basis for distinguishing public enterprises from non-public enterprises, and even to regard the shareholding system solely held by private ownership as "new public ownership" enterprises. The practical experience of the reform of state-owned enterprises demonstrated that the joint stock system was a modern enterprise system and an effective form of capital organization, not privatization, and should be vigorously promoted. However, in the process of implementation, it was important to have laws to abide by and strict supervision. Otherwise, things might move in the opposite direction and become a shortcut to covert and gradual privatization in the hands of some people.

Scholars held that public ownership and the joint stock system were not on the same level. Public ownership, as a form of ownership, reflected the social attributes of economic relations and belonged to the scope of institutional level, and private ownership was the opposite. As

---

36. Hu Jintao, *Holding High the Great Banner of Socialism with Chinese Characteristics and Striving for the New Victory in Building a Moderately Prosperous Society in All Aspects: Report on the Seventeenth National Congress of the Communist Party of China* (People's Publishing House, 2007).

37. Li Yining, "On New Public Enterprises," *Economics Trends*, no. 1 (2004).

38. Xiang Qiyuan, "We Can't Equate the Stock System with Public Ownership: A Discussion with Professor Li Yining," *Economics Trends*, no. 4 (2004).

an organizational and operational mode of an enterprise, the shareholding system belonged to the scope of the operational level. Its typical feature was the separation of ownership and management rights. Corresponding to the joint stock system was a self-supporting enterprise with a highly unified ownership and management rights. Whether a joint stock enterprise was a public enterprise depended on who controlled the shares. Only the joint stock enterprises or mixed ownership enterprises which were wholly owned, controlled, or jointly controlled by public ownership were public enterprises, while joint stock enterprises with private or foreign capital were not public enterprises. There were also views that stock making was a form of capital organization of modern enterprises and an indirect operation mode of investors, or as a realization form of ownership at the level of capital organization form and management mode, and both capitalism and socialism could use it. The ownership nature of the joint stock system should not be discussed in general, but the characteristics of the specific ownership system analyzed in connection with the realization form of the specific ownership system at the system level.[39]

From the analysis of the relationship between the perfection of the socialist market economy and the adjustment of the ownership structure, the irrationality of China's ownership structure was mainly manifested in two aspects. First, the realization of the state-owned economy was relatively singular, and its efficiency was relatively low, but it occupied relatively more resources (including financial resources). Second, it failed to form a mixed ownership economy with diversified property rights and investors as the mainstream economic form. In an economic society, the growth of the market, the reform of the enterprise system, and the adjustment of the ownership and property rights system were interrelated processes. The adjustment of the ownership and property rights system aimed to meet the requirements of the socialist market economic system and improve the efficiency of the economic system and economic activities. According to this goal, it was necessary to adjust the layout and structure of the state-owned economy, deepen the reform of state-owned holding companies and large enterprise groups, and improve the management system of state-owned assets, so as to integrate the scale of state-owned assets, optimize the quality, and improve the efficiency of operations and management. It was important to vigorously develop the non-public economy and make the private economy become the micro foundation of the social economy. It was the main form and source of growth for national wealth. The development of the mixed ownership economy was a meeting point of the state-owned economic layout and structural adjustment and the vigorous development of the private economy. State-owned capital could be linked with other capital through the mechanisms of advance and retreat and reasonable flow, and it could be concentrated in advantageous industries and key fields, so as to improve the leading competitiveness of the state-owned economy. Private capital participated in the assets reorganization and shareholding system transformation of state-owned enterprises, and it entered all industries and fields not prohibited by laws and regulations.

---

39. Zheng Zhiguo, "Integration and Sublation of the Shareholding System and Corporate Factors," *Economics Trends*, no. 10 (2008); Huang Fanzhang, "Reflections on the Shareholding System and Socialization," *Economics Trends*, no. 12 (2008); Wang Lu, "Scientific Development and the Sinicization of Marxist Economics," *Economics Trends*, no. 1 (2011).

State-owned capital and private capital infiltrated and merged with each other to form the greater capital strength of mixed ownership and jointly supported the sustainable development of China's economy and society.

The discussion of private economy and enterprises should be connected with enriching the people and strengthening the country. The economic prosperity and wealth growth of a country or region is based on efficient enterprises. After thirty years of Reform and Opening Up in China, small and medium-sized enterprises (mainly private or non-public enterprises) became an important foundation of the national economy. According to statistics from 2007, the added value created by small and medium-sized enterprises accounted for 60% of the national GDP, the taxes paid accounted for 50%, the invention patents of small and medium-sized enterprises accounted for 66% of the country's total, and research and development products accounted for 82%, absorbing 75% of the urban population's employment. However, the number of Chinese enterprises was much less than that of international levels. China had less than 10 enterprises per 1,000 people, far less than the average level of 50 enterprises per 1,000 people in developed countries and 20–30 enterprises per 1,000 people in developing countries. The small number of enterprises directly limited the employment capacity of the economy and the growth of residents' income. However, the difficulties in starting a business and in operating and various forms of "discrimination against ownership" put a large number of private and private enterprises in trouble and even forced them to withdraw from the market. With this national economic pattern, there were still obstacles to improving people's livelihood. However, China's concept and social ecology determined that the survival and growth of small enterprises, mainly private enterprises, were difficult to overcome.

In June 2009, at the International Forum on Solving the Financing Difficulties of Small and Medium Enterprises held in Beijing, the main leaders of the Ministry of Industry and Information Technology pointed out that in the first three months of 2009, the total credit in China increased by 4.8 trillion yuan, of which the increase in loans for small and medium enterprises only accounted for less than 5%. Small and medium enterprises created 60% of China's total economic volume, created nearly 1 trillion yuan of fiscal and tax revenue, and provided nearly 80% of the employment. According to the regulations issued in September 2007, state-owned enterprises paid dividends in the form of the capital operating budget. The contribution ratio was that tobacco, petroleum and petrochemical, electric power, telecommunications, five coal resource industries paid 10%, while steel, transportation, and other general competitive industries to paid 5%. There were reports that state-owned enterprises did not pay dividends in the 14 years before 2007. Even when state-owned enterprises began to pay 5 to 10% of the annual dividend since 2007, the aim was not to improve people's livelihood, but mainly to "promote the strategic adjustment of the layout and structure of the state-owned economy and cultivate large enterprise groups with international competitiveness," that is, the dividends turned in were used for the self-strengthening closed cycle of state-owned enterprises.[40]

---

40. *Jiefang Daily*, June 12, 2009, 9.

Research indicated that in China, the biggest distortion of the economic system was the distortion of resource allocation. Low efficiency state-owned enterprises obtained most of the resource input, which led to the low efficiency of economic investment. In 2007, the marginal income of state-owned enterprises was 25 to 50% lower than that of private enterprises. In the manufacturing industry, if the investment could be allocated effectively, the actual output in 2007 could be increased by 30%.[41] Therefore, it was important to provide a favorable business environment and conditions for small and medium private enterprises and support them to enhance their competitiveness and efficiency, which was an important policy to enrich the people and strengthen the country. On April 29, 2009, the executive meeting of the State Council adopted in principle the Opinions on Deepening the Reform of the Economic System in 2009, which determined the ten reform tasks to be promoted that year. The first was to change the government's economic management functions, continue to reduce and adjust administrative examination and approval items, and stimulate the vitality of market investment. The aim was to deepen the reform of monopoly industries and broaden the fields and channels of private investment. The secondary goal was to deepen the reform of state-owned enterprises, further optimize the ownership structure, and promote the development of the non-public economy and small and medium enterprises. The reform measures of the central government were in line with the requirements of the international and domestic economic situation. This reform path was an important guarantee for China's economic growth and modernization.

In 2008, the US subprime mortgage crisis triggered the global financial crisis, and developed market economies in Europe and the United States fell into a financial and economic crisis. In the context of economic globalization, countries with emerging market economies were also seriously impacted. In response to the crisis, China adopted a proactive fiscal policy to stimulate aggregate demand and maintain steady economic growth through large-scale infrastructure construction and fixed asset investment. In this process, the inherent function of the state-owned economy to comply with the state's macro-control goal to deal with the economic crisis became more prominent. In addition, the state-owned economy had a strong ability to obtain loans, and the state-owned and private economies underwent mergers and acquisitions, which led some in economic and ideological circles to believe that this was a phenomenon of "the state advancing and the people retreating," and even that it was a retrogression of reform. There were different opinions. Statistics showed that since the beginning of Reform and Opening Up, although the total amount of the state-owned economy had expanded, the proportion of the state-owned economy had declined. Therefore, from the general situation of China's ownership structural changes, the situation in which "the state advances and the people retreat" did not exist. On the contrary, there was a trend of "the people advancing and the state retreating." In recent years, the expansion of state-owned enterprises in some fields had been related to three factors. The first was the special role of the state-owned economy in dealing with the crisis, the second, the special advantages

---

41. "Improving Investment Efficiency an Urgent Issue in China," *Reference News*, May 29, 2009.

of large enterprises in the crisis, and the third, the improvement of the competitiveness of the state-owned economy. From the micro level, there was the advance and retreat of the state-owned economy or the private economy as normal phenomena of the market economy in a specific period and in some fields. However, from the perspective of the basic system and development trend, if the proportion of the public ownership economy continued to decline, it would eventually affect the dominant position of public ownership and the leading role of the state-owned economy and disintegrate the basic socialist economic system. This was the real danger China faced.[42]

At the level of national legislation and policy, the idea of developing the non-public economy was clear. According to the report of the Seventeenth National Congress of the Communist Party of China, it was important to adhere to and improve the basic economic system with public ownership as the main body and the common development of various types of ownership economies, unswervingly consolidate and develop the public ownership economy, and unswervingly encourage, support, and guide the development of the non-public sector of the economy, while adhering to the principle of equal protection of property rights and forming a new pattern of equal competition and mutual promotion among all sectors of the economy. In February 2005, the State Council issued Several Opinions on Encouraging, Supporting, and Guiding the Development of Non-public Sectors of the Economy, including the individual and private sectors to relax market access to the non-public sectors and create a market environment of fair competition. In March 2007, the Fifth Session of the Tenth National People's Congress passed the Property Law to guarantee the equal legal status and development rights of all market entities. In May 2010, the State Council issued Several Opinions on Encouraging and Guiding the Healthy Development of Private Investment, which encouraged and guided private capital to enter the fields of basic industries and infrastructure, municipal public utilities and policy housing construction, social undertakings, financial services, trade circulation, and the national defense science and technology industry, and it encouraged and guided private capital to reorganize, unite, and participate in state-owned enterprise reform, actively participate in international competition, and promote private enterprises to strengthen independent innovation, transformation, and upgrading. However, in actual economic life, the development of the private economy was faced with internal obstacles such as a weak ability in self-accumulation and capital strength, backward technology research and development, a low degree of operations and management modernization, and low market competitiveness. There were also external obstacles such as system, concept, investment and financing policy, government supervision, market access, and other such areas. Many government departments still followed the management concepts and methods developed under the planned economic system and were accustomed to taking the public economy as the main service object. They had not realized that the government's function

---

42. Zhang Yu, "Current Controversial Issues Regarding the State-Owned Economy," *Economics Trends*, no. 6 (2010); Wei Xinghua and Zhang Fujun, "The Theory that 'the State Advancing and the People Retreating' Cannot Be Established: A Review of the Debate on 'the State Advancing and the People Retreating,'" *Marxism Research*, no. 3 (2010).

was to provide a fair and just market environment for all kinds of enterprises and economic entities under various ownership systems. In view of this situation, some theorists proposed that China further emancipate the people's minds, change their concepts, and realize that the development of the private economy was the requirement for adhering to and improving the basic economic system. It was important to improve relevant laws and regulations and optimize various supporting measures to promote the development of the private economy. It was likewise necessary to change government functions and improve the government's service to the non-public economy and the supervision of fair market competition.[43]

Some scholars believed that "the state advancing and the people retreating" was not a pseudo or false proposition, but reflected the objective reality of the 2008 to 2010 economic cycle. In response to the international financial crisis, the Chinese government launched a stimulus package with 4 trillion yuan of investment and revitalization in ten major industries. In the process of implementing the package plan, although the government partly used market means, it more habitually used administrative means to allocate most investment projects and credit shares to state-owned enterprises. From 2008 to 2009, the proportion of the state-owned holding economy relative to the private holding economy increased. According to the standard of productivity, it was important to adhere to the policy idea of public ownership as the main body and the common development of various ownership economies. At the same time, it was necessary to vigorously develop the private economy and improve the institutional environment of equal competition between the state-owned and private economies.[44]

In November 2013, the Third Plenary Session of the Eighteenth CPC Central Committee proposed the active development of the mixed ownership economy. The mixed ownership economy with cross shareholding and mutual integration of state-owned capital, collective capital, and non-public capital was an important form for realizing the basic economic system. It was conducive to the amplification of the state-owned capital function, the maintenance and appreciation of value, the improvement of competitiveness, and the advantages and disadvantages of various ownership capitals, mutual promotion, and common development, allowing for the state-owned economy and other ownership economies to develop into a mixed ownership economy. Non state-owned capital was allowed to participate in state-owned capital investment projects. The mixed ownership economy was to be allowed to implement employee stock ownership and form the interest community of capital owners and workers.[45]

---

43. Zhang Zhuoyuan et al., *An Outline of the History of New China's Economics, 1949–2011* (China Social Sciences Press, 2012), 253.

44. Wang Haibo, "My Views on the Issue of 'the State Advancing and the People Retreating,'" *Economics Trends,* no. 1 (2011); Zhou Xincheng, "Unswervingly Adhere to Public Ownership as the Main Body and the Common Development of the Multiple Ownership Economy: Comment on the Debate on 'the State Advancing and the People Retreating,' and 'the State Retreating and the People Advancing,'" *Journal of Contemporary Economic Research,* no. 4 (2010).

45. *Decision of the CPC Central Committee on Several Major Issues Concerning Comprehensive Deepening of the Reform* (People's Publishing House, 2013).

After the Third Plenary Session of the Eighteenth Central Committee of the Communist Party of China, a new round of discussion on the status, role, and efficiency of the state-owned economy was launched in economic circle. Some held the view that state-owned enterprises were not conducive to narrowing the income distribution gap and solving the employment problem. The more areas of state-owned enterprises, the greater the income distribution gap, and the more difficult it was for people to find employment. Moreover, state-owned enterprises monopolized most of the resources and became the largest rent-seeking field in China, but they created little value. There were two negative externalities in state-owned enterprises. One was that state-owned enterprises occupied the dominant position and seriously restrained Chinese entrepreneurship, and the other was that state-owned enterprises enjoyed privileges, leading to a serious moral crisis. Therefore, the investment boundary of state-owned enterprises needed to be strictly limited. Moreover, the proportion of state-owned enterprises was too high, making it impossible for China to form a real market economy, which meant that state-owned enterprises had become an obstacle to the further development of China's economy. It was necessary to take the means of privatization to reduce the proportion of state-owned enterprises.[46]

Another point of view was that China's current basic economic system required the adherence to public ownership and the development of the state-owned economy. It was necessary to "make a broader and stronger state-owned economy and collective economy, and give full play to the leading role of the state-owned economy and the main role of the public ownership economy." In the socialist economy, the state-owned economy was not mainly engaged in the departments in which private enterprises were not willing to operate, as in the capitalist system, to supplement the deficiencies of private enterprises, but to realize the sustained, stable, and coordinated development of the national economy and to consolidate and improve the socialist economic, political, and cultural systems. Therefore, the state-owned economy needed to have "absolute control" in key industries and key fields related to the lifeline of the national economy. As a great socialist country, China's bottom line of the state-owned economy could not be based on the "international experience" of privatization in capitalist countries.[47] It was suggested that China must correctly understand and reasonably promote the mixed ownership reform of state-owned enterprises. It was important to prevent the proportion of the public sector of the economy from declining because of an excessive focus on the development of the mixed ownership economy and neglect of the development of the public sector economy.[48]

On September 13, 2018, the general office of the CPC Central Committee and the general office of the State Council issued the Guiding Opinions on Strengthening the Asset Liability Constraint of State-Owned Enterprises, which required improvement of the self-restraint mechanism of assets

---

46. Zhang Weiying, "Rational Thinking on China's Reform," *New Finance*, no. 8 (2013).

47. Liu Guoguang, "Further Discussion on the Direction of China's Economic System Reform," *Entrepreneur Daily*, September 14, 2013.

48. Jian Xinhua, "Correct Understand and Reasonable Promotion of the Mixed Ownership Reform of State-Owned Enterprises," *Financial Science*, no. 12 (2017).

and liabilities of state-owned enterprises and strengthening of supervision and management, so as to make the asset liability ratio of high debt state-owned enterprises return to a reasonable level as soon as possible and promote the average asset liability ratio of state-owned enterprises to reduce it by 2% of 2017 rates by the end of 2020. After that, the asset liability ratio of state-owned enterprises basically remained at the average level of enterprises in the same industry and the same scale.[49] This was a policy measure to strengthen the constraint mechanism of assets and liabilities of state-owned enterprises, promote the state-owned enterprises to become stronger, better, and bigger, and improve the quality of development.

13.4 The Evolution of the Socialist Market Economy and Income Distribution Theory

1. The Socialist Market Economy, Distribution According to Work Theory, and Labor Value Theory

Against the backdrop of socialist market economic system reform, economic and ideological circles carried out a more in-depth study on distribution according to work and labor value theory. These academic circles mainly put forward new views on the meaning of distribution according to work, the application scope of distribution according to work, the realization form of distribution according to work, the relationship between distribution according to work and commodity currency, and labor measurement.

Some studies pointed out that the core content of Marx's idea of distribution according to work had two points. One took labor as the sole measure of income distribution throughout society. The other provided equal amount of labor and obtained equal remuneration across society. On this basis, there was additional content on the meaning of distribution according to work, which included the notion that the object of distribution according to work was the consumption material part of the total social products, that distribution according to work was determined by the public ownership of means of production, that the basis of distribution according to work was labor time, that the implementation subject of distribution according to work was social consumer goods reserve management organs or social organs, and that distribution according to work was divided according to work. The main beneficiary of distribution was the laborer in the material production department, and the historical change of distribution according to work developed with the advancement of society. Another point of view was that in Marx's theory of distribution according to work, there were four main points in the connotation of distribution

---

49. General Office of the CPC Central Committee and General Office of the State Council, "Guiding Opinions on Strengthening the Restraint of Assets and Liabilities of State-Owned Enterprises," *Xinhua News Agency* (Beijing), September 13, 2018.

according to work: only labor force, a kind of production factor, participated in product distribution, and other factors of production did not participate in product distribution; the object of distribution was the consumption materials that were left for personal consumption after six deductions of total products. Chinese economists called this part of consumption materials personal consumption. The scale of distribution was the amount of labor provided by individuals to society or the collective, and the amount of consumption materials shared by individuals was proportional to the amount of labor provided by individuals to society or the collective. More work was more, less work was less, and the same amount of labor obtained the same number of products. Among these four points, the latter three could be found in Marx's relevant expositions. The first key point was from Marx's distribution theory and China's practice of distribution according to work under the planned economic system.

In a long period of time, it is generally believed that distribution according to work is the distribution principle of personal consumer goods. But in the 1990s, the theoretical circle began to make some new explanations on the application scope of distribution according to work. Some commentators believe that the scope of distribution according to work does not include the distribution of all personal consumer goods in the whole society, but only applies to the distribution of personal labor income, which means that distribution according to work is only the distribution principle of personal labor income, not any non-labor income distribution principle. On the one hand, the principle of distribution according to work should be followed when an individual obtains income through labor; on the other hand, every individual who obtains income through non-labor means is not bound by the principle of distribution according to work.

As for the realization form of distribution according to work, the economic and ideological circles agree that to adhere to the principle of distribution according to work, the most important thing is to find a realization form that can fully reflect the objective requirements of distribution according to work. Generally speaking, this realization form is expressed through the distribution system and mechanism of labor income, which should include three aspects of policy, system and mechanism of labor wage, labor welfare and labor security. According to the practice of establishing modern enterprise system, some theorists think that the realization of distribution according to work in China also reflects some new characteristics. According to Marx's assumption, the distribution according to work is that society as a unified distribution center directly distributes to individuals. Under the condition of market economy, it is not for the state to directly distribute the individual, but for the state to implement macro-control over the total wage, so that enterprises can form a self-restraint profit distribution mechanism. The individual labor of the laborer is not the direct social labor, but the individual labor of the enterprise. Therefore, distribution according to work can be realized within enterprises only after commodity exchange between enterprises according to relevant national policies and enterprise regulations.[50]

In the socialist market economy, the personal labor of workers was not directly social labor. This kind of personal labor still needed to go through an arduous road, that is, from "famous value intervening in the process" to social labor. In the socialist market economy, the individual labor of workers in state-owned enterprises did not directly provide commodities to society, but condensed in the products of enterprises as a part of their joint labor. As an independent commodity producer, an enterprise needed to sell all its products at value in the market. Only the joint labor of the enterprise and the individual labor of the laborers who are part of the joint labor could be recognized by society and transformed into social labor and be compensated accordingly. Equivalent exchange in general was an abstraction of the law of value. In the socialist market economy, the general equivalent exchange between labor was shown as equal labor exchange of workers, "that is, a certain amount of labor in one form can be exchanged with the same amount of labor in another form."[51] The "equal quantity" was essentially equivalent, because in the commodity economy, everyone's labor did not become direct social labor from the beginning, and the amount of social labor contained in products could not be directly or absolutely known. Therefore, these quantities of labor could only be "relative, vacillating, and inadequate, and as a last resort, the measure that had to be adopted was time"[52]

The formation and realization of commodity value were two inseparable links in the process of value movement. Marx said, "Only the amount of social necessary labor, or the time used by social necessary labor to produce use value, determines the value of the use value."[53] However, regardless whether the commodity value formed in the production process could be realized, it was still important to examine the circulation process. Marx stated, "If the output of a certain commodity exceeds the needs of society at that time, a part of the social labor time will be wasted. At this time, the social labor volume represented by the commodity volume in the market is much

---

50. Hu Jichuang, *An Analysis of the Differences in Economic Theories* (Fudan University Press, 1991); Zhang Qingren, "Distribution According to Work is a Hypothesis," *Shandong Social Sciences*, no. 2 (1998); Lu Lijun, "Thoughts on the Commodity Economy, Distribution According to Work, and the Labor Force Commodity," *Economic Research*, no. 10 (1989); Xiang Qiyuan, "On the Issue of Labor Measurement in Distribution According to Work," *Economic Research*, no. 2 (1990); Song Yangyan, "The Law, Mode and Form of Distribution According to Work," *Academic Monthly*, no. 2 (1990); Chen Dehua, "Comments on Several Views of Distribution According to Work," *Seeking the Truth*, no. 5 (1990); Cao Lei and Guo Fei, "Summary of Disputes on Distribution According to Work," *Journal of Renmin University of China*, no. 2 (1991); Fan Yunping, "On Distribution According to Work in the Socialist Commodity Economy," *East China Economic Management*, no. 3 (1991); Gao Weiwu, "A New Understanding of Distribution According to Work," *Academic Monthly*, no. 2 (1993); Shi Luming, "On Distribution According to Work in Socialism," *Journal of Guizhou University of Finance and Economics*, no. 3 (1993); Hu Peizhao, "Public Ownership and Distribution According to Work in the Market Economy," *Economic Research*, no. 4 (1993); Jiang Xuemo, "Several Controversial Theoretical Issues in the Socialist Market Economy," *Social Science Front*, no. 1 (1994).

51. Marx and Engels, *Selected Works of Marx and Engels*, vol. 3 (People's Publishing House, 1972), 11.

52. Marx and Engels, *Complete Works of Marx and Engels*, vol. 26 (People's Publishing House, 1972), 348.

53. Marx, *Das Kapital*, vol. 1 (People's Publishing House, 1975), 52.

smaller than the actual social labor amount contained in it."[54] He further pointed out, "If the amount of social labor time spent by a certain department is too large, it can only be paid equivalent according to the amount of social labor time that should be spent. Therefore, in this case, the total product, that is, the value of the total product, is not equal to the labor time contained in itself, but to the labor time that should be spent proportionally when the total product of this field keeps its due proportion with the products of other fields."[55] That is to say, it was not the sum of the combined labor of any enterprise that naturally constituted the social necessary labor time, but the part of the enterprise labor recognized by society in the market (completing the exchange) was a part of the social necessary labor time, realizing its value.

In the socialist market economy, every laborer was an independent interest subject, and the equal amount of labor exchange existed among them. The law of value covered the entire society, that is, the workers passed through the intermediary of enterprises with their own personal labor, undergoing the test of the market and carrying out equal amount of labor exchange according to the principle of equivalent exchange. Whether or to what extent the laborer's personal labor could be transformed into social labor was related to whether their labor was effective, whether their labor consumption could or to what extent it could be compensated, and to what extent their material interests were satisfied. This was ultimately attributed to the economic efficiency of enterprises. The economic efficiency of enterprises determined the income of enterprise members, and the economic efficiency of enterprises was closely related to the labor of each worker, such as the amount of labor provided by workers, the level of labor productivity, the quality of products, and so on. Here, there was a mechanism that linked the labor of workers with their economic interests, and then with the economic efficiency of enterprises.

The so-called distribution according to production factors referred to a means of income distribution according to the amount of production factors input in the production of material means. It was pointed out that there was a close relationship between distribution according to production factors and distribution according to work in the primary stage of socialism. The neutrality of the market economy determined the neutrality of distribution according to production factors. The integrity of the combination of socialism and market economy and the systematic nature of socialist economic theory innovation determined the mode of distribution and the innovation of distribution theory. All the operation modes and organizational forms reflecting the law of social production were neutral. In terms of distribution, it was possible to learn from and use the distribution mode of the market economy. Distribution according to production factors was the distribution mode generally followed by the market economy. In this way, the combination of China's socialism and the market economy and the innovation of socialist economic theory demonstrated the integrity of the system and the unity of content. In the process of the development of the market economy, distribution according to production

---

54. Marx and Engels, *Complete Works of Marx and Engels*, vol. 25 (People's Publishing House, 1972), 205.

55. Marx and Engels, *Complete Works of Marx and Engels*, vol. 26, vol. 1 (People's Publishing House, 1972), 235.

factors was naturally linked with the market economy. No matter what kind of social system the market economy was combined with, as long as it was a market economy, distribution according to production factors would inevitably exist and play a role. Therefore, if the market economy had a neutral nature, then the distribution according to the production factors would naturally have a neutral nature, that is, the neutrality of the market economy determined the neutrality of the distribution according to the production factors, and if the concept of the socialist market economy was established, then the socialist distribution according to the production factors was also established.[56]

Distribution according to work as Marx conceived it was that in the narrow sense, that is, the distribution according to work in which the material production factors did not participate in the distribution of products. The distribution according to work conceived by Marx was consistent with the productivity level and public ownership of means of production in the first stage of a communist society. Some held that if a society did not have the conditions to implement distribution according to work as envisaged by Marx, it should not be implemented. If it were forced to do so, it could not really realize distribution according to work as conceived by Marx. If it had the conditions for implementing the distribution according to work conceived by Marx, it would inevitably implement the distribution according to work envisaged by Marx, because under the conditions envisaged by Marx, productivity had not yet reached the level of "distribution according to needs." Material production factors belonged to all members of society and did not participate in product distribution. Only the labor force was a kind of production factor owned by individuals, and personal consumption materials could only be distributed according to work, because in this case, only the distribution of personal consumption materials according to work could promote enthusiasm among workers and the development of productivity. Therefore, the distribution according to work conceived by Marx was the law of distribution according to work, which was not transferred by human will. Marx's assumption of distribution according to work was consistent with the conditions of implementing distribution according to work. It recognized the difference in human ability. After the necessary deduction of total social products, distribution according to work for consumer goods merely reflected the interest requirements and differences of people under the assumed conditions. There was no inherent contradiction in theory. Although Marx's idea of distribution according to work had not been correctly verified by practice so far, it could be regarded as an abstract inference. However, the earlier unsuccessful practice of distribution according to work had at least proved the correctness of Marx's theory of distribution according to work, which meant that without the conditions for implementing

---

56. Wu Mengjiao and Shi Qinghong, "On the Compatibility of Distribution According to Work and the Socialist Market Economy," *Research World*, no. 4 (1995); Chen Xiaobing, "A Review of the Theory of Distribution According to Work," *Social Science Trends*, no. 7 (1996); Gao Linyuan, "Rethinking Several Theoretical Issues on Distribution According to Work," *Journal of Sichuan Normal University (Social Science Edition)*, no. 2 (1996); Tang Zaixin, "On the Distribution Mode of the Socialist Market Economy," *Economist*, no. 2 (1997); Liu Jielong, "The Neutral Nature of Distribution According to Production Factors," *Economics Trends*, no. 6 (1999).

the distribution according to work conceived by Marx, it would not succeed.[57] Some held that socialist political economics with Chinese characteristics adhered to the basic class position and historical values of Marxist labor theory of value and should adhere to its attitude of historical materialism and dialectical materialism that actively echoed the progress and development of social productive forces.[58]

The Fourteenth National Congress of the Communist Party of China established the goal of socialist market economy reform. In the distribution system, distribution according to work was the main body, and other distribution methods were complementary. It allowed individual capital and other production factors to participate in income distribution. In 1997, the Fifteenth National Congress of the Communist Party of China proposed that capital, technology and other production factors be allowed and encouraged to participate in income distribution, and it explicitly proposed the combination of distribution according to work with distribution according to factors. The Seventeenth National Congress of the Communist Party of China further proposed that it was necessary to adhere to and improve the distribution system with distribution according to work as the main body with various distribution modes coexisting, improve the system of distribution of production factors such as labor, capital, technology and management according to their contributions, and create conditions for more people to have property income. In 2013, the Third Plenary Session of the Eighteenth CPC Central Committee pointed out that it was necessary to improve the compensation mechanism determined by the factor market, such as capital, knowledge, technology and management. According to the report of the Nineteenth National Congress of the Communist Party of China, it was necessary to adhere to the principle of distribution according to work, improve the distribution according to factors, and promote more reasonable, fair, and orderly income distribution. In the socialist market economy, distribution according to work was transformed into distribution according to work and distribution according to factors.[59]

The theory of labor value was a scientific theory to prove that commodity value was created by abstract labor. Plato in ancient Greece, Cicero in ancient Rome, and Augustine and Magnus in the Middle Ages all emphasized the role of labor in the formation of commodity value or price. In the late 17th and early 18th century, William Petty, the founder of British classical political economics, put forward some basic arguments on the relationship between labor and value, while Boisguillebert, the founder of French classical political economics, actually attributed

---

57. Cheng Baoping, "A Preliminary Study on Marx's Theoretical System of Distribution According to Work," *Economic Review*, no. 2 (1995); Shen Bo, "The Conditions of Productive Forces for the Distribution According to Work," *Exploration*, no. 4 (1995); Su Xing, "On the Monism of Labor Value Theory," *Economic Overview*, no. 7 (1995); Xiao Yuming, "On the Evolution and Essence of the Connotation of Distribution According to Work," *The Party and Government Cadres Forum*, no. 11 (1998); Dong Quanhai, "Some Understanding of Distribution According to Work," *Journal of Hebei University of Economic and Trade*, no. 12 (1998).

58. Liu Wei, "Socialist Political Economics with Chinese Characteristics Should Adhere to Marx's Labor Value Theory," *Management World*, no. 3 (2017).

59. Hong Yinxing, "Major Breakthroughs in the Logic of Economic Reform and Political Economics in the Past Forty Years," *Economist*, no. 12 (2018).

the exchange value of goods to labor time when he explained the reasons for determining "real value." Later, Adam Smith, the founder of the British classical political economics system, further elaborated the theory of labor as the source of wealth and the yardstick of value and contributed to the establishment of the theory of labor value. However, there were some defects in Smith's theory of labor value, such as his idea that value is composed of wages, profits, and land rent. Starting from the analysis of Smith's theory, David Ricardo insisted on and extended his basic proposition, refuted and corrected some fallacies that deviated from this proposition, established the most thorough labor value theory that could be achieved in the bourgeois field of vision, and offered a beneficial exploration to explain the internal relations of capitalist production relations and the conflicts of interests of various social classes. However, his understanding of the nature of labor, the relationship between value and exchange value and production price remained vague.

Marx's theory of labor value was a scientific theoretical system established through the study of the political and economic development of European capitalism and summary of the experience of European workers' movement on the basis of critically absorbing their predecessors' views. Starting from the analysis of the commodity economy, the economic cell of capitalist society, Marx found the factors of commodity, namely, the use value and value of the commodity and the duality of labor, that is, the dual attribute of concrete labor and abstract labor in the production of a commodity, and proved that concrete labor created use value, abstract labor created value, and the amount of value depended on the socially necessary labor time needed to produce the commodity. At the same time, it was proved that in the commodity economy based on private ownership, the duality of labor reflected the contradiction between private labor and social labor, while in a capitalist commodity economy, this contradiction developed into the contradiction between the socialization of production and the form of capitalist private ownership. This scientific theory was "the key to understand political economics." It was the first time that economics had revealed the law of the development of human value and a commodity's value, which laid the foundation for the development of human value and commodity.

After the beginning of China's Reform and Opening Up, under the guidance of the ideological line of seeking truth from facts and with the deepening of socialist market economic practice, people's understanding of labor and labor value theory also deepened. This was a new theoretical exploration and innovation process combining Marxism with China's reality. It showed that, since China was in and would remain in the primary stage of socialism for a long time, it implemented the basic economic system with public ownership as the main body and the common development of various ownership economies. The goal of economic system reform was to establish a socialist market economy. This national condition determined that in distribution, it was necessary to adhere to the system of distribution according to work as the main body with various modes of distribution. It was important to combine distribution according to work with distribution according to production factors, adhere to the principle of giving priority to efficiency with due consideration to fairness, allow some areas and some people to become wealthy first, drive and later help enrich all the people, and gradually move towards common prosperity. These important theoretical achievements were breakthroughs in the traditional theoretical model and contributions to contemporary economic science. They embodied the theoretical vitality of extricating from rigid ideological bondage, adhering to reality, and applying the basic view and stands of Marxism to study new situations and new problems.

2. Discussion on the Fairness and Efficiency in the Socialist Market Economy

(1) Egalitarianism and Fairness

Egalitarianism is a concept of fairness based on the small-scale peasant economy. Its typical representatives include the ideas of "balancing the rich and the poor," "equalizing the noble and the humble," "sharing food and clothing," and other similar concepts. Such fairness pays little attention to the improvement of the overall living standard of all members of a society, but only pays attention to the wealth distribution among members, and there is no difference in the results, that is, as Confucius said, "no concern for scarcity, but for inequality." The emergence of this view of fairness is generally mainly the result of a low level of productivity and the mode of production of a small-scale peasant economy. Under the condition of an extreme lack of material goods, people mainly pursue the value of life. Equalitarianism and fairness can ensure the equality of survival opportunities of society or its members, but because this kind of fairness only focuses on equality and excludes the reasonable gap brought about by justice, it lacks a dynamic mechanism to increase wealth and has a weak ability to promote the development of productive forces. In fact, it is only with some difficulty that it exists for a long time in practice. For a long time, due to some defects in China's system and the deviation of people's subjective understanding, fairness was simply understood as the average, and the reasonable income gap required by different personal abilities was completely excluded, which stifled the enthusiasm of workers and caused long-term low efficiency. Equalitarianism was unfairness in distribution, not fairness. The responsibility of inefficiency caused by equalitarianism could not be attributed to fairness, nor could equalitarianism be discussed as fairness in theory.

(2) Equality of Opportunity and Fairness

The equality of opportunity corresponds to equalitarianism, which comes into being in the period of the commodity economy. Its basic proposition is "natural selection, survival of the fittest," and its core is equal opportunity for competition. The effect of this type of fairness in promoting the progress of productivity is obvious. Historically, capitalism can create such huge material wealth over time, to a large extent, due to the role of this value of fairness. Therefore, relatively speaking, this idea of fairness is more advanced than that of equalitarianism. However, under the condition of capitalism, this idea of fairness serves the vested interests, and "equality of opportunity" is only formal equality. Different competitors are faced with de facto inequality of opportunity due to different conditions.

(3) Appropriate Fairness of the Income Gap

This view of equity regards the income gap as the standard to judge whether the social distribution is fair or not, which is a popular view in Western theoretical circles. According to this theory, if the income gap is small, it is considered to be fair or at least close to fair, but if the income gap is large, it is considered unfair. Therefore, the essence of the equality of income gap lies in the equality of distribution as the criterion to judge whether it is fair or not. This view of equity envisages the negative consequences of the excessive income gap and requires that the excessive income gap be narrowed in order to maintain social stability. However, its defects are also obvious, especially the income brought by an unfair economy, such as monopoly income, differential income, income from the exchange of power and money, and the income brought by the ownership of the means of production, as well as the income caused by different personal ability, obscures the qualitative difference between the three.

(4) Fair View of Distribution According to Work

This view of fairness acquiesces on the fact that different incomes formed by "different personal gifts" are "natural privileges," and it requires the abolition of egalitarianism in distribution and the effective implementation of the distribution principle of "more work for more, less work for less, no labor for no food," so it has enjoyed great historical progress. In fact, distribution according to work is fair in itself. However, it is not correct to regard distribution according to work as the whole content of the concept of equality under the condition of a socialist market economy. First of all, there are two prerequisites for the realization of the principle of fair distribution according to work. First, the workers within the scope of the application of the principle of distribution according to work have more real equality in front of the means of production. Second, there should be a sound labor market, so that workers can freely move and choose jobs, allowing their different "natural privileges" to be effectively exerted. Only under these conditions is the principle of distribution according to work fair. Further, at present, there are many kinds of ownership structures in China and the corresponding distribution according to capital, as well as the allocation according to position to ensure the living conditions of all the people in society. If their existence is fair, then the scope of distribution according to work is too narrow, and if they are unfair, what is to be done? Should it be eliminated or perhaps regulated? The answer to such questions cannot be found in the principle of fair distribution according to work.

In the discussion on the priority of efficiency, the view of efficiency supremacy regards whether it is conducive to the improvement of efficiency as the standard of fairness. It holds that only when efficiency is improved and the social wealth is greatly increased can the social welfare be increased and the welfare between individuals become fair. According to the theory of efficiency priority, the optimal allocation of resources should be placed in the first position, and the premise of achieving the optimal allocation of resources is free market competition. In the market economy, the enterprise's goal is to pursue profit maximization, and the individual's goal is to pursue utility maximization. This is an internal incentive mechanism. Free competition in the market produces a kind of external restriction mechanism, which forces enterprises and individuals to improve their efficiency in order to maximize their own interests. Under the effect of such an incentive constraint mechanism, the efficiency of economic activities can be improved, social wealth can be increased, and society will be more able to pay attention to the issue of equity. The theory of efficiency supremacy pursues the efficiency principle of economics, which is conducive to the development of the market economy at a given time. However, the affirmation of the theory of efficiency supremacy is conditional, that is, it only takes the development of the market economy as the reference system. If it goes beyond this scope (for example, taking the development of the overall society as the reference system), the theory of efficiency supremacy will have its defects and become one-sided.

Efficiency priority and equality are the mainstream views in China. The reason China advocates "efficiency first" and "gives consideration to equality" is that efficiency and equality are not always easily taken into account at the same time. In general, efficiency and equality are contradictory. In order to improve efficiency, it is necessary to emphasize the role of the market mechanism and implement distribution according to work. The result of the market mechanism and distribution according to work is the expansion of people's income gap and the degree of wealth and even polarization. This widening income gap, the extent of the rich and the poor, and polarization are a form of inequality. In order to eliminate or reduce this kind of inequality, it is necessary to regulate people's income through the state, so that the gap between the rich and the poor will not be too wide. The state's regulation of people's income serves to restrain and offset the efficiency and its results under the prevailing market conditions, to a certain extent. But generally speaking, efficiency and equality are in contradiction and conflict. The task of a society is to balance the two, to obtain more equality at the expense of certain efficiency, or to achieve higher efficiency on the premise of giving up certain equality. This is a dilemma.

The report of the Sixteenth National Congress of the Communist Party of China clearly put forward the principle of "establishing the distribution principle of labor, capital, technology, and management and other production factors according to their contribution." Economic and ideological circles discussed the objective necessity, theoretical basis, and realization mechanism of distribution according to the contribution of production factors. Some theorists believed that the theoretical basis of distribution according to the contribution of production factors was the ownership relationship or property rights relationship of production factors. Because different factors of production made different contributions in the process of creating and using value, the owners of these factors participated in income distribution by virtue of the ownership requirements of elements. This was the realization of ownership of production factors in the economy, and also the need for rational utilization of production factors and effective allocation of resources. As to whether the "contribution" of production factors was the contribution of creating value or producing wealth (i.e. use value), some scholars thought that different factors of production should be treated differently. For example, in the production process, the "contribution" of workers' labor, scientific and technological labor, or management labor in commodity production served to create both wealth and new value. The contribution of capital as a non-labor factor referred to its contribution in the production of wealth. It was true that in a sense, capital was the necessary condition for creating value and wealth, and it played an objective role in creating value, which could also be called a contribution. Another view was that the "contribution" here referred to those made by various factors of production in the production process of use value or wealth. As to how to measure the contribution of factors of production and how to determine the amount of income from distribution according to those contributions, some held that the determination of factor remuneration by the market price of factors was only a reflection of the most superficial phenomenon of things, but not the essence. Some believed that the realization mechanism of the contribution distribution of production factors could be solved through the combination of factor equity and factor marketization. It was pointed out that due to historical and institutional reasons, the number, quality, and types of production factors owned by individual residents were different. Therefore, income distribution according to the ownership of factors would inevitably lead to the widening of the income gap among residents, which was an objective reality in China at the time.[60]

The positive sum relationship between labor and capital in the process of value creation was also discussed. The theory that labor productivity was directly proportional to the value created per unit time was applied to analyze the process of value formation based on technological change and improvement of labor complexity. Based on this theory, the economic conditions for the realization of the positive sum relationship between labor and capital were discussed. This positive sum relationship in different levels constituted the counteracting factor of the law of relative surplus value.[61]

At the beginning of the 21st century, the discussion on fairness and efficiency mainly centered on the different understandings of the policy concept of "giving priority to efficiency with due consideration to fairness" and the so-called "reflection." In particular, statements from the Seventeenth National Congress of the Communist Party of China concerning the efficiency and fairness of some new terms triggered a new round of debate in economic and ideological circles. At the 21st Annual Meeting of the National Symposium on Socialist Economic Theory and Practice of Colleges and Universities held in November 2007, some scholars pointed out that the new formulation of the relationship between efficiency and equity in the report of the Seventeenth CPC National Congress was an important adjustment to the formulation of "efficiency first, and fairness in consideration." Some people held that the relationship between fairness and efficiency was not mutually exclusive, nor should they be ordered. In the process of building a harmonious society, it was important to gradually transform from "giving priority to efficiency with due consideration to fairness" to "paying attention to both efficiency and fairness." In fact,

---

60. Chen Shizhong and Zhang Yunwei, "The Starting Point of the Combination of Distribution According to Work and Distribution According to Production Factors," *Economics Trends*, no. 6 (1999); Wei Min, "A Theoretical Approach to Distribution According to Factors," *Economics Trends*, no. 6 (1999); Chen Ximin and Bai Yongxiu, "On the New Contribution of the Report of the Sixteenth CPC National Congress to the Theory of Income Distribution," *Economics Trends*, no. 1 (2003).

61. Meng Jie, "Research on the Positive Sum Relationship Between Labor and Capital in Value Creation," *Economic Research*, no. 4 (2011).

before the Seventeenth National Congress of the Communist Party of China, some commentators had "reconsidered" the idea of "giving priority to efficiency with due consideration to fairness." Some point out that "efficiency first, and fairness in consideration" had been the value judgment basis of policy recommendations for many years, but this was a "view with major defects or even mistakes." This sort of opinion leading policy proposal bore great responsibility for many unfair phenomena in practice, and even provided an excuse for some bad behaviors that did not consider justice in practice. The reason that this view was wrong lay in its narrow, inappropriate understanding of "fairness," which endowed efficiency with a position completely superior to any other social and economic goals. Some commentators claimed to "give priority to fairness and give consideration to efficiency." An article published in *China Youth Daily* on December 23, 2005, asked, "At the beginning of the formulation of our various policies, were there serious moral defects? For example, the policy-making concept of giving priority to efficiency with due consideration to fairness has led to the failure of various policies since then."

There were many scholars who held positive opinions on "giving priority to efficiency with due consideration to fairness." According to Wu Jinglian, "efficiency first, fairness in consideration" was put forward in the 1980s as a pushback against the dominant equalitarianism at that time. The premise was that when people's opportunities were equal, there would be a negative correlation between efficiency and equality. At the time, the main cause of income inequality in China was most likely unequal opportunity rather than efficiency. The elimination of inequality of opportunity was complementary to the improvement of efficiency. Therefore, it was believed that the excessive income gap was mainly due to overemphasizing efficiency and conflating of various problems. In a society where the rich were reasonably rich and the poor still had hope and security, people could accept the gap between the rich and the poor.[62]

Some research results analyzed the relationship among technological progress, educational income, and income inequality. In the framework of skill biased technological progress, the analysis showed that skill biased technological progress could well explain the phenomenon in which the proportion of highly skilled workers increased and the relative income of high skilled workers increased. The increase of the average educational level of workers reduced income inequality, while the skill biased technological progress improved the marginal return rate of education to a greater extent.[63]

It was pointed out that the problem of income distribution in the process of China's marketization was largely caused by the distribution of production conditions. Therefore, the solution to the problem of income distribution needed to be combined with the problem of distribution of production conditions. Some commentators believed that the lack of collective bargaining system was an important reason for the relatively low income (labor share) of workers. Only when trade unions could truly represent workers, be relatively independent of

---

62. Wei Xinghua and Sun Yongmei, "Hot issues in Theoretical Economics Research in 2008," *Economics Trends*, no. 2 (2009).

63. Xu Shu, "Technological Progress, Educational Income, and Income Inequality," *Economic Research*, no. 9 (2010).

the government, and conduct equal negotiations with employers and their organizations could the collective bargaining mechanism be effectively established and the labor share in national income be expanded. According to this analysis of some research results, and according to the principle of factor contribution participating in income distribution, without considering the government tax revenue, the contribution of capital factor was higher than that of the labor factor, the capital income of enterprises with capital factor was much higher than that of labor factor provider, and the gap between capital factor income and labor income was also expanding.[64] Some discussed the new characteristics of the labor force commodity value in the socialist public ownership enterprises. It was first noted that the labor force value had the inherent attribute of meeting the needs of both survival and development. In addition, the surplus labor was constantly transformed into necessary labor, which had become a new law of economic development. These two characteristics were the inevitable requirements of the theory of people's shared development and the overall development of socialist political economics with Chinese characteristics.[65]

It is my view that the problem of income distribution should be discussed on the basis of economic development. The adjustment of interest relations represented by income distribution is related to economic development, and the expansion of income gap occurs under the condition of the overall increase of absolute income level and the continuous decrease of the impoverished population. In other words, without the sustained growth of China's economy, there will be no obvious income gap. Further, when the economy develops to a certain level, society should pay more attention to the problem of the income gap, adjust the income distribution relationship with economic ability and economic means, and promote common prosperity. Finally, it is important to avoid abandoning the principle of efficiency and damaging the basis of economic development, because the purpose of income distribution regulation is common prosperity, not common poverty. Therefore, in the economic framework to discuss income distribution (including industry income differences), the key link is building a fair competition market system. In the process of promoting the system reform, it is necessary to strengthen policy regulation, mainly to improve the social security system and financial transfer payment system, limit the income gap within a certain range, and ensure social stability and security.

From the analysis of the requirements of promoting the transformation of economic development, it is important to increase the proportion of labor share (wages) in the national income and make the actual wage level close to the level of labor productivity, so as to achieve a large increase in residents' disposable income. This is also an effective mechanism for increasing the ratio of household consumption to GDP, expanding domestic demand, and transforming economic growth from being investment driven to being consumption driven. In terms of system arrangement, it is necessary to have support from corresponding laws and regulations and to establish a trade union power balance.

---

64. Wang Lu, "Scientific Development and the Sinicization of Marxist Economics: A Summary of the Fourth China Political and Economic Annual Meeting," *Economics Trends,* no. 1 (2011).

65. Liu Fengyi, "A New Understanding of Labor Force Commodity Theory in the Socialist Market Economy," *Economics Trends,* no. 10 (2017).

3. An Economic Analysis of the Widening Income Gap in China

National income distribution is a concept of macroeconomics which reflects the interest relationship and distribution relationship among residents, enterprises, and government. The distribution of the national income is closely related to such macroeconomic variables as the disposable income of residents, after tax income of enterprises, government revenue, national savings, residents' savings, consumption, and investment, so it has an important impact on the operation of the national economy. What is even more deeply felt is that the distribution pattern of the national income is the embodiment of social and economic interest relations, so it is related to the change of production relations and the whole mode of production. In fact, China's economic system reform started from the change of distribution pattern, and the development process of economic system reform and the operation quality of the national economy also interacted with the change of the income distribution pattern. Therefore, from the perspective of the change of the income distribution pattern, it is possible to grasp the changes of China's social and economic interest relations since the beginning of Reform and Opening Up and essentially explain the development requirements of China's advanced productive forces represented by the economic system reform and the fundamental interests of the overwhelming majority of the Chinese people.

With the deepening of economic system reform and the development of the social economy, the pattern of national income distribution has undergone fundamental changes. In terms of the relationship between production and distribution and between accumulation and consumption, the unreasonable practice of emphasizing production, neglecting distribution, valuing accu-mulation, and neglecting consumption in the period of planned economy has changed. Most of the newly increased national income has been used to increase personal income, and the distribution pattern of national income has changed from the sequence of government-enterprise and business unit-resident to resident-enterprise and institution-government. The change of the distribution pattern reflects the major adjustment of the social and economic interest relations, and it demonstrates the change of understanding of the essence of socialism and the re-identification of the purpose of socialist production.

The change of the income distribution relationship is intrinsically related to the development of the social economy. The development of the social economy leads to an increase in income level, which leads to a change of the income distribution and national savings patterns. Income distribution is inclined to individuals, and the main body of national savings is residents' savings, which not only reflects the internal requirements of the development of the market economy, but also constitutes an important economic condition for the expansion of the income gap.

Since the beginning of Reform and Opening Up, China's distribution theory and distribution mode have undergone an evolution process from a singular distribution according to work to distribution according to work supplemented by other distribution methods, and then to the combination of distribution according to work and distribution according to various factors. This changed the egalitarian distribution management system dominated by administrative means in the period of the planned economy and introduced the incentive and competition mechanism of the market economy, especially the establishment of the concept of distribution according to factors, so that the supply-demand relationship of the production factor market gradually became the basic adjustment mechanism of individual income distribution. After the reform of the theory, concept, and method, the income sources of Chinese residents were increasingly diversified, and the income gap gradually expanded.

Whether income distribution pursues egalitarianism or allows for a gap is primarily related to the issue of fairness and efficiency in the sense of economics. Deng Xiaoping's policy of allowing some regions, some enterprises, and some people to first increase their income and improve their lives by their hard work and great achievements aimed precisely to improve the efficiency of production and economic activities through effective incentives. Facts showed that the policy of giving priority to efficiency, giving consideration to fairness, encouraging advancement, and emphasizing competition were conducive to stimulating people's initiative, enthusiasm, and creativity, to the growth of the social economy and the improvement of people's living standards, and to the development of socialist modernization.

Before the beginning of Reform and Opening Up, the income gap between urban and rural residents was quite small. According to the estimation of the National Bureau of Statistics, the Gini coefficient of China's urban areas in 1978 was 0.16, and 0.21 in rural areas. The income gap caused by the equalitarian distribution system became smaller, which seriously suppressed the workers' enthusiasm for production and innovation and covered up many actual unequal distribution phenomena. After the beginning of Reform and Opening Up, the income gap of rural residents continued to expand, mainly because of the sustainable development of rural economy, especially the development of rural industrialization and urbanization. The widening income gap of urban residents was due to the long-term rapid economic development, the establishment of a reward and punishment mechanism, and the diversification of income sources caused by economic system reform. With the effective implementation of the principle of distribution according to work, China changed the absolute egalitarian practice of "rewarding laziness and punishing diligence," meaning doing more and doing less and doing and not doing were the same, which greatly mobilized the enthusiasm and innovation willingness of the majority of workers and made workers with different abilities obtain different incomes. As wealth and production factors were also used as the basis for distribution, wealth income and element income became an important part of personal income, which made individuals with both wealth and factor advantages get a higher income. In addition, some studies showed that the level of education had also become an important factor affecting the level of personal income. The income of residents with a college education or above was significantly higher than that of residents without a higher education. The impact of human capital on income distribution was also reflected in the widening income gap between professional and technical personnel and ordinary workers. The practice in China had proven that it was a kind of historical progress from equalitarianism to efficiency priority. Equalitarianism was actually unfair in distribution. It excluded reasonable income differences required by different personal abilities and factor productivity, stifled the enthusiasm of workers, and inhibited the improvement of economic activity efficiency. The fairness view of efficiency priority did not pursue the average of distribution results, but emphasized different abilities and productivity as the basis of income distribution and allowed the existence of an income gap within a reasonable range. Efficiency priority meant improving the efficiency of economic activities and increasing social wealth and social welfare through the incentive of increasing income. In a market economy, efficiency priority was not only manifested as "more work, more gain," but more importantly, as the optimal allocation of resources. The flow of economic resources and factors of production aimed to pursue higher returns. According to the law of market competition, in order to get higher rewards, it was important to improve efficiency. Economic resources and factors of production thus flowed to places with high returns, that is, they were allocated to more efficient uses. Under such a mechanism, the efficiency of social and economic activities could be improved and social wealth could be increased. However, the distribution mechanism of efficiency priority would lead to the widening of the income gap and even the polarization between the rich and the poor, which was contrary to socialist values. In order to prevent the polarization caused by the excessive expansion of the income gap, it was necessary to "give consideration to fairness," that is, the government used economic means to adjust income distribution, so that the gap between the rich and the poor would not be too wide.

Research on the relationship between the widening of the income gap and economic growth aimed mainly to analyze the impact of income gap expansion on consumption demand and investment demand. There were many views in economic circles that suggested that the widening income gap suppressed consumption and investment demand, which was the root cause of insufficient aggregate demand. This analysis was not very accurate in theory. According to the theory of absolute income, consumption was an increasing function of income. When income increased, consumption also increased, but the extent of consumption increase was less than that of income, that is, when the income level increased, the average propensity to consume tended to decrease and the average propensity to save tended to rise. In other words, the higher the income, the lower the average propensity to consume, but this did not mean that the absolute amount of consumption would decrease, and the absolute consumption volume would continue to increase with the increase of income level. Therefore, the decline of average propensity to consume was not caused by the widening of the income gap, but by the rise of income level. The decline of average propensity to consume was not related to the decline of consumption demand, but to the absolute increase of consumption demand. In fact, what was more directly related to the actual consumption level was the marginal propensity to consume (referring to the proportion of consumption increment in income increment). When income increased, the proportion of the income increment was used to increase consumption determined how much consumption demand would increase. The marginal propensity to consume was positively correlated with the absolute level of disposable income and wealth holding. In addition, the main factor affecting marginal propensity to consume was not the income gap, but income level, income expectation, and consumption habits. The income gap only exerted some indirect influence on marginal propensity to consume through income expectation. Specifically, the widening income gap made the income expectation of the lower income class tend to be pessimistic, leading to the decline of their marginal propensity to consume. However, the factors influencing income expectation were complex and diverse, and the influence of income gap on it was only indirect and uncertain. Generally speaking, the widening of the income gap did not directly lead to a decline in the overall level of social consumption, but only caused changes in the consumption structure.

The widening of the income gap did not directly restrain investment demand. The average propensity to consume was lower, and the average propensity to save was higher. The savings of the high-income group were generally not motivated by preventive motives, so most of the savings could be used for investment. In fact, according to Kuznets' inverted U-model and Lewis' two-sector model, in a certain stage of economic development, the expansion of the income gap was positively related to economic growth. According to a large number of empirical data, Kuznets concluded that the income gap would show a regular change trend from gradually expanding to gradually narrowing with the improvement of economic development. This theory could be confirmed by experience, to a certain extent. The comparison of economic growth and the Gini coefficient before and after China launched its Reform and Opening Up could also prove this theory. Kuznets believed that economic growth was a function of savings and accumulation. The expansion of the income gap concentrated savings and accelerated accumulation, thus expanding the scale of investment and promoting further economic growth. Lewis divided the economy into the traditional and modern sectors. Economic growth depended on the continuous expansion of the modern sector. The expansion of the income gap was conducive to the concentration of capital, thus promoting the expansion of the modern sector and economic growth, so that the surplus labor force in the traditional sector was gradually absorbed by the modern sector. With the expansion of the modern sector and economic growth, the income distribution situation had gradually improved.

However, if the continuous growth of savings could not be smoothly converted into investment, the macroeconomic process would be hindered. From the perspective of the market economy, there were three basic conditions for the smooth transformation of savings into investment. The first was optimistic expectations of the economy, the second, a standardized and efficient capital market, and the third was a legal system for strict protection of property rights. If these three conditions were not met, the savings of the rich class could not be smoothly converted into investment. These savings were either accumulated into the banking system or flowed abroad.

This analysis indicates that the widening income gap did not directly lead to the decline of either consumption or investment demand, so it was not directly related to the decline of economic growth. The key to solving the macro-economic problems at the time was to break through the obstruction of the smooth transformation of savings into investment, so as to increase the demand for investment. The increase of investment would promote economic growth, and economic growth could improve the absolute income level. The increase of the income level would lead to the rise of the consumption level, which would shift the entire economy to a positive cycle.

Although the expansion of the income gap was an inevitable phenomenon in the process of economic development and had the positive significance of stimulating efficiency and promoting growth, and it could not be generalized. First of all, the means of increasing income needed to be proper and should be made rich through honest labor and management. It would endanger the normal development of society and economy if unreasonable income was gained through unfair competition conditions and improper management means, or even gaining wealth by using power for personal gain, trading power and money, and embezzling state-owned assets. Secondly, excessive disparity in income would lead to polarization and affect the stability of the social order. China's income gap was rapidly widening, and the Gini coefficient had exceeded that of other countries at the same development stage in the world, so it was necessary to carry out some governance.

It was crucial to adhere to the principle of giving priority to efficiency with due consideration to fairness and to have a scientific understanding of the widening income gap. The pursuit of the efficiency priority would inevitably lead to an income gap, and the incentive of the income gap would further promote the efficiency of resource allocation and use, and it would promote economic growth. Therefore, from the law of economic growth, the expansion of income gap at a certain stage and to a certain extent was the necessary condition and inevitable result of economic growth. With the social and economic changes of China's Reform and Opening Up over more than forty years, there was a positive correlation between the expansion of the income gap and economic growth. Without the adjustment of both interest and distribution relations represented by income distribution, China's long-term sustained economic growth was impossible. Since the expansion of the income gap was fundamentally related to the process of economic development, the basic way to narrow the income gap was to continue to deepen the reform of the economic system, follow the law of the market economy, and form a unified national market through the free flow of production factors (capital, labor, technology, etc.), so as to improve the speed and quality of economic growth. At the same time, there was also the development and maturity process of socialist market economy.

In addition, it was important to establish and improve the property rights protection system to protect legitimate income according to the law. The long-term growth of an economy needed the support of the accumulation of wealth and savings, and the accumulation of wealth and savings came from the formation and expansion of society's wealthy class. On the premise of legitimate income, the bigger the rich class, the better, which was also in line with the essence and purpose of socialist production. China had a long-term accumulation of social psychology and cultural concepts of small-scale peasant economic equalitarianism. The wave of equalitarianism could easily wash away the accumulation of wealth and savings, making it difficult for economic growth to move onto the track of stable, sustained growth. Therefore, it was important to reasonably explain the social function of the wealthy class who got rich by legal income both theoretically and culturally and to effectively protect the property rights of all citizens in the system. This was the basic condition for building a democratic, prosperous, powerful country.

Further, in order to prevent the serious polarization caused by the excessive expansion of income gap, the government needed to reasonably adjust the distribution relationship and distribution pattern of the entire society through effective macro-control, appropriately restrict the excessive income by economic means, and improve the income and welfare of the low-income class. In the aspect of properly limiting the excessive income, it was important to primarily use reasonable, effective tax tools to reduce the disposable income of the high-income population. There were two main points in this operation. The first was that the means of regulation should be economic, with high transparency that was legal and standardized. The second was that the intensity of regulation should be moderate, because maintaining a high-income class that had become rich on legitimate income was beneficial to social and economic development. In terms of improving the income and welfare of the low-income class, the main measures were to improve the social security and financial transfer payment systems, ensure the basic living conditions of the low-income class, strive to improve their income and welfare, limit the gap between the rich and the poor within a certain range, and ensure social stability and security.

Finally, it was necessary to rely on the legal system to control the behavior of seizing wealth by improper or illegal means (including power and money trading, unfair competition, improper management, etc.). Primarily, through deepening the reform of economic and political systems, the construction of a clean and honest government needed to be strengthened and the space for "power and money trading" and rent-seeking activities reduced. Further, it was important to improve the laws and regulations against economic crimes, improve the efficiency of law enforcement, and ban illegal income. Finally, anti-monopoly laws needed to be formulated to break industrial monopolies (including natural monopolies and administrative monopolies) and rectify unreasonable monopoly income, building a fair competition market environment. Achieve income equity, first of all, required fair opportunity, that is, fair, and open competition among market subjects at the same starting point. Fair competition was the soul of the market mechanism and the source of the efficiency of the market economy. The market environment of fair competition was not only an important condition for income fairness, but also an important condition for the establishment of the socialist market economic system.

CHAPTER 14

Exploration and Development of Socialist Political Economics with Chinese Characteristics

14.1 Research on the Construction of Socialist Political Economics with Chinese Characteristics

1. The Construction Process of Socialist Political Economics with Chinese Characteristics

Before the 1980s, the study of socialist political economics was mainly based on the combination of some fundamental principles, categories, and concepts of Marxist economic theory with the socialist political economics system of the Soviet Union. There was no "Chinese" political economics. According to the research, Mao Zedong once proposed writing a textbook of political economics. He thought that the research object of political economics was mainly the relations of production, but to study the relations of production clearly, it was necessary to study the productive forces on the one hand and the positive and negative effects of the superstructure on the relations of production on the other. The balance and imbalance between productive forces and the relations of production and between the relations of production and the superstructure needed to be taken as the key points in the study of social and economic issues.[1] Mao believed that in order to promote China's socialist economic construction, it was necessary to not only adhere to the basic principles of Marxist political economics, but also to root it in China's national conditions, sum up China's experience, constantly promote the innovations of Marxist theory,

---

1. Wang Lisheng and Deng Guanqing, "On the Theoretical Sources of Political Economics of Socialism with Chinese Characteristics," *Economics Trends*, no. 5 (2016).

produce China's own theorists, create its own economic theory, and form a theory of political economics with Chinese characteristics. When reading the Soviet Union's political economics textbook, he noted, "Marxist books by our predecessors should be read, and their basic principles should be observed. This is primary. However, the Communist Party of any country and its ideological circles should create new theories, write new works, and produce its own theorists to serve its own current politics. It is impossible to rely on our predecessors alone."[2] In October 1984, the Third Plenary Session of the Twelfth Central Committee of the Communist Party of China adopted the Decision of the CPC Central Committee on Economic System Reform. Deng Xiaoping proposed that this document served as "a first draft of political economics, which is a political economics combining the basic principles of Marxism with the practice of socialism in China."[3]

From the 1980s to the beginning of the 21st century, China's academic circles compiled several political economics textbooks, including *Political Economics (Socialism)* compiled by thirteen colleges in the north (1979, 1980), *Political Economics (Capitalism)* compiled by sixteen universities in the south (1979, 1980), *Political Economics Coursebook* (1980) edited by Jiang Xuemo, *Political Economics Coursebook* (1982) edited by Song Tao, *Political Economics (Socialism)* (1993) edited by Wu Shuqing, Gu Shutang, and Wu Xuangong, *Political Economics (Capitalism)* (1993) edited by Wu Shuqing, Wei Xinghua, and Hong Wenda, and *Political Economics* (2002) edited by Pang Jinju, Hong Yinxing, Lin Gang, and Liu Wei.[4] These textbooks were basically the integration of Marx's *Das Kapital,* Soviet Socialist political economics, Western economics, and China's economic system reform policies (such as the socialist commodity economy and the socialist market economy). Some scholars believed that it was after the beginning of Reform and Opening Up that China really began to study and compile its thinking on socialist political economics, but based on the requirements of socialist political economics as a science, there was still a big gap it practice. It was unrealistic to explore the laws of socialist economic development before the socialist mode of production had been developed and finalized. There were many versions of socialist political economics, but none could put forward a core category of the whole book as solid evidence. It was important to proceed from the actual situation and conduct a practical, realistic study on the existing economic problems and development direction. It was only possible to study one problem at a time, and a system could not be formed immediately. Thus, this was not a "systematic theory."[5]

In April 2004, the project of Marxist theoretical research and construction was launched, and the textbook compilation project for *Introduction to Marxist Political Economics* was established and a research group set up. The textbook was put into use in colleges and universities nationwide

---

2. Mao Zedong, *Collected Works of Mao Zedong,* vol. 8 (People's Publishing House, 1999), 109.

3. Deng Xiaoping, *Selected Works of Deng Xiaoping,* vol. 3 (People's Publishing House, 1994), 93.

4. Liu Shucheng, "Infrastructure Construction of Political Economics with Chinese Characteristics," *Economic Research,* no. 10 (2012).

5. Gu Shutang, "My Experience on Political Economics (Especially the Socialist Part)," *Economics Trends,* no. 11 (2010).

in 2011. The compilation and publication of the textbook was regarded as a basic work on the theoretical research and textbook construction of political economics with Chinese characteristics. The framework structure of the textbook was divided into four parts, covering 1) commodity and currency, or a general theory of the market economy, 2) the capitalist economy, 3) the socialist economy, and 4) economic globalization and opening up, or international economic relations. This framework fully absorbed and reflected the latest research results.[6]

On November 23, 2015, at the collective learning meeting of the Political Bureau of the CPC Central Committee, Xi Jinping pointed out that it was necessary to be rooted in China's national conditions and development practice, reveal new characteristics and new laws, refine and summarize the regular results of China's economic development practice, and upgrade practical experience to systematic theory in an effort to constantly open up a new realm of contemporary Marx's political economics.[7] On December 18, 2015, when Xi Jinping presided over the Central Economic Work Conference, he emphasized once again that China should adhere to the principle of socialist political economics with Chinese characteristics.[8]

On May 17, 2016, Xi Jinping hosted a forum on philosophy and the social sciences, emphasizing the need to accelerate the construction of philosophy and the social sciences with Chinese characteristics. In accordance with the ideas of establishing a foothold in China, learning from other countries, digging into history, grasping the contemporary, caring for humanity, and facing the future, it was important to strive to build China's philosophy and social sciences with a Chinese guiding ideology, discipline system, academic system, and discourse. The system fully embodied Chinese characteristics, Chinese style, and Chinese features.[9]

Regarding the development of the new realm of political economics of contemporary Marxist doctrine in China, Xi Jinping pointed out that since the Third Plenary Session of the Eleventh CPC Central Committee, the party had combined the basic principle of Marx's political economics with the new practice of Reform and Opening Up, enriching and developing Marxist political economics and forming many important theoretical achievements of contemporary China's Marxist political economics. Examples included the theory of the essence of socialism, the theory of the basic economic system in the primary stage of socialism, the theory of establishing and implementing the development concept of innovation, coordination, green, openness, and sharing, the theory of developing the socialist market economy, making the market play a decisive role in the allocation of resources and giving better play to the role of the government, the emergence of China's economic development, the theory of the new normal, the theory of making good use of the two markets and resources at home and abroad, the theory of promoting social equity and justice, and the importance of gradually realizing the common prosperity of all

6. Liu Shucheng, "Infrastructure Construction of Political Economics with Chinese Characteristics," *Economic Research*, no. 10 (2012).

7. Xi Jinping, "Based on China's National Conditions and Development Practice in China, Develop the Political Economics of Marx Doctrine in Contemporary China," *People's Daily*, November 25, 2015.

8. "Central Economic Work Conference Held in Beijing," *People's Daily*, December 22, 2015.

9. Xi Jinping, "Speech at the Symposium on Philosophy and Social Sciences," *People's Daily*, May 19, 2016.

the people, among others. These theoretical achievements were a political economics that adapted to the national conditions and characteristics of contemporary China. They not only effectively guided the practice of China's economic development, but also opened up a new realm of Marxist political economics. Practice was thus the source of theory. The process of China's economic development was magnificent, and its achievements attracted worldwide attention. It contained great power, vitality, and great potential for theoretical creation. It was important to study the new situation and new problems faced by both the world economy and China's own economy and contribute Chinese wisdom to the innovative development of Marxist political economics.[10]

On July 8, 2016, when Xi Jinping held a forum among experts on the economic situation, he pointed out that in adhering to and developing socialist political economics with Chinese characteristics, it was important to take Marx's political economics as the guide, summarize and refine the great achievements of China's Reform and Opening Up and socialist modernization, and draw lessons from the useful elements of Western economics.[11] After the publication of a series of speeches by Xi Jinping on Chinese political economics and Marxist philosophy and social sciences with Chinese characteristics, there was a heated discussion among economic circles on China's socialist political economics. According to statistics, there were 305 papers on the political economics of socialism with Chinese characteristics in 2016 and 379 in 2017 (according to the CNKI database). The research focused on the research object, logical starting point, fundamental method, theoretical attributes, guiding principle, historical orientation, theoretical source, practical basis, scientific connotation, direction for theoretical innovation, system construction evolution, and similar areas.[12] The general understanding in the literature was that the development performance, development path, and structural contradictions in the development of China's Reform and Opening Up and the construction of socialism with Chinese characteristics were difficult to explain with the theories and paradigms of Western economics. It was thus necessary to combine China's development practice, national characteristics, and institutional conditions, develop Marxist economics under the guidance of Marxist economic principles, scientifically learn from Western economics, and construct socialist political economics with Chinese characteristics.

2. The Characteristics of Socialist Political Economics with Chinese Characteristics

Xi Jinping's speech at the symposium on philosophy and social sciences outlined the characteristics of China's characteristic philosophy and social sciences including China's socialist political

---

10. Xi Jinping, "Based on China's National Conditions and Development Practice in China, Develop the Political Economics of Marx Doctrine in Contemporary China," *People's Daily*, November 25, 2015.

11. "Xi Jinping's Speech at the Symposium Held by Experts at the Economic Situation," *Xinhua News Agency* (Beijing), July 8, 2016.

12. Research Group of the Economic Editorial Department of the Book and Newspaper Data Center of Renmin University of China, "An Analysis of Research Hotspots of China's Economics and Management in 2017," *Economics Trends*, no. 4 (2018).

economics. The characteristics, style, and approach of philosophy and social sciences were the product of development to a certain stage, a symbol of maturity, a symbol of strength, and a manifestation of self-confidence. The characteristics of philosophy and social sciences with Chinese characteristics needed to grasp three main aspects.

First, it was important to embody the inheritance and national characteristics of China. The nation needed to effectively integrate the resources of Marxism, the excellence of Chinese traditional culture, foreign philosophy, and social sciences and adhere to the principle of not forgetting the original, absorbing foreign resources, and facing the future. Strengthening self-confidence in the path, theory, and system of socialism with Chinese characteristics aimed, in the final analysis, to strengthen cultural confidence, which was a deeper, more basic, and more lasting force.

The second aspect was to embody the originality and the times. Whether China's philosophy and social sciences had Chinese characteristics ultimately depended on subjectivity and originality. Only by taking the reality of China as the starting point, putting forward subjective, original theoretical viewpoints, and constructing a discipline system, academic system, and discourse system with its own characteristics could the philosophy and social sciences of China form its own characteristics and advantages. China's philosophy and social sciences should focus on what China was doing, excavate new materials, discover new problems, put forward new ideas, and construct new theories from the practice of China's reform and development, strengthen the systematic summary of the practical experience of Reform and Opening Up and socialist modernization, and strengthen the development of the socialist market economy, democratic politics, advanced culture, a harmonious society, and ecology. It was important to strengthen the research and interpretation of the new ideas and new strategies of the Party Central Committee in the fields of civilization and the construction of the Party's ruling ability, refine the new theory with academic rationality, and summarize the new practice with regularity.

The third priority was to embody a systematic approach and professionalism. Philosophy and social sciences with Chinese characteristics should cover history, the economy, politics, culture, society, ecology, military affairs, Party building, and other fields, including traditional disciplines, emerging disciplines, frontier disciplines, interdisciplinary fields, non-military subjects, and many other disciplines. It was important to constantly promote the construction and innovation of the discipline, academic, and discourse systems and strive to build an all-round, all-field, and all-factor system of philosophy and social science. China needed to effectively construct teaching materials and form a complete teaching system of philosophy and social sciences that met the requirements of the development of socialism with Chinese characteristics and was based on cutting edge international academic materials.[13]

In the construction of socialist political economics with Chinese characteristics, or philosophy and social sciences with Chinese characteristics, a fundamental orientation would reflect a nation's thinking ability, spiritual character, and civilization quality, as well as its comprehensive

---

13. Xi Jinping, "Speech at the Symposium on Philosophy and Social Sciences," *People's Daily*, May 19, 2016.

national strength and competitiveness in the process of human historical development and social progress.[14] In the progress and development of world civilization and culture, this mindset had the corresponding right of discourse and international status. In the 2010s, Chinese academic circles discussed and studied the independent construction of the contemporary Chinese academic discourse system. It was pointed out that the discussion and debate on the contemporary construction of China's academic discourse system would have a unique, influence and far-reaching significance in the history of academic development in China. Although there were different opinions, the exploration process of this topic itself aimed to open up a kind of positive consciousness, that is, self-consciousness through self-examination of its own academic discourse system. In fact, this kind of self-consciousness had a dual orientation. On the one hand, it was critical, that is, it required a critical review of the academic discourse of contemporary Chinese humanities and social sciences, while on the other, it was constructive, which required constructive guidance for the reconstruction of the contemporary Chinese academic discourse system. What was more important was that the research on the humanities and social sciences in China aimed to eliminate its "apprenticeship" under foreign learning and put forward its own "self-discipline" requirements. The contemporary construction of China's academic discourse system could only be carried out and actively formed on the basis of China's own national language.[15] Some commentators considered the contradiction and integration of universalism and nationalism in values and discourse system against the backdrop of globalization. Globalization supported universalism. In the era of globalization, information convergence, economic convergence, lifestyle convergence, and cultural convergence gradually formed the universal cultural principles generally recognized by humankind. In fact, since the beginning of Reform and Opening Up, China had gradually accepted some foreign values, consciously or unconsciously. For example, in the past, China believed that bourgeois human rights were a typical manifestation of bourgeois legal rights, which were hypocritical, deceptive, and anti-socialist. In the 1980s, there was heated debate about humanitarianism. Some people only recognized revolutionary humanitarianism, that is, they recognized humanitarianism in the sense of saving the dying and helping the wounded. They thought that being "people-oriented" violated the principle of materialism, which was the manifestation of an idealistic view of history. In the early part of the 21st century, scientific development and being people-oriented became the mainstream values of society, marking a huge ideological change.[16]

Some critics believed that socialist political economics with Chinese characteristics had three characteristics. The first was the theory of the socialist market economy, which was the most important achievement of the integration of contemporary Marxist political economics into China. In a large country, the realization of the combination of socialism and the market

---

14. Xi Jinping, "Speech at the Symposium on Philosophy and Social Sciences," *People's Daily*, May 19, 2016.

15. Wu Xiaoming, "On the Independent Construction of Contemporary Chinese Academic Discourse System," *Chinese Social Sciences*, no. 2 (2011).

16. Bing Zheng, "Contemporary Cultural Contradiction and Transformation of Philosophical Discourse System," *Chinese Social Sciences*, no. 2 (2011).

economy was a great groundbreaking task which had epoch-making significance both in theory and in practice. Second, based on China's national conditions, China's development economics gradually moved toward modernization. China's gradual industrialization and modernization from poverty and backwardness was based on China's national conditions under the guidance of the continuous development of Marxist political economics in China. The third was that it was important to adhere to the people-centered approach and share the fruits of development with the people. Taking the people as the center in the economic field meant allowing them to share the fruits of reform and development and take the path of common prosperity.[17] Some people held that the characteristics or qualities of socialist political economics with Chinese characteristics could be grasped from three aspects: practicality, human nature, and purpose. Practice was the source of theory. The practice of China's Reform and Opening Up and economic development was the only correct way to develop contemporary Chinese Marxist political economics. Through the understanding of the new economic phenomenon, it was important to further explore the new economic law, and then rise to a new economic concept and economic theory. The study of Marxist political economics was for humans, while the "human" in Marxist political economics was totally different from what it implied in Western economics. In Western economics, "human" referred to abstract "economic man," while Marxism held that "human" referred to a group of people, and social people were the masses. The view of Marxist political economics was that people in the economic process were the unity of producers and consumers. Therefore, the broad masses of the people were the main body of economic development. The main line or purpose of socialist political economics with Chinese characteristics was to develop social productive forces. Productivity was the fundamental driving force for the change and development of human society. The relations of production should adapt to productive forces, and the superstructure should adapt to the economic base. This was the general law of the development of human society and a basic principle of Marxism. In the effort to promote the development of social productive forces as the logic to expand the structure and system of socialist political economics, the overall picture of socialist economic development needed to be fully displayed.[18]

Some critics proposed that China had the realistic foundation and ability to construct an economic discourse system. Since the beginning of Reform and Opening Up, China's economy had contributed more than 20% to world economic growth. Based on China's economic development trend, China would become an important engine to drive the recovery of the world economy. China's economy had the energy to lead the world economy. These two aspects laid a realistic foundation for the construction of the "discourse system" of China's economics. China should and had the ability to gain a greater voice in the development of the world economy, and China's development experience was the basic core of China's economic discourse system. The experience

---

17. Zhang Zhuoyuan, "Three Issues Concerning the Development of Contemporary Chinese Marxism," *Chinese Social Sciences*, no. 3 (2016).

18. Ding Renzhong, "On the Quality of Contemporary Chinese Marxist Political Economics," *Economic Research*, no. 3 (2016).

of China's development had rich connotations and multi-dimensional levels, with inexhaustible economic elements far beyond the curve and model description of Western economic theory.[19]

Some held that the most fundamental meaning of the "characteristics" of "economics with Chinese characteristics" was solving China's problems under the guidance of Marxism and based on China's practice. Chinese characteristics should be reflected not only in the major principles of the nation's economics, but also in the list of topics brought into the purview of its economics research. One of the basic tasks of constructing economics with Chinese characteristics was to adhere to the orientation of the problem, focus on the major issues facing both China and global economic development, and focus on putting forward ideas, propositions, and plans that could reflect China's position, wisdom, and values.[20]

The biggest difference between the socialist market economy with Chinese characteristics and the Western capitalist market economy was the mixed economic system dominated by public ownership and the extent and depth of the government's intervention and influence on the economy through laws and various economic policies. Therefore, in the allocation and distribution of scarce resources, the relationship between public and personal interests, as well as the relationship between the government and the market, were the most significant characteristics of China's economy. Under the conditions of the market economy, important fields of research included finding ways to explore the respective regulatory boundaries of the government and the market and their interactive relationship to achieve the optimal allocation of scarce resources and to explore the best combination of public and personal interests in each historical period to achieve the ultimate socialist goal of common prosperity. These were fields in which China's economics were most likely to make major theoretical contributions, greatly enriching the theory of both the market economy and the socialist economy. However, there were different opinions on whether it was necessary to construct a Chinese discourse system, whether to use "international language" (research paradigms and methods generally recognized by international peers) or "Chinese language" to tell Chinese stories. Naturally, it was likely to be difficult to spread the economic thought and theories of Chinese economists over a long period of time, and it was likely to become very inward focused, not to mention enhancing the international discourse power and influence of Chinese economists.[21] However, there were other views that held that China's economics should have Chinese characteristics and its own discourse system, discipline system, and academic system. History proved that the idea that China's economics could be brought to the world with the words of Western economics was not feasible, because the development of China's economics itself relied on the world's second largest economy. China needed to display self-confidence in its theory, not restoring Chinese economic theory to the Western economic paradigm or publishing models and data in international journals, but rather

---

19. Zhou Wen, "The Times Call for China's Economic Discourse System," *Economic Research*, no. 3 (2016).

20. Gao Peiyong, "Institute of Economics, Institute of Economics and the Construction of Economics with Chinese Characteristics," *Economic Research*, no. 5 (2017).

21. Hong Yongmiao, "Standing on the Position of Chinese People, Studying China's Problems with Modern Methods, Telling China's Stories in International Language," *Economic Research*, no. 5 (2017).

translating the research paradigm of China's economics into English and popularizing it across the world.[22]

Some scholars held that the greatest characteristic of socialist political economics with Chinese characteristics was the combination of the social characteristics of socialism with the market characteristics of the market economy. As the social characteristics of socialism and the market characteristics of the market economy had their own regulations, integrating the two became the top priority in the study of socialist political economics with Chinese characteristics. Moving from a material-oriented to human-oriented approach meant solving the problems of who and what was the purpose of development, which was the foundation of socialist political economics with Chinese characteristics. Moving from capital logic as the main axis to labor logic as the main axis was the concrete embodiment of the practical implementation of being people-oriented, because capital logic was material-oriented, and only labor logic could truly embody the concept of being people-oriented. Moving from private ownership as the basis to public ownership as the main body, the common development of multiple ownership was not only an internal requirement of following labor logic, fully reflecting labor differences, advocating labor equity, and giving full play to the enthusiasm of all kinds of labor, but also an inherent provision of China's socialist characteristics. Moving from the idea of a free market to the idea of the "double haves" of market efficiency and government's action, which was insisted on by macro-control, was a correction of the poor practice of market factors and omnipotent government after the combination of socialism and the market economy. Therefore, the source of theoretical innovation of socialist political economics with Chinese characteristics could be explored from the perspective of being human-centered, with labor logic as the main axis, public ownership as the main body, the common development of multiple ownership, and the concept of market efficiency and government performance.[23]

Some scholars believed that the characteristic of socialist political economics with Chinese characteristics was the innovation of scientific socialist theory and practice. After forty years of Reform and Opening Up, China had successfully constructed a socialist market economic system with public ownership as the main body and with various economic components developing together and giving full play to the function of the market mechanism. With the conditions of backward production technology, it was important to realize the great leap forward in the development of the economy and society. These theoretical and practical innovations needed in-depth theoretical survey and summary to form the Chinese version of socialist political economics.[24]

---

22. Hong Yinxing, "Building Socialist Political Economics with Chinese Characteristics," *Economist*, no. 1 (2019).

23. Huang Hua and Cheng Chengping, "On the Theoretical Innovation Direction of Socialist Political Economics with Chinese Characteristics," *Economist*, no. 6 (2017).

24. Hong Yinxing, "Building Socialist Political Economics with Chinese Characteristics," *Economist*, no. 1 (2019).

On December 4, 2018, the academic journal *China Political Economics* (English edition), founded by the School of Economics of Nanjing University, was officially published. The journal adhered to the concept of "Chinese issues, global vision, inclusiveness, and cohesion, and a Chinese voice." It focused on Chinese issues and actively absorbed excellent research results including both Chinese and international scholars. It was an important part of the earnest exploration of the reference significance of China's economic development path to world economic development, and it actively explored the developmental contribution of various innovative practices in China's economy to global economic theory.[25]

3. On the Subject Orientation and Category System of Socialist Political Economics with Chinese Characteristics

Xi Jinping pointed out that it was only by taking China's actual situation as the starting point and putting forward the theoretical viewpoints of subjectivity and originality and constructing a disciplinary system, academic system, and discourse system with its own characteristics that the nation's philosophy and social sciences could form its own characteristics and advantages.[26] A key issue in the discussion was the subject orientation and the construction of a category system of socialist political economics with Chinese characteristics. Some scholars held that the discipline orientation of socialist political economics with Chinese characteristics at different stages was part of the political economics of the primary stage of socialism in terms of production relations and the political economics of the middle-income development stage in terms of productivity. The research object of the political economics of socialism with Chinese characteristics was extended to productive forces, and its task was to establish a systematic economic theory on the liberation, development, and protection of productive forces.[27] Some commentators believed that the core proposition of socialist political economics with Chinese characteristics was that it was necessary to adhere to the direction of socialist market economic reform. The ideological and theoretical vitality of socialist political economics with Chinese characteristics lay in summing up the experience of China's reform and forming a systematic theory.

There were three main topics in the reform practice and the systematization of ideological theory. The first was that the fundamental significance of socialist economic reform with Chinese characteristics lay in the unification of socialist public ownership and the market economic system. This was not only a fundamental feature of China's socialist market economic reform, but also a fundamental breakthrough in traditional Marxist economic theory and reform practice and socialist political economics with Chinese characteristics. The notion that economic theory needed to be studied, summarized, and developed thoroughly was an important proposition. The second topic was the main line of the reform of the economic operation mechanism and its role in

---

25. "China Political Economics (First Issue)," *Economics State*, no. 2 (2019).

26. Xi Jinping, "Speech at the Symposium on Philosophy and Social Sciences," *People's Daily*, May 19, 2016.

27. Hong Yinxing, "Building the Theoretical system of Socialist Political Economics with Chinese Characteristics with Innovative Theory," *Economic Research*, no. 4 (2016).

making the market play a decisive part in the allocation of resources, with the key lying in handling the relationship between the government and the market from the perspective of the economic system. The third was the improvement of the quality of the market economic order, including the internal competition order and the external environment order.[28] It was a basic understanding that the foundation of socialist political economics with Chinese characteristics was the reform practice of China's socialist market economy. Some held that the conditions for creating a Chinese school of economics could be found in several key areas, including China's industrialization road, the role of the government in economic development, the shift from population burden to demographic dividend, breaking the "domestic savings gap" and "foreign exchange gap" in development, the urbanization road, the Internet economy, and Internet finance. These aspects were mature enough to form a theoretical system of economics with Chinese characteristics.[29]

The economic theory of socialism with Chinese characteristics rose from empirical knowledge to systematic theory, and it became a science. Its scientific connotation included the idea that socialist political economics with Chinese characteristics was the contemporary Marxist political economics of China, and that socialist political economics with Chinese characteristics was the summary of the practical experience of socialist economic construction with Chinese characteristics. Socialist political economics with Chinese characteristics was an important part of the theoretical system of socialism with Chinese characteristics. It was the new development and new form of socialist political economics, and it was the political economics of the people and of the developing socialist market economy.[30] Some commentators emphasized that the most fundamental meaning of the "characteristics" of "economics with Chinese characteristics" was solving China's problems under the guidance of Marxism and based on China's practice. As a science, the results of economics needed to be refined by objective laws and formed by a theoretical system. This meant that only by raising the practice of China's economic reform and development to the level of law could the features of economics with Chinese characteristics make their due contribution to world economics.[31] Some pointed out that China's economics was not the Chinese version of Western economics, nor was it a "mixture" of Chinese and Western economic thought "with Chinese as the body," but a concept system which was really different from Western economics, based on Chinese practice and Chinese experience.[32]

There were also many discussions on the research methods of socialist political economics with Chinese characteristics. Some thought that the research object of socialist political economics with Chinese characteristics was the mode of production in the primary stage of socialism in

28. Liu Wei, "Developing Socialist Political Economics with Chinese Characteristics in the Combination of Marxism and Chinese Practice," *Economic Research*, no. 5 (2016).

29. Li Yang, "Political Economics with Chinese Characteristics Is Rooted in China's Practice," *Economic Research*, no. 5 (2017).

30. Zhang Yu, "The Scientific Connotation of Socialist Political Economics with Chinese Characteristics," *Economic Research*, no. 4 (2017).

31. Gao Peiyong, "Institute of Economics, Institute of Economics and the Construction of Economics with Chinese Characteristics," *Economic Research*, no. 5 (2017).

32. Zhou Wen, "China's Road and China's Economics," *Economist*, no. 7 (2018).

China and the corresponding relations of production and exchange. The research task could be summarized as revealing the law of socialist economic movement, providing theoretical guidance for improving the socialist economic system, promoting the development of productive forces, satisfying the improvement of people's material and cultural living standards, and realizing people's all-round development and common prosperity. Historical materialism and dialectical materialism were the fundamental methodology of socialist political economics with Chinese characteristics.[33] Some further deduced the analytical norms of Marxist political economics from the methodological principles of dialectical materialism and historical materialism. The first was to explain the change of the social and economic system with the inevitable adaptation of production relations with the development of productive forces. The second was to make all means of production the basis for analyzing the whole system of production relations. The third was to understand the political and legal systems and moral norms according to the economic relations corresponding to a certain historical stage of the development of productive forces, and the fourth was the analysis of human economic behavior in the overall restriction of the social and economic structure formed throughout history.[34] According to the relationship between value orientation and quantitative analysis in economic research, it was argued that the tendency of "valuing quantity over vector" in recent years in China's economic research had actually weakened creativity in economic research. In economic research, quantitative relations (including absolute numbers, relative numbers, and quantitative models) served to demonstrate theoretical viewpoints. Without an ideological nature, quantitative relations lost the direction and value of argumentation. Mathematical analysis was based on many hypothetical conditions, omitting condition analysis, process analysis, and effect analysis, which would naturally lead to misunderstanding.[35]

Some believed that economics had a general paradigm in research methods and expressions. There were three sources for the theoretical innovation of China's economics: China's practical experience, the basic principles of Marxist historical materialism, and the research paradigm of modern economics. Researchers focused on China's economic theory needed to follow the research paradigm of modern economics so that scholars in other countries could understand and accept it. Not only did the theory need internal logic and self-consistency, but the inference of the theory should likewise be consistent with empirical facts. The mathematical model and econometric analysis were the general methods international economic circles used to ensure logical rigor and to test whether the various inferences of theoretical models were consistent with empirical facts. Only by passing these two tests could a theory be said to explain the causal logic behind the phenomenon, and only in this way could it communicate and be accepted by the international economic community. The results obtained by Chinese economic circles in studying local

---

33. Pang Jinju, "Learning How to Make Good Use of and Develop Socialist Political Economics with Chinese Characteristics," *Economics Trends*, no. 4 (2016).

34. Lin Gang, "An Analysis of Marxist Political Economics Methodology," *Economics Trends*, no. 4 (2016).

35. Wang Guogang, "Adhering to the Problem Orientation and Promoting the Innovative Development of China's Economic Research," *Economic Research*, no. 5 (2017).

economic phenomena and problems with international standard methods naturally contributed to the development of modern economics and international achievements.[36] Some commentators pointed out that the new development concept was the main content of systematic economic theory with Chinese characteristics and also the main line running through the internal relations of socialist political economics with Chinese characteristics. A set of institutional frameworks to promote the sustained and healthy development of China's economy, which was led by the new development concept, was the realistic basis that allowed the new development concept to become the main content and line of systematic economic theory with Chinese characteristics.[37]

As a social science, economics had some basic ideological elements and categories. These basic ideological elements and categories constituted the basis for communication and dialogue among different cultures and social systems, and also provided a path for the pursuit of scientific universality. Therefore, in terms of basic assumptions, basic theoretical models, and the basic analytical tools of the market economy, scientifically, economics was characteristically general or universal.

14.2 Theory of Socialism with Chinese Characteristics and Socialist Political Economics with Chinese Characteristics

1. The Formation of the Theory of Socialism with Chinese Characteristics

On September 1, 1992, at the Twelfth National Congress of the Communist Party of China, Deng Xiaoping said in the opening speech, "Our modernization construction should proceed from China's actual situation. In both revolution and construction, we should learn from foreign experience. However, duplicating other countries' experiences and models will never succeed. We have learned much in this respect. Combining the universal truth of Marxism with the concrete reality of our country, taking our own road and building socialism with Chinese characteristics, are the basic conclusions drawn from our long-term historical experience."[38] This was the first time after the beginning of Reform and Opening Up that the CPC Central Committee plenary session clearly put forward the idea of "building socialism with Chinese characteristics." This idea was based on a deep understanding of the theory of scientific socialism, a profound understanding of the essence of socialism, a careful summary of China's historical experience, and a careful study of China's actual situation and development requirements.

In October 1984, the Third Plenary Session of the Twelfth Central Committee of the Communist Party of China adopted the Decision of the Central Committee of the Communist Party

---

36. Lin Yifu, "Thoughts on the Development and Innovation of China's Economic Theory," *Economic Research*, no. 5 (2017).

37. Gu Hailiang, "Introduction to Political Economics of Socialism with Chinese Characteristics," *Economist*, no. 3 (2019).

38. Deng Xiaoping, *Selected Works of Deng Xiaoping*, vol. 3 (People's Publishing House, 1993).

of China on the Reform of the Economic System. It was suggested that China should further implement the policy of invigorating the domestic economy and opening up to the outside world in accordance with the general requirements of combining the basic principles of Marxism with China's actual situation and building socialism with Chinese characteristics to accelerate economic system reform with cities as the focus, so as to contribute to the creation of a new situation of socialist modernization.[39] The Central Committee of the Communist Party of China held that it was the fundamental task of the economic system reform to further emancipate the mind, take its own path, establish a socialist economic system with Chinese characteristics, full of vigor and vitality, and promote the development of social productive forces, in accordance with the principle of combining the basic principles of Marxism with China's reality and the principle of correctly treating foreign experience.[40] The fundamental task of socialism was to develop social productive forces, that is, to further generate social wealth and constantly meet the people's growing material and cultural needs. In order to eliminate poverty in socialism, it was important not to regard poverty as socialism. In the process of reform, all the comrades in the party needed to grasp this basic viewpoint of Marxism and consider whether it was conducive to the development of social productive forces as the main criterion to test the success or failure of all reforms.[41]

Issued in October 1987, the title of the report of the Thirteenth National Congress of the Communist Party of China was "Advancing Along the Socialist Road with Chinese Characteristics." For the first time, socialism with Chinese characteristics was directly addressed as the report topic of the Party Congress. The report of the Thirteenth National Congress of the Communist Party of China had determined the primary stage of socialism and the basic line of building socialism with Chinese characteristics. The conclusion of the primary stage of socialism had two implications. First, Chinese society was already a socialist society. Second, China's socialist society was still in its infancy. It was important to proceed from this reality and not go beyond this stage. In the primary stage of socialism, the Party's basic line of building socialism with Chinese characteristics involved leading and uniting the people of all ethnic groups throughout the country, taking economic construction as the center, adhering to the four basic principles, adhering to Reform and Opening Up, self-reliance, and hard work, and striving to build China into a prosperous, strong, democratic, and civilized modern socialist country.[42] The socialist economy with Chinese characteristics was a planned commodity economy based on public ownership. The system of the socialist planned commodity economy was to be the internal unity of planning and market. The basic framework of the new system of the planned commodity

---

39. *Decision of the Central Committee of the Communist Party of China on the Reform of the Economic System* (People's Publishing House, 1984).

40. *Decision of the Central Committee of the Communist Party of China on the Reform of the Economic System* (People's Publishing House, 1984).

41. *Decision of the Central Committee of the Communist Party of China on the Reform of the Economic System* (People's Publishing House, 1984).

42. Zhao Ziyang, *Advancing Along the Socialist Road with Chinese Characteristics: Report on the Thirteenth National Congress of the Communist Party of China* (People's Publishing House, 1987).

economy was to invigorate enterprises owned by all the people in accordance with the principle of separation of ownership and management rights. It was important to promote the further development of horizontal economic union. China aimed to accelerate the establishment and cultivation of a socialist market system and gradually improve the macroeconomic regulation system with indirect management as the main factor. Based on the premise of public ownership as the main body, it was necessary to continue to develop the diversified ownership economy and adopt a variety of distribution methods and correct distribution policies, with distribution according to work as the main body. Socialism with Chinese characteristics needed to carry out political system reform, and the process of developing the socialist commodity economy needed to be a process of building socialist democratic politics. Without reform of the political system, reform of the economic system would not succeed. The purpose of the reform of the political and economic systems was to better develop social productive forces and give full play to the superiority of socialism under the leadership of the party and the socialist system.[43]

The Fourteenth National Congress of the Communist Party of China was held on October 12, 1992. The title of the report of the Fourteenth National Congress of the Communist Party of China was "Accelerating Reform, Opening Up, and Modernization and Striving for Greater Victory in the Cause of Socialism with Chinese Characteristics." The report of the Fourteenth National Congress of the Communist Party of China elevated the thought of socialism with Chinese characteristics into a theory and systematically summarized the main contents of the theory of building socialism with Chinese characteristics for the first time. It established the guiding position of Deng Xiaoping's theory of building socialism with Chinese characteristics throughout the Party.

On the path of socialist development, it was necessary to follow China's own path, rather than take books as dogma. China needed to avoid copying foreign models, instead taking the guidance and practice of Marxism as the only standard to test truth, emancipate the mind, seek truth from facts, respect the initiative of the masses, and build socialism with Chinese characteristics.

On the issue of the development stage of socialism, the scientific conclusion that China is still in the primary stage of socialism was drawn, stressing that this was a very long historical stage of at least a hundred years. All principles and policies should be formulated on the basis of this basic national condition, and they could not be divorced from reality and go beyond the stage.

On the basic task of socialism, the essence of socialism was to liberate and develop productive forces and eliminate exploitation and polarization for the ultimate common prosperity. It emphasized that the main contradiction of Chinese society at that stage was the contradiction between the people's growing material and cultural needs and the backward social production in China. It was important to put the development of productive forces in the primary position, take economic construction as the center, and promote all-round social progress. In the final analysis, it was crucial that the merits and demerits of the reform and various aspects of work be judged

---

43. Zhao Ziyang, *Advancing Along the Socialist Road with Chinese Characteristics: Report on the Thirteenth National Congress of the Communist Party of China* (People's Publishing House, 1987).

according to whether they were conducive to developing the productive forces of a socialist society, enhancing the comprehensive national strength of socialist countries, and improving the people's living standards. Science and technology were the primary productive forces. Economic construction had to rely on the progress of science and technology and the improvement of the quality of workers.

On the issue of the motivating force of socialist development, it was emphasized that reform was also a revolution, and it was the only way to liberate productive forces, and thus there was no room for ossification and stagnation. The goal of economic system reform was to establish and improve the socialist market economic system on the basis of adhering to and improving the basic economic system with socialist public ownership as the main body and multiple ownership economies developing together and with the distribution system with distribution according to work as the main body and various distribution modes coexisting. The goal of political system reform was to further expand socialist democracy, improve the socialist legal system, rule the country according to law, and build a socialist legal system with the main content of improving the system of the people's Congress and of multi-party cooperation and political consultation under the leadership of the Communist Party. To adapt to the economic and political reform and development, it was necessary to strive to improve the ideological and moral quality and the scientific and cultural quality of the whole nation and to build a socialist spiritual civilization with the goal of cultivating citizens with "ideals, morality, culture, and discipline."

On the external conditions of socialist construction, it was pointed out that peace and development were the two major themes in the world at that time. It was important to adhere to the independent foreign policy of peace and strive for a favorable international environment for China's modernization. It was emphasized that opening to the outside world was essential for reform and construction, and it was necessary to absorb and make use of all the achievements of advanced civilization created by all countries in the world, including developed capitalist countries, to develop socialism, as continued isolation could only lead to backwardness.

On the issue of political guarantees for socialist construction, it was important to adhere to the socialist path, to the people's democratic dictatorship, to the leadership of the Communist Party of China, and to Marxist Leninism and Mao Zedong Thought. These four basic principles were the foundation of China, a guarantee of the healthy development of Reform and Opening Up and modernization, and a means for obtaining new current content from Reform and Opening Up and modernization.

On the issue of strategic steps in socialist construction, it was proposed that modernization should be basically realized in three steps. In the process of modernization, it was important to seize the opportunity and strive for the emergence of several stages of rapid development and good efficiency and to step up every few years. Poverty was not socialism, and yet simultaneous prosperity was impossible. It was important to allow and encourage some regions and some people to prosper first, so as to drive more regions and people to steadily achieve common prosperity.

On the issue of the leadership and dependence of socialism, as the vanguard of the working class, the Communist Party was the leading core of the socialist cause. The Party needed to adapt to the needs of reform, opening up, and modernization, constantly improve and strengthen its leadership in all aspects of work, and improve and strengthen its own construction. The working style of the ruling party and the relationship between the party and the masses were issues concerning the survival of the party. It was necessary to rely on the broad masses of workers, peasants, and intellectuals, the unity of the people of all nationalities, and the broadest united front of all socialist workers, patriots who supported socialism, and patriots who supported the reunification of the motherland. The people's army under the leadership of the Communist Party was the defender of the socialist motherland and an important force in building socialism.

On the issue of the reunification of the motherland, the creative idea of "one country, two systems" was put forward. Under the premise of one China, the main body of the state adhered to the socialist system, while Hong Kong, Macao, and Taiwan would be allowed to maintain their original capitalist systems for a prolonged period, so as to promote the accomplishment of the great cause of peaceful reunification of the motherland in accordance with this principle.

There were many other ideas in the theory of building socialism with Chinese characteristics, which was to be enriched, perfected, and developed in the process of studying new situations and solving new problems. Under the guidance of the theory of building socialism with Chinese characteristics, the party formed the basic line of the primary stage of socialism, which included leading and uniting the people of all ethnic groups in the country, taking economic construction as the center, adhering to the four basic principles, and adhering to Reform and Opening Up, self-reliance, and hard work to build China into a prosperous, strong, democratic, and civilized socialist modern country. "One center, two basic points" was a concise summary of this line. In line with this thought, the Party formed a complete set of principles and policies covering the economy, politics, science and technology, education, culture, military affairs, and foreign affairs. This line and these principles and policies were to be enriched, improved, and developed in practice.

The theory of building socialism with Chinese characteristics gradually formed and developed under the historical conditions in which peace and development had become the theme of the times in the practice process of China's Reform and Opening Up and socialist modernization construction, on the basis of summing up the historical experience of China's socialist victories and setbacks and drawing on the historical experience of the rise and fall of socialism in other countries. It was the product of the combination of the basic principles of Marxist Leninism with the reality of contemporary China and the characteristics of the times, the inheritance and development of Mao Zedong Thought, the crystallization of the collective wisdom of the Party and the people, and the most precious spiritual wealth of the Communist Party of China and the Chinese people. Comrade Deng Xiaoping was the chief designer of China's socialist reform, opening up, and modernization. He respected practice, respected the masses, always paid attention to the interests and wishes of the overwhelming majority of the people, was good at summarizing the experience and creation of the masses, keenly grasped the pulse and opportunity of the development of the times, inherited from his predecessors, and broke through the old rules. He showed the great political courage to open up a new road of socialist construction and the great theoretical courage to open up a new realm of Marxism, making a historically great contribution to the establishment of the theory of constructing socialism with Chinese characteristics.

The experience of fourteen years of excellent practice concentrated on unswervingly adhering to the Party's basic line guided by the theory of building socialism with Chinese characteristics. This was the most reliable guarantee that China's business could withstand the test of risks and successfully achieve its goal.[44]

On November 14, 1993, the Third Plenary Session of the Fourteenth CPC Central Committee deliberated and passed the Decision of the CPC Central Committee on Several Issues Concerning the Establishment of a Socialist Market Economic System. The communique of the plenary session pointed out that under the guidance of Deng Xiaoping's theory of building socialism with Chinese characteristics, great changes had taken place in China's economic system after fifteen years of reform. China's Reform and Opening Up and modernization drive had entered a new stage of development. New steps had been taken in Reform and Opening Up, and it was important to now accelerate the process of establishing a socialist market economic system and realize the sustained, rapid, and healthy development of the national economy.[45]

2. Development of the Theory of Socialism with Chinese Characteristics

The Fifteenth National Congress of the Communist Party of China was held on September 12, 1997. On the basis of establishing the guiding position of Deng Xiaoping's theory of building socialism with Chinese characteristics throughout the party at the Fourteenth National Congress of the Communist Party of China, the Fifteenth National Congress further clarified the historical position and guiding significance of Deng Xiaoping Theory. Deng Xiaoping Theory was a new stage in the development of Marxism in China. Deng Xiaoping Theory adhered to emancipating the mind, seeking truth from facts, inheriting from China's predecessors on the basis of new practice, breaking through the old rules, and opening up a new realm of Marxism. Similarly, it adhered to the basic achievements of the theory and practice of scientific socialism, grasped the fundamental problem of "what is socialism and how to build it," profoundly revealed the essence of socialism, and raised the understanding of socialism to a new scientific level. Deng Xiaoping Theory persisted in observing the world with a broad vision of Marxism and offered a new scientific evaluation of the characteristics of the times and the overall international situation.

Generally speaking, Deng Xiaoping Theory constituted a new scientific system for the construction of socialism with Chinese characteristics. Under the historical conditions in which peace and development had become the theme of the times, and in the practice of China's Reform and Opening Up and modernization, it gradually formed and developed on the basis of summing

---

44. Jiang Zemin, *Accelerating Reform, Opening Up, and Modernization and Striving for Greater Victory in the Cause of Socialism with Chinese Characteristics: Report on the Fourteenth Plenary Session National Congress of the Communist Party of China* (People's Publishing House, 1992).

45. Refer to the *Communique of the Third Plenary Session of the Fourteenth Central Committee of the Communist Party of China* (November 14, 1993).

up the historical experience of China's socialist victories and setbacks and learning from the success or failure of other socialist countries. For the first time, it systematically and preliminarily answered a series of basic questions concerning the development path, stage, fundamental task, motivating force, external conditions, political guarantees, strategic steps, leadership, and reliability of the Party and the reunification of the motherland, guiding the CPC to formulate the basic line in the primary stage of socialism. It was a relatively complete scientific system covering the fields of philosophy, political economics, scientific socialism, finance, politics, science and technology, education, culture, nationality, military, diplomacy, the united front, and Party building, and it was a scientific system that needed to be further enriched and developed in all aspects.[46]

The Fifteenth National Congress of the Communist Party of China established the basic line and program for the primary stage of socialism, which was to unify economic construction as the center and the four basic principles and Reform and Opening Up into the great practice of building socialism with Chinese characteristics. According to Deng Xiaoping Theory and the basic line of the primary stage of socialism, centering on the goal of building a prosperous, democratic, and civilized modern socialist country, it was important to clarify the economy, politics, and culture of socialism with Chinese characteristics in the primary stage of socialism and form the basic program for the primary stage of socialism.

To build a socialist economy with Chinese characteristics was to develop the market economy under socialist conditions and constantly liberate and develop productive forces. It was important to adhere to and improve the basic economic system with socialist public ownership as the main body and the common development of various ownership economies, and to adhere to and improve the socialist market economic system so that the market could play a fundamental role in the allocation of resources under the state's macro-control. It was likewise important to adhere to and improve the various distribution methods with distribution according to work as the main body, allowing some regions and some people to prosper first, so as to drive and promote the development of the socialist market economy. Those who prospered first had to help those who prospered later to gradually move toward common prosperity, adhere to and improve opening up, and actively participate in international economic cooperation and competition. It was necessary to ensure the sustained, rapid, and healthy development of the national economy and the people's sharing of the fruits of that economic prosperity.

The construction of socialist politics with Chinese characteristics aimed to rule the country according to law and develop socialist democracy under the leadership of the Communist Party of China and on the basis of the people being masters of the country. Therefore, it was imperative that China adhere to and improve the people's democratic dictatorship led by the working class and based on the alliance of workers and peasants and adhere to and improve the system of the

---

46. Jiang Zemin, *Holding High the Great Banner of Deng Xiaoping Theory and Pushing the Cause of Building Socialism with Chinese Characteristics Into the 21st Century: Report on the Fifteenth National Congress of the Communist Party of China* (People's Publishing House, 1997).

People's Congress, the system of multi-party cooperation, and political consultation under the leadership of the Communist Party, as well as the system of regional national autonomy. It was important to develop democracy, improve the legal system, and build a socialist country ruled by law so as to build a lively, harmonious political environment with social stability, a clean, efficient government, and a united people of all ethnic groups across the country.

To build a socialist culture with Chinese characteristics was to develop a national, scientific, and popular socialist culture oriented toward modernization, the world, and the future, with Marxism as the guidance and the cultivation of citizens with ideals, morality, culture, and discipline. It was necessary to persist in arming the entire party with Deng Xiaoping Theory and educate the people and strive to improve the ideological and moral quality of the whole nation and the level of education, science, and culture. It was important to adhere to the direction of serving the people and socialism and the principle of letting a hundred flowers bloom and a hundred schools of thought contend, focusing on construction and prosperity of learning and literature and art. A socialist spiritual civilization based on China's reality needed to be built, inheriting the excellent traditions of history and culture and absorbing the beneficial achievements of foreign cultures.

These economic, political, and cultural objectives and policies for building socialism with Chinese characteristics were organically unified and inseparable, and they constituted the Party's basic program in the primary stage of socialism.[47]

The Sixteenth National Congress of the Communist Party of China proposed that an affluent society in all aspects be built and a new situation in the cause of socialism with Chinese characteristics be created. The goal of building an affluent society in all aspects meant, on the basis of optimizing the structure and improving efficiency, the gross domestic product (GDP) would quadruple by 2020 compared with that in 2000, and the comprehensive national strength and international competitiveness would be significantly enhanced. Industrialization would be basically realized and a more open, more dynamic, sound socialist market economic system would be built. The proportion of urban population would increase by a large margin, and the trend of widening differences between workers and peasants, between urban and rural areas, and between regions would be gradually reversed. The social security system would be relatively sound, social employment would be sufficient, family property would generally increase, and the people would live a more prosperous life. Socialist democracy would be improved, the socialist legal system more complete, the basic strategy of governing the country according to law fully implemented, and the people's political, economic, and cultural rights and interests earnestly respected and protected. Democracy at the grassroots level would be improved, with a good social order in which the people lived and worked in peace and contentment. The ideological and moral quality, scientific and cultural quality, and health quality of the entire nation would significantly improve,

---

47. Jiang Zemin, *Holding High the Great Banner of Deng Xiaoping Theory and Pushing the Cause of Building Socialism with Chinese Characteristics Into the 21st Century: Report on the Fifteenth National Congress of the Communist Party of China* (People's Publishing House, 1997).

forming a relatively complete modern national education system, a scientific and technological and cultural innovation system, and a national fitness, medical, and health system. The people would enjoy the opportunity to receive a good education, popularizing high school education and eliminating illiteracy. It was necessary to form a learning society in which all people learned and studied throughout their lives and the all-round development of humans was promoted. The ability of sustainable development was continuously enhanced, the ecological environment improved, the efficiency of resource utilization significantly improved, the harmony between humans and nature promoted, and the overall society put on the path of civilized development with advanced production, a rich life, and a good ecology.[48]

The goal of building an affluent society in all aspects, established at the Sixteenth National Congress of the Communist Party of China, was the goal of the all-round economic, political, and cultural development of socialism with Chinese characteristics, accelerating modernization, and ensuring concrete, practical development of the basic program for the primary stage of socialism, as proposed by the Fifteenth National Congress of the Communist Party of China.

The Seventeenth National Congress of the Communist Party of China systematically summarized the path and the theoretical system of socialism with Chinese characteristics. The path of socialism with Chinese characteristics meant, under the leadership of the Communist Party of China and based on the basic national conditions, centering on economic construction, adhering to the four basic principles, adhering to Reform and Opening Up, liberating and developing social productive forces, consolidating and improving the socialist system, and building a socialist market economy, socialist democratic politics, advanced socialist culture, and a harmonious socialist society. It was important to build a prosperous, strong, democratic, civilized, and harmonious modern socialist country. The reason the path of socialism with Chinese characteristics was completely correct and could lead China's development and progress lay in that it not only adhered to the basic principles of scientific socialism, but also endowed it with distinctive Chinese characteristics according to China's reality and the characteristics of the times. In contemporary China, to adhere to the road of socialism with Chinese characteristics was to truly adhere to socialism.

The theoretical system of socialism with Chinese characteristics was a scientific theoretical system including Deng Xiaoping Theory, the important thought of the Three Represents, and the scientific outlook on development. This theoretical system adhered to and developed Marxist Leninism and Mao Zedong Thought and condensed the wisdom and painstaking efforts of several generations of Chinese Communists to lead the people in unremitting exploration and practice. It was the latest achievement of the localization of Marxism in China, the most valuable political and spiritual wealth of the party, and the common ideological basis for the unity and struggle of the people of all ethnic groups in China. The theoretical system of socialism with

---

48. Jiang Zemin, *Building a Well-off Society in All Aspects and Creating a New Situation in the Cause of Socialism with Chinese Characteristics: Report on the Sixteenth National Congress of the Communist Party of China* (People's Publishing House, 2002).

Chinese characteristics was a continuously developing and open theoretical system. The practice of nearly 160 years since *The Communist Manifesto* was published had proven that only when Marxism was combined with the national conditions, progressing with the development of the times, and sharing a common destiny with the people could it radiate its strong vitality, creativity, and appeal. In contemporary China, to adhere to the theoretical system of socialism with Chinese characteristics was to truly adhere to Marxism.

To continue to build a prosperous society in all aspects and develop socialism with Chinese characteristics in the new stage of development, it was necessary to adhere to Deng Xiaoping Theory and the important theory of the Three Represents and to thoroughly implement the scientific outlook on development.

The scientific outlook on development was the inheritance and development of the important thought on development from the three generations of the central leading groups of the party, the concentrated embodiment of the world outlook and methodology of Marxism on development, and a scientific theory that was in the same line as Marxist Leninism, Mao Zedong Thought, Deng Xiaoping Theory, and the important theory of the Three Represents, and it was the development of China's economy and society. The important guiding principle was a major strategic thought that had to be adhered to and carried out in the development of socialism with Chinese characteristics.

The scientific outlook on development was based on the basic national conditions of the primary stage of socialism. It summarized China's development practice, drew lessons from foreign development experience, and adapted to the new development requirements. In the scientific concept of development, the key idea was development, the core was people-oriented, the basic requirement was that it be comprehensive, coordinated, and sustainable, and the fundamental method involved overall consideration. According to the scientific outlook on development, development should be regarded as the first priority of the Party in governing and rejuvenating the country, people-oriented, comprehensive, coordinated, and sustainable development, with overall planning and consideration.[49] On the basis of the goal of building a prosperous society in all aspects established by the Sixteenth National Congress of the Communist Party of China, the Seventeenth National Congress of the Communist Party of China put forward new, higher requirements for the development of socialism with Chinese characteristics, including enhancing the coordination of development and striving to achieve sound, rapid economic development. It was important to expand socialist democracy and better protect people's rights and interests and social equality and justice. Strengthening cultural construction and significantly improving the quality of civilization throughout the nation were also core concerns. It was necessary to accelerate the development of social undertakings and improve people's living standards in all aspects. To build an ecological civilization, it was necessary to basically form an industrial structure, growth

---

49. Hu Jintao, *Holding High the Great Banner of Socialism with Chinese Characteristics and Striving for the New Victory of Building a Moderately Prosperous Society in All Aspects: Report on the Seventeenth National Congress of the Communist Party of China* (People's Publishing House, 2007).

mode, and consumption mode that could save energy and resources and protect the ecological environment.[50]

The Eighteenth CPC National Congress further developed and established the path of socialism with Chinese characteristics, the theoretical system of socialism with Chinese characteristics, and the socialist system with Chinese characteristics. The road of socialism with Chinese characteristics included, under the leadership of the Communist Party of China and based on the basic national conditions, centering on economic construction, adhering to the four basic principles, adhering to Reform and Opening Up, liberating and developing social productive forces, building a socialist market economy, socialist democratic politics, an advanced socialist culture, a harmonious socialist society, a socialist ecological civilization, and promoting the overall progress of humans. It was important to gradually realize the common prosperity of all the people and build a prosperous, strong, democratic, civilized, and harmonious modern socialist country. The theoretical system of socialism with Chinese characteristics was a scientific theoretical system including Deng Xiaoping Theory, the important theory of the Three Represents, and the scientific outlook on development. It was the adherence to and development of Marxism, Leninism, and Mao Zedong Thought. The socialist system with Chinese characteristics was the fundamental political system of the People's Congress system, the basic political systems of multi-party cooperation and political consultation under the leadership of the Communist Party of China, the regional ethnic autonomy system, the grassroots people's autonomy system, the socialist legal system with Chinese characteristics, the basic economic system with public ownership as the main body, the common development of various ownership economies, and the economic, political, cultural, and social systems based on all these systems. The road of socialism with Chinese characteristics was the way to realize this goal, the theoretical system of socialism with Chinese characteristics was the guide to action, and the system of socialism with Chinese characteristics was the fundamental guarantee. The three were unified in the great practice of socialism with Chinese characteristics. The general basis for building socialism with Chinese characteristics was the primary stage of socialism, the general layout was Five in One, and the general task was to realize socialist modernization and the great rejuvenation of the Chinese nation. When the People's Republic of China was founded a century earlier, it strove to build a strong, prosperous, democratic, civilized, harmonious modern socialist country. The entire party needed to be firmly confident in its path, theory, and system.[51]

The Nineteenth National Congress of the Communist Party of China announced that after long-term effort, socialism with Chinese characteristics had entered a new era, which was a new historical orientation in China's development. The Nineteenth National Congress of the

---

50. Hu Jintao, *Holding High the Great Banner of Socialism with Chinese Characteristics and Striving for the New Victory of Building a Moderately Prosperous Society in All Aspects: Report on the Seventeenth National Congress of the Communist Party of China* (People's Publishing House, 2007).

51. Hu Jintao, *Unswervingly Advancing Along the Road of Socialism with Chinese Characteristics and Striving for Building a Moderately Prosperous Society in All Aspects: Report on the Eighteenth National Congress of the Communist Party of China* (People's Publishing House, 2012).

Communist Party of China established the basic strategy and strategic arrangement of socialism with Chinese characteristics in the new era.

The main task of socialism with Chinese characteristics in the new era was to realize socialist modernization and the great rejuvenation of the Chinese nation. On the basis of building a prosperous society in all aspects, it was important to take two steps to build a strong, prosperous, democratic, civilized, harmonious, and beautiful modern socialist country by the middle of the century and make it clear that the main social contradiction in the new era was that between the people's growing needs for a better life and the unbalanced, inadequate development. It was important to adhere to people-centered development, constantly promote the all-round development of the people and their common prosperity, and make it clear that the overall layout of the cause of socialism with Chinese characteristics was "five in one" and the strategic layout was "four comprehensives," highlighting confidence in the path, theory, system, and culture. It was clear that the overall goal of comprehensively deepening the reform was to improve and develop the socialist system with Chinese characteristics and promote the modernization of the national governance system and governance capacity, and that the overall goal of comprehensively promoting the rule of law was to build a socialist legal system with Chinese characteristics and a socialist country ruled by law. The Party's goal of building a strong army in the new era was to build a competent, disciplined army following the Party's command, i.e., a first-tier army. It was important to make it clear that diplomacy with Chinese characteristics should promote the construction of a new type of international relations and promote the construction of a community of shared destiny for humankind, that the most essential feature of socialism with Chinese characteristics was the leadership of the Communist Party of China, and that the greatest advantage of the socialist system with Chinese characteristics was the leadership of the Communist Party of China, which was the highest political leadership. It put forward the general requirements of party building in the new era and highlighted the important position of political construction in the Party's construction. The thought of socialism with Chinese characteristics in the new era was the inheritance and development of Marxism, Leninism, Mao Zedong Thought, Deng Xiaoping Theory, the important theory of the Three Represents, and the scientific outlook on development. It was the latest achievement of the localization of Marxism in China and the crystallization of the practical experience and collective wisdom of the party and the people.[52]

There were fourteen basic strategies for upholding and developing socialism with Chinese characteristics in the new era, which involved adhering to the Party's leadership in all work, to ensuring that people were the center, to the comprehensive deepening of reform, to the new development concept, to the people as masters of the country, to the comprehensive rule of law, to the socialist core value system, to the guarantee and improvement of people's livelihoods in development, to the harmonious coexistence of man and nature, to the overall national security

---

52. Xi Jinping, *Winning the Victory in Building a Moderately Prosperous Society in All Respects and Socialism with Chinese Characteristics in the New Era: Report on the Nineteenth National Congress of the Communist Party of China* (People's Publishing House, 2017).

concept, to the party's absolute leadership over the people's army, to "one country, two systems," to promoting the reunification of the motherland, persistently promoting the construction of a community with a shared future for mankind, and persistently, comprehensively, and strictly administering the Party.[53]

The strategic arrangement for the development of socialism with Chinese characteristics in the new era was to build a prosperous society with a more developed economy, more sound democracy, more advanced science and education, more prosperous culture, more harmonious society, and a more affluent life for the people on the basis of the overall affluent level of the general public in the country. By the centennial of the founding of the People's Republic of China, modernization would be basically realized and China would be built into a modern socialist country. Comprehensive analysis of the international and domestic situation and China's development conditions suggested that the development could be divided into two stages from 2020 to the middle of the 21st century. In the first stage, from 2020 to 2035, on the basis of building a moderately prosperous society in all respects, China would strive for another fifteen years to basically realize socialist modernization. In the second stage, from 2035 to the middle of the 21st century, on the basis of basically realizing modernization, China would strive for another fifteen years to build itself into a strong, prosperous, democratic, civilized, harmonious, and beautiful modern socialist country.[54]

3. The Relationship Between the Theory of Socialism with Chinese Characteristics and the Political Economics of Socialism with Chinese Characteristics

The concept and theory of socialism with Chinese characteristics, especially in the new era, included the leadership of the Party, taking the people as the center, comprehensively deepening reform, the new development concept, comprehensively ruling the country according to law, the socialist core value system, improving people's livelihood, harmonious development, the concept of overall national security, the Party's absolute leadership over the people's army, promoting the reunification of the motherland, building a community of a shared future for humankind, and strict management of the Party. The political economics of socialism with Chinese characteristics was to be the systematization, disciplinarization, and scientification of the theoretical thought on economic construction and development in the theory of socialism with Chinese characteristics, especially in the new era. It was a professional theoretical discipline system of the theory of socialism with Chinese characteristics in the new era. The idea of socialism with Chinese characteristics in the new era had rich connotations. The overall strategic layout of the cause of socialism with

---

53. Xi Jinping, *Winning the Victory in Building a Moderately Prosperous Society in All Respects and Socialism with Chinese Characteristics in the New Era: Report on the Nineteenth National Congress of the Communist Party of China* (People's Publishing House, 2017).

54. Xi Jinping, *Winning the Victory in Building a Moderately Prosperous Society in All Respects and Socialism with Chinese Characteristics in the New Era: Report on the Nineteenth National Congress of the Communist Party of China* (People's Publishing House, 2017).

Chinese characteristics and the basic strategy and strategic arrangement for upholding and developing socialism with Chinese characteristics in the new era were comprehensive, but the main line of its general task and goal was development, from building a moderately prosperous society in all aspects to basically realizing modernization, and then to building a powerful socialist country in all aspects. Therefore, the political economics of socialism with Chinese characteristics was to be an important part of the theoretical and professional discipline system of the concept and theory of socialism with Chinese characteristics in the new era. According to the report of the Nineteenth National Congress of the Communist Party of China, in order to realize the "two centenary" goals, realize the Chinese dream of great rejuvenation of the Chinese nation, and constantly improve people's living standards, it was necessary to unswervingly take development as the first priority of the Party's ruling and rejuvenating the country, adhere to the liberation and development of social productive forces, adhere to the direction of socialist market economic reform, and promote sustained, healthy economic development.[55] This was the connotation of the combination of the theory and practice of socialist political economics with Chinese characteristics. The development of socialism with Chinese characteristics in the new era was in the stage of China's economic development from high-speed development to high-quality development, and it was in the crucial period of transforming the development mode, optimizing the economic structure, and transforming the driving force of growth. To cross this threshold, it was necessary to implement the new concept of development and build a modern economic system.

The path or practical content of implementing the new development concept and building a modern economic system was to deepen the supply side structural reform, accelerate the construction of an innovative country, implement the rural revitalization strategy and the regional coordinated development strategy, accelerate the improvement of the socialist market economic system, and promote the formation of a new pattern of comprehensive opening up. The construction of a modern economic system embodied the essential requirement of emancipating and developing social productive forces. Through policy design and practical plan, the aim was to achieve higher quality, more efficiency, more fairness, and more sustainable development. It was also the converging point between theory and practice of the political economics of socialism with Chinese characteristics, the theory of socialism with Chinese characteristics, and the thought of socialism with Chinese characteristics in the new era. It was observed that "the modern economic system is an organic whole composed of the interrelations and internal relations among various links, levels, and fields of social activities."[56] It provided a disciplinary framework combining theory and practice for socialist political economics with Chinese characteristics.

---

55. Xi Jinping, *Wining the Victory in Building a Moderately Prosperous Society in All Respects and Socialism with Chinese Characteristics in the New Era: Report on the Nineteenth National Congress of the Communist Party of China* (People's Publishing House, 2017).

56. Xi Jinping, "Profoundly Understanding the Importance of Building a Modern Economic System, and Promoting China's Economic Development to a New Level," *People's Daily*, February 1, 2018.

14.3 The Guidance of Marxist Economics and the Reference of Western Economics

1. Adhering to and Developing Marxist Economics

At the beginning of the 21st century, finding ways to uphold and develop Marxism in the new milieu was an important topic in the study of Marxist economics in China. In the teaching and research process of theoretical economics, some scholars worried about the rising influence of Western economics and the weakening of the guilding position of the Marxist economics. These theorists raised this issue to the ideological level in the notion of "two interrelated tendentious problems in the field of ideology," one of which was two types of dogmatism, and the other, left and right leaning tendencies. The two wrong kinds of dogmatism were superstitious and empty talk about Marxism, rather than developing Marxism with the times, and superstitious worship of Western developed countries' ideological theories, reflecting the mainstream ideology of the bourgeoisie. The first dogmatism has persisted even until today, but it is not the main issue at present, and its influence is declining. The second kind of dogmatism, namely Western dogmatism, was on the rise in the field of ideology and economic society. Here, I will expound the relationship between Marxist political economics and Western economics, the correct treatment of Western economic theory and neo-liberal economics, the question of whether economic education is ideological education or analytical tool education, the internationalization and localization of economics, and what theory should be taken as the guidance for China's economic reform and development.[57]

After this section was published as an article, it caused certain repercussions in theoretical circles. Around the problems and views raised in the article, some media made relevant reports and published several articles in response. Some universities, scientific research institutions, and societies held seminars to discuss the issue. Looking at some relevant materials from the second half of 2005 to 2006, some scholars expressed their views on adhering to the guiding position of Marxist economics. They believed that only the basic economic theory of Marxism could illuminate its essence from the movement of economic phenomena and analyze some important characteristics of the process of social and economic development. Since China's economic construction and Reform and Opening Up were socialist economic construction, reform, and opening up, only under the guidance of the basic theory of Marxism could scientific conclusions be drawn. Some theorists adhered to the guiding position and development of Marxist economics. They believed that Marxist economics should keep pace with the times, correctly understand and handle the relationship between Marxism's persistence, development, inheritance, and innovation, and unify the adherence and development of Marxism with the practice of building socialism with Chinese characteristics.

---

57. Liu Guoguang, "Some Issues in Economics Teaching and Research," *Economic Research*, no. 10 (2005).

In the discussion, some scholars put forward specific opinions. Adhering to the guiding position of Marxist economics was not a simple quantitative concept, but instead aimed to emphasize its basic position, views, and methods, as well as its position and role in the teaching and research of economics. As for the division of "mainstream economics" and "non-mainstream economics," it was thought to be very difficult to distinguish between the two in China at this stage, because the standard was not clear. I believe that this was just popular terminology for economists who had returned from overseas studies in the previous twenty years, as their academic views were very different. They were not all bourgeois neo-liberalists, and definitely not "anti-Marxist economists." With regard to the tendency of China's current economic circles, I believe that it was "leftist" to regard Reform and Opening Up as the introduction and development of capitalism, and that the main danger of peaceful evolution came from the economic field. With regard to the meaning of socialist market economy and "market-oriented reform," I have pointed out that Deng Xiaoping made it very clear that the concept of the socialist market economy was not that the market economy was categorized as "socialism," but that the market economic system could be implemented under the socialist system. Therefore, the so-called "market-oriented reform" only referred to the transformation from a planned economic system to a market economic system. The problem was not a question of "turning public into private affairs." With regard to the issue of "efficiency first and fairness in consideration," I believe that "fairness" was only "low-level equalitarianism" that failed to highlight "efficiency first." It was precisely because of the adherence to "efficiency priority" that China's economy greatly developed and reached a new level. Therefore, although the income gap was expanded, it was greatly improved, and the middle-income class was expanding.[58]

The topic of adhering to Marxist economics originated from some phenomena in economic research, not against any different opinions or objections. From these phenomena, the proposer pointed out that the guiding position of Marxist economics had been shaken, and the influence of Western economics, especially Western neo-liberal economics, was expanding day by day. However, in the media, there were no comments against adhering to Marxist economics, and there were no commentators standing on the opposite side of adhering to Marxist economics to participate in the debate. In addition, the language used in this discussion had a strong political and ideological color, using phrases such as "who is in charge of the leadership of economic circles, including the economics departments and economic research institutions in universities," and, "where is China going?" It was noted that "this was a clarion call for fighting against neo-liberalism and defending the dominant position of Marxism in economics." Further, "The key is to distinguish the two views of reform, and to determine whether to hold or deny the four basic principles was the standard to distinguish the two views of reform. In doing so, it was not possible to deceive people with the banner of reform in the bourgeois liberalization reform view" and "in the public opinion, we should tear open the gap in neo-liberalism that encircles us on the ideological and theoretical front." This was not an academic debate, but a debate between

---

58. He Liancheng, "Where Does China's Economics Go?" *Economics Trends*, no. 9 (2006).

right and wrong in the ideological and political fields. Therefore, this discussion was basically a statement of a point of view, not a debate on different views.

China's economic and ideological circles adhered to the link between Marxism and the development of Marxism and believed that only by developing Marxism was it possible to better adhere to it and develop it on that premise. A common view was that Marxism was a science, not a fixed dogma, and the scientific system was open and developing. The vitality of Marxism lay in the continuous innovation and development of later generations according to practice. Under the new historical conditions, in order to develop Marxism, it was necessary to adhere to the basic principles and methods of Marxism, master the theoretical system and essence of Marxism as a whole from the original classics, and avoid taking a pragmatic and out of context attitude toward Marxism. It was important to regard Marxism as a think tank and a method system.

On the path of developing Marxist economics, the direction of development needed to be the application and guidance of the basic principles of Marxist economics in contemporary practice. According to many viewpoints, traditional Marxist economics held that the decentralized decision-making of economic subjects in the market economy would lead to a capitalist economic crisis. There was obviously a contradiction between the negative evaluation of the market economy and the requirements of the times for the development of the socialist market economy. Researchers of traditional Marxist economics only discussed the contradictory movement of productivity and production relations at the abstract level, but in order to develop Marxist political economics, it was necessary to study the new changes of contemporary capitalist labor relations from the perspective of how specific productive forces change the specific labor process.

In August 2008, the theme of the Fourteenth Symposium of the China *Das Kapital* Research Association was Marxist Economics and Contemporary China. At the meeting, many views were expressed on the innovation and development of Marxist economics. There were two problems that needed to be solved in the development of contemporary Marxist economics: putting things back in order, rectifying the source, and inheriting the scientific tradition of Marxist economics; and realizing the modern innovation of Marxist economics. In order to realize the modern innovation of Marxist economics, it was necessary to put forward new viewpoints on the new characteristics of the modern capitalist production mode, realize the major innovation of socialist economic theory, and construct a new system of Marxist economics. On May 4, 2018, Xi Jinping delivered a speech at the 200th anniversary commemorative celebration of Marx's birthday. He pointed out that "Marxist doctrine is a constantly developing and open theory and always stands at the forefront of the times. Marx repeatedly warned that Marxist theory is not a dogma, but a guide to action, and it should develop with the change of practice. A history of the development of Marxism is the history that Marx, Engels, and their successors have developed according to the times, practice, and understanding. It is a history that constantly absorbs all the excellent ideological and cultural achievements in human history and enriches their own history. Therefore, Marxism can always maintain its wonderful youth, constantly explore the new issues raised by the development of the times, and respond to the new challenges faced by human society." He continued, "We should adhere to the use of Marxism to observe, interpret, and lead the times, promote the development of Marxism with rich, fresh contemporary Chinese practice, absorb all the excellent achievements of civilization that have been created by humankind with a broad vision, adhere to the principle of keeping the right out of the new and constantly surpass ourselves in reform, learn from others' strong points in opening up, constantly improve ourselves, and constantly deepen the ruling law of the Communist Party. The understanding of the law of socialist construction and the law of human social development will constantly open up new realms of Marxism in contemporary China and Marxism in the 21st century."[59]

At the International Symposium on *Das Kapital* and its Contemporary Value, held in November 2007, the basic point of view was that although *Das Kapital* was a topic drawn from the capitalist mode of production and its laws, it revealed many universal laws of the market economy, so it was an important foundation of socialist market economic theory. In the practice of socialist economic development and reform, further enriching and developing Marxist institutional economic thought and theory was a basic task in the construction of contemporary Marxist institutional economics.[60]

The 150th anniversary of the publication of the first volume of *Das Kapital* was in 2017. That year theoretical circles launched a heated discussion on the contemporary value of *Das Kapital*. It was generally believed that whether it was to understand modern capitalism or to build modern socialism, the basic principles of Marxist economics expounded in *Das Kapital* published more than a century earlier still held important theoretical value and practical guiding significance for contemporary times. Although a series of great changes had taken place in the world in the 150 years since the publication of *Das Kapital*, it was still important to follow the basic principles and laws revealed in it in order to better understand capitalism and its development in contemporary times.

By the 21st century, the development of contemporary capitalism presented many new characteristics. The development of capitalism had fallen into a new predicament, which led to many global problems. The materialist dialectics used in the analysis of capitalist relations of production in *Das Kapital* were applicable to promoting the economic construction of socialism with Chinese characteristics in the new era and the construction of the theoretical system of socialist political economics with Chinese characteristics. It was an important guideline for the construction of socialism with Chinese characteristics under the new historical conditions.[61] Some

---

59. Xi Jinping, "Speech at the 200th Anniversary Commemorative Meeting of Marx's Birthday," *People's Daily*, May 5, 2018.

60. Tang Juelan and Liu Zhiguang, "A Review of the International Symposium on Capital and its Contemporary Value," *Economics Trends*, no. 12 (2007).

61. Zhang Xu, "Contemporary Value of *Das Kapital*," *Marxist Studies*, no. 10 (2017); Wei Xinghua and Tian Chaowei, "The Guiding Significance of *Das Kapital* to Socialism with Chinese Characteristics," *Journal of the Party School of Fujian Provincial Committee of the Communist Party of China*, no. 7 (2017); He Yuanfeng and Li Xiangju, "The Practical Significance and Important Value of *Das Kapital* in Contemporary China," *Gansu Social Sciences*, no. 1 (2014).

scholars discussed the guiding significance of the great theoretical contribution of *Das Kapital* to China's socialist cause. For example, Marx's theory of ownership could be understood from ten aspects: clarifying the key to socialist revolution and construction through understanding the important position and role of ownership, understanding the basis and nature of capitalist production relations from the role of ownership in the process of surplus value production, correctly understanding the predictions of the future society, and establishing and improving the basic experience of the primary stage of the socialist economic system, studying the systematic analysis of the internal property rights structure of ownership and exploring the ways and forms of public ownership reform, correctly understanding the discussion of joint stock companies and seeing clearly the transition form of capitalist private ownership, understanding the relationship between ownership and commodity exchange and improving the socialist market economy with Chinese characteristics, recognizing the decisive role of ownership in distribution and dealing with the initial stage of socialism, understanding the relationship between ownership and social contradictions and correctly handling the main social contradictions and their changes in the primary stage of socialism, and taking the ownership theory of *Das Kapital* as the basis for analyzing the social, political, and economic relations, in order to better understand the basic characteristics of socialism with Chinese characteristics. Under the guidance of the Marxist theory of ownership, the Chinese people attached great importance to the role of ownership. After gaining power, they immediately carried out land reform, followed by the socialist transformation of ownership, and they established socialist ownership by all the people and collective ownership by laborers. For socialist countries, a correct understanding of the important position and decisive role of ownership and upholding and improving the public ownership of the means of production were the primary conditions related to economic development, stable political power, and people's happiness and well-being.[62] Based on the bibliometric analysis of material in Chinese journals from 2011 to 2017, a total of 2,301 papers with the theme of *Das Kapital* were published, and the number of relevant papers published each year was on the rise. However, there were still some problems in the study of *Das Kapital*, such as imperfect tiers, a relatively one-dimensional perspective, and weak empirical research.[63]

After the Eighteenth National Congress of the Communist Party of China, academic discussion on socialist political economics with Chinese characteristics gradually deepened, and there was heated discussion and in-depth study on *Das Kapital* and the construction of socialist political economics with Chinese characteristics. The basic point of view was that *Das Kapital* could provide guidance and reference for the construction of socialist political economics with Chinese characteristics, but it was important to remain rooted in Chinese practice and innovate

---

62. Wu Xuangong, "The Important Guiding Significance of the Ownership Theory of *Das Kapital* to the Socialist Cause," *Economist*, no. 11 (2017).

63. Wang Jun and Li Ping, "The Current Situation, Characteristics and Prospects of *Das Kapital* Research," *Western China*, no. 1 (2019).

on the basis of reference. *Das Kapital* provided a fundamental position for the construction of and a fundamental methodology for the construction of socialist political economics with Chinese characteristics.[64]

The system of socialist political economics with Chinese characteristics needed to be guided by the theory and the method of Marx's *Das Kapital*, especially the spirit of keeping pace with the times in its creation. Only by staying rooted in the reality of socialist economic relations with Chinese characteristics was it possible to establish a theoretical system.[65] The discourse system of socialist political economics with Chinese characteristics had to be based on the Marxist economic paradigm provided by *Das Kapital*, including the systematic economics category established in it.[66] The system structure of *Das Kapital* could provide an important reference for the construction of the theoretical system of socialist political economics with Chinese characteristics, which focused on innovation and could not blindly copy others. It was important to build a structure on the basis of inheriting Marxism, drawing lessons from the achievements of human civilization, especially on the basis of summarizing China's practical experience and theoretical progress.[67] The enlightenment of *Das Kapital* to the construction of socialist political economics with Chinese characteristics was that the establishment of socialist political economics with Chinese characteristics needed to have a clear goal and a clear logical point of study. At the same time, it had to not only be based on reality, but also surpass it, starting from the practice of the contemporary Chinese economy, but not limited to the issues of contemporary socialist political economics with Chinese characteristics. Rather, it needed to foresee the future trend of China's economic development.[68] Some held to the modern significance of Marx's competition theory. According to Marx's competition theory, the development and perfection of the market competition mechanism was an important guarantee for the law of value to play its role. Meanwhile, different competition systems and modes had different influences on capital accumulation, technological progress, and macroeconomic performance, which had important guiding significance for the construction of China's modern economic system.[69]

Adhering to and developing Marxist economics had two levels of theoretical construction. One was to adhere to the guiding position of Marxism, and the other was to develop Marxism and its localization. Adhering to the guidance of Marxism was the fundamental sign that contemporary

---

64. Pang Jinju, "*Das Kapital* and Socialist Political Economics with Chinese Characteristics," *Nankai Academic Journal (Philosophy and Social Edition)*, no. 4 (2017).

65. Gu Hailiang, "*Das Kapital* and Socialist Political Economics with Chinese Characteristics," *Political Economics Review*, no. 3 (2017).

66. Hong Yinxing, "*Das Kapital* and Discourse System of Socialist Economics with Chinese Characteristics," *Economist*, no. 1 (2016).

67. Pang Jinju, "The Relationship Between the System Structure of *Das Kapital* and the Political Economics of Socialism with Chinese Characteristics," *Political Economics Review*, no. 3 (2017).

68. Wang Chaoke, "The Enlightenment of *Das Kapital* on the Construction of Socialist Political Economics with Chinese Characteristics," *Political Economics Review*, no. 3 (2017).

69. Zhao Feng and Duan Yuchen, "Marx's Competition Theory and its Modern Significance," *Economist*, no. 3 (2019).

Chinese philosophy and social sciences were different from other philosophy and social sciences, and it was important to adhere to it with a clear-cut stand. Marxism profoundly revealed the universal law of the development of nature, human society, and human thinking, and pointed out the direction for the development and progress of human society. In the history of human thought, no theory had had such a broad, intense impact on the progress of human civilization as had Marxism. The entry of Marxism into China not only triggered profound changes in Chinese civilization, but also went through a process of gradual localization. In various historical periods of revolution, construction, and reform, the Party adhered to the combination of the basic principles of Marxism with China's specific situation, used the Marxist stand, viewpoint, and method to study and solve various major theoretical and practical problems, and constantly promoted the localization of Marxism. The localization of Marxism in China made great achievements, but it was far from over. One important task of philosophy and social sciences in China was to continue to promote the localization, modernization, and popularization of Marxism and to continue to develop it in the 21st century and contemporary China.[70]

2. The Influence of and Reference to Western Economics

In the 1990s and the 2010s, Chinese scholars introduced the frontier theories of Western economics and its latest research results. It included information asymmetry, information economics and game theory, neo-liberal economic theory represented by Hayek, new economic growth theory (including frontier theoretical research on endogenous growth and frontier theory on the relationship between trade and economic growth, etc.), behavioral economics, new economic geography, public economics, and other fields, as well as new research results in micro- and macro-economics, behavioral welfare research on the frontier theory of economics, the frontier theory of industrial organization and regulation, and new developments in contract theory. The foreign economic theories introduced included the latest research achievements of some famous economists and Nobel Prize winners' economic theories. Since then, China's introduction of Western economics has basically grasped the current situation and theoretical innovation of Western modern economics.

The introduction of Western economics had an impact on the study of Chinese socialist political economics. Most important was the influence of empirical methods of Western economics on the definition of the discipline and research methods of economics. The mainstream view of China's socialist political economics had for a long period of time held that political economics was a social science that studied social and economic relations and production relations, or mainly normative economics. Normative economics referred to a certain value judgment as the basis, put forward some standards as the analysis scale, established the premise of economic theory, and studied how to meet these standards. Its primary characteristic was that it did not consider how the economy actually operated, but was concerned with how it should operate, that is, answering

---

70. Xi Jinping, "Speech at the Symposium on Philosophy and Social Sciences," *People's Daily*, May 19, 2016.

the question of "what it should be." In addition, the content of its research lacked objectivity, and the opinions or conclusions it produced could not pass the empirical test. Western economics called itself an "economic science," that is, positive economics. Empirical economics attempted to transcend or exclude all value judgments, only considered the laws of establishing the relationship between economic variables, and analyzed and forecasted the effect of economic activities under the influence of these laws. Empirical economics also had two characteristics. First, it only expressed and analyzed the actual situation, and it made accurate quantitative description as far as possible, that is, it mainly answered the question of "what it is." Second, its research content was objective, and the conclusions derived from it could generally be tested by empirical facts.

In the history of economic theory, the definition of economics had always been controversial. Western classical political economics was a tradition of normative economics, and some disciplines such as welfare economics were normative economics. But the mainstream of Western economics or modern economics was empirical economics. The definition of positive economics in Western economics, especially its function of explaining economic reality, had a great influence on China's socialist political economics. Some scholars analyzed papers published in *Economic Research* from the 1990s to the end of the 2010s. They believed that by the end of the decade, the published papers had absorbed the commonly used mathematical models in Western economics to express causal logic and empirical tests with econometric methods. They were not much difference from the articles published in mainstream international economic journals.[71]

Some scholars believed that China's socialist political economics had made innovations in the analysis of economic operations. The economic operations level mainly involved the analysis of the mode of resource allocation and the relationship between supply and demand. Over a prolonged period, the discourse power of economic operations analysis had rested in Western economics. China's market-oriented reform had extended the study of political economics to the field of economic operations, which was a major contribution of socialist political economics with Chinese characteristics.[72] Many scholars engaged in empirical research in China had basically mastered the corresponding analytical tools, and the number of papers published in mainstream international economic journals increased. They believed that economics, as an empirical science, studied people's economic behavior and its influence under the conditions of a given value standard by assuming that individual's preferences were given. However, the definition of empirical economics and the hypothesis of "moral neutrality" in economics had always been controversial in China. Especially in the discussion of the political economics of socialism with Chinese characteristics, some commentators emphasized that the most important thing in Marxist political economics was politics. Economic issues could not be regarded only as the pure relationship between things, as it reflected the economic and social relations between people, especially ownership relations and distribution relations, and it included the relationship

71. Lin Yifu, "Thoughts on the Development and Innovation of China's Economic Theory," *Economic Research*, no. 5 (2017).

72. Hong Yinxing, "Building the Theoretical System of Socialist Political Economics with Chinese Characteristics with Innovative Theory," *Economic Research*, no. 4 (2016).

between people in all aspects of production, circulation, and consumption. Marxist political economics mainly started from the analysis of production relations and the fundamental problem of ownership of the means of production. The real purpose of Western economics was to cover up the essence of capitalist exploitation, to defend the private ownership of means of production, and to defend the capitalist system.[73] Classical Western political economics and Marxist political economics both took social production relations as the main research objects and discussed the relationship between social production and distribution and value theory. Marxist political economics studied the evolution of social formation from the perspectives of production relations, productive forces, and production modes. However, the transformation of Western economics since the "marginal revolution" in the 1870s not only offered much analysis of the reasons for ideological and class defense, but also presented the technical reasons for economic development. Classical political economics made economics an independent discipline and had classical economic theories. However, some basic categories of classical political economics, such as value and price, work and labor force, interest and profit, free competition and the "invisible hand," lacked strict definitions and logical arguments, which caused ambiguity and divergence in expression and understanding.[74]

Influenced by Darwin's *Origin of Species,* published in 1859, there appeared in Western humanities and social sciences a trend of pursuing accurate scientific analysis, especially in the field of economics. After the marginal revolution, Western economics transformed from classical political economics to the effective allocation of resources from the basic proposition of production relations, exchange relations, and value theory, and it demonstrated the movement and realization of equilibrium price through "scientific analysis" and sought to make the analysis technology closer to the standard of scientific analysis, allowing economics to become an empirical science. In fact, normative economics and empirical economics could not be completely separated. Marxist political economics was quite empirical in the investigation and analysis of the division of labor, production, exchange, profit, interest, and land rent, many of which were supported by practical cases. Western economics was not absolute positivism either. With the development of welfare economics integrated into microeconomics and institutional analysis, empirical and normative economics were also integrated in Western economics to a certain extent. However, China's economic thought or political economics research had a tradition of normative research, and it was difficult to form a general standard and discourse in the aspects of the "scientific community," the "discipline paradigm," and the "analytical technology and path." The arguments, inferences, and conclusions in the research and discussion were broad and scattered, and they also restricted the connection and explanatory power of the real economy. Therefore, it was necessary to pay attention to the introduction of empirical factors in the discipline definition and research methods of economics and to pay attention to the combination of norms and empirical studies.

---

73. Wang Weiguang, "Marxist Political Economics is a Necessary Course to Uphold and Develop Marxism," *Economic Research*, no. 3 (2016).

74. Hu Jichuang, *Western Economic Theories Since 1870* (Economic Science Press, 1988), 1.

After the end of the 1980s, China's economic structure adjustment research, macroeconomic analysis, and other fields shifted to structural theory. This phenomenon continued into the 1990s and through the 2010s. It was generally believed that the different development heights of industrial structure and the structural benefits associated with it determined the stage characteristics of economic growth. Structuralism also influenced the government's industrial policy and macro-control policy and the formulation of the Five-Year Plan for national economic and social development. For example, the Proposal of the CPC Central Committee on formulating the Twelfth Five-Year Plan for National Economic and Social Development clearly adhered to the strategic adjustment of the economic structure as the main direction of accelerating the transformation of the mode of economic development, and it took making significant progress in the strategic adjustment of the economic structure as one of the main objectives of social and economic development.[75] The Proposal of the CPC Central Committee on Formulating the Thirteenth Five-Year Plan for National Economic and Social Development further intensified structural reform, accelerated the transformation of the economic development mode, and realized higher quality, more efficient, fairer, and more sustainable development as one of the principles that should be followed.[76]

The institutional analysis of Western economics and new institutional economics were of special significance to China's economic reality. The new institutional economics took transaction as the analysis unit, transaction cost as the main analysis tool, property rights as the core of resource allocation, and the economic system as an important variable of economic growth, and it held that the level of transaction costs was related to the efficiency of economic system operations. All of these had certain reference significance for China's economic theory and economic reform.

The relationship between the construction and development of Chinese socialist political economics and Western economics was a long-term topic of discussion. The mainstream view of political economics was that modern Western economics was the product of the Western capitalist system. Due to the fundamental difference in social system, modern Western economics, as a system, could not be duplicated or become the guiding theory of China's national economy and economic reform. However, in some major aspects, modern Western economics had something to learn from and make use of in promoting economic modernization and market-oriented reform. Some held that Western economics was basically useless for China's economy except for the data and measurement methods used to describe economic phenomena. Especially in the discussion of the political economics of socialism with Chinese characteristics, some believed that the fundamental difference between mainstream Western economics and Marxist economics and between the political economics of socialism with Chinese characteristics lay in the differences of standpoint and epistemology. Western economics maintained a capitalist mode of production and its economic system, and its epistemology was idealistic transcendentalism, while socialist

---

75. *Proposal of the CPC Central Committee on Formulating the 12th Five-Year Plan for National Economic and Social Development* (People's Publishing House, 2010).

76. *Proposal of the CPC Central Committee on Formulating the 13th Five-Year Plan for National Economic and Social Development* (People's Publishing House, 2015).

political economics with Chinese characteristics revealed the development law of the socialist economy in China, and its epistemology was the practice and theory of dialectical materialism. However, the analytical framework and research paradigm of Western economics had formed a relatively mature discourse system. Under the strong influence of the academic system of Western economics, there was indeed a long way to go before Chinese economic research could find a theoretical development path that reflected the law of the economic development of socialism with Chinese characteristics and Chinese style.[77] Some scholars investigated the new trends of Western economic thought against the background of the global financial crisis in 2007, and they began to reflect on the new liberalism and free market economic system, queried Western economics, and understood Marxist economics afresh.[78]

From the end of 1980s to the 2010s, there was a certain integration trend between Chinese socialist political economics and Western economics. This integration was reflected in the fact that some scholars engaged in the study of socialist political economics were involved in Western economics, and some scholars engaged in Western economic research were also interested in the construction of Chinese political economics. The concepts, categories, and methods of Western economics were widely used by socialist political economics, and the principles and methods of Marxist economics were also used to review and comment on Western economic theory. Socialist political economics and Western economics were two theoretical systems. The basic category of the former was commodity, value, capital, and surplus value, while the latter was demand, supply, utility, and profit. There were great differences in the basic premises, methods, and contents of the two systems, so it was impossible to integrate them into one. The current textbooks of political economics added the categories of equilibrium price, cost-benefit, and monopolistic competition into the "capitalist part," and the categories of consumption function, multiplier principle, and market equilibrium were added to the "socialist part." However, as long as socialist political economics was based on the evolution of social production relations rather than on actual social and economic operations, then this theoretical system could not be integrated with Western economics.

In fact, in terms of discipline definition and theoretical framework, socialist political economics with Chinese characteristics included not only social production relations, productivity, and mode of production, but also market economy operations, resource allocation, and social welfare growth. Economics, as a social science which studied the social economic relations and economic behaviors of human beings, had its own general provisions. Its basic principles and methods were not different because of the differences between countries, because the scarcity of resources and its effective allocation were the problems that any society would encounter. The maximization of economic welfare was the purpose of any social development, and there were similarities between different countries and different societies in the purpose and means of optimal allocation of

---

77. Pei Changhong, "Theoretical Research Outline of Open Economy with Chinese Characteristics," *Economic Research*, no. 4 (2016).

78. Wu Yifeng, "New Trends of Western Economic Thoughts in the Context of the Current Financial Crisis and Economic Crisis," *Economics Trends*, no. 3 (2010).

scarce resources. In China, there was a tendency to overemphasize the specific class attribute of economics while ignoring the generality of economics. In fact, in the social sciences, the generality of economics was obvious. From the development trend of China, as long as the market-oriented reform did not reverse, some basic theories and analysis methods of Western economics could be incorporated into the theoretical framework of its socialist political economics.

Western economics and its "empirical science" positioning and analysis tools had a wide impact on China's economic research. In order to avoid the tendency of extremism, it was important to study it from two aspects. First, economics was after all a social science. Unlike a natural science, it could not test its theories with "scientific methods" (controlled experiments). Because economics studied people's behavior, and because preferences and behaviors were not always like chemical elements in a test tube, their utility could not be measured and compared absolutely by mathematical methods. It was possible to test by statistical or other means and determine that the demand for a commodity would increase after its market price decreased, but it could not be absolutely determined that the demand would increase by a certain number of percentage points. Any "law" described in economics could only be a kind of "trend," reflecting the general direction of economic activities, but not with 100% certainty. The requirement of the application of mathematics was very strict. Mathematics required a weaker hypothesis, a stronger argument, and wider applicability. Under such demands, economics hoped to pursue stronger universality, accuracy, and conciseness. But after all, mathematics could not replace economics, and mathematical principles could not be widely applied to people's economic behavior. Economics always needed some basic assumptions, though they should be proved or falsified by experience and logic. Further, for China's economic theoretical research, it seemed that more emphasis needed to be placed on the transformation of analytical methods and theoretical paradigms. One of the biggest differences between economics and other social sciences lay in its strong experimental nature. Economics was directly produced in real economic life, and it needed to be able to withstand the test of real economic life. However, one of the traditional defects of Chinese socialist political economics lay in its inability to explain economic life. On the one hand, theory could not explain the real economic relationship in essence, and on the other, the real economic life in many places did not match the theory. The fundamental reason was that economic theory, in many cases, did not take real economic life as the starting point, but derived its conclusions within the framework of abstract concepts, without empirical practice. Changing this situation required learning from Western economics in the discipline orientation, theoretical paradigm, and analytical methods of economics and making corresponding changes.

3. An Analysis of the Relationship Between "Disciplinary Generalization" and "Framework Constraint" in Economic Research

At the beginning of the 21st century, with the evolution of China's reform process, there was a complex situation in the development of the socialist market economy and the social structure, social concepts, traditional culture, social interest relations, and other contradictory movements, with the supply of public goods being scarce, the basic social security system imperfect, the income gap expanding, the growing conflict between vested interests and reform, and the edge of institutional change diminishing international benefits. The interweaving of many problems formed a social mindset of questioning reform, dissatisfaction with the distribution pattern of social interests, and criticizing "elite consciousness" with "popular emotion." The embodiment of this social mindset in the field of economic thought was criticism of economists who lacked a discipline framework, and such criticism mainly came from academic circles. This led to a consideration of how to define the value judgment and moral concept in economic research, and whether economic research and criticism should tend toward "subject generalization" or "analytical framework constraint."

After 1979, China began to reform its economic system with economic construction as the center, and the national economy continued to grow at a rapid pace. In this process, the social demand of economics increased, and economics gradually became a strong discipline of social science, that is, the so-called "prominent learning." The research results, academic viewpoints, and policy suggestions of economics affected the government's reform policy choices and even the direction of economic and social development, to a certain extent. Due to the increase of social demand, finance and economics in universities became popular majors. Almost all comprehensive universities, even universities focused on science and engineering, set up departments and specializations in finance and economics. In the expansion of the "demand" and "supply" of economics, the nature, definition, and standard of economics were quite confused. China's economic thought originally lacked the tradition of empirical thinking. In addition, the demarcation of disciplines was not clear, and the theoretical training was not regular, resulting in a lack of scientific research and economic analysis. Some critics pointed out that it was inappropriate for China's current academic and subject classification system to confuse "humanities" and "social science" with "humanities and social sciences" (liberal arts). Humanities did not belong to "science," but was a "value system" with "human science" as its purport. Its mode of thinking was non-empirical, that is, "normative," and the proposition studied was a "value proposition," while social sciences (economics, political science, sociology, law, etc.) belonged to the category of "science," which was a kind of knowledge with "material science" as its purport. The mode of thinking of its "knowledge system" was empirical, and it studied "fact propositions" rather than "value propositions."[79] According to the requirements of scientific thinking, social science research needed to be committed to value neutrality and eliminate the "value load," so as to conform to positivity and falsification.

According to the scientific methodology, science was a conditional cognitive human process, and scientific theory was an axiomatic system. Theoretical language, basic theorems, and corresponding rules had to have unified epistemological significance. Scientific research involved selection and orientation standards for knowledge background, knowledge structure, and

---

79. Wang Xinyan, "The Distinction Between Humanities and Social Sciences," *Guangming Daily*, June 16, 2009.

theoretical training. Theory had to be clear and recognizable, and it had to provide information, which were the requirements of paradigm and falsification. In terms of methodology, economics accepted falsificationism and a scientific research program (refined falsificationism), realizing the "progress of research framework," which made the theoretical research of economics more axiomatic, systematic, and logical. However, China's economic research had a tendency toward disciplinary generalization, which lacked the generality of methods and paradigms, the agreement of basic statements, and the technical provisions of a discipline in terms of knowledge background and theoretical training. Anyone could focus on some hot economic issues or even some specialized economic issues (such as interest rate, exchange rate, capital market, international trade) to make their own "economic analysis" and carry out endless debates, research, and discussion of various kinds, so that economics was "generalized" in a way that appeared colorful, scattered, and disorderly.

For example, a hot topic in economics was the real estate market. Some discussed the real estate market from the perspective of a harmonious society, some from the perspective of living rights, some from the perspective of the gap between rich and poor, and some even from the perspective of building the Party for the public and ruling the people. People from all walks of life participated in this discussion. They delivered speeches from their own professional backgrounds, theoretical perspectives, and interest relationships, and they offered "economic analysis" on the real estate market. Browsing the relevant newspapers and magazines, the discourse of analyzing the real estate market was varied. Some commentators use the harsh words such as "plundering society," "firmly attacking," and "substantive infringement." Some scholars made it their duty to meet the needs of the low-income class. Some "real estate economics experts" even used poetic language to describe real estate prices as being "like a runaway horse," especially for the real estate markets in Shanghai, Beijing, and other first-tier cities, where local commentators were more interested and published many lengthy, empty research articles.

In fact, the real estate market was strongly regional and professional, and the research work had requirements for information and theoretical training. If it was to achieve solid economic analysis, it needed an analytical framework with constraints. People's housing problem was not only economic issue, but also social, political, and cultural issue which could be discussed from a variety of disciplines. But if it was the real estate market, it was basically an economic topic, which required discussion within the framework of economics. In the face of almost unlimited improvement of the housing demand of all the people, the screening mechanism of the market was the ability to pay. The market set the price. When the price was set, nothing else would work, regardless of the class, level, and social status. It depended only on the ability to pay, which was the essence of equality in the market economy. As long as the price was not manipulated and distorted, it contained the most complete information and guided the most efficient allocation of resources. The market was flawed in the balance between fairness and efficiency, but the market mechanism was fairer than any other mechanism. As the screening mechanism of the market was the ability to pay, it would encourage people to strive to improve their ability to pay, which led to the development of the social economy.

It was true that the market could not solve all of the problems. The real estate market could not fully meet the needs of low-income people to improve their housing, which was market failure. Therefore, improving housing conditions for low income people was not a market problem, but a social security and government function issue. The government could also use some market means to help address this problem, such as real estate financial institutions such as Freddie Mac and Fannie Mae, established by the US government.

If there were no discipline framework constraint in economic research, it would be nothing but a kind of "debate" or word game which had nothing to do with science or application. However, by the beginning of the 21st century, Chinese academia had not yet established such academic norms and thinking, and analysis, discussion, and criticism were basically not subject to discipline framework constraints. In the framework of economics, the market was the market. It had no interest orientation of a special class, and it could not be "regulated" to serve the interests of a special class. Otherwise, it would not be called the market. Similarly, in its framework, economics assumed that both income and wealth accumulation were legal, and it was on this premise that income distribution was discussed. If the accumulation of income and wealth were caused by illegal activities, it was beyond the framework of economics. It was not an economic problem, but a legal and political issue. After the world financial crisis in 2008, many countries put forward reform requirements for the role and voting mechanism of the International Monetary Fund (IMF) based on the US dollar. Before and after the G20 summit in London in April 2009, some economists proposed the "creation of an international reserve currency that is decoupled from sovereign countries and can maintain the long-term stability of currency value to replace the US dollar." But in the IMF, all other countries had less voting power than the United States, which had the largest share. If developing countries wanted to increase their voting rights, they needed to first increase their equity. This was the capital rights mechanism of economics, which had nothing to do with morality. The framework of economics was very strict. If the framework were relaxed, the explanatory power of economics would be greatly reduced, unless there was progress in theory (such as transaction cost theory, rational expectation theory, information economics, etc.). It was true that humans were not an economic animal. Their behavior was multifaceted, their spiritual world was rich, and their thoughts were complicated. Economics only analyzed people's economic behavior. In the framework of economics, people's economic behavior could be basically treated as the calculation of income and cost price comparison. However, criticizing the utilitarianism of economics with other social behavioral norms, and even accusing economics of being "immoral," was a totally different matter.

Economics was more dynamic and scientific because it attached great importance to drawing methodological nourishment from other disciplines, especially the natural sciences. Economics held that the natural sciences and the social sciences should have common ground as sciences and have unity in epistemology and methodology. It was precisely because economics was a scientific theoretical system, meaning that there was a strict framework constraint, that it was impossible to spread it all over the world. In the same way, the criticism of economists could not be without discipline framework constraints, training of a kind of "professional matrix" and agreement of discourse and concept system of a "scientific community." Otherwise, it could not be discussed at all.

From the beginning of the 21st century, and especially from 2005, many scholars in the social sciences and humanities in China published many articles on moral appeals in view of the widening income distribution gap. The scholars who participated in the discussion had different academic backgrounds, so the analysis perspectives and methods were also different, and the conclusions drawn were very different. It was true that income distribution was not only an economic problem, but also a social problem. Every member of society could make a speech on this issue based on their own interests, knowledge background, and information acquisition, but income distribution was basically an economic problem, and the discussion of it should be carried out in the framework of economics. Academic discussion with a discipline framework ensured the scientificity of academic form, led research and analysis meet the requirements of scientific thinking to the maximum extent, and ensured the conclusions were as accurate and close to science as possible. Otherwise, an "academic discussion" which was pan-disciplinary and emotional lacked objective judgment criteria, and it could not reach consensus in the scientific sense, but also affected public opinion, thus affecting the process of political, economic, and social development. The divergence of views and ideas between economics and other social humanities lay not in moral principles or moral goals, but in epistemology and methodology.

Efficiency in economics was economic efficiency. Economic efficiency included efficiency of production and of exchange. The standard of the efficiency of production was unique, which was production at the minimum cost. The standard of exchange efficiency was also unique, which was that no one could benefit himself without harming others (Pareto efficiency). The general equilibrium theory of economics proved that the competitive market system could achieve economic efficiency and achieve long-term economic growth under the framework of two constraints: the maximum rationality of producers and consumers and complete market price information. According to economic logic, efficiency was the source of net wealth growth, and the competitive market system was the channel to achieve efficiency. But if fairness were introduced, the analysis became more complicated.

Defining fairness and determining how it operated was a difficult problem. Four definitions of equity were given in economics textbooks. Equalitarianism meant that all members of a society got the same number of products. The Rawls doctrine maximized the utility of the worst-off people in a society. Utilitarianism maximized the total utility of all members of society. Market dominance was the fairest result. If a society were allowed to choose the four definitions of fairness, there were no more than two criteria: equalitarianism and efficiency. According to the economic method, any choice had a cost. The cost of extreme equalitarianism was to make society fall into overall poverty, and the cost of the extreme efficiency doctrine was the gap between the rich and the poor among the members of society, which put society in an unstable state. Comparing the cost of various options, most economists chose the utilitarian definition of fairness. There were also some economists who chose the market-oriented view of fairness and believed that the outcome of the competitive market process was fair, because it rewarded those who were most capable if they worked hard.

Most economists chose the utilitarian welfare function because its definition of fairness was consistent with the efficiency standard of economics. Economics held that the increase of a person's wealth was not conditional on the loss of other people's wealth (or utility), and the increase of personal wealth would lead to the net growth of total social welfare, so it was efficient. This criterion was often used in economics, called "Pareto optimality." Pareto optimality was achieved through free and fair trade.

This analysis was simple and clear. The economic system was directly related to the growth of social wealth, and efficient social institutional arrangements would lead to the net growth of social wealth. An efficient system had to be one that could ensure free and fair trade, or that only through free and fair trade could wealth growth be achieved. In the economy, the smaller the space for the use of non-free and unfair trade meant to benefit, the more efficient the system was. An increase of personal wealth would lead to a net growth of social wealth. By contrast, if personal wealth could be obtained through non-free and unfair trade, then the system was inefficient. According to this idea, a society could greatly improve the growth rate of social wealth and promote the progress its economic society through institutional reform under the condition of unchanged resource endowment conditions. This was the institutional value of the market economy revealed by economics.

CHAPTER 15

Research on the Transformation of Economic System and Development Economics

15.1 A Study of China's Economic System Reform and Institutional Change

1. Research on China's Reform and Opening Up and Institutional Change

The American economist Samuel Bowles pointed out that institutions provide incentives and constraints to explain individual behavior and aggregate results. Institutions influence individual's preferences and beliefs, and individual's preferences and beliefs change together with the institutional environment. From the perspective of the institutional change process, an institution should not be described as an exogenous constraint, but as the result of individual interactions. The process of institutional change is the transformation from one result to another.[1] Generally speaking, China's economic and ideological circles believed that Reform and Opening Up was essentially a process of institutional change, the essence of which was the transformation from a planned economy to a market economy. The performance of economic system transformation was reflected in economic growth and social and economic modernization. In line with this process of social development, institutional transformation, economic development, and economic growth became important areas of economic research.

Economic circles in China and abroad summed up China's economic reform path as gradualism or gradual reform, compared with Russia's "shock therapy." From the early to mid-1990s, academic circles began discussing the path of gradual reform.

---

1. Samuel Bowles, *Microeconomics: Behavior, Institution and Evolution* (China Renmin University Press, 2006), 273.

Some scholars discussed the economic model and system characteristics of China, the Soviet Union, and Eastern European countries before reform. They believed that the different initial conditions determined the different reform paths. When analyzing the institutional characteristics of China before reform, some held that the organizational structure of Eastern Europe and the Soviet Union was a single form (U-type economy) based on the principle of functional and professional "rules." By contrast, China's hierarchical system was a multi-level, multi-regional (M-type economy) form that had been based on the regional "block" principle since 1958. They particularly stressed that the M-type referred to the hierarchical system of multi-level and multi-regional reform rather than the hierarchical system of multiple departments. Some theorists analyzed the preconditions of China's economic system reform from the perspective of system reform or institutional change. Some held that the prerequisite for the actual occurrence of institutional change was not only that the net income (total revenue minus operating cost) provided by the new system was greater than that of the old system after it was put into operation, but also that the condition of $Wn - Tc > Wo$ should be met. Among them, Wn referred to the expected benefits that the new system could provide for the people (this generation) who were carrying out institutional change. Tc represented the various costs paid by the same group for reforming the system, that is, "reform cost." Wo represented the net benefits that the old system could provide for them. Inequality showed that only when the "reform cost" was taken into account would the new system achieve higher benefits than the old system, and the reform would then take place. According to this analysis, the theorists further believed that under the given initial conditions (represented by Wo) and target mode (represented by Wn), the choice of reform path would be reduced to the minimization of reform cost Tc. According to the theory of new Western institutional economics, some theorists held that the necessary condition of institutional change was the change of technical constraints such as the motivation of institutional change and the production capacity, and the old system was in an unbalanced state, which led to new potential profit opportunities. In order to obtain the profit opportunities that could not be obtained under the old system, the relevant actors would produce the potential demand and supply of institutional change.[2]

As for the reasons for China's gradual reform, some scholars put forward a theoretical model, pointing out that "reform cost" could be divided into "implementation cost" and "friction cost." The former included the loss of efficiency caused by incomplete information, incomplete knowledge, and an unstable system expectations after the beginning of the reform process (taking the ideal "optimal state" as the reference system), while the latter was the economic loss caused by some people who realized that their interests would be damaged in the process of reform and oppose the reform. If an economy had the conditions to develop a new system first, other things

2. Zheng Hongqing, "Reflections on Economic System Reform in the 1990s," *China's Economic System Reform*, no. 10 (1990); Wang Dingding, "General Theory of System Innovation," *Economic Research*, no. 5 (1992); Fan Gang, *The Path of Gradual Progress* (China Social Science Press, 1993); Qian Yingyi, "Why China's Economic Reform Is Different," *Comparative Study of Economic and Social Systems*, no. 1 (1993); Zhou Xiaochuan, "Different Paths of Economic System Reform," *Reform*, no. 2 (1993).

being equal, people would generally prefer not to take the road of radical reform.[3]

Some scholars concluded that China's gradual reform had three characteristics: incremental reform, experimental promotion, and non-radical reform. Incremental reform was the introduction of increasing degrees of the market mechanism into the allocation of asset increment. When correcting the unreasonable industrial structure, this path avoided the adjustment cost, and the incremental reform was also conducive to maintaining the balance between stability and speed in the process of reform. However, incremental reform was a suboptimal choice, and economic parties tended to obtain income through rent-seeking. The advantages of experimental promotion included reducing the risk of reform as much as possible, combining with incremental reform, by which there was timely signaling of which areas of reform had the greatest benefit and a process for the construction and development of the market was created. The defects of the experiment and promotion were the friction caused by the artificial isolation between the reformed and the unmodified, a series of problems such as unbalanced regional development and uneven income distribution, a vacuum in the adjustment mechanism formed by the lag of supporting reform measures, and the relative lag of the reform of the macro policy environment caused by partial reform, which was the fundamental reason the reform fell into the "flexibility-chaos" cycle. As for the implementation of non-radical reform, it could make full use of the existing organizational resources and maintain the relative stability and effective connection of the system in the process of institutional innovation. Further, it could avoid great social unrest and waste of resources. Finally, it could avoid the unfairness and conflicts in the process of asset stock redistribution.[4]

According to the literature of new institutional economics, institutional change was the process of institutional substitution, transformation, and transaction. North believed that the term "change" referred to the establishment, change, and the way of breaking with time. The basic motive force of institutional change was that the actor pursued the maximization of interests. The inducement factor of institutional change lay in the economic subject's expectation of obtaining the maximum potential profit, that is, obtaining the potential profit that could not be obtained in the existing institutional arrangements through institutional innovation. If there was potential profit in a kind of institutional arrangement, it meant that the institutional arrangement had not reached Pareto optimality and was in an unbalanced state. The emergence of institutional disequilibrium pointed to the objective inevitability and basic motive force of institutional change, but the change itself depended on the benefit cost analysis of institutional change. Only when the expected income was greater than the expected cost would the economic behavior subject as the main body of institutional change promote the change.

According to the analysis of some critics, the mode of institutional change (reform mode) referred to the sum of the form, speed, breakthrough, and timing of institutional change adopted by the institutional innovation subject to achieve a certain goal, while the objective of institutional

---

3. Fan Gang, "Two Reform Costs and Two Reform Methods," *Economic Research*, no. 1 (1993).

4. Liu Shijin, "Conditions, Process, and Cost of Economic System Innovation," *Economic Research*, no. 3 (1993); Miao Zhuang, "On the Path of China's Steady Reform," *Economics Trends*, no. 1 (1993); Lin Yifu, "On the Steady Path of China's Economic Reform," *Economic Research*, no. 3 (1993).

selection (reform goal) referred to the future institutional arrangement expected by the institutional innovation subject under the given utility function and constraint conditions. Since China had clearly set the socialist market economic system as the goal of system selection, the focus of theoretical circles at the time was on determining how to evaluate the existing system change mode and what kind of system change mode could be selected to achieve the market economic system with the lowest implementation and friction costs and the fastest possible speed under the given realistic constraints. The transition of China's economic system from a planned economy to a market economy was a kind of "structural institutional change," which was different from institutional changes within an economic system. To that point, the information from the existing literature on institutional economics showed that its main focus was to study several institutional changes in the same system, which was a kind of "non-structural institutional change." Structural institutional change was much more complicated than non-structural institutional change, and the cost was much higher. The choice of the path of institutional change was mainly controlled by the power and social preference structure among various interest groups in a society. Institutional change could be roughly divided into demand-induced and supply-led. China's current choice was a government-led mode of institutional change. Under the constraints of the existing social order and ideology, the main body of the government usually preferred gradual reform.

Some scholars concluded that China was experiencing a great era of reform. Reform, or the transition from a planned economy to a market economy, was a major process of institutional change. It was self-evident that this process was path dependent. That is to say, first of all, the initial system selection would provide stimulation and inertia to strengthen the existing system, because it was more convenient to move forward along the original path of institutional change and the established direction than to find another way. In addition, after a system was formed, it would form a pressure group with vested interests in the existing system. They sought to consolidate the existing system and hinder further reform, even where the new system was more efficient than the existing one. Even if they accepted further change, they would try to make it beneficial to consolidate and expand their vested interests. Therefore, the initial reform tended to delimit the scope for the subsequent reform. In this way, the success of the reform, the realization of the goal of establishing a socialist market economy, and the establishment of an efficient economic system depended not only on the reformers' subjective desire and ultimate goal, but also on the path chosen at the beginning. Even if the goal was clear and the general direction of specific measures was correct, as long as there were some slight errors in the initial path selection, future development would deviate from the original goal according to its own logic and evolve into another system far from the original design.[5] It was pointed out that China's economic path was unique, because as a developing country and a country in transition, China's reform was accompanied by two important changes in the process of economic reform and promoting economic development. One was the transformation of a dual economic structure as a process of economic development,

---

5. Wu Jinglian, "Path Dependence and China's Reform," in *Economics and China's Economic Reform* (Shanghai People's Publishing House, 1995).

and the other was the system shift from a planned economy to a market economy as an economic transition process. In addition to the particularity of each transformation, the interweaving of these two changes also formed a series of characteristics of China's development path.[6]

In the late 1990s, with the deepening of China's economic system reform, all kinds of social contradictions grew increasingly complex, and the reform grew increasingly difficult. Especially, the impact of the economic system and the political system put forward urgent requirements for the overall reform of the social system, leading economic and ideological circles to reflect on China's gradual reform.

Some scholars compared China's steady reform with Russia's and Eastern Europe's radical reform. They believed that the fundamental difference between China's steady reform and the radical reform lay in the basic feature of China's gradual reform, which was that when the old system "was yet to be changed" due to great resistance, new systems or new economic components (market pricing mechanism, various forms of non-state-owned economy, etc.) could be developed close to or around it. With the development of these economic components, the continuous change of economic structure and the improvement of institutional environment, the old system would be steadily reformed. In comparison, the basic feature of radical reform was that the old system must (could only) be reformed from the very beginning so as to pave the way for the growth of the new system. In this sense, the basic meaning of "progressive reform" was "incremental reform." It was more accurate to use North's concept of "incremental reform" (but this concept was generally translated as "gradual reform"), rather than the concept of "steady reform" with more "speed." China's gradual reform involved developing the new system through incremental reform when the stock was not changed, and with the accumulation of incremental reform, the whole economic system's structure was gradually reformed to create the conditions for the final reform of "stock"; while Russia's radical reform was carried out directly (in the absence of conditions for incremental reform) to promote the increment of a new system. Gradual reform required a long transition period for the disintegration of the old system and the formation of the new system, which led to the long-term dual system and the popularization of the dual track system of price, income, and economic operations. It led to many distortions and inefficiencies in the economy for a long period, which delayed the process of reforming the old system and hindered the rapid growth of the new system. The friction between the old and new systems in the process of the "double track transition" would produce new inefficiency, the long-standing problems of corruption, inflation, and economic instability would aggravate social instability, and the transitional system would become a transitional entity. The system would produce new vested interest groups, which would become a new resistance rather than a motive force for further reform, making further reform not easier but more difficult.

There were different opinions on whether China's gradual reform had the nature of a "Pareto improvement." Many scholars believed that it was reasonable to emphasize the loss of interests

---

6. Cai Fang, "The Gap Between Neoclassical Economic Thinking and China's Reality," *Economics Trends*, no. 2 (2010).

and social resistance in the process of reform, but it was not possible to regard the reform as a process of "non-Pareto improvement." According to the concept of "Pareto efficiency" and "Pareto improvement," China's reform process had the nature of "Pareto improvement." Reform was not only a static process of interest pattern adjustment or redistribution, but a dynamic process associated with economic growth and development. The reform created conditions for the optimization of the behavior of various economic entities and the improvement of efficiency by eliminating various factors that inhibited the efficiency of the original system. The more the economy developed, the stronger the bearing capacity of social members for institutional change and interest adjustment, which was more conducive to the promotion of reform. Therefore, in the short run, the "substitution effect" of interest relations caused by the reform might be more obvious, and some people's absolute and relative income would increase, while others' income would decrease, but in the long run, the "diffusion effect" of social wealth enhancement brought about by the improvement of the whole social efficiency level would increase and penetrate into all levels of society, which indicated that in the long run, the "substitution effect" of interest relations caused by the reform would be increasingly obvious, indicating that in the long run, the "substitution effect" of social wealth enhancement would be more and reform was thus a process of Pareto improvement.[7]

2. Research on the Path to Institutional Change of the "Washington Consensus" and the "Beijing Consensus"

At the end of the 20th century and the beginning of the 21st century, the two concepts of the "Washington consensus" and the "Beijing consensus" were gradually formed in international academic circles, referring to the path of neoclassical economics and the path of "Chinese characteristics" respectively. In this framework, economic and ideological circles conducted a more in-depth study on the path of institutional change.

In 1989, John Williamson, of the American Institute of International Economics, first proposed the term the "Washington consensus" to reflect the economic system and values of the United States. Stiglitz noted that the basic connotation of the Washington consensus included

7. Zhang Yu, "Contradictions and Choices Facing Steady Reform," *Economics Trends*, no. 11 (1994); Gao Haiyan, "System Selection and Reform," *Comparative Study of Economic and Social Systems*, no. 2 (1995); Lin Yifu, Cai Fang and Li Zhou, "Why China's Economic Reform Has Been Successful," *Comparative Study of Economic and Social Systems*, no. 4 (1995); Xu Jingyong, "On China's Gradual Reform," *Financial Treatise*, no. 6 (1995); Zou Wei and Zhuang Ziyin, "The Nature, Characteristics and Dynamic Optimization of China's Reform Process," *Economic Research*, no. 9 (1995); Fan Gang, *A Political and Economic Analysis of Gradual Reform* (Shanghai Far East Publishing House, 1996); Wen Li, "Cost Analysis of Institutional Change," *Learning and Exploration*, no. 1 (1996); Yu Zuyao, "Historical Experience of China's Economic Reform," *New Horizon*, no. 2 (1996); Zhang Jun, *Dual Track Economics: China's Economic Reform (1978–1992)* (Shanghai Sanlian Bookstore, 1998); Cui Rubo, "Theory of Institutional Change and the Establishment of Socialist Market Economic System in China," *Exploration*, no. 4 (1998); Xiong Yingwu, "Institutional Analysis of China's Reform," *Research on Financial Issues*, no. 9 (1998).

the development strategy with privatization, liberalization, and macroeconomic stability (price stability) as the main content and a series of policies based on the firm belief in the free market and aimed at weakening or even minimizing the role of the government.[8] The Washington consensus, or the post-Washington consensus, was a path of institutional change or transition derived from neoclassical economics. Its core elements were the establishment of a free market, competitive system, the rationalization of market relations, and the construction of political and social systems compatible with the free market. The Beijing consensus referred to the mode or path of institutional change in China's Reform and Opening Up. This concept was more a practice than a theoretical system or analytical method. Its core element was a gradual transformation under the constraints of national conditions (practical basis) to achieve the performance goals of economic growth or development.

Some scholars concluded that the research method of the Washington consensus was to set the transition target in advance and transform this goal into certain observable indicators for classification and judgment. The implied logic was that as long as the main indicators improved, the efficiency of the market mechanism could be brought into play. There were two defects in this research method. One was that the evaluation standard itself was quite dogmatic, and the existence of consensus itself was questioned. The other was that even if there was a consensus, it could not ensure that transitional countries could automatically establish the system determined by the target mode based on such a consensus. The Beijing consensus was only put forward as a concept and had not become a complete, systematic analysis method, so it lacked universal guiding significance for practice. However, critics believed that the essence of the Beijing consensus was to always take the people's livelihood as the fundamental purpose of the transition and take public opinion as the basic direction of the transition path selection. These two principles determined that performance was the core of the evaluation of the transition. Performance included two aspects: the performance of system transition and the performance of economic development. The performance of the system transition was ultimately evaluated by the performance of economic development, that is, the performance of economic development was the most real and meaningful, and it should be directly reflected in the improvement of people's livelihood. In this process, adaptability, path selection, and innovation ability constituted an evaluation system, which was also the basic framework to ensure the success of the transition process. The core of its evaluation was performance. The conclusion was that, compared with the planned system, the market was the most effective mechanism to maximize the allocation of resources and social welfare, and that the market economy was more efficient than the planned economy was the premise of the transition. As far as economics was concerned, what was studied was the equilibrium between different goods, behaviors, and systems, not the absolute judgment of value. The purpose of institutional change was to provide an efficient, balanced institutional arrangement for economic growth. The performance of transition could be judged by the improvement of

---

8. Stiglitz, *The Consensus of the Post Washington Consensus;* Huang Ping and Cui Zhiyuan, *China and Globalization: the Washington Consensus or the Beijing Consensus* (Social Science Academic Press, 2005).

efficiency at different equilibrium points in the process. The institutional change that led to this efficiency improvement should be placed in the specific social and historical background of countries in transition.[9]

Regarding the market economy as an indivisible whole or a hierarchical system construction was the fundamental difference between the Western theory of the transition economy and the practical rationality of China's transformation. Janos Kornai, who had a great influence on the study of transformation in China and abroad, famously stated that unlike supermarkets, an economic system could not guarantee that the best of two worlds, planning and the market, would be put together in one basket, and that the economic systems could not be separated or replace each other, but could only be taken as a whole. The conclusion of the transition was the radical reform path of a big explosion. This was the representative view of comparative economic system theory, which was regarded as an important theoretical basis of the Washington consensus by Gerard Roland. In fact, whether the best part of planning and the market could be "put into one basket" was the essence of the target model of China's economic transformation. How to explain this problem in theory was perhaps the most valuable theoretical contribution that China's economic transformation model could make.

Empirical research indicated that the hierarchical institutional arrangement of a market economy from micro to meso and onto macro formed the logical clue of the sequential reform of economic transformation. The main line of logic was the cultivation of the market operation mechanism, and the focus of reform was the formation of a micro level price mechanism, the standardization of a medium level enterprise system, and the improvement of a macro level economic system, which could be regarded as the basic order of economic transformation. According to different transformation practices, there could be different levels of fine-tuning, but neither the radical model nor the Chinese path was divorced from the basic development context of transformation practice. However, different transformation and reform orders had resulted in different transformation consequences. This sequential institutional arrangement was completely determined by the essential characteristics of the market economy. It was also pointed out that the core issue of the Chinese model was whether sustainable development could be achieved, harmony between humans and nature realized in development, and the distribution of development achievements reflected in social equity and justice. The Chinese model could also be used for international reference, but it needed corresponding institutional conditions, including

---

9. Fan Gang and Hu Yongtai, "Gradual or Parallel Advance: On the Theory and Reform of the Optimal Path of System Transition," *Economic Research*, no. 1 (2005); Lv Wei, "Research on the Analysis Method Based on China's Economic Transition Practice," *Economic Research*, no. 2 (2005); Mao Tianqi, "Different Institutional Arrangements and Value Orientations of Transition Countries: A Comparison of China Russia Transition Theory and Practice," *Economic Research*, no. 8 (2007); Tang Jijun and Guo Yanli, "The Transformation of Economic System Dynamic Evolution Analysis: A Sunk Cost Method," *Nanjing University Business Review*, no. 14 (2007); Liu Shibai, *On System Transformation* (Sanlian Bookstore, 2008); Yao Yang, *Economic Reform as a Process of Institutional Innovation* (Truth and Wisdom Press, 2008); Jiang Ying and Wei Zhong, "International Research on China's Economic Transformation and Development," *Economics Trends*, no. 8 (2008); Hu Jiayong, "China Path and China Economists, *Economic Research*, no. 5 (2010).

a central government with strong control, continuity of ideology, an imbalance of interest groups, and a strong public ownership system.[10] Some commentators pointed out that the Washington consensus, which overemphasized liberalization, privatization, and marketization, could not take into account the overall national interests and was seriously divorced from the actual national conditions of various countries. Many transitional countries quickly destroyed the traditional planned economic system and the omnipotent national governance model. However, due to the excessive weakening of the government's governing ability, the neglect of system construction, and the coordination of the relationship between the government, the market, and society, most of these transitional countries fell into an "order division" institutional trap, which led to serious economic recession and social unrest. As early as 1998, after the Asian financial crisis, some international economists, represented by American economist Stiglitz, began to criticize the Washington consensus. They thought that the Washington consensus ignored some important factors in economic development, such as the role of the government and the improvement of human capital and technological progress, which had "misleading" consequences, and thus called for "exceeding the Washington consensus" with the "post-Washington consensus," the nature of which remained neo-liberalism. However, it began to attach importance to state intervention, advocated a new understanding of the relationship between the government and the market, highlighted the positive role of the government in promoting development, stressed the institutional factors and reform order of economic transformation and development, and tried to seek the coordination between justice and efficiency.[11]

Some commentators concluded that in the late 1980s and early 1990s, the transition from the traditional planned economy to the market economy formed two different paths, namely, the radical reform of the Soviet Union and Eastern Europe and the gradual reform of China. The success of China's economic reform was not only that it showed the world that socialism and the market economy could be combined, but also that it had explored a progressive reform road or reform mode with Chinese characteristics in practice. The main characteristics of this reform mode were the combination of top-down and bottom-up under the premise of adhering to unified leadership and giving full play to the enthusiasm and creativity of grassroots units in system innovation. In the dual track transition, the increment should be first. On the premise of retaining the coordination of the plan, it was important to gradually expand the proportion of market regulation in the newly added resources and make a steady transition to the market economy. On the premise of adhering to the one game of the entire country, it was important to make breakthroughs in various sectors, enterprises, and regions to realize the overall transformation of the economic system from point to surface. Consideration needed to be given

10. Zhang Jianjun, "Theoretical Innovation of China Model," *Economic News*, March 13, 2009; Tang Xiao, "Evaluation and Enlightenment of European and American Media on 'China Model'," *Xinhua Digest*, no. 10 (2010); Huang Zhiqi and Zhao Jingfeng, "Institutional Interpretation of 'China Model': Comparison and Evaluation Based on Two Theories," *Economist*, no. 9 (2010).

11. Liu Yan, Xue Rong, and Fu Chunguang, "Transformation Path and Risk of Chinese Society," *Research on Financial Issues*, no. 12 (2011).

to reform, development, and stability, the intensity of reform unified, the pace of development and the degree of social affordability raised, reform and development promoted in social stability, and social stability promoted through reform and development. It was important to proceed systematically, experiment first, and then popularize. According to the needs of practice and the development of understanding, it was necessary to constantly adjust and improve the specific objectives and ideas of reform.[12]

3. Research on the Performance of China's Path to Institutional Change

By 2008, China had been reforming and opening up for thirty years. After that, economic and ideological circles published a series of research results to analyze the performance of China's institutional change. In 2008, Shanghai People's Publishing House published *Thirty Years of China's Reform and Opening Up: Reflections of Ten Economists*, compiled by Zhang Weiying, which collected speeches and related articles by ten influential Chinese economists at the Peking University Guanghua New Year Forum, where the achievements of China's economic system reform and the future development direction from various perspectives had been discussed. Some commentators proposed that the thirty-year reform had only taken the first step of economic transformation, and there was still a long way to go. There were many problems to be solved and many things to be done. However, the key lay in two transformations, namely, the market-oriented transformation and the transformation of the mode of economic growth. The reason market-oriented transformation was important was that China was not a complete market economy, but was at best, a market economy dominated by the government, and the government still played a crucial role in the allocation of resources. There were three key points in the market-oriented transformation. The first was the need to allow state-owned enterprises to become real enterprises, the second was the need to liberalize prices, especially the prices of production factors, and the third was the need to liberalize finance and promote financial deepening. The transformation of economic growth mode was not a scientific and technological problem, but an institutional problem. Without market-oriented transformation, there would be no transformation of the economic growth mode. According to the analysis of some scholars, there were five key changes to understand China's thirty-year economic system reform and its achievements. First, the signal of resource allocation had shifted from planned indicators to market prices. Second, the main body of economic decision-making had changed from government officials to entrepreneurs. Third, the basis of individual rights and interests had shifted from government posts to private property. Fourth, the driving force of economic development had shifted from central government to local competition. Fifth, the economic operation system had shifted from closed to open. However, after thirty years of Reform and Opening Up, some public opinions and policies issued by the government ran counter to these changes. People's trust in the price mechanism was not

---

12. Zhang Yu, Zhang Chen and Cai Wanhuan, "Political Economics Analysis of China's Economic Model," *Chinese Social Sciences*, no. 3 (2011).

increasing, but declining. Various forms of price intervention were frequently introduced under the support of public opinion. The government's grasp of social resources was not decreasing, but increasing. The business environment and entrepreneurial conditions of enterprises were not improving, but deteriorating. The employment of enterprises was less free and the new "iron rice bowl" had again become the guidance of social employment. The institutional innovation of local governments was not encouraged, but criticized. The media and public opinion blamed the root causes of most economic problems on local governments. The policy of opening to the outside world was questioned, while there was a growing market for populist and parochial nationalist rhetoric. These indicators suggested that the prospect of China's market-oriented reform was still full of uncertainty. In the social system reform, it was the choice of political leaders that played a key role in the short term, but the ideology and value orientation of the masses played a decisive role in the long term. The work of Chinese economists would help build a good mass concept and promote China's reform to continue to move forward toward marketization.[13]

On the evaluation of the performance of China's economic system reform and the path of further reform, some commentators concluded that on the one hand, almost everyone admitted that the reform had greatly promoted the development of China's productive forces and accelerated China's integration into the world's modernization trend. But on the other hand, the process of reform was accompanied by all kinds of debates, especially in the new round of reform disputes, in which not only the intellectual circles but also the public participated widely through the Internet. Although the relevant parties consciously used the media and high-level publicity to guide public thought, they were not able to settle the dispute as before. Why was the institutional change that had greatly promoted China's economic growth and social progress still facing controversy and questioning? Some scholars pointed out that as long as the reform conformed to the Kaldor-Hicks standard of welfare economics, the government should promote it. The Kaldor-Hicks standard referred to a state in which the total outcomes of the reform to all members of society, after compensating the total cost of reform, still resulted in net benefits. However, this standard did not consider "the distribution of net income among different members society." Whether different members of society supported the reform or not was closely related to the distribution of the net income of the reform. Therefore, the new institutional economics provided a standard, the Davis-North standard, which stated that only when the expected benefits of supporting the reform exceeded the expected cost of supporting it would the members support it. However, Davis and North introduced uncertainty, and it was concluded that because of the great uncertainty in the process of institutional change, and members of all social strata had different discount rates relative to the "expected consumption" of the system, and thus different "expected" time limits of the "expected net income" of the system. The basic conclusion was that the low-income group had a higher discount rate and was more inclined to choose the current payment flow arrangement, while the high-income group had a lower discount rate and was more inclined to choose the

---

13. Zhang Weiying, "Understanding China's Economic Reform," in *Thirty Years of China's Reform and Opening-up: Reflections of Ten Economists* (Shanghai People's Publishing House, 2008); Mao Tianqi, "Review and Prospect of Theoretical Research on Transition Economy," *Economist*, no. 10 (2010).

arrangement of expected return flow. The most difficult issue to deal with in the reform was that the institutional reform arrangements that could greatly improve productivity and social wealth might not be adopted and implemented smoothly because of the inconsistent interests caused by the distribution. In other words, the key to the smooth progress of institutional change was not whether the reform could greatly enhance productivity and social wealth, but whether it could deal with the interests in the process of reform. In dealing with the problem of "inconsistent interests," China's gradual institutional change could bypass it, and if it could not, it would adopt various transitional plans to minimize the degree of interest conflict and unify the strength of reform with the degree of social affordability. This was one of the important experiences of China's reform. However, it was precisely these strategies adopted by China's reform to deal with the problem of "inconsistent interests" which inevitably led to the accumulation of "inconsistent interests." In addition, due to the untimely compensation, with the deepening of the system transformation, contradictions also accumulated, and China's social equity situation deteriorated.

This was all in contrast to Russia's radical reform. There was now a "complex conspiracy" in China. Not only were those whose interests in the previous stage of reform were relatively damaged unwilling to support the reform, but those who had vested interests in the reform in the previous stage were likewise not willing to push it forward. The plan given by theorists was that in order to continue to promote this "acceptable reform," the most urgent task was to transform the reform to conform it to the Kaldor-Hicks standard into the reform of "sharing results" by implementing the policy of income redistribution boldly, so that those who felt that their relative interests had been damaged in the reform could get due compensation, allowing the reform to be regained by the people, especially those at the bottom. The government needed to change its functions, turn to "social management" and "public service," coordinate the interests of all walks of life, and improve the social security and social welfare system.[14]

From the above analysis, the profound influence of the traditional Chinese cultural norm of "worrying not about scarcity but about inequality" and the thinking of China's ancient sages can be felt. This sort of national cultural mentality was an important constraining condition in China's institutional change. In a sense, a "harmonious society" and a "scientific outlook on development" were the policy choices for continuing to promote reform under this constraint. However, if "worrying not about scarcity but about inequality" was a definite constraint, continuing to deepen the market-oriented reform under such a constraint was indeed a great test of China's political wisdom. By 2009, China's institutional change and economic and social transformation process had been going on for thirty years. Compared with international experience, the time was not short, but it was still far from the goal of "enriching the people and strengthening the country." Unless it continued to promote Reform and Opening Up, China would return to the historical cycle of poverty and backwardness.

Some commentators found that the efficiency improvement in China's economic system transition came from the incremental and stock reforms, which enabled the incremental and stock

---

14. Lu Zhoulai, "The New Political Economics of China's Reform," *Reading*, no. 5 (2009).

resources to be allocated vertically and horizontally according to the opportunity cost principle. It also came from the improvement of adaptive efficiency brought by institutional innovation. China carried out a series of reforms and innovations, mainly including the combination of basic system innovation and its realization form innovation, the combination of enterprise reform innovation and government reform innovation, and the combination of the development of the public ownership economy and the development of the non-public ownership economy. The reform and innovation in these aspects, to a large extent, solved the problem of the failure of the original system, released the potential of production efficiency, and improved the efficiency of the system. There were also those who held that the effect of the reform should be to pay attention to social equity and move toward common prosperity and harmonious social development. This was one of the characteristics of China's reform model.[15]

The research group of the Chinese Academy of Social Sciences (CASS), active for thirty years, published the research results On the Path of Economic System Reform with Chinese Characteristics in the 9th and 10th issues of *Economic Research* in 2008.[16] It summarized the reform path of the economic system with Chinese characteristics from nine aspects and summarized the core of the "China model." The theoretical guidance of reform involved paying attention to the leading role of theoretical innovation. The nature of reform was the unity of the second revolution and the self-improvement of the socialist system. The direction of reform was to take the establishment of the socialist market economic system as the goal. The path of reform was to advance marketization gradually. The relationship between reform and development involved taking development as the purpose of reform. The relationship between reform and stability involved taking stability as the guarantee of reform. The relationship between reform and opening up involved paying attention to the mutual promotion between marketization and internationalization. The coordination and matching of reform aimed to promote all-round reform. The driving force of the reform gave attention to the joint effort of the grassroots and the leadership. With the affirmation of the thirty-year reform performance, the research report pointed out that in the face of the future, China's reform and development was in a critical stage, and it faced many new challenges. First, the reform would be further advanced in depth, with increasing difficulties and heavy tasks. Second, the reform would further expand in the direction of comprehensive system innovation, and the reform would become increasingly systematic.

---

15. Zhang Peili and Chen Liang, "Review of the Forum on the Road and Mode of Socialist Market Economy with Chinese Characteristics and Commemorating the 30th Anniversary of Reform and Opening Up," *Economics Trends*, no. 9 (2008); Sun Shengmin, "Research and Progress on the Relationship Between Institutional Change and Economic Performance," *Economics Trends*, no. 10 (2008); Chen Xiangguang, "The Logic and Path of Efficiency Increase in China's Economic Transition," *Economics Trends*, no. 1 (2009); Lv Wei, "Chinese-style Transition: Internal Characteristics, Evolution Logic and Prospects," *Research on Financial Issues*, no. 3 (2009); Research Center of Quantitative Economy, Shanghai Academy of Social Sciences, "Research on Sustainable Growth and Transformation of China's Economy under the Financial Crisis," *Economic Research*, no. 1 (2010); Li Bingyan, "Outline of Economic Reform of 'China Model,'" *Economics Trends*, no. 2 (2010).

16. Research Group of the Chinese Academy of Social Sciences on the 30-Year Economic System Reform, "On the Road of Economic System Reform with Chinese Characteristics," *Economic Research*, no. 9, 10 (2008).

It needed not only coordination among various links in the economic system reform, but also comprehensive matching between the economic system reform and the political, cultural, and social system reform. Third, in order to realize the transformation of the economic development mode, the new development framework, including economic development, social development, coordinated development between humans and nature, and humankind's all-round development, should also be taken into account. The requirements for reform were always rising. Fourth, it was necessary to coordinate the interests of all aspects in China under the condition of diversified stakeholders and to seek advantages and avoid disadvantages in a more complex, changeable international environment. The risks of reform could not be ignored. Fifth, as far as the leaders of reform were concerned, they were faced with the important mission of unswervingly adhering to the direction of reform, improving the mode of reform, enhancing the driving force of reform, further improving the scientificity of reform decision-making, and enhancing the coordination of reform measures. In the face of these challenges, more wisdom and greater courage in building a dynamic, efficient, more open approach that was conducive to the scientific development system and mechanism was needed. It was important to continue to explore the road of economic system reform with Chinese characteristics and to continue to strive for the goal of perfecting and finalizing the socialist market economic system. Some scholars empirically studied the contribution of China's marketization process to economic growth. From 1997 to 2007, the contribution of the marketization process to economic growth reached 1.45% per year. The market-oriented reform promoted the improvement of resource allocation efficiency. In this period, 39.2% of total factor productivity was contributed by marketization.[17]

Some commentators used the "China model" to explain the "China miracle" of China's rapid economic growth after the beginning of Reform and Opening Up and summed up several conditions for China's transition to a market economy and its economic growth. First, the central government of a country should have strong control. It could not only maintain social, economic, and political stability, but also have a strong ability of macro-control, and it would not make systematic mistakes. Second, the dominant ideology could maintain continuity. Ideology has always played an important role in the institutional change of human society. Institutional change could not be understood without considering ideology. Before and after the beginning of the reform of China's economic system, the consistency of ideology in Chinese society reduced the cost of incremental reform. Third, there was no vested interest group with balanced power in the political market of a country. If there were more than two interest groups in a country and there was no consistent goal among them, each interest group would act according to their own interests, which would not only lead to the proliferation of rent-seeking political activities and rampant corruption, but also consume the limited economic resources. Fourth, it was important to have basic material production conditions. Before the economic system reform launched in 1978, China had established a relatively perfect industrial system through the strategy of giving priority to the

---

17. Fan Gang, Wang Xiaolu and Ma Guangrong, "Contribution of China's Marketization Process to Economic Growth," *Economic Research*, no. 9 (2011).

development of heavy and chemical industry. Although the system lacked economic efficiency, various sales channels, production equipment, and technical networks had laid the foundation for the reform of the economic system. Fifth, it had a strong public ownership system. If the governments of developing countries wanted to effectively regulate and intervene in the economy, they needed to have strong public resources. The foundation and dominant position of China's state-owned economy was not only reflected in its total social assets, but also in the operating assets, which provided the basis for the state to effectively regulate and control the economy.[18]

Studies showed that at the beginning of the 21st century, China faced the challenge of determining how it might overcome the "middle income trap." In 2010, China's GDP per capita reached 4,382 US dollars, while China's total economic output leapt to the second place in the world, and it had just entered the ranks of upper-middle income countries as defined by the World Bank. According to the Madison standard adopted by many authors, in terms of purchasing power parity, China had exceeded the deceleration point of US$7,000. If the annual GDP growth rate of 9% were maintained, China would meet the conditions of a higher deceleration point of US$17,000 in 2015. According to the international experience and lessons, China needed to carry out reforms in improving total factor productivity, expanding the accumulation of human capital, and deepening the transformation of system and government functions, so as to maintain sustainable economic growth.[19] Some people believed that China's rapid economic growth had greatly enhanced its overall economic strength and the people's material living standards. However, China's development model also brought about some side effects. Therefore, it was necessary to accelerate system reform, including political and economic system reform. The main point of political system reform was to introduce external supervision to curb corruption. The direction of further reform of the economic system was to eliminate all discriminatory systems and establish an institutional environment of fair competition.[20] The gradual characteristics of the "China model" ensured the steady progress of China's economic development and social prosperity. At the beginning of the reform, China's development involved the "dual synchronization" of modernization and marketization, so there were risks of internal deepening adjustment and external environment changes. Therefore, the "China model" faced new challenges and was poised to undergo a long-term process of structural adjustment and system improvement. The further transformation included the in-depth promotion of political system reform, the proper positioning of the role of market and government, the improvement of government governance efficiency, the continuous promotion of market-oriented reform, and the cultivation of civil society to generate "benign social capital."[21]

---

18. Huang Ziqi and Zhao Jingfeng, "Institutional Interpretation of the 'China Model': Comparison and Evaluation Based on Two Theories," *Economist*, no. 9 (2010).

19. Cai Fang, "Theory, Experience and Pertinence of 'Middle Income Trap,'" *Economics Trends*, no. 12 (2011).

20. Guo Xibao, "On China's Economic Development Model and its Transformation," *Contemporary Finance and Economics*, no. 3 (2011).

21. Liu Yan and Li Wenzhen, "'China Model': Challenges and Promotion Strategies," *Research on Financial Issues*, no. 2 (2014).

From 1978 to 2017, China's economy achieved an average annual growth rate of 9.5% for 39 consecutive years. In 2009, China's economy surpassed Japan to become the second largest economy in the world. In 2010, China's export volume surpassed that of Germany to become the world's largest exporter. In 2013, China's total trade volume surpassed that of the United States to become the world's largest trading country. In 2017, China's per capita GDP exceeded US$8,000, making it an upper-middle income country. In this process, more than 700 million people were lifted above the international poverty line. The practice of China's Reform and Opening Up proved that the gradual dual track system was an important means of maintaining economic stability and rapid development. However, the market distortion and improper intervention in the process of gradual dual track reform also led to corruption and a widening income gap, which were the challenges to continuing the deepening of economic reform.[22] Gradualism was the appropriate strategy for China's economic transformation. The gradual reform process meant that many state-owned enterprises would remain inefficient for a period of time. In order to accelerate economic growth, power and support were needed. The vigorous development of non-state-owned enterprises could be used as the engine of growth. Once given the opportunity, the appropriate economic system would naturally form and develop, which was the case in China.[23]

Entrusted by the central leading group on finance and economics of the CPC Central Committee and the National Development and Reform Commission, Professor Michael Spencer, Nobel Laureate in economics, and others led the writing of *China's Economy: Medium and Long-term Development and Transformation* and studied the medium and long-term strategy of China's economy and the Twelfth Five-Year Plan. The book collected more than twenty economists from all over the world who worked in different renowned international institutions and had different backgrounds. The summary of the "China miracle" focused on the summary of the "China experience," which could be summarized as making full use of the world economy, maintaining macroeconomic stability, maintaining high savings and investment rates, allocating resources through the market, and having a responsible, credible, competent government.[24]

4. Research on "China's Transitional Economics" and Evolutionary Economics

The "transitional stage" involved a process of changing the social system. This sort of process might include a change in the social, economic, or political system. The change of any social form or system requires a process and time, and it is not managed in a single step. Instead it constitutes a special stage in the process of social development. This special stage has an impact on the nature of historical development. During this historical period, China was facing a transition from a

---

22. Lin Yifu, "40 Years of Reform and Opening Up and China's Economic Development," *Economics Trends*, no. 8 (2018).

23. Zou Zhiqing, "Important Experience of China's Economic Reform and Development," *China Economic Report*, no. 2 (2019).

24. Liu He, *Important Experience of China's Economic Reform and Development* (CITIC Press, 2011); Xia Bin, "China Miracle: An Economist's Thinking on Theoretical Innovation," *Economics Trends*, no. 3 (2019).

planned economy to a market economy. It was thus the task of "China's transition economics" to systematically study the approaches and methods of transition from a planned economy to a market economy, to complete the transition with the lowest cost and in the shortest possible time, and to realize the benign transformation of society and the economy. "China's transition economics" needed to pay special attention to the research on the process of China's market-oriented reform, analyze different reform paths in the transition process, compare costs and benefits, and design an optimal path to guide the reform to success. Some critics pointed out that the concept of reform cost could be deduced from the analysis of benefit distribution in the process of reform. With the concept of reform cost, it was impossible to use the cost-benefit analysis method of economics to study the transition process and reform path of China's reform. Generally speaking, the benefits of reform were clear, focusing on the improvement of resource allocation efficiency brought about by institutional change. As for the reform cost, some people emphasized "social cost," while others emphasized "individual cost." This reflected the difference between the "collectivist methodology" and the "individualist methodology." The cost of reform was not only the cost caused by the conflict of interest, but also the "implementation cost" of reform, that is, the cost of searching and learning new institutional arrangements and renegotiating and signing contracts to change the system. No matter how the extension of reform cost was defined, it was common to extend the concept of reform cost from the interest conflict of economic subjects.[25]

Generally speaking, China's transitional economics was an institutional economics, or a theory of institutional change. It gave greater attention to the system and the change of the system. The basic logic of institutional change theory was to emphasize the important influence of the institution on economic efficiency and the decision-making role of institutional change on economic development. China's institutional change theory, which studied the process of economic transition, seemed to focus more on issues such as how to realize the replacement of the new institutional arrangement with the old one without changing the initial income distribution pattern. In the specific research of the reform process, the basic institutional change and the secondary institutional change had a strong explanatory power, and the public choice theory was used to study the basic institutional change, while the property rights transaction theory was used to study the secondary institutional change, or the change of contract form. The mutual influence and intersections of these two kinds of institutional changes constituted the main substance of the transition process. The challenge of China's transitional economics to orthodox economics was not so much its own, but the challenge to orthodox economics from the relative success of institutional economics and China's marketization. The suboptimal theory derived from the

25. Hu Ruyin, "Political Economics of China's Reform," *Economic Development Research*, no. 4 (1992); Jiang Yuezhong, "Practice Calls for Transitional Economics," *Academic Research*, no. 6 (1995); Sheng Hong, "Research on the Transition Process of China's Market-oriented Reform," *Economic Research*, no. 1 (1996); Jiang Chunze, "Transition Economics and the Characteristics of China's Economic System," *World Economic Journal*, no. 2 (1996); Feng Tao, "China's Progressive Reform Model and China's Transitional Economics," *Contemporary Economic Science*, no. 1 (1996).

general equilibrium theory held that local improvement might lead to worse results from the overall situation. Therefore, it was impossible or unnecessary to achieve market-oriented reform through "gradual" reform or local marginal change. China's reform proved that far from bringing negative externalities, local marginal reform would lead to positive external effects, which made the reform easier. The efforts to explain China's market-oriented path could further enrich the theory of institutional change and bring about theoretical breakthroughs relative to orthodox economics.[26]

According to analysis, at the beginning of the reform, the demonstration of the goal of the market-oriented reform and the choice of the reform path and plan mainly depended on the theoretical resources available at that time—Marxist economics and the classical political economics, which was very similar to it. This included the discussion on "the purpose of production," the defense of "commodity production," the reaffirmation of "the law of value," and the advocacy of "rebuilding individual ownership." More importantly, it was the preliminary application of the economic analysis method. After that, the reform theory of Eastern Europe had an impact on economic theory circles. Representatives of this theory included Bruce of Hungary, Sikh of Czechoslovakia, Lange of Poland, and Kornai of Hungary. Although they were all regarded as Eastern European theorists, their theoretical backgrounds were different. The former two were mainly rooted in Marxist economics, while the latter two had moved from Marxist economics to modern Western economics, mainly microeconomics, were specifically, analyzing the planned economy with the method of microeconomics. Although the influence of Bruce, Sikh, and Langer's theories did not last for long, they still played a considerable role in the direction of decentralization reform. Comparatively speaking, Kornai's *Economics of Shortage* achieved considerable success in the field of Chinese economic theory because of its great explanatory power.

As these Eastern European theories gained attention, orthodox Western economic theory— neoclassical economics—was introduced into the study of reform. At the time, this theory was no longer used to prove the correctness of the goal of market-oriented reform, but was used more as an analytical method. Therefore, what it faced was not one or two abstract concepts, but many practical economic issues. As a result, every branch of orthodox economics was introduced and applied to the study of China's market reform process. With the application of more academic economists in analysis, neoclassical economics achieved considerable success. In the mid-1980s, the theory called new institutional economics or new political economics came into the view of Chinese economists. Among them, there were three schools of thought that had great influence on China's economic circles. One was the new institutional economics led by Coase, or the theory of property rights or transaction costs. The second was the public choice theory headed by Buchanan. The third was Olsen's "logic of collective action." Although the new

---

26. Sheng Hong, "How Economics Challenges History," *Oriental*, no. 1 (1996); Li Xiao, "Several Issues on China's Transitional Economics," *Economic News*, July 19, 1996; Wang Zhicheng and Shi Xuejun, "Institutional Change and China's Reform," *Economist*, no. 5 (1998).

institutional economics was based on the method of neoclassical economics, its characteristics of emphasizing institutional factors and conflicts of interest made it the most powerful critic of the latter. Neoclassical economics assumed that the system was an unchangeable factor, that the transaction cost was zero, and that people had perfect rationality, while ignoring the study of interest factors, which made it impossible to correctly explain many practical economic problems, especially those in the transitional period. The spread of new institutional economics in China helped foster understanding of the limitations of neoclassical economics and avoided coming to wrong conclusions. The explanatory power of the new institutional economics to the transition process, together with its research methods in line with the needs of China's market-oriented reform, made it perhaps the most popular economic theory in China in the late 1980s and the first half of the 1990s.[27]

"China's transition economics" was formed through the comparison of different reform paths and their consequences among China, the Soviet Union, and the Eastern European socialist countries. The so-called transitional economics referred to an economic theory that studied how to transition from a planned economy to a market economy. Transitional economics in China referred to the research literature and thought of Chinese scholars in this field combined with China's reform practice. The book *Transition Economics in China* collected analytical articles on the process of China's reform, as well as the comparative analysis of this process with the reform of the Soviet Union and Eastern European countries. There was no systematic theoretical system in transitional economics. If it was "China's transitional economics," it could only be said that the tools and methods used by these scholars to analyze problems had great similarity. Even the editor in chief of *Transition Economics in China* said that it seemed that there was no consensus on who first proposed the term "transitional economics." At the time, only some theoretical documents and the economists who wrote these documents constituted this school of economics. But it was difficult to say who the "transition economist" were because there was no one specializing in this theoretical research. Moreover, by the end of the 20th century, in 1998 and 1999, "transition economics" research seemed to have declined.

In the analysis of the reform process with institutional change as the main content, "China's transitional economics" took the distribution of interests, conflicts of interests, and the resolution of conflicts of interests as the central issues and put forward the concept of reform costs related to the loss of interests. According to the logic of reform cost, "transitional economics" had two understandings of the process of reform. First, the improvement of resource allocation brought about by replacing the old institutional arrangement with a new institutional arrangement was the benefit of this reform, which was also recognized by neoclassical economics. But the difference was that "transition economics" held that because the reform involved the change and distribution of interests, the replacement process of the old and new systems could not be

---

27. Sheng Hong, *Transition Economics in China* (Shanghai Sanlian Bookstore, 1994); Wu Jinglian et al., *Gradualness and Radicalness: the Choice of China's Reform Path* (Economic Science Press, 1996); Han Zhiguo, *Institutional Effect of China's Reform and Development* (Economic Science Press, 1998); Hu Jizhi, "The Stages of China's Economic Transition and its Realization," *Economist*, no. 2 (1998).

completed "instantaneously" under the condition of zero transaction costs, but a process of constantly overcoming resistance. In order to make the reform go smoothly, it was necessary to maintain the strength of supporting the reform (those who obtained benefits from it) at a level greater than those who opposed the reform (those who may lose their vested interests after it). The task of the reformers was to find the reform path with the lowest cost. Second, the reason the early effect of Russia's radical reform was not good was that the reform caused those with vested interests to lose their interests quickly, which led to opposition to the reform that was far greater than the reform advocated, making the resistance and cost of reform too large, and ultimately leading to the poor effects of the reform.[28] The hypothesis of "China's transition economics" in the reform process had a strong explanatory power for China's gradual reform, but it was not convincing to use it to explain Russia's reform. Whether the failure of Russia's reform was due to the strong opposition to reform was a question that needed further study. Moreover, whether Russia's market-oriented reform had "failed" could not be concluded. After the implementation of political reform in Russia, decision-making in connection with the reform generally went through a democratic decision-making process, but Russia's reform was still in progress, and it could not support the judgment that "the forces against reform were strong." If this judgment was difficult to establish, then the inference that "the cost of radical reform was too high" based on cost-benefit analysis was groundless.

The theoretical and practical value of "China's transitional economics" research was evident in the fact that the essence of China's economic system reform was the marketization of the economy, or the establishment of the "socialist market economy." The marketization of the economy referred to the transition from a non-market economy to a market economy. Therefore, China's economy was in the stage of "transformation" or "transition." This characteristic determined the particularity of economics in this period, that it was neither covered by traditional socialist economics nor represented by modern Western economics as a theoretical description of a mature market economic system. In fact, China's current economics could be called "transition economics," with "transition" referring to the transition from a non-market economy to a market economy. The content of transitional economics included the cultivation and perfection of the market system, the shaping of the market subject, the generation of the market operation mechanism and its micro foundation, the adjustment of the interest relationship, the transformation of people's ideas and behavior standards, and even the reform of the social and political system. None of them had an example to follow. It was only possible to carry out scientific research and theoretical innovation according to the basic national conditions, the social and cultural characteristics, the inherent law of economic development, and the specific practice of social change, so that economic theory could explain the real economy and guide social and economic activities.

China's market-oriented reform had an essential provision, the establishment of a socialist market economy. This essential regulation had two implications. First, China was changing and

---

28. Zhang Jun, "Transition Economics: Review and Controversy of Theory," *Shanghai Economic Research*, no. 4 (1997); Yuan Zhigang and Lu Ming, "Several Theoretical Issues in Transitional Economy," *Economist*, no. 3 (1997); Zhang Pu, "The Limitations of China's Transition Economics," *Economist*, no. 2 (1998).

transiting from the socialist planned economic system to the market economic system. Second, China needed to transition to the market economy without changing the basic socialist production relations and social systems. These two implications, especially the second one, meant that China's reform was a historical institutional innovation. To that point, economic theories could not provide the analytical framework of a category system for this innovation. China's transitional economics would go through a difficult process of exploration in order to establish a market operation mechanism based on the incentive and restriction of individual interests on the basis of socialist production relations, and to solve the long-standing problem of fairness and efficiency in economics. Once this system innovation was realized, it would be a great contribution to human civilization.

At the beginning of the 21st century, evolutionary economics, a branch of Western economics, began to be introduced into China. China's economic circles gradually attached importance to the study of evolutionary economics, and the theoretical description of the economic and social evolution of evolutionary economics, such as the institutional background and artificial selection mechanism, was related to China's economic and social transformation. In the study of China's institutional change, evolutionary economics gradually replaced transitional economics.

Darwin's *The Origin of the Species,* published in the 1860s, had a great impact on social sciences and economics. In 1898, American economist Thorstein Veblen published *Why Economics Is Not an Evolutionary Science,* followed by *The Theory of the Leisure Class,* for the first time applying Darwinist variation, inheritance, and selection to economics. Joseph Schumpeter published *The Theory of Economic Development* in 1912, and *Capitalism, Socialism, and Democracy* in 1942, putting forward the evolutionary theory and the endogenous technological progress theory to explain the change. Later, Friedrich Hayek put forward the theory of "independent order" to study the formation of social order from the perspective of evolutionary economics. Beginning in the 1990s, the theory of evolutionary economics was applied to the fields of technological change, institutional change, and industrial evolution.[29] In China, literature on the theory, ideas, and methods of evolutionary economics was increasingly published to allow for greater study of China's institutional change and economic system transformation.

Some studies discussed evolutionary economics from the perspective of the economic paradigm or philosophical basis. Evolutionary economics was the product of the new world outlook produced by Darwin's revolution and the physics revolution at the end of the 19th century, while neoclassical economics was based on the Newtonian world outlook produced by classical physics. There were essential differences between evolutionary economics and neoclassical economics in the area of philosophy. The study of evolutionary economics was not to be limited to specific economic issues, but needed to embody its dynamic, organic, systematic, and open world outlook, so as to realize the creative synthesis of various schools of evolutionary economics.[30] Some scholars re-examined the incomplete contract theory from the perspective of evolutionary

---

29. Chen Liuqin, "Booming Evolutionary Economics," *China Social Sciences Journal,* September 14, 2010.

30. Jia Genliang, "Ontological Hypothesis of Evolutionary Economics and its Practical Guiding Value," *Contemporary Finance and Economics,* no. 7 (2010).

economics, emphasizing that the incompleteness of contract should be explained from the perspective of knowledge incompleteness, and the limited cognition of the individual was the important theoretical basis of incomplete contract.[31] Theorists sought to promote the construction of the general theoretical framework of institutional evolution economics by studying the core concepts, methodology, and analysis mechanism of institutional evolution theory. It was pointed out that the essence of China's economic transformation and upgrading was institutional change and evolution, not merely the non-evolutionary growth of quantitative expansion. The theory of institutional evolution could provide important theoretical enlightenment for the transformation of China's economic system.[32]

15.2 The Transformation of China's Economic System and the Evaluation of Western Neo-liberal Economics

1. A Review of Neo-liberal Economics

Beginning in the 1980s, the two terms "neo-liberalism" and "neo-liberal economics" appeared frequently in China. Academic and economic circles began to introduce, study, and discuss the philosophical, political, and economic thought of neo-liberalism. In the 21st century, with the development of economic globalization and the deepening of China's Reform and Opening Up, the discussion on neo-liberal economics became increasingly heated, and there were even fierce debates on the direction of China's economic system reform. Many commentators did not grasp the theoretical origin, school formation, analytical framework, and main points of neo-liberal economics accurately, with some even having a wrong understanding, and some of the controversial topics and views were ideological, but this was the scene in China's economic thought at the time, and it was necessary to offer a description and an analysis.

Some researchers commented that neo-liberal economic thought, also known as neo-conservative economic thought, was a contemporary Western economic theory gradually formed and developed in the process of anti-Keynesianism after the 1930s. From 1929 to 1933, the capitalist world economic crisis had a great impact on classical liberal economics, and the dominant position of classical liberal economics was replaced by Keynesianism. However, there were still a few economists who adhered to the creed of the liberal economy, opposed Keynesianism, advocated a return to the laissez faire market economy, and opposed state intervention. In the 1970s, especially after the economic crisis of 1974–1975, the "stagflation" of unemployment and inflation coexisted in capitalist countries, which put Keynesianism in a dilemma. It was in this context that the economic trend of neo-liberalism rose and gained a certain market.

---

31. Huang Kainan, "A New Perspective of Incomplete Contract Theory: An Analysis Based on Evolutionary Economics," *Economic Research*, no. 2 (2012).

32. Huang Kainan, "Theoretical Development and Construction of Institutional Evolutionary Economics," *Chinese Social Sciences*, no. 5 (2016).

Neo-liberal economic thought mainly included the London school, the modern currency school, the rational expectation school, the supply school, the Freiburg school, the public choice school, and the property rights economic school. Among them, the London school was the most thoroughly liberal, and the modern monetary school was the most influential school in the new liberalism. The reason these schools fell into the scope of neo-liberalism was that they had something in common in terms of their basic ideas. For example, they advocated a liberal economy, opposed state intervention, advocated individual freedom, advocated privatization and private ownership, advocated global liberalization and free trade, advocated welfare individualization, and opposed the welfare state. Neo-liberal economics was the connection between private ownership and individual freedom. Hayek said, "It is the only reason that the means of production is in the hands of many independent people. Only because no one controls our property rights can we decide what we want to do as individuals. If all the means of production fall into the hands of one person, whether it belongs to the whole 'society' in name or belongs to a dictator, whoever holds the power of management will have full control over us."[33] Some commentators commented that the essential feature of neo-liberal economic thought was the modern liberalism of "retrogression" and "return" on the basis of Keynesianism, or "rightist" neo-conservatism.

Neo-liberal economics did not refer to a set of independent economic theories. It was mainly reflected in the theoretical paradigm and value concept of neoclassical economics, which was the mainstream economics. Compared with Keynesian theory and state interventionism, neo-liberal economics advocated the values of "economic freedom" and "personal choice." Up to that time, most Nobel laureates were advocates and promoters of neo-liberal economics, such as Hayek, Stigler, Friedman, Buchanan, Becker, Coase, North, and Lucas. Neo-liberalism was the inheritance of classical liberalism. In the 18th century England, Locke, Mandeville, and Hume developed the initial expression of economic liberalism, but its economic meaning was not clear. Adam Smith systematically expounded the economic thought of "laissez faire" in *An Inquiry into the Nature and Causes of the Wealth of Nations* published in 1776, and put forward the basic concepts of the "economic man" and "invisible hand," which laid the ideological foundation for economic liberalism. The theoretical basis of classical liberalism was individualism. It took the independent, free, and equal individual as the starting point for political philosophy and regarded this abstract individual as the foundation and origin of the state, while the state was just a collection of individuals, which endowed individuals with ultimate value, made the individual the end, and made the state the tool to protect individual rights. The core of liberalist theory was to define individual rights and state (government) power. Liberals held that individuals had some natural basic rights, such as life, freedom, property, or the pursuit of happiness. This was the inherent requirement of human nature. They call it "natural rights." The central idea of economic liberalism was that a market society organized on the basis of everyone's private interests was the natural state of human beings. As long as there was no external barrier, this type of society would undoubtedly prosper through the "invisible hand." Capitalism had always existed. All human

---

33. Hayek, *The Path to Slavery* (China Social Science Press, 1997), 101.

history was just the gradual liberation of market relations, and what this universal, rational social form needed was to eliminate its bondage.[34]

As an economic trend of thought, neo-liberalism was formed in the 1930s and developed rapidly after the 1960s, when it began to penetrate into the field of international trade. The representative figures of neo-liberalism who had great influence in this field included Balassa, Bagwati, Kruger, Lal, Ritter, and Srinivasan. Starting from the study of trade strategy and the trade system, neo-liberalism explored a series of related trade policy issues and gradually formed the main viewpoints of its trade policy theory, including protection cost theory, trade distortion theory, neutral trade system theory, and trade liberalization theory. The theory of protection cost evaluated the effect of the import substitution strategy and pointed out that import substitution was accompanied by a high degree of effective protection measures. This high degree of protection involved the overestimation of local currency, the suppression of exports, and the huge cost of domestic resources, resulting in the misplacement of resources, dependence on the import of capital goods, and low economic efficiency. On the issue of trade, neo-liberalism adhered to the dogma of classical international trade theory and believed that free trade without intervention was an ideal state. However, it was difficult to meet the strict conditions required by the laissez faire of the Pareto optimality. Distortion was defined as the deviation of economic activities from the Pareto optimal state. The root cause of the distortion was market failure, and it was also the result of government policies. The new liberal economy required the implementation of a "neutral trade system," the core of which lay in the equivalence of judgment on import and export. Both import substitution and extreme export promotion depended on the biased policies of the government, which were important reasons for the distortions. Trade liberalization needed to be carried out in a world with distortions and trade protection, and a neutral trade system needed to be established to return to free trade. Trade liberalization was a process in which more price mechanisms were used to make the trade system more transparent and domestic prices closer to world market prices. Trade liberalization required the reform of trade policy, which included the change of the trade system to a neutral incentive structure, the tendency to freer trade system, or both. It was generally believed that the typical order of trade policy reform first included that adjusting the exchange rate to be realistic through the devaluation of the local currency could make the import quantity restrictions redundant, and at the same time, it would help to remove these restrictions quickly and increase the relative interests of exporters. Further, export policy reforms (e.g., temporary export licensing or export tax rebate) needed to be carried out before the import reform, which would provide support for the unification of tariffs. In addition, quantitative restrictions needed to be transformed into equivalent tariff measures, because tariffs were generally less disruptive and could bring tax benefits to the government. Finally, in order to

---

34. Henry Lepage, *American Neo-liberal Economics* (Peking University Press, 1985); Noam Chomsky, *Neo-liberalism and Global Economy* (Jiangsu People's Publishing House, 2000); Zuo Dapei, "Reflections on the Evolution of Neoliberal Economic Theory," *Theoretical Frontier*, no. 16, 2005; Zhuo Yue, "New Development of New Institutional Economics: Historical Comparative Institutional Analysis," *Economist*, no. 6 (2006).

further liberalize, the total tariff needed to be reduced.[35]

Neo-liberal policy theory of the world economy and economic globalization were embodied in the Washington consensus. In 1989, Latin American countries were still in a debt crisis, and their domestic economies were in urgent need of reform. In view of the problems existing in Latin American countries, the American Institute of International Economics invited representatives of Latin American countries and researchers from the World Bank, the International Monetary Fund, the Inter-American Development Bank, and the US Department of Finance to hold a seminar on economic adjustment and reform in Latin American countries in Washington. At the end of the conference, John Williamson, a senior researcher at the American Institute of International Economics, proposed ten policy measures for the reform of Latin American countries, claiming that they had reached an agreement with these international institutions headquartered in Washington and the US Treasury Department, so it was called the Washington consensus. The Washington consensus included strengthening fiscal discipline, shifting the focus of government spending to areas with high economic returns and conducive to improved income distribution, such as basic health care, basic education, and infrastructure, tax reform to reduce marginal tax rates and expand the tax base, interest rate liberalization, the adoption of a competitive exchange rate system, trade liberalization, capital entry, especially foreign direct investment (FDI) entry liberalization, privatization, deregulation of the government to eliminate barriers to entry and exit, and protection of property rights. However, based on the international economic relations situation, the Washington consensus was basically unilateral, that is, it required emerging economies to open their markets and almost all economic fields to developed market economy countries, meet the requirements of multinational companies' capital internationalization and production system internationalization expansion, and maintain the seigniorage interests of the US dollar in the international financial field. The policy recommendations of the Washington consensus on the transformation of public expenditure, tax reform, open economy, and other policy recommendations had some reference value for the reform of emerging economies.

2. Critique of Neo-Liberal Economics

At the beginning of the 21st century, China's economic theory circles criticized neo-liberal economics or economic thought from various angles, and many scholars refuted the viewpoint of neo-liberalism. They believed that neo-liberalism was the ideology of the right wing of the modern bourgeoisie. Its theory of the omnipotence of private property rights was essentially the partition of state-owned assets by the power system, while its theory of the omnipotence of the market was essentially a defense for polarization, which had led to great disaster in some developing countries in practice. Some scholars pointed out that the manifestations of

---

35. Huang Jingbo, "Neoliberal Trade Policy and Its Evolution," *Economics Trends*, no. 11 (2003); Fu Yincai, *Neoconservative Economics* (China Economic Press, 1994); Zhao Wei and Guan Hanhui, "A Review of the Relationship Between Trade Growth," *Economics Trends*, no. 12 (2004).

neo-liberalism in China's theoretical circles were the emergence of the views of privatization of ownership reform and multi factor creation value distribution, the reform view completely denying the state plan, and an advocacy of the idea that all industries need not be protected. These views could only mislead China's reform practice. Some scholars believed that the establishment of the socialist market economy and the solution of China's economic problems should be guided by Marxism and based on China's specific situation. Neo-liberalism advocated non-regulation, advocated market fundamentalism, and opposed state intervention. It advocated privatization, propagated the eternal role of the "deification of private property rights," and opposed public ownership. It advocated global liberalization, upheld the free economy dominated by the United States, and opposed the establishment of a new international economic order. It advocated the individualization of welfare and emphasized the transfer of the responsibility of protection from the state to the individual. Compared with Marxist economics, Western radical economics, and new and old Keynesian economics, neo-liberal economic thought was generally conservative and backward. Neo-liberalism was an economic liberalism formed in the 1930s, which was opposite to state interventionism. Neo-liberalism advocated the omnipotence of the market and did not recognize the existence of "market failure." For example, there was no macro-economic stability. Neo-liberalism opposed state intervention and advocated a laissez faire approach. At the time, Neo-liberalism was a theoretical weapon for Western countries to induce the peaceful evolution of socialist countries. It was also a theoretical weapon for Western countries to pursue neo-colonialism in developing countries.[36]

Some people held that the new liberal economic theory was keen on complete privatization and publicized the idea that the efficiency of private ownership was higher than that of public ownership and that fairness and efficiency were alternative relations, thus belittling social equity. Private ownership pursued the maximization of personal interests, which inevitably led to the accumulation of the wealth of the minority and the poverty of the majority and brought about various unfair phenomena. Without exception, the gap between the rich and the poor and the polarization between the rich and the poor were highlighted and deepened in the countries that implemented neo-liberal economic theory. Neo-liberal economic theory on the use of monetary policy for macro-control, the reduction of inflation, and the reduction of the fiscal deficit proposition had a certain reference. However, it was not advisable to advocate the full liberalization of finance and price, the absolute marketization of industry and capital, and the complete privatization of state-owned enterprises and collective enterprises, which served the transformation of capitalism from a state monopoly to an international monopoly.

Some critics criticized the fact that neo-liberalism advocated private ownership but belittled public ownership, advocated market regulation and belittled government intervention, advocated

---

36. Fang Fuqian, "On the Two Sides of Neo-liberal Economics," *Economics Trends*, no. 6 (2004); Pan Shengwen, "How to Look at Neo-liberal Economics," *Economic Overview*, no. 9 (2005); Shen Yue, "The New Development of Western Economics and China's Practice: A Summary of the Sixteenth Annual Meeting of the China Society for the Study of Foreign Economic Theories," *Economist*, no. 5 (2009); Liu Fengyi, "New Liberalism, Financial Crisis and Adjustment of Capitalist Model," *Economist*, no. 4 (2001).

globalization and belittled national interests, advocated efficiency and belittled fairness, advocated individual freedom and belittled social cooperation, advocated capital sovereignty but belittled labor sovereignty, advocated comparative advantage and belittled independent innovation, and advocated Western democracy and belittled social democracy. These ideas included advocating the universality and belittling the particularity of China and advocating the historical mode of Western capitalist development and belittling the history and experience of socialist construction with Chinese characteristics. In fact, the "backwardness" of China's economic system, which was strongly criticized by liberalism, such as the leading role of the state-owned economy, the socialist political system, strong government regulation, and effective control of capital liberalization, was not only the key factor for the success of China's model, but also an effective weapon and powerful guarantee for China to resist the impact of the global financial crisis and get out of that predicament.[37]

The global financial crisis, which began in 2007 and 2008, stimulated criticism of neo-liberalism and the transformation paradigm in China's economic and ideological circles. Some believed that the Washington consensus based on neo-liberal theory and policy propositions promoted market fundamentalism in developing countries. If the capitalist economic crisis in the 1930s proved the failure of neoclassical economic liberalism, then the global financial crisis triggered by the US subprime mortgage crisis declared the complete bankruptcy of neo-liberal economic thought and policies. This crisis not only had a serious impact on developed Western market economies, but also brought disaster to developing countries. According to the data provided by the World Economic Outlook released by the International Monetary Fund in April 2010, the growth rate of global GDP in 2009 was −0.6%, of which the economic growth rate of developed economies was −3.2%, and that of emerging market economies and developing economies was 2.4%. The outbreak of the crisis reflected the inherent defects of the transition strategy of extreme privatization and the absolute liberalization of neo-liberalism. The abnormal economic system it caused had serious instability, fragility, and ineffectiveness in the market order, property rights system, financial system, economic structure, development mode, and state governance, which became the root in a system leading to the aggravation of the crisis. After the advent of the crisis, it was necessary for transitioning countries to make major adjustments to the neo-liberalism paradigm guiding their own transformation and to explore an effective transformation and development path beyond neo-liberalism.[38] Some theorists analyzed that the essential cause of the financial crisis was that in the stage of new liberalism, the economic practice

---

37. Wei Xinghua and Sun Yongmei, "Some Hot Issues of Theoretical Economics in 2005," *Economics Trends*, no. 4 (2006); Ding Weimin, "Contradictions and Crisis of Economic Growth Under the New Liberalism System," *Economics Trends*, no. 3 (2009); Zhang Yu, "Financial Crisis, New Liberalism and China's Road," *Economics Trends*, no. 4 (2009); He Bingmeng, "The Profound Background and Institutional Roots of the Outbreak of the Financial Crisis in the United States," *Marxist Studies*, no. 3 (2009); He Bingmeng, "The US Financial Crisis and International Financial Monopoly Capitalism," *Chinese Social Sciences*, no. 2 (2010).

38. Huang Qiuju and Jing Weimin, "The Harm and Reflection of New Liberalism Paradigm to Transition Countries," *Journal of Hebei University of Economics and Trade*, no. 1 (2011).

and theory of capitalism returned to its essential motivation and original form, leading to the intensification of the basic contradictions of capitalism. The collapse of the financial system was only the fuse of the crisis, and the potential crisis of the real economy was the root cause. It was the result of system dynamics, which included the interaction between productive forces and production relations, and between economic base and superstructure. These categories supported the production, realization, and accumulation of surplus value harmoniously, and at the same time, they caused the accumulation of contradictions until the collapse came as a result of the concentrated outbreak of contradictions.[39] There were two important concepts of neo-liberal theory and neo-liberal policy. Theoretically, the premise and hypothesis of the "perfect market" on which neo-liberalism relied had been strongly refuted, so it could be said to be a "failure" to some extent. However, from the policy point of view, neo-liberalism had not obviously failed. Neo-liberal policy continued to be implemented in many major countries, and even if it did not produce the expected effect and was criticized by many social levels, it still had the support at the state power level. This showed that the ideology of neo-liberalism (including superstition in connection with neo-liberalism) still played an important role in a specific social context.[40]

3. Evaluation of the Ideological System of New Liberalism

From the perspective of the history of economic theory, neo-liberal economics did not have a strict definition like neoclassical economics. Van Buren first used the term "neoclassical" to describe Marshall economics in 1900. More precisely, it was Marshall and other marginal economists who use the concept of marginal analysis and differential tools to once again elaborate the subjective value theory and utility concept contained in classical economics to make it more "mature." In this process, it abandoned the theoretical elements of objective value theory and labor value theory contained in classical economics and completed the "transformation" from classical economics to neoclassical economics. Neoclassical synthesis was proposed by Samuelson in the third edition of *Economics* published in 1955. It referred to the macroeconomics that integrated Keynesian economics and some anti-Keynesian economics, as there was a theoretical connection between neoclassical synthesis and neoclassical economics. The neoclassical synthesis did not hold that full employment would be realized automatically with a laissez faire approach, but it believed that the ideal state of a free market economy advocated by classical and neoclassical economics could be achieved by properly applying monetary and fiscal policy.

The theoretical core of neo-liberalism was still neoclassical, in that it assumed a completely competitive market structure or economic environment. In this economic scenario, prices could float freely, and investment only accounted for a small proportion of the total economic volume. The criterion of economic behavior was to pursue the maximization of interests. As far as possible,

---

39. Liu Dun, Yuan Lunqu and Lin Daidai, "The Double Crisis and Reconstruction of Capitalist Economy and Economics: The Perspective of Historical Materialism," *Economist*, no. 7 (2013).

40. Chen Renjiang, "Neo-liberalism after Neo-liberalism," *Journal of Hebei University of Economics and Trade*, no. 1 (2018).

the market and price mechanism could solve the problem of economic equilibrium. The best governance mode was small government and a large market (society). The problem was that there were few successful cases in the world to advance economic policies based on the assumptions used in the construction of the model and to apply them to various real economies. The capitalist economic system of the UK and the US was the closest to the liberal economics concept, but they had an important condition—either they had a global colonial system or they controlled the global monetary and financial system. In other words, the external economic conditions of the rich and poor could be eased to the maximum extent by the transfer of wealth from the rich to the poor. But not all countries had such conditions. Therefore, the theoretical or academic value could not be equal to the value of economic policy and the value of practice. Economic policy needed not only theoretical guidance, but also an appropriate economic reality, which was also a scientific principle.

Neo-liberal economics, basically regarded as a school of economics, believed in liberalism, that is, the idea of a free market economy. In 1947, Hayek invited 38 liberal economists to hold a meeting at the Hotel du Parc in Switzerland's Mont Pelerin and decided to establish a group aimed at upholding Smith's "system of natural liberty," upholding liberal civilization, opposing all forms of totalitarianism, and fighting against the Keynesianism prevailing at that time and against socialist thought. This academic group was known as the Mont Pelerin Society. The Mont Pelerin Society brought together liberal economists from Europe and the United States, mainly including Mises, Hayek, Machlup, and Brent of the Austrian school and Friedman, Stigler, Buchanan, and Becker of the Chicago school. Generally speaking, the aggregation of liberal economists marked the formation of neo-liberal economics. In fact, based on its theoretical origin, neo-liberal economics was essentially the inheritance of Smith's economics by the Austrian school founded by Carl Menger in 1870's and the Chicago school headed by Friedman and Stigler in the middle of the 20th century. Menger published *The Principles of National Economics* in 1871 and translated it into English in 1950. The theoretical framework put forward by Menger inherited the theoretical core of Smith's "system of natural liberty," but used the marginal utility and opportunity cost principles to "repair" the value price theory of classical economics, making up for the "defect" of "separating production and distribution" in classical economics, and it combined production and distribution, thus combining class and other various types of interests. The conflict turned to Smith's Harmony of Interest theory, which put the system of natural liberty and the Harmony of Interest theory into "perfect" unity.

The Austrian school, inherited by Bohm-Bawerk and Wiesel, was called the modern Austrian school in Mises. Hayek was considered the most famous student of Mises. He won the Nobel Prize in economics in 1974, the first liberal economist to win the prize. Friedman was elected president of the American Economic Society in 1967 and won the Nobel Prize in economics in 1976. In the 1990s, a group of Chicago school economists won the Nobel Prize in economics, including Coase, Becker, Vogel, and Lucas. In fact, Hayek also taught at the University of Chicago from 1950 to 1962. Neo-liberal economics revised some "paradoxes" and even some assumptions of classical liberal economics, such as "correcting" the price theory of classical economics with marginal analysis tools, modifying the complete information hypothesis of classical economics with "decentralized knowledge" and incomplete information, and modifying the hypothesis of "rational man" with limited rationality. Adopting the system of natural liberty in classical economics was a smoother, more universal approach to this theoretical revision and repair. After the middle of the 20th century, the ideas and policies of neo-liberal economics began to be valued by Western countries and became the mainstream in the field of world economics. After the launch of China's Reform and Opening Up, classical Western economics, neoclassical economics, Keynesian economics, and neo-liberal economics were introduced into China, which had an impact on the development of China's economic thought. Neo-liberalism was not only economic thought, but also ideology. Some of the representative works of neo-liberal economists were devoted to the research and exploration of their life's work, which condensed the essence of Western political culture. The neo-liberal thought system closely revolved around the pursuit of self-interest under the conditions of free competition and the system of natural liberty, which was the core of classical economics. It linked this behavior and order with the growth of national wealth and "general prosperity" and demonstrated the superiority of the capitalist market economy system in morality and efficiency. This academic thought system was not only systematic in theory, but also confirmed by the practice of countries with a developed market economy. The evaluation and criticism of it needed to be based on an in-depth, systematic research, and the reasonable scientific ideological and theoretical elements in this system needed to be absorbed and used for reference.

15.3 The Research on China's Development Economics and New Development Concept

1. Chinese Scholars' Early Research on Development Economics and the Current Situation

Development economics began to form after the mid-1940s, studying the process and law of economic development in underdeveloped conditions by comparing various development theories and strategies, economic systems, and feasible countermeasures. Generally speaking, this theory included ideas such as economic growth theory, income distribution theory, capital accumulation theory, human capital theory, industrialization theory, technological progress theory, equilibrium-disequilibrium growth theory, international trade theory, and macro-control theory. These aspects constituted the theoretical framework of development economics, and its core aim was to elaborate how to make backward dual socio-economic countries become developed countries through industrialization. Western economist Rostow's theory of economic growth stage, Lewis's theory of dual economic structure, Schumpeter's theory of technological innovation, Knox's theory of vicious circle of poverty, Rosenstein-Rodan's great promotion theory, Hirschman's unbalanced growth theory, Myrdal's structuralist development theory, and Tinbergen's theory of economic development likewise discussed the design of a "long-term development plan." Schultz's research on agricultural problems and Chenery's research on economic growth and structural transformation made important contributions to the establishment of development economics. Among them, Tinbergen, Lewis, Schultz, and Myrdal were awarded the Nobel Prize in economics for their outstanding contributions to the theory of economic development.

In the evolution of development economics itself, there were three trends. First of all, there was a tendency toward subdivision, that is, some subjects studied in the past under the academic discipline of development economics were now independent in several sub-disciplines, such as labor economics, human capital economics, industrial organization theory, population economics, and education economics. In addition, there were studies on the progress of developing countries. Secondly, they were micro-empirical. This was because economists put forward a number of hypotheses mainly based on logical reasoning, but due to the limitations of conditions, they were not tested. Now, with the more sufficient practice of economic development, it was possible to carry out empirical tests on the hypothesis. For example, the hypothesis of the irrational behavior of farmers and the assumption of full employment of urban industry had been questioned in recent years. Finally, the internal schools of development economics tended to merge. There were three schools of development economics: the neoclassical school, which advocated market regulation, complete competition, maximization of interests, and general equilibrium; the neo-Marxist school, which emphasized class relationship, institutional change, and the dominant / dependent relationship between developed and developing countries; and the structuralist school, which gave attention to structural rigidity (such as the dual economy), oligopoly, and industry. The behavior of the subject was irrational, and the rigidity was determined by the system, habit, custom, culture, and other factors. On the surface, the three schools were separated by a clear line, but in fact they had some common ground. There was even a school called "new neoclassicism," which integrated the main characteristics of the three schools. Its main idea was that all the actors in the economy were the subjects of maximizing interests (neoclassicism), and the most important means to pursue the maximization of interests was perfect information, but the transmission and acquisition of information had costs, and the cost was mainly constrained by the system and restricted by the rigidity of the system (neo-Marxism). The solution, therefore, was to allow changes in the system (neo-Marxism), thereby changing the cost of searching for information. In short, from the perspective of the latest development, the integration of various schools of development economics was obvious.

From the global perspective, the earliest research on the industrialization of agricultural countries was Wilhelm Ropke's "The Industrialization of Agricultural Countries: A Scientific Issue," which was published in French in the *International Economic Review* in July 1938. Later, there was Rosenstein-Rodan's "Industrialization in Eastern and Southeast Europe" published in the *Journal of Economics* in 1943. The earliest monograph on the industrialization of agricultural countries was the doctoral dissertation written by Zhang Peigang of Harvard University at the end of 1945, which was selected into Volume 85 of *Harvard Economic Series* by the university. In 1949, *Agriculture and Industrialization* was published in English by Harvard University Press.

After the founding of the People's Republic of China, from the 1950s to the end of the 1970s, some theories about economic development emerged, including the theory of realizing national industrialization through a catching up strategy, the theory of giving priority to the development of heavy industry (the core of the catching up strategy), the theory of realizing industrialization by relying on internal accumulation, the theory of industrialization based on agriculture, the theory of an industrialization development road led by industry, the theory of correctly handling the relationship among speed, proportion, and benefit in a planned, proportional way, and the theory of the industrial division of the two major categories of the means of production and consumption and the three sectors of agriculture, heavy industry, and light industry. Other ideas included the concept of attaching importance to material production and ignoring non-material production, dividing economic development stages according to the proportion of industrial output value, the theory that balance was relative, imbalance was absolute, or positive and negative balance, the idea of self-reliance as the main idea and foreign aid as the supplement, the theory of implementing the planned economy and denying market regulation, the notion of "the greater the population, the better," and that of the "population restraining theory" and of "balance between population and resources," among others.

There were some outstanding innovations in these theories, such as the relationship between industrialization and agricultural modernization, population control and economic development, and the industrialization development path based on agriculture and led by industry. However, research and discussion in this period was carried out under the condition of being basically isolated from the outside world, so some of the latest international research results and new theories could not be introduced into China, and some of China's innovative theories and ideas could not be recognized by the international community, which seriously hindered the progress and modernization of China's development economics research.

In 1979, at a lecture on "foreign economic theory" held by Peking University, Fan Jiaxiang and other scholars delivered a lecture on economic development theory, which was the first time a theory of Western economic development was systematically introduced in China. In 1984, Zhang Peigang's Chinese version of *Agriculture and Industrialization* was published by Huazhong Institute of Technology Press. In 1988, Tao Wenda's *Development Economics* was published, which was the first development economics work produced as a textbook for colleges and universities in China. In the same year, *An Introduction to Western Development Economics* by Yang Jingnian was published. In July 1989, entrusted by the State Education Commission and funded by the Ford Foundation in the United States, the National College Development Economics Teacher Training Course was held in Renmin University of China. Development economists such as Zhang Peigang, Tan Chongtai, Tao Wenda, and various American development economists taught the course. The training session was held three times and trained more than a hundred teachers, and it played an important role in promoting the teaching and research of development economics in China.

In 1992, *Development Economics*, the core course material for finance and economics majors in colleges and universities, was published by the State Education Commission. It was the first development economics textbook approved by the state. Its publication marked the completion of the first stage of the introduction and establishment of the discipline of development economics in China, and new efforts were made to establish a multi-level, multi-disciplinary, high-level comprehensive research framework for economic development theory.

From the perspective of the current situation and development trend of the theoretical research on development economics in colleges and universities, it was mainly divided into the north and the south. The south, represented by Zhang Peigang of Huazhong University of Science and Technology and Tan Chongtai of Wuhan University, formed a development theory research center. In 1989, Tan Chongtai published *Development Economics*, which introduced Western development economic theory. In 1991, the expanded edition of Zhang Peigang's *General Theory of Development Economics*, Volume I, *Agriculture and Industrialization*, was published. And in 1993, Tan Chongtai published *The History of Western Economic Development Thoughts*, which was the first systematic discussion on the theoretical foundation of Western development theory and a source and development of academic works.

The north was centered around Renmin University of China and Nankai University. Yang Jingnian of Nankai University completed two monographs: *Selected Readings of Development Economics* and *A Comprehensive Analysis of Economic Development Practice of Third World Countries*. Tao Wenda of the economic development research center in Renmin University of China took the establishment of the disciplinary theoretical system of Marxist development economics as the goal of struggle. His monograph *Development Economics* and the textbooks he edited were not translated or rewritten versions of Western development theories, but adhered to the Marxist stands, views, and methods, starting from the national conditions of developing countries and absorbing them. From the theoretical framework and expression to the content tailoring and case analysis, they all expressed the theoretical views of Chinese development economists on economic development.

To sum up, in the early 1990s, development economics in China initially formed a situation in which the north and the south echoed and spread in every aspect. In colleges and universities, development economics was listed as a core economics course, and a master's program (Renmin University of China) and doctoral program (Wuhan University) in development economics were established.

According to the analysis of some critics, the concept of development should be the basic concept and core content of development economics. However, most of the works on development economics did not clearly put forward the concept of the development view, and some even lacked research and discussion on the scientific concept of development. Although Francois Perroux, a French scholar, wrote a book called *New Outlook on Development,* he did not clearly define the connotations of the concept of development. His "new development concept" was only an "overall, endogenous, and comprehensive" development concept. It lacked overall coordination and sustainable development, and it did not put forward a complete, accurate scientific development concept. Therefore, the comprehensive, coordinated, and sustainable scientific development concept innovated the concept of development, enriched the content of development economics, and made up for the deficiency of development theory.

The scientific outlook on development not only improved development economics in terms of defining what development was and why it mattered, but also developed development economics in the area of deciding how to develop. Although development economics summarized and put forward a variety of development paths, development models, and development strategies, such as export of primary products, import substitution, export orientation, priority of light industry, priority of heavy industry, balanced development of industry, unbalanced development of industry, and sustainable development, many of which played a certain role in the development of some countries and achieved certain results, it did not put forward a more rational, comprehensive development path or strategy. In the discussion on how to correctly deal with the important relations and problems between industry and agriculture and urban and rural areas, regional economic development, economy and society, domestic development and opening to the outside world, and the harmonious development of man and nature, there were major defects in terms of overall view, a lack of a big-picture perspective, and a lack of a coordinated outlook. It either emphasized industrialization while belittling agricultural development or focused on urban areas while neglecting rural ones, and it either emphasized unbalanced development of regions while neglecting coordinated development of regional economy, or it paid attention to the balanced development of regions and industries while neglecting overall coordinated development of other aspects. There were other problems, such as the emphasis on the development of the export-oriented economy while neglecting the development of the inward-oriented economy, or affirming self-reliance and denying opening to the outside world. It put forward a sustainable development model and emphasized the coordination of social and economic development with the population, resources, and environment, but it failed to put forward a model of overall planning and coordinated development. The scientific outlook on development overcame the defects in this respect, put forward a complete overall planning and coordinated development model, emphasized that development should correctly handle "seven relations," implemented "five overall plans," and enriched the theory of the development mode in development economics.[41]

2. Chinese Scholars' Research on Development Economics

It was more difficult to divide the thought or schools of thought in development economics than in the orthodox macroeconomics and microeconomics. The reason was not only that the researchers in development economics came from different countries (developed or developing countries), had different knowledge backgrounds, used different analytical tools, and had different degrees of participation in development practice, but also that the research objects of

41. *According to the Editorial Department of Theoretical Trends: Establishing and Implementing the Outlook on Scientific Development* (CPC Central Committee Party School Press, 2004); Wen Jiabao, "Enhancing Understanding, Unifying Ideas, Firmly Establishing and Earnestly Implementing the Scientific Outlook on Development," *Economic Daily*, March 1, 2004; Jian Xinhua and Zeng Xianming, "On the Formation, Contribution and Implementation of the Scientific Outlook on Development," *Economics Trends*, no. 1 (2005); Wang Xiaolin, "On the Theoretical Program of China's Scientific Development Economics," *Economist*, no. 6 (2008); Tang Jijun, "Marxist Economic Interpretation of the Scientific Outlook on Development," *Economist*, no. 4 (2010).

development economics were developing countries with great differences in economy, political system, culture, and religious customs. Therefore, it was difficult to find economics schools with common academic origin, analysis tools, and policy propositions in development economics. Even so, a certain degree of division could be achieved. The key lay in what kind of division standard to choose. According to the research by economic circles, three classification criteria had become more significant in recent years.

Hirschman standard. In 1980, Albert Hirschman, a development economist, used two criteria to divide development theory in his paper entitled *Rise and Fall of Development Economics,* which included affirming or denying the proposition that North-South relations were mutually beneficial and affirming or denying the existence of single economics (that is, an economic theory applicable to any country and any time). He believed that four theories could be drawn from this standard: orthodox economics, which held a positive attitude toward both issues; new Marxist economics, which held a negative attitude toward both issues; development economics, which affirmed the idea of mutual benefit and denied single economics; and Marxist economics, which denied the proposition of mutual benefit and affirmed single economics. Hirschman's criterion was to distinguish development economics from other economics. It was not only a fundamental understanding of the nature of economic theory, but also a fundamental understanding of the nature of international relations.

Ritter standard. In 1971, Todaro, a development economist, pointed out in his book *Economic Development in the Third World* that in the previous thirty years, development works had been dominated by three main and sometimes contradictory ideological clues: linear stage economic growth theory, neoclassical structural change theory, and international dependence model. Todaro did not distinguish structuralism from neoclassicism, and he brought economic growth theory into development economics. Ritter did not believe that the growth stage theory was very important or overwhelming. The standard for his choice was the basic assumption of individual behavior in economics. In his opinion, those who believed that factors of production responded to normal stimulus and flowed smoothly and rapidly from one industry to another at a minimum cost were neoclassicism while those which belonged to structuralism believed that the economy was rigid, that it was made up of special capital currency, and that the individuals with special training in certain areas could be transformed only at high costs or after a long period of time, or perhaps that they could not be transformed at all. Ritter's criterion pointed out a key difference between structuralism and neoclassicism.

Myint standard. In 1987, Hyla Myint divided development economics into four situations according to whether they accepted the orthodox neoclassical theory and supported a free market and free trade. First, free neoclassical economists accepted neoclassical theory and supported a free market and free trade policy. Second, the opponents of neoclassical economics rejected neoclassical economic theory and opposed free market and free trade policies. Third, neoclassical welfare economists accepted neoclassical economic theory, but had doubts about the optimal allocation of resources caused by free market forces. Fourth, the economists inclined to neoclassicism but relatively independent doubted the application of neoclassical economics theory to developing countries, but supported a free market and free trade.

The differences between development economics and other economics and the different theories within development economics mainly focused on three issues: single economics or non-single economics, trust in price mechanism and the market economy or emphasis on state intervention, and finally, whether international trade was beneficial to development.[42]

The term structuralism first appeared in the debate between structuralism and monetarism centering on inflation in Latin America in the 1950s. It was widely used by Chenery in 1965. The development economists known as structuralists included Paul Rosenstein-Rodan, Ragnar Nurkse, Arthur Lewis, Paul Prebisch, Hans Singh, Karl Gunnar Myrdal, and Hollis Chenery. According to Chenery, the basic hypothesis of structuralism was formed in the 1950s. Structuralism held that development was a determinable process of growth and change. The characteristics of development in all countries were similar, so there were rules to follow. The direction of structural change could be obtained from empirical cross-country statistical analysis. However, this did not deny that due to the specific environment of different countries, the speed and specific mode of development could be different. Therefore, structuralism held that the central issue in the study of development economics was what kind of economic mechanism an underdeveloped economy could use to transform the domestic economic structure from a traditional economy that could only survive in a modern, urbanized, and diversified manufacturing and service economy. Structuralism purported that in order to achieve development, the structure should change, and in order to achieve rapid development, the structure should change rapidly. The task of structuralism was to study how this transformation took place.

Some studies pointed out that in the early stage of development economics, structuralism was dominant, and a series of influential structuralist theories emerged. Examples included Rosenstein-Rodan's big push theory, Hirschman's balanced growth theory, Lewis's dual structure analysis, Nurkse's vicious circle of poverty theory, Myrdal's cycle accumulation causal principle, and Prebisch's center-periphery theory. The basic policy propositions derived from these theories were to use central planning to promote large-scale investment in material capital, to realize domestic industrialization with surplus agricultural labor force, to make up for the shortage of domestic capital with foreign aid, and to support the development of the import substitution industry with trade protection policies. These policy propositions greatly influenced the economic development process of most developing countries from the 1950s to the 1960s. The dominant position of structuralism changed in the 1960s. Neoclassicism, which was the opposite of structuralism, gradually revived and became a prominent feature of the second development stage of development economics.

---

42. Zhang Peigang, "Where Does Development Economics Go," *Economic Research*, no. 6 (1989); Hong Yinxing and Chen Zhibiao, "Evolution of Development Economics in China," *Economics Trends*, no. 5 (1992); Tan Chongtai, *The History of Western Economic Development Thoughts* (Wuhan University Press, 1993); Hu Jingbei, "On the Definition of Development Economics," *Economic Research*, no. 11 (1995); Gu Shutang and Liu Zhannian, "Economics in China: Research on Development and Development Economics," *Economics Trends*, no. 11 (1995).

Some theorists concluded that the influence of neoclassicism on development theory was mainly reflected in several aspects. The first was the understanding of the price mechanism and its function. Neoclassical development economists opened up a new field of development economics, the theory and method of "shadow price," aimed at correcting the defects of market operations. The second aspect was the emphasis on the quality of capital. Neoclassical development economists put forward the theory of human capital for the first time, and they placed agriculture in the primary position of development. Finally, the role of international trade in development was reevaluated. Neoclassical development economists put forward the theory of "surplus outlet" to explain the effect of trade on developing countries' economies and the theory of protection cost to analyze the distortion of public policy.[43]

At the end of 1997, the World Bank and the MacArthur Foundation held a seminar on development economics attended by the world's leading economists in Washington. The main focus of the conference was to explore and plan the key directions of development economics research in the early 21st century. As the most remarkable outcome of the meeting, experts at the meeting agreed that the relationship between the government and the market was no longer so important. What would really challenge policy makers and economists in the 21st century was the clarification of the behavioral characteristics of the government and the market from the practical level on the premise of accelerating development and the formulation and implementation of the effective coordination between the two development policies. This might also be the main defect of the development economics research with neoclassical theory as the mainstream. In short, the development economics of the 21st century would be pragmatic, not impractical.

This new research direction was different from the previous research on development economics in three ways. First, it further affirmed the limitations of the market. Second, the extreme importance of technological knowledge to development was further recognized, especially the widening technical knowledge gap between developing and industrial countries, which needed closer attention. Third, it needed to emphasize the key lasting effects of the institutional factors in the development, such as the improvement of the factor market, the adjustment of macro policy, the grasp of the process of trade, and investment liberalization, all of which should be based on the improvement and innovation of the system, with the core content of organizational capacity and political adaptability. The government needed to also keep pace with technological changes and globalization in terms of institutions and policies. Experts from the World Bank pointed out that development economists needed to pay more attention to the system and its individual incentives, and to the interaction between economic policy and the social and political environment. Any policy that could not clearly identify institutional constraints might be ineffective, or even lead to serious negative effects. This type of example promoted capital too early, before the capital market was fully developed, and it could be easily found in liberalized countries. In fact,

---

43. Hu Jian, "On Structuralism and Neoclassicism in Development Economics," *Economic Science*, no. 2 (1992); Liao Shixiang, *Economic Methodology* (Shanghai Academy of Social Sciences Press, 1991); Tan Chongtai, *The History of Western Economic Development Thoughts* (Wuhan University Press, 1993); Chen Zongsheng, "On Development Economics Current Situation and Trend," *Economist*, no. 4 (1995).

the attention to the system naturally led the attention of development economists to some more practical issues, among which was the related issue of the distribution and implementation of development aid in the 21st century. Experts from the World Bank believed that although foreign aid had promoted the economic and social development of recipient countries, there were still a large number of aid projects that were inefficient, and the key was that the recipient countries lacked appropriate and effective economic policies and institutional environments. Therefore, development institutions needed to provide economic policy assistance and system-building support to less developed countries.[44]

3. New Development Economics and Comparative Development Research

In the late 1980s, Zhang Peigang proposed establishing a new type of development economics. After several years, he edited and published *New Development Economics* (Henan People's Publishing House, 1992).

Although traditional development economics took "low-income countries," or developing countries, as research objects, it did not include socialist developing countries. "New development economics" held that since it was "development economics," it did not include all developing countries in its research scope, which was regretful in terms of discipline construction. What's more, developing socialist countries occupied a considerable proportion of the developing countries in terms of population and land area. The successful experience and failure lessons they had gained in the process of economic take-off and economic development could have brought beneficial reference guidance to other developing countries, and they could and should have been inspired by the development experience of other developing countries. Therefore, only by taking all the developing countries, including socialist countries, as the research objects was it possible to reveal the general law of economic development and help human society eliminate poverty. In development economics, it was only in this way that the limitations of the original narrow vision could be overcome and the plight of its poor theory be eliminated, allowing it to become a true development economics.

New development economics held that industrialization should be the theme of development economics research, which was an important part of the reform of economic development theory and the theoretical main line of new development economics.

The meaning of industrialization advocated by Zhang Peigang was broader than the popular one. He described industrialization as "a process in which a series of production functions (or combinations of production factors) in the national economy continuously undergo breakthrough changes from low level to high level." Industrialization had three basic characteristics. The first was that the primary essential feature was the replacement of manual production with machine

---

44. Refer to World Bank, *World Development Report of 1997* (Tianjin University Press, 1997); Liu Enchuan, "New Research Directions of Development Economics in the 21st Century," *Foreign Economy and Management*, no. 6 (1998); Xu Changsheng and Zhang Yin, "On the Strategic Adjustment of 'East Asian Model,'" *Economics Trends*, no. 3 (1999).

production or mechanized processes. The second was that it included not only the mechanization and modernization of industry itself, but also the mechanization and modernization of agriculture. Finally, industrialization needed to first promote the innovation of agricultural production technology and the growth of agricultural production. Industrialization first manifested itself in the change of production technology and social productive forces, and then in the adjustment and change of national economic structure caused by it. Finally, it would inevitably lead to a change in the people's ideology and cultural quality. Under certain circumstances, it would lead to the reform of the whole economic and social system. From this concept of industrialization, it was possible to define industrialization as the center of development.

As for the export-oriented economy, new development economics held that large developing countries should not unilaterally emphasize and comprehensively implement an export-oriented economic strategy, but should adopt the overall development strategy of combining import substitution with export orientation. That is to say, such countries had a huge domestic market, and their economic development should be mainly based on the domestic market. It was unnecessary and impossible to carry out the overall export-oriented strategy. But at the same time, all effective means should be adopted to encourage and support the development of export-oriented enterprises, vigorously developing export-oriented economies in all regions where conditions permitted, in other words, the implementation of an export-oriented development strategy, so as to actively and steadily increase the export-oriented component of domestic economy. At the same time, it was important to maintain a proper balance among regions.[45]

In 2008, Wuhan University Press published *A Comparative Study on the Economic Development of the Developed Countries at Early Stage and the Developing Countries Today*, edited by Tan Chongtai, which opened up a new research field for development economics. The comparative study of economic development referred to the comparative analysis of the early economic development of developed countries and the economic development of developing countries, so as to discover the rules and characteristics. The comparative analysis was carried out from three aspects: comparing the economic development practice of two kinds of countries, expounding the theoretical basis for these countries to adopt various strategies and policies from the perspective of economic theory history, and making a comparative analysis between the theory of contemporary economic development and early economic development thought. According to the summary of researchers, Tan Chongtai put forward some new theoretical viewpoints in the research of development economics in the previous thirty years. In the research on development, the two concepts of growth and development were generally confused. Tan Chongtai believed that the two concepts of economic growth and economic development were different. Economic growth meant that the national economy had more output, and economic development meant not only the increase of output, but also the structural change of output and input and the change

---

45. Zhang Peigang, *New Development Economics* (Henan People's Publishing House, 1992); Yang Yonghua, "Pioneering Research of New Development Economics," *Economist*, no. 1 (1995); Hong Yinxing and Chen Zhibiao: "Evolution of Development Economics in China," *Economics Trends*, no. 2 (1992).

of general economic conditions with the increase of output. In other words, the meaning of economic growth was narrow and generally referred to the pure sense of production growth, while the meaning of economic development was broader, generally including economic structure and even some changes in the system of economic progress. However, the basic driving force for economic development was economic growth, which was the primary necessary material condition for all economic progress. Growth without development had happened in some developing countries, but it was generally impossible to have development without growth. Even if it occurred, it was short-term and partial, but it could not be sustained and comprehensive. He believed that development should include the change of industrial structure, the decline of income distribution inequality, the alleviation of poverty, the improvement of people's living standards, the improvement of education and health conditions, and the protection of the ecological environment.

In development economics, the characteristics of the first and second stages were clearly summarized and a consensus was reached. The first stage of development economics was dominated by structuralism, and the second stage by the revival of neoclassicism. After the 1980s, the research on development economics had entered a new stage, but there was no authoritative summary on the theoretical research characteristics of this new stage. After a detailed investigation and analysis of the development theory of the new historical stage, Tan Chongtai proposed the theoretical characteristics of the third stage of development economics, which not only inherited the analytical methods of neoclassicism in the second stage, but also corrected some theoretical defects of neoclassicism in the second stage, such as ignoring the key role of government and institutional factors in economic development. According to these theoretical characteristics, the third stage of development economics was summarized as the stage of neoclassical political economics, and the new institutional economics, new growth theory, and sustainable development research in this stage of development economics were logically linked together to offer academic analysis and evaluation.[46]

In the 2010s, economic and ideological circles studied industrialization from a new perspective. Some studies suggested that after the 1990s, developed countries had entered the era of "post-industrialization" and transformed to a knowledge-based economy. The invention and application of new technology became an important driving force for the development of the knowledge economy. Society presented economic characteristics different from those in the early stage of industrialization, such as a widening income gap, different contribution rate of factors, frequent mergers and acquisitions of enterprises,[47] and so forth. Some theorists studied the applicability of "de-industrialization" in China. De-industrialization was an economic

---

46. Tan Chongtai, *A Comparative Study on the Economic Development of the Developed Countries at Early Stage and the Developing Countries Today* (Wuhan University Press, 2008); Guo Xibao, "Mr. Tan Chongtai's Contribution to the Development of China's Development Economics," *Economic Review*, no. 6 (2008).

47. Huo Wenhui and Yang Yunjie, "New Progress of Industrialization Theory Research," *Economics Trends*, no. 3 (2010).

phenomenon that occurred after the completion of industrialization.[48] Some believed that de-industrialization was an imbalance of economic structure in the process of industrialization, which was reflected in the elements allocation structure, industrial structure, regional economic structure, value chain structure, and other areas. This imbalance had serious consequences for the development of the national economy. Industrial structure theory, industrial transfer theory, structuralism development theory, and polarization theory were important theoretical sources for studying the problem of de-industrialization. From the perspective of structural imbalance, there was not only a certain form of overall de-industrialization, but also an obvious regional de-industrialization in China.[49]

Some critics pointed out that de-industrialization was an inevitable economic phenomenon that a country's economy would inevitably face when it developed to a certain extent. Different modes of de-industrialization had different impacts on a country's economy. A negative consequence of total de-industrialization was industrial hollowing, which was also a problem faced by many developed countries in the process of economic development, while structural de-industrialization could better preserve a country's manufacturing industry and the power source of its economic growth. At the time, China was in the stage of de-industrialization. The manufacturing industry faced some unfavorable factors, such as rising costs, the disappearance of demographic dividends, the rise of the exchange rate, and competition from Southeast Asian countries. At the same time, the re-industrialization of developed countries posed a great challenge to China's manufacturing industry. Structural de-industrialization was the model that China needed to adopt.[50] Some commentators point out that there was a tendency toward early de-industrialization in China. After China entered the middle- and upper-income stage, the proportion of the manufacturing industry and total factor productivity decreased at the same time. In theory and experience, there was a tendency toward "premature de-industrialization," which increased the risk of falling into the "middle income trap." Accelerating the construction of a manufacturing power, developing an advanced manufacturing industry, and improving the quality and efficiency of the development of traditional industries was a realistic option for China's industrialization development strategy.[51]

It was pointed out that "over-industrialization" was a result of excessive industrial upgrading. It was not unreasonable for the government to promote the upgrading of industrial structure, but it need not go beyond the stage of development and pursue excessively high proportion of service industry, whether artificially or deliberately. In fact, in the formulation of the Thirteenth

---

48. R. Rowthorn and R. Ramaswamy, "Growth, Trade, and De-industrialization," *IMF Staff Papers* 1, no. 46, (1999): 18–24.

49. Wang Zhanxiang and Wei Lin, "Research on De-industrialization and its Adaptability in China," *Contemporary Finance and Economics*, no. 6 (2012).

50. Wang Qiushi and Wang Yixin, "De-industrialization, Economic Development and China's Industrial Path Selection," *Contemporary Finance and Economics*, no. 3 (2014).

51. Huang Qunhui, Huang Yanghua, He Jun et al., "Research on China's Industrialization Strategy for the Middle and Upper Income Stage," *China Social Sciences*, no. 12 (2017).

Five-Year Plan, this tendency existed to a certain extent, both at the national and local levels. The harm over-industrialization did to China's economic development included restraining economic growth and productivity, hindering the development of the modern service industry, and not being conducive to urbanization and agricultural labor transfer. In order to ensure the stable, sustained growth of the national economy, it was necessary to implement a strategy of deep industrialization, rely on the modern scientific and technological revolution, vigorously promote the transformation of industrial quality, efficiency, and power, comprehensively improve the industrial quality and competitiveness, and maintain the industrial added value and employment proportion in a reasonable range corresponding to the development stage.[52]

4. Research on Economic Structural Adjustment and the New Development Concept

Adjusting economic structure and promoting sustainable development was a long-term topic in the process of China's economic growth and economic development. In the 21st century, the Seventeenth National Congress of the Communist Party of China clearly put forward the strategic task of accelerating the transformation of the mode of economic development. The Central Economic Work Conference in 2009 stressed that accelerating the transformation of the mode of economic development was a profound change in China's economic field, which was related to the overall situation of Reform and Opening Up and socialist modernization. The adjustment of the economic structure was an important part of the transformation of the development mode, which was of decisive significance to accelerating the transformation of the economic development mode. China had entered a critical period in which only adjusting the economic structure could promote sustainable development. It was important to expanding domestic demand on this basis to adjust the structure and enhance the ability of sustainable development. It was necessary to take urbanization as the strategic focus of expanding domestic demand and expand the space for sustainable development. The optimization and upgrading of the industrial structure needed to be accelerated to improve the level of sustainable development. It was likewise important to coordinate the population, resources, environment, and economic and social development to solve the issue of sustainability in development.[53]

In the 2010s, some studies proposed that whether China could break through the "trap of middle-income countries" would depend on its ability to correctly grasp its own development stage and promote structural adjustment and development transformation. It was argued that the stage of national economic development needed to be defined from the perspective of industrial development and pointed out that China was currently in the stage of investment orientation. Investment driving economy was a key feature of China's economy. Labor productivity was the main driving factor in a country's economic structural transformation, so the structural

---

52. Wei Houkai and Wang Songji, "Analysis and Theoretical Reflection on China's Excessive De-industrialization," *China Industrial Economy*, no. 1 (2019).

53. Li Keqiang, "Several Issues on Adjusting Economic Structure and Promoting Sustainable Development," *Qiushi*, no. 11 (2010).

transformation needed to be guided by efficiency. The primary problem in China's structural transformation was that the economic stage it was in inevitably determined that it was investment oriented. So far, the characteristics of economic growth were still in the traditional mechanism. Therefore, China's future structural transformation needed to be implemented through efficiency guidance, human behavior, enterprise behavior, and industrial change. Through the guidance of the market-oriented reform and the realization of structural adjustment, the competitive advantage of the manufacturing industry needed to be maintained rather than be immediately driven out of the city to shift swiftly from labor-intensive industry to the service economy. It was important to vigorously promote the combination of the service industry and heavy industry, improve the trade level of the service industry, and increase policy guidance and structural adjustment, especially the support of special government policies, such as financial and tax support, so that enterprises and individuals could play an active role in economic transformation and move the structure in a benign direction. Some scholars pointed out that the current development stage of China was that there were not many surplus labor forces, and economic growth was led by investment. In fact, with the digestion of surplus labor force, the contradiction between economic growth and inflation in the future could become increasingly intense. Therefore, the only driving force of economic growth was the improvement of labor productivity, which could only come from technological progress. At this time, the role of macro-control was perhaps not be very sizeable, but it was particularly important for generating a sufficient incentive mechanism through institutional guarantees.[54]

Against the backdrop of adjusting the economic structure and changing the development mode, some scholars advanced "new structural economics." Some commented that the starting point of new structural economics was that the essence of modern economic growth was the continuous upgrading of industrial and technological structure, and the most competitive industrial and technological structure of a country at any time point was determined by its factor endowment structure. Because the factor endowment structure determined a country's factor relative price system, this factor price system was the main parameter and basis for the enterprise's industrial and technological selection. According to these factor price signals, the enterprise decided what to produce and how to produce it. Only in this way could its products be competitive in the domestic and foreign markets at the lowest cost. For example, in an economy with a relatively rich labor force, the price of labor force was obviously relatively cheap, so there was a cost advantage to producing labor-intensive products by adopting labor-intensive technology, while in an economy relatively rich in capital, labor was relatively expensive and capital was relatively cheap. Therefore, the use of capital-intensive technology to produce capital-intensive products would have a cost advantage. Competitiveness was the basis for rapid economic development. If a country wanted to achieve rapid economic development, it should follow the development strategy of comparative advantage, so as to ensure that its competitiveness was always at the maximum state.

---

54. Lang Lihua and Zhou Mingsheng, "Structural Reform and Macroeconomic Stability: A Summary of the International Summit Forum on China's Economic Growth and Cycle (2012)," *Economic Research*, no. 8 (2012).

Developing countries were often poor, lacking capital but having a relatively abundant labor force, so developing countries needed to give priority to the development of labor-intensive industries. However, in order to pursue profits, enterprises should have a fully competitive market in order to encourage a country's enterprises to choose industries and technologies according to the comparative advantages determined by the factor endowment structure. Only in this way could factor prices fully reflect the relative richness of factors in the economy and guide enterprises to make correct industrial and technological choices.[55]

The Eighteenth National Congress of the Communist Party of China proposed the acceleration of the transformation of the mode of economic development as the main line and a shift in the foothold of promoting development to improving quality and efficiency. The main direction of accelerating the transformation of economic development aimed to promote the strategic adjustment of the economic structure. The Nineteenth National Congress of the Communist Party of China suggested that China's economy had changed from a high-speed growth stage to a high-quality development stage, and it was then in a critical period of transforming the development mode, optimizing the economic structure, and transforming the growth momentum. It emphasized that China needed to deepen the structural reform of the supply side, put the economic development focus on the real economy, and take improving the quality of the supply system as the main direction of attack, so as to significantly enhance China's economic quality advantage. During this period, economic growth and development under the new normal became a hot field in economics research. According to research data in 2015, economic growth and development in the new normal were the areas of greatest concern in China's economics research that year. Among them, the frequency of the three keywords (economic growth, new normal, and economic development) ranked the top five. There were 2,874 CSSCI source journals that included the keywords of the cluster members.

The economic growth under the new normal had three characteristics. The first was that in terms of growth rate, it changed from high-speed growth to medium high-speed growth, from low-value-added to high-value-added, and from factor and investment driven to innovation driven. Through a detailed analysis of the keyword co-occurrence knowledge map in this field, it was noted that these three characteristics were the main research directions in 2015. The high-frequency keywords of economic growth rate were economic downward pressure, potential economic growth rate, per capita income of residents, GNP, and middle-income trap, among others. There were many discussions on the prediction of China's economic growth trend in the new normal, the cyclical factors of economic growth slowdown, the realization conditions of stable growth goals, and the macro-control policies of economic growth. The evaluation of the middle income trap and whether China could surmount it were still controversial. The new normal urged China to pay greater attention to the quality and efficiency of economic development, and the quality of economic development had become a hot topic in academic circles. The research

---

55. Su Jian, "Internal Logic and Correct Path of Economic Development," *Economic Research*, no. 11 (2012); Lin Yifu, *New Structural Economics* (Peking University Press, 2012).

in this direction analyzed the impact of industrial transformation and upgrading, renewable resource industries, environmental regulation, service export complexity, financial and insurance structure, and institutional changes on the quality of China's economic growth.[56]

According to some views, although the Chinese style of the new normal was formed by the structural slowdown of the economy, it was not and should not be a low-speed growth state, but a long-term stable state in which the speed changed from high-speed growth to medium high-speed growth, from unbalanced growth to optimized growth in structure, and from factor input to an innovation driven mode. To promote the optimization of economic structure and realize the transformation of growth mode in the new normal, it was necessary to break through the constraints of the unreasonable distribution structure, slow accumulation of human capital, high financing costs of enterprises, resource shortage, and environmental deterioration in the development process, so as to effectively enhance independent innovation and promote technological progress. It was important to take the opportunity of international multilateral cooperation to promote the steady development of foreign trade and foreign investment, take the new urbanization as the carrier to promote the further benign expansion of investment and consumption demand, focus on deepening the institutional reform, further improve the effective incentive mechanism of the system, release the huge dividend of the institutional reform, and effectively cultivate new and innovative growth points with the support of strategic emerging industries to expand the space for employment.[57] Some held that the supply side structural reform of China's socialist market economy was mainly aimed at the crux of the main problems existing at the present stage of China's economic development, based on the needs of deepening reform and further development of China's economy, rather than from a ready-made economic theory. In fact, since the beginning of Reform and Opening Up, the major reform measures and policy adjustments of the Chinese government had all been based on China's national conditions and the actual needs at that time. The practice of China's Reform and Opening Up in establishing a socialist market economic system on the basis of breaking the planned economic system was an unprecedented initiative. Contemporary supply side structural reform in China needed not only the ideological resources including classical economics, but also the guidance of supply theory provided by Marxist economics, so as to innovate the socialist supply theory with Chinese characteristics in combination with China's actual situation, and then to design a set of structural reform programs and policy combinations aiming at the crux of China's economic problems.[58] Some scholars analyzed the innovation of China's economic development theory. As China said farewell to the low-income development stage and entered the middle-income development stage, a series of innovations appeared in its development theory.

56. Luo Rundong and Li Chao, "Analysis of Hot Spots in China's Economic Research in 2015," *Economics Trends*, no. 4 (2016).

57. Li Zilian and Hua Guihong, "China's Economic Growth Under the New Normal," *Economist*, no. 6 (2015).

58. Fang Fuqian, "Looking for the Theoretical Source of Supply Side Structural Reform," *China Social Sciences*, no. 7 (2017).

Accordingly, it was necessary to change the traditional view of economic development to fit the new development concept, including the idea that the task of development should shift from eliminating poverty to focusing on affluence, the engine of development should shift from external demand to domestic demand, the main driving force of growth should shift from investment to consumption, and the focus of reform to release vitality should shift from the demand side to the supply side. In addition, the principle pursued by economic growth needed to shift from efficiency to inclusiveness. The path of economic development had changed from relying on material resources input to being innovation driven. The strategy of economic development had changed from an unbalanced strategy to a balanced strategy, the path of dual structure modernization had changed from non-agricultural driving "agriculture, rural areas, and farmers" to facing the development of "agriculture, rural areas, and farmers," and China's position in the global economy had changed from integrating comparative advantage into globalization to leading globalization with a competitive advantage.[59] Some studies measured China's potential economic growth rate. Based on the theoretical analysis of the impact mechanism of supply side structural reform on China's potential economic growth rate, the key factors of supply side structural reform, such as institutional change, structural adjustment, overcapacity, and population structure, were embedded in the analysis framework of the model. On the basis of measuring the potential growth rate of China's economy from 1993 to 2015, the potential growth rate of China's economy from 2016 to 2040 was further predicted. Research indicated that the main reason for China's sustained economic decline since 2010 was the decline of the potential growth rate itself. Structural reform needed to be carried out from the supply side to improve the potential growth rate. In the base scenario and a pessimistic scenario, the average potential growth rates of 2016 to 2020 were 6.9% and 6.5%, the average potential growth rates from 2021 to 2025 were 6.3% and 5.8%, the average potential growth rates from 2026 to 2030 were 6.0% and 5.7%, the average potential growth rates from 2031 to 2035 were 4.9% and 4.4%, and the average potential growth rates from 2036 to 2040 were 4.6% and 4.3% respectively. Promoting supply side structural reform was an important measure to promote economic development in the new normal. It was important to realize the optimal allocation of production factors, especially to accelerate the reform of labor, land, capital, system, innovation, and other elements.[60] Other scholars estimated that by 2028, China would have an average annual growth potential of 8%. In order to achieve this growth, China needed to deepen reform at home and eliminate all kinds of distortions left over from the dual track system. It also needed to look at the external environment of the global economy, which was beyond China's control. Since the outbreak of the subprime mortgage crisis in the United States in 2008, the global economy had developed slowly, and it was likely that growth would be sluggish for a long time. However, as long as China continued to emancipate its mind, seek truth from facts, make use of its favorable domestic conditions, and devote itself to supply side structural reform, it

59. Hong Yinxing, "Major Innovation of China's Economic Development Theory after Entering the New Stage," *China Industrial Economy*, no. 5 (2017).

60. Guo Xueneng and Lu Shengrong, "An Analysis of China's Potential Economic Growth Rate against the Background of Supply Side Structural Reform," *Economist*, no. 1 (2018).

was believed that China would maintain a growth rate of at least 6% over the next ten years. What did a 6% growth rate mean? In 2016, China's economy accounted for 18.6% of the world economy in terms of purchasing power parity and 14.9% in terms of market exchange rate. A growth rate of 6% meant that China would contribute about 1% to the world economy every year. The world economy was growing at 3%. China contributed about 30% of the world economic growth rate every year. In the next ten years, China would still be the engine of world economic growth.[61]

Some commentators pointed out that it was necessary to implement the new concept of development in order to overcome the problem of the middle income trap. Economic development had entered a new stage, and socialism with Chinese characteristics had entered a new era. The basic conditions restricting social and economic development had undergone profound, systematic changes. The comparative advantage of the supply side, low factor cost (including labor cost, land and natural resource prices, ecological environment bearing capacity, technological innovation, progress cost, etc.) had undergone profound changes. It was necessary to cultivate new advantages through innovation, adopt new methods, develop new power, and adjust new structure. The potential broad space on the demand side was the fundamental change of the pattern in the market with a long-term economic shortage, which required innovation and capability improvement to adapt to and lead the changes in market demand. The historic changes in these conditions brought new opportunities and challenges to China's development.[62] According to some viewpoints, China's gradual economic liberalization process was of great significance to development. Reform and Opening Up made possible the free flow of goods, capital, technology, and personnel and the improvement of the efficiency of resource allocation and acceleration of economic growth. The efficiency of state-owned enterprises was improved in the competition with imported products and foreign-funded enterprises, and the management level and technology likewise improved. China's economic liberalization process was gradual and prudent, which to a certain extent eased the impact of the financial crisis on China and helped China play an important role in leading the world economic recovery.[63] Through the analysis of the theoretical framework of high-quality development, some studies observed that the concepts of innovation, coordination, green, openness, and sharing were embedded in high-quality development and had a strong cross impact and comparative advantage stimulation on the economic operation process, economic power transformation, economic form evolution, and economic structural adjustment of high-quality development.[64]

61. Lin Yifu, "Needham Puzzle and China's Revival: A Perspective of New Structural Economics," *China Reform*, no. 1 (2018).

62. Liu Wei, "New Development Concept and Overcoming the 'Middle Income Trap,'" *China Economic Report*, no. 2 (2019).

63. Zou Zhiqing, "An Important Path for China's Economic Reform and Development," *China Economic Report*, no. 2 (2019).

64. Li Mengxin and Ren Baoping, "Comprehensive Evaluation and Path Selection of China's High-quality Development in the New Era," *Financial Science*, no. 5 (2019).

15.4 Risk in Development: Theory and Experience

1. Cyclical Risk

(1) Growth Cycle

In economics, the two concepts of growth and cycle were closely linked. From the development history of the world economy, almost any economy would have cyclical fluctuations. An economic boom was followed by depression and recession, the decline of national output and employment, and the fall of prices and profits. When the recession reached the bottom, it would become a recovery, and then there would be a new upsurge. It could be analyzed by change in the inventory cycle model and the durable goods cycle. Primarily, the example of negative feedback control was given. Assuming that the productivity was determined by the inventory of finished products required to be maintained, then if the actual inventory quantity S_t was greater than the required inventory quantity S^*, the output q should be reduced

$$q = -\beta (S_t - S^*), \beta > 0$$

The difference between demand and output was the rate of change in inventory. If the output was expressed as the deviation from the equilibrium level caused by external demand, the linear storage function was used

$$S = S_t - S^* = Q - \alpha Q, 1 > \alpha > 0$$

to get

$$q = -\beta S = -\beta (1 - \alpha)Q$$

This formula reflected a simple turning motion, which indicated that there was periodic unemployment in economic activities.

When the output was higher than the previous level, it was necessary to expand investment in order to expand production capacity. The growth of demand caused by investment would further demand the expansion of production capacity, thus promoting economic growth. Due to the rapid change in demand, the growth of production capacity was relatively slow. Therefore, when the production capacity was finally in line with the output, according to certain structural parameters, the economic upsurge would automatically stop and the investment demand would decline, leading to a rapid decline in consumption demand and output. If this internal effect failed to curb prosperity, then the shortage of existing resources, especially the restriction of skilled labor supply, would lead to the decline of economic development speed and the decrease of demand. In the depression stage, because of the rising unemployment rate, the increase of wage rate was lower than that of labor productivity. Therefore, with the increase of production, the profit per unit output increased. The growth of profits provided incentives and capital conditions for investment in technological innovation and expansion of existing production capacity, and the economy began to recover and soar at a certain speed.

Empirical research on the world economy indicated that the length of the business cycle was eight to ten years. Although the increase of labor productivity brought about by the "new economy" made the economy grow for a long period, the new economy could only deform the cycle, but not make the cycle disappear. In particular, due to the fluctuation of technology industry cycle and the volatility of venture capital, the potential impact of the new economy was great.

(2) Currency, Expectation, and Cycle

The monetary school and the neoclassical school held that the interference factors leading to economic fluctuation mainly came from the government's economic policy, especially its monetary policy. In the long run, due to the existence of rational expectations, the change of money supply was expected, the price level would change correspondingly, and the actual money supply would remain unchanged, so the policy would be invalid. However, in the short term, the change of money supply was not expected by manufacturers, which would cause economic fluctuations. This theory could be represented by the model in Figure 15-1.

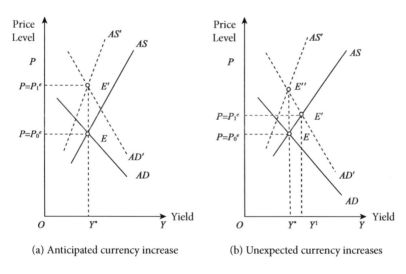

(a) Anticipated currency increase   (b) Unexpected currency increases

FIGURE 15-1

(a) The expected increase in money was fully reflected in the expected price and supply curve. In the face of this expected monetary increase, the AS and AD curves both moved up by the same proportion at the production level Y^*. Therefore, at the new equilibrium point E', the yield was maintained at the level of Y^*. Therefore, the expected increase in money had no real effect.

(b) An unexpected increase in currency would not be reflected in the expected price. Therefore, at first, only the AD curve moved, and a short-term equilibrium of higher yield appeared at Point

E'. However, because the price was greater than the expected price, the expectation would be an upward correction, the AS curve would move upward, and the economy would eventually move to E''. Therefore, the unexpected monetary increase had a real effect, but its effect was only temporary.

However, it is worth noting that under the conditions of rational expectation, the state of Point E' could not last for long. If the price were higher than expected, residents and manufacturers would revise their expectations. For example, when households and manufacturers expected the increase in money stock to be sustained, they would revise their price expectations and raise them to P_1^e. At this time, the AS curve moved up to AS'. Therefore, changes in money only worked when they were not expected, but an increase in money could not always be expected. Money had only a short-term effect and would soon be fully reflected in prices. In other words, monetary policy was neutral as long as the economic entities discovered the monetary changes and used the new information to recalculate the equilibrium wages and prices corresponding to full employment. The core assumption leading to this result was that expectations were formed rationally and the market was clear.

(3) Bubble Economy and Capital Asset Prices

According to *The New Palgrave Dictionary of Economics and the Law*, a bubble economy referred to a sudden rise in price of a series of capital assets in a continuous process. When the asset price rose to a certain limit, expectations reversed, then the price fell sharply, finally ending in a financial crisis. Further analysis shows that the bubble in the economy at that time was related to people's earning expectations or to the process of expansion of capital asset prices deviating from their underlying values driven by earnings expectations. The cause of the bubble economy was the frenzy of investment in some capital assets. People believed that buying these capital assets could make money and chase them vigorously with the expectation of huge profits, resulting in a sharp rise in the prices of these capital assets. The essence of the bubble economy was that the rise in capital asset price deviated from its basic value. These basic value factors included the normal return of capital assets, the risk premium of assets, the long-term interest rate, and the net present value of capital assets. However, this analysis seemed suspiciously like a circular argument, because the pricing of any capital asset depended on the expected effect (such as the prediction of future profits). The key to the problem, then, seemed to be whether the expectation of future profits of capital assets was based on real information and rational calculation, or based on distorted information and speculative psychology. The school of rational expectation pointed out that the price of a certain capital asset was formed by market participants using the standard economic model suitable for the specific local conditions at that time within the scope of the information available. They believed that the market price of capital assets could not deviate from its basic value unless market participants received the wrong information. In this way, the essence of the bubble economy could be more precisely defined as the expectation of future earnings of capital assets based on distorted information and speculative psychology, and the investment driven by this expectation led to a sharp rise in the price of capital assets. Here, distorted information could also be understood as incomplete information. So, if the hypothesis of complete information could not be satisfied, especially when people offered false information artificially for profiteering, bubbles would often occur in the economy. When the bubble expanded, the book price of capital assets rose sharply, the market was extremely active, and people's confidence grew stronger. This price rise was not supported by real performance returns, but by expectations. The financial system was under great pressure and became very fragile. Once a certain financial link failed to offer support, the whole financial system would collapse. When public confidence was frustrated, the expectation was reversed, and the bubble economy would soon be overturned.

Mainstream economics analyzed the risk of a bubble economy. From the economic point of view, there were two fatal defects in stock market speculation. The first was that stock market speculation merely transferred money or wealth between individuals without creating more wealth, but consumed resources and time, and the second was that stock market speculation tended to increase income inequality and instability. Speculation mania made people lose their senses and rush into the tide of driving up asset prices, eventually leading to the total collapse of the market, which was an inevitable result. Stock market bubbles meant that stock prices and price earnings ratios were unusually high due to speculation expectations, which were out of the performance base of listed companies. In the theory of modern enterprise value evaluation, a core formula of company value evaluation system was market value = net profit × P / E ratio. Here, the net profit was the achievement of the company, while the P / E ratio reflected the expectation of the company's future performance. Investors predicted the company's future performance by evaluating the company's realized performance, and then gave different P / E ratios. In this evaluation system, market value was an important index to judge the internal value of a company. But if there was no basis for performance, only an absorption of social capital to boost market value through anticipation, then consideration needed to be given to the fact that there was a stock market bubble. Network stocks and high-tech stocks were high risk and high return, so the P / E ratio was very high, which was the procedure of venture capital operations. But if in the stock market dominated by traditional industries the P / E ratio and market value were not supported by actual performance, the risk of a bubble would be high. World economic history indicated that speculation could not be avoided in the economy, so there were always bubbles. But if speculation became a social atmosphere and "universal behavior," the rapid expansion of bubbles would lead to the collapse of the national economy.

2. Risk of Industry Hollowing Out

(1) The Law of Industrial Gradient Transfer
In regional economics, the concept of a "gradient" is used to show the difference of regional economic development level and the spatial change process from a low level area to a high level region. In the study of modern productivity distribution, it is common to draw a gradient map of regional economic development, which shows the gradient change of a country's economic development level from high to low. The basic theory of industrial gradient transfer can be

expressed as: within a country, the economic and technological development is unbalanced, and there is an objective economic and technological gradient. If there is a gradient, there is a space shift. The general law of spatial evolution of productivity is that advanced technology is introduced and mastered first by a high gradient area, and then it is gradually transferred to a second and third grade gradient area. With the development of the economy, the process accelerates, gradually narrowing the gap between regions and realizing the relative balance of productivity distribution and economic development. An empirical study indicates that the direction of productivity shift mainly depends on the "gravitational field" of the receiving area. In the sense of economics, a gravity field mainly refers to a labor field, resource field, location field, market field, technology field, and capital field. Generally speaking, the gravity intensity of a market field, technology field, capital field, and location field is larger than that of a labor field or resource field. The formation of a technology field, capital field, and market field with a strong gravity intensity is related to the degree of economic development, that is, it is mainly distributed in developed areas. Therefore, new technologies and new productive forces are often produced in developed areas and gradually move to underdeveloped areas. Even in developed countries, the spatial distribution of industries is also the main function of the gradient.

(2) Cost Comparison and Investment Conditions

From the perspective of developed regions, there are two main reasons for the outward transfer of industries. One is that the life cycle of the original products is shortened due to the application of new technologies and the introduction of new products, and the other is the decline of comparative benefits due to the rise of production costs. The first is industrial upgrading, so there is no risk of industrial hollowing out. The second is the relocation of industries. If there is no growth of new industries, there will be a risk of industry hollowing out. When the developed areas develop to a certain extent, due to the factors such as population density, traffic congestion, rising labor costs, environmental pollution, lack of natural resources, and other factors, production costs will rise and the expansion of production scale will become relatively uneconomical. Therefore, enterprises will transfer capital, technology, and other elements to other regions. This kind of industrial gradient transfer is the diffusion effect of developed areas, which is beneficial to backward areas. However, this process also shows that developed regions are in a disadvantageous position in cost comparison, and investment conditions are deteriorating. If the cost structure is not adjusted or new industries are not developed, the result will be the hollowing out of industries and the economic growth rate will be slowed down.

(3) Industry Hollowing Out and Economic Virtualization

Industry hollowing out refers to the economic phenomenon in which a country or region's existing industries enter a recession period due to the product life cycle or the rise of production costs, and at the same time, the new industries do not grow, resulting in the shrinkage of economic pillars and economic growth points, and then the economic growth rate decreases. For a region or a central city, industrial hollowing implies the risk of regional economic recession. If there is no effective innovation mechanism and favorable investment conditions, the new industry cannot develop rapidly and the industrial structure cannot be smoothly transformed, and the region will decline. There are many such examples in the world economy.

Industrial hollowing is often associated with economic virtualization. When the investment conditions worsen and the industrial structure is out of gear, attractive investment projects are scarce, and the demand for industrial investment will decline. At this time, a savings rate higher than the investment rate becomes the norm. A large amount of idle capital is stranded in the financial system, becoming "interest bearing capital," and it is invested in high-risk areas in order to pursue profits. This situation leads to the shrinking of the real economy and the expansion of the false economy. The strong demand for speculation induces a bubble economy, causing the financial system and even the whole economic system to risk an increase. In China's situation, the change of economic situation made the investment mode change. The general processing industry was generally in excess, and the new investment fields, such as the high-tech industry, the advanced manufacturing industry, and the modern service industry, had a relatively high entry threshold and a high investment risk. Therefore, it would take some time to form the industrial scale. This situation prevented the new industry from fully developing and the industrial structure from advancing naturally, and industry hollowing was caused by the fracture of the industrial chain. Therefore, to avoid the risk of industry hollowing out, it was important not only to optimize industrial policy, but also to deepen economic system reform.

3. Institutional Risk

The essence of China's economic system reform was the marketization of the economy, that is, the establishment of a socialist market economic system. It was a process of moving from a non-market economy to a market economy, which was called an economic transition period. China's economy in transition or transition period had its own characteristics in terms of system, mainly including the characteristics of economic foundation and economic conditions in the transition from a planned economy to a market economy; the characteristics of competition, growth, and decline and coordination between a traditional economy and a modern economy in the transformation of a dual economic structure; the contradiction, combination, and growth and decline of a planned mechanism and a market mechanism in economic operations, and system transformation. The characteristics of economic behavior such as production, distribution, exchange, consumption, and investment were changed, and the relationship between government and market in system transformation was also discussed. Determined by these characteristics, China's economic system had a "double failure," that is, market failure and government failure. The market system was not developed, the market mechanism was not mature, and the market could not fully and effectively regulate the economic operation. The regulatory effect of the planned mechanism gradually weakened, but the government had not fully adapted to the reasonable positioning in the market economy, and the government's function of managing and regulating the economy could not be brought into full play. This "double failure" was a unique institutional risk in the period of economic transition. Especially in the deepening of market-oriented reform, if the government's function orientation was not adjusted reasonably, this risk would be strengthened.

(1) Government Regulation and Government Failure

The characteristics of government regulation were that the government controlled resources, interfered in the economy, and even directly performed economic functions. The system of the government regulating the economy was considered the general system characteristic of late developing industrialized countries (regions), which had the powerful function of starting industrialization and promoting the industrialization process. However, facts indicated that the return of this system increased at first, but with the development of the economy, the cost rose, efficiency decreased, and returns decreased, which hindered economic development. Because the market economy was a bottom-up economy, the demand for institutions was also bottom-up. When the market economy developed to a certain extent, it was necessary to have a democratic procedure from the bottom up to adapt to it.

According to the economic policy theory, the root cause of government failure was the "agency problem." In democratic politics, government officials were the agents of public interests, and there was a principal-agent relationship between the government and the public. If government officials had their own special interests which were inconsistent with public interests, there would be an agency problem. The way to solve the agency problem was to strengthen the supervision and incentive for the government. In theory, by establishing a control and incentive system for the government, the formulation and implementation of public policies could be in line with public interest. But the cost of such supervision and incentive was high, and it would be inefficient due to a large number of "free riding" behaviors. Moreover, the operation of a huge bureaucracy also had a high cost, and sometimes the cost was so high as to make the bureaucratic system run inefficiently. Therefore, many economic theories held that the government's economic behavior should be clearly defined within the scope of market failure, that is, the government should intervene where the market failed, but it should not otherwise intervene in the economy. The approach of system reform should be to cultivate the main market body and promote free economic development. Government intervention, however important, was not the fundamental driving force of economic development.

(2) "Demographic Dividend" Risk

"Demographic dividend" referred to a situation in which a country's working age population accounted for a large proportion of the total population, and its dependency ratio was relatively low, which created favorable demographic conditions for economic development. Generally, the dependency ratio was regarded as the proxy variable of demographic dividend. According to this standard definition, some scholars believed that China's demographic dividend would end in 2015. But some foreign scholars used the working population rather than the working age population to measure the actual demographic dividend. Here, the total labor force of the whole society was obtained by constructing the labor participation rates of different age and gender groups, and then totaling them up. For example, extending the retirement age could improve the labor participation rate of the elderly group, which would lead to an increase of the total labor force. According to this new definition (labor force) and through simulation analysis, China's demographic dividend could last until 2030. This was to increase the number of labor force through the increase of labor participation rate, thus prolonging the period of demographic dividend. According to the data of the sixth national census in 2010, if the population aged between 25 and 59 was defined as producers and those under 25 and above 59 as consumers, the ratio of producers to consumers in China was 117%, that is, 117 producers per 100 consumers. If the retirement age were extended to 65, the producer to consumer ratio in China would be 142%, and it was possible this ratio would begin to decline after reaching its peak in 2015. From 2012, the number and proportion of China's working age population dropped for seven consecutive years, with a decrease of more than 26 million. At the end of 2018, there were 775.86 million employees nationwide, 540,000 less than at the end of the previous year, with the number dropping for the first time. It was expected that the number of employees would continue to decline over the next few years.

In addition, in terms of quality, especially from the perspective of human capital, this was a more important way to obtain demographic dividend. Due to the development of education, China was gaining a large-scale human resource dividend, which could not only effectively offset the negative effect of the decreasing demographic dividend, but also maintain the continuous increase of the total amount of human capital, so as to support the long-term sustained high growth rate of the entire Chinese economy. Since 2000, China had seen a net human capital dividend, and the human capital dividend would continue increasing until 2030. There were limitations to measuring human capital in terms of average years of education, and because the gap between China's current average length of education and that of developed countries (such as the United States) was not very large (the difference in 2010 was more than three years), it could be inferred that the future growth space of human capital was limited. However, considering that the average length of schooling could not measure the quality of education well, China's human capital growth would have greater potential in the future if focus was placed on improving the quality of education rather than simply starting from the length of education.

4. China's Policies and Measures for Adhering to the New Development Concept and Promoting High Quality Development in 2019

In December 2018, the Central Economic Work Conference deployed economic work in 2019. The meeting determined that several key tasks should be performed effectively in 2019. The first was to promote the high-quality development of the manufacturing industry. It was important to promote the deep integration of the advanced manufacturing industry and the modern service industry and unswervingly build a powerful manufacturing country. China needed to steadily promote the survival of the fittest enterprises, speed up the disposal of "zombie enterprises," formulate exit implementation measures, and promote the formation and development of new technologies, new organizational forms, and new industrial clusters. It was necessary to enhance the technological innovation ability of the manufacturing industry, build an open, collaborative, and efficient R & D platform for generic technology, improve the demand- and enterprise-oriented integrated innovation mechanism, pay close attention to the layout of national laboratories, restructure the system of key national laboratories, increase the support for innovation of small and medium enterprises, strengthen the protection and application of intellectual property rights, and form an effective innovation incentive mechanism system.

The second task was to promote the formation of a strong domestic market. China's market scale ranked first in the world, with even greater potential in the future. It was important to strive to meet the final demand, improve the quality of products, accelerate the development of education, child care, pension, medical care, culture, tourism, and other service industries, improve the consumption environment, implement the special additional deduction policy of personal income tax, and enhance consumption ability, so that the people could eat, dress, and use resources comfortably. At the current stage of China's development, there was still a huge potential for investment demand. China needed to play a key role in investment, increase technological transformation and equipment update of manufacturing industry, speed up the pace of 5G business, strengthen the construction of new infrastructure such as artificial intelligence, industrial Internet, and the Internet of things, increase investment in intercity transportation, logistics, and municipal infrastructure, and make up for the construction of rural infrastructure and public service facilities. Short boards needed to be set up and capacity building of natural disaster prevention and control strengthened.

The third task was to promote the strategy of rural revitalization. It was important to give priority to the development of agriculture and rural areas, act effectively in agriculture, especially grain production, promote the implementation of grain storage in land and technology, rationally adjust the structure of the "grain, forage, and industrial crops," and strive to increase the supply of high-quality green agricultural products. It was important to pay attention to the cultivation of new business entities such as family farms and farmers' cooperatives, pay attention to solving the difficulties faced by small farmers in production and operations, and introduce them to a pattern of modern agricultural development. To improve the rural living environment, it was necessary to focus on garbage and sewage treatment, upgrading of public restrooms, and the improvement of village appearance. The experience of the three pilot projects of rural land system reform needed to be summed up, the achievements of the reform consolidated, and the reform of the rural land system continued and intensified.

The fourth task was to promote coordinated regional development. It was important to make overall plans to promote the development of the west, the overall revitalization of the northeast, the rise of the central region, and the leading development of the east. At present, the development of Beijing-Tianjin-Hebei, Guangdong-Hong Kong-Macao Greater Bay Area, the Yangtze River Delta, and other regions displayed many new characteristics. Economies of scale effect were beginning to appear, infrastructure density and network degree were comprehensively improved, innovation factors were rapidly gathered, and new leading industries were developing rapidly. These areas needed to be promoted to become important power sources leading to high-quality development. It was necessary to enhance the power of the radiation belt of central cities and form an important driving force for high-quality development. The development of the Yangtze River Economic Belt needed to be promoted, the systematic protection and restoration of the Yangtze River ecological environment implemented, and high-quality development promoted vigorously. It was important to promote the development of urbanization, effectively settle the agricultural transfer population who were already employed in cities and towns, urge the implementation of the goal of 100 million people settling down in 2020, and improve the fine management level of big cities.

The fifth task was to accelerate the reform of the economic system. It was necessary to deepen the reform of the nature of "four beams and eight pillars," focus on enhancing the vitality of micro subjects, and promote the relevant reform to go deep and become solid. The reform of state-owned assets and state-owned enterprises needed to be accelerated, principles of separation of government and enterprise adhered to, along with the separation of government and capital and fair competition. China needed to be stronger and better, a big country with capital, accelerating the transformation from enterprise management to capital management, reorganizing and establishing a number of state-owned capital investment companies, setting up a number of state-owned capital operation companies, actively promoting the mixed ownership reform, and accelerating the joint-stock reform of the China Railway Corporation. It was important to support the development of private enterprises, create a legal system environment, and protect the personal and property safety of private enterprises. Focus needed to be placed on the structural adjustment and optimization of the financial system, the reform of the financial system needed to be deepened and private banks and community banks developed, gradually returning the business of urban commercial banks, rural commercial banks, and rural credit cooperatives. It was important to improve the financial infrastructure and strengthen the ability of supervision and service. The capital market played an important role in financial operations. Through deepening reform, it was important to create a standardized, transparent, open, dynamic, and resilient capital market, improve the quality of listed companies, improve the trading system, guide more medium and long-term capital to enter the economy, promote the establishment of the science and technology innovation board in the Shanghai Stock Exchange, and implement the pilot registration system as soon as possible. It was necessary to promote the reform of the fiscal and taxation system, improve the local tax system, and standardize the government's debt financing mechanism. It was likewise necessary to effectively transform the functions of the government, substantially reduce the direct allocation of resources by the government, and strengthen supervision during and after the event. If the market could adjust itself, it should be allowed to regulate itself, and enterprises should be allowed to do what enterprises could do.

The sixth task was to promote all-round opening up. It was necessary to adapt to the new situation and grasp the new characteristics, promoting the transformation from the flow type of commodity and factor toward a rule-based opening up. It was necessary to relax market access, fully implement the pre-admission national treatment plus negative list management system, protect the legitimate rights and interests of foreign investors in China, especially intellectual property rights, and allow more fields to implement sole proprietorships. It was important to expand import and export trade, diversify export markets, and reduce institutional costs in import links. The Belt and Road and the other programs needed to be promoted, and it was important that the government play the role of the main body of enterprises and effectively control all kinds of risks. It was similarly important to carefully manage the second Belt and Road International Cooperation Summit Forum. The construction of a community with a shared future for humankind needed to be promoted, and China needed to actively participate in the WTO reform and promote trade and investment liberalization and facilitation. It was necessary to implement the consensus reached at the meeting between China and the US heads of state in Argentina and promote Sino-US economic and trade consultations.

The seventh task was to strengthen the protection and improvement of people's livelihoods. It was necessary to improve the system, keep the bottom line, and effectively manage the people's livelihoods. Stable employment needed to be given a prominent position and focus placed on solving the employment problems of college graduates, migrant workers, ex-servicemen, and other groups. It was important to increase investment in pre-school education, early development of children in poor rural areas, and vocational education. It was necessary to improve the elder care system and strive to solve the problem of providing for the aged in large cities. Greater effort needed to be made to ensure food and drug safety, production safety, and traffic safety. It was important to deepen the reform of the social security system, promote the overall planning of endowment insurance across the country on the basis of speeding up the overall planning at the provincial level, and include more good medicines for saving lives and addressing emergencies into medical insurance. It was important to continue to transfer part of the state-owned capital to replenish the social security fund, and it was necessary to build a long-term mechanism for the healthy development of the real estate market, adhere to the position that housing was for living, not for speculation, implement policies and classified guidance in cities, consolidate the main responsibility of the city government, and improve the housing market and housing security systems.

The meeting stressed that China's development had sufficient toughness and huge potential, and its long-term economic growth would not change. It was important to comprehensively and correctly grasp the orientation of macro policy, structural policy, and social policy to ensure that economic operations were within a reasonable range. It was necessary to implement a positive fiscal policy and a prudent monetary policy, implement the employment priority policy, and promote a larger scale of tax reduction and more obvious reduction of fees, so as to effectively alleviate the problem of financing difficulties and the high financing costs of enterprises. Effort needed to be made to optimize the business environment, deepen the reform of "streamlining administration, reinforcing supervision, and optimizing service," and promote the development of new driving forces. It was necessary to implement the innovation driven development strategy, comprehensively improve innovation ability and efficiency, and improve the level of mass entrepreneurship and innovation. It was important to aim at the difficult task of building a moderately prosperous society in all aspects and promote poverty alleviation and rural revitalization. China needed to continuously release the potential of domestic demand and promote coordinated regional development. It was important to deepen the reform of finance, taxation, state-owned enterprises, and other key areas, resolutely break down barriers to the development of private enterprises, and enhance endogenous driving forces for development. Opening up to the outside world at a higher level needed to be promoted and effort made to stabilize foreign trade and investment. It was important to work together to promote economic development and environmental protection, and to strengthen pollution prevention and ecological construction. It was necessary to highlight the basic guarantee and the bottom line, so as to better guarantee and improve people's livelihoods.[65]

---

65. "Bulletin of the Central Economic Work Conference in 2018," *Xinhua News Agency* (Beijing), December 21, 2018.

CHAPTER 16

An Overview of Economic Thought Works of the People's Republic of China

16.1 The History of Economic Thought and Technical Statistics

Technical statistics have been an important part of the research basis for this book and a main method for acquiring information in the study of the history of economic thought. According to the *National General Bibliography* compiled by the Information Center of the National Press and Publication Administration and the China Archives of Publications, the *National New Bibliography* sponsored by the Information Center of the National Press and Publication Administration, the *National Bibliography of China* compiled by Beijing Library, and the *General Bibliography of National Economic Science* compiled by Liaoning University Library, the catalogue of economic theoretical works included in the "General Bibliography" provides the total statistics and classification statistics of economic theoretical works and economic journals in each era.

1. Statistical Caliber

In technical statistics, the works classified as economic theory include those on Marxist economics and the socialist and communist modes of production, works and textbooks on political economics, works and textbooks on Western economics, works on Chinese socialist economic theory, works in Chinese and in translation on the history of Chinese and foreign economic thought, and famous works on economics, including works on macro-economic management and enterprise management, theoretical works on development economics, regional economics, and productivity economics, theoretical works on the world economy, and various broad, comprehensive economic reference books. During the period of the Great Leap Forward, the anti-rightist movement, and the Cultural Revolution, some publications that were not theoretical works were basically omitted, but it was difficult to deal with them if they were omitted completely. In addition, the standard of "theoretical works" was relatively vague. Some anthologies, teaching materials, popular reading materials, reference books, and reference materials could not be strictly regarded as theoretical works. However, as long as the title or content of the book was related to economic theory, they could be classified as works on economic theory.

If a book was published by several publishing houses at the same time (more common in the 1960s–1970s), it was counted as one book, but if it was a different edition (reprinted, revised, minority language edition), it was counted by edition. Some books were published in separate volumes, which were generally counted by volume, but if they were published in chapters, lectures, and sub-volumes and the publication time was within the same year, the whole set was counted as a unit. In terms of subject classification, the works counted here generally belonged to basic economic theories. Other theoretical works on such subjects as industry, agriculture, finance, commerce and trade, accounting, and statistics were not included in the statistics. However, these statistics classify enterprise management into economic management for the sake of comprehensiveness.

From 2000, there was a rapid rise in the number of enterprise management texts related to business, operations, finance, strategy, and other sub-item management issues, and because of the emphasis on practical operations, these statistics only included the introductory works according to the narrow definition of enterprise management, which did not involve the specialized works on business operation, finance, strategy, and other sub-item management issues. In addition, with the increase in the number of works on industrial economics and yearbooks, these two types of works were listed separately beginning in 2000.

Of the materials on which the statistics were based, the bibliography of the *National General Bibliography* was the most complete. However, its publication was temporarily suspended beginning in 1992. The *National General Bibliography* was not published in 1993, 1994 and 1995, but was published again beginning in 1996. In order to make up for the lack of information, it is necessary to turn to the *National Bibliography of China*, the *General Bibliography of National Economic Science*, and the *National New Bibliography* (monthly). However, the *National Bibliography of China* and the *General Bibliography of National Economic Science* were not available from 1995, and the *National New Bibliography* (monthly) did not include all the bibliographies from 1998, instead introducing items selectively. At the same time, *China's New Catalogue Express* (weekly) was set up in 1999 to collect the full catalogue of new books. This situation reflects that fact that the statistics for publications in China remain relatively rough, and the publication of statistical data lacks continuity, bringing certain difficulties to research work. For this reason, the statistics on the economic theory works in this book may have overlaps and omissions, and the figures given may lack accuracy. However, it basically reflects the overall situation of the publication of economic theory works of the People's Republic of China after certain deletions and selections. In particular, beginning in 1998, the publication of the *National General Bibliography* was normalized, so the statistics after 1998 are mainly based on the *National General Bibliography*.

The National Press and Publication Administration issued a notice on March 8, 1999, requesting that the national standard of cataloging data in print be popularized and implemented in China from April 1, 1999. Cataloging in Publication (CIP) is the international common bibliographic data compiled for books in the process of publication. China issued the national standard of cataloging data in publication on July 31, 1990, which was first implemented in various publishing houses in Beijing in 1993. After five years of practice and preparation, the basic conditions for popularization and implementation in China were met. The National Press and Publication Administration decided to extend the implementation of the national standard cataloging data in publication to all publishing houses in China. This was an important work plan for realizing the modernization and internationalization of book cataloguing, strengthening standardized management, promoting foreign exchange, and enriching and developing China's publishing industry.

2. Statistics for All Economic Theory Works from 1949 to 1997

From 1949 to 1997, China (mainland, here and below) published about 10,487 economic theory works. Among them, 390 were published from 1949 to 1959, 123 from 1960 to 1969, 179 from 1970 to 1979, 4,040 from 1980 to 1989, and 5,755 from 1990 to 1997. Among the 10,487 economic theory works, there are not only works written and edited by Chinese economists, but also translated works on foreign economic theory. See Table 16-1 for the status of writing and translation in each era.

TABLE 16-1 1949–1997 Statistics for Economic Theory Works and Translations

Year	Total	Works	Translations
1949–1959	390	227	163
1960–1969	123	76	47
1970–1979	179	166	13
1980–1989	4,040	3,463	577
1990–1997	5,755	5,193	562
Total	10,487	9,125	1,362

Note: Compiled by the author.

According to the statistical data, the ratio of works on economic theory written and compiled by Chinese economists in the 1950s to the translated works was generally 2:1, reflecting the fact that at that time, China's socialist economics was in the initial stage, and to a large extent still relied on the introduction and absorption of foreign theories, especially the theories of the Soviet Union. In the 1960s, the ratio of writing to translation remained 2:1, but the number of both decreased significantly. In the 1970s, the number of translated works decreased sharply. By the 1980s, the total number of works written and translated increased by a large margin, but the proportion of translated works in the total amount decreased significantly compared with that in the 1950s and 1960s. In the 1990s, the total number of published works on economic theory increased greatly compared with that in the 1980s, while the proportion of writing and translation was not different.

From 1949 to 1997, there were about 1,362 economic theoretical works translated (excluding the translated works of various applied economics disciplines), which was not much in absolute terms. In fact, since the founding of the People's Republic of China, it was after the 1980s that foreign economic theories were introduced in a large-scale, comprehensive way. Before that, the introduction of works on foreign economic theory was seriously affected by the political climate and foreign policy. In the thirty years from 1949 to 1979, 223 foreign economic theoretical works were translated and published, and most were introduced from the Soviet Union. There is no doubt that the lack of normal international exchange in economic theory was a major reason for the sluggish development of China's economic thought. The translated and published works on economic theory are listed in Table 16-2 by country, region, and organization.

TABLE 16-2 1949–1997 Statistics for Translated Works on Economic Theory by Country, Region, and Organization

Country \ Year	1949–1959	1960–1969	1970–1979	1980–1989	1990–1997	Total
Soviet Union, Russia	136	14	1	87	13	251
USA	8	12	6	153	206	385
UK	12	10	4	83	82	191
Japan		1		140	83	224
France		4	1	18	26	49
Germany	3	3		21	27	51
European Community					7	7
International Monetary Fund				3	10	13
World Bank				5	15	20
UN				2	16	18
Italy				8	15	23
Sweden	1			9	4	14

(Continued)

Year Country	1949–1959	1960–1969	1970–1979	1980–1989	1990–1997	Total
Former Yugoslavia				8	5	13
Austria	2			4	3	9
Hungary				7	2	9
Romania			1	3	3	7
Switzerland	1			9	4	17
Netherlands				3	4	7
New Zealand				1	1	2
Australia				2	8	10
North Korea		1				1
The Republic of Korea					11	11
Belgium				1	1	2
Mexico				1		1
Egypt				1	1	2
Trinidad and Tobago				1		1
Poland	1	1		9	2	13
Canada					4	4
Peru					1	1
Vietnam					1	1
Argentina					1	1
Norway					3	3
Iceland					1	1
Singapore					2	2
Uzbekistan					1	1
Czech Republic				5		5
India					1	1

Note: Compiled by the author.

According to these statistics, in the 1950s, the translated economic works mainly came from the Soviet Union, and a large number were related items of economics in Soviet political economics textbooks and encyclopedias. Due to the deterioration of Sino-Soviet relations in the

1960s, the number of works imported from the Soviet Union decreased sharply, and it did not start to increase again until the 1980s. From 1949 to 1989, most of the works on economic theory introduced from Western countries were from the UK and the US, with more coming from the United States. This situation was in line with the actual development of world economics, since classical Western economics was mainly developed in England, and in modern times, Western economics developed mainly in the UK and the United States became the center of development for Western economics in the 20th century and after.

In the 1980s, most of the economic works translated and introduced into China were British and American. Japanese economic management, enterprise management, and industrial policies also began to be introduced into China at this time. The Soviet Union played an important role in the study of the socialist economy as well. At the same time, the number of economic works translated and introduced from China in the 1980s into various other countries grew, including not only major countries in Eastern Europe, Western Europe, and the United States, but also many small and medium-sized countries and some developing countries. This was an important factor and a manifestation of China's economic development and prosperity in the 1980s.

In the 1990s, the United States accounted for the absolute majority of the works on economic theory translated and introduced into China, while works from Russia decreased significantly. The number of works from other countries with a developed market economy changed little, while the literature from the United Nations, the International Monetary Fund, the World Bank and other international organizations were introduced with greater frequency. This situation reflected the fact that with the deepening of China's market-oriented reform and the expansion of opening up to the outside world, China had a greater demand for the literature on market economy theory and from international economic organizations.

3. Statistical Classification of Economic Works from 1949 to 1997

The purpose of classified statistics was to explain the emphasis of China's economic theory research in different periods, as well as the scope of disciplines involved in economic theory research. Table 16-3 shows the classification and statistics of economic theory works in different years.

TABLE 16-3 1949–1997 Classification and Statistics of Works on Economic Theory

Subject classification \ Year	1949–1959	1960–1969	1970–1979	1980–1985	1986–1989	1990–1997	Total
Political Economics	138	16	74	176	452	810	1,666
Socialist Economy and Chinese Economy	99	33	35	147	493	1,758	2,565

(Continued)

Subject classification \ Year	1949–1959	1960–1969	1970–1979	1980–1985	1986–1989	1990–1997	Total
Capitalist Economy	56	5	24	20	20	110	235
Economic Management	27	4	12	293	1,452	634	2,422
History of Western Economics and Economic Theories	43	51	24	107	152	491	868
National Economy and World Economy	4	2	2	2	248	318	576
Urban and Regional Economy				3	241	776	1,020
Labor Economy and Human Capital	2	3	3	39	88	120	255
Mode of Production and Productivity	10	1	2	8	27	73	121
Development Economics and Economic Growth						164	164
Others	11	8	4	71	315	186	595

Note: Compiled by the author.

In these statistics, the category of political economics mainly refers to relevant courses, works, and translations. The category of the socialist economy and the Chinese economy mainly includes academic works on socialist economic theory and contemporary economic development and reform in China. The category of the capitalist economy refers to theoretical and translated works on the study of capitalism, imperialism, and the history of capitalist development. Economic management includes theoretical works and translated works on national economic management, planned economics, enterprise management, econometrics, and mathematical economics. The history of Western economics and economic theory includes the works, translations, and teaching materials of the history of Western economics, Chinese and foreign economic theory, the history of Marxist economic theory, monographs and translations on economic development, and economic histories of countries and regions other than China. Urban economy and regional economy includes theoretical works and translated works on the urban economy, municipal construction, real estate, productivity distribution, and domestic regional economy. Labor economy and human capital includes labor economics, labor resources, labor productivity, and human capital. The category of mode of production and productivity mainly includes the evolution of social mode of production, productivity, and production relations, and works on productivity economics. The category of development economics and economic growth includes the translated works and treatises on development economics and the works on economic growth in China and abroad. Before the 1990s, such works were classified as "others" because there were so few. In the "other" category, the works on economic theory that are not included in the above categories are grouped together. This mainly includes some disciplines and research fields newly introduced or produced after the 1980s, such as material economics, comparative economics, national defense economics, national economics, consumption economics, ecological economics, technical economics, information economics, circulation economics, the international economy, and works and translations on science, economic geography, and practical economics. The number of theses and translated works in these fields increased each year, suggesting that the branches of economic theory research covered in China were quite extensive, a manifestation of the prosperity and development of domestic economics. In addition, in the "other" category, there are also collected works by some famous domestic economists, dictionaries, handbooks, and other reference books.

In Table 16-3, the 1980s are divided into two stages in order to more accurately reflect the general situation of the development of economic theory in this period. In the 1980s, the total number of works in various categories increased greatly compared with previous years, but most of these works were published between 1986 and 1989. In particular, works on political economics, the socialist economy and China's economy, economic management, the national economy and the world economy, the urban economy and the regional economy, and the mode of production and productivity published after 1986 account for the vast majority published. Among other kinds of works, a large number of new economic disciplines were published after 1986. Counting the works published from 1986 to 1989 by year, it is evident that more works have been published each year than in the previous year, reflecting the normal development of economic science.

4. Classified Statistics for All Works on Economic Theory from 1998 to 2007

Since 1998, the *National New Bibliography* (monthly) has no longer included all bibliographies. Since January 2000, only the new book bibliography of the council units of the journal has been published. The original *National New Bibliography* (monthly) was suspended at the same time. Therefore, the statistics of this period are based on the publication information of the *National General Bibliography*.

(1) Statistics for All Works on Economic Theory

From 1998 to 2007, China published 17,007 theoretical works on economics. Among them, 1,587 were published in 1998, 1,736 in 1999, 1,831 in 2000, 1,326 in 2001, 1,441 in 2002, 1,532 in 2003, 2,104 in 2004, 1,842 in 2005, 1,321 in 2006, and 2,287 in 2007. The 17,007 works on economic theory include not only the works written and edited by Chinese economists, but also imported foreign translated works and original works. See Table 16-4 for the description and introduction of works in each period.

TABLE 16-4 Statistics for New Writings and Introduced Works on Economic Theory
from 1998 to 2007

Year	Total	Works	Introduced
1998	1,587	1,510	77
1999	1,736	1,586	150
2000	1,831	1,662	169
2001	1,326	1,207	119
2002	1,441	1,347	94
2003	1,532	1,381	151
2004	2,104	1,890	214
2005	1,842	1,654	188
2006	1,321	1,230	91
2007	2,287	2,104	183
Total	17,007	15,571	1,436

Note: Compiled by the author.

From the data, it is evident that in 1998, the proportion of works on economic theory written and compiled by Chinese economists was about 20:1, indicating that at that time, China's economic theory research was in a period of vigorous development, while the introduction of foreign theories was less significant. In 1999, there was a sharp increase in the number of introduced works, and the ratio of works to imported works decreased to 11:1. In 2000 and 2001, the number of works written and introduced remained at the level of 10:1, but the number of works written and introduced in 2001 decreased greatly. The publishing volume of the two kinds of works in 2002 increased compared with that in 2001, but it still did not reach the level seen in 2000, and the ratio of the two categories was about 14:1. In 2003, 2004, and 2005, the proportion of the two types of works was maintained at the level of 9:1. In 2004, the publication volume of the two types of works exceeded previous levels. In 2005, publication volume decreased, but it was slightly higher than 2000 levels. In 2006, the number of the two types of works decreased again, to a ratio of 14:1. In 2007, the number of publications reached a ten-year high, and the ratio of two types of works was about 11:1.

From 1998 to 2007, about 1,436 economic theoretical works were introduced (excluding translation works of various applied economic disciplines, which includes original foreign works), which exceeded the total of 1,362 translated works from 1949 to 1997. The translated and published works on economic theory are listed by country, region, and organization in Table 16-5.

TABLE 16-5 Statistics for Works Introducing Economic Theory by Country, Region, and Organization, 1998–2007

Country \ Year	1998	1999	2000	2001	2002	2003	2004	2005	2006	2007	Total
Russia	1	1	3	1	1	1	1		1	1	11
USA	47	90	103	64	60	102	142	121	56	118	903
UK	14	34	23	20	19	22	31	43	15	29	250
Japan	4	12	16	6	7	5	6	10	3	6	75
France	1		2	5		4	3	2		5	22
Germany	4	4	11	6	2	1	15	1	7	5	56
Denmark									2		2
International Monetary Fund					1		1				2
World Bank					1	1	3	1	1	1	8
UN				2							2
Italy		2		1		2			1		6
Sweden	1			2		1	1	1	1	2	9
Former Yugoslavia		1									1
Croatia				1							1
Austria		1		2		2		1	1	2	9
Hungary						1					1
Switzerland			1			1	1				3
Netherlands		1		1	1	1	2		2	1	9
New Zealand							1				1
Australia	2	1	6	1			1	2		1	14
North Korea											
The Republic of Korea		1		1			1	2	1	2	8
Belgium	1										1
Egypt				1							1
Ireland					1		1				2
Poland	1					1					2

(Continued)

Country \ Year	1998	1999	2000	2001	2002	2003	2004	2005	2006	2007	Total
Canada	1	1	3	1		5	2		1	2	16
Peru				1				1		1	3
Norway				1		1	1			2	5
Iceland							1			1	2
Singapore								1			1
India				1				1	1	2	5
Kazakhstan		1									1
Chile			1								1
Uruguay					1						1
Israel						1					1
Finland								1			1

Note: Compiled by the author.

It can be seen from the above data that the United States accounted for the absolute majority of the economic theoretical works introduced from 1998 to 2007, and the United Kingdom and Japan ranked second and third. In 2000, 2003, 2004, 2005, and 2007, American works were introduced more, especially those related to economic management, Western economics, and the history of economic theories. There was little change in the number of books introduced from UK and Japan from 1998 to 2007. Of these, the majority of British works were translations of Western classical economics, business management, and world economy, while most of the Japanese works were about the world economy.

(2) Classified Statistics for Works on Economic Theory
See Table 16-6 for the classification and statistics of economic theory works in this period.

TABLE 16-6 Classification Statistics for Works on Economic Theory from 1998 to 2007

Subject Classification \ Year	1998	1999	2000	2001	2002	2003	2004	2005	2006	2007	Total
Political Economics	60	72	65	73	63	86	61	25	9	18	532
Socialist Economy and Chinese Economy	309	334	259	188	244	206	234	160	140	312	2,386
Capitalist Economy	14	7	7	10	5	8	13	12	2	7	85
Economic Management	365	422	542	135	151	158	415	362	136	360	3,046

(Continued)

Subject Classification / Year	1998	1999	2000	2001	2002	2003	2004	2005	2006	2007	Total
History of Western Economics and Economic Theories	81	87	112	83	100	160	161	141	100	147	1,172
National Economy and World Economy	74	83	105	84	66	98	64	68	58	117	817
Urban Economy and Regional Economy	295	339	417	315	311	351	611	506	419	687	4,251
Labor Economy and Human Capital	43	55	45	50	62	67	127	119	97	175	840
Mode of Production and Productivity	18	1	2	12	8	11	6	3		4	65
Development Economics and Economic Growth	24	22	30	29	22	30	22	17	13	43	252
Economic History	22	45	39	37	65	32	47	39	25	85	436
Industrial Economics				28	21	13	29	29	24	35	179
Yearbook				23	18	40	35	33	50	81	280
Others	282	269	208	259	305	272	279	328	248	216	2,666

Note: Compiled by the author.

5. Statistics for Economic Journals from 1950 to 2008

(1) Statistical Caliber

The journals included in the statistics are mainly economic journals (Chinese library classification number F). In statistics, different editions of the same journal are counted according to different types of journals, renamed journals and their predecessors are counted as the same journal, with the first year of publication traced back to the original year of the former title, combined journals and their predecessors are counted separately according to different kinds of journals, English versions of domestic journals are not included, copies of newspapers and periodicals and yearbook journals are not counted, and journals of the same name with different publishing places and authors are counted as different journals.

This statistical data is mainly based on the *National Index of Newspapers and Periodicals* and its predecessor, the *Index of Important Materials of Major National Journals* (1951–1955), and the *Index of Major National Newspapers and Periodicals* (Philosophy and Social Sciences) (1955–1964). In addition, it refers to the *China Journal Full Text Database*, the National Library of China's Chinese and Foreign Language Catalogue Index, the *China Contemporary Journals Overview*, and the List of Academic Journals of Economic Science in the *Overview of Core Chinese Journals*.

(2) Statistics for All Economic Journals from 1950 to 2008

From 1950 to 2008, China published about 1,330 kinds of economic journals (including some journals that have been discontinued). The statistics for the total number of economic journals are shown in Table 16-7.

TABLE 16-7 1950–2008 Statistics for Economic Journals

Year of Publication	Total
1950–1959	84
1960–1969	6
1970–1979	63
1980–1989	691
1990–1999	315
2000–2008	171

Note: Compiled by the author.

From this statistical data, it is evident that the 1950s was the initial period for the establishment of economic journals. In the 1960s, the publication of journals was almost completely interrupted, and it began to recover in the 1970s. In the 1980s, the height of journal establishment was ushered in. Since the 1990s, due to the increasingly standardized publication of journals, the number of new journals has gradually increased, reflecting the fact that China's periodical industry is gradually moving from quantitative development to quality-oriented development.

(3) Classified Statistics for Economic Journals from 1950 to 2008

In these statistics, theoretical economics mainly includes political economics, the history of economic thought, economic history, Western economics, the world economy, population, resources, and environmental economics, and other areas. Applied economics mainly includes national economics, regional economics, finance (including taxation), finance (including insurance), industrial economics, international economics, economic journals of trade, labor economics, statistics, quantitative economics, and the national defense economy. Economic journals on business administration mainly include statistical accounting, enterprise management (including financial management, marketing, human resource management), tourism management, the technical economy, and management. In practice, some comprehensive journals are also included in the journal of theoretical economics category. The specific classification statistics are shown in Table 16-8.

From these statistics, it is evident that the number of journals of applied economics is the largest. The proportion of theoretical economics, applied economics, and business administration journals is about 1:15.91:3.55, while in the 1980s and 1990s, the proportions of the three journals were 1:20.27:5.31 and 1:22.73:4.91, which was higher than the overall level, indicating that the

1980s and 1990s were a period of great development in applied economics journals.

TABLE 16-8 1950–2008 Classified Statistics for Economic Journals

Year \ Classification	Theoretical Economics	Applied Economics	Business Management	Total
1950–1959	7	71	6	84
1960–1969	1	3	2	6
1970–1979	9	45	9	63
1980–1989	26	527	138	691
1990–1999	11	250	54	315
2000–2008	11	138	22	171
Total	65	1,034	231	1,330

Note: Compiled by the author.

16.2 A Summary of Works on Economic Theory from 1949 to 2007

1. A Summary of Works on Economic Theory in the 1950s through the 1970s

In the 1950s, most of the economic works were political economics course books and related dictionaries and reference books, many of which were translated from the Soviet Union. Most of the other works not belonging to the textbook of political economics category were based on Marx's *Das Kapital* and Lenin and Stalin's theories studying the topics of commodity production, law of value, labor theory of value, capital accumulation and distribution consumption, and other related topics, characterized by pure theoretical research. In addition, in line with the debate on political economics at that time, some works on the research object and method of political economics were also published. In addition to political economics, the economic theoretical problems studied in the theoretical works at that time included the mode of social production, the modern capitalist economy, national economic planning, productivity economics, and economic accounting. The works on Western economics introduced in this period were mainly scattered in the fields of economic policy, employment, monopoly competition, interest and price, capital and labor, foreign trade, the planned economy, and the history of economic theory. There were also some systematic introductions, such as Keynes' *The General Theory of Employment, Interest, and Money*, Malthus's *Theory of Population*, and Menger's *Principles of Economics*.

In the 1960s, political economics courses, reference books, popular books, and handbooks still accounted for the main share. As China's socialist construction had much experience and many lessons by this time, economic theorists began to use the principles of political economics to study and analyze real economic problems, and they published many works on socialist economic theory, such as finance and commerce under the socialist system, labor and wages under the socialist system, differential land income under the socialist system, the law of value and commodity production under the socialist system, the relations of production under the socialist system, and social products under the socialist system. In addition, more attention was paid to the study of the capitalist economy during this period, and many works on the topic were published in China.

In the 1960s, with the increase in political movements and the Cultural Revolution, which began in the mid-1960s, the study of economic theory in this decade was not very active and there were few works produced. However, in the first half of the 1960s, there was a noticeable phenomenon in the translation and introduction of foreign economic theories. In this period, the total amount of translated works of Western economic theory was more than that in the 1950s, and the quality had greatly improved. Many of the Western economics books introduced at that time were the original works of classical Western economics and vulgar economics. At the same time, some Chinese economists also devoted themselves to the study of classical Western economics and published works such as *British Classical Political Economics, Keynesianism, Vulgar Political Economics of France and Britain in the First Half of the 19th Century*, and *Critique of Modern Bourgeois Economic Theory*. There were two main reasons for this situation. One was that since the end of 1950s, there were cracks in the relationship between China and the Soviet Union, so the economic works translated and introduced from the Soviet Union in the 1960s declined greatly, while the introduction of economic theory from Western countries was more important. The second was the introduction of economic theory itself from Western countries from the 1950s to 1960s. There was also a process of development, from a scattered approach in the 1950s to a systematic, focused comparison in the 1960s, indicating that the understanding and research of Western economic theories by Chinese theorists had deepened. Judging from the situation in the 1960s, if the Cultural Revolution had not interrupted the international exchange on economics, the development of China's economic thought could have been greatly accelerated.

The 1970s included the later part of the Cultural Revolution and "bringing order out of chaos" after the Cultural Revolution. Economic theory research was inevitably disrupted during this time. The theoretical works published in this period were not only small in number, but also addressed a small range of topics. Most were popular books and critical works, and there was little real theoretical research. From the perspective of political economics, some popular reading materials, such as *Political Economics on the Slipway, Political Economics on the Wharf, Popular Political Economics, Some Knowledge of Political Economics, Basics of Political Economics*, and *Questions and Answers on Political Economics*, accounted for a large proportion. Among the major categories of the socialist economy and the Chinese economy, a large number of publications were pamphlets such as *Transforming Small Production, Revolution and Production*, and *On the Relationship Between Politics and Economy*, and some were critical publications produced after the Cultural Revolution ended. During this period, there were a large number of works on the capitalist economy, most of which focused on the comments on the capitalist economic crisis and criticism of the capitalist economic system. Examples included *The Doom of Imperialism*,

Economic Crisis as an Incurable Disease of the Capitalist System, Speech on the Economic Crisis, Knowledge of the Economic Crisis, and *What is Economic Crisis: On the Capitalist Economic Crisis.* It was the need of the political climate and propaganda at that time and an objective reflection of the development of the world capitalist economy. In the 1970s, the world's capitalist countries had one economic crisis after another, and many countries were still trapped in "stagflation," which provided a subject for domestic capitalist economic research.

Most of the domestic works and translated works on the history of Western economics and economic theories were published in 1978 and 1979. They were basically similar to those produced in the 1960s in terms of topics and content, that is, they mainly introduced classical Western economic theories. For examples, Adam Smith's works, Quesnay's works, Ricardo's works, Sismondi's economic thought, and Galbraith's theory of institutional economy were all translated and introduced in this period.

2. A Summary of Works on Economic Theory in the 1980s

Of the economic theory works published in the 1980s, although there were a number of political economics publications, their proportion had greatly decreased, and they were replaced by economic management and Chinese economic works. Other works, such as the history of Western economics and economic theory, the national economy, the urban economy, and the regional economy, also increased significantly.

The works on political economics published in 1980s not only increased in absolute quantity, but also in academic quality. The political economics in this period was different from the Soviet Union system in the 1950s and 1960s, nor was it a part of the popular and critical nature of the 1970s. Instead, it devoted itself to the scientific study and mastery of Marxist economic principles and widely absorbed the experience and lessons from global socialist economic practice combined with China's economic reform and development. There were some innovations in theory. Therefore, the work in this period was basically divided into two categories. The first concerned the research and development of Marxist economics, such as *An Introduction to Marxist Political Economics, Exploration of Marxist Economic Theory, Marx's Theory of Social Reproduction and Its Application,* and some related works translated from the Soviet Union and Eastern European countries. The second category was political economics coursebooks, which greatly expanded and improved in content and style compared with earlier ones. For example, in the coursebooks on political economics before the 1980s, the main body was capitalism, and the socialist part was almost non-existent, except for a few "laws" of Soviet theory. In the coursebooks on political economics in the 1980s, especially in the second half of the 1980s, the content was equally divided between the capitalist part and the socialist part, and some were called "socialist political economics." By the end of the 1980s, China's socialist political economics course system had been basically formed. In this system, there were many theories, viewpoints, and ideas that were a combination of Marxist principles with socialist economic development and reform practice, among which there were some valuable theoretical innovations. There were also some courses that adopted the concepts and content of Western economics in order to be innovative, but practice proved that this approach was not very desirable. Marxist political economics and contemporary Western economics were two theoretical systems. It was beneficial to both to compare, learn from, and absorb each other in theoretical research. However, it was not suitable to confuse the two systems and methods in teaching. This was not only difficult to deal with in teaching, but also not conducive to students' systematic and complete study and mastery of the two subjects.

In the 1980s, there were a large number of works on the socialist economy and the Chinese economy. This sort of treatise generally involved some specific content. First was the research and elaboration of socialist ownership, distribution according to work, the law of planned, proportional development, and the essence and law of the socialist economy. Second was the theoretical discussion of economic growth, value and price, macroeconomic benefits and national income, the socialist commodity economy, and the primary stage of socialism. The third addressed theoretical and policy research on China's economic system reform. These works were more concerned with the overall theoretical research on the socialist economy. Strictly speaking, it fell into the category of socialist political economics. However, compared with the course of political economics, these works were more theoretical and academic. They included specialized research on socialist economic theory, so they were classified separately from textbooks.

In the 1980s, the largest number of works addressed the economy and management. Such works were roughly divided into three parts. One addressed the planning and management of the national economy, such as *An Introduction to National Economic Management, Socialist Planning Work*, and *An Introduction to Modern Economic Management*. The other focused on economic management technology, such as *Economic Cybernetics, Application of Econometrics Principles, Compilation and Application of the Input-Output Table*, and *Economic Quantitative Analysis, Input-Output Analysis, Network Planning Technology, System Economics*. There were a large number of works in this category, and a considerable number were translated works. The third part addressed enterprise management, such as *Enterprise Strategy, Target Management, Decision-making Technology, Production Management, Production Organization*. It included the largest number of works and formed the largest proportion of translated works.

During this period, there were not only a large number of works and translations on the history of Western economics and economic theories, but also a wide range of content covered. In addition to continuing to introduce and study Western classical economics, it introduced many works on contemporary Western economics and started to involve some branches of it, such as comparative economics, development economics, new institutional economics, the monetary school, and the supply school. At the same time, there were many Western macroeconomics and microeconomics coursebooks compiled by Chinese economists.

The economic works and translated works of various countries mainly covered the economic development and economic growth history of the developed countries of Europe, the United States, Japan, and the "Four Asian Tigers," as well as the Soviet Union and Eastern European countries and regions. Among them, the works describing the economic situations of Japan, Europe, the United States, and other major capitalist countries accounted for a large proportion, and the number of books introducing the economic take-off of newly industrialized countries and regions was also large. In addition, there were some works on international economic organizations, such as the EU and ASEAN.

The number of other works on topics such as the urban economy, the regional economy, the labor economy, and human capital increased significantly in the 1980s. Before that, the works on the urban economy were almost non-existent, and the works on the labor economy basically only reproduced the theories of the Soviet Union, and their number was very small. In the 1980s, these disciplines gradually emerged and developed from scratch, growing from small to large and from lower level to higher level, and all became a branch of economics with a relatively complete framework system. But on the whole, the theoretical research of these subjects was relatively weak. In particular, most of the works on the urban economy and the labor economy were limited to the practical level, such as real estate development, housing system reform, urban construction management, wage management, labor management, labor economics course, and other similar topics, and they lacked comprehensive, high-level empirical research on urban development, urbanization, regional development, labor transfer, and human capital from the perspective of economic theoretical research. Moreover, compared with other disciplines, there were fewer translated works on the urban economy and the labor economy. In brief, from the perspective of publishing, the theoretical research power of the urban economy, the regional economy, the labor economy, and human capital was not very strong and still needed further development.

3. A Review of Works on Economic Theory from the 1990s to 2007

From the early to the mid-1990s, works on political economics, the socialist economy, and China's economy still accounted for the largest portion of theoretical works on economics. In textbooks on political economics, the capitalist part and the socialist part were often combined into one book, such as the *Newly Compiled Political Economics,* which was published widely at that time. In addition, the number of textbooks on "socialist political economics" or the "socialist part of political economics" continued to increase as it had in the late 1980s. Some textbooks on political economics were directly named "Marxist political economics," indicating that their style was to get rid of the traditional mode of the Soviet Union and refer to the framework system of Marx's *Das Kapital.* During this period, there were also numerous books on the methodology of political economics, which studied the theoretical framework, analytical methods, and category system of Marxist economics. The theoretical works on the socialist economy and China's economy mainly focused on research on the combination of Marxist economic theory and Chinese socialist economic practice, the study of the primary stage of socialism, the study of economic system reform, and the study of hot social and economic issues. After 1993, a large number of works on the socialist market economy emerged, such as *The Theory of the Socialist Market Economy, Socialist Market Economics, Lectures on the Socialist Market Economy, An Introduction to the Socialist Market Economy,* and *A Collection of China's Socialist Market Economy Law.* This situation continued until the mid and late 1990s. Other research on the construction of the socialist market economic system involved Marxist economic theory and the socialist market economy, the development form of a socialist society, the market economy and macro-control, the market economy and system reform, the market economy and state-owned enterprise reform, and the market economy and reform of state-owned assets and the market economy, among others topics.

Before the mid-1990s, Western economics and the history of economic theory also accounted for a significant share. During this period, a large number of Western economics textbooks were published by Chinese scholars, which may have been related to the fact that economics majors in colleges and universities generally attached importance to the teaching of Western economics. In order to rapidly improve the teaching level of Western economics, China translated and introduced original Western economics courses, such as Samuelson's *Economics*, which was constantly cited. Others included *An Introduction to Western Macroeconomics* by Christie, *Neoclassical Macroeconomics* by Hoover, *Price Theory* by Stigler, *Economics* by Stiglitz, *Macroeconomics: An Advanced Coursebook* by Blanchard and Fisher, *Microeconomic Theory: Mathematical Analysis Method* by Henderson, and *Macroeconomic Theory in the Context of Free Economy* by Paul Crowe. In addition, a large number of specialized research results were introduced, such as Ronald Coase's *Property Rights and Institutional Evolution*, Schumpeter's *The History of Economic Analysis*, Solow's *Capital Theory and the Rate of Return*, Mead's *Efficiency, Equity, and Property Rights*, Atkinson's *Public Economics*, Miller's *Public Choice Theory*, and Demsetz's *The Economic Legal*, and *Political Systems of Competition*, Scheffrin's *Rational Expectations*, and Samuelson's *The Basis of Economic Analysis*.

After 1991, the number of works on urban economics, regional economics, and economic management increased sharply, while theoretical works on production mode and productivity decreased by a large margin, indicating that with the rapid growth of China's economy, research on economic theory was more focused on fields closely related to the real economy, and scholars' interest in purely speculative research topics was significantly weaker. Even theoretical studies on productivity and production relations mainly focused on productivity system theory, productivity distribution, science and technology, and productivity. In addition, from 1994, "productivity and relations of production" was no longer listed separately in the column of "cataloging books in publication" in the *National New Bibliography*. Most works on the urban economy and the regional economy were about the real estate economy and regional development, which seemed to be related to the "real estate fever," "development zone fever," and housing system reform. The theoretical nature of the works in this respect was not strong, and they were more inclined to practical operation. From the perspective of theoretical research, the regional economy, the urban economy, and other fields were still relatively weak.

In the second half of the 1990s, especially at the end of the 1990s, new changes took place in the publication of works on economic theory. First of all, the number of textbooks on political economics was greatly reduced. In 1997, the column of "national latest published books monthly report" (changed to "national latest book publishing monthly report" in 1998 and changed to "national new bibliography monthly report" in 1999) no longer set a "political economics" column in the *National New Bibliography*. Secondly, in the category of the socialist economy and the

Chinese economy, there were many books about the establishment of China's economic system, such as *The Outline of Contemporary China's Economics, China's Market Economics*, and *Socialist Market Economics*. The growth of such books and political economics textbooks may have been a reflection of the important changes in the textbook system and teaching content of socialist political economics in China, that is, from the original textbook system and teaching content based on the concept category of *Das Kapital* to the framework system and teaching content combining the socialist category with the market economy category. Finally, the introduction of Western economics in this period paid more attention to application and new research results, such as Stiglitz's *Why Government Intervenes in the Economy*, Ethridge's *Methodology of Applied Economics*, Hall's *Economics: Theory and Application*, Edith's *Enterprise Life Cycle*, Ellerman's *The Democratic Corporation*, Levy's *Economics in Daily Life*, Hart's *Enterprise, Contract, and Financial Structure*, Dornbusch's *Macroeconomics*, Pindyck's *Microeconomics*, and Taylor's *Industrial Organization Theory*.

Of the economic works published from 1998 to 2007, there were more works on the socialist economy and China's economy, economic management, the urban economy, and the regional economy, while those on political economics, the capitalist economy, mode of production, and productivity accounted for only a small proportion.

In 1998, the works on political economics were basically divided into two categories: political economics that included both the capitalist and socialist economy, and political economics based on Marx's *Das Kapital*. The works on the socialist economy involved the theory of the primary stage of socialism, socialist ownership, and the socialist market economy, while those on the Chinese economy involved socialism with Chinese characteristics, economic system reform, and macro management. The works on the category of the capitalist economy mainly included the introduction to the capitalist economy, capitalist ownership, and the capitalist economic cycle. That year, Western economic books translated and introduced from the West were mainly works on macroeconomics, such as *Macroeconomics: An Advanced Coursebook* by Blanchard and Fisher and *Macroeconomics of Rational Expectation* by Minford. There were many works on Western economics written by domestic scholars, most of which covered microeconomics, macroeconomics, and the history of Western economics. In addition, the history of economic theory and the history of economic thought were published. There were many studies on the East Asian economy and the Japanese economy in the works on the economy of various countries and the world economy. Most of the works on economic management were about enterprise management, while those on national economic management mainly involved state-owned assets management and macroeconomic management. Econometrics was introduced, but there were few works on mathematical economics written by Chinese scholars. There were more works on the urban and regional economy, more works on real estate finance, real estate economics, and real estate market science were published, and there were more works on the regional economy in China. Of the works on the labor economy, the translation and treatise on human resource management was a relatively new research field.

In 1999, there was a slight increase in the number of works on political economics, and the main topics covered were political economics and Marxist political economics. The number of works on the socialist economy and China's economy also increased, mainly involving the theory of the socialist market economy, China's economy against the backdrop of economic globalization and the knowledge economy, and the reform of China's economic system. Of the works on the history of Western economics and economic theories, the works introduced from the West included not only micro- and macroeconomics, but also representative works of Western economics schools and the history of economic theories, such as Stevens' *Economics of Collective Choice*, Mueller's *Theory of Public Choice*, Williamson's *Economics of Antitrust*, Schumpeter's *From Marx to Keynes*, Howe's *The Rise of Marginal Utility School*, and Rutherford's *Institution in Economics: Old and New Institutionalism*. The number of works on economic management increased significantly, mainly due to the increase in the publication of books on enterprise production management, quality management, financial management, and the management practice of various enterprises. Of the urban economic works, there were many on real estate appraisal, real estate management, and real estate finance. The number of works on the capitalist economy, productivity, and mode of production was greatly reduced.

In 2000, the number of works on political economics fell. Of the works on political economics and Marxist political economics, the latter accounted for a larger proportion. The publication of books on the socialist economy and China's economy decreased, covering the socialist market economy, economic system reform, macro-control, and the World Trade Organization. There were more works on Western economics and the history of economic theories. There were more publications of works on macroeconomics, microeconomics, and general Western economics written by domestic scholars. The number of works on the world economy increased, as did the number of countries studied. The number of books on the urban economy, the regional economy, and economic management increased significantly. Of these, the number of books on Western development in works on regional economics increased significantly, the number of econometrics works in works on economic management increased, and the number of books on enterprise financial management and management practice of various types of enterprises in enterprise management books increased even more.

In 2001, in addition to political economics and Marxist political economics, some foreign scholars' related works were translated and published. The number of theses on the socialist economy and China's economy was greatly reduced. The main topics covered were socialist economic theory, economic system reform, and hot social issues. That year, China's accession to the WTO was imminent, and a large number of theoretical works on this event sprang up. The books on Western economics and the history of Western economics introduced that year were mainly classical works of Western economists, textbooks on Western economics, and anthologies by Western economists. There were many Western economics works compiled by domestic scholars as well. The number of economics and management works published that year decreased significantly, which is mostly due to the fact that the statistics did not include enterprise management works related to enterprise operation, finance, strategy, and other sub-management items. Only introductory works were used to reflect the publishing situation of enterprise management texts. The number of books on the urban and regional economy decreased compared with the previous year. Most of the works on the regional economy were about the development of the west, such as *The Theory of Western Development* and *The Mode Selection of Western Development*. This was probably related to the implementation of the strategy of western development in 2000.

Works on political economics in 2002 continued to focus on political economics and Marxist political economics. Those addressing the socialist economy and China's economy offered theoretical explorations of the socialist market economy and economic transformation. The introduced works on the history of Western economics and economic theories were mainly economics textbooks and works by well-known economists, such as Tulowitzki's *International Macroeconomic Dynamics* and *Macroeconomic Dynamics Methods* and Williamson's *Capitalist Economic System*. Domestic scholars not only published a large number of works on Western economics, but also a series of works on the history of economic theories, such as Yan Zhijie's *A Coursebook of Western Economic Theories*, Ding Bing and Zhang Liancheng's *Modern Western Economic Theories*, and Wang Zhiwei's *Schools of Modern Western Economics*. The number of works on the urban economy, the regional economy, and the labor economy that year was basically the same as that of the previous year. The translation of works on labor economics mainly came from the United States. That year, there were many economic history books published, including general historical works, ancient and modern history works, and the ten-volume *A General History of China's Economy* edited by Zhao Dexin.

In 2003, the publication volume of political economics books was the highest in ten years, but the content was still centered on political economics and Marxist political economics. Works on the socialist economy studied the new development of socialist economic theory, the socialist market economy, and income distribution. China's economic works gave more attention to the open economy, and a large number of books on China's accession to the World Trade Organization were published. The number of works on the history of Western economics and economic theories increased greatly. There were more works on microeconomics, macroeconomics, and Western economics introduced and written by Chinese scholars. There were a large number of domestic works on the history of economic theories of new institutional economics. The number of works on the urban economy, the regional economy, and the labor economy published that year did not increase significantly. There were more theoretical works on the urban economy, such as *Urban Economics* by O'Sullivan and *Real Estate Economics* by McKenzie, as well as relevant works written by Chinese scholars, such as *Modern Urban Management*, *Real Estate Economics*, and *A General Theory of Real Estate Economics*. There were also more general works on the regional economy, such as *The Theory of Regional Differences*, *The Research on the Coordinated Development of Urbanization and Regional Economy*, and *The Micro-mechanism of Regional Economic Development*. The number of regional economics works related to the development of the West decreased.

In 2004, political economics works were still dominated by the introduction of political economics and Marxist political economics. There was a large number of works on the socialist economy and China's economy, which mainly involved 1) a course or special topic study on socialist economic theory concerning ownership and market economy, 2) theoretical research on private economic development and foreign economic cooperation, and 3) theoretical and policy research on China's economic system reform. The introduction of Western economics and the history of theory accounted for not only a large number of books, but also a wide range of content. In addition to the introduction of Western economics textbooks and learning guides, Western economists' works were also introduced, such as Friedman's *Capitalism and Freedom* and Zimmerman's *Frontier Issues of Economics*. Western economics textbooks compiled by Chinese scholars and introductions to Western economic schools were likewise published. That year, the number of publications on economic management, the urban economy, the regional economy, and the labor economy increased significantly compared with that in 2003. Of these three categories of works, most translated works were from the United States, and the number of labor economics books compiled by domestic scholars began to increase.

In 2005, the number of published works on political economics decreased significantly compared with previous years, and the topics covered were still mainly Marxist political economics and political economics textbooks. The number of theses on the socialist economy and China's economy decreased by a large margin. The contents included 1) monographs on socialist economic theory, with a focus on the socialist market economy, 2) books on economic development, among which were more studies on the private economy, and 3) works on the reform of the economic system, focusing on the reform of state-owned enterprises. There were many theoretical explorations in this field. The books on the history of Western economics and economic theories introduced that year were mainly textbooks on Western microeconomics and macroeconomics, such as *Macroeconomics* (5th Edition) by Mankiw, *Microeconomics* by Robert Frank, and *An Introduction to Dynamic Economics* by Ronald Shone. With the improvement of English proficiency of domestic readers, more works were introduced in the form of photocopies, such as Tucker's *Microeconomics for Today* (3rd edition) and Mankiw's *Principles of Microeconomics*. In addition, there were works on the history of Western economic thought, such as Pressman's *Fifty Major Economists* and Mills' *A Critical History of Economics*. That year, the number of works on the urban economy, the regional economy, and the labor economy decreased compared with that in 2004, but the number of other types of works increased significantly, indicating that the breadth of economic research had expanded.

Among the economic theoretical works published in 2006, works on political economics, the socialist economy, and China's economy decreased compared with those in 2005. More works on political economics took a certain theoretical category of Marxist economics as the research object. There were also works that expressed the basic principles of Marxist economics with modern social science research methods, such as *Mathematical Political Economics*. Theoretical works on the socialist economy and the Chinese economy mainly focused on research on economic system reform and hot issues in the social economy. Western economics and histories of economic theory published in 2006 accounted for a large proportion of the total publications that year. Among them, Western economics textbooks compiled by Chinese scholars, histories of

Marxist economic theory, and works introducing Western economists were the most frequently published. In 2006, the number of publications of economic management, urban economics, and regional economics decreased to varying degrees, and there were no clear works on "productivity and production relations" published.

There are many kinds of economic works published in 2007, and the number of works on political economics increased compared with that in 2006. They mainly covered Marxist political and economic theory, and there were works that studied from a macro perspective, such as *Marxist Economics and Classical General Equilibrium Theory* and *Research on the Marxist Macroeconomic Analysis System*. The theoretical works on the socialist economy and the Chinese economy gave more attention to the problems of China's economic development against the backdrop of economic system reform and globalization. Of the works on the history of Western economics and economic theories, textbooks on microeconomics, macroeconomics, Western economics, the history of Marx's economic theory, and the history of Western economic theory compiled by domestic scholars were mainly introduced, including Van Buren's *Theory of the Leisure Class*, Hiller's *Market Fluctuation*, Eggertsson's *Economic Behavior and System,* and Steven Medema's *Coase Economics: Law, Economics, and New Institutional Economics*. In 2007, the number of works on economic theory published in the categories of the national economy and the world economy, the urban economy and the regional economy, the labor economy and human capital, development economics and economic growth, economic history, industrial economics, and yearbooks reached the highest level in ten years.

16.3 Statistics for Works on Economic Theory from 2008 to 2011

1. Introduction of the National General Bibliography

The basic statistical data of works on economic theory from 2008 to 2011 that is recorded here is mainly based on the *National General Bibliography*. The *National General Bibliography* is the only annual bibliography in China. It has been compiled each year since 1949. Based on the samples collected by the China Archives of Publications, it includes the first edition and revised books (excluding reprinted books) published in China in the year of public and domestic circulation only, as well as teaching books for primary and secondary schools, normal schools, and trade schools. It is a necessary reference book for publishing house, library, information materials, scientific research, and teaching departments.

From 1949 to 1955, the *National General Bibliography* was edited by the head office of Xinhua Bookstore. It mainly reflected the books distributed by Xinhua Bookstore, with only some select books from private bookstores. After 1956, it was edited by the China Archives of Publications. In 1966, the editing work was interrupted, only to be resumed in 1971, when the *National General Bibliography* for 1970 was published. Later, the *National General Bibliography* was published for various years from 1972 to 1982. In 1987, the *National General Bibliography* for 1966–1969 was published, along with the *National General Bibliography* for 1971, published in 1988.

The classified catalogue is the main part, which includes books published in Chinese. The special catalogue mainly includes technical standards, Braille books, translated books, series of books, and other similar works. The appendix includes a list of domestic newspapers, magazines, publishers, book title indices, and statistical table of all kinds of books. The title, author, translator, publication time, number of pages, format, binding, and pricing of the revised books are described separately. Since 1982, a synopsis was included for most of the books. In the early stages, the catalogue was arranged according to the Book Classification of the Library of Renmin University of China. Since the 1960s, 22 categories have been redesigned, and since 1973, the Chinese Library Classification has been used.

From 2001 to 2003, efforts were made to publish a CD version with the printed edition. Since 2004, the printed version has no longer been published, and the catalogue was published only in the form of CD-ROM. Before 2004, the printed edition was published by Zhonghua Book Company once a year. Since 2004, the CD-ROM version has been published by the Electronic Publications Data Center of the National Press and Publication Administration.

The interface format of the CD-ROM includes the Chinese Library Classification Index and the national publishing house Index. Each bibliographic data in the CD-ROM includes book title, author, publisher, key words, subject headings, classification number, ISBN number, and a summary of the contents. Users can conduct comprehensive combination searches and single item searches.

According to the information obtained, when this book was published, only the 2004–2011 *National General Bibliography* CD-ROM could be purchased, with the annual price of 550 yuan. There was no CD-ROM published information after 2011, only data from 2012 to 2018, with the price of 1 yuan per piece. It is estimated that there are more than 170,000 pieces of published information related to economics, so the data purchase cost is about 170,000 yuan. The research funds of this project are insufficient to support it, so these statistics can only rely on the CD-ROM version through 2011. If a CD-ROM is published in the future, this material will be revised and supplemented.

2. Classified Statistics for All Works on Economic Theory from 2008 to 2011

(1) Statistics for All Works on Economic Theory

The statistics from this period are based on the published information of the *National General Bibliography*. From 2008 to 2011, China published 8,524 economic theory books. Of them, 1,809 were published in 2008, 2,150 in 2009, 2,211 in 2010, and 2,354 in 2011. Of the 8,524 economic theoretical works, there were not only works written and edited by Chinese economists, but also imported foreign translated works and original works. See Table 16-9 for a description and introduction for each year.

TABLE 16-9 Statistics for Economic Theory and Introduction from 2008 to 2011

Year	Total	Works	Translations
2008	1,809	1,665	144
2009	2,150	1,977	173
2010	2,211	2,006	205
2011	2,354	2,184	170
Total	8,524	7,832	692

Note: Compiled by the author.

From 2008 to 2011, there about 692 economic theory works were introduced. The translated and published economic theory works are listed by country, region, and organization in Table 16-10.

TABLE 16-10 Statistics for Works on Economic Theory in Translation by Country, Region, and Organization from 2008 to 2011

Country \ Year	2008	2009	2010	2011	Total
Soviet Union	1				1
Russia	4	4			8
USA	92	115	127	106	440
UK	19	29	29	30	107
Japan	7	4	7	9	27
France		2	8	4	14
Germany	5		10	4	19
IMF	1		1		2
World Bank		5	4	1	10
UN	1			2	3
Italy	1	4	3	1	9
Sweden	1	1	1		3
Austria			3		3
Hungary		1			1
Switzerland			1		1

(Continued)

Country \ Year	2008	2009	2010	2011	Total
Netherlands	1	1	2		4
New Zealand					
Australia		1	1	2	4
The Republic of Korea	1	2	1	1	5
Belgium			1	1	2
Egypt	1				1
Ireland	1	1			2
Canada	2	2	3	2	9
Peru					
Norway	1	1			2
Iceland					
Singapore					
India	4			2	6
Finland				1	1
South Africa	1			2	3
Span			2		2
Zambia			1		1
Mexico				1	1
Malaysia				1	1

Note: Compiled by the author

From this data, it is evident that of the works on economic theory introduced from 2008 to 2011, the United States accounted for the absolute majority, and Britain and Japan ranked second and third. Most of the books introduced from the United States were Western economics course books and works on neoclassical economics. The majority of British works were classical Western economics, and the majority of Japanese works were on the world economy. The number of books imported from France and Germany increased significantly in 2010 and 2011.

(2) Classified Statistics for Works on Economic Theory
Table 16-11 shows the classification and statistics of economic theory works in this period.

TABLE 16-11 Classified Statistics for Works on Economic Theory from 2008 to 2011

Subject Classification / Year	2008	2009	2010	2011	Total
Political Economics	17	17	33	16	83
Socialist Economy and Chinese Economy	198	188	133	180	699
Capitalist Economy	11	8	10	9	38
Economic Management	142	183	158	127	610
History of Western Economics and Economic Theories	135	155	180	158	628
National Economy and World Economy	121	132	112	110	475
Urban Economy and Regional Economy	640	723	805	927	3,095
Labor Economy and Human Capital	110	145	151	183	589
Mode of Production and Productivity	0	6	5	5	16
Development Economics and Economic Growth	19	22	10	37	88
Economic History	39	27	50	50	166
Industrial Economics	52	74	88	99	313
Yearbook	31	21	49	60	161
Others	294	449	427	393	1,563

Note: Compiled by the author

3. Review of Works on Economic Theory from 2008 to 2011

Works on economic theory in 2008–2011 are categorized under political economics, the socialist economy and the Chinese economy, the capitalist economy, economic management, the history of Western economics and economic theory, the national economy and the world economy, the urban economy and the regional economy, the labor economy and human capital, the mode of production and productivity, development economics and economic growth, economic history, industrial economics, yearbooks, and others (mainly including circulation economics, consumption economics, virtual economics, behavioral economics, experimental economics, social economics, public economics, ecological economics, technical economics, network economics, circular economics, international economics, logistics management, and other similar topics).

Of the works on economic theory published in 2008, the largest number were on the urban economy and the regional economy, with a total of 640. This category included the regional economy, the urban economy, local economic development, the real estate economy, the industrial park economy, the county economy, and other related topics. It covered a relatively large scope and reflected the reality of vigorous economic development in China in the previous thirty years of Reform and Opening Up. The number of publications ranked second was in the category of "others," with a total of 294 books, including those on the circulation economy, consumption economics, behavioral economics, information economics, circular economics, experimental economics, competitiveness evaluation, public economics, the knowledge economy, ecological economics, technological economics, international economics, economic geography, asset appraisal, the logistics economy, and other similar topics. There were numerous publications on the socialist economy and the Chinese economy (198), the national economy and the world economy (121), and the labor economy and human capital (110). The number of publications in other categories was less than 100, and 17 works were published in the category of political economics.

Of the translated works published in 2008, there were 92 translated works from the United States, 19 from Britain, 7 from Japan, 5 from Russia and Germany, 4 from India, and less than 4 from all other countries. Of the translated works in the United States, many were economics courses, such as macroeconomics, microeconomics, and econometrics. The others included works on economic history, human resource management, economic growth, and international economics. There were many works on the history of economic theory, human resource management, and similar topics.

Of the works on economic theory published in 2009, the largest number were those on the urban economy and the regional economy, with a total of 723. This was not only related to the formulation and implementation of China's regional development strategy, but also to the change in China's economic and industrial development pattern and the rapid development of the regional and urban economy, including the real estate economy. The number of publications that ranked second was in the category of "others," with a total of 449 books. Most of these were works on the service economy, the technological economy, the circular economy, the information economy, international economics, logistics, and supply chain. There were numerous publications on the socialist economy and the Chinese economy (188), economic management (183), the history of Western economics and economic theory (155), the labor economy and human capital (145), and the national economy and the world economy (132). The number of publications in other categories was less than 100, and 17 works were published in the category of political economics.

Of the translated works published in 2009, the United States accounted for the majority of the translated works, with a total of 115. There were 29 English translations, four in Russian, Italian, and Japanese, and five on the World Bank, while only a few came from other countries. Most of the translated works from the United States were economics courses, while others were on the world economy, international economics, human resource management, econometrics, game theory, labor economics, and economic management. Of the English translations, there were many versions of Adam Smith's *An Inquiry into the Nature and Causes of the Wealth of Nations* and Keynes' *The General Theory of Employment, Interest and Money*.

Among the economic theoretical works published in 2010, 805 books were published in the categories of the urban economy and the regional economy. In addition to the textbooks and theoretical works in the field of the regional and urban economy, a large number of books are about local economic research and regional economic development strategies. There were also a considerable number of books in the field of land and real estate. The second category was "others," with 427 books, with topics including technological innovation, experimental and behavioral economics, the circular economy, the public economy, the ecological economy, the knowledge economy, the Internet economy, the technological economy, international economics, global integration, economic geography, the resource economy, consumption economics, asset evaluation, the logistics economy, and other similar topics. There were more than 100 works on Western economics and the history of economic theories (180), economic management (158), the socialist economy and the Chinese economy (133), the labor economy and human capital (151), the national economy and the world economy (112). There were 33 published books on political economics, including political economics courses, Marxist economics research, and related translated works.

Of the translations published in 2010, 127 were from the United States, 29 from the United Kingdom, 10 from Germany, 8 from France, 7 from Japan, and 4 or less from other countries and international organizations. Works on macroeconomics and microeconomics made up the majority of American translations. Others topics included international economics, antitrust and regulatory economics, behavioral economics, public economics, social choice theory, economic growth theory, econometrics, human capital management, urban economics, and the history of economic theories. Selected topics for English translations were scattered, and the translations of classical economics and Keynesian economics still made up the bulk of translations published. Most of the translated works from Japan focused on the study of the capitalist economy.

Of the economic theoretical works published in 2011, 927 were published on the urban economy and the regional economy. Most of the research covered the economic development of provinces, cities, and regions in China, including some series of regional development strategies, regional economic development reports, county economic research, and other similar works, and there were a large number of works on regional coordinated development, economic development in the central and western regions, and urbanization. There were quite a number of works in the field of the real estate economy. The second category was "others," with 393 publications. There were a large number of studies on the consumer economy. Others included books and translations on the circular economy, the network economy, information economics, experimental economics, public economics, the low-carbon economy, the resource economy, the technological economy, engineering economics, international economics, economic globalization, and circulation economics. There were more than 100 works on the labor economy and human capital (183), the socialist economy and the Chinese economy (180), Western economics and the history of economic theory (158), economic management (127), the national economy and the world economy (110). There were 16 books on political economics published, mainly on the study of Marxist economics.

Of the translations published in 2011, there were 106 from the United States, 30 from the UK, 9 from Japan, and 4 or less from other countries. There were no Russian translations published in 2010 and 2011. There were many textbooks and works on the principles of economics, macroeconomics, microeconomics, and growth economics in the translated works from the United States. There was also some research on the frontier disciplines of economics, such as experimental economics, public choice theory, supply school theory, evolutionary economics, and similar topics, as well as some aspects of economic history, the history of economic theory, management economics, human resource management, and related topics. There were a number of classical economics and works by or on Keynes among the books translated from English. The topics of translated Japanese works fell in the fields of the consumer economy, industrial agglomeration, the world economy, management, and similar areas.

Bibliography

BOOKS

A Guide to "The Decision of the Central Committee of the Communist Party of China on Several Issues Concerning the Improvement of the Socialist Market Economy." People's Publishing House, 2002.

Bai, Yongxiu and Ren Baoping. *60 Years of New China Economics.* Higher Education Press, 2009.

Bai, Yongxiu, and Ren Baoping. *Modern Political Economics.* Higher Education Press, 2008.

Beijing Research Center of Deng Xiaoping Theory and the Important Thought of the Three Represents. *Collected Works on the Sinicization of Marxism.* Red Flag Press, 2006.

Beijing Tianze Economic Research Institute. *China's Economics (1994, 1995, 1996).* Shanghai People's Publishing House, 1995, 1996, 1997.

Book Compilation Group. *Guidance Book for the Report of the Nineteenth National Congress of the Communist Party of China.* People's Publishing House, 2017.

Book Compilation Group. *Guidance Reading of the Report of the Eighteenth CPC National Congress.* People's Publishing House, 2012.

Central Archives. *Selected Documents of the CPC Central Committee.* Vol. 11. CPC Central Party School Press, 1991.

Chen, Daisun. *A History of Political Economics.* Jilin People's Publishing House, 1981.

Chen, Daisun. *From Classical Economic School to Marx: A Brief Introduction to the Development of Some Major Theories.* The Commercial Press, 2014.

Chen, Yun. *Selected Works of Chen Yun (1949–1956).* Shanghai People's Publishing House, 1980.

Chen, Zhang, Chen Guodong, and Liu Xiahui. *Western Economic Theory and Empirical Methodology.* Peking University Press, 1993.

Chen, Zhan'an. *The New Progress of Marxism in China since the Sixteenth National Congress of the Communist Party of China.* Peking University Press, 2008.

Chen, Zongsheng, Wu Zhe, and Xie Siquan. *Research on the Marketization Process of China's Economic System.* Shanghai People's Publishing House, 1999.

China Economic Research Center of Peking University. *Economics and China's Economic Reform.* Shanghai People's Publishing House, 1995.

China Encyclopedia Editorial Department. *Encyclopedia of China: Philosophy Volume.* China Encyclopedia Press, 1987.

China Industrial Development Research Institute. *2015 China Industrial Development Report: New Normal and New Strategy.* Shanghai University of Finance and Economics Press, 2015.

China National Economic Accounting and Economic Growth Research Center of Peking University. *China Economic Growth Report.* China Economic Press, 2004.

Compilation Group of Political Economics Textbook of 13 Universities in North China. *Socialist Part of Political Economics.* Shaanxi People's Publishing House, 1979.

Compilation Group of Political Economics Textbook of 13 Universities in South China. *Socialist Part of Political Economics.* Sichuan People's Publishing House, 1979.

China Archives of Publications. *National General Bibliography.* Zhonghua Book Company, 1960–1979.

Dai, Yuanchen. "Macro-management in Socialist Market Economy." In *Yearbook of China Economic Sciences (1993),* edited by Li Jingwen. China Statistics Press, 1993.

Deng, Xu. *A Dictionary of China's System Reform and Opening-up: Volume of Economic System Reform.* Sichuan Science and Technology Press, 1992.

Dong, Fureng. *A Study of Economic Development Strategy.* Economic Science Press, 1988.

Dong, Fureng. *On Market and Socialist Market Economy.* People's Publishing House, 1993.

Dong, Jiancai. *A New Theory of Marxist Economics.* Economy and Management Publishing House, 2006.

Editorial Board of *China Economic Science Yearbook. China Economic Science Yearbook* (1984). Hebei People's Publishing House, 1988.

Editorial Board of *National Bibliography of China,* Beijing Library. *China National Bibliography.* Bibliography and Literature Publishing House, 1985.

Editorial Department of *Economic Research* and *Economics Trends. Debates on Important Issues of Political Economics Since the Founding of the People's Republic of China (1949–1980).* China Financial and Economic Publishing House, 1981.

Editorial Department of *Economic Research. Debates on China's Economic Theory* (1990–1999). China Financial and Economic Publishing House, 2002.

Editorial Department of *Economic Research. Debates on the Theoretical Issues of China's Socialist Economy* (1985–1989). China Financial and Economic Publishing House, 1991.

Editorial Department of *Economic Research. Review and Prospect of China's Socialist Economic Theory.* China Economic Press, 1986.

Fan, Gang. *A Political and Economic Analysis of Gradual Reform.* Shanghai Far East Publishing House, 1996.

Fan, Gang. *Comparison and Synthesis of Three Modern Economic Theory Systems.* Shanghai People's Publishing House and Shanghai Sanlian Bookstore, 1995.

Fan, Gang. *The Road of Gradual Progress.* China Social Sciences Press, 1993.

Fan, Jiaxiang. "Development Economics." In *Lectures on Foreign Economics.* Vol. 1. China Social Sciences Press, 1980.

Fang, Fuqian. *Major Schools of Contemporary Western Economics*. China Renmin University Press, 2004.

Fu, Yincai. *Neoconservative Economics*. China Economic Press, 1994.

Gregory, Paul, and Robert Stewart. *Comparative Economic System*. Shanghai Sanlian Bookstore, 1988.

Gu, Hailiang, and Yan Pengfei. *A New History of Economic Thought*. Economic Science Press, 2016.

Gu, Hailiang. *A Study on the Theoretical System of Socialism with Chinese Characteristics*. China Renmin University Press, 2009.

Gu, Hailiang. *Contemporary Vision of Marx's Economic Thought*. Economic Science Press, 2005.

Gu, Shutang. *The Germination and System Transformation of China's Market Economy*. Tianjin People's Publishing House, 1993.

Gu, Zhun. *Collected Works of Gu Zhun*. Guizhou People's Publishing House, 1994.

Gu, Zhun. *From Idealism to Empiricism*. Guangming Daily Press, 2013.

Guiding Committee for the Compilation and Review of National Cadre Training Materials. *Basic Issues of Deng Xiaoping Theory*. People's Publishing House, 2002.

Han, Yongjin. *Methodology of Western Economics: A Study on the Methodology of Philosophy of Science and the Methodology of Economics*. China Social Sciences Press, 2000.

He, Jianzhang, and Wang Jiye. *Issues of China's Planned Management*. China Social Sciences Press, 1984.

He, Liancheng, and Li Zhongmin. *Research on the Economic Issues of Socialism with Chinese Characteristics*. People's Publishing House, 2010.

He, Liancheng. *Deepening the Research and Understanding of Labor and Labor Value Theory*. Economic Science Press, 2002.

He, Liancheng. *The Theory and Practice of China's Market Economy*. Northwestern University Press, 1992.

Hong, Yinxing. *An Analysis of Equilibrium and Disequilibrium of Economic Operation*. China Social Sciences Press, 1997.

Hu, Angang. *China's Economic Fluctuation Report*. Tsinghua University Press, 1994.

Hu, Daiguang, and Gao Hongye. *A Dictionary of Western Economics*. Economic Science Press, 2000.

Hu, Daiguang, Zhou Shulian, and Wang Haibo. *The Essence of Western Economics*. Economy and Management Publishing House, 1997.

Hu, Daiguang. *Selected Papers on Modern Foreign Economics*. The Commercial Press, 1982.

Hu, Daiguang. *The Evolution and Influence of Western Economics*. Peking University Press, 1998.

Hu, Daiguang. *The New Trend of Foreign Economics and the Development of China's Economics*. Economic Science Press, 1998.

Hu, Jichuang, and Tan Min. *An Outline of the History of New China's Economic Thought*. Shanghai University of Finance and Economics Press, 1997.

Hu, Jichuang. *An Analysis of Differences in Economic Theories*. Fudan University Press, 1991.

Hu, Xiaofeng, and Han Shuying. *An Outline of Discussion on China's Socialist Economic Issues*. Jilin People's Publishing House, 1983.

Huang, Taiyan. *The Frontier Hot Issues of China Economy*. Economic Science Press, 2010.

Information Center of the Press and Publication Administration. *China Copy Library*. Zhonghua Book Company, 1980–1996.

Institute of Economics of Chinese Academy of Social Sciences. *A Dictionary of Modern Economy.* Jiangsu People's Publishing House, 2004.

Institute of Economics of Chinese Academy of Social Sciences. *The Gang of Four's Tampering with Marxist Political Economics.* Shanxi People's Publishing House, 1978.

Institute of Economics of the Soviet Academy of Sciences. *Textbook of Political Economics.* Sanlian Bookstore, 1960.

Jiang, Xuemo. *Political Economics.* 10th ed. Shanghai People's Publishing House, 1999.

Jiang, Xuemo. *Socialist Political Economics.* Fudan University Press, 1987.

Jiang, Zemin. *On Socialism with Chinese Characteristics.* Central Literature Publishing House, 2002.

Li, Jianping et al. *Analysis Report on Economic Hot Spots of the G20 (2016–2017).* Economic Science Press, 2016.

Li, Jingwen et al. *The Yearbook of China's Economic Sciences.* China Statistics Press, 1990, 1991, 1992, and 1993.

Li, Jingwen, and Zheng Youjing. *Technical Progress and Economic Benefits.* China Financial and Economic Publishing House, 1989.

Li, Wuwei. *Volume of Applied Economics of Chinese Social Sciences in the 20th Century.* Shanghai People's Publishing House, 2005.

Li, Yining. *An Empirical Analysis of China's Macroeconomy.* Peking University Press, 1992.

Li, Yining. *Science of National Economic Management.* Hebei People's Publishing House, 1988.

Li, Zezhong. *The Theory of Socialist Economy in Contemporary China.* China Social Sciences Press, 1989.

Li, Zhancai. *A History of Contemporary Chinese Economic Thoughts.* Henan University Press, 1999.

Liao, Shixiang. *Economic Methodology.* Shanghai Academy of Social Sciences Press, 1991.

Lin, Yifu, Cai Fang, and Li Zhou. *China's Miracle: Development Strategy and Economic Reform.* Shanghai Sanlian Bookstore, 2002.

Lin, Yifu, Cai Fang, and Li Zhou. *China's Miracle: Development Strategy and Economics.* Shanghai Sanlian Bookstore, 1994.

Lin, Yifu. *On Economic Methods.* Peking University Press, 2005.

Lin, Zili. *Modern Market Economy and Modern Socialism.* People's Publishing House, 1993.

Lin, Zili. *On the New Equivalent Exchange.* Economic Science Press, 1987.

Liu, Guoguang, and Dai Yuanchen. *The Rigid Reality and the Relaxing Reality: Macromanagement Under the Dual Systems.* Shanghai People's Publishing House, 1991.

Liu, Guoguang, and Li Jingwen. *A Comprehensive Study on the Transformation of China's Economic Growth Mode.* Guangdong People's Publishing House, 1999.

Liu, Guoguang. *Stable Economic Growth in System Reform.* China Planning Economy Press, 1990.

Liu, Rongqin. *Contemporary Economics.* China Prospect Publishing House, 1988.

Liu, Shibai. *A New Theory of Property Rights.* Southwest University of Finance and Economics Press, 1993.

Liu, Shibai. *On System Transformation.* Sanlian Bookstore, 2008.

Liu, Shibai. *Selected Works of Liu Shibai: Research on Socialist Political Economics.* Vol. 1, vol. 2. Sichuan People's Publishing House, 2018.

Liu, Shijin. *An Introduction to the Analysis of Economic System Efficiency.* Shanghai Sanlian Bookstore, 1993.

Lü, Wei. *An Outline of Economic Transition Theory*. The Commercial Press, 2006.

Ma, Hong et al. *Reform and Development*. Economy and Management Publishing House, 1989.

Ma, Yinchu. *Selected Economic Papers of Ma Yinchu*. Peking University Press, 1981.

Ma, Yinchu. *Selected Works of Ma Yinchu*. Tianjin People's Publishing House, 1988.

Mao, Zedong. *Selected Works of Mao Zedong*. Vol. 3. People's Publishing House, 1991.

Meng, Jie. *Creative Transformation of Marxist Political Economics*. Economic Science Press, 2001.

National Economic System Reform Commission. *Ten years of China's Economic System Reform*. Economy and Management Publishing House, Reform Press, 1988.

Newman et al. *New Palgrave Dictionary of Economics*. Economic Science Press, 1992.

Norton, Barry. *China's Economy: Transformation and Growth*. Shanghai People's Publishing House, 2010.

Ouyang, Yao. *Theory of Economic Development of Great Powers*. China Renmin University Press, 2014.

Pang Jinju. *Economic Innovation in the Process of Marxism Sinicization*. Economic Science Press, 2011.

Pei, Xiaoge. *Economics of Construction: A Study on the Sinicization of Marxist Economics*. China Social Sciences Press, 2011.

Ri, Shan. *Distinguished Scholars on Socialist Market*. People's Publishing House, 1992.

Sheng, Hong. *Modern Institutional Economics*. Peking University Press, 2003.

Sheng, Hong. *Transition Economics in China*. Shanghai Sanlian Bookstore, 1994.

Shi, Yuequn, Yuan Enzhen, and Cheng Enfu. *Volume of Theoretical Economics of Chinese Social Sciences in the 20th Century*. Shanghai People's Publishing House, 2005.

Song, Tao. *Exploration of Socialist Economic Theory*. Beijing University of Technology Press, 1994.

Sun, Yefang. *Research on Socialist Economic Issues*. People's Publishing House, 1985.

Sun, Yefang. *Selected Works of Sun Yefang*. Shanxi Economic Publishing House, 1984.

Sun, Yefang. *Sequel to Some Theoretical Issues of Socialist Economy*. People's Publishing House, 1983.

Tan Min. *Looking Back on History: The Pre-history of Marxist Economics in China*. Shanghai University of Finance and Economics Press, 2008.

Tan, Chongtai. *A Comparative Study on the Economic Development of the Developed Countries at Early Stage and the Developing Countries Today*. Wuhan University Press, 2008.

Tan, Chongtai. *The History of Western Economic Development Thoughts*. Wuhan University Press, 1993.

Tan, Chongtai. *Development Economics*. Shanghai People's Publishing House, 1989.

The Editorial Department of the Commercial Press. *Selected Papers on Modern Foreign Economics (Issue 14)*. The Commercial Press, 1992.

The Guiding Committee for the Compilation and Review of National Cadre Training Textbooks. *Basic Issues of Marxism and Leninism*. People's Publishing House, 2002.

The Publicity Department of the CPC Central Committee. *A Reader on General Secretary Xi Jinping's Important Speech*. Learning Press, People's Publishing House, 2016.

The Theory Bureau of the Propaganda Department of the CPC Central Committee. *A Learner's Book on An Outlook on Scientific Development*. Learning Press, 2006.

Theory Dynamic Editorial Department. *Establishing and Implementing the Scientific Outlook on Development*. CPC Central Committee Party School Press, 2004.

Wang Yanan. *Selected Works of Wang Yanan*. Vol. 1. Fujian Education Press, 1988.

Wang, Fuyu. *An Introduction to Social Science Methodology*. Yanshan Press, 1993.

Wang, Hongchang et al. *China Economic Science Yearbook (1994)*. China Statistics Press, 1994.

Wang, Lisheng, and Pei Changhong. *Exploration of Socialist Political Economics with Chinese Characteristics*. China Social Sciences Press, 2016.

Wang, Wenyin. *A Study on the Sinicization of Marxist Economics*. Shanxi Economic Publishing House, 2009.

Wang, Yuanzhang. *A History of Marxist Economic Development Thought*. Xinjiang People's Publishing House, 2006.

Wang, Zhenzhong. *A Research Report on Political Economics*. Social Sciences Academic Press, 2001.

Wei, Xinghua, and Huang Taiyan. "Constraints on the Relationship Between Planning and Market under the New Economic System." In *China Economic Science Yearbook (1993)*, edited by Li Jingwen. China Statistics Press, 1993.

Wei, Xinghua. *Research on the Economic Theoretical System of Socialism with Chinese Characteristics*. China Financial and Economic Publishing House, 2015.

Wei, Xun, and Gu Shutang. *The Role and Manifestation of the Law of Value at Various Stages of Capitalism*. Shanghai People's Publishing House, 1956.

Wu, Jinglian et al. *Gradualness and Radicality: the Choice of China's Reform Path*. Economic Science Press, 1996.

Wu, Jinglian. "Historical Evolution and Practical Significance of Socialist Market Economy." In *Distinguished Scholars on Socialist Market Economy*, edited by Jia Chunfeng. People's Publishing House, 1993.

Wu, Jinglian. "Path Dependence and China's Reform." In *Economics and China's Economic Reform*, edited by China Economic Research Center of Peking University. Shanghai People's Publishing House, 1995.

Wu, Jinglian. *Economic Reform in Contemporary China*. Shanghai Far East Publishing House, 2004.

Wu, Jinglian. *Modern Company and Enterprise Reform*. Tianjin People's Publishing House, 1994.

Wu, Jinglian. *Reform of Large and Medium-sized Enterprises: Establishing Modern Enterprise System*. Tianjin People's Publishing House, 1993.

Wu, Jinglian. *The Road to Market Economy*. Beijing University of Technology Press, 1992.

Wu, Shuqing, and Hu Naiwu. *Macro-management of National Economy*. Peking University Press, 1993.

Wu, Shuqing, and Wang Mengkui. *Research on Some Issues of Political Economics*. Economic Science Press, 1991.

Wu, Yifeng et al. *Research on Mathematical Model of Marxist Economics*. China Renmin University Press, 2011.

Xiang, Qiyuan et al. *Review and Reflection on Socialist Economic Theory*. Jiangsu People's Publishing House, 1988.

Xiao, Liang. *China's Economic Research in 1993: Hot Issues, Debates, and Progress*. China Statistics Press, 1994.

Xiao, Liang. *Yearbook of China's Economic Sciences (1985, 1986)*. Economic Science Press, 1985, 1986.

Xin, Ming, and Yang Haiying. *The Latest Achievements of Marxism in China*. CPC Central Committee Party School Press, 2007.

Xu, Dixin. *On Socialist Production, Circulation and Distribution*. People's Publishing House, 1997.

Xue, Muqiao. *China Economic Yearbook*. Economic Management Press, China Economic Yearbook Press, 1981–1997.

Xue, Muqiao. *Memoirs of Xue Muqiao*. Tianjin People's Publishing House, 1996.

Xue, Muqiao. *On the Issues of Socialist Market Economy*. People's Publishing House, 1993.

Xue, Muqiao. *Selected Works of Xue Muqiao*. Shanxi Economic Publishing House, 1985.

Xue, Muqiao. *Theoretical Issues in the Socialist Economy*. People's Publishing House, 1979.

Yan, Zhijie. *A New Exploration of Labor Value Theory*. Peking University Press, 2001.

Yang, Chengxun. *Economics of Socialism with Chinese Characteristics*. People's Publishing House, 2009.

Yang, Chunxue. *Breaking Through the Ideological Bottleneck: Political Economics in the Past Forty Years of Reform*. Capital University of Economics and Business Press, 2018.

Yang, Jianbai. *On Socialist Macroeconomy*. Dongbei University of Finance and Economics Press, 1990.

Yang, Wenhan. *An Outline of the History of Socialist Economic Theory*. Shaanxi People's Publishing House, 1988.

Yao, Yang. *Economic Reform as a Process of Institutional Innovation*. Truth and Wisdom Press, 2008.

Yong, Wenyuan et al. *The Exploration of Socialist Political Economics: The Theory of Social Necessary Products*. Shanghai People's Publishing House, 1985.

Yu, Guangyuan. *A History of Theoretical Economics in China* (1949–1989). Henan People's Publishing House, 1996.

Yu, Guangyuan. *Exploration of the Socialist Part of Political Economics (1)*. People's Publishing House, 1980.

Yu, Guangyuan. *Theory and Practice of Socialist Market Economy*. China Financial and Economic Publishing House, 1992.

Yu, Jinfu. *Classical Theory and Modern Viewpoint of Marxist Economics*. China Social Sciences Press, 2008.

Yu, Shaobo, and Xiang Qiyuan. *On the Rule that Production Relations Must be Suitable for the Nature of Productive Forces*. Shandong People's Publishing House, 1980.

Zhang, Jun. *Dual Track Economics: China's Economic Reform* (1978–1992). Shanghai Sanlian Bookstore, 1998.

Zhang, Peigang. *New Development Economics*. Henan People's Publishing House, 1992.

Zhang, Weiying. *Political Economics*. Higher Education Press, 2000.

Zhang, Wenmin et al. *The Great Debate on China's Economy*. Vol. 1, vol. 2. Economy and Management Publishing House, 1997.

Zhang, Wuchang. *The Future of China*. Hong Kong Letters Limited, 1989.

Zhang, Xu. *An Analysis of Economics in the 20th Century*. China Social Sciences Press, 2000.

Zhang, Xunhua. *The Contending Department of Social Sciences: Volume of Socialist Economic Theory*. Shanghai People's Publishing House, 1991.

Zhang, Yu. *An Introduction to Transitional Political Economics*. Economic Science Press, 2001.

Zhang, Yu. *Political Economics of Socialism with Chinese Characteristics*. China Renmin University Press, 2016.

Zhang, Zhuoyuan et al. *An Outline of the History of New China's Economics* (1949–2011). China Social Sciences Press, 2012.

Zhang, Zhuoyuan. *60 Years of China's Economics*. China Social Sciences Press, 2009.

Zhang, Zhuoyuan. *Experts on China's Economic Issues in the 21st Century*. Henan People's Publishing House, 1999.

Zhao, Xiaolei. *Development of Modern Economic Thought in China.* Economic Science Press, 2016.

Zheng, Shao, and He Xiaoxing. *A Chronicle of 20 Years' of China's Economic System Reform.* Shanghai Dictionary Publishing House, 1998.

Zhongnan University of Finance and Economics. *A Dictionary of Economic Sciences.* Economic Science Press, 1987.

Zhou, Qiren, Du Ying, and Qiu Jicheng. *The Theme of Development.* Sichuan People's Publishing House, 1987.

Zhou, Shaodong et al. *Division and Innovation: Marxist Revival of Development Economics.* Economic Science Press, 2015.

Zhou, Shulian. *Economic Structure and Economic Effect.* Guangdong People's Publishing House, 1989.

Zhou, Xiaochuan, Wang Lin, and Xiao Meng et al. *Enterprise Reform: Mode Selection and Matching Design.* China Economic Press, 1994.

Zhuo, Jiong. *On Socialist Commodity Economy.* Guangdong People's Publishing House, 1981.

JOURNAL ARTICLES

Cai, Fang. "Leading the New Normal Leads to Medium High Speed." *Economic Research*, no. 12 (2015).

Cai, Fang. "How China's Economic Growth Becomes TFP Driven." *China Social Sciences*, no. 1 (2013).

Chen, Changbing. "Research on the 'Characteristics' of the Sinicization of Marxist Political Economics." *Learning and Exploration*, no. 11 (2016).

Chen, Qing. "Research Progress of Political Economics of Socialism with Chinese Characteristics." *Economics Trends*, no. 8 (2017).

Chen, Renjiang. "Neo-liberalism after Neo-liberalism." *Journal of Hebei University of Economics and Trade*, no. 1 (2018).

Chen, Xiangguang. "A Summary of the Fifteenth National Symposium on Socialist Economic Theory and Practice in Colleges and Universities." *Economics Trends*, no. 4 (2002).

Chen, Xiaobing. "A Review of the Theory of Distribution According to Work." *Social Science Trends*, no. 7 (1996).

Dong, Shuancheng, and Zhao Haihong. "A Summary of the National Symposium on Distribution Theory and Income Gap." *Economics Trends*, no. 7 (2002).

Du, Hui. "A Review of the Debates on the Periodicity of Socialist Economic Fluctuations in Recent Years." *Economics Trends*, no. 8 (1990).

Duan, Mei, and Li Keqiang. "Economic Policy Uncertainty, Financing Constraints, and Total Factor Productivity." *Contemporary Finance and Economics*, no. 6 (2019).

Editorial Department of the Economist. "Talks on Innovation of China's Political Economics." *Economist*, no. 2 (2017).

Fan, Liangcong, and Zhou Minghai. "The Road of the Socialist Market Economy with Chinese Characteristics: A Summary of the Theoretical Seminar on Commemorating the 40th Anniversary of Reform and Opening Up." *Economic Research*, no. 8 (2018).

Fang, Songhua, and Chen Xiangqin. "Review of Theoretical Research on the Primary Stage of Socialism Since 2003." *Research on Mao Zedong and Deng Xiaoping Theory*, no. 7 (2014).

Gao, Fan, and Li Huizhong. "30 Years of China's Economic Reform and Opening Up: Experience Summary and Theoretical Interpretation—Summary of the 22nd Annual Meeting of the National Symposium on Socialist Economic Theory and Practice in Colleges and Universities." *Economics Trends*, no. 1 (2009).

Gao, Peiyong et al. "Study and Implement the Spirit of the May 17 Speech and Build a Written Talk on Economics with Chinese Characteristics." *Economic Research*, no. 5 (2017).

Gao, Shangquan. "Review and Reflection on China's Reform and Opening Up in the Past 40 Years." *Xinhua Digest*, no. 9 (2018).

Ge, Yang and Shen Kunrong. "Discussion on the Development and Theoretical Innovation in the era of Marxist Economics: A Summary of the Fifth National Forum on the Development and Innovation of Marxist Economics." *Economic Research*, no. 1 (2012).

Gu, Hailiang. "Introduction to the Political Economics of Socialism with Chinese Characteristics." *Economist*, no. 3 (2019).

Gu, Hailiang. "Theoretical Innovation of Socialist Economics with Chinese Characteristics." *Frontline*, no. 8 (2011).

Guo, Xiaoming, and Guan Ying. "A Summary of the Discussion on the Transformation of China's Economic Growth Mode." *Contemporary Economic Science*, no. 2 (1996).

Guo, Xueneng, and Lu Shengrong. "An Analysis of China's Potential Economic Growth Rate against the Background of Supply Side Structural Reform." *Economist*, no. 1 (2018).

He, Yuanfeng, and Li Xiangju. "The Practical Significance and Important Value of *Das Kapital* in Contemporary China." *Gansu Social Sciences*, no. 1 (2014).

Hong, Yinxing. "Building Socialist Political Economics with Chinese Characteristics." *Economist*, no. 1 (2019).

Hong, Yinxing. "Constructing the Theoretical System of Socialist Political Economics with Chinese Characteristics with Innovative Theory." *Economic Research*, no. 4 (2016).

Hong, Yinxing. "Innovation of Marxist Economics and Sinicization of Marxist Economics." *Economics Trends*, no. 9 (2007).

Hong, Yinxing. "Major Breakthroughs in the Logic of Economic Reform and Political Economics in the Past Forty Years." *Economist*, no. 12 (2018).

Hong, Yinxing. "On the New Normal of Medium and High-speed Growth and its Supporting Normal." *Economics Trends*, no. 11 (2014).

Hong, Yuanpeng. "The Development of Socialist Political Economics with Chinese Characteristics in the New Era." *Economic Research*, no. 11 (2017).

Hu, Delong et al. "Theoretical Exploration and System Construction of Socialist Political Economics with Chinese Characteristics: A Summary of the 10th National Forum on the Development and Innovation of Marxist Economics and the 6th Symposium on Capital and Contemporary Economic Issues." *Economic Research*, no. 11 (2016).

Hu, Jiayong. "A Review of Political Economics Research in 2008." *Economics Trends*, no. 1 (2009).

Hu, Jiayong. "Summary of the Nineteenth Annual Meeting of the Forum on Socialist Political Economics with Chinese Characteristics." *Economics Trends*, no. 3 (2018).

Hu, Jun. "The Theory of the Socialist Market Economy is the Sinicization of Marxism." *Fujian Forum (Humanities and Social Sciences Edition)*, no. 11 (2008).

Hua, Sheng, Zhang Xuejun, and Luo Xiaopeng. "Ten Years of China's Reform: Review, Reflection, and Prospect." *Economic Research*, no. 11 (1988).

Huang, Guitian, Li Ping, and Jiang Shaolong. "A Summary of the National Symposium on the Transformation of Economic Growth Mode in Colleges and Universities." *China Social Sciences*, no. 2 (1997).

Jian, Xinhua. "Major Achievements in Economic Theory of Socialism with Chinese Characteristics and Innovation and Development in the New Era." *Economic Research*, no. 12 (2017).

Jiang, Nanping. "Why Should We Study the Sinicization of Marxist Economics." *Journal of Chengdu University of Technology*, no. 1 (2011).

Jiang, Yonghong et al. "Innovating Marxist Economics and Promoting Comprehensive, Deepening Economic Reform—A Summary of the Eighth National Forum on the Development and Innovation of Marxist Economics." *Economic Research*, no. 9 (2014).

Jin, Wei, and Cui Xuelian. "The Historical Process and Basic Law of the Formation and Development of Socialist Economic Theory with Chinese Characteristics." *Learning Forum*, no. 9 (2010).

Jin, Weiping and Xiong Chai. "A Summary of the Sixth National Forum on the Development and Innovation of Marxist Economics." *Economic Research*, no. 10 (2012).

Li Yi. "A Review of the Discussion of Some Issues in China's Economic Research." *Academic Trends*, no. 3 (1990).

Li Yiping and Zhang Wenduo. "A Summary of the Symposium on the Combination of Socialist Public Ownership and Commodity Economy." *Economics Trends*, no. 7 (1991).

Li, Junru. "Research on Some Problems of Marxism in China." *Journal of the Party School of the CPC Central Committee*, no. 1 (2008).

Li, Mengxin, and Ren Baoping. "Comprehensive Evaluation and Path Selection of China's High-quality Development in the New Era." *Financial Science*, no. 5 (2019).

Lin, Jue. "A Summary of the Symposium on the Development of China's Economics." *Social Sciences*, no. 2 (1996).

Lin, Yifu. "40 Years of Reform and Opening Up and China's Economic Development." *Economics Trends*, no. 8 (2018).

Lin, Yifu. "A Review of China's Economic Research in 1999." *Economic Research*, no. 11 (2000).

Lin, Yifu. "The Joseph Needham Puzzle and China's Revival: The Perspective of New Structural Economics." *China Reform*, no. 1 (2018).

Lin, Yifu. "The Path of China's Stable Economic Growth." *People's Daily*, July 11, 2014.

Liu, Can, Wu Yin, and Gai Kaicheng. "A Summary of the Fourth National Forum on the Development and Innovation of Marxist Economics." *Economic Research*, no. 2 (2012).

Liu, Wei. "New Development Concept and Overcoming the 'Middle Income Trap.'" *China Economic Report*, no. 2 (2019).

Liu, Wei. "The Logic of Xi Jinping's New Socialist Economic Thought in China's New Era." *Economic Research*, no. 5 (2018).

Liu, Yongji. "Practice Calls for the Sinicization of Political Economics." *Economic Research*, no. 6 (1989).

Lu, Yangchun. "A Review of the Theoretical Research on the Economic Development of Socialism with Chinese Characteristics." *Discussion on Modern Economy*, no. 11 (2008).

Lu, Yunbin. "An Overview of the Research on the Stock System." *Jiangxi Social Sciences*, no. 3 (1998).

Luo, Rundong, and Li Chao. "Analysis of Hot Spots in China's Economic Research in 2017." *Economics Trends*, no. 4 (2018).

Ma, Jiantang. "A Summary of the Viewpoints of the Research Association on Inflation Control Policy." *Price Theory and Practice*, no. 5 (1989).

Niu, Tiansheng. "Debate and Discussion on Methodology Research of Marxism Sinicization." *Changbai Academic Journal*, no. 2 (2010).

Qiao, Gang, and Chen Gongyan. "Causes and Countermeasures of Inflation in China: A Summary of the Symposium on Inflation Control." *Economics Trends*, no. 5 (1989).

Qin, Xiaoqing. "A Summary of the Viewpoints on Joint Stock System in Past Two Years." *Reform*, no. 3 (1991).

Research Group of Economic Editorial Department of Book and Newspaper Data Center of Renmin University of China. "Analysis of Hot Spots of China's Economics and Management Research in 2017." *Economics Trends*, no. 4 (2018).

Research Group of Economic Research Institute of National Development and Reform Commission. "Development Environment Changes at Home and Abroad in the Next 30 Years and Prospects for the Second Centennial Goal." *Xinhua Digest*, no. 16 (2018).

Secretary Group of the Seminar. "A Summary of the Seminar on the Theory and Practice of China's Shareholding System Reform." *Economics Trends*, no. 8 (1998).

Shen, Kaiyan. "Conception of Building the Theoretical System of Political Economics of Socialism with Chinese Characteristics." *Research on Mao Zedong and Deng Xiaoping Theory*, no. 1 (2017).

Shen, Yue. "New Progress of Foreign Economic Theory and New Trend of World Economic Development: A Summary of the Ninth Symposium of the Chinese Association for the Study of Foreign Economics." *Economics Trends*, no. 4 (2002).

Shen, Yue. "The New Development of Western Economics and China's Practice: A Summary of the Sixteenth Annual Meeting of the China Society for the Study of Foreign Economic Theories." *Economist*, no. 5 (2009).

Su, Jian, and Chen Yang. "Macro Control Policy System with Chinese Characteristics and its Application." *Economist*, no. 6 (2019).

"Summary of the Symposium on the Principal Agent Relationship in the Reform of State-owned Enterprises." *Economic Research*, no. 8 (1995).

Sun, Liang. "A Review of the Theoretical Research on China's Institutional Change." *Economics Trends*, no. 2 (2002).

The Research Group of China's *Socialist Political Economics with the Central Party School*. "The Reference and Transcendence of Western Economic Theories–Learning from General Secretary Xi Jinping's Exposition on China's Socialist Political Economics." *Management World*, no. 7 (2017).

Wang, Chaoke. "The Enlightenment of *Das Kapital* on the Construction of Socialist Political Economics with Chinese Characteristics." *Political Economics Review*, no. 3 (2017).

Wang, Hong. "A Review of Different Views on the Transformation of Economic Growth Mode." *Economic Issues*, no. 10 (1996).

Wang, Jun, and Li Ping. "The Current Situation, Characteristics, and Prospects of *Das Kapital* Research." *Western China*, no. 1 (2019).

Wang, Lei, Liu Hongtao, and Li Yuan. "A Review of the Theoretical Basis of Contemporary Enterprise Strategy Research." *Economics Trends*, no. 2 (1998).

Wang, Lu. "Scientific Development and the Sinicization of Marxist Economics: A Summary of the Fourth China Political and Economic Annual Meeting." *Economics Trends*, no. 1 (2011).

Wang, Mingyi, and Shi Lijing. "Path Analysis of the Impact of Government Intervention in the Market Exit of Chinese Manufacturing Enterprises." *Economics Trends*, no. 6 (2018).

Wang, Wenbing. "On the Dual Identity of Marxism in China." *Journal of Wuhan University (Philosophy and Social Sciences Edition)*, no. 1 (2012).

Wang, Xiaoyong. "A Review of the Research on the Historical Starting Point of the Sinicization of Marxism." *Marxism Research*, no. 6 (2012).

Wang, Xiongjian and Gong Liutang. "A Summary of the Second Forum of Young Chinese Economists." *Economic Research*, no. 12 (2002).

Wei, Houkai, and Wang Songji. "Analysis and Theoretical Reflection on China's Excessive De-industrialization." *China's Industrial Economy*, no. 1 (2019).

Wei, Xinghua. "Adherence, Development, and Innovation of the Economic Theory of Socialism with Chinese Characteristics." *Marxism Research*, no. 10 (2015).

Wu, Xuangong. "The Important Guiding Significance of the Ownership Theory of *Das Kapital* to the Socialist Cause." *Economist*, no. 11 (2017).

Wu, Zhong. "A Summary of the Theoretical Seminar on 'Adhering to the Dominant Position of Public Ownership.'" *Qiushi*, no. 6 (1997).

Xia, Bin. "China Miracle: An Economist's Thinking on Theoretical Innovation." *Economics Trends*, no. 3 (2019).

Xiang, Jiuyu. "New Development Concept and Cultural Confidence." *Chinese Social Sciences*, no. 6 (2018).

Xiao, Qiong. "A Summary of the Discussion on Labor Commodity in China's Theoretical Circles in Recent Years." *Contemporary Economic Science*, no. 5 (1996).

Xiao, Xia. "A Summary of the Symposium on Behavioral Science Facing Market Economy." *Economics Trends*, no. 2 (2002).

Xiao, Yu. "A Summary of the Symposium on the Operation Law of Socialist Market Economy." *Economics Trends*, no. 11 (1995).

Xu, Jiajun. "A Review of China's Political Economics Research in 2009." *Economics Trends*, no. 1 (2010).

Yang, Yonghua. "A Review of the Research on the History of Socialist Economic Theory." *Economics Trends*, no. 4 (1989).

Yang, Yonghua. "A Summary of the First National Symposium on the History of Socialist Political Economics." *Economics Trends*, no. 8 (1989).

Yang, Zhimin. "On the Sinicization of Marxist Economics and Chinese Traditional Culture." *Qiushi*, no. 11 (2000).

Yin, Heng, Gong Liutang, and Zou Hengfu. "New Development of Contemporary Income Distribution Theory." *Economic Research*, no. 8 (2002).

Yu Zuyao. "A Review of the Discussion on the Relationship Between Planning and Market in Recent Years." *Economics Trends*, no. 3 (1991).

Yu, Chunhui. "A Review of the Theoretical Development of Western Development Economics." *Economics Trends*, no. 8 (1997).

Zhang Delin. "Exploration and Contention of Aggregate Analysis, Structural Analysis, and Institutional Analysis." *Economics Trends*, no. 6 (1990).

Zhang, Leisheng. "On the Development and Innovation of Socialist Political Economics with Chinese Characteristics." *Marxism Research*, no. 5 (2017).

Zhang, Shuguang, and Sheng Hong. "A Review of the Theoretical Research of China's Institutional Economics in 1995." *Economics Trends*, no. 12 (1996).

Zhang, Tianlei, and Ren Baoping. "A Review of the Main Research Methods of Contemporary Western Economics." *Economic Review*, no. 3 (2002).

Zhang, Xinning. "A Review of the Research on Socialist Political Economics with Chinese Characteristics." *Political Economics Review*, no. 2 (2017).

Zhang, Zhidong and Hua Deya. "A Summary of the First National Symposium on Textbook and Curriculum Reform of Political Economics." *Economics Trends*, no. 6 (2009).

Zhang, Zhuoyuan, Fan Gang, Wang Tongsan, Pei Changhong, and Gao Peiyong. "Theory and Practice of Economic System Reform in the Past Forty Years of Reform and Opening Up." *Economics Trends*, no. 7 (2018).

Zhang, Zhuoyuan, Li Yining, Su Xing, Chen Xiwen, and Liu Shijin. "China's Economic Reform and Development in the New Century." *Economic Research*, no. 12 (2002).

Zhang, Zhuoyuan. "A Review of China's Market-oriented Economic Reform in the Past 40 Years." *Economic and Management Research*, no. 3 (2018).

Zhang, Zhuoyuan. "Realizing the Organic Combination of Socialism and the Market Economy–The Main Line of Building Socialist Political Economics with Chinese Characteristics." *People's Daily*, November 21, 2016.

Zhang, Zhuoyuan et al. "On the Development and Innovation of Socialist Political Economics with Chinese Characteristics." *Economic Research*, no. 3 (2016).

Zhao, Feng, and Duan Yuchen. "Marx's Competition Theory and its Modern Significance." *Economist*, no. 3 (2019).

Zhao, Junjie. "Giving Full Play to the Role of 'Cornerstone'—A Summary of the National Working Conference on the Transformation of Enterprise Management Mechanism." *Economic Work Bulletin*, no. 17 (1993).

Zhao, Xuezeng, Zhang Fengchao, and Chen Biaohong. "A Summary of the Sixteenth Symposium of China Das Kapital Research Association." *Economics Trends*, no. 10 (2012).

Zheng, Bingwen. "A Review of the Development of Western Economics in the 20th Century." *Chinese Social Sciences*, no. 3 (2001).

Han, Zhiguo. "A Summary of the Views of the Seminar on the Theory of Distribution According to Work in the Primary Stage of Socialism." *Chinese Social Sciences*, no. 1 (1988).

Zheng, Wen. "A Summary of Discussion on the Nature of Labor in the Public Economy." *Reference for Ideological and Political Courses*, no. 6 (1995).

Zhong, Peihua. "A Summary of the Symposium on Ethical Issues in the Socialist Market Economy." *Economics Trends*, no. 9 (1996).

Zhou, Wen, and Bao Weijie. "Further Discussion on the Socialist Market Economic System with Chinese Characteristics." *Economist*, no. 3 (2019).

Zhou, Wen. "China's Road and China's Economics." *Economist*, no. 7 (2018).

Zou, Zhiqing. "An Important Path for China's Economic Reform and Development." *China Economic Report*, no. 2 (2019).

Zuo, Dapei. "A Review of Contemporary Western Economics and its Main Schools." *Economics Trends*, no. 12 (1996).

Index

ABOUT THE AUTHOR

Born in Shanghai in May 1955, Zhao Xiaolei is a Doctor of Economics and a professor and doctoral advisor at Shanghai University of Finance and Economics, where he currently holds the position of Director of the Free-Trade Zone Research Institute/Shanghai Development Research Institute. He has also received the Sun Yefang Economic Science Award and holds the position of Vice President at the Chinese Society for the History of Economic Thought. He specializes in theoretical economics, macroeconomics, urban economic planning, and urban agglomeration economics.